E
F
G
H
1
2
3
4
5
6
7
8
Allen
Forest Grove
Estates Pkwy.
Winningkoff
Snider Ln.
Branch
New Mesquite
Lavon Shores Estates
Bethany Dr.
Lucas Rd.
Lucas
Clear Lake
Copeville
Beverly Hill
Lavon Lake
Little Ridge
Jupiter Rd.
Curtis
Stinson Rd.
Parker
Parker Rd.
Country Club Rd.
E Parker Rd.
COLLIN COUNTY
Betsy
E Park Blvd.
Plano
Murphy
Shiloh Rd.
E Plano Pkwy.
Maxwell Creek Rd.
Hooper Rd.
Murphy Rd.
Lavon Pkwy.
Ballard Ave.
E Stone St.
Elm Dr.
Milwood
Smith
Plano Rd.
Sachse
Sachse Rd.
Pleasant Valley Rd.
Whitley Rd.
E Campbell Rd.
E Collins Blvd.
Arapaho Rd.
Apollo Rd.
Belt Line Rd.
Naaman
Miles Rd.
Liberty Grove
Pleasant Valley
Goliad St.
Dalton
Shores Blvd.
Quail Run
ROCKWALL COUNTY
Williams St.
Rockwall
Buckingham Rd.
Garland Ave.
Lavon Dr.
Northeast Pkwy.
Castle Dr.
Hickox Rd.
Merritt Rd.
Princeton Rd.
Chiesa Dr.
W Walnut St.
Garland
Audelia
Forest Ln.
Lakeview Pkwy.
Dalrock
Bethard
Rowlett
Miller Rd.
W Miller Rd.
1st St.
E Miller Rd.
Rowlett Rd.
Dalrock Rd.
Glen Hill
Stodghill
Goliad St. S.
Horizon
Ridge Rd.
White Rock
Saturn Rd.
Centerville Rd.
Centerville
Lake Ray Hubbard
Buffalo Way
Pullens Rd.
Garland Rd.
Ferguson Rd.
Rose Hill
Oates Dr.
Reinhardt
Gus Thomasson Rd.
Lyndon B Johnson Frwy.
Barnes Bridge Rd.
Heath
McLendon
McDonald
King St.
Stevens
Neal Rd.
Buckner Blvd.
Lakeland Dr.
John West Rd.
North Galloway Ave.
New Hope
Town East Blvd.
Belt Line Rd.
Ray Hubbard
Bois D'Arc
RL Thornton Fwy.
N Town East Blvd.
Tripp Rd.
Sunnyvale
Valley View
University Dr.
Ranch Rd.
Samuell Blvd.
Ridgeview St.
Hillcrest St.
Tripp
Rebecca Rd.
Forney Rd.
Skyline Dr.
Cross Rd.
Military Pkwy.
Sam Houston Rd.
Kearney St.
Ridge E.
Mesquite
Clay Rd.
Berry Rd.
Lawson Rd.
Reeder Rd.
Colquitt
Bruton Rd.
N Prairie Creek Rd.
St Augustine Dr.
Masters Dr.
S Peachtree Rd.
Hickory Tree Rd.
Forney
Pleasant Dr.
Buckner Blvd.
Hillburn Dr.
Jim Miller Rd.
Lake June Rd.
Pioneer Rd.
Clay Mathis Rd.
Cartwright Rd.
Faithon P Lucas Sr Blvd.
Bois D'Arc St. S
Talty Rd.
College
Balch Springs
Elam Rd.
Belt Line Rd.
Lawson Rd.
Walnut Ln.
Pleasant Grove
Pioneer Rd.
Helms Tr.
Lawson
Markout
Seagoville Rd.
Rylie
Crest Dr.
Fireside Dr.
Ravenview Rd.
Lasater Rd.
Rylie
Edd Rd.
Belt Line Rd.
Woody Rd.
Lyndon B. Johnson Fwy.
Teagarden Rd.
Jordan Valley Rd.
Kleberg
Ard Rd.
Simonds Rd.
Alto Rd.
KAUFMAN COUNTY
Cleveland Rd.
Perry Rd.
Dowdy
Bobwyn
N
DALLAS COUNTY
Beckett Rd.
Seagoville
S. Kaufman St.
Bowers Rd.
Combine Rd.
Crandall
Fulghum Rd.
Post Oak Rd.
Pleasant Run Rd.
Trinity River
Bilindsay Rd.
Hunter Ln.
Gastonia
Run Rd.
Belt Line Rd.
Malloy Bridge Rd.
Bois D'Arc Rd.
Combine
Wilmer
Mars Rd.
Gravel Slough
Combine
Patrick
0 1 MILE
0 1 KILOMETER

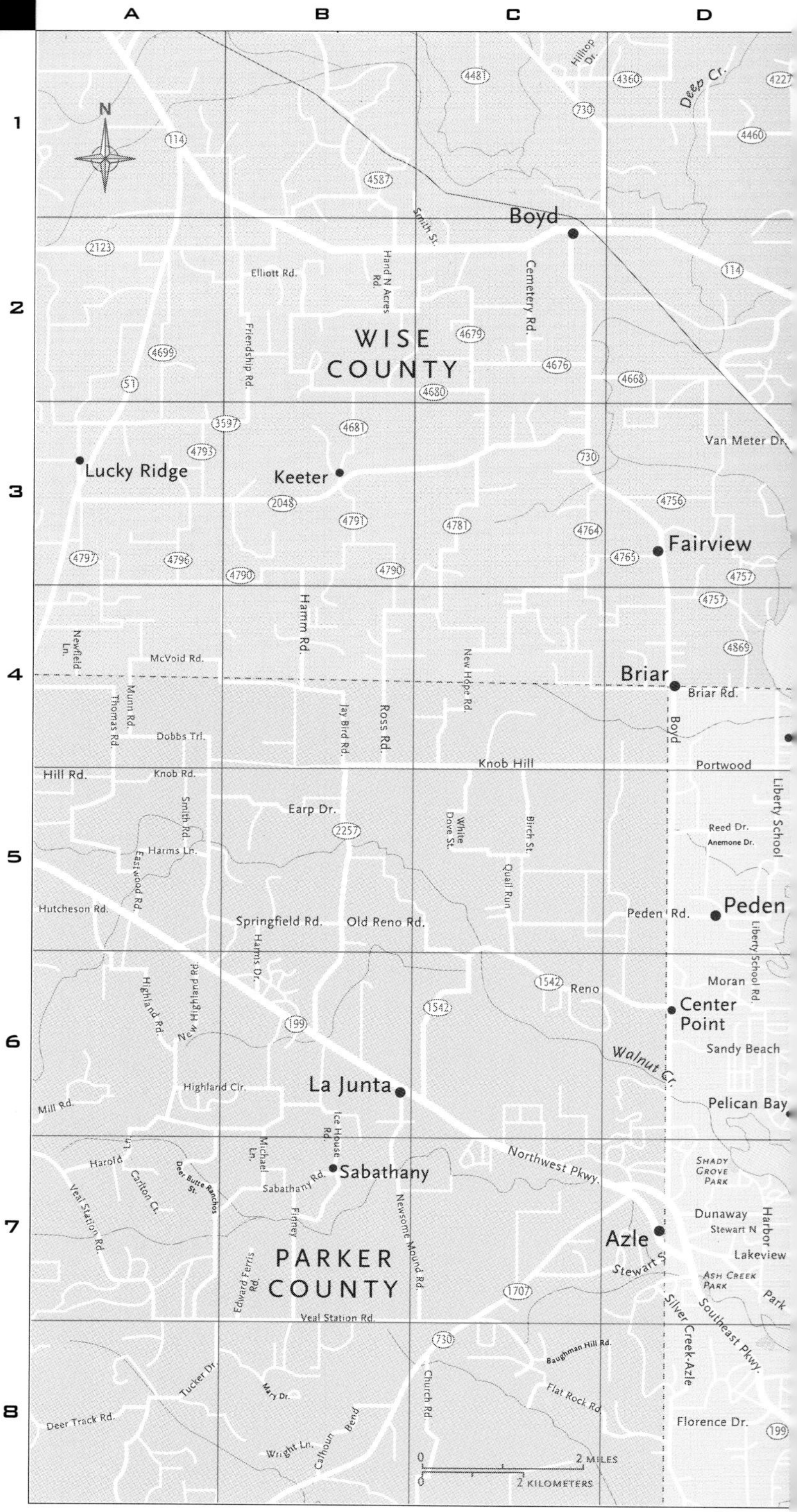
A
B
C
D
1
2
3
4
5
6
7
8
N
Boyd
WISE COUNTY
Lucky Ridge
Keeter
Fairview
Briar
Peden
Center Point
La Junta
Sabathany
Azle
PARKER COUNTY
Reno
Moran
Sandy Beach
Pelican Bay
Dunaway
Stewart N
Lakeview
Shady Grove Park
Ash Creek Park
Harbor Park
Deep Cr.
Walnut Cr.
Hilltop Dr.
Smith St.
Elliott Rd.
Hand N Acres Rd.
Cemetery Rd.
Friendship Rd.
Van Meter Dr.
Newfield Ln.
McVoid Rd.
Munn Rd.
Thomas Rd.
Dobbs Trl.
Hamm Rd.
Jay Bird Rd.
Ross Rd.
New Hope Rd.
Briar Rd.
Boyd
Hill Rd.
Knob Rd.
Knob Hill
Portwood
Liberty School
Smith Rd.
Earp Dr.
White Dove St.
Birch St.
Reed Dr.
Anemone Dr.
Harms Ln.
Eastwood Rd.
Quail Run
Hutcheson Rd.
Springfield Rd.
Old Reno Rd.
Peden Rd.
Liberty School Rd.
Harms Dr.
Highland Rd.
New Highland Rd.
Highland Cir.
Mill Rd.
Harold
Ln.
Carlton Ct.
Deer Butte Ranchos St.
Michael Ln.
Ice House Rd.
Sabathany Rd.
Northwest Pkwy.
Veal Station Rd.
Finney
Newsome Mound Rd.
Edward Ferris Rd.
Stewart St.
Silver Creek-Azle
Southeast Pkwy.
Veal Station Rd.
Baughman Hill Rd.
Flat Rock Rd.
Tucker Dr.
Church Rd.
Mary Dr.
Deer Track Rd.
Wright Ln.
Calhoun Bend
Florence Dr.
0
2 MILES
0
2 KILOMETERS
4481
4360
4227
730
4460
114
4587
2123
114
4679
4699
4676
4668
51
4680
3597
4681
4793
730
2048
4756
4791
4781
4764
4797
4796
4790
4790
4765
4757
4757
4869
2257
1542
1542
199
1707
730
199

Fodor's

CITYGUIDE DALLAS FT. WORTH AND THE MID-CITIES

Dear Terry,
I hope this guide leads to some fun times in your new home.
Love,
Sharon

FODOR'S TRAVEL PUBLICATIONS
NEW YORK • TORONTO • LONDON • SYDNEY • AUCKLAND
WWW.FODORS.COM

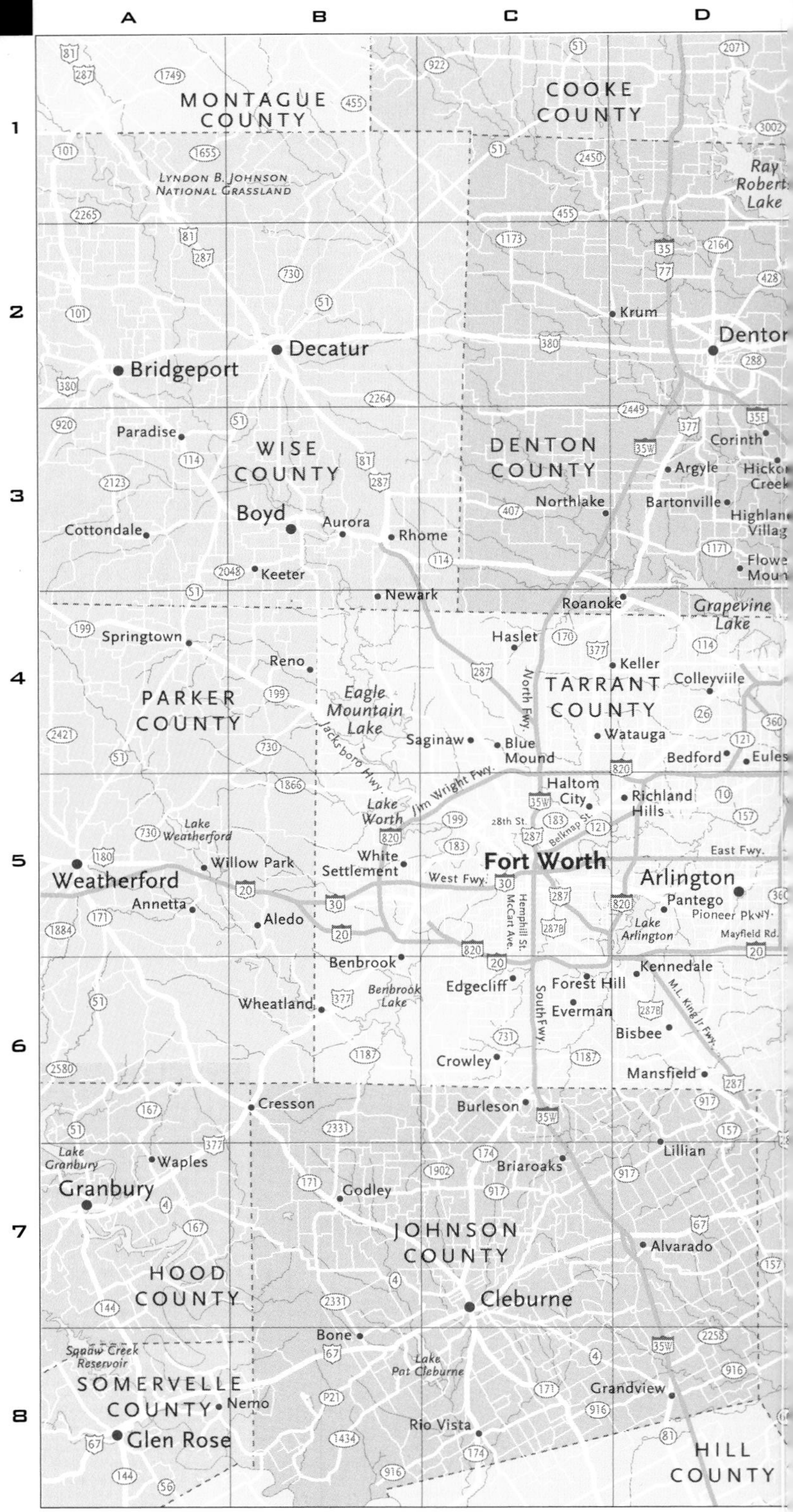
A
B
C
D
1
2
3
4
5
6
7
8
MONTAGUE COUNTY
COOKE COUNTY
LYNDON B. JOHNSON NATIONAL GRASSLAND
Ray Roberts Lake
Krum
Denton
Decatur
Bridgeport
WISE COUNTY
DENTON COUNTY
Paradise
Corinth
Argyle
Bartonville
Northlake
Boyd
Aurora
Rhome
Cottondale
Keeter
Newark
Roanoke
Grapevine Lake
Springtown
Haslet
Keller
Reno
Colleyville
PARKER COUNTY
Eagle Mountain Lake
TARRANT COUNTY
Jacksboro Hwy.
Saginaw
Blue Mound
Watauga
Bedford
North Fwy.
Jim Wright Fwy.
Haltom City
Richland Hills
Lake Worth
Lake Weatherford
28th St.
Belknap St.
East Fwy.
Weatherford
Willow Park
White Settlement
Fort Worth
Arlington
West Fwy.
Annetta
Pantego
Pioneer Pkwy.
Aledo
Hemphill St.
McCart Ave.
Lake Arlington
Mayfield Rd.
Benbrook
Kennedale
Edgecliff
Forest Hill
Wheatland
Benbrook Lake
Everman
South Fwy.
M.L. King Jr. Fwy.
Bisbee
Crowley
Mansfield
Cresson
Burleson
Lillian
Lake Granbury
Waples
Briaroaks
Granbury
Godley
JOHNSON COUNTY
Alvarado
HOOD COUNTY
Cleburne
Bone
Squaw Creek Reservoir
Lake Pat Cleburne
SOMERVELLE COUNTY
Grandview
Nemo
Glen Rose
Rio Vista
HILL COUNTY

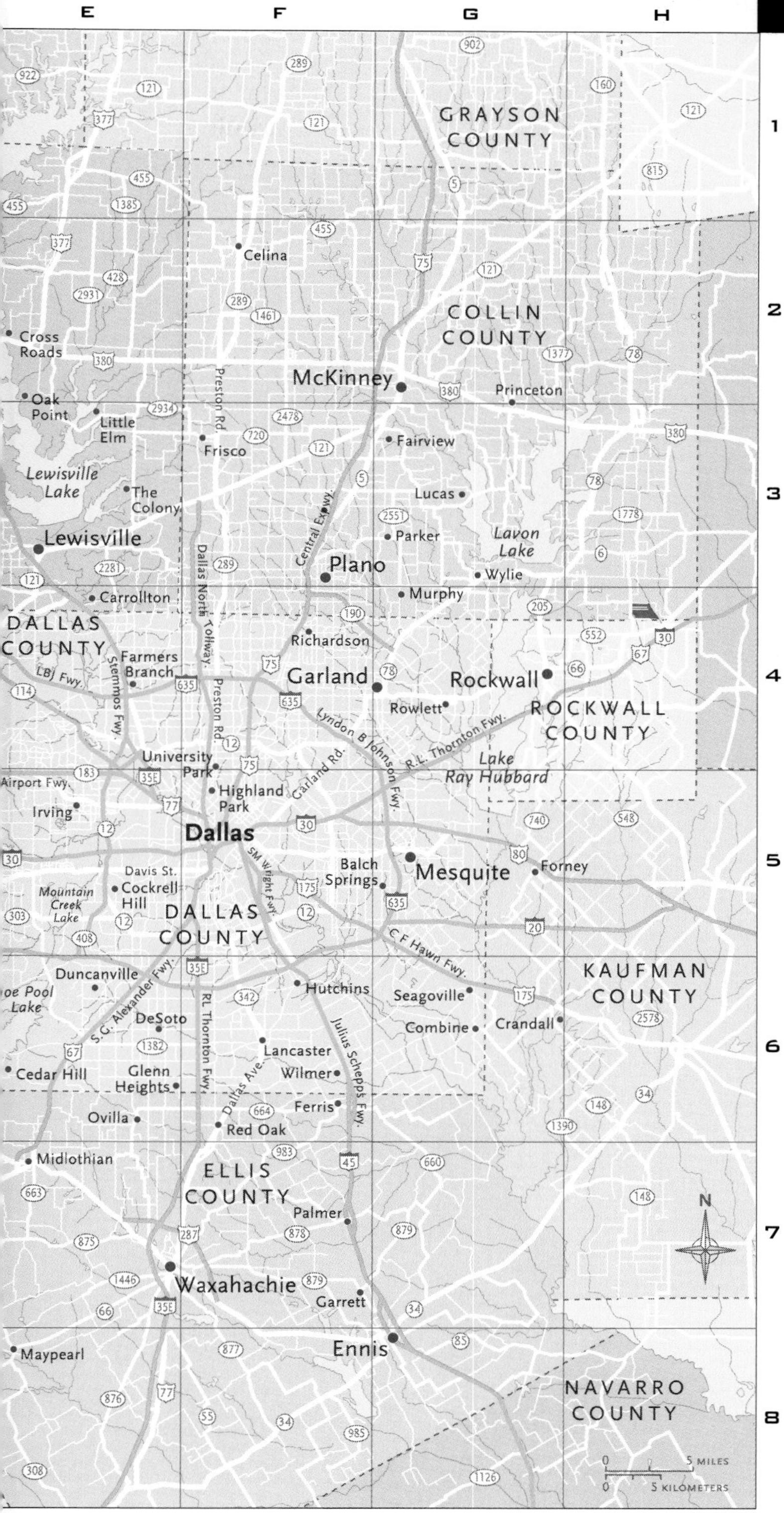
E
F
G
H
1
2
3
4
5
6
7
8
GRAYSON COUNTY
COLLIN COUNTY
DALLAS COUNTY
ROCKWALL COUNTY
KAUFMAN COUNTY
ELLIS COUNTY
NAVARRO COUNTY
Celina
Cross Roads
McKinney
Princeton
Oak Point
Little Elm
Frisco
Fairview
Lewisville Lake
The Colony
Lucas
Lewisville
Parker
Lavon Lake
Plano
Wylie
Carrollton
Murphy
Richardson
Farmers Branch
Garland
Rockwall
Rowlett
University Park
Highland Park
Lake Ray Hubbard
Irving
Dallas
Balch Springs
Mesquite
Forney
Cockrell Hill
Mountain Creek Lake
Duncanville
Hutchins
Seagoville
Combine
Crandall
DeSoto
Lancaster
Wilmer
Cedar Hill
Glenn Heights
Ferris
Ovilla
Red Oak
Midlothian
Palmer
Waxahachie
Garrett
Ennis
Maypearl
Preston Rd.
Dallas North Tollway
Central Expwy.
LBJ Fwy.
Stemmons Fwy.
Lyndon B Johnson Fwy.
R.L. Thornton Fwy.
Garland Rd.
Airport Fwy.
SM Wright Fwy.
Davis St.
C F Hawn Fwy.
S.G. Alexander Fwy.
R.L. Thornton Fwy.
Dallas Ave.
Julius Schepps Fwy.
N
0 5 MILES
0 5 KILOMETERS

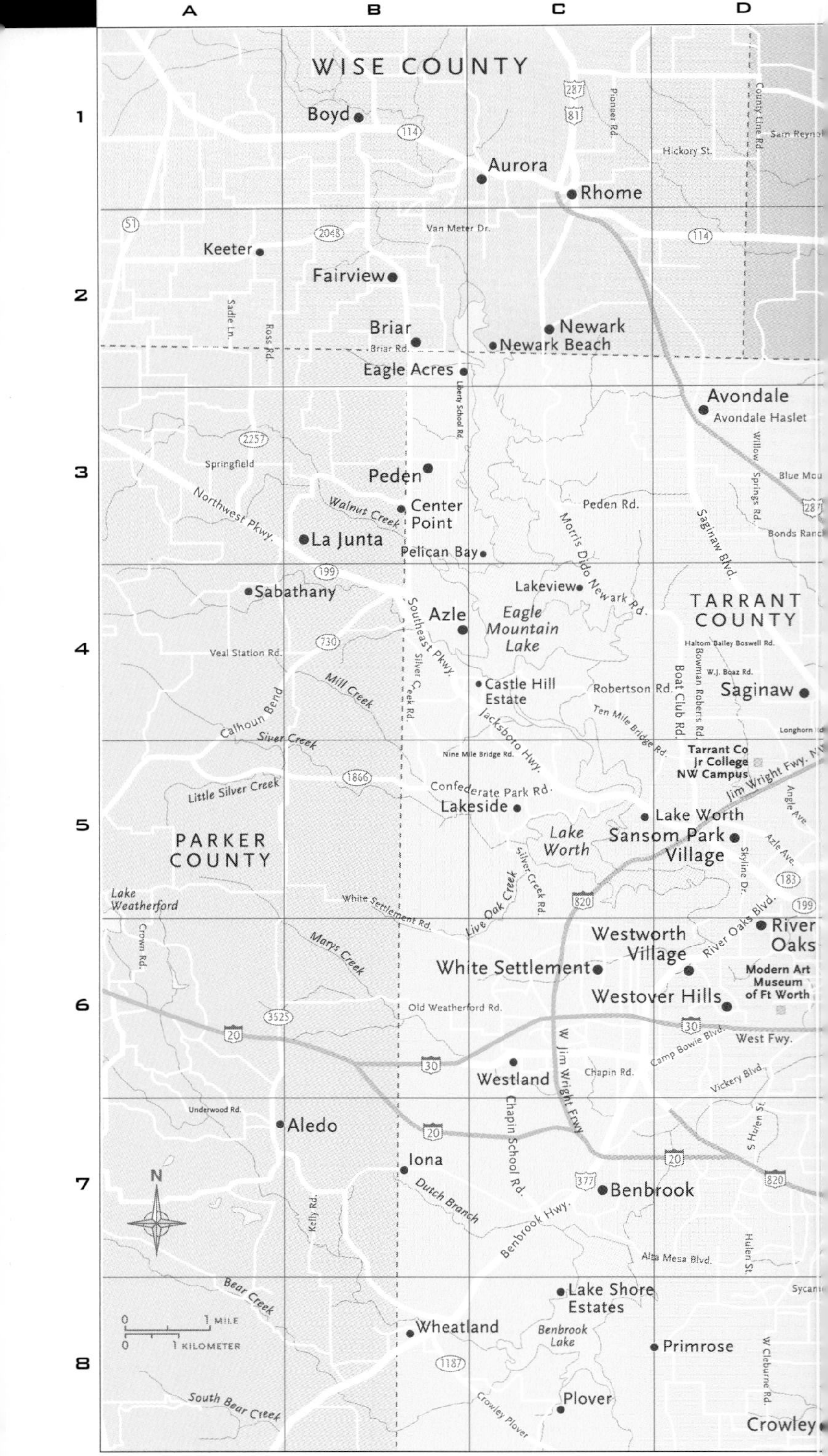
A
B
C
D
1
2
3
4
5
6
7
8
WISE COUNTY
Boyd
Aurora
Rhome
Keeter
Fairview
Briar
Newark
Newark Beach
Eagle Acres
Avondale
Avondale Haslet
Springfield
Peden
Center Point
La Junta
Pelican Bay
Sabathany
Lakeview
Azle
Eagle Mountain Lake
TARRANT COUNTY
Saginaw
Castle Hill Estate
Tarrant Co Jr College NW Campus
Lakeside
Lake Worth
Sansom Park Village
Lake Worth
PARKER COUNTY
Lake Weatherford
River Oaks
Westworth Village
White Settlement
Modern Art Museum of Ft Worth
Westover Hills
Westland
Aledo
Iona
Benbrook
Lake Shore Estates
Wheatland
Benbrook Lake
Primrose
Plover
Crowley
Van Meter Dr.
Hickory St.
Pioneer Rd.
County Line Rd.
Sam Reynol
Sadie Ln.
Ross Rd.
Briar Rd.
Liberty School Rd.
Northwest Pkwy.
Walnut Creek
Peden Rd.
Morris Dido Newark Rd.
Saginaw Blvd.
Willow Springs Rd.
Blue Mou
Bonds Ranc
Southeast Pkwy.
Silver Creek Rd.
Veal Station Rd.
Mill Creek
Halton Bailey Boswell Rd.
Bowman Roberts Rd.
W.J. Boaz Rd.
Boat Club Rd.
Robertson Rd.
Ten Mile Bridge Rd.
Jacksboro Hwy.
Calhoun Bend
Silver Creek
Longhorn
Nine Mile Bridge Rd.
Jim Wright Fwy. NW
Confederate Park Rd.
Little Silver Creek
Angle Ave.
Azle Ave.
Skyline Dr.
Silver Creek Rd.
Live Oak Creek
White Settlement Rd.
River Oaks Blvd.
Crown Rd.
Marys Creek
Old Weatherford Rd.
Camp Bowie Blvd.
West Fwy.
W Jim Wright Frwy
Chapin Rd.
Vickery Blvd.
Underwood Rd.
Chapin School Rd.
Hulen St.
S Hulen St.
Dutch Branch
Kelly Rd.
Benbrook Hwy.
Alta Mesa Blvd.
Sycam
Bear Creek
W Cleburne Rd.
South Bear Creek
Crowley Plover
N
0
1 MILE
0
1 KILOMETER
287
81
114
51
2048
2257
199
730
1866
183
820
3525
20
30
377
1187

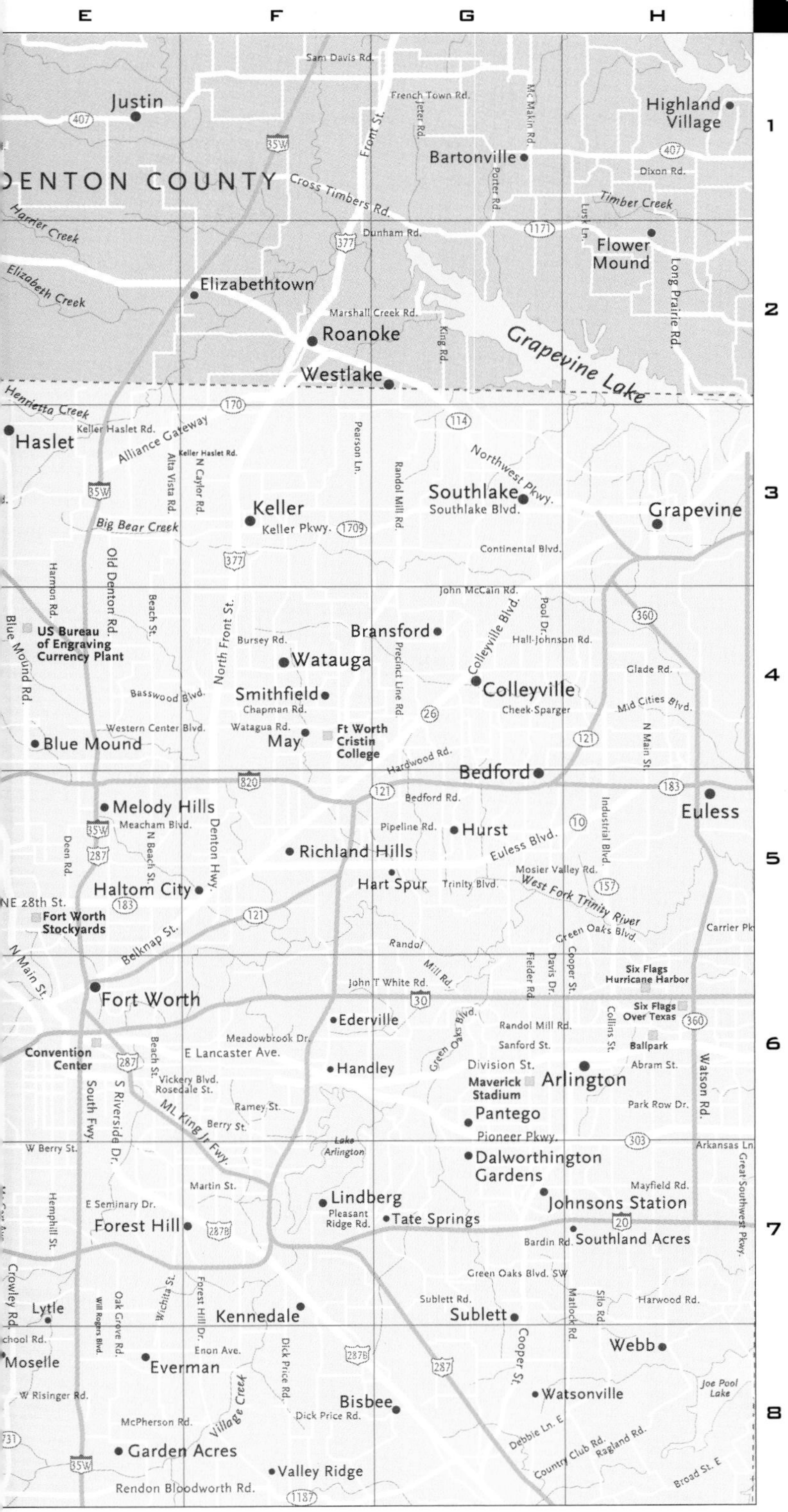
E
F
G
H
1
2
3
4
5
6
7
8
DENTON COUNTY
Justin
Highland Village
Bartonville
Flower Mound
Elizabethtown
Roanoke
Westlake
Grapevine Lake
Haslet
Keller
Southlake
Grapevine
Bransford
Watauga
Colleyville
Smithfield
May
Blue Mound
US Bureau of Engraving Currency Plant
Ft Worth Cristin College
Bedford
Euless
Melody Hills
Hurst
Richland Hills
Hart Spur
Haltom City
Fort Worth Stockyards
Fort Worth
Ederville
Convention Center
Handley
Arlington
Maverick Stadium
Pantego
Six Flags Hurricane Harbor
Six Flags Over Texas
Ballpark
Dalworthington Gardens
Johnsons Station
Lindberg
Tate Springs
Southland Acres
Forest Hill
Lake Arlington
Lytle
Kennedale
Sublett
Webb
Moselle
Everman
Bisbee
Watsonville
Joe Pool Lake
Garden Acres
Valley Ridge
Sam Davis Rd.
French Town Rd.
Jeter Rd.
Mc Makin Rd.
Front St.
Cross Timbers Rd.
Dixon Rd.
Timber Creek
Porter Rd.
Lusk Ln.
Dunham Rd.
Harrier Creek
Elizabeth Creek
Long Prairie Rd.
Marshall Creek Rd.
King Rd.
Henrietta Creek
Keller Haslet Rd.
Alliance Gateway
Pearson Ln.
Randol Mill Rd.
Northwest Pkwy.
Southlake Blvd.
Alta Vista Rd.
N Caylor Rd.
Big Bear Creek
Keller Pkwy.
Continental Blvd.
Old Denton Rd.
Harmon Rd.
Beach St.
North Front St.
John McCain Rd.
Colleyville Blvd.
Pool Dr.
Hall-Johnson Rd.
Blue Mound Rd.
Bursey Rd.
Precinct Line Rd.
Glade Rd.
Mid Cities Blvd.
Basswood Blvd.
Chapman Rd.
Cheek-Sparger
Western Center Blvd.
Watagua Rd.
N Main St.
Hardwood Rd.
Bedford Rd.
Meacham Blvd.
Denton Hwy.
Pipeline Rd.
Industrial Blvd.
Euless Blvd.
Deen Rd.
N Beach St.
Mosier Valley Rd.
Trinity Blvd.
West Fork Trinity River
NE 28th St.
Green Oaks Blvd.
Carrier Pk
Belknap St.
Randol
Mill Rd.
John T White Rd.
Fielder Rd.
Davis Dr.
Cooper St.
Meadowbrook Dr.
Green Oaks Blvd.
Randol Mill Rd.
Collins St.
E Lancaster Ave.
Sanford St.
Division St.
Abram St.
Vickery Blvd.
Rosedale St.
South Fwy.
S Riverside Dr.
ML King Jr Fwy.
Ramey St.
Berry St.
Park Row Dr.
Watson Rd.
Pioneer Pkwy.
W Berry St.
Arkansas Ln.
Great Southwest Pkwy.
Martin St.
Mayfield Rd.
E Seminary Dr.
Hemphill St.
Pleasant Ridge Rd.
Bardin Rd.
Green Oaks Blvd. SW
Crowley Rd.
Will Rogers Blvd.
Oak Grove Rd.
Wichita St.
Forest Hill Dr.
Sublett Rd.
Matlock Rd.
Silo Rd.
Harwood Rd.
Enon Ave.
Dick Price Rd.
W Risinger Rd.
McPherson Rd.
Village Creek
Debbie Ln. E
Country Club Rd.
Ragland Rd.
Broad St. E
Rendon Bloodworth Rd.
407
35W
1171
377
170
114
1709
360
26
121
820
183
10
287
157
30
303
287B
20
1187
731

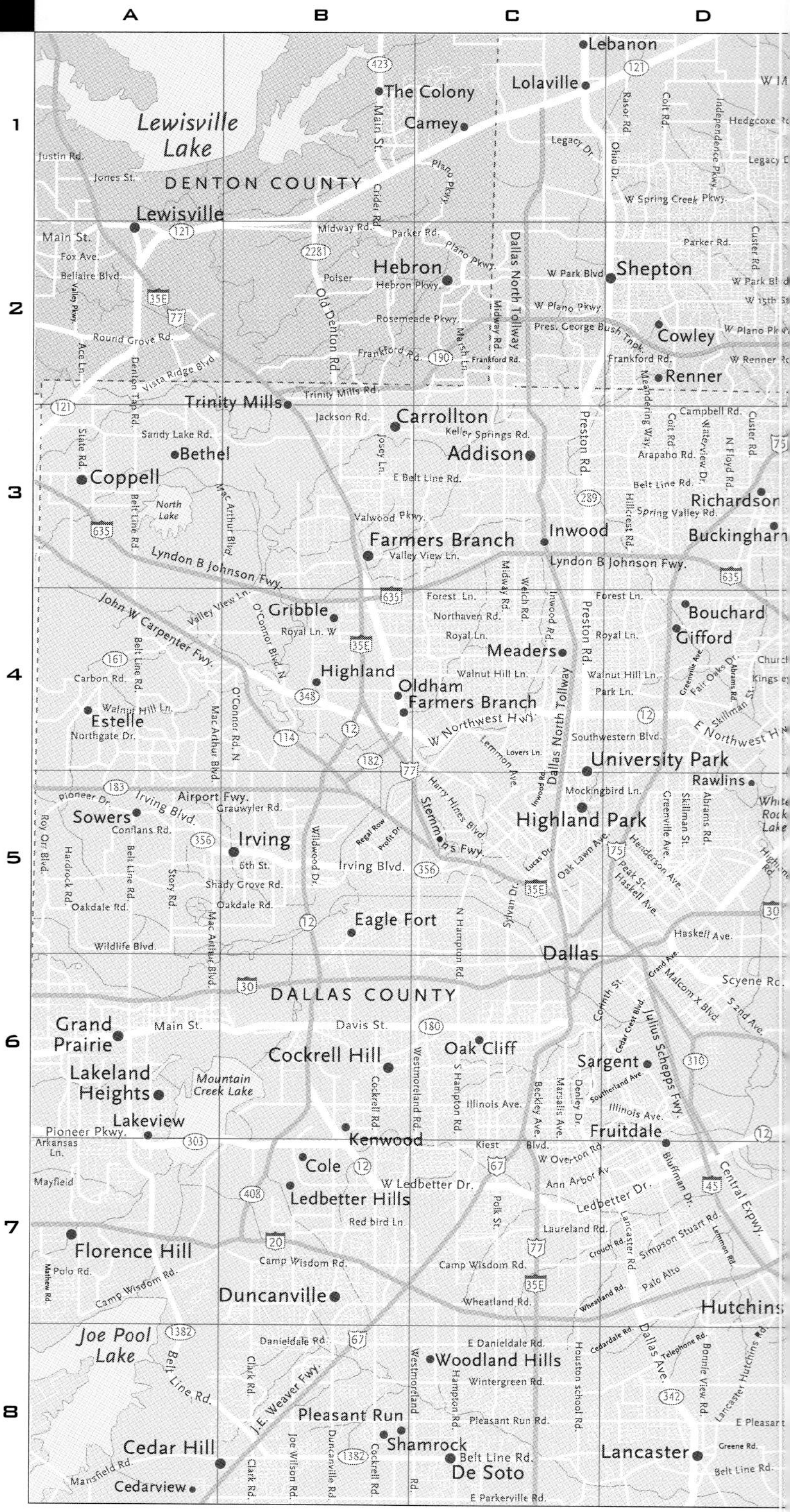
A
B
C
D
1
2
3
4
5
6
7
8
Lewisville Lake
DENTON COUNTY
Lebanon
Lolaville
The Colony
Carney
Lewisville
Hebron
Shepton
Cowley
Renner
Trinity Mills
Carrollton
Addison
Bethel
Coppell
North Lake
Farmers Branch
Inwood
Richardson
Buckingham
Gribble
Bouchard
Gifford
Meaders
Highland
Oldham
Farmers Branch
Estelle
University Park
Rawlins
White Rock Lake
Sowers
Irving
Highland Park
Eagle Fort
Dallas
DALLAS COUNTY
Grand Prairie
Oak Cliff
Cockrell Hill
Sargent
Lakeland Heights
Mountain Creek Lake
Lakeview
Fruitdale
Kenwood
Cole
Ledbetter Hills
Florence Hill
Duncanville
Hutchins
Joe Pool Lake
Woodland Hills
Pleasant Run
Shamrock
Cedar Hill
De Soto
Lancaster
Cedarview
Justin Rd.
Jones St.
Main St.
Fox Ave.
Bellaire Blvd.
Valley Pkwy.
Round Grove Rd.
Ace Ln.
Denton Tap Rd.
Vista Ridge Blvd.
Midway Rd.
Parker Rd.
Plano Pkwy.
Crider Rd.
Main St.
Polser
Hebron Pkwy.
Old Denton Rd.
Rosemeade Pkwy.
Frankford Rd.
Marsh Ln.
Midway Rd.
Dallas North Tollway
Legacy Dr.
Rasor Rd.
Ohio Dr.
Coit Rd.
Independence Pkwy.
Hedgcoxe Rd.
W Spring Creek Pkwy.
W Park Blvd
W Plano Pkwy.
Pres. George Bush Tnpk.
Frankford Rd.
Meandering Way
Custer Rd.
W Renner Rd
Trinity Mills Rd.
Jackson Rd.
Sandy Lake Rd.
Keller Springs Rd.
Josey Ln.
State Rd.
Belt Line Rd.
Mac Arthur Blvd.
E Belt Line Rd.
Valwood Pkwy.
Valley View Ln.
Lyndon B Johnson Fwy.
Preston Rd.
Campbell Rd.
Coit Rd.
Waterview Dr.
N Floyd Rd.
Arapaho Rd.
Belt Line Rd.
Hillcrest Rd.
Spring Valley Rd.
John W Carpenter Fwy.
Valley View Ln.
O'Connor Blvd. N
Royal Ln. W
Forest Ln.
Northaven Rd.
Royal Ln.
Midway Rd.
Welch Rd.
Inwood Rd.
Walnut Hill Ln.
Park Ln.
Greenville Ave.
Fair Oaks Dr.
Abrams Rd.
E Skillman St.
Carbon Rd.
Walnut Hill Ln.
Northgate Dr.
O'Connor Rd. N
W Northwest Hwy.
E Northwest Hwy
Lemmon Ave.
Lovers Ln.
Southwestern Blvd.
Harry Hines Blvd.
Stemmons Fwy.
Mockingbird Ln.
Skillman St.
Abrams Rd.
Pioneer Dr.
Irving Blvd.
Airport Fwy.
Grauwyler Rd.
Conflans Rd.
Roy Orr Blvd.
Hardrock Rd.
Story Rd.
6th St.
Shady Grove Rd.
Oakdale Rd.
Wildwood Dr.
Regal Row
Profit Dr.
Irving Blvd.
Lucas Dr.
Oak Lawn Ave.
Peak St.
Haskell Ave.
Henderson Ave.
Sylvan Dr.
N Hampton Rd.
Haskell Ave.
Wildlife Blvd.
Scyene Rd.
Grand Ave.
Malcom X Blvd.
S 2nd Ave.
Corinth St.
Cedar Crest Blvd.
Julius Schepps Fwy.
Main St.
Davis St.
Westmoreland Rd.
S Hampton Rd.
Cockrell Rd.
Illinois Ave.
Beckley Ave.
Marsalis Ave.
Denley Dr.
Southerland Ave.
Pioneer Pkwy.
Arkansas Ln.
Mayfield
Kiest Blvd.
W Overton Rd.
Bluffman Dr.
Central Expwy.
W Ledbetter Dr.
Ann Arbor Av
Ledbetter Dr.
Red bird Ln.
Polk St.
Laureland Rd.
Crouch Rd.
Lancaster Rd.
Simpson Stuart Rd.
Lemmon Rd.
Polo Rd.
Mathew Rd.
Camp Wisdom Rd.
Camp Wisdom Rd.
Camp Wisdom Rd.
Wheatland Rd.
Wheatland Rd.
Palo Alto
Danieldale Rd.
E Danieldale Rd.
Cedardale Rd.
Telephone Rd.
Bonnie View Rd.
Lancaster Hutchins Rd.
Belt Line Rd.
Clark Rd.
J.E. Weaver Fwy.
Westmoreland
Hampton Rd.
Wintergreen Rd.
Houston school Rd.
Dallas Ave.
Pleasant Run Rd.
E Pleasant Run
Greene Rd.
Mansfield Rd.
Joe Wilson Rd.
Duncanville Rd.
Cockrell Rd.
Belt Line Rd.
E Parkerville Rd.
Belt Line Rd.
Church
Kingsley

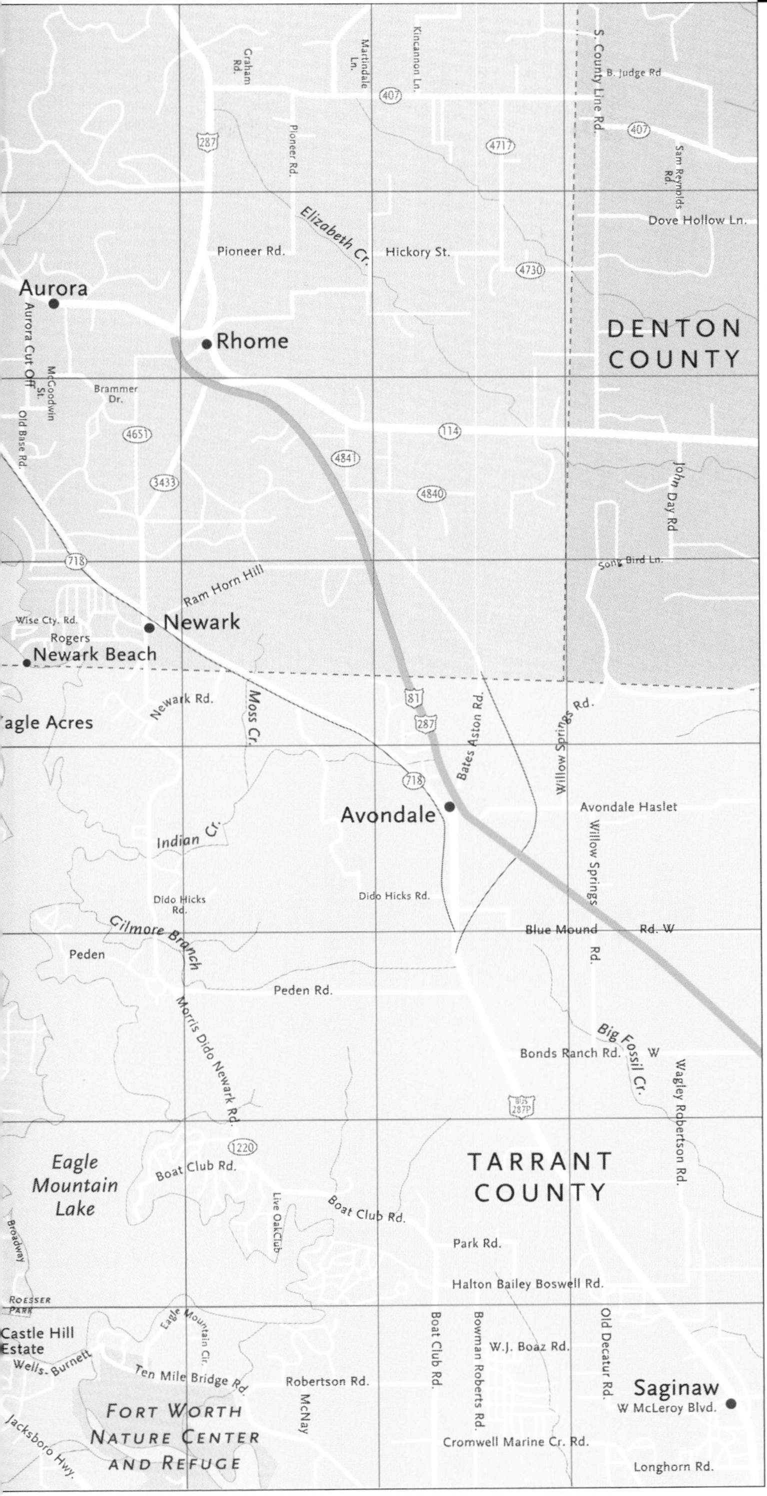
E
F
G
H
1
2
3
4
5
6
7
8
Graham Rd.
Martindale Ln.
Kincannon Ln.
S. County Line Rd.
B. Judge Rd
407
287
Pioneer Rd.
4717
Sam Reynolds Rd.
Dove Hollow Ln.
Elizabeth Cr.
Pioneer Rd.
Hickory St.
4730
Aurora
Aurora Cut Off
Rhome
DENTON COUNTY
McGoodwin St.
Brammer Dr.
Old Base Rd.
4651
114
4841
3433
4840
John Day Rd
718
Song Bird Ln.
Ram Horn Hill
Wise Cty. Rd.
Newark
Rogers
Newark Beach
Newark Rd.
Moss Cr.
81
287
Bates Aston Rd.
Willow Springs Rd.
'agle Acres
Avondale
Avondale Haslet
Willow Springs Rd.
Indian Cr.
Dido Hicks Rd.
Dido Hicks Rd.
Gilmore Branch
Blue Mound Rd. W
Peden
Peden Rd.
Morris Dido Newark Rd.
Big Fossil Cr.
Bonds Ranch Rd. W
Wagley Robertson Rd.
BUS 287P
1220
Eagle Mountain Lake
Boat Club Rd.
TARRANT COUNTY
Live Oak Club
Boat Club Rd.
Broadway
Park Rd.
Halton Bailey Boswell Rd.
ROESSER PARK
Castle Hill Estate
Eagle Mountain Cir.
Boat Club Rd.
Bowman Roberts Rd.
W.J. Boaz Rd.
Old Decatur Rd.
Wells-Burnett
Ten Mile Bridge Rd.
Robertson Rd.
Saginaw
W McLeroy Blvd.
FORT WORTH NATURE CENTER AND REFUGE
McNay
Cromwell Marine Cr. Rd.
Jacksboro Hwy.
Longhorn Rd.

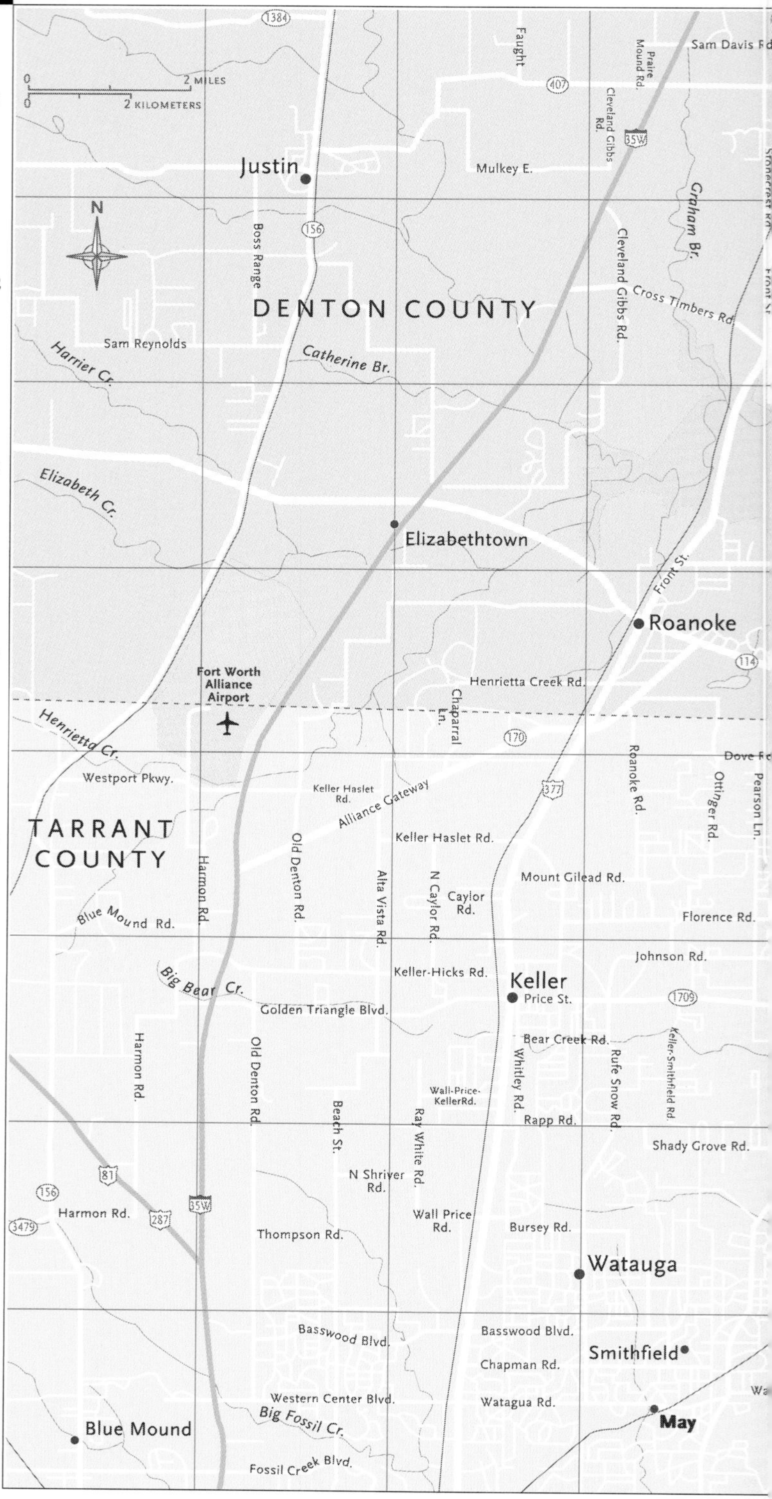
A
B
C
D
1
2
3
4
5
6
7
8
0
2 MILES
0
2 KILOMETERS
N
Justin
DENTON COUNTY
Elizabethtown
Roanoke
Fort Worth Alliance Airport
TARRANT COUNTY
Keller
Watauga
Smithfield
May
Blue Mound
Faught
Prairie Mound Rd.
Sam Davis Rd
Cleveland Gibbs Rd.
Mulkey E.
Graham Br.
Boss Range
Cleveland Gibbs Rd.
Cross Timbers Rd
Sam Reynolds
Harrier Cr.
Catherine Br.
Elizabeth Cr.
Front St.
Henrietta Creek Rd.
Chaparral Ln.
Henrietta Cr.
Westport Pkwy.
Keller Haslet Rd.
Alliance Gateway
Dove Rd
Roanoke Rd.
Ottinger Rd.
Pearson Ln.
Keller Haslet Rd.
Harmon Rd.
Old Denton Rd.
Alta Vista Rd.
N Caylor Rd.
Caylor Rd.
Mount Gilead Rd.
Florence Rd.
Blue Mound Rd.
Johnson Rd.
Big Bear Cr.
Keller-Hicks Rd.
Price St.
Golden Triangle Blvd.
Bear Creek Rd.
Harmon Rd.
Old Denton Rd.
Wall-Price-Keller Rd.
Whitley Rd.
Rufe Snow Rd.
Keller-Smithfield Rd.
Beach St.
Ray White Rd.
Rapp Rd.
Shady Grove Rd.
N Shriver Rd.
Harmon Rd.
Wall Price Rd.
Bursey Rd.
Thompson Rd.
Basswood Blvd.
Basswood Blvd.
Chapman Rd.
Western Center Blvd.
Watagua Rd.
Big Fossil Cr.
Fossil Creek Blvd.
1384
407
35W
156
170
377
114
1709
81
156
287
3479
35W

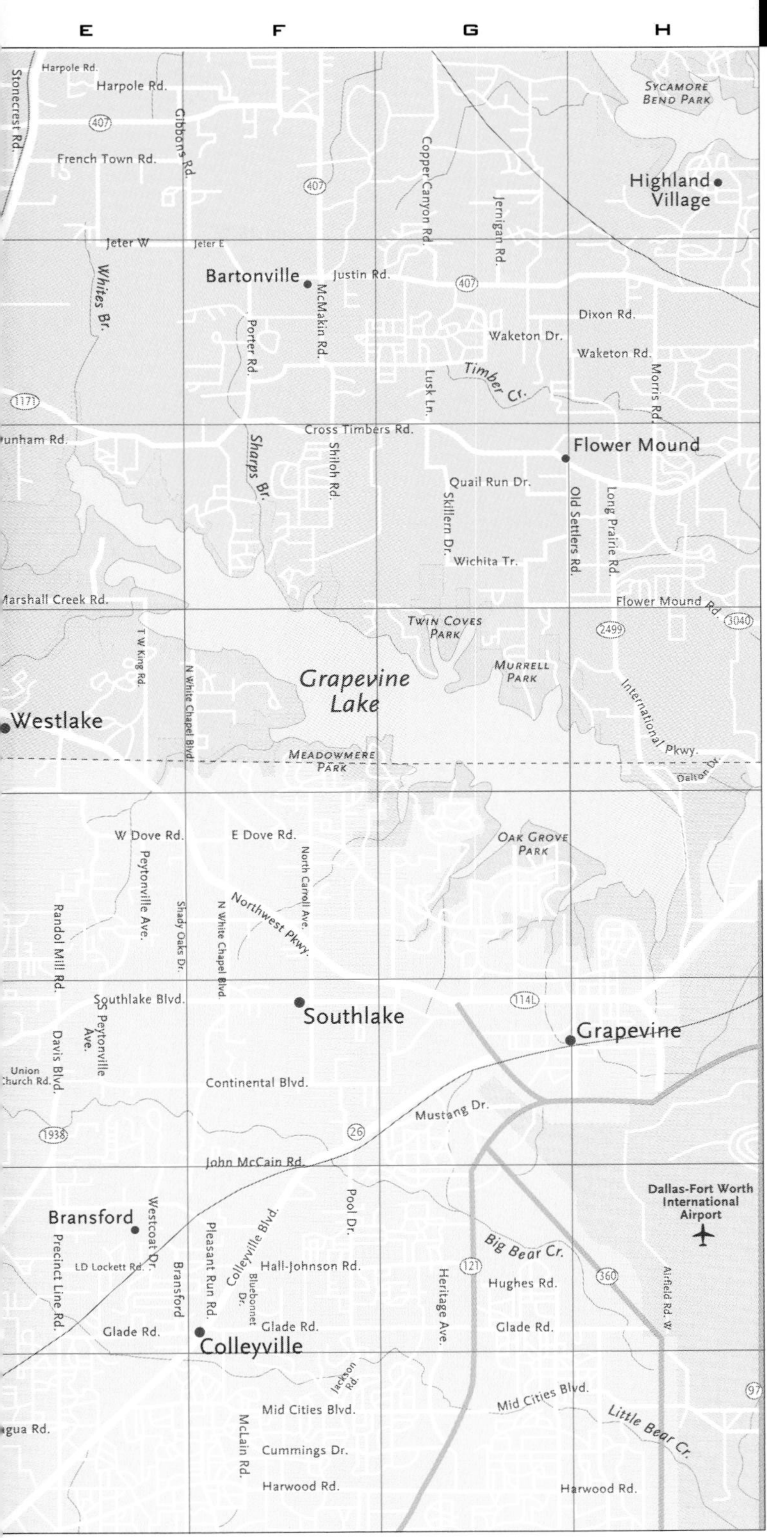
E
F
G
H
1
2
3
4
5
6
7
8
Harpole Rd.
Stonecrest Rd.
French Town Rd.
Gibbons Rd.
Copper Canyon Rd.
Jernigan Rd.
Sycamore Bend Park
Highland Village
Jeter W
Jeter E
Whites Br.
Bartonville
Justin Rd.
McMakin Rd.
Porter Rd.
Dixon Rd.
Waketon Dr.
Waketon Rd.
Timber Cr.
Lusk Ln.
Morris Rd.
Dunham Rd.
Cross Timbers Rd.
Sharps Br.
Shiloh Rd.
Flower Mound
Quail Run Dr.
Skillern Dr.
Old Settlers Rd.
Long Prairie Rd.
Wichita Tr.
Marshall Creek Rd.
Flower Mound Rd.
Twin Coves Park
Murrell Park
T W King Rd.
N White Chapel Blvd.
Grapevine Lake
International Pkwy.
Westlake
Meadowmere Park
Dalton Dr.
W Dove Rd.
E Dove Rd.
Oak Grove Park
Peytonville Ave.
North Carroll Ave.
Randol Mill Rd.
Shady Oaks Dr.
Northwest Pkwy.
Southlake Blvd.
Southlake
Grapevine
S Peytonville Ave.
Davis Blvd.
Union Church Rd.
Continental Blvd.
Mustang Dr.
John McCain Rd.
Pool Dr.
Dallas-Fort Worth International Airport
Bransford
Westcoat Dr.
Pleasant Run Rd.
Colleyville Blvd.
Big Bear Cr.
Precinct Line Rd.
LD Lockett Rd.
Hall-Johnson Rd.
Heritage Ave.
Hughes Rd.
Airfield Rd. W
Bluebonnet Dr.
Glade Rd.
Colleyville
Jackson Rd.
Mid Cities Blvd.
Little Bear Cr.
Cummings Dr.
McLain Rd.
Harwood Rd.
407
1171
2499
3040
114L
26
1938
121
360
97

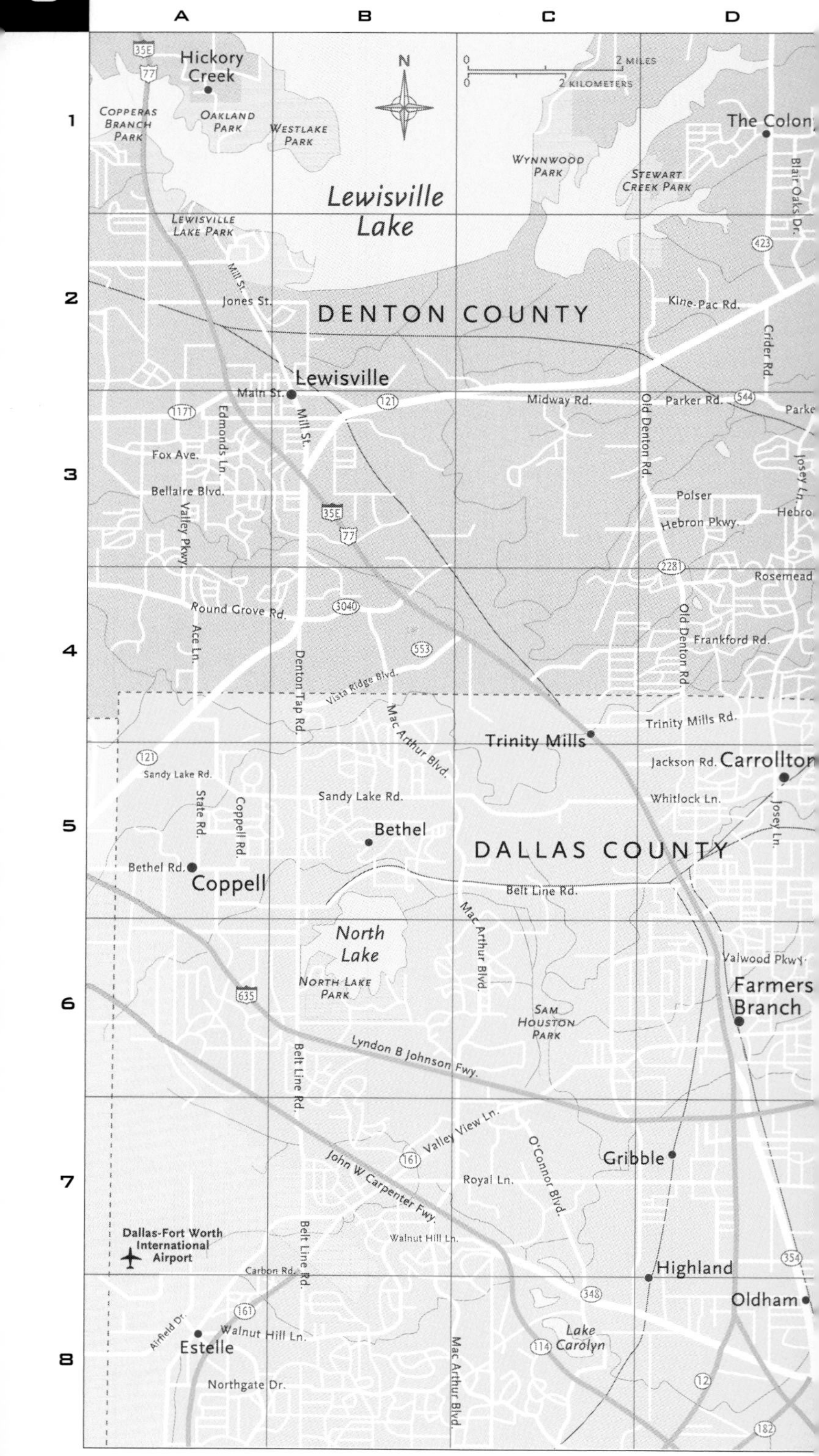
A
B
C
D
1
2
3
4
5
6
7
8
N
0 2 MILES
0 2 KILOMETERS
Hickory Creek
Copperas Branch Park
Oakland Park
Westlake Park
Lewisville Lake
Wynnwood Park
Stewart Creek Park
The Colony
Blair Oaks Dr.
Lewisville Lake Park
Mill St.
Jones St.
DENTON COUNTY
Kine-Pac Rd.
Crider Rd.
Lewisville
Main St.
Midway Rd.
Old Denton Rd.
Parker Rd.
Edmonds Ln.
Fox Ave.
Bellaire Blvd.
Valley Pkwy.
Polser
Hebron Pkwy.
Josey Ln.
Rosemead
Round Grove Rd.
Ace Ln.
Denton Tap Rd.
Frankford Rd.
Vista Ridge Blvd.
Mac Arthur Blvd.
Trinity Mills
Trinity Mills Rd.
Jackson Rd.
Carrollton
Sandy Lake Rd.
State Rd.
Coppell Rd.
Whitlock Ln.
Bethel
DALLAS COUNTY
Bethel Rd.
Coppell
Belt Line Rd.
North Lake
North Lake Park
Valwood Pkwy.
Farmers Branch
Sam Houston Park
Lyndon B Johnson Fwy.
Valley View Ln.
O'Connor Blvd.
Gribble
John W Carpenter Fwy.
Royal Ln.
Dallas-Fort Worth International Airport
Walnut Hill Ln.
Highland
Oldham
Carbon Rd.
Airfield Dr.
Estelle
Lake Carolyn
Northgate Dr.
35E
77
121
1171
423
544
2281
3040
553
635
161
348
114
354
12
182

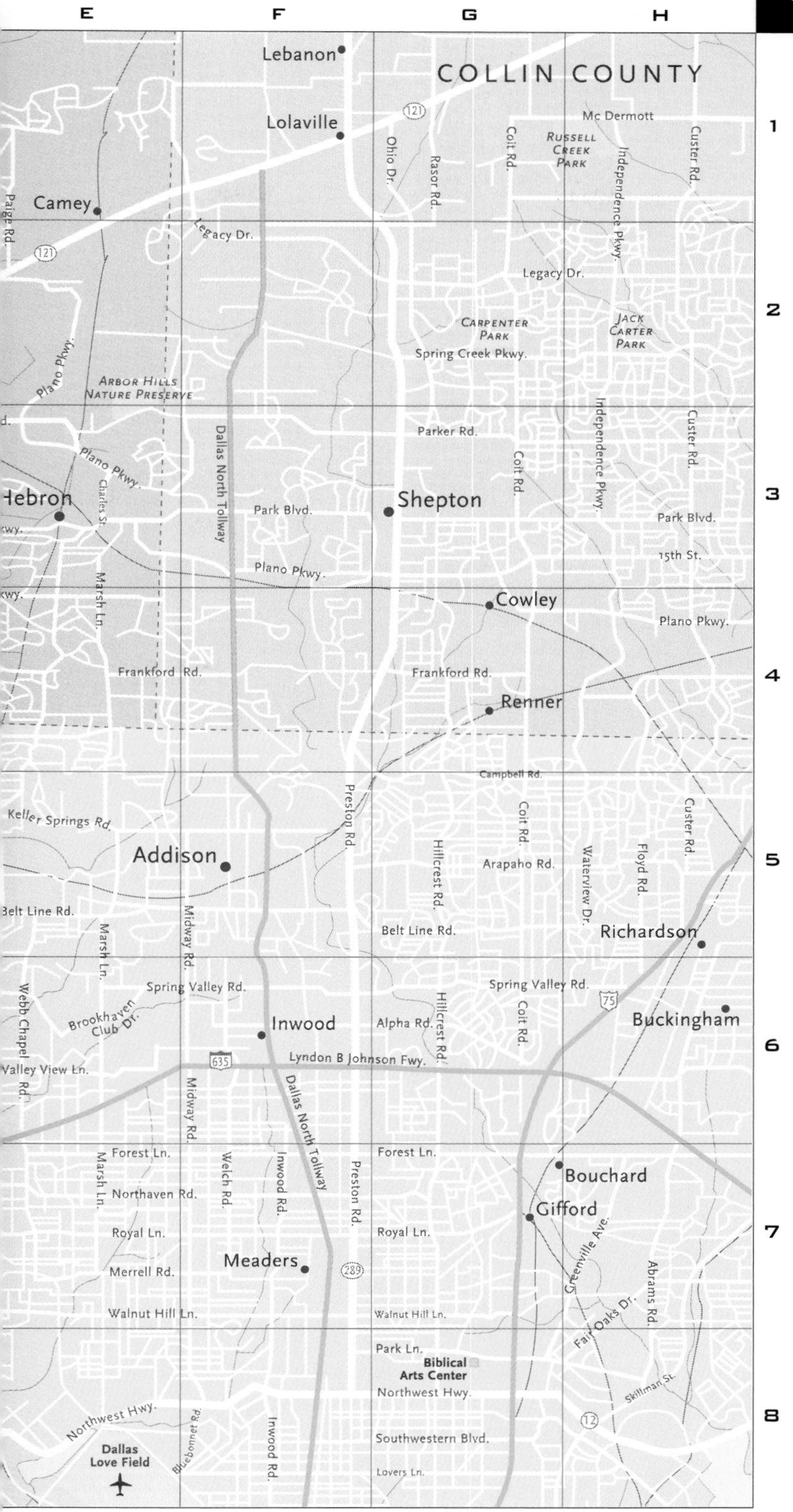
E
F
G
H
1
2
3
4
5
6
7
8
COLLIN COUNTY
Lebanon
Lolaville
Camey
Mc Dermott
Russell Creek Park
Ohio Dr.
Rasor Rd.
Coit Rd.
Independence Pkwy.
Custer Rd.
Paige Rd.
Legacy Dr.
121
Carpenter Park
Jack Carter Park
Spring Creek Pkwy.
Plano Pkwy.
Arbor Hills Nature Preserve
Parker Rd.
Dallas North Tollway
Hebron
Charles St.
Shepton
Park Blvd.
15th St.
Plano Pkwy.
Marsh Ln.
Cowley
Frankford Rd.
Renner
Campbell Rd.
Keller Springs Rd.
Preston Rd.
Hillcrest Rd.
Waterview Dr.
Floyd Rd.
Addison
Arapaho Rd.
Belt Line Rd.
Midway Rd.
Richardson
Spring Valley Rd.
Webb Chapel Rd.
Brookhaven Club Dr.
Inwood
Alpha Rd.
Buckingham
75
635
Lyndon B Johnson Fwy.
Valley View Ln.
Forest Ln.
Northaven Rd.
Welch Rd.
Inwood Rd.
Bouchard
Gifford
Royal Ln.
Greenville Ave.
Abrams Rd.
Meaders
289
Merrell Rd.
Walnut Hill Ln.
Fair Oaks Dr.
Park Ln.
Biblical Arts Center
Northwest Hwy.
Skillman St.
12
Southwestern Blvd.
Lovers Ln.
Bluebonnet Rd.
Dallas Love Field

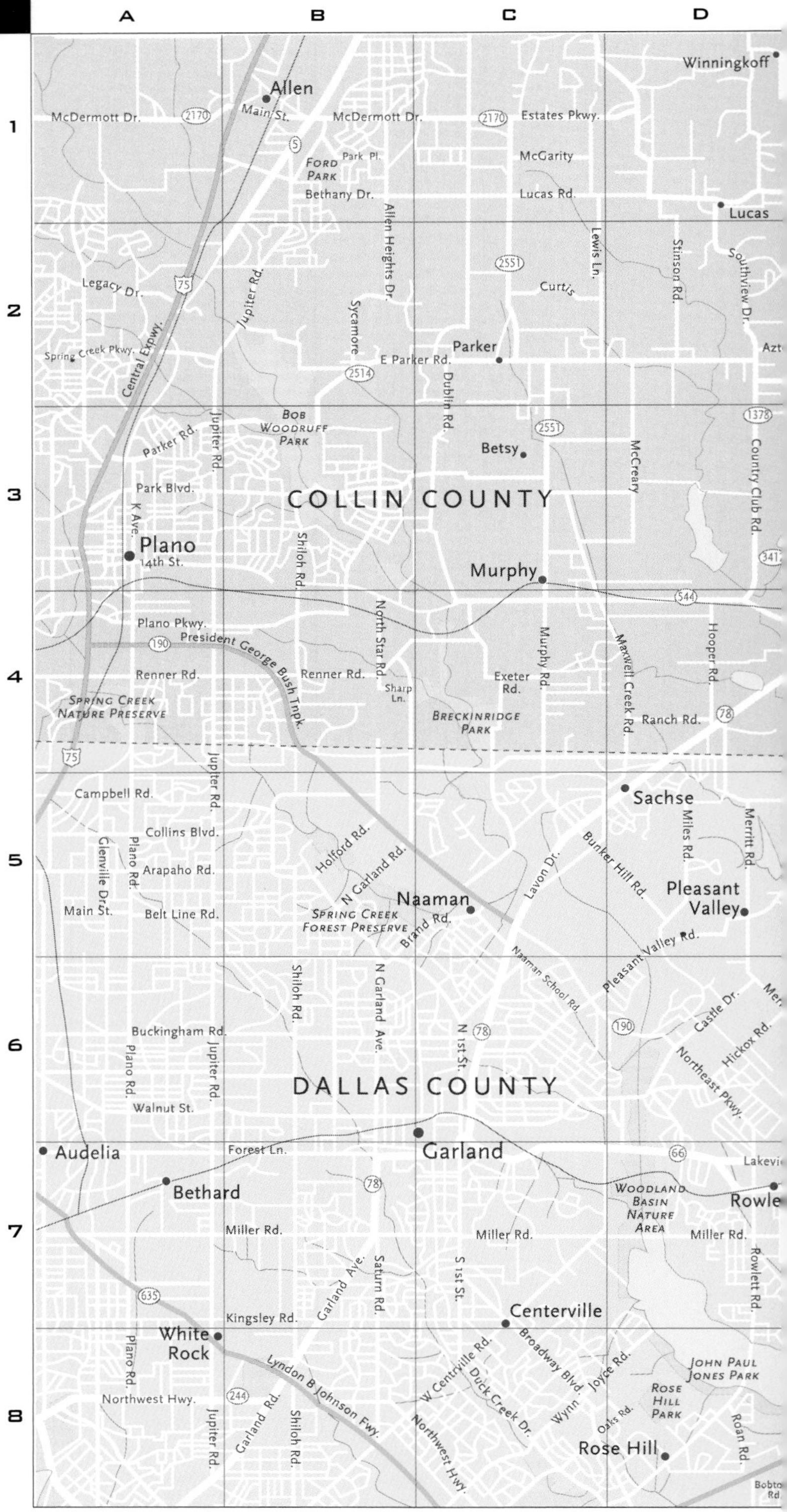
A
B
C
D
1
2
3
4
5
6
7
8
Allen
Winningkoff
McDermott Dr.
2170
Main St.
McDermott Dr.
2170
Estates Pkwy.
5
Ford Park
Park Pl.
McGarity
Bethany Dr.
Lucas Rd.
Lucas
Allen Heights Dr.
Lewis Ln.
Stinson Rd.
Southview Dr.
2551
Legacy Dr.
75
Jupiter Rd.
Curtis
Sycamore
Central Expwy.
Spring Creek Pkwy.
Parker
E Parker Rd.
2514
Dublin Rd.
Bob Woodruff Park
2551
1378
Jupiter Rd.
Parker Rd.
Betsy
McCreary
Country Club Rd.
Park Blvd.
COLLIN COUNTY
K Ave.
Plano
14th St.
Shiloh Rd.
Murphy
544
North Star Rd.
Plano Pkwy.
President George Bush Tnpk.
190
Murphy Rd.
Maxwell Creek Rd.
Hooper Rd.
Renner Rd.
Renner Rd.
Exeter Rd.
Sharp Ln.
Spring Creek Nature Preserve
Breckinridge Park
Ranch Rd.
78
75
Jupiter Rd.
Campbell Rd.
Sachse
Collins Blvd.
Holford Rd.
Miles Rd.
Merritt Rd.
Glenville Dr.
Plano Rd.
Arapaho Rd.
N Garland Rd.
Bunker Hill Rd.
Lavon Dr.
Pleasant Valley
Main St.
Belt Line Rd.
Naaman
Spring Creek Forest Preserve
Brand Rd.
Pleasant Valley Rd.
Naaman School Rd.
Shiloh Rd.
N Garland Ave.
Castle Dr.
190
N 1st St.
78
Buckingham Rd.
Hickox Rd.
Plano Rd.
Jupiter Rd.
Northeast Pkwy.
DALLAS COUNTY
Walnut St.
Audelia
Forest Ln.
Garland
66
Bethard
78
Woodland Basin Nature Area
Rowle
Miller Rd.
Miller Rd.
Miller Rd.
Garland Ave.
Saturn Rd.
S 1st St.
Rowlett Rd.
635
Kingsley Rd.
Centerville
White Rock
Plano Rd.
Lyndon B Johnson Fwy.
W Centerville Rd.
Broadway Blvd.
Joyce Rd.
John Paul Jones Park
Duck Creek Dr.
Wynn
Rose Hill Park
Northwest Hwy.
244
Garland Rd.
Shiloh Rd.
Jupiter Rd.
Northwest Hwy.
Oaks Rd.
Rose Hill
Roan Rd.

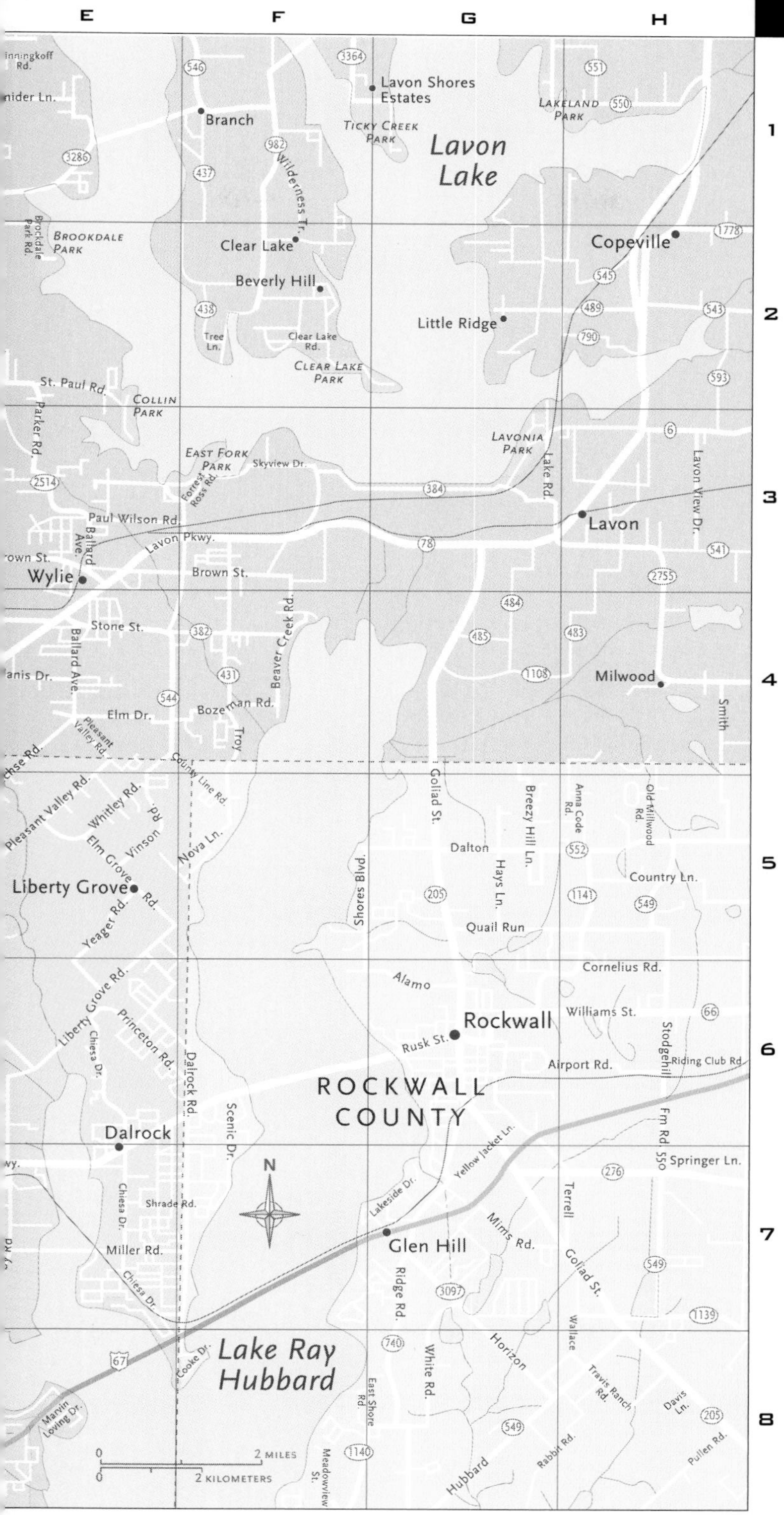
E
F
G
H
1
2
3
4
5
6
7
8
Lavon Shores Estates
Branch
Ticky Creek Park
Lakeland Park
Lavon Lake
Wilderness Tr.
Brookdale Park Rd.
Brookdale Park
Clear Lake
Beverly Hill
Copeville
Little Ridge
Tree Ln.
Clear Lake Rd.
Clear Lake Park
St. Paul Rd.
Collin Park
Parker Rd.
Lavonia Park
East Fork Park
Skyview Dr.
Forrest Ross Rd.
Lake Rd.
Lavon View Dr.
Paul Wilson Rd.
Ballard Ave.
Lavon Pkwy.
Lavon
Wylie
Brown St.
Beaver Creek Rd.
Stone St.
Ballard Ave.
Milwood
Elm Dr.
Bozeman Rd.
Pleasant Valley Rd.
Troy
Smith
County Line Rd.
Goliad St.
Breezy Hill Ln.
Anna Code Rd.
Old Millwood Rd.
Pleasant Valley Rd.
Whitley Rd.
Vinson Rd.
Nova Ln.
Elm Grove Rd.
Dalton
Hays Ln.
Country Ln.
Liberty Grove
Yeager Rd.
Shores Blvd.
Quail Run
Cornelius Rd.
Alamo
Liberty Grove Rd.
Princeton Rd.
Chiesa Dr.
Williams St.
Rockwall
Rusk St.
Stodgehill
Riding Club Rd
Airport Rd.
Dalrock Rd.
Scenic Dr.
ROCKWALL COUNTY
Fm Rd. 550
Dalrock
Yellow Jacket Ln.
Springer Ln.
N
Chiesa Dr.
Shrade Rd.
Lakeside Dr.
Terrell
Mims Rd.
Miller Rd.
Glen Hill
Goliad St.
Ridge Rd.
Chiesa Dr.
Wallace
Horizon
White Rd.
Cooke Dr.
Lake Ray Hubbard
Travis Ranch Rd.
East Shore Rd.
Davis Ln.
Marvin Loving Dr.
Rabbit Rd.
Pullen Rd.
Hubbard
Meadowview St.
0 2 MILES
0 2 KILOMETERS
3364
546
551
550
982
3286
437
1778
545
489
543
438
790
593
6
2514
384
78
541
2755
484
382
485
483
431
1108
544
552
205
1141
549
66
276
3097
549
1139
740
67
549
205
1140

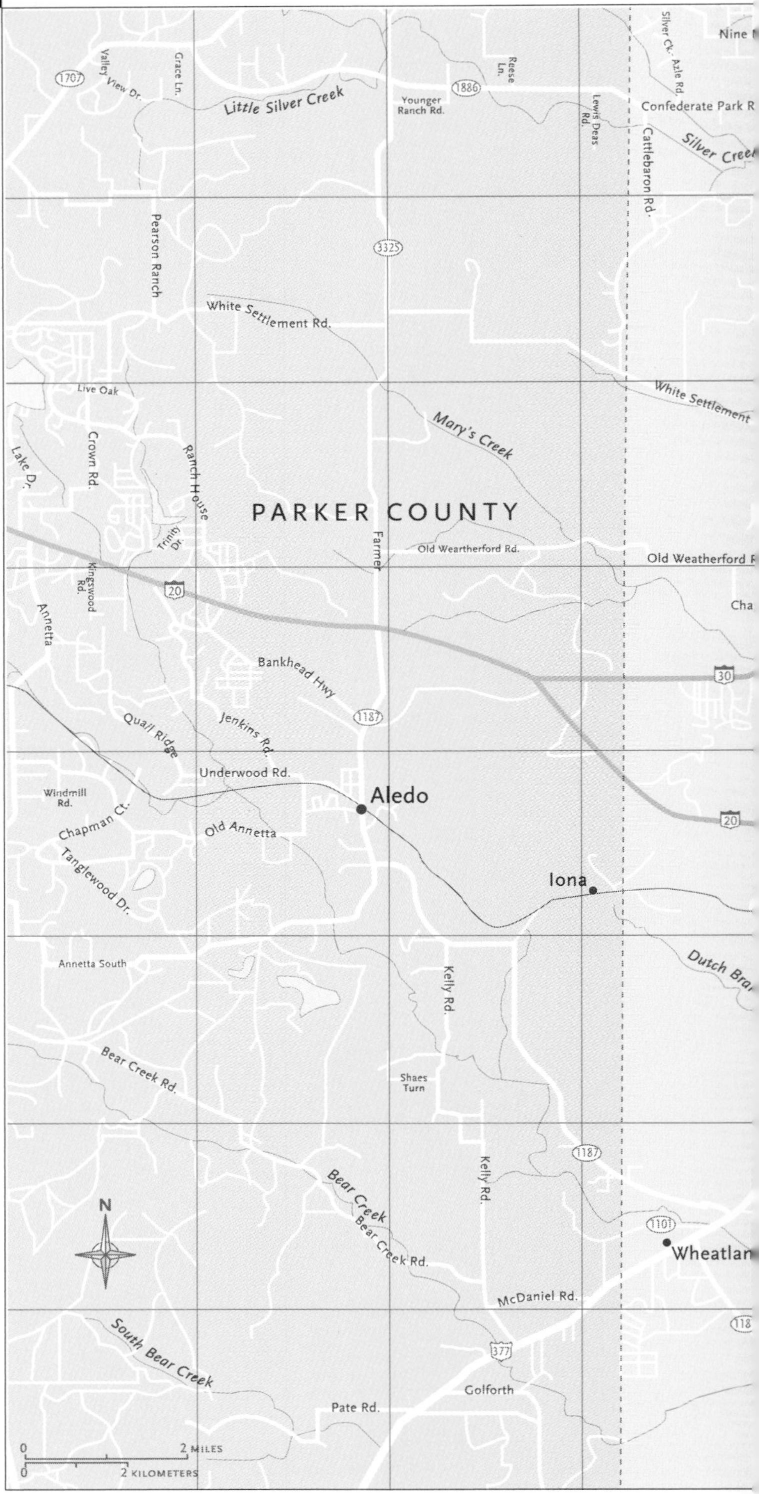
A
B
C
D
1
2
3
4
5
6
7
8
1707
Valley View Dr.
Grace Ln.
Little Silver Creek
Younger Ranch Rd.
1886
Reese Ln.
Lewis Deas Rd.
Silver Ck.-Azle Rd.
Nine
Confederate Park R
Silver Cree
Cattlebaron Rd.
3325
Pearson Ranch
White Settlement Rd.
Live Oak
White Settlement
Mary's Creek
Crown Rd.
Lake Dr.
Ranch House
PARKER COUNTY
Trinity Dr.
Farmer
Old Weartherford Rd.
Old Weatherford R
Kingswood Rd.
20
Annetta
Cha
Bankhead Hwy
30
1187
Jenkins Rd.
Quail Ridge
Underwood Rd.
Windmill Rd.
Aledo
Chapman Ct.
Old Annetta
20
Tanglewood Dr.
Iona
Dutch Bra
Annetta South
Kelly Rd.
Bear Creek Rd.
Shaes Turn
1187
Kelly Rd.
Bear Creek
N
Bear Creek Rd.
1101
Wheatlan
McDaniel Rd.
118
South Bear Creek
377
Golforth
Pate Rd.
0
2 MILES
0
2 KILOMETERS

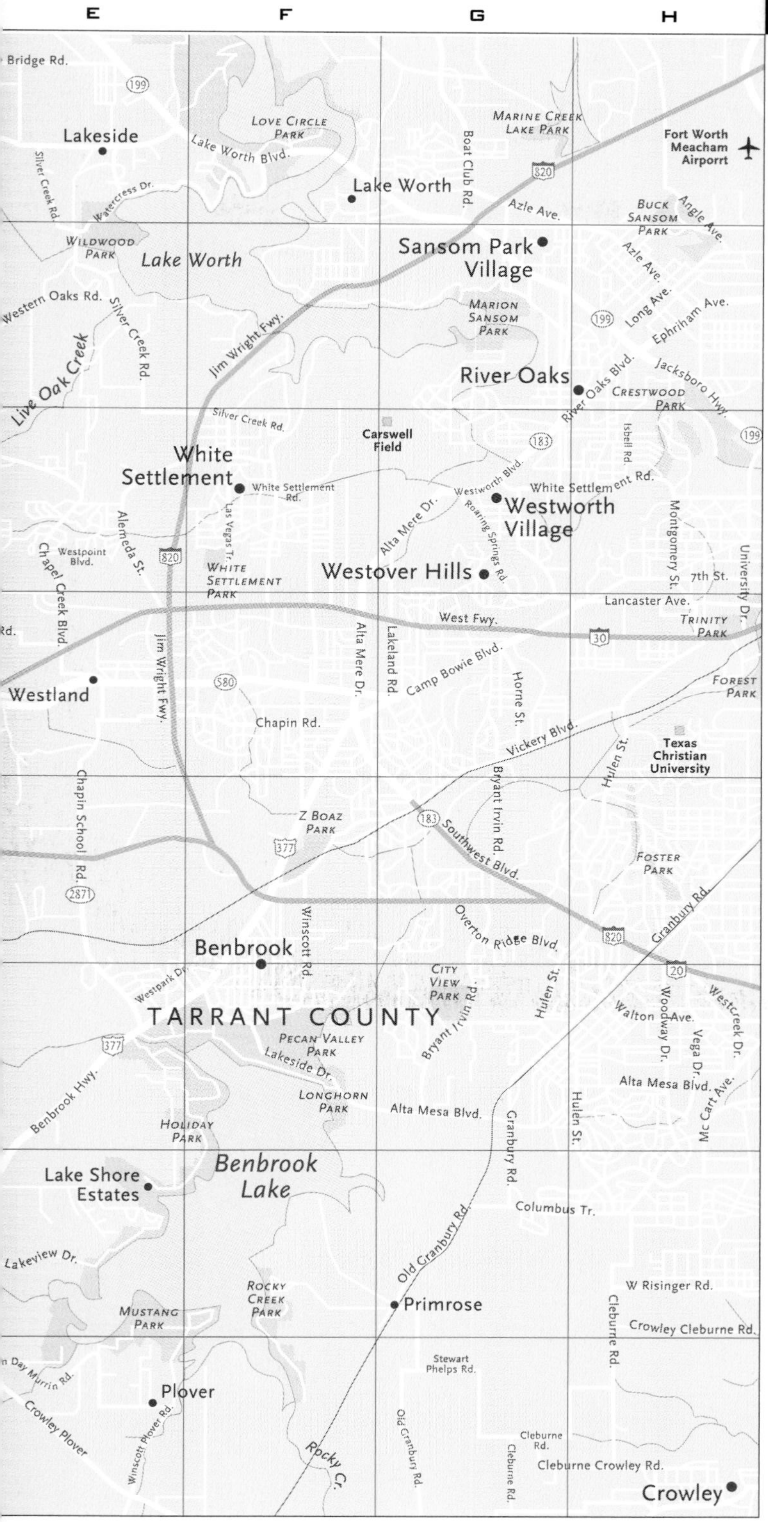
E
F
G
H
1
2
3
4
5
6
7
8
Bridge Rd.
Lakeside
Silver Creek Rd.
Watercress Dr.
Love Circle Park
Lake Worth Blvd.
Lake Worth
Boat Club Rd.
Marine Creek Lake Park
Fort Worth Meacham Airporrt
Azle Ave.
Buck Sansom Park
Angle Ave.
Wildwood Park
Lake Worth
Sansom Park Village
Western Oaks Rd.
Silver Creek Rd.
Marion Sansom Park
Long Ave.
Ephriham Ave.
Live Oak Creek
Jim Wright Fwy.
River Oaks
River Oaks Blvd.
Jacksboro Hwy.
Crestwood Park
Silver Creek Rd.
Carswell Field
Isbell Rd.
White Settlement
White Settlement Rd.
Westworth Blvd.
White Settlement Rd.
Westworth Village
Alta Mere Dr.
Roaring Springs Rd.
Montgomery St.
Alemeda St.
Las Vegas Tr.
Westpoint Blvd.
Chapel Creek Blvd.
White Settlement Park
Westover Hills
7th St.
University Dr.
Lancaster Ave.
West Fwy.
Trinity Park
Alta Mere Dr.
Lakeland Rd.
Jim Wright Fwy.
Camp Bowie Blvd.
Horne St.
Forest Park
Westland
Chapin Rd.
Vickery Blvd.
Texas Christian University
Hulen St.
Chapin School Rd.
Bryant Irvin Rd.
Z Boaz Park
Southwest Blvd.
Foster Park
Granbury Rd.
Winscott Rd.
Overton Ridge Blvd.
Benbrook
Westpark Dr.
City View Park
Hulen St.
Westcreek Dr.
Walton Ave.
TARRANT COUNTY
Bryant Irvin Rd.
Woodway Dr.
Vega Dr.
Pecan Valley Park
Lakeside Dr.
Mc Cart Ave.
Alta Mesa Blvd.
Benbrook Hwy.
Longhorn Park
Alta Mesa Blvd.
Hulen St.
Granbury Rd.
Holiday Park
Lake Shore Estates
Benbrook Lake
Columbus Tr.
Old Granbury Rd.
Lakeview Dr.
W Risinger Rd.
Rocky Creek Park
Mustang Park
Primrose
Cleburne Rd.
Crowley Cleburne Rd.
Stewart Phelps Rd.
Day Murrin Rd.
Plover
Crowley Plover
Winscott Plover Rd.
Old Granbury Rd.
Cleburne Rd.
Cleburne Rd.
Cleburne Crowley Rd.
Rocky Cr.
Crowley

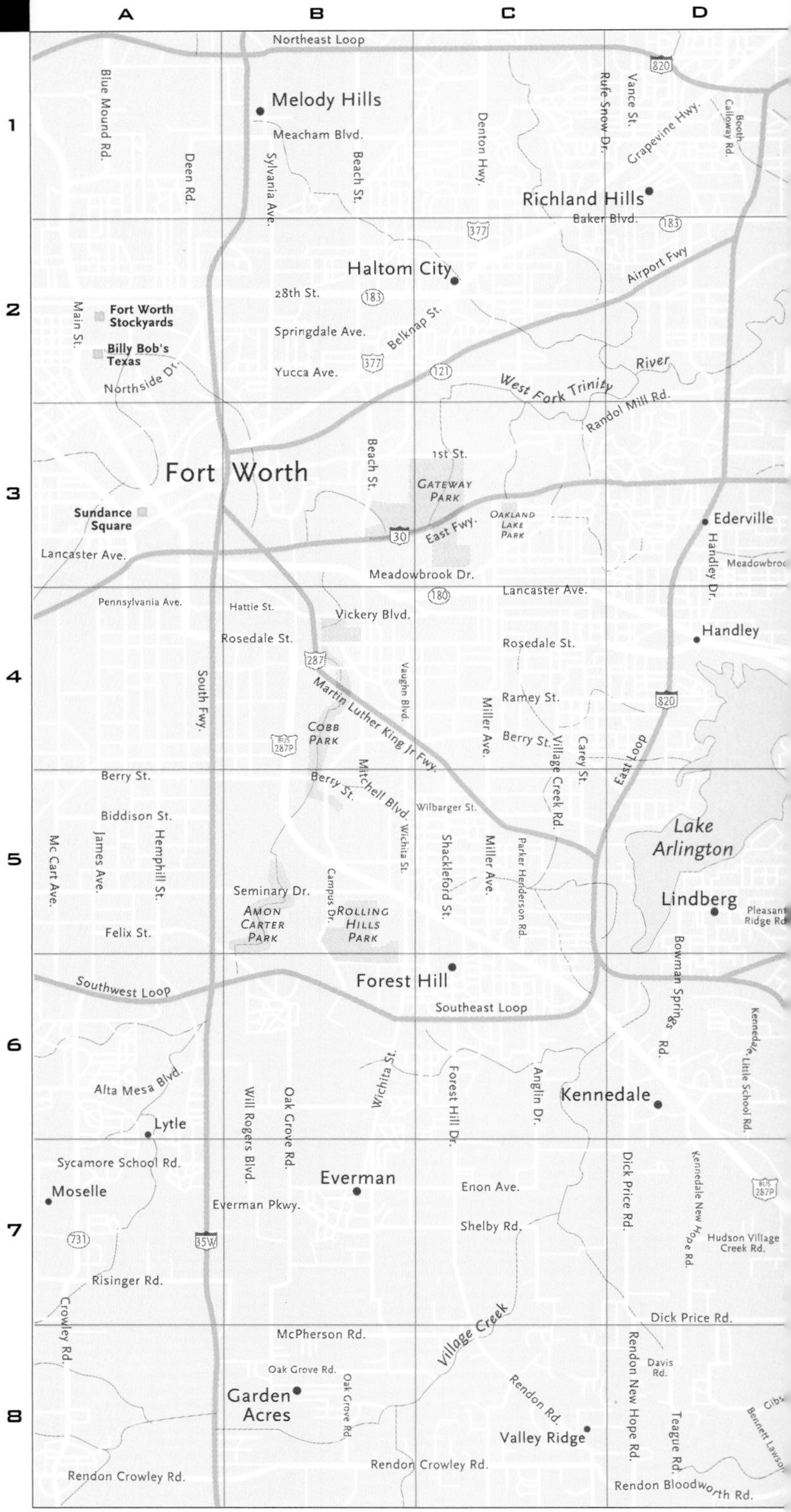
A
B
C
D
1
2
3
4
5
6
7
8
Northeast Loop
820
Melody Hills
Meacham Blvd.
Blue Mound Rd.
Deen Rd.
Sylvania Ave.
Beach St.
Denton Hwy.
Rufe Snow Dr.
Vance St.
Crapevine Hwy.
Booth Calloway Rd.
Richland Hills
Baker Blvd.
377
183
Haltom City
Airport Fwy
28th St.
Main St.
Fort Worth Stockyards
Billy Bob's Texas
Springdale Ave.
Belknap St.
Yucca Ave.
121
West Fork Trinity
River
Randol Mill Rd.
Northside Dr.
Fort Worth
1st St.
Gateway Park
Sundance Square
Oakland Lake Park
Ederville
30
East Fwy.
Lancaster Ave.
Handley Dr.
Meadowbrook Dr.
Meadowbroo
180
Lancaster Ave.
Pennsylvania Ave.
Hattie St.
Vickery Blvd.
Rosedale St.
Rosedale St.
Handley
287
Vaughn Blvd.
Martin Luther King Jr Fwy.
South Fwy.
Ramey St.
Miller Ave.
Cobb Park
Bus 287P
Berry St.
Village Creek Rd.
Carey St.
East Loop
Berry St.
Berry St.
Mitchell Blvd.
Wilbarger St.
Biddison St.
Lake Arlington
Mc Cart Ave.
James Ave.
Hemphill St.
Wichita St.
Shackleford St.
Miller Ave.
Parker Henderson Rd.
Seminary Dr.
Campus Dr.
Lindberg
Amon Carter Park
Rolling Hills Park
Pleasant Ridge Rd
Felix St.
Bowman Springs Rd.
Forest Hill
Southwest Loop
Southeast Loop
Kennedale Little School Rd.
Wichita St.
Forest Hill Dr.
Anglin Dr.
Alta Mesa Blvd.
Kennedale
Will Rogers Blvd.
Oak Grove Rd.
Lytle
Dick Price Rd.
Kennedale New Hope Rd.
Sycamore School Rd.
Everman
Bus 287P
Moselle
Enon Ave.
Everman Pkwy.
Shelby Rd.
Hudson Village Creek Rd.
731
35W
Risinger Rd.
Crowley Rd.
Village Creek
Dick Price Rd.
McPherson Rd.
Davis Rd.
Oak Grove Rd.
Oak Grove Rd.
Rendon Rd.
Rendon New Hope Rd.
Garden Acres
Teague Rd.
Gibs
Bennett Lawson
Valley Ridge
Rendon Crowley Rd.
Rendon Crowley Rd.
Rendon Bloodworth Rd.

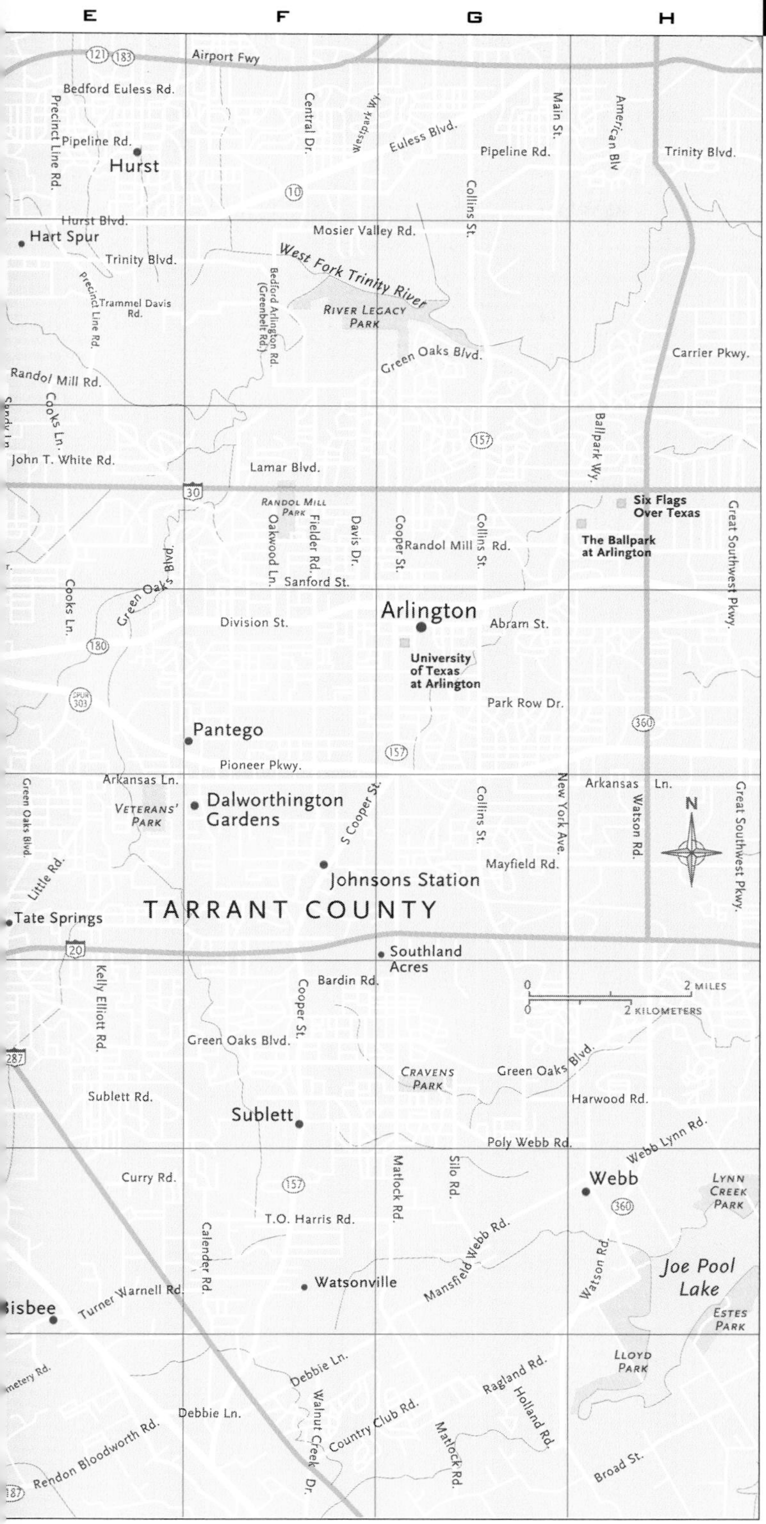
E
F
G
H
1
2
3
4
5
6
7
8
Airport Fwy
Bedford Euless Rd.
Precinct Line Rd.
Pipeline Rd.
Hurst
Central Dr.
Westpark Wy.
Euless Blvd.
Pipeline Rd.
Main St.
American Blv
Trinity Blvd.
Collins St.
Hurst Blvd.
Hart Spur
Mosier Valley Rd.
Trinity Blvd.
West Fork Trinity River
Precinct Line Rd.
Trammel Davis Rd.
Bedford Arlington Rd. (Greenbelt Rd.)
River Legacy Park
Green Oaks Blvd.
Carrier Pkwy.
Randol Mill Rd.
Cooks Ln.
Ballpark Wy.
John T. White Rd.
Lamar Blvd.
Randol Mill Park
Six Flags Over Texas
Great Southwest Pkwy.
Oakwood Ln.
Fielder Rd.
Davis Dr.
Cooper St.
Randol Mill Rd.
Collins St.
The Ballpark at Arlington
Green Oaks Blvd.
Sanford St.
Cooks Ln.
Division St.
Arlington
Abram St.
University of Texas at Arlington
Park Row Dr.
Pantego
Pioneer Pkwy.
Arkansas Ln.
Arkansas Ln.
Green Oaks Blvd.
Veterans' Park
Dalworthington Gardens
S Cooper St.
Collins St.
New York Ave.
Watson Rd.
Great Southwest Pkwy.
N
Little Rd.
Mayfield Rd.
Johnsons Station
Tate Springs
TARRANT COUNTY
Southland Acres
Kelly Elliott Rd.
Bardin Rd.
Cooper St.
0
2 MILES
0
2 KILOMETERS
Green Oaks Blvd.
Cravens Park
Green Oaks Blvd.
Sublett Rd.
Harwood Rd.
Sublett
Poly Webb Rd.
Webb Lynn Rd.
Curry Rd.
Matlock Rd.
Silo Rd.
Webb
Lynn Creek Park
T.O. Harris Rd.
Calender Rd.
Mansfield Webb Rd.
Watson Rd.
Joe Pool Lake
Watsonville
Turner Warnell Rd.
Bisbee
Estes Park
Lloyd Park
Debbie Ln.
Ragland Rd.
Holland Rd.
Debbie Ln.
Walnut Creek Dr.
Country Club Rd.
Matlock Rd.
Rendon Bloodworth Rd.
Broad St.

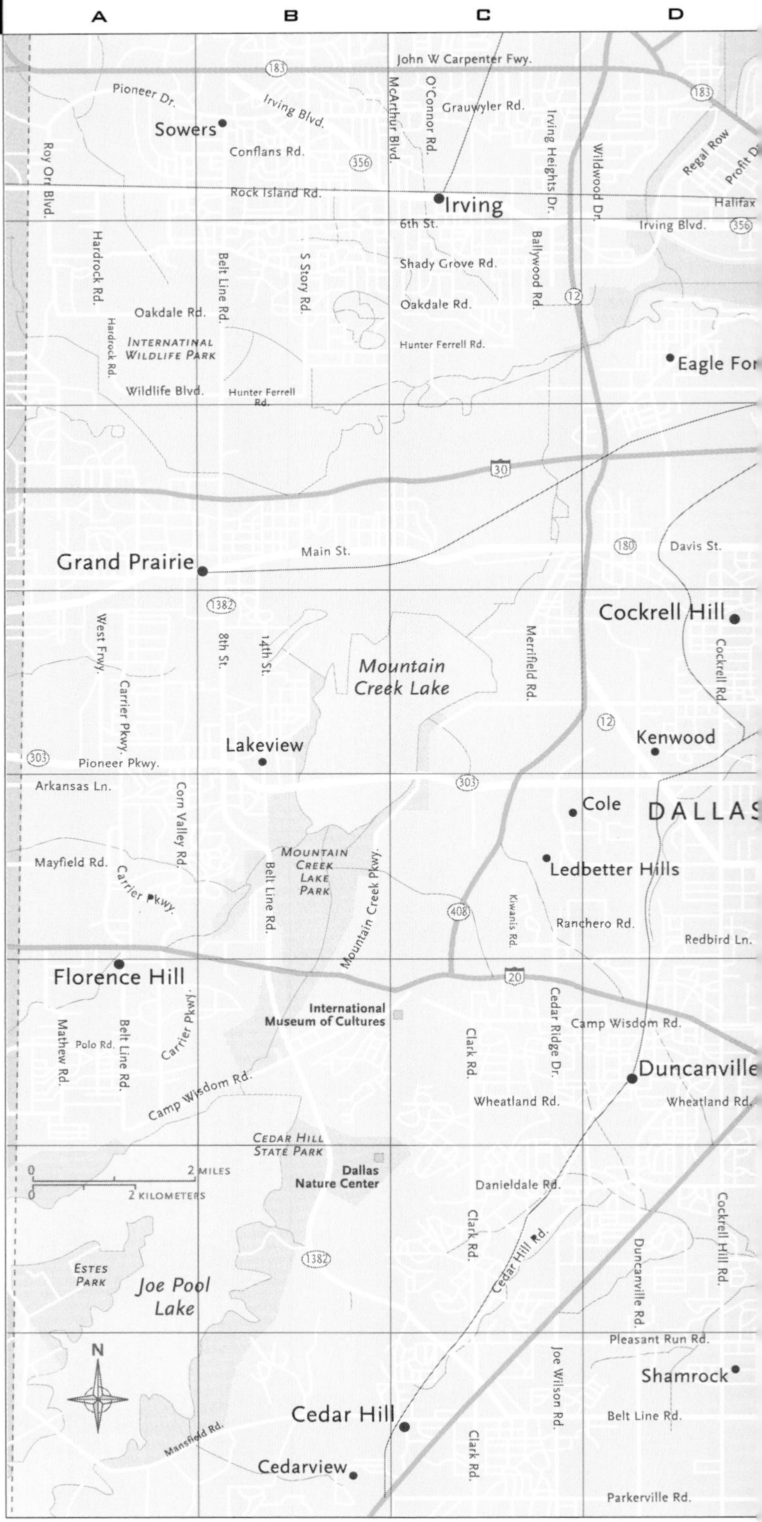

A
B
C
D
1
2
3
4
5
6
7
8
John W Carpenter Fwy.
183
Pioneer Dr.
Irving Blvd.
McArthur Blvd.
O'Connor Rd.
Grauwyler Rd.
Irving Heights Dr.
Wildwood Dr.
Regal Row
Sowers
Conflans Rd.
356
Roy Orr Blvd.
Rock Island Rd.
Irving
Halifax
6th St.
Irving Blvd.
Hardrock Rd.
Belt Line Rd.
S Story Rd.
Shady Grove Rd.
Ballywood Rd.
12
Oakdale Rd.
Oakdale Rd.
Hardrock Rd.
INTERNATINAL WILDLIFE PARK
Hunter Ferrell Rd.
Eagle For
Wildlife Blvd.
Hunter Ferrell Rd.
30
Main St.
180
Davis St.
Grand Prairie
1382
Cockrell Hill
West Frwy.
8th St.
14th St.
Mountain Creek Lake
Merrifield Rd.
Cockrell Rd.
Carrier Pkwy.
Kenwood
303
Lakeview
Pioneer Pkwy.
Arkansas Ln.
Corn Valley Rd.
Cole
DALLAS
Mayfield Rd.
Carrier Pkwy.
MOUNTAIN CREEK LAKE PARK
Belt Line Rd.
Mountain Creek Pkwy.
Ledbetter Hills
408
Kiwanis Rd.
Ranchero Rd.
Redbird Ln.
Florence Hill
20
Cedar Ridge Dr.
International Museum of Cultures
Camp Wisdom Rd.
Mathew Rd.
Polo Rd.
Belt Line Rd.
Carrier Pkwy.
Clark Rd.
Duncanville
Camp Wisdom Rd.
Wheatland Rd.
Wheatland Rd.
CEDAR HILL STATE PARK
0
2 MILES
0
2 KILOMETERS
Dallas Nature Center
Danieldale Rd.
Cockrell Hill Rd.
Clark Rd.
Cedar Hill Rd.
Duncanville Rd.
ESTES PARK
Joe Pool Lake
Pleasant Run Rd.
N
Joe Wilson Rd.
Shamrock
Cedar Hill
Belt Line Rd.
Mansfield Rd.
Clark Rd.
Cedarview
Parkerville Rd.

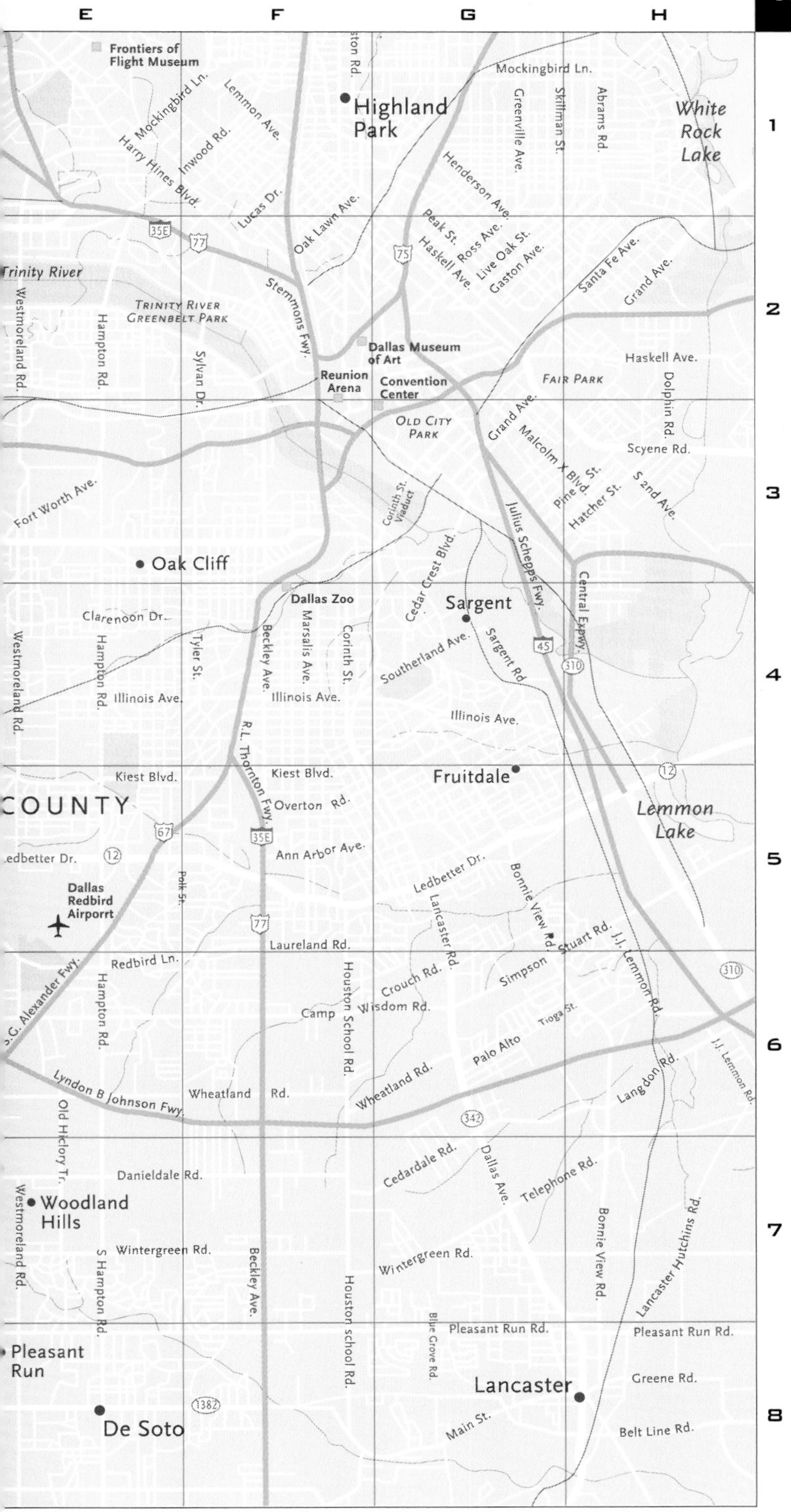
E
F
G
H
1
2
3
4
5
6
7
8
Frontiers of Flight Museum
Mockingbird Ln.
Lemmon Ave.
Inwood Rd.
Harry Hines Blvd.
Lucas Dr.
Highland Park
Mockingbird Ln.
Greenville Ave.
Skillman St.
Abrams Rd.
White Rock Lake
Henderson Ave.
Oak Lawn Ave.
Peak St.
Ross Ave.
Haskell Ave.
Live Oak St.
Gaston Ave.
Santa Fe Ave.
Grand Ave.
35E
77
75
Trinity River
Westmoreland Rd.
Trinity River Greenbelt Park
Hampton Rd.
Stemmons Fwy.
Sylvan Dr.
Dallas Museum of Art
Reunion Arena
Convention Center
Haskell Ave.
Fair Park
Dolphin Rd.
Old City Park
Grand Ave.
Malcolm X Blvd.
Scyene Rd.
Pine St.
Hatcher St.
S 2nd Ave.
Fort Worth Ave.
Corinth St. Viaduct
Julius Schepps Fwy.
Cedar Crest Blvd.
Oak Cliff
Dallas Zoo
Sargent
Central Expwy.
Clarenoon Dr.
Westmoreland Rd.
Hampton Rd.
Tyler St.
Beckley Ave.
Marsalis Ave.
Corinth St.
Southerland Ave.
Sargent Rd.
45
310
Illinois Ave.
Illinois Ave.
Illinois Ave.
R.L. Thornton Fwy.
Kiest Blvd.
Kiest Blvd.
Fruitdale
12
COUNTY
Overton Rd.
Lemmon Lake
67
35E
Ledbetter Dr.
12
Ann Arbor Ave.
Ledbetter Dr.
Bonnie View Rd.
Dallas Redbird Airporrt
Polk St.
Lancaster Rd.
77
Laureland Rd.
Stuart Rd.
J.J. Lemmon Rd.
Redbird Ln.
S.G. Alexander Fwy.
Hampton Rd.
Houston School Rd.
Crouch Rd.
Simpson
310
Camp Wisdom Rd.
Tioga St.
Palo Alto
J.J. Lemmon Rd.
Langdon Rd.
Lyndon B Johnson Fwy.
Wheatland Rd.
Wheatland Rd.
342
Old Hickory Tr.
Cedardale Rd.
Dallas Ave.
Telephone Rd.
Danieldale Rd.
Westmoreland Rd.
Woodland Hills
Bonnie View Rd.
Lancaster Hutchins Rd.
Wintergreen Rd.
S Hampton Rd.
Beckley Ave.
Wintergreen Rd.
Houston school Rd.
Blue Grove Rd.
Pleasant Run Rd.
Pleasant Run Rd.
Pleasant Run
Greene Rd.
Lancaster
1382
De Soto
Main St.
Belt Line Rd.

A
B
C
D
1
2
3
4
5
6
7
8
Garland Rd.
Reinhardt
Ferguson Rd.
Thomasson Rd.
Oates Dr.
Oates Dr.
Belt Line Rd.
Barnes Bridge
Lakeland Dr.
Buckner Blvd.
La Prada Dr.
Eastfield College
30
New Hope
Town East Blvd.
John West Rd.
Motley Dr.
Town East Blvd.
Thomasson Rd.
Galloway Ave.
Highland Rd.
R.L. Thornton Fwy.
Sunnyvale
Tripp Rd.
Samuell Blvd.
80
Town East Blvd.
Gross Rd.
Ridgeview St.
Galloway Ave.
Royal Crest Dr.
Hillcrest St.
Eastpoint Dr.
Skyline Dr.
Kearney St.
352
Forney Rd.
Peachtree Rd.
Sam Houston Rd.
Prairie Creek Rd.
Long Creek Rd.
Military Pkwy.
Military Pkwy.
Kearney St.
352
Mesquite
Buckner Blvd.
Pleasant Dr.
St Augustine Dr.
Masters Dr.
Peachtree Rd.
Hickory Tree Rd.
Pioneer Rd.
Hillburn St.
635
Jim Miller Rd.
Bruton Rd.
Pioneer Rd.
Lake June Rd.
Balch Springs
Faithon P Lucas Sr Blvd.
175
Pleasant Grove
Belt Line Rd.
Elam Rd.
Pioneer Rd.
12
Murdock Rd.
Seagoville Rd.
Lawson
Fireside Dr.
Rylie Crest Dr.
Lasater
Rylie
Ravenview Rd.
Seagoville Rd.
Edd Rd.
Belt Line Rd.
Kleberg Rd.
20
Oakwood Dr.
Stark Rd.
Teagarden Rd.
Woody Rd.
Dowdy Ferry Rd.
Haymarket Rd.
Kleberg
175
Ard Rd.
St Augustine Rd.
Jordan Valley
Cleveland Rd.
Cloverhill Rd.
Bobwyn
Jordan Valley
Beckett Rd.
Trout Rd.
DALLAS COUNTY
Wintergreen Rd.
Simonds Rd.
Bowers Rd.
Fulghum Rd.
Post Oak Rd.
Belt Line Rd.
Bilindsay Rd.
Pleasant Run Rd.
45
Trinity River
Belt Line Rd.
Geller Rd.
Malloy Bridge Rd.
Bois D'Arc Rd.
Wilmer
Gravel Slough
Mars Rd.
Mars Rd.
Cook Rd.
Nokes Rd.

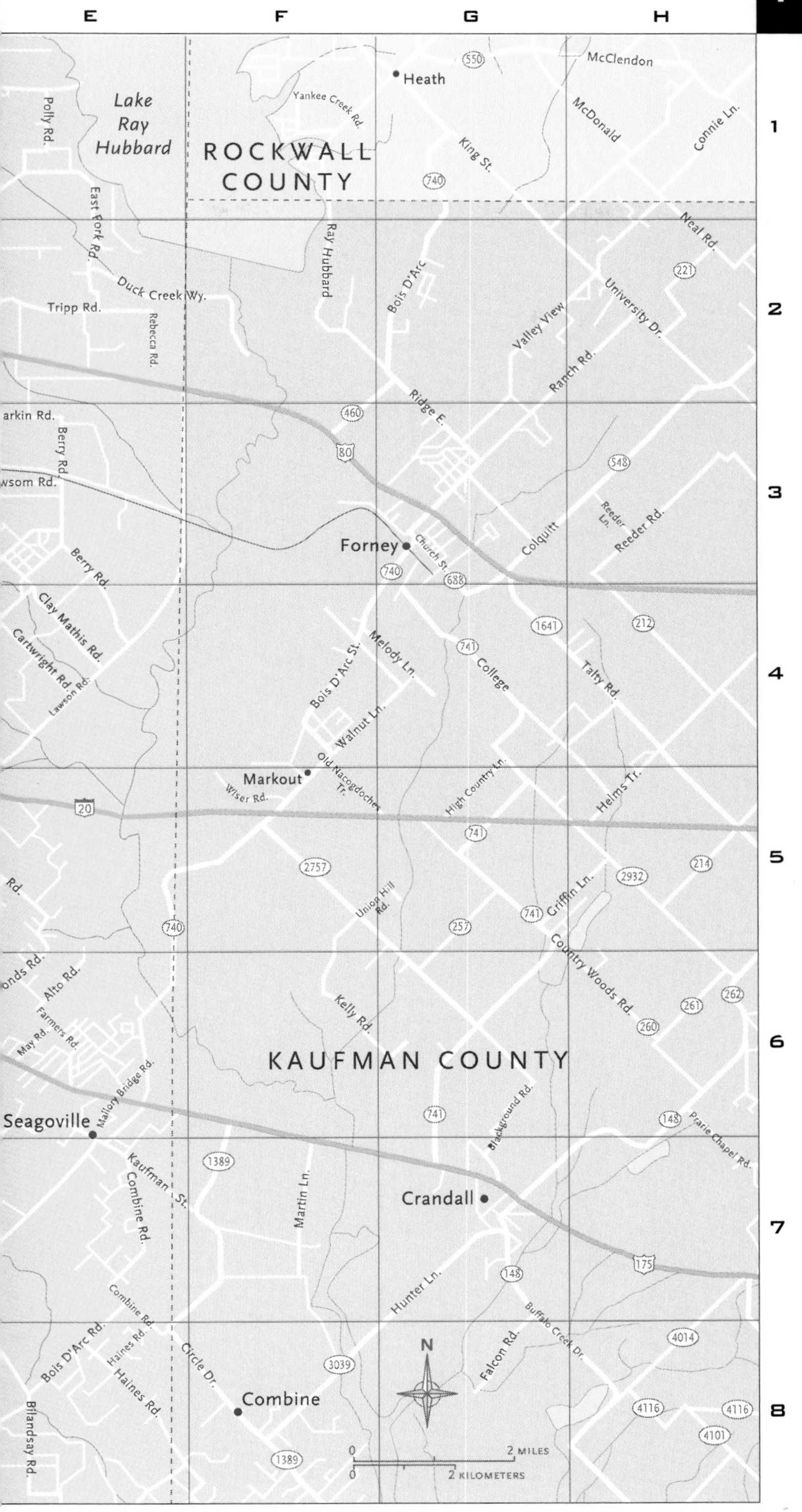
E
F
G
H
1
2
3
4
5
6
7
8
Lake Ray Hubbard
ROCKWALL COUNTY
KAUFMAN COUNTY
Heath
McClendon
McDonald
Connie Ln.
Yankee Creek Rd.
King St.
Polly Rd.
East Fork Rd.
Duck Creek Wy.
Tripp Rd.
Rebecca Rd.
Ray Hubbard
Bois D'Arc
Neal Rd.
University Dr.
Valley View
Ranch Rd.
Ridge E.
arkin Rd.
Berry Rd.
wsom Rd.
Forney
Church St.
Colquitt
Reeder Ln.
Reeder Rd.
Berry Rd.
Clay Mathis Rd.
Cartwright Rd.
Lawson Rd.
Bois D'Arc St.
Melody Ln.
Walnut Ln.
College
Talty Rd.
Markout
Wiser Rd.
Old Nacogdoches Tr.
High Country Ln.
Helms Tr.
Union Hill Rd.
Griffin Ln.
Country Woods Rd.
Rd.
onds Rd.
Alto Rd.
Farmers Rd.
May Rd.
Mallory Bridge Rd.
Kelly Rd.
Seagoville
Blackground Rd.
Prarie Chapel Rd.
Kaufman St.
Combine Rd.
Martin Ln.
Crandall
Hunter Ln.
Buffalo Creek Dr.
Falcon Rd.
Combine Rd.
Haines Rd.
Bois D'Arc Rd.
Haines Rd.
Circle Dr.
Combine
Blandsay Rd.
550
740
221
460
80
548
740
688
1641
212
741
20
741
2757
214
2932
740
741
257
262
261
260
741
148
1389
175
148
4014
3039
4116
4116
4101
1389
N
0
2 MILES
0
2 KILOMETERS

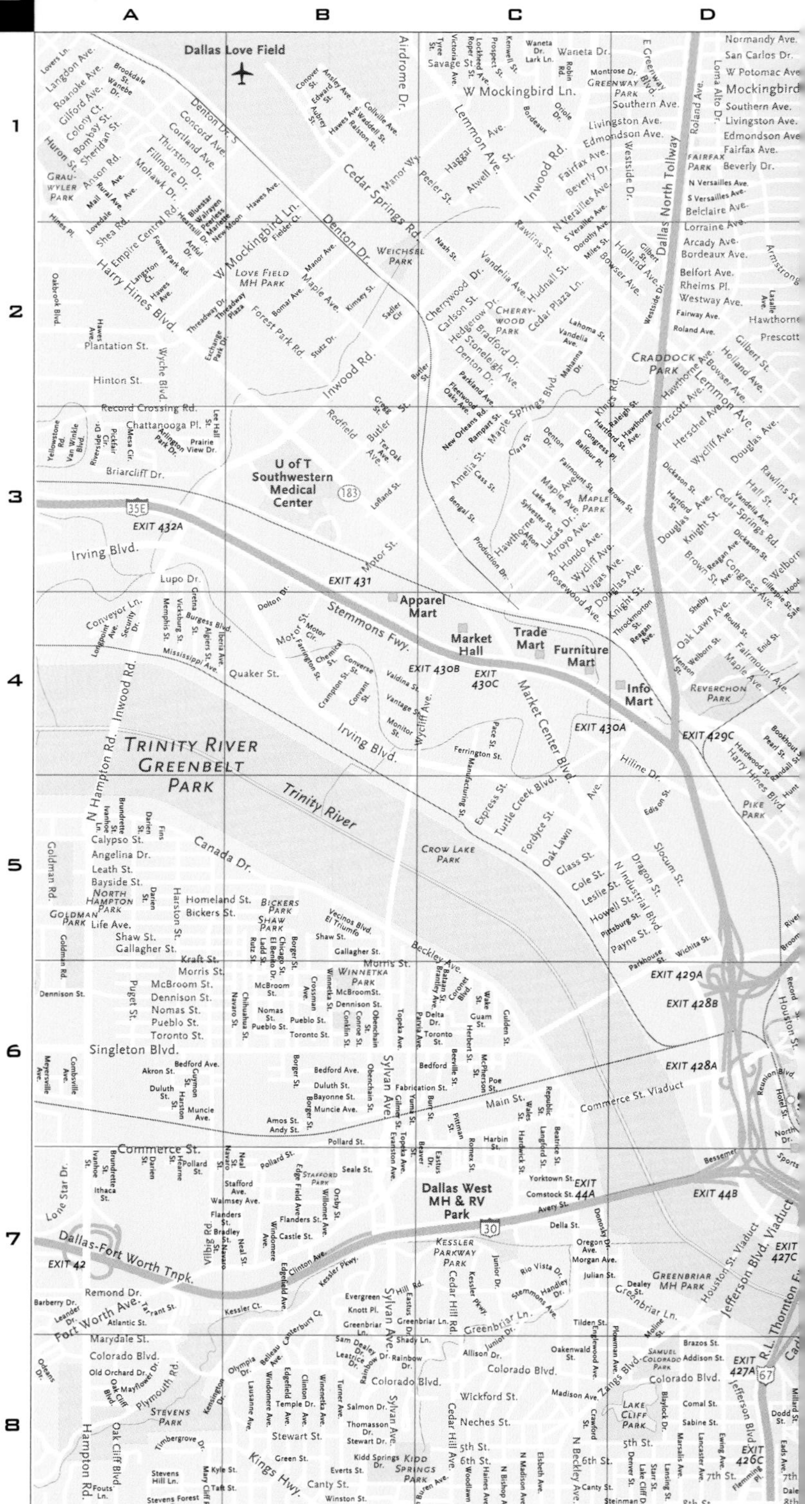
A
B
C
D
1
2
3
4
5
6
7
8
Dallas Love Field
Lovers Ln.
Langdon Ave.
Roanoke Ave.
Gilford Ave.
Colony Ct.
Bombay St.
Sheridan St.
Huron St.
Anson Rd.
GRAUWYLER PARK
Denton Dr. S
Concord Ave.
Cortland Ave.
Thurston Dr.
Fillmore Dr.
Mohawk Dr.
Shea Rd.
Empire Central Rd.
Harry Hines Blvd.
Oakbrook Blvd.
Plantation St.
Hinton St.
Wyche Blvd.
Record Crossing Rd.
Chattanooga Pl.
Briarcliff Dr.
W Mockingbird Ln.
LOVE FIELD MH PARK
Forest Park Rd.
Inwood Rd.
Denton Dr.
Cedar Springs Rd.
Manor Wy.
WEICHSEL PARK
Maple Ave.
Airdrome Dr.
Savage St.
W Mockingbird Ln.
Lemmon Ave.
Haggar Ave.
Atwell St.
Peeler St.
Inwood Rd.
Waneta Dr.
GREENWAY PARK
Southern Ave.
Livingston Ave.
Edmondson Ave.
Fairfax Ave.
Beverly Dr.
Westside Dr.
Dallas North Tollway
Roland Ave.
Normandy Ave.
San Carlos Dr.
W Potomac Ave.
Mockingbird
Southern Ave.
Livingston Ave.
Edmondson Ave.
Fairfax Ave.
Beverly Dr.
FAIRFAX PARK
Belclaire Ave.
Lorraine Ave.
Arcady Ave.
Bordeaux Ave.
Belfort Ave.
Rheims Pl.
Westway Ave.
Fairway Ave.
Roland Ave.
Hawthorne
Prescott
Armstrong
Cherrywood Dr.
Vandelia Ave.
CHERRYWOOD PARK
Cedar Plaza Ln.
Rawlins St.
Bowser Ave.
Holland Ave.
CRADDOCK PARK
Lemmon Ave.
Hawthorne Ave.
Prescott Ave.
Herschel Ave.
Wycliff Ave.
Douglas Ave.
Rawlins St.
Hall St.
Cedar Springs Rd.
Maple Springs Blvd.
U of T Southwestern Medical Center
183
35E
EXIT 432A
Irving Blvd.
Lupo Dr.
EXIT 431
Motor St.
Apparel Mart
Stemmons Fwy.
Market Hall
Trade Mart
Furniture Mart
Info Mart
EXIT 430B
EXIT 430C
EXIT 430A
EXIT 429C
Market Center Blvd.
MAPLE AVE. PARK
REVERCHON PARK
Oak Lawn Ave.
Maple Ave.
Fairmount Ave.
Conveyor Ln.
Mississippi Ave.
Quaker St.
Irving Blvd.
Inwood Rd.
TRINITY RIVER GREENBELT PARK
Trinity River
N Hampton Rd.
Canada Dr.
CROW LAKE PARK
Turtle Creek Blvd.
Hi Line Dr.
PIKE PARK
Harry Hines Blvd.
Slocum St.
N Industrial Blvd.
Dragon St.
Goldman Rd.
Calypso St.
Angelina Dr.
Leath St.
Bayside St.
NORTH HAMPTON PARK
GOLDMAN PARK
Life Ave.
Shaw St.
Gallagher St.
Homeland St.
Bickers St.
Harston St.
BICKERS PARK
SHAW PARK
Kraft St.
Morris St.
McBroom St.
Dennison St.
Nomas St.
Pueblo St.
Toronto St.
Singleton Blvd.
Puget St.
WINNETKA PARK
Beckley Ave.
Sylvan Ave.
EXIT 429A
EXIT 428B
EXIT 428A
Commerce St. Viaduct
Main St.
Commerce St.
Houston St.
Lone Star Dr.
Dallas West MH & RV Park
30
STAFFORD PARK
EXIT 44A
EXIT 44B
Dallas-Fort Worth Tnpk.
EXIT 42
Fort Worth Ave.
Remond Dr.
Clinton Ave.
KESSLER PARKWAY PARK
Cedar Hill Rd.
GREENBRIAR MH PARK
Greenbriar Ln.
Houston St. Viaduct
Jefferson Blvd. Viaduct
R.L. Thornton Fwy.
EXIT 427C
Colorado Blvd.
Marydale St.
Atlantic St.
Plymouth Rd.
STEVENS PARK
Hampton Rd.
Oak Cliff Blvd.
Kings Hwy.
KIDD SPRINGS PARK
Canty St.
Winston St.
Wickford St.
Neches St.
5th St.
6th St.
Cedar Hill Ave.
N Beckley Ave.
Zangs Blvd.
SAMUEL COLORADO PARK
LAKE CLIFF PARK
Colorado Blvd.
Jefferson Blvd.
EXIT 427A
67
EXIT 426C
7th St.
8th St.

E
F
G
H
1
2
3
4
5
6
7
8
HIGHLAND PARK
DALLAS COUNTRY CLUB
Preston Rd.
Town Hall
PRATHER PARK
LAKESIDE PARK
CHURCH PARK
DYCKMAN PARK
ABBOTT PARK
MOCKINGBIRD
E Mockingbird Ln.
EXIT 8
GLENCOE PARK
EXIT 7
EXIT 6
EXIT 5
EXIT 4
EXIT 3
EXIT 2
EXIT 1
LAKEWOOD
TIETZ PARK
Greenville Ave.
Skillman St.
N Central Expwy.
McKinney Ave.
Turtle Creek Blvd.
OAK LAWN
ROBERT E LEE PARK
COLE PARK
CITY PLACE
GARRETT PARK
EMANUEL CEMETERY
GREENWOOD CEMETERY
GRIGGS PARK
BUCKNER PARK
EXALL PARK
Live Oak St.
Gaston Ave.
Swiss Ave.
Columbia Ave.
N Munger Blvd.
Abrams Pkwy.
PARRY PARK
EXIT 47B
FAIR PARK
Texas State Fair Grounds
Starplex Auditorium
Main St.
Commerce St.
Elm St.
Good-Latimer Expwy.
ASTON PARK
City Hall
EXIT 47A
EXIT 46A
OLD CITY PARK
Griffin St.
Lamar St.
Harwood St.
Akard St.
Ervay St.
Martin Luther King Blvd.
MARTIN LUTHER KING JR PARK
WHEATLEY PARK
OAKLAND CEMETERY
EXLINE PARK
Malcolm X Blvd.
Grand Ave.
Robert B Cullum Blvd.
S Industrial Blvd.
EXIT 427B
EXIT 283A
TRINITY RIVER GREENBELT PARK
Trinity River
Corinth St. Viaduct
Colonial Ave.
S Harwood St.
N
0
1000 FEET
1 KILOMETER

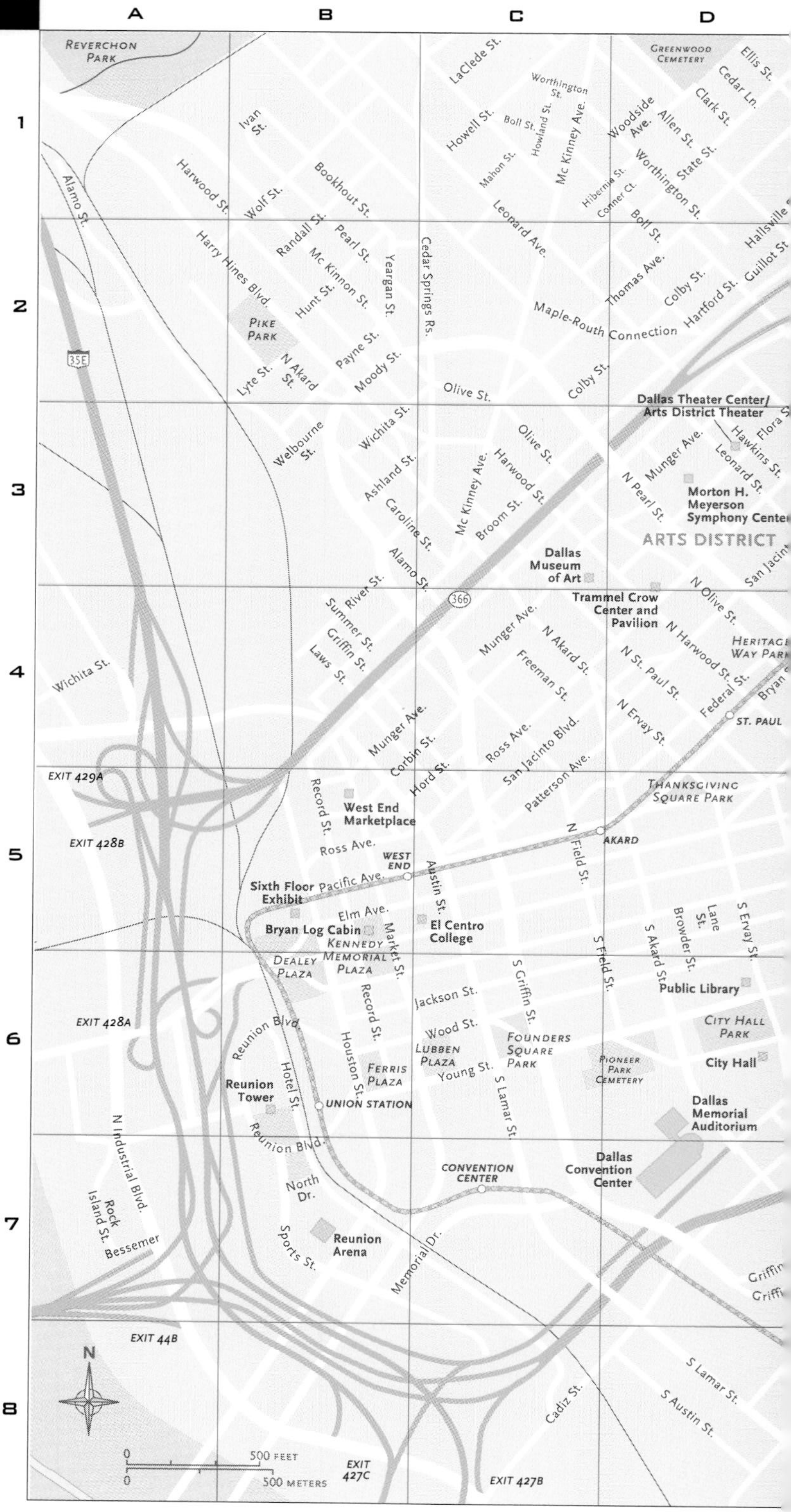
A
B
C
D
1
2
3
4
5
6
7
8
Reverchon Park
Greenwood Cemetery
Pike Park
Dallas Theater Center/ Arts District Theater
Morton H. Meyerson Symphony Center
ARTS DISTRICT
Dallas Museum of Art
Trammel Crow Center and Pavilion
Heritage Way Park
St. Paul
Thanksgiving Square Park
West End Marketplace
Akard
West End
Sixth Floor Exhibit
Bryan Log Cabin
Kennedy Memorial Plaza
Dealey Plaza
El Centro College
Public Library
City Hall Park
City Hall
Founders Square Park
Lubben Plaza
Ferris Plaza
Pioneer Park Cemetery
Reunion Tower
Union Station
Dallas Memorial Auditorium
Convention Center
Dallas Convention Center
Reunion Arena
Exit 429A
Exit 428B
Exit 428A
Exit 44B
Exit 427C
Exit 427B
N
0
500 feet
500 meters

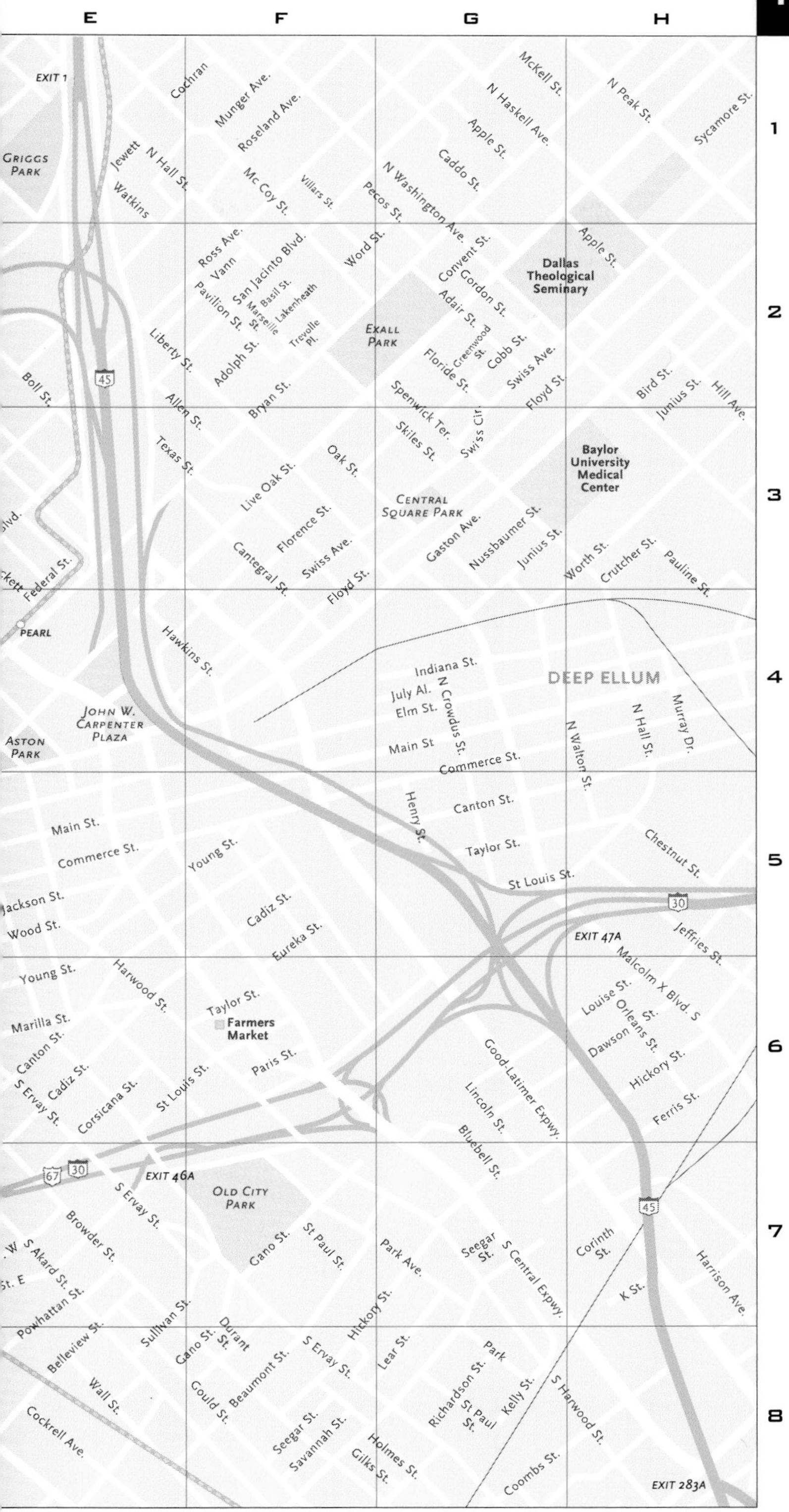
E
F
G
H
1
2
3
4
5
6
7
8
EXIT 1
Griggs Park
Cochran
Munger Ave.
Roseland Ave.
Jewett
N Hall St.
Watkins
Mc Coy St.
Villars St.
Pecos St.
N Washington Ave.
McKell St.
N Haskell Ave.
Apple St.
Caddo St.
N Peak St.
Sycamore St.
Ross Ave.
Vann
San Jacinto Blvd.
Basil St.
Marseille St.
Lakenheath
Pavilion St.
Trevolle Pl.
Word St.
Exall Park
Convent St.
Gordon St.
Adair St.
Greenwood St.
Cobb St.
Floride St.
Swiss Ave.
Floyd St.
Dallas Theological Seminary
Apple St.
Liberty St.
Adolph St.
Boll St.
Bryan St.
Allen St.
Spenwick Ter.
Skiles St.
Swiss Cir.
Bird St.
Junius St.
Hill Ave.
Texas St.
Oak St.
Live Oak St.
Baylor University Medical Center
Central Square Park
Florence St.
Gaston Ave.
Nussbaumer St.
Junius St.
Cantegral St.
Swiss Ave.
Floyd St.
Worth St.
Crutcher St.
Pauline St.
Federal St.
Pearl
Hawkins St.
Indiana St.
July Al.
Elm St.
N Crowdus St.
Main St
Deep Ellum
N Hall St.
Murray Dr.
N Walton St.
Commerce St.
John W. Carpenter Plaza
Aston Park
Main St.
Commerce St.
Young St.
Henry St.
Canton St.
Taylor St.
Chestnut St.
St Louis St.
Jackson St.
Wood St.
Cadiz St.
Eureka St.
EXIT 47A
Jeffries St.
Malcolm X Blvd. S
Young St.
Harwood St.
Taylor St.
Farmers Market
Louise St.
Orleans St.
Dawson St.
Marilla St.
Canton St.
Cadiz St.
S Ervay St.
Corsicana St.
St Louis St.
Paris St.
Good-Latimer Expwy.
Lincoln St.
Hickory St.
Ferris St.
Bluebell St.
67
30
EXIT 46A
Old City Park
S Ervay St.
45
Browder St.
S Akard St.
Powhattan St.
Cano St.
St Paul St.
Park Ave.
Seegar St.
S Central Expwy.
Corinth St.
K St.
Harrison Ave.
Sullivan St.
Belleview St.
Gano St.
Durant St.
S Ervay St.
Hickory St.
Lear St.
Park
Richardson St.
St Paul St.
Kelly St.
S Harwood St.
Wall St.
Beaumont St.
Gould St.
Cockrell Ave.
Seegar St.
Savannah St.
Holmes St.
Gilks St.
Coombs St.
EXIT 283A

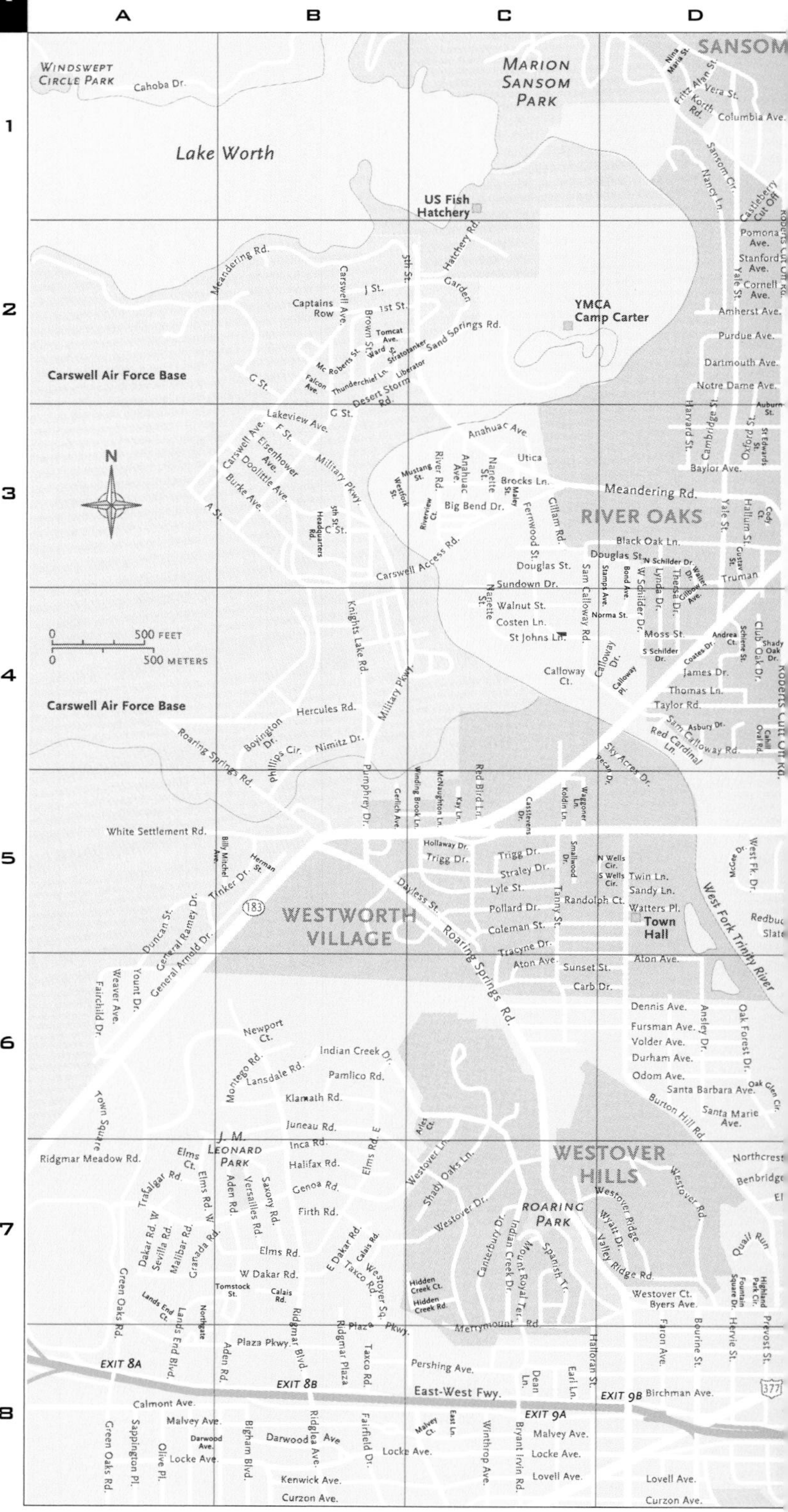
A
B
C
D
1
2
3
4
5
6
7
8
Windswept Circle Park
Cahoba Dr.
Lake Worth
Marion Sansom Park
Sansom
US Fish Hatchery
Hatchery Rd.
Meandering Rd.
Carswell Ave.
5th St.
J St.
Garden
Captains Row
1st St.
Brown St.
Tomcat Ave.
Ward St.
Stratotanker
Sand Springs Rd.
Mc Roberts St.
Thunderchief Ln.
Liberator
Falcon Ave.
Desert Storm Rd.
YMCA Camp Carter
Carswell Air Force Base
G St.
Lakeview Ave.
F St.
Eisenhower Ave.
Doolittle Ave.
Burke Ave.
A St.
Military Pkwy.
Anahuac Ave.
Utica
Mustang St.
Westfork St.
River Rd.
Anahuac Ave.
Nanette St.
Maley St.
Brocks Ln.
Riverview Ct.
Big Bend Dr.
Fernwood St.
Cillam Rd.
Meandering Rd.
River Oaks
5th St.
Headquarters Rd.
C St.
Carswell Access Rd.
Black Oak Ln.
Douglas St.
Douglas St.
N Schilder Dr.
Sundown Dr.
Nanette St.
Walnut St.
Costen Ln.
St Johns Ln.
Sam Calloway Rd.
Stamps Ave.
Bond Ave.
W Schilder Dr.
Lynda Dr.
Theesa Dr.
Gilbow Ave.
Walker Dr.
Norma St.
Moss St.
S Schilder Dr.
Calloway Dr.
Calloway Ct.
Calloway Pl.
Coates Dr.
James Dr.
Thomas Ln.
Taylor Rd.
Asbury Dr.
Sam Calloway Rd.
Red Cardinal Ln.
Sky Acres Dr.
Pecan Dr.
N
0 500 Feet
0 500 Meters
Knights Lake Rd.
Military Pkwy.
Hercules Rd.
Bovington Dr.
Phillips Cir.
Nimitz Dr.
Roaring Springs Rd.
Pumphrey Dr.
Gerlich Ave.
Winding Brook Ln.
McNaughton Ln.
Kay Ln.
Red Bird Ln.
Casstevens Dr.
Koldin Ln.
Waggoner Ln.
White Settlement Rd.
Billy Mitchel Ave.
Herman St.
Tinker Dr.
183
Hollaway Dr.
Trigg Dr.
Trigg Dr.
Straley Dr.
Lyle St.
Smallwood Dr.
N Wells Cir.
S Wells Cir.
Twin Ln.
Sandy Ln.
Randolph Ct.
Watters Pl.
Town Hall
Pollard Dr.
Coleman St.
Tanny St.
Westworth Village
Dayless St.
Roaring Springs Rd.
Duncan St.
General Ramey Dr.
General Arnold Dr.
Tracyne Dr.
Aton Ave.
Aton Ave.
Sunset St.
Carb Dr.
West Fork Trinity River
West Fk. Dr.
McCee Dr.
Redbud
Slate
Yount Dr.
Weaver Ave.
Fairchild Dr.
Dennis Ave.
Fursman Ave.
Volder Ave.
Durham Ave.
Odom Ave.
Ansley Dr.
Oak Forest Dr.
Newport Ct.
Indian Creek Dr.
Montego Rd.
Lansdale Rd.
Pamlico Rd.
Klamath Rd.
Santa Barbara Ave.
Oak Glen Cir.
Burton Hill Rd.
Santa Marie Ave.
Town Square
Juneau Rd.
Inca Rd.
Halifax Rd.
Elms Rd. E
Aries Ct.
Westover Ln.
Shady Oaks Ln.
Westover Hills
Northcrest
Benbridge
Ridgmar Meadow Rd.
Elms Ct.
J. M. Leonard Park
Trafalgar Rd.
Elms Rd. W
Aden Rd.
Versailles Rd.
Saxony Rd.
Genoa Rd.
Firth Rd.
Westover Dr.
Roaring Park
Canterbury Dr.
Indian Creek Dr.
Mount Royal Ter.
Spanish Tr.
Westover Ridge
Wyatt Dr.
Valley Ridge Rd.
Westover Rd.
Quail Run
Dakar Rd. W
Sevilla Rd.
Malibar Rd.
Granada Rd.
Elms Rd.
E Dakar Rd.
Calais Rd.
Westover Sq.
W Dakar Rd.
Taxco Rd.
Hidden Creek Ct.
Hidden Creek Rd.
Westover Ct.
Byers Ave.
Green Oaks Rd.
Lands End Ct.
Lands End Blvd.
Northgate
Tomstock St.
Calais Rd.
Ridgmar Blvd.
Ridgmar Plaza
Plaza Pkwy.
Merrymount Rd.
Square Dr.
Fountain Square Dr.
Highland Park Cir.
Hervie St.
Prevost St.
Faron Ave.
Bourine St.
Plaza Pkwy.
Aden Rd.
Taxco Rd.
Pershing Ave.
Exit 8A
Exit 8B
East-West Fwy.
Dean Ln.
Earl Ln.
Halloran St.
Exit 9B
Birchman Ave.
377
Exit 9A
Calmont Ave.
Malvey Ave.
Malvey Ct.
East Ln.
Winthrop Ave.
Bryant Irvin Rd.
Malvey Ave.
Darwood Ave.
Darwood Ave.
Ridglea Ave.
Fairfield Dr.
Locke Ave.
Locke Ave.
Locke Ave.
Green Oaks Rd.
Sappington Pl.
Olive Pl.
Bigham Blvd.
Kenwick Ave.
Lovell Ave.
Lovell Ave.
Curzon Ave.
Curzon Ave.
Nina Maria St.
Fritz Alan St.
Vera St.
Korth Rd.
Columbia Ave.
Sansom Cir.
Nancy Ln.
Castleberry Cut Off
Roberts Cut Off Rd.
Pomona Ave.
Stanford Ave.
Yale St.
Cornell Ave.
Amherst Ave.
Purdue Ave.
Dartmouth Ave.
Notre Dame Ave.
Auburn St.
Harvard St.
Cambridge St.
Oxford St.
St Edwards St.
Baylor Ave.
Yale St.
Hallum St.
Cody Ct.
Gustav St.
Truman
Club Oak Dr.
Andrea Ct.
Schiene St.
Shady Oak Dr.
Cahill Oval Rd.
Roberts Cut Off Rd.

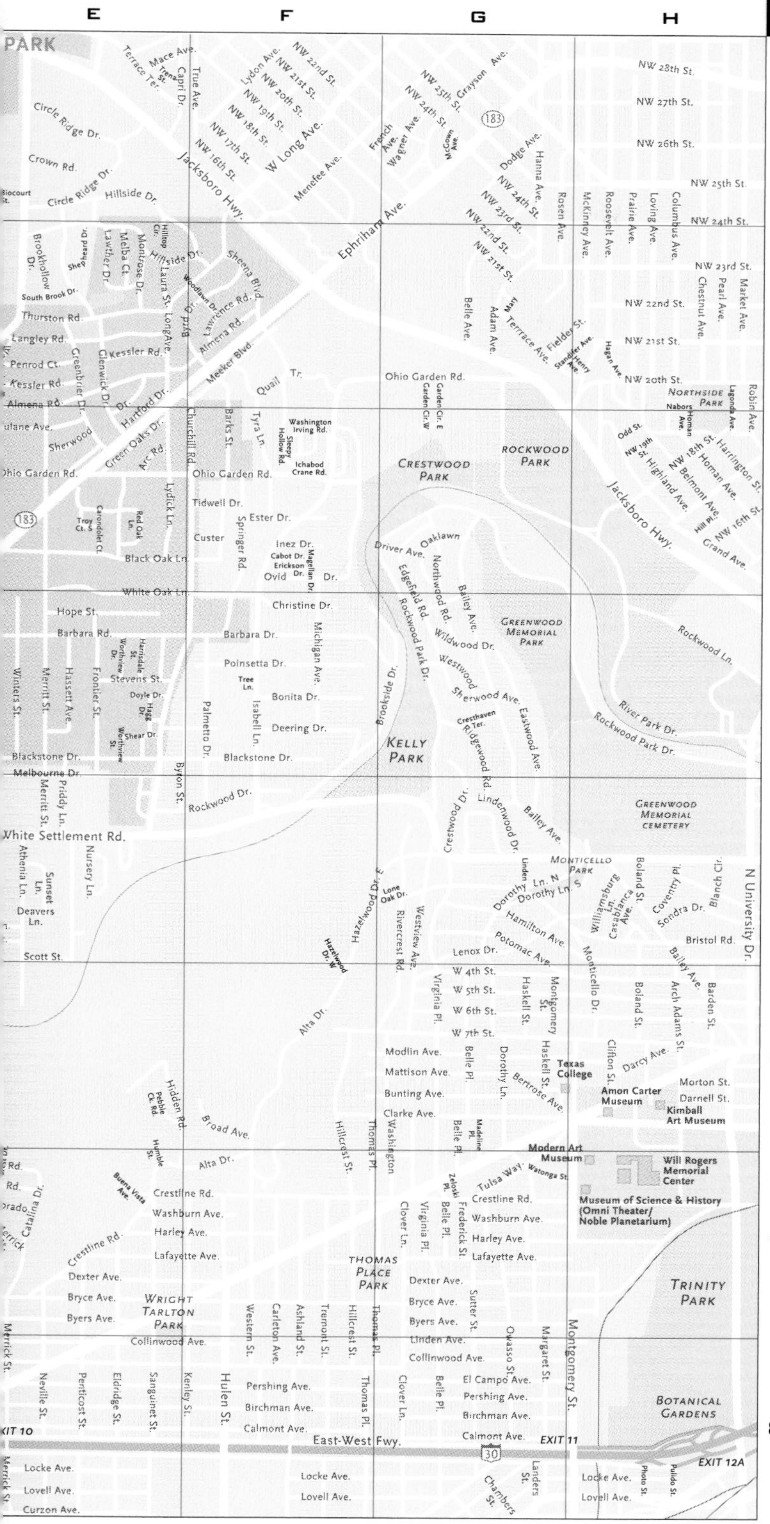
E
F
G
H
1
2
3
4
5
6
7
8
PARK
Terrace Ter.
Mace Ave.
Trena St.
Capri Dr.
True Ave.
Lydon Ave.
NW 22nd St.
NW 21st St.
NW 20th St.
NW 19th St.
NW 18th St.
NW 17th St.
NW 16th St.
W Long Ave.
Menefee Ave.
Jacksboro Hwy.
Circle Ridge Dr.
Crown Rd.
Circle Ridge Dr.
Hillside Dr.
Biocourt St.
NW 25th St.
Grayson Ave.
NW 24th St.
French Ave.
Wagner Ave.
McGown Ave.
183
Dodge Ave.
NW 24th St.
NW 23rd St.
NW 22nd St.
NW 21st St.
Hanna Ave.
Rosen Ave.
McKinley Ave.
Roosevelt Ave.
Prairie Ave.
Loving Ave.
Columbus Ave.
NW 28th St.
NW 27th St.
NW 26th St.
NW 25th St.
NW 24th St.
NW 23rd St.
Pearl Ave.
Chestnut Ave.
Market Ave.
NW 22nd St.
NW 21st St.
NW 20th St.
Ephriham Ave.
Brookhollow Dr.
Shepherd Dr.
Lawther Dr.
Melba Ct.
Montrose Dr.
Hilltop Cir.
Hillside Dr.
Laura St.
Long Ave.
Byrd Dr.
Woodlawn Dr.
Lawrence Rd.
Sheena Blvd.
Almena Rd.
Meeker Blvd.
South Brook Dr.
Thurston Rd.
Langley Rd.
Penrod Ct.
Kessler Rd.
Almena Rd.
Greenbrier Dr.
Glenwick Dr.
Kessler Rd.
Hartford Dr.
Quail Tr.
Belle Ave.
Adam Ave.
Mary Terrace Ave.
Fielder St.
Standifer Ave.
Henry Ave.
Hagan Ave.
Ohio Garden Rd.
Garden Cir. E
Garden Cir. W
Northside Park
Nabors
Homan Ave.
Lagonda Ave.
Robin Ave.
Tulane Ave.
Sherwood
Green Oaks Dr.
Arc Rd.
Churchill Rd.
Barks St.
Tyra Ln.
Washington Irving Rd.
Sleepy Hollow Rd.
Ichabod Crane Rd.
Crestwood Park
Rockwood Park
Odd St.
NW 19th St.
Highland Ave.
NW 18th St.
Belmont Ave.
Homan Ave.
Harrington St.
Hill Pl.
NW 16th St.
Grand Ave.
Jacksboro Hwy.
Ohio Garden Rd.
Ohio Garden Rd.
Tidwell Dr.
Lydick Ln.
183
Troy Ct. S
Carondolet Ct.
Red Oak Ln.
Ester Dr.
Custer
Springer Rd.
Inez Dr.
Cabot Dr.
Erickson Dr.
Ovid Dr.
Magellan Dr.
Black Oak Ln.
White Oak Ln.
Driver Ave.
Oaklawn
Northwood Rd.
Edgefield Rd.
Rockwood Park Dr.
Bailey Ave.
Greenwood Memorial Park
Rockwood Ln.
Hope St.
Barbara Rd.
Harrisdale St.
Worthview Dr.
Stevens St.
Christine Dr.
Barbara Dr.
Poinsetta Dr.
Michigan Ave.
Wildwood Dr.
Westwood
Brookside Dr.
Winters St.
Merritt St.
Hassett Ave.
Frontier St.
Doyle Dr.
Hagg Dr.
Shear Dr.
Worthview St.
Tree Ln.
Bonita Dr.
Isabell Ln.
Palmetto Dr.
Deering Dr.
Sherwood Ave.
Cresthaven Ter.
Ridgewood Rd.
Eastwood Ave.
River Park Dr.
Rockwood Park Dr.
Kelly Park
Blackstone Dr.
Melbourne Dr.
Blackstone Dr.
Byron St.
Merritt St.
Priddy Ln.
Rockwood Dr.
Crestwood Dr.
Lindenwood Dr.
Bailey Ave.
Greenwood Memorial Cemetery
White Settlement Rd.
Nursery Ln.
Athenia Ln.
Sunset Ln.
Deavers Ln.
Hazelwood Dr. E
Lone Oak Dr.
Westview Ave.
Rivercrest Rd.
Linden
Dorothy Ln. N
Dorothy Ln. S
Monticello Park
Williamsburg Ln.
Casablanca Ave.
Boland St.
Coventry Pl.
Sondra Dr.
Blanch Cir.
N University Dr.
Hamilton Ave.
Bristol Rd.
Scott St.
Hazelwood Dr. W
Potomac Ave.
Lenox Dr.
Monticello Dr.
Bailey Ave.
Virginia Pl.
W 4th St.
W 5th St.
W 6th St.
W 7th St.
Haskell St.
Montgomery St.
Boland St.
Arch Adams St.
Barden St.
Alta Dr.
Modlin Ave.
Mattison Ave.
Belle Pl.
Dorothy Ln.
Haskell St.
Texas College
Clifton St.
Darcy Ave.
Bertrose Ave.
Amon Carter Museum
Morton St.
Darnell St.
Kimball Art Museum
Bunting Ave.
Clarke Ave.
Hidden Rd.
Pebble Ck. Rd.
Broad Ave.
Hillcrest St.
Thomas Pl.
Washington
Belle Pl.
Madeline Pl.
Modern Art Museum
Will Rogers Memorial Center
Humble St.
Alta Dr.
Tulsa Way
Watonga St.
Buena Vista Ave.
Catalina Dr.
Crestline Rd.
Washburn Ave.
Harley Ave.
Lafayette Ave.
Zeloski Pl.
Belle Pl.
Frederick St.
Virginia Pl.
Clover Ln.
Crestline Rd.
Washburn Ave.
Harley Ave.
Lafayette Ave.
Museum of Science & History
(Omni Theater/
Noble Planetarium)
Crestline Rd.
Dexter Ave.
Bryce Ave.
Byers Ave.
Wright Tarlton Park
Thomas Place Park
Dexter Ave.
Bryce Ave.
Byers Ave.
Linden Ave.
Sutter St.
Trinity Park
Merrick St.
Collinwood Ave.
Western St.
Carleton Ave.
Ashland St.
Tremont St.
Hillcrest St.
Thomas Pl.
Collinwood Ave.
Owasso St.
Margaret St.
Montgomery St.
Neville St.
Penticost St.
Eldridge St.
Sanguinet St.
Kenley St.
Hulen St.
Pershing Ave.
Birchman Ave.
Calmont Ave.
Thomas Pl.
Clover Ln.
Belle Pl.
El Campo Ave.
Pershing Ave.
Birchman Ave.
Calmont Ave.
Botanical Gardens
Exit 10
East-West Fwy.
30
Exit 11
Exit 12A
Merrick St.
Locke Ave.
Lovell Ave.
Curzon Ave.
Locke Ave.
Lovell Ave.
Chambers St.
Landers St.
Locke Ave.
Lovell Ave.
Photo St.
Pulido St.

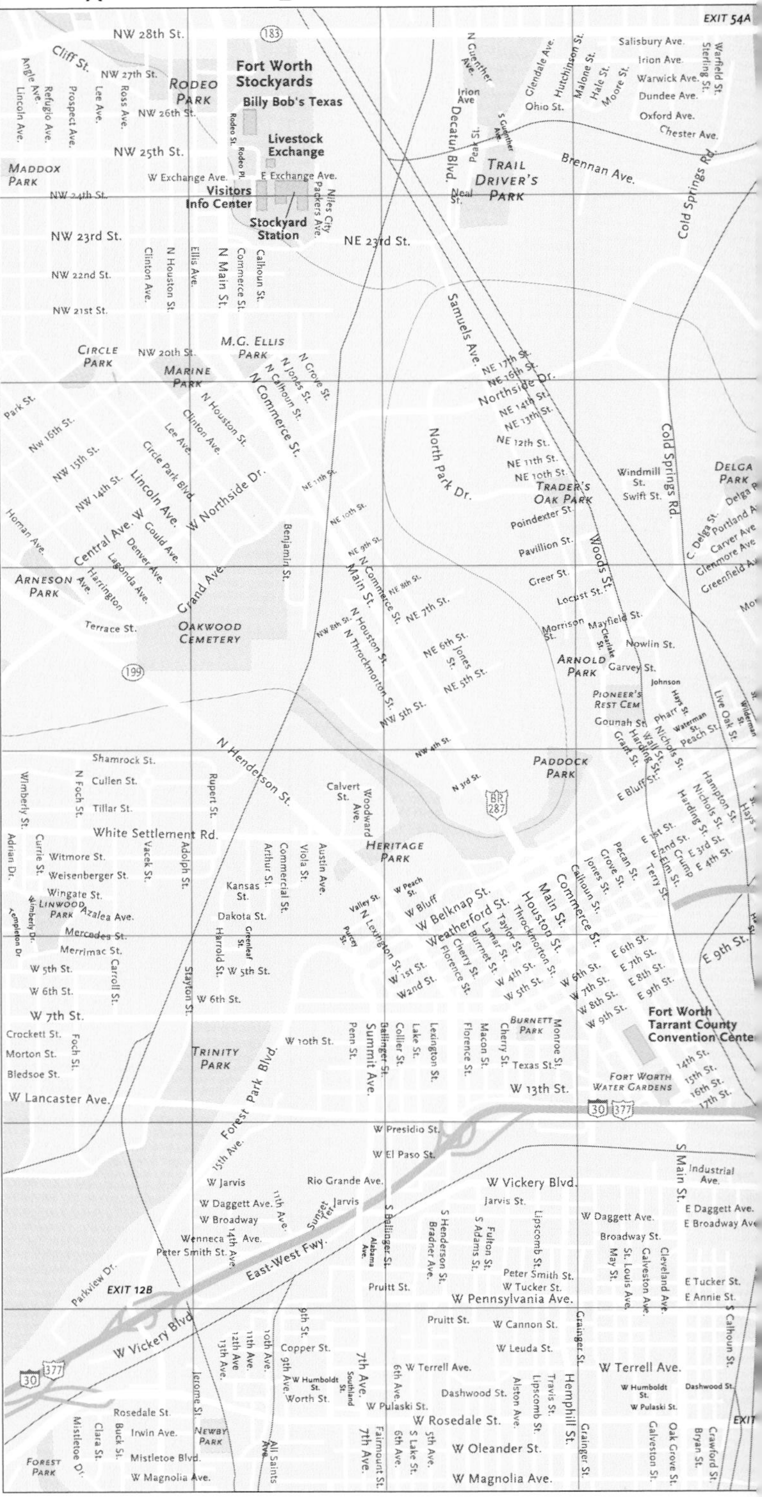
A
B
C
D
1
2
3
4
5
6
7
8
EXIT 54A
NW 28th St.
183
Cliff St.
NW 27th St.
Angle Ave.
Lincoln Ave.
Refugio Ave.
Prospect Ave.
Lee Ave.
Ross Ave.
Rodeo Park
NW 26th St.
Fort Worth Stockyards
Billy Bob's Texas
Rodeo St.
Rodeo Pl.
Livestock Exchange
NW 25th St.
Maddox Park
W Exchange Ave.
E Exchange Ave.
Visitors Info Center
Niles City
Packers Ave.
Stockyard Station
NW 24th St.
NW 23rd St.
NE 23rd St.
NW 22nd St.
NW 21st St.
Clinton Ave.
N Houston St.
Ellis Ave.
N Main St.
Commerce St.
Calhoun St.
N Guenther Ave.
Irion Ave.
Decatur Blvd.
Peach St.
S Guenther Ave.
Neal St.
Trail Driver's Park
Glendale Ave.
Hutchinson St.
Ohio St.
Malone St.
Hale St.
Moore St.
Brennan Ave.
Salisbury Ave.
Irion Ave.
Warwick Ave.
Dundee Ave.
Oxford Ave.
Chester Ave.
Warfield St.
Sterling St.
Cold Springs Rd.
Samuels Ave.
M.G. Ellis Park
Circle Park
NW 20th St.
Marine Park
N Grove St.
N Jones St.
N Calhoun St.
N Commerce St.
N Houston St.
Clinton Ave.
Lee Ave.
Park St.
NW 16th St.
NW 15th St.
NW 14th St.
Circle Park Blvd.
Lincoln Ave.
W Northside Dr.
NE 11th St.
NE 10th St.
NE 9th St.
Benjamin St.
Central Ave.
Gould Ave.
Denver Ave.
Homan Ave.
Lagonda Ave.
Harrington Ave.
Arneson Park
Grand Ave.
Terrace St.
Oakwood Cemetery
199
NE 17th St.
NE 16th St.
Northside Dr.
NE 14th St.
NE 13th St.
NE 12th St.
NE 11th St.
NE 10th St.
North Park Dr.
Trader's Oak Park
Windmill St.
Swift St.
Cold Springs Rd.
Delga Park
Poindexter St.
Pavillion St.
Woods St.
Delga St.
Portland Ave.
Carver Ave.
Glenmore Ave.
Greenfield Ave.
Greer St.
Locust St.
Morrison St.
Mayfield St.
Nowlin St.
Clearlake St.
Arnold Park
Garvey St.
Johnson
N Commerce St.
NE 8th St.
Main St.
NE 7th St.
NW 8th St.
N Houston St.
N Throckmorton St.
NE 6th St.
Jones St.
NE 5th St.
NW 5th St.
NW 4th St.
N 3rd St.
Pioneer's Rest Cem
Gounah St.
Pharr St.
Hays St.
Waterman St.
Peach St.
Live Oak St.
Wilderman St.
Grant St.
Harding St.
Wall St.
Nichols St.
Paddock Park
BR 287
E Bluff St.
Hampton St.
Nichols St.
Harding St.
Hays St.
N Henderson St.
Shamrock St.
Cullen St.
Tillar St.
N Foch St.
Wimberly St.
White Settlement Rd.
Rupert St.
Calvert St.
Woodward Ave.
Adrian Dr.
Currie St.
Witmore St.
Vacek St.
Adolph St.
Weisenberger St.
Wingate St.
Linwood Park
Azalea Ave.
Wimberly Dr.
Templeton Dr.
Arthur St.
Commercial St.
Viola St.
Austin Ave.
Kansas St.
Dakota St.
Heritage Park
W Peach St.
Valley St.
W Bluff
W Belknap St.
N Lexington St.
Purcey St.
Weatherford St.
Houston St.
Main St.
Commerce St.
Calhoun St.
Jones St.
Grove St.
Pecan St.
E 1st St.
E 2nd St.
E 3rd St.
E 4th St.
Elm St.
Crump
Terry St.
Mercedes St.
Merrimac St.
W 5th St.
W 6th St.
W 7th St.
Carroll St.
Harrold St.
Greenleaf St.
W 5th St.
W 6th St.
Stayton St.
W 1st St.
W 2nd St.
Florence St.
Cherry St.
Burnett St.
Lamar St.
Taylor St.
Throckmorton St.
W 4th St.
W 5th St.
W 6th St.
W 7th St.
W 8th St.
W 9th St.
E 6th St.
E 7th St.
E 8th St.
E 9th St.
E 9th St.
Crockett St.
Morton St.
Bledsoe St.
Foch St.
Trinity Park
W 10th St.
Penn St.
Summit Ave.
Ballinger St.
Collier St.
Lake St.
Lexington St.
Florence St.
Macon St.
Cherry St.
Burnett Park
Monroe St.
Texas St.
W 13th St.
Fort Worth Tarrant County Convention Center
Fort Worth Water Gardens
14th St.
15th St.
16th St.
17th St.
W Lancaster Ave.
Forest Park Blvd.
30
377
W Presidio St.
W El Paso St.
15th Ave.
W Jarvis
Rio Grande Ave.
W Vickery Blvd.
Jarvis St.
S Main St.
Industrial Ave.
W Daggett Ave.
W Broadway
11th Ave.
Jarvis
Sunset Ter.
S Ballinger St.
S Henderson St.
S Adams St.
Bradner Ave.
Fulton St.
Lipscomb St.
W Daggett Ave.
E Daggett Ave.
E Broadway Ave.
Wenneca Ave.
14th Ave.
Peter Smith St.
East-West Fwy.
Alabama Ave.
Broadway St.
May St.
St. Louis Ave.
Galveston Ave.
Cleveland Ave.
Parkview Dr.
EXIT 12B
Pruitt St.
Peter Smith St.
W Tucker St.
W Pennsylvania Ave.
E Tucker St.
E Annie St.
W Vickery Blvd.
Pruitt St.
W Cannon St.
Grainger St.
S Calhoun St.
9th St.
11th Ave.
12th Ave.
13th Ave.
10th Ave.
Copper St.
W Leuda St.
9th Ave.
W Humboldt St.
Southland St.
7th Ave.
6th Ave.
W Terrell Ave.
W Terrell Ave.
30
377
Jerome St.
Worth St.
W Pulaski St.
Dashwood St.
Alston Ave.
Lipscomb St.
Travis St.
Hemphill St.
W Humboldt St.
W Pulaski St.
Dashwood St.
EXIT
Rosedale St.
W Rosedale St.
Mistletoe Dr.
Clara St.
Buck St.
Irwin Ave.
Newby Park
All Saints Ave.
7th Ave.
Fairmount St.
6th Ave.
S Lake St.
5th Ave.
W Oleander St.
Grainger St.
Galveston St.
Oak Grove St.
Bryan St.
Crawford St.
Forest Park
Mistletoe Blvd.
W Magnolia Ave.
W Magnolia Ave.

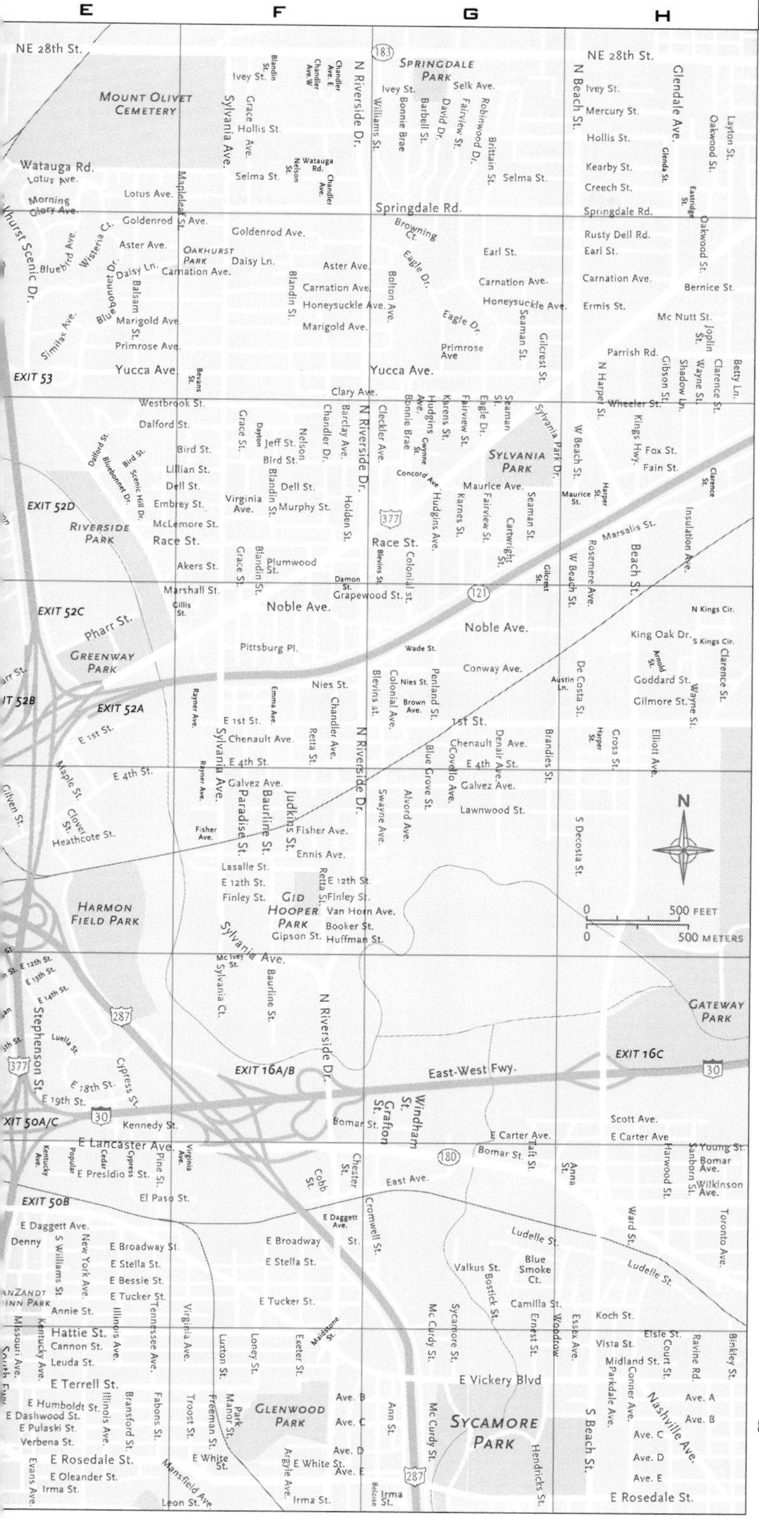
E
F
G
H
1
2
3
4
5
6
7
8
NE 28th St.
Mount Olivet Cemetery
Springdale Park
Selk Ave.
Ivey St.
Grace St.
Hollis St.
Sylvania Ave.
N Riverside Dr.
Williams St.
Bonnie Brae
Barbell St.
David Dr.
Fairview St.
Robinwood Dr.
Brittain St.
N Beach St.
Mercury St.
Glendale Ave.
Oakwood St.
Layton St.
Watauga Rd.
Lotus Ave.
Morning Glory Ave.
Selma St.
Kearby St.
Creech St.
Springdale Rd.
Goldenrod Ave.
Rusty Dell Rd.
Earl St.
Aster Ave.
Oakhurst Park
Daisy Ln.
Carnation Ave.
Honeysuckle Ave.
Marigold Ave.
Primrose Ave.
Yucca Ave.
Ermis St.
Bernice St.
Mc Nutt St.
Parrish Rd.
Oakhurst Scenic Dr.
Bluebird Ave.
Wisteria Ct.
Bluebonnet Dr.
Balsam St.
Similax Ave.
Exit 53
Browning Ct.
Eagle Dr.
Bolton Ave.
Blandin St.
Seaman St.
Gilcrest St.
Wheeler St.
Clary Ave.
Westbrook St.
Dalford St.
Bird St.
Lillian St.
Dell St.
Embrey St.
McLemore St.
Race St.
Akers St.
Marshall St.
Exit 52D
Riverside Park
Jeff St.
Nelson St.
Chandler Dr.
Barclay Ave.
Cleckler Ave.
Hudgins Ave.
Karens St.
Eagle Dr.
Sylvania Park
Sylvania Park Dr.
W Beach St.
N Harper St.
Kings Hwy.
Fox St.
Fain St.
Maurice Ave.
Concord Ave.
Virginia Ave.
Murphy St.
Holden St.
Karnes St.
Cartwright St.
Marsalis St.
Beach St.
Insulation Ave.
Plumwood St.
Colonial St.
Grapewood St.
Noble Ave.
Exit 52C
Pharr St.
Greenway Park
Pittsburg Pl.
Wade St.
Conway Ave.
De Costa St.
King Oak Dr.
N Kings Cir.
S Kings Cir.
Goddard St.
Gilmore St.
Clarence St.
Wayne St.
Exit 52A
Exit 52B
Nies St.
Penland St.
Brown Ave.
Rayner Ave.
E 1st St.
Chenault Ave.
E 4th St.
Galvez Ave.
Retta St.
1st St.
Denair Ave.
Brandies St.
Cross St.
Elliott Ave.
Maple St.
Clover St.
Heathcote St.
Gilvin St.
Paradise St.
Baurline St.
Judkins St.
Fisher Ave.
Ennis Ave.
Blue Grove St.
Covello Ave.
Swayne Ave.
Alvord Ave.
Lawnwood St.
S Decosta St.
N
Lasalle St.
E 12th St.
Finley St.
Gid Hooper Park
Van Horn Ave.
Booker St.
Gipson St.
Huffman St.
Harmon Field Park
0
500 feet
500 meters
Mc Ivey St.
Sylvania Ct.
Stephenson St.
Luella St.
Cypress St.
E 18th St.
E 19th St.
Exit 16A/B
Exit 16C
Gateway Park
East-West Fwy.
Exit 50A/C
Kennedy St.
Bomar St.
Grafton St.
Windham St.
Scott Ave.
E Carter Ave.
Taft St.
E Lancaster Ave.
E Presidio St.
Pine St.
El Paso St.
Exit 50B
Cobb St.
Chester St.
East Ave.
Anna St.
Harwood St.
Sanborn St.
Young St.
Bomar Ave.
Wilkinson Ave.
E Daggett Ave.
Denny
S Williams St.
New York Ave.
E Broadway St.
E Stella St.
E Bessie St.
E Tucker St.
Cromwell St.
Ludelle St.
Valkus St.
Blue Smoke Ct.
Bostick St.
Camilla St.
Ward St.
Toronto Ave.
VanZandt Inn Park
Annie St.
Hattie St.
Cannon St.
Leuda St.
E Terrell St.
Missouri Ave.
Kentucky Ave.
Illinois Ave.
Tennessee Ave.
Virginia Ave.
Luxton St.
Loney St.
Exeter St.
Maidstone St.
Mc Curdy St.
Sycamore St.
Ernest St.
Woodrow
Essex Ave.
Koch St.
Vista St.
Elsie St.
Court St.
Midland St.
Ravine Rd.
Binkley St.
E Vickery Blvd
Parkdale Ave.
Conner Ave.
Nashville Ave.
E Humboldt St.
E Dashwood St.
E Pulaski St.
Verbena St.
E Rosedale St.
E Oleander St.
Irma St.
Evans Ave.
Bransford St.
Fabons St.
Troost St.
Freeman St.
Park Manor St.
Glenwood Park
Ave. B
Ave. C
Ave. D
Ave. E
Ann St.
Sycamore Park
Hendricks St.
S Beach St.
Ave. A
E White St.
Argyle Ave.
Mansfield Ave.
Leon St.
Belzise
183
377
121
287
30
180

FROM THE EDITORS OF

TexasMonthly®

MANY MAPS • WHERE & HOW

FIND IT ALL • NIGHT & DAY

ANTIQUES TO ZIPPERS

BARGAINS & BAUBLES

ELEGANT EDIBLES • ETHNIC EATS

STEAK HOUSES • BISTROS

DELIS • TRATTORIAS

CLASSICAL • JAZZ • COMEDY

THEATER • DANCE • CLUBS

COCKTAIL LOUNGES

COUNTRY & WESTERN • ROCK

COOL TOURS

HOUSECLEANING • CATERING

GET A LAWYER • GET A DENTIST

GET A NEW PET • GET A VET

BASEBALL TO ROCK CLIMBING

FESTIVALS • EVENTS

DAY SPAS • DAY TRIPS

HOTELS • HOT LINES

GET A LAWYER • GET A DENTIST

PASSPORT PIX • TRAVEL INFO

HELICOPTER TOURS

DINERS • DELIS • PIZZERIAS

BRASSERIES • TAQUERÍAS

BOOTS • BOOKS • BUTTONS

BICYCLES • SKATES

SUITS • SHOES • HATS

RENT A TUX • RENT A COSTUME

BAKERIES • SPICE SHOPS

SOUP TO NUTS

Fodor's

CITYGUIDE DALLAS FT. WORTH

AND THE MID-CITIES

FODOR'S TRAVEL PUBLICATIONS

NEW YORK • TORONTO • LONDON • SYDNEY • AUCKLAND

WWW.FODORS.COM

FODOR'S CITYGUIDE DALLAS/ FORT WORTH AND THE MID-CITIES

EDITOR
William Travis

EDITORIAL CONTRIBUTORS
Cathy Casey, Mark Magilow, Betty Plumlee, Christina Patoski, June Rodriguez, Pat Gordon, Kate Lorenz

EDITORIAL PRODUCTION
Kristin Milavec

MAPS
David Lindroth, Inc., *cartographer;* Bob Blake, *map editor*

DESIGN
Fabrizio La Rocca, *creative director;* Allison Saltzman, *text design;* Tigist Getachew, *cover design;* Jolie Novak, *senior picture editor;* Melanie Marin, *photo editor*

PRODUCTION/MANUFACTURING
Angela L. McLean

COVER PHOTOGRAPH
Randy Wells

COPYRIGHT

First Edition

ISBN 0-679-00461-0

ISSN 1533-0508

SPECIAL SALES

Fodor's Travel Publications are available at special discounts for bulk purchases for sales promotions or premiums. Special editions, including personalized covers, excerpts of existing guides, and corporate imprints, can be created in large quantities for special needs. For more information, contact your local bookseller or write to Special Markets, Fodor's Travel Publications, 280 Park Avenue, New York, NY 10017. Inquiries from Canada should be directed to your local Canadian bookseller or sent to Random House of Canada, Ltd., Marketing Department, 2775 Matheson Boulevard East, Mississauga, Ontario L4W 4P7. Inquiries from the United Kingdom should be sent to Fodor's Travel Publications, 20 Vauxhall Bridge Road, London SW1V 2SA, England.

PRINTED IN THE UNITED STATES OF AMERICA

10 9 8 7 6 5 4 3 2 1

CONTENTS

METROPOLITAN LIFE

On a bad day in a big city, the little things that go with living shoulder-to-shoulder with a few million people wear us all down. But the special pleasures of urban life have a way of keeping us around town—and thankful, even, for every second of stress. The field of daffodils in the park on a fine spring day. The perfect little black dress that you find for half price. The markets—so fabulously well stocked that you can cook any recipe without resorting to mail-order catalogs. The way you can sometimes turn a corner and discover a whole new world, so foreign you can hardly believe you're only a few miles from home. The never-ending wealth of possibilities and opportunities.

If you know where to find it all, the city cannot defeat you. With knowledge comes power. That's why Fodor's has prepared this book, with the editors at *Texas Monthly*. It will put phone numbers at your fingertips. It'll take you to new places and remind you of those you've forgotten. It's the ultimate urban companion—and, we hope, your **new best friend in the city.**

It's the **Dallas/Fort Worthwise shopaholic,** who always knows where to find something, no matter how obscure. We've made a concerted effort to bring hundreds of great shops to your attention, so that you'll never be at a loss, whether you need a special birthday present for a great friend or some obscure craft items to make Halloween costumes for your kids.

It's the **restaurant know-it-all,** who's full of ideas for every occasion—you know, the one who would never send you to the slick chain joint where the tortillas taste like cardboard and the steaks don't taste like anything at all. In this book we'll steer you around the corner, to a perfect little place with five tables, a chalkboard menu, and the family matriarch in the kitchen.

It's a **hip barfly buddy,** who can give you advice when you need a charming nook, not too noisy, to take a friend after work. Among the dozens of bars and nightspots in this book, you're bound to find something that fits your mood.

It's the **sagest nightlife maven you know,** the one who always has the scoop on what's on that's worthwhile after dark. In these pages, you'll find dozens of jazz clubs, concert venues and arts organizations.

It's also the **city whiz,** who knows how to get you where you're going, wherever you are.

It's the **best map guide** on the shelves, and it puts **all the city in your briefcase** or on your bookshelf.

Stick with us. We lay out all the options for your leisure time—and gently nudge you away from the duds—so that you can truly enjoy your Dallas/Fort Worth life.

YOUR GUIDES

No one person can know it all. To help get you on track around the city, a stellar group of local experts are sharing their wisdom.

Texas Monthly magazine plugged Fodor's directly into everything going on around Dallas/Fort Worth. Winner of eight National Magazine Awards, it has chronicled life in Texas since 1973 and is every Texan's last word on the Texas scene. Music, the arts, travel, restaurants, museums, and cultural events—the Texas Monthly staff has all the bases covered.

Pat Gordon, a former reporter for *The Dallas Morning News*, now freelances for such publications as *The Boston Globe.* She also teaches journalism at the University of Texas at Arlington.

A native Dallasite, **Betty Plumlee** divides her time between singing with the Dallas Symphony Chorus and freelance writing about food. Her well-honed skills in the kitchen, formal culinary training, and ample forays through New York, California, Italy, Germany, and France qualify her as a keen observer of the local restaurant scene.

Lawyer, musician and Renaissance Boy, **Mark Magilow** has been writing about food for more than 17 years. Quick with the sharp barb but easily neutralized by the greenest of Italian chefs, he especially enjoys exploring the funky ethnic places of Dallas' remote regions.

Peripatetic writer and photographer **Christina Patoski** has explored the dining scene in Fort Worth for more than 30 years. An enthusiastic cook and self-professed bon vivant, her work has appeared in *The New York Times*, *Harper's Bazaar*, *Metropolis*, *American Way Magazine*, *USA Today*, *Texas Monthly*, and on National Public Radio's "All Things Considered." Her book *Merry Christmas America: A Front Yard View of the Holidays* is a Christmas classic. Christina's photographs have been exhibited at museums throughout the United States from the Smithsonian's National Museum of American History to the Weisman Art Museum in Minneapolis.

June Naylor Rodriguez is a sixth-generation Texan and a life-long resident of the Dallas/Fort Worth area. A contributing food, dining and travel writer for the *Fort Worth Star-Telegram* where she spent many years as assistant travel editor, June is also the author of several Texas travel books.

HOW TO USE THIS BOOK

The first thing you need to know is that everything in this book is **arranged by category and by alphabetical order** within each category.

Now, before you go any farther, check out the **city maps** up front. Each map has a number, in a black box at the top of the page, and grid coordinates along the top and side margins. On the text pages, nearly every listing in the book is keyed to one of these maps. Look for the map number in a small black box preceding each establishment name. The grid code follows in italics. For establishments with more than one location, additional map numbers and grid codes appear at the end of the listing. To locate a museum that's identified in the text as 7 *e-6*, turn to Map 7 and locate the address within the e-6 grid square. To locate restaurants that are nearby, simply skim the text in the restaurant chapter for listings identified as being on Map 7.

Where appropriate throughout the guide, we name the neighborhood or town in which each sight, restaurant, shop, or other destination is located. We also give you complete opening hours and admission fees for sights; closing information for shops; and credit-card, closing hours, reservations, and price information for restaurants.

At the end of the book, in addition to an **alphabetical index,** you'll find **directories of shops and restaurants by neighborhood.**

Chapter 7, City Sources, lists essential information, such as entertainment hot lines (for those times when you can't lay your hands on a newspaper), and resources for residents—everything from vet and lawyer-referral services to caterers worth calling.

We've worked hard to make sure that all of the information we give you is accurate at press time. Still, time brings changes, so always confirm information when it matters—especially if you're making a detour.

Feel free to drop us a line. Were the restaurants we recommended as described? Did you find a wonderful shop you'd like to share? If you have complaints, we'll look into them and revise our entries in the next edition when the facts warrant. So send us your feedback. Either e-mail us at editors@fodors.com (specifying *Fodor's CITYGUIDE Dallas/Fort Worth and the Mid-Cities* on the subject line), or write to the *Fodor's CITYGUIDE Dallas/Fort Worth and the Mid-Cities* editor at Fodor's, 280 Park Avenue, New York, New York 10017. We look forward to hearing from you.

Karen Cure
Editorial Director

chapter 1

RESTAURANTS

A triumvirate of diversity, the Metroplex—Dallas, Fort Worth, Mid-Cities—ranks high among its contenders as the region of the Millennium. High tech, financial and professional services, retailing, and petroleum shape the business life in Dallas while high fashion, trendiness, and the endless grasp for the brass ring drive the cultural and entertainment lives of Fort Worth and the sprawling Mid-Cities. "Big D" flaunts its extremes of down-home friendliness juxtaposed with sophistication, urbanity, and cosmopolitan glitter; Fort Worth and Mid-Cities favor earthy complexity over glitz; and underneath them all is a rich dining culture that reflects its surroundings.

Without the benefit of urban density and generations of ethnic texture, Dallas restaurateurs have relied on importing the finest from the world's largest cities to create a hub for homegrown southwestern cuisine—an amalgamation of earthy Texas, Mexican, and New Mexican flavors. Second to none in ubiquitous and economical Tex-Mex, Dallas affords plenty of opportunities for hot dogs and foie gras, steaks and lobster, and green mussels in oriental black bean sauce. Large, active Asian communities thrive in both northeast Dallas and the near east inner city areas. Many humble establishments offer ethnic dining experiences you won't soon forget.

In the city to the west you will find the high points of dining to be more earthy, reflecting Fort Worth's laid-back character. Not that fine dining opportunities lack here, but you are more likely to find heaven by sticking to what native Dan Jenkins lovingly refers to as "brown food"—chicken-fried steak, Tex-Mex, barbeque, hamburgers, and chili. Let the chase-your-tails trends bypass the Fort Worth city limits altogether because most of the locals here value basic, hearty, and even downright humble cuisine. Although a number of national franchised chains, such as Romano's Macaroni Grill, Pappadeaux's, and Uncle Julio's, consistently serve up excellent food, the listings here focus on local independents, unless a franchise is locally-based.

As the "Mid-Cities"—that thick cluster of towns connecting Dallas with Fort Worth—has exploded, so has the complexity of its dining scene. Once a hallowed ground for chicken-fried steak and enchiladas, Tarrant County now offers a variety of Vietnamese, Thai, and Japanese restaurants. Of course, a worthy debate among barbecue joint owners as to whether beef, sausage, ribs, and chicken should be smoked over hickory, oak, or mesquite still prevails. Diners in the Mid-Cities are lucky enough to decide for themselves while sorting through the pleasing depth of places from Grapevine to Arlington serving goodies from calamari to tabbouleh.

Wherever you choose to dine in the Metroplex, diversity awaits. Gaze, partake, enjoy.

general information

NO SMOKING

Most restaurants have a designated area for smoking. Some restaurants have smoking/dining areas near the bar. Restaurants seating 50 or more patrons have a non-smoking section.

RESERVATIONS

It's common courtesy to make reservations at a restaurant: when you call you might discover that the restaurant is closed for a private party, the air-conditioning is on the blink, or some other important consideration. Likewise, if you can't make it at your reserved time (give or take 20 minutes), or if you can't make it at all, definitely call the restaurant. Believe it or not, cumulative no-shows can seriously hurt a restaurant.

TIPPING

Tipping in Texas is 15% of the total, excluding tax; additional compensation is based on your judgment of service and overall experience. A simple guideline for judging the baseline is doubling the 8.5% tax on your check. Most restaurants add a service charge for large parties, so if you are dining with a group of six or more, be sure to check the bill carefully before leaving a tip.

PRICE CATEGORIES

Restaurant price categories are based on the average cost of a dinner that includes appetizer, entrée, and dessert.

CATEGORY	COST*
$$$$	over $45
$$$	$30–$45
$$	$18–$30
$	under $18

**per person, excluding drinks, service, and sales tax (8.25%)*

restaurants by cuisine: dallas

AMERICAN

12 *g-4*

BROTHERS' FRIED CHICKEN

When those midnight Saturday cravings for fried okra or a fried chicken gizzard sandwich on white bread, washed down with a grape soda, come a knockin', time to head to Brothers. Variations include mix-and-match gizzards and livers with a few jalapeño peppers. For more traditional fare, try the well-battered, crispy golden thighs and breasts. This is authentic Southern fried chicken. Tables are few, and the drive-through resembles a twisted Monaco grand prix route, moving at an escargot's pace. *4839 Gaston Ave., at Fitzhugh Ave., East, 214/370–0800. Reservations not accepted. No credit cards. No smoking. $*

10 *g-1*

BUBBA'S

This 50-seat, Art Deco diner in Snider Plaza serves catfish fillets, country veggies, homemade rolls, a home-style breakfast, and fried chicken locals swear by. *6617 Hillcrest Ave., University Park, 214/373–6527. No credit cards. $*

10 *g-1*

CELEBRATION

From its late '60s origins as two separate houses—one serving family-style home cooking, and the other selling handmade sandals—this earthy establishment bridges the two and provides a fresh, clean look. From those earthy origins, both houses have been bridged together by a pleasant bar. Copper-covered tables adorn the inside and the all-you-can-eat menu has grown in variety and sophistication. Salmon and roasted chicken are popular, as well as mainstays of meat loaf and pot roast. Service is exemplary and the tab is still a bargain for what you get. *4503 W. Lovers La., at Inwood Rd., North, 214/358–0612. Reservations not accepted. AE, D, MC, V. $–$$*

10 *h-1*

DIXIE HOUSE

This Lakewood stalwart serves economical Southern food in a casual, barnlike space. Familiar favorites include fried chicken livers with cream gravy and yeast rolls. "Mom's meat loaf" and cooked-to-order fried chicken puts the chain versions to shame. Side dishes include bubba favorites pinto beans, stewed greens, and mashed potatoes. *6400 Gaston Ave., at Abrams Rd., East, 214/826–2412. AE, D, MC, V. $*

12 *e-8*

GENNIE'S BISHOP GRILL

Across the virtual Trinity River in Oak Cliff, the venerable Gennie's greets throngs of pilgrims each weekday seeking the ultimate "home cookin'" lunch. The lauded chicken-fried steak strikes the proper balance of meat and gravy. The soothing monster proves the truth of the sign posted over the counter: "We cook for Texans, not Frenchmen." Choose a grapefruit-size yeast roll, mashed spuds, and bitter stewed greens to finish out your authentic heaping plate. No right-minded diner can pass up a slice of chocolate, banana cream, or lemon meringue pie. *321 N. Bishop, at 8th St., Oak Cliff, 214/946–1752. Reservations not accepted. No credit cards. Closed Sat.–Sun. No dinner. $*

6 *d-8*

MAMA'S DAUGHTERS' DINER

"Purt'near perfect" describes in local parlance the comfort food consistently emerging from this kitchen. Chicken-fried chicken (smothered in gravy) is a traditional Southern home-style mainstay; so are the well-cooked squash, mashed potatoes, and greens. The peach cobbler à la mode is as close to a "state dessert" as you can get. It's the stuff from which dreams are made. *2610 Royal La., at Harry Hines Blvd., Northwest, 972/241–8646. Reservations not accepted. AE, D, MC, V. Closed Sun. No dinner Sat. $*

6 *e-8*

SURREY CAFÉ

A cluster of cars at this shopping center parking lot is not unusual on weekend mornings. Breakfast feasts adhere to the classics: two eggs, crisp bacon, and a short stack of hearty pancakes. Eggs Benedict with hash browns sets you back a mere five-spot. Predictable and tasty lunch sandwiches include ham-and-cheese, turkey, and tuna, plus whopping 8-ounce burgers. *232 Webbs Chapel Village, at Forest La., North, 972/247–9021. AE, D, DC, MC, V. No dinner Sun. $*

13 *d-2*

TRACI'S

A beautifully restored old house provides a warm, soft setting for the upscale Southern cooking prepared at this eatery. It's the kind of haven that evokes good feelings, both from the ambiance and the availability of comfort foods such as mashed potatoes and fried chicken. Diners raised on such food will find the pork tenderloin familiar but the sweet cherry sauce novel. The filet mignon with wild mushroom sauce rates high in both flavor and texture. *2403 Thomas Ave., at Maple Ave., Uptown, 214/849–0007. AE, MC, V. Closed Sun. No lunch Sat. No dinner Mon. $$–$$$*

AMERICAN/CASUAL

13 *g-5*

ANTARES

Revolving on top of the Downtown Hyatt Regency, this restaurant attracts more than its share of out-of-towners. Like its rotating skyline views of the city below, the rotating specials menus—one month seafood, another pasta—ensure a lively dining experience. *300 Reunion Blvd., Reunion Tower, Downtown, 214/712–7145. AE, D, DC, MC, V. $–$$*

10 *g-1*

BALL'S HAMBURGERS

Linebacker-size burgers and thick milk shakes are necessities of life for some folks, and Ball's provides admirable versions. You'll find plenty of zest in the tangy hickory sauce burger, and a few items from south of the border add a dash of spice to the menu. Lean meat patties, consummate freshness, and accurate execution of doneness make Ball's a reliable, family-oriented venue. *3404 Rankin St., at Lovers La., Snider Plaza, University Park, 214/373–1717. Reservations not accepted. AE, D, MC, V. $*

4343 W. Northwest Hwy., Preston Hollow Shopping Center, North, 214/352–2525.

7 *b-8*

BARBEC'S

Here's an east Dallas institution for ranch-hand breakfasts and country lunches. Daily specials include baked chicken, rice and giblet gravy, and beef tips on noodles, all reminiscent of mom's kitchen and quite good. Still, they don't command attention like the fabled beer biscuits or the endearingly named "Flap and Cluck with Oink"—a pair of eggs your way, sausage, ham or bacon, and two pancakes. *8949 Garland Rd., at Buckner Blvd., East, 214/321–5597. Reservations not accepted. No credit cards. No dinner Sun. $*

6 *f-5*

BENEDICT'S

Look no further for a hearty breakfast with traditional favorites such as waffles and eggs, enlivened with some novel variations such as omelet du jour and Italian frittatas. The light, bright and cheery setting and courteous staff are ideal for a wholesome family dining experience. Tried and true lunch items include salads, soups, and sandwiches. *4800 Belt Line Rd., at Inwood Rd., North Suburbs, 972/490–0500. AE, DC, MC, V. No dinner. $*

12 *e-4*

BREADWINNERS CAFÉ & BAKERY

The complimentary breads, such as tomato-basil, make for delightful munching at this perennially popular café. Breakfast and lunch are its specialties, and throngs of people fill its tables on weekends. A favorite entrée is the exceptionally tasty grilled chicken salad, distinguished by mango slivers juxtaposed with crunchy celery and almonds and sparingly doused with a delicate mustard sauce. *3301 McKinney Ave,. at Hall St., Uptown, 214/754–0099. Reservations not accepted. AE, D, MC, V. No dinner Mon.–Tues. $$*

12 *d-3*

THE BRONX

The slightly funky neighborhood feel of this bustling Oak Lawn institution is especially appealing for Sunday brunch or late-night dining. Dishes range from such simple pleasures as chicken fettuccine Alfredo to more elaborate culinary creations such as rosemary glace on an ambitious roasted pork loin with a wild rice blend and crisp veggies. For dessert, try a wedge of satisfying Viennese apricot pie with whipped cream. Service is friendly and obliging. *3835 Cedar Springs Rd., Oak Lawn, 214/521–5821. AE, DC, MC, V. Closed Mon. No dinner Sun. $$*

10 *g-1*

BURGER HOUSE

There may be funkier places in town, but the tilted concrete floor places this institution right up with the prize-winners. The burgers with the secret salty spices have been passed over the counter for at least 50 years. The Southern Methodist University community crowds this tiny space to order burgers and hot dogs, Jack's famous fries, and "real" malts and shakes. The meat patty in the chili cheeseburger isn't the ¼-pounder type, but they'll create pizzazz with the added tomato, lettuce, and pickle that's necessary for every Texas-bred burger. *6913 Hillcrest, at Lovers La., University Park, 214/361–0370. Reservations not accepted. No credit cards. $*

THE CHEESECAKE FACTORY

This heralded California chain blasted into Dallas big time, opening an enormous space across from fashionable NorthPark. The encyclopedic menu draws heavily on Asia and Italy. Entrees include *Paglia e fieno*, a creamy Florentine pasta dish, and piping hot barbecued duck spring rolls with a tangy citrus dipping sauce. Like everything else, the Portobello mushroom burger is larger than life. Be conservative in ordering earlier courses if you plan to have any capacity left for the myriad of cheesecake flavors. *7700 Northwest Hwy., Lincoln Park Shopping Center, University Park, 214/373–4844. Reservations not accepted. AE, D, DC, MC, V. $$*

CHIP'S OLD FASHIONED HAMBURGERS

Chips's serves up classic thin burgers and tasty sides, especially the renowned calorie-fueled onion rings. It's said that no one is able to resist the infamous banana milk shakes. When you want to take the family for burgers without frills, this is the spot. *4530 W. Lovers La., University Park, 214/691–2447. AE, MC, V. $*

4501 Cole Ave., Oak Lawn, 214/526–1092. AE, MC, V. $

CITY CAFÉ

This popular Park Cities brunch spot promises to serve up eggs "as you like them." Other standout favorites include an open-faced omelet with spinach, herbs, tomatoes, pesto, and mozzarella, and a chicken Caesar salad with smoked bacon, red onion, tomatoes, sourdough croutons, and Parmesan. Leave room for the chocolate strawberry shortcake—an absolute must. *5757 W. Lovers La., at Dallas Tollway, University Park, 214/351–2233. Reservations essential. AE, D, DC, MC, V. $$$*

CLUB SCHMITZ

Despite its weathered, funky exterior, this circa 1946 establishment draws upstanding doctors and lawyers and other cordial young professionals. Service is down-home Texas friendly. Juicy burgers and hot French fries are the mainstays, but you can also score a mean bowl of chili, thick with molten cheese and chopped onions. Clam or shrimp baskets, Polish sausage, fried stuffed jalapeños, and chicken fried steak make this a "one stop covers it all" place for Texas' native food treasures. Take note that the parking lot is best navigated by pickups and SUVs. *9661 Denton Dr., at Webb Chapel, Northwest, 214/350–3607. No credit cards. Closed Sun. $*

12 *d-3*

EATZI'S

Besides its extensive selection of breads and pastries, the bakery for all seasons serves hot-off-the-stove entrées such as roasted chicken, built-to-order sandwiches, soups, salads, and even sushi. A small eating area is in the front of the store but most people prefer take-out. *3403 Oak Lawn Ave., Oak Lawn, 214/526–1515. AE, D, MC, V. $–$$*

13 *g-4*

FAT TED'S

The lure of this Deep Ellum eatery used to be the offbeat atmosphere, but nowadays the typical brick-walled storefront complete with aged wooden bar has become a cliché. What sets this place apart? Juicy hamburgers, griddle-fried to your satisfaction—a reminder why franchise burgers will never make the grade. *2713 Commerce St., Deep Ellum, 214/747–8337. AE, DC, MC, V. Closed Sun. $*

10 *g-1*

GOFF'S

As well-known for its eccentric management personalities as its burgers, Goff's is a Dallas fixture. Proprietor Harvey Goff is known for such antics as refusing service to long-haired male customers and indignantly pouring drinks to-go directly into a paper sack. The locals keep coming back, though, for the old-fashioned hamburgers and to see what Harvey will do next. *5702 W. Lovers La., University Park, 214/351–3336. No credit cards. $*

6 *g-5*

THE GOOD EGG

This comfortable unpretentious breakfast-and-lunch eatery is as homey as your neighbor's kitchen. Settle in for breakfast with an Eye Opener—eggs, bacon, and French toast made with cinnamon bread—among other simple favorites. If lunchtime is tight, sandwiches and salads can be prepared as wraps for those on the go. *1930 N. Coit Rd., at Campbell Rd., North Suburbs, 972/783–4663. Reservations not accepted. AE, MC, V. No smoking. No dinner. $*

13 *d-5*

GUTHRIE'S

At his off-the-beaten-path location near new City Hall, renowned chef William Guthrie returns to basics by preparing simple, delectable meals at reasonable prices. Economical creations include juicy, bronze roasted chicken with assorted vegetables and mashed potatoes in a hearty egg gravy. Other entrées range from hamburgers to fish and chips. Breakfast choices include a giant apple pancake and a boneless pork chop with eggs. Step up to the counter to place your order. *400 S. Ervay St., Downtown, 214/760–7900. AE, MC, V. Closed Sun. $–$$*

10 *e-1*

HOLE IN THE WALL

After sundown, blues bands wail away on the rear deck and come as close as Dallas will ever get to Austin's legendary Armadillo World Headquarters. Inside its funky den, bikers and lawyers, highbrows and lowlifes, convene for classic Texas greasy burgers, a bowl of red, chicken-fried steak, and RC Cola. Yankee visitors note: this is as good as it gets. *11654 Harry Hines Blvd., at Forest La., Northwest, 972/247–2253. Reservations not accepted. D, MC, V. Closed Sun. $*

10 *g-1*

HOUSTON'S

Though part of a chain, its lavish new digs in tony Preston Center have spawned an immediate destination scene. The sparse menu includes distinctively flavored chicken topped with a salad dressed with lime vinaigrette, and a chuck roast jumbo burger served with skins-on fries and baked beans. Coarse slaw, heavy on the mayo, delightfully balance smoky, sauce-basted ribs. *8300-A Preston Rd., at Northwest Hwy., University Park, 214/691–8991. Reservations not accepted. AE, MC, V. $$–$$$*

6 *g-6*

HUNGRY JOCKEY

When plain old breakfast oatmeal just won't do, make tracks for this oasis of comfort food. Two eggs, two sausages or three strips of bacon, and two fluffy, plate-size pancakes is a hearty ticket. If conscience awakens early, a grapefruit, two poached eggs, and whole-wheat toast will satisfy. *12829 Preston Rd., at LBJ Fwy., North, 972/661–0134. Reservations not accepted. MC, V. No dinner. $*

6 *f-5*

J'S BREAKFAST AND BURGERS

This all-American spot serves just about anything anytime. J's menu includes burgers, chili, chicken-fried steak, and breakfast 24 hours. *14925 Midway Rd., Suite 105, North Suburbs, 972/239-7619. No credit cards. Open 24 hours. $*

12 *h-2*

JOHN'S CAFÉ

This is the type of friendly neighborhood eatery where John says "hi" from behind the counter when you walk in and people order "the usual." A favorite place for a burger or a big, home-style egg-and-bacon breakfast. *2724 Greenville Ave, East, 214/827-4610. No credit cards. No dinner Sun. $*

6 *g-6*

LEMMON AVE. BAR & GRILL

Much more cozy and comfy than its funky exterior suggests, "LaBar" serves its loyal devotees economical country home cooking. At $6.95 it's hard to beat the juicy baked chicken on rice with your choice of two side dishes. Lovers of southern fried chicken or fried chicken livers with cream gravy will think they have found the promised land. The veggie plate with yeast rolls and honey-drenched corn bread is a wonderful, healthful, and satisfying alternative. *4330 Lemmon Ave., at Wycliff Ave., Oak Lawn, 214/521-4730. Reservations not accepted. AE, D, MC, V. $-$$*

6 *g-6*

MECCA RESTAURANT

Funky, older than the hills, and staffed with waitresses straight from Old South Central Casting, this stalwart eatery serves the stuff of legends. Eggs can be ordered every which way, and biscuits and creamy gravy make breakfast the real occasion. Mecca also serves great country lunches such as chicken-fried steak and greens. *10422 Harry Hines Blvd,. at Walnut Hill, Northwest, 214/352-0051. Reservations not accepted. AE, D, MC, V. Closed Sun. No dinner. $*

6 *g-7*

PURPLE COW

Remember those soda fountains from the 1940's movies where wholesome teens hung out in a wholesome environment and exchanged banter that wouldn't be out of place in a church? In this retro ice cream parlor, the average age of patrons is probably six. Adults will find amenities, too, such as all-beef hot dogs peeking out from a tangle of briny sauerkraut and a tasty cappuccino shake. Individually wrapped Alka-Seltzers (50¢) inspire culinary courage. *110 Preston Rd., at Royal La., Preston Royal Shopping Center, North, 214/373-0037. Reservations not accepted. AE, MC, V. $*

12 *h-2*

SAN FRANCISCO ROSE

This relaxed, comfortable neighborhood hangout has survived and modernized, appearing today as a fern bar, complete with funky antique sofas. The champagne brunch is a treat, serving such attractive choices as a Belgian waffle, grapefruit juice, and a hot muffin. Predictably enough, eggs Benedict, omelets, and breakfast tacos are tasty alternatives. *3024 Greenville Ave., East, 214/826-2020. Reservations not accepted. AE, D, DC, MC, V. $-$$*

6 *g-5*

SNUFFER'S

Casual and straightforward, Snuffer's has countless fans who declare its thick hamburger to be the city's best. A cheeseburger plus onion fries is just the ticket for a casual Saturday meal at the Midway location, especially if accompanied by a vanilla milk shake, heavy on the Blue Bell ice cream (a Texas favorite). The mysterious spices on the onion fries (known only to the owner) will leave your taste buds tingling. *14910 Midway Rd., at Belt Line Rd., North Suburbs, 972/991-8811. Reservations not accepted. AE, D, MC, V. $*

3526 Greenville Ave., at Martel Ave., East, 214/826-6850.

12 *d-4*

STONELEIGH P

Recreating the feel of an old pharmacy soda fountain that once occupied the site, this Dallas institution serves as a local watering hole, pool hall, political forum, and back fence. No less a burgermeister than *The New York Times* has praised P's fine, cooked-to-order hamburger. It's served exclusively on a pumpernickel bun with provolone and spicy mustard. Tasty fajitas, soups, and salads are good alternatives to the burgers. *2926 Maple Ave., at Wolf St., Turtle Creek, 214/871–2346. Reservations not accepted. AE, D, DC, MC, V. Closed Mon. $–$$*

13 *d-1*

THOMAS AVENUE BEVERAGE CO.

Beyond the ubiquitous pool tables and TV sports, you'll find an able and ambitious chef at work. Sun-dried tomatoes provide inspiration to deep red hummus with pita chips, kalamata olives, and artichoke hearts. Boston lettuce, wilted on the grill, is sprinkled with warm, creamy blue cheese. A shared appetizer of roasted artichoke hearts in Chardonnay Beurre blanc sauce is voluptuous, as is the roasted chicken breast stuffed with herbed goat cheese. A plus is the welcoming service. *2901 Thomas Ave., at Allen St., Uptown, 214/979–0452. Reservations not accepted. AE, MC, V. Closed Sun. No lunch Sat. $$*

13 *c-1*

TIN STAR

Slick and spirited, this southwestern-inspired newcomer gives new meaning to "fast food." The industrial modern setting provides a cool and incongruous backdrop for greaseless *chile relleno* (stuffed peppers), enhanced by avocado pesto, roasted corn and black beans—a distinctive vegetarian dish. Daily soft taco specials run the gamut from a version of cheese steak, bulging with roast beef, mushrooms, jack cheese, mild peppers, and onions to a spicy Buffalo wing flavor. Those in the know squeeze fresh lime into the house salsa. *2626 Howell St., at Worthington, Turtle Creek, 214/999–0059. Reservations not accepted. AE, MC, V. $–$$*

12 *f-2*

WILD ABOUT HARRY'S

They said it couldn't be done: serve only one entrée and one dessert on the trendiest shopping strip in Dallas. But wily Harry knew better. Offer real Chicago all-beef hot dogs on a fresh bun and out-of-this world frozen custard (soft ice cream) from a St. Louis recipe, and Texans will stampede to your door. Since then, veggie dogs, chili topping, Polish sausage, and jalapeños for those with cast iron innards have spiced up the menu, and the array of custard flavors (made fresh daily) includes German chocolate cake and pistachio. *3113 Knox St., at McKinney Ave., Highland Park, 214/520–3113. Reservations not accepted. No credit cards. No dinner Sun. $*

ARGENTINE

6 *f-5*

FOGO DE CHAO

This frenzied, high profile Brazilian steakhouse grills endless skewers of sizzling meats, sliced directly onto your plate by gaucho-garbed servers who are more comfortable with Portuguese than English. Although it's primarily a meat-lover's paradise, the eye-popping salad bar is a wonderful surprise. The price is fixed, and not for timid wallets, but the experience can only be described as "epic." *4300 Belt Line Rd., at Midway Rd., North Suburbs, 972/503–7300. Reservations essential. AE, D, MC, V. No lunch weekends. $$–$$$*

AUSTRIAN

10 *g-1*

HOFSTETTER'S SPARGEL CAFÉ

Dining is a delight in this quietly sophisticated restaurant, with its airy and minimal setting. From signature cream of asparagus (*spargel*) soup to toothsome linguine with sautéed sea scallops in Dijon-tarragon sauce to traditional plate-size Wiener schnitzel, the entrées are often truly exceptional. Little explosions of flavor emerge from the capers, olives, and tomatoes adorning the chicken Provençal. Only its master Viennese baker/owner can create the hazelnut *baiser* ("kiss") meringues with ice cream in between and chocolate sauce on top. *4326 Lovers La., at Douglas Ave., University Park, 214/368–3002. AE, D, DC, MC, V. No dinner Sun. $$$*

BARBECUE

12 *f-2*

DICKEY'S

Dating back to the 1940s, this dressed-down, caféteria-style barbecue joint is a local favorite. About as traditional as barbecue can get (though turkey breasts and fresh fruit salad have managed to find their way onto the menu), Dickey's has some of the best-tasting sides in Dallas. When you go, it's possible you'll see Ross Perot, a frequent customer. *4610 N. Central Expressway, East University Park, 214/823–0240. Reservations not accepted. AE, D, DC, MC, V. $*

10 *g-1*

PEGGY SUE BBQ

Forget the Texas myth of authentic barbecue being only available in funky smoke-filled shanties on back roads. At this laid-back, '50s-style place, brisket quesadillas cross Tex with Mex. The ribs are ultimately lean and fall easily from the bone, while smoky turkey breast is a healthy treat. For a side, try the fresh steamed spinach doused in lemon butter and the fine squash-and-corn casserole. A fresh, hot apricot fried pie is the de rigueur dessert, improved only by a ball of vanilla ice cream. *6600 Snider Plaza, at Hilcrest Rd., University Park, 214/987–9188. Reservations not accepted. MC, V. No smoking. $*

13 *c-2*

SAMMY'S

When the cashier calls out, "Mother, bring a piece of pecan pie to go," you know the place is family-run. Locals call this the best BBQ in town, and the chopped barbecued-beef sandwich and spinach salad flecked with carrots and blue cheese proves it. Along with a side of fried okra and a slice of pecan pie, BBQ doesn't get much better than this. *2126 Leonard, at Maple Ave. and McKinney Ave., Downtown, 214/880–9064. Reservations not accepted. AE, D, MC, V. No smoking. Closed Sun. No dinner. $*

12 *b-3*

SONNY BRYAN'S SMOKEHOUSE

Since Sonny's opened its first smokehouse more than 40 years ago, satellite Sonny's have sprouted up all over the Metroplex. However, the heart and soul and true taste of classic Texana is still best experienced at the original ramshackle hut, which offers well-worn school desk seating and generations of smoke suffusing everything. Barbecued po' boys call for a two-fisted appetite—good pulled pork piled high, with brisket and cheese, and festooned with onions and relish. Be sure to spike it with the sauce in that little bottle on the table. The ribs are absolutely the best, and those black-eyed peas dotted with jalapeños pack quite a punch. Cold beer is virtually a necessity. *2202 Inwood Rd., at Harry Hines Blvd., Northwest, 214/357–7120. Reservations not accepted. AE, D, MC, V. No dinner. $*

BRAZILIAN

12 *f-2*

SAMBA ROOM

Well prepared, offbeat Latin-fusion dishes nourish the prosperous, young, and noisy in this setting designed for the grandchildren of Ricky Ricardo and Carmen Miranda. For starters, try the Lulu frita (Brazilian fried calamari) with tartar sauce. A whole fried red snapper, skillfully despined and stuffed with herbed rice, with an elusive sweet ingredient, is a delightful entrée. And talk about "sweet"—juicy rubbed chicken straddling rum-vanilla mashed potatoes can almost serve as a dessert substitute. *4514 Travis St., at Knox St., Highland Park, 214/522–4137. Reservations essential. AE, D, DC, MC, V. No lunch Mon.–Sat. No dinner Sun. $$$*

12 *e-4*

TEXAS DE BRAZIL

Brazilian-style churrasco reigns here, with endless skewers of grilled beef, chicken, lamb, and pork available for one price. Vegetarians, however, should beware that the salad bar is their only option. Attentive staff and a warm, relaxed atmosphere complete the experience. *2727 Cedar Springs Rd., Turtle Creek, 214/720–1414, AE, D, DC, MC. $$$*

15101 Addison Rd., North Suburbs, 972/385–1000. $$$

CAFÉS

12 *d-3*

CAFÉ TUGOGH AT MARTY'S

Whether you want to relax in front and sip a glass of wine or grab a takeout, this cozy café belies its upscale feel with its down-to-earth prices. Highlights include the mildly-flavored chicken salad and salmon (cooked on a cedar plank) sparked with a zippy horseradish sauce. The fresh fruit salad is a delight to behold, and desserts range from simple to spectacular. *3316 Oak Lawn Ave., at*

Lemmon Ave., Oak Lawn, 214/526–4070. AE, D, DC, MC, V. Closed Sun. $$

12 *e-4*

DREAM CAFÉ AND BAKERY

With origins in '70s hippie-healthy counterculture, the Dream Café has evolved into a trendy venue of great popularity (especially for breakfast) that has expanded its horizons without totally forsaking its heritage. Lunchtime favorites include Austin Tacos: whole-wheat tortillas enfolding scrambled eggs, potatoes, cilantro, and bacon with toppings of picante cream sauce and jack cheese. Leave room for the final indulgence—pumpkin flan. *2800 Routh St., at Laclede St., Turtle Creek, 214/954–0486. AE, D, DC, MC, V. No smoking. $$*

10 *g-1*

EMPIRE BAKING CO.

If you're looking for something a little more imaginative in a sandwich, this upscale bakery is the ticket. A thick but excellent olive-cauliflower relish adds zip to the Sicilian Square sandwich of ham, salami, and provolone on rustic Italian bread. For fun, munch on some of "Bob's Vinegar-Dill Polish-Style" potato chips or an order of rice salad with a few artichoke hearts and a surfeit of Kalamata olives. *5450 W. Lovers La., at Inwood Rd., University Park, 214/350–0007. AE, MC, V. No smoking. $*

12 *h-3*

LEGAL GROUNDS, LAW AND COFFEE

Even though the lawyer's office on the premises charges $25 for a traffic ticket consultation, the food is a deal. A cilantro-lime chicken sandwich with grilled red onions and jack cheese on a toothsome grilled whole wheat bun satisfies for a mere $5.95. A special iced "Legalitea" and fine estate teas are also available. *2015 Abrams Rd., at Gaston Ave., East, 214/953–2200. AE, D, MC, V. No dinner Sun. $*

10 *g-1*

ROLY POLY SANDWICHES

Come see frat boys entertain customers with big, rolled flour tortillas. The countless menu choices might arouse skepticism, but the results are fresh, flavorful, and packaged to arrive home hot and intact. Try the Philly Melt with its payload of hot, pink, thinly shaved beef as well as onions, green peppers, and lava-like cheese. *3038 Mockingbird La. at N. Central Expressway and Airline Rd., University Park, 214/363–0522. Reservations not accepted. DC, MC, V. No smoking. No dinner Sun. $*

12 *e-3*

WEB CORNER CAFÉ

Instead of starting the morning at the office, sit down in front of a computer at this web café and have a cup of steaming coffee with a banana-nut muffin. Aside from a fast Internet connection, it also serves up bagels, sandwiches, desserts, beer, and wine. Hourly computer rates range from $6.50 to $8. After surfing, chill out on one of the sofas. *3028 N. Hall St., at McKinney Ave., Suite 179, Oak Lawn, 214/303–0869. AE, D, DC, MC, V. $*

CAJUN/CREOLE

13 *c-2*

MARGAUX'S

Though stylish and charming, this New Orleans-inspired café somehow maintains a low profile. The sparse menu brims with Cajun/Creole flavors including a lightly creamed mushroom soup with garlic and a turkey muffaletta dressed with puckery olive relish. Its intimate surroundings and personal touch is a taste of pure Crescent City comfort. *2404 Cedar Springs Rd., at Maple Ave., Uptown, 214/740–1985. AE, MC, V. No smoking. Closed weekends. No dinner Fri.–Wed., Fri.–Sun. $$*

12 *g-1*

SHUCK 'N' JIVE

Stop here for a relaxed and friendly slice of the bayou. From appetizers to entrées, gumbo, crawfish, catfish, and oysters, everything is seasoned to perfection. Down-home dining at its best. *5315 Greenville Ave., East, 214/369–9471, AE, D, MC, V. $–$$.*

3940 Rosemeade Pkwy., Northwest, 972/307–8064.

CHINESE

10 *g-1*

CAFÉ PANDA

Despite its understated typical Chinese restaurant décor—none of the usual reds and golds—tuxedoed waiters happily serve upscale mandarin dishes. Such delights as chicken mimosa with tangerine sauce, chicken Kung Pao, and beef marengo populate its menu. A bargain lunch menu is a bonus; so is its excellent take-out service. *7979 Inwood Rd., at Lovers La., University Park, 214/902–9500. AE, D, MC, V. $–$$*

12 *g-3*

JADE GARDEN

This restaurant is the winner of both the funky (a recycled old Dairy Queen) and fabulous (green-lipped mussels in spicy black bean sauce) awards. The extensive menu includes deep-fried whole fish with ginger garlic sauce, oysters on a sizzling platter, and sliced pork on a tangle of pan-fried noodles with Chinese cabbage and broccoli. The chef's special shrimp suffer only from the need to shell the delicious critters. *4800 Bryan St., at Fitzhugh Ave., East, 214/821–0675. Reservations not accepted. D, MC, V. BYOB. $$*

10 *g-1*

P.F. CHANG'S CHINA BISTRO

Bypass glamorous Chang's if you're prowling for economical egg rolls and egg drop soup. Here you will see the beautiful and the rested dining in highly visible and lavishly decorated rooms. The popular lettuce wraps—a bird's portion of flash-cooked, spiced bird enfolding chilled iceberg lettuce leaves—re-invent tacos with a fresh, healthy twist and great flavor. Other favorites include the flavorful crispy honey shrimp and garlicky Mongolian beef with scallions. Service may be leisurely, but if you have the time, who cares? *225 N. Park Center, at Northwest Hwy. and Central Expressway, University Park, 214/265–8669. Reservations not accepted. AE, D, DC, MC, V. Closed Sun. $$*

18323 Dallas Pkwy., at Frankford Rd., North Suburbs, 972/818–3336.

6 *h-5*

ROYAL CHINA

Yellow lanterns, colorful streamers, paper butterflies, and friendly service are the backdrop for generous portions of wonton soup, sautéed shrimp, pork, chicken, beef with baby corn, broccoli, snow peas, carrots, and onions in seasoned brown sauce plus steamed rice. It's easy to see why neighborhood regulars have been faithfully eating here since 1974. All entrées are MSG-free. *201 Preston Royal Center, Preston Rd. at Royal La., University Park, 214/361–1771. Reservations not accepted. AE, D, MC, V. Closed Sun. No lunch Sat. $$*

11 *a-1*

SZECHUAN PAVILION

Szechuan Pavilion is well known for its classic Chinese cuisine. Its extensive menu and unfailingly speedy service has earned the restaurant a strong local following. *1152 N. Buckner Blvd., East, 214/321–7599. AE, MC, V. $$*

12 *g-2*

7402 Greenville Ave., East, 214/369–9822.

6 *g-6*

8411 Preston Rd., North, 214/368–4303.

CONTEMPORARY

12 *e-2*

AL BIERNAT'S

Although holding a conversation amid its active social scene is a challenge, this upscale, owner-on-the-spot eatery is still worth the trip. Standout beginners include a rich, intense mushroom soup and Al's Special Salad, with hearts of palm, avocado, and shrimp. A fresh horseradish crust adds zest to the oven-roasted pork tenderloin entrée. *4217 Oak Lawn Ave., at Herschel Ave., Oak Lawn, 214/219–2201. AE, D, DC, MC, V. No lunch weekends. $$$$*

12 *e-5*

BEAU NASH

Amid tranquil, gardenlike surroundings, this elegant eatery serves soothing starters including a variation on hearty navy bean soup, surprisingly based on a piquant tomato-based broth. Entrées include angel-hair pasta with lump crab meat, tomatoes, pine nuts, and pesto; and grilled Atlantic salmon propped atop a mound of horseradish mashed potatoes and baby carrots with mustard sauce. Service is first-rate, seamless and professional. *400 Crescent Ct. at Cedar Springs Rd., Uptown, 214/871–3240. AE, D, DC, MC, V. $$–$$$*

13 *e-5*

CHAPARRAL CLUB

Friendly service and a top-of-the-world view highlight this landmark Downtown eatery. Standout entrées include cream of roasted eggplant soup with goat cheese crostini, and an enticing sugarcane-cured pork tenderloin. *400 N. Olive St., at Pearl St., Adam's Mark Hotel, Downtown, 214/922–8000. Reservations essential. AE, D, DC, MC, V. No smoking. Closed Sun.-Mon. No lunch Sat. $$$–$$$$*

13 *d-4*

DAKOTA'S

It's hard to concentrate on the contemporary American menu in architectural surroundings so striking and clever. Colorful art punctuates the elegant dark-wood decor, and a below-the-street patio with a waterfall brings a pocket full of the outdoors inside. Popular with the business set, lunch ranges from a New York strip steak sided by a tasty house-made steak sauce to an enormous triple-decker club sandwich, bulging with grilled ham, tender chicken breast, cheddar and Swiss cheeses, and loads of bacon. Dinner is pricey and features dishes flaunting innovative and earthy flavors of the Southwest. *600 N. Akard, Downtown, 214/740–4001. AE, D, DC, MC, V. No lunch Sun. $$$*

13 *g-14*

GREEN ROOM

Despite its obscure Deep Ellum location and ultra-hip waitstaff, the Green Room is listed by *Gourmet* magazine as one of "America's Top Tables." Innovative creations such as ethereally light black-bean soup and a martini glass of spicy scallop-and-shrimp cocktail (with chunks of tomato and avocado in a cilantro-lime sauce); pork tenderloin, accompanied by goat cheese risotto with tarragon accents; and New Zealand venison on beluga lentils in a potato-leek sauce highlight its menu. Desserts are just as creative: caramelized-mango cake and Grand Marnier sauce is a perfect finale. *2715 Elm St., at Crowdus St., Deep Ellum, 214/748–7666. Reservations essential. AE, D, DC, MC, V. No lunch. $$–$$$*

12 *e-4*

THE MANSION ON TURTLE CREEK

A favorite of local and national celebrities, this former cotton-baron residence retains much of its Italian-renaissance opulence. A varied menu includes a white-cheddar soup chunky with lobster, asparagus, and red pepper; "bronzed" sea scallops on potato puree; and a tower of pineapple parfait atop banana cake surrounded by fresh plums. You can order a four-course fixed-price meal, and choose from a varied selection of wine. *2821 Turtle Creek Blvd., at Gillespie Ave., Turtle Creek, 214/526–2121. Reservations essential. Jacket required. AE, D, DC, MC, V. $$$$*

6 *h-6*

THE MERCURY

Sleek and streamlined, casual yet sophisticated, Mercury was voted hands down as 1998's Best New Restaurant. A small, intimate bar helps the wait seem shorter. Don't be deceived by the sparse menu; each dish is meticulously and artfully prepared. Yellow tomato salad with its vinaigrette of apple-wood bacon, basil, and Roquefort is an ideal blending of flavors. A side of guacamole perfectly enhances an entrée of crisp polenta, sandwiched between two thin slices of the grilled swordfish. Be sure to try one of delectable dessert soufflés. *11909 Preston Rd., at Forest La., North, 972/960–7774. Reservations essential. AE, D, MC, V. No lunch weekends. $$$*

13 *d-4*

SEVENTEEN SEVENTEEN

As you would expect in any major urban art museum, presentation is paramount. At this eatery, equal attention is lavished on the cuisine, including such artfully prepared creations as lobster ravioli with goat cheese and a tomato-basil sauce. Dessert includes a sweetly tangy *panna cotta*—"cooked cream" enlivened with a splash of buttermilk—with mixed berries. *1717 N. Harwood, at Ross St., Dallas Museum of Art, Downtown, 214/880–0158. Reservations essential. AE, D, MC, V. No smoking. Closed Mon. No dinner. $$$*

6 *g-8*

SEVY'S GRILL

Like its lively ever-changing upscale atmosphere, the food here continues to evolve and improve, and throngs of beautiful people congregate at the bar. What's not to like? Appetizers such as fried calamari and crunchy pork wontons with a tangy soy-ginger dipping sauce rate very high. Entrées display skill and creativity: garlic shrimp lay atop fettuccine intermingled with Swiss chard, tomatoes, and a subtle garlic-tarragon butter sauce. Although the bar is a bit noisy, the ample dining room is conducive for leisurely dining and conversation. *8201 Preston Rd., University Park, 214/265–7389. Reservations essential. AE, D, DC, MC, V. No smoking. No lunch weekends. $$$*

12 *f-2*

SIPANGO

Trendy singles pack this pulsating bar like designer-dressed sardines. Meanwhile, the kitchen puts its best food forward, succeeding with such creations as margherita pizza, a simple preparation made more interesting by a quartet of Italian cheeses, and an ambitious red snapper on creamy mashed potatoes. *4513 Travis St., at Knox St., Highland Park, 214/522–2411. Reservations essential. AE, D, MC, V. Closed Sun. No lunch. $$–$$$*

10 *e-4*

TILLMAN'S CORNER

Tillman's casual, offbeat quarters and varied menu boasts that all-important ingredient that seems to elude so many restaurants: consistency. They don't mess with success, although changing daily specials—usually one poultry, one fish, and a pizzette—sustain the interest of regulars. From one of the city's best cheeseburgers to fabulous crab cakes in spicy ginger sauce and smoky chicken corn chowder, innovative flavors abound. Exotic edible flower-flavored sorbets offer a memorable finale. *324 W. 7th St., at Bishop Ave., Oak Cliff, 214/942–0988. AE, DC, MC, V. Closed Sun. No lunch Mon. $$*

12 *e-5*

TRULUCK'S

The sign says it all: Steak and Stone Crab. Delicious, sweet, and tender, a quartet of medium-size crab claws easily separates from the cracked shell, and a remoulade-like sauce proves the perfect companion. Other specialties include a sizeable open-faced prime rib sandwich, augmented with Parmesan potatoes. A smart staff and a lively bar scene add to your dining pleasure. *2401 McKinney Ave., at Maple Ave., Uptown, 214/220–2401. Reservations essential. AE, D, DC, MC, V. $$$–$$$$*

6 *f-5*

5001 Belt Line Rd., at Quorum, Addison, 972/503–3079.

12 *h-3*

YORK ST.

This tiny jewel of a restaurant only seats about 30 diners, and has a long-standing and loyal clientele who rave about its eclectic offerings. The menu continually changes, but its culinary creations consistently please palates. Appetizers include velvety chicken mousse truffle pâté with Montrachet cheese and wonderful coarse mustard and tiny cornichons. Grilled Pacific sea bass with lump crabmeat, shallots, and saffron sauce can only be called a wonder. The gracious owner-hostess is always on the scene to assure the finest in comfort and quality. The wine list is inviting, drawing from both European and domestic choices, and service is attentive. *6047 Lewis St., at Skillman St., East, 214/826–0968. Reservations essential. D, DC, MC, V. No smoking. Closed Sun.–Mon. No lunch. $$$*

CONTINENTAL

13 *d-5*

THE FRENCH ROOM

Surely the most elaborate and perhaps the most expensive restaurant in Texas, the French Room conjures up images of folks wearing white powdered wigs and satin ruffles. Lots of marble and gold leaf, as well as lofty dome ceilings with frescoes of cherubs create a one-of-a-kind place for this side of the pond. The menu includes classical French and saucy Continental choices, but also recognizes contemporary culinary trends. Highlights include a sizzling, seared foie gras surrounded by cool ruby plums, and juicy rack of lamb. *1321 Commerce St., at Field St., The Adolphus Hotel, Downtown, 214/742–8200. Reservations essential. Jacket required. AE, D, DC, MC, V. No Smoking. Closed Sun.–Mon. No lunch. $$$$*

12 *g-2*

THE GRAPE

For years, this eatery has proven that "funky can be romantic" when it's warm, dark, and cozy. A veritable who's who of prominent local chefs have passed through the kitchen, leaving such legacies as the house salad with red and green lettuces, dressed in cranberry vinaigrette, that seem to sprout flowerlike from a "vase" of fried garlic wonton wrappers. The eclectic menu is best described as "Continental with exotic influences," with such specialties as almond roasted quail with apricot glaze and carrot-curry couscous. A commitment to quality, yet affordable, wines contribute to the popularity of the excellent selection of pâtés and cheeses. *2808 Greenville Ave., at Vickery Blvd., East, 214/828–1981. Reservations not accepted. AE, D, DC, MC, V. No lunch weekends. $$$*

6 *g-5*

LAUREL'S

High atop the Sheraton Park Central Hotel on LBJ Freeway, this showcase restaurant serves Continental and New American cuisine—an oft-changing menu masterminded by eminent chefs. Sophisticated and complex, beef and seafood dishes are innovative culinary creations. A panoramic view of the affluent north area of town sparkles like a black velvet blanket speckled with gleaming stars. It's a first-rate venue for a leisurely romantic dinner. *12720 Merit Dr. at LBJ Fwy., North, 972/851–2021. Reservations essential. AE, D, MC, V. Closed Sun.–Mon. No lunch. $$$–$$$$*

12 *b-4*

NANA GRILL

One of Texas' largest and grandest hotels—the Anatole—puts its best foot forward in this renowned penthouse restaurant with a sweeping view of the city below. Suave servers and well-experienced maître d'hotels serve scrumptious Continental and New American type dishes. *2201 N. Stemmons Fwy., at I–35 E, Wyndham Anatole Hotel, Northwest, 214/761–7479. Reservations essential. AE, D, MC, V. No dinner Sun. $$$–$$$$*

12 *e-4*

OLD WARSAW

Ever the grande dame of Dallas' fine restaurants, Old Warsaw seems to have changed little in 20 years. The professional waitstaff still takes pride in their craft, and the venerable entrées never seem to go out of fashion. The monster New York strip pepper steak is as good as it gets, and deft waiters assemble Caesar salads from fresh ingredients at tableside. The asparagus soup is light and creamy, and braised salmon arrives stylishly in a lush pool of basil beurre blanc. Dessert highlights include cherries jubilee and classic crepes flambé. *2610 Maple Ave., at Cedar Springs, Uptown, 214/528–0032. Reservations essential. AE, D, DC, MC, V. No lunch. $$$–$$$$*

13 *c-4*

PYRAMID GRILL

Many of the city's most prominent chefs and restaurateurs earned their culinary wings at the Fairmont Hotel's premier dining room. The setting is plainly stated, "first class." The preparations are often complex, the ingredients rare, but the results are deliciously accessible. Memorable starters include the lovely Napoleon, with red and yellow tomatoes, mozzarella, and roasted-garlic coulis, or scallops and snails in puff pastry with fresh herbs. For those who love salmon, a braise of leeks and shitake mushrooms accompanied by spinach and tomato flan is otherworldly. The dense chocolate marquise is an extravagant finale. *1717 N. Akard St., at Ross Ave., Fairmont Hotel, Downtown, 214/720–5249. AE, D, DC, MC, V. No dinner Sun. $$$–$$$$*

DELICATESSENS

6 *g-7*

CINDI'S

Central Expressway is now at full speed but Cindi's still offers a perfect pit stop. Alongside bacon, eggs, or pig-in-a-blanket standards, you can pick your bagel du jour from 15 varieties. Fuel up with crepelike German pancakes or their American banana-pecan cousins, topped with delicious banana syrup. Add a bottomless coffee pot and fresh squeezed juices and you're ready for the on-ramp. For lunch or dinner, check out the full array of generous deli sandwiches and hot entrées. *11111 N. Central Expressway, at Forest La., North, 214/739–0918. AE, D, MC, V. $–$$*

6 *g-8*

CORNER BAKERY

This fast, fresh deli/bakery has become a Dallas favorite but thankfully has not lost that "hello, neighbor" attitude its name implies. Apart from its garden-fresh gourmet salads and flavorful sandwiches, the true treasure of the bakery is the bread, baked daily in-house. *4019 Villanova Dr., University Park, 214/368–7101. AE, D, DC, MC, V. $*

6 *g-7*

GILBERT'S NEW YORK DELI AND RESTAURANT

On a cool day, few things are more satisfying than settling back in a comfy booth with a bowl of Grandma's hot soup. Gilbert's thick lima-barley recreates that warm feeling, and pairs it with one of the great culinary concoctions of modern time: a fluffy egg salad sandwich. The standard New York style fare is readily available, from matzo balls to hot pastrami and chopped liver. *11661 Preston Rd., at Forest La., North, 214/373-3333. AE, D, DC, MC, V. $–$$*

6 *h-5*

MICHAEL'S ORIGINAL DELI–NEWS RESTAURANT & CLUB

This Russian-owned deli serves the best chopped liver and apple-sauced potato latkes within a 500-mi radius. The menu, with its newspaper-inspired combo sandwiches, has endless possibilities and permutations. Hearty soups such as the absolutely-necessary matzo ball and virile beef and barley are meals in themselves. The lox plate for two with capers, onions, cream cheese, and bagels is a challenge for the most hard-core smoked salmon lovers. *7615 W. Campbell Rd., at Coit Rd., North Suburbs, 972/392–3354. AE, D, MC, V. No smoking. No dinner Sun. $$*

EASTERN EUROPEAN

6 *g-6*

CAFÉ ATHENÉE

This cozy and surprisingly handsome sleeper of a restaurant, set in an easy-to-bypass strip mall, fills its menu with delicious Hungarian and Romanian recipes such as sautéed cabbage with onions, tomatoes, and parsley, and a charbroiled rack of lamb. Indulge in a mountain of mousaka—eggplant with ground meat—or stuffed cabbage rolls, and you'll be happily satisfied. *5365 Spring Valley Rd., at Montfort Rd., North Suburbs, 972/239–8060. AE, D, MC, V. Closed Sun. No lunch Sat. $$–$$$*

6 *h-5*

LIZA'S

For a city with few Eastern Europeans, Liza's serves creative Eastern European comfort food. Polish vegetable soup with cauliflower, carrots, and potatoes in a clear broth is the sort that sticks to your ribs, while tender vegetarian cabbage rolls bathed in tomato sauce and dotted with sour cream are deliciously homey. Try Fanya's Napoleon—a slice of seven-layer cake with vanilla custard cream. *7517 Campbell Rd., at Coit Rd., North Suburbs, 972/248–2246. AE, D, MC, V. Closed Sun.–Mon. $–$$*

ECLECTIC

12 *f-2*

ABACUS

This new restaurant was created to give diners a total food experience. The decor soothes guests by surrounding them with warm, rich colors accentuated by metal and glass sculptures and dim lighting. Although the restaurant's beautiful design is reason enough to visit, its wildly creative menu of Asian cuisine with a Southwestern flare truly stimulates. *4511 McKinney Ave., Oak Lawn, 214/559–3111. AE, D, DC, MC, V. Closed Sun. $$–$$$*

CAFÉ BRAZIL

Open 24 hours, this popular chain restaurant draws younger crowds for big portions and bottomless cups of coffee. Sandwiches, crepes, and delicious desserts populate the menu. The original location near Southern Methodist University has live music on the weekends. *6420 N. Central Expressway, University Park, 214/691–7791. AE, D, DC, MC, V. $–$$*

10 *h-1*

2221 Abrams Rd., East, 214/826–9522.

10 *g-1*

2071 S. Central Expressway, East, 972/783–9011.

13 *g-4*

2815 Elm St., Deep Ellum, 214/747–2730.

6 *g-5*

OBZEET COFFEE BAR & CAFÉ

This café serves pitas with such fillings as spinach, mushrooms, asparagus, and black olives. You can enjoy coffee or a glass from the café's South African wine selection in the tropical garden patio, amid the soothing ambiance of its fish pond and waterfall. *19020 Preston Rd., at Frankford Rd., North Suburbs, 972/867–6126. Reservations not accepted. AE, D, MC, V. No dinner Mon. $$*

6 *g-6*

SUZE

Sophisticated dishes at this cozy, romantic spot draw primarily on the culinary traditions of Italy, America, and France. Risotto, enriched with Asiago and Parmesan cheeses, are endowed with marvelously fresh shrimp. Zambezi, an African beer, is a fine companion with the chicken-and-Monterey-jack quesadillas accented with mango-tequila salsa. Specialties from New England, Morocco, and India are also served. Delicious and creative desserts—prepared by owner Suze herself—include Kahlua-laced tiramisu and tangy apple-cranberry crumb cake. *4345 W. Northwest Hwy., at Midway Rd., Suite 270, University Park, 214/350–6135. MC, V. No smoking. Closed Sun.–Mon. No lunch. $$–$$$*

ENGLISH

6 *h-5*

BRITISH ROSE PUB

With darts, pool, dark woods, green felt walls, plaid wingback chairs, and Bass Ale and Guinness on draught, you'll find a taste of Britain in Texas. Classic Brit staples such as fish-and-chips and deep-fried cod sprinkled with malt vinegar are served along with garlicky coleslaw and chips. *8989 Forest La., at Greenville Ave., Suite 100, North, 972/690–8340. AE, DC, MC, V. No lunch. $–$$*

12 *e-4*

JENNIVINE

Reminiscent of a rustic cottage in the English countryside, this charming pub accompanies its British theme with a suitable menu. An appetizer sampler of two cheeses and one pâté serves three easily, and chunky broccoli soup is mellow and savory. More elaborate entrées include baked mahimahi nestled beneath mango-red pepper salsa and served with basmati rice studded with pecans. It's all part of its trademark hospitality, consistency, and congenial service. *3605 McKinney Ave., at W. Lemmon Ave., Turtle Creek, 214/528–6010. AE, D, MC, V. No dinner Sun. $$–$$$*

FRENCH

13 *c-1*

BISTRAL

This new neighborhood bistro with youthful demographics boasts one of the city's most prominent chefs. The innovative kitchen—albeit far from classic French cuisine—creates artfully prepared exotica such as crispy Parmesan calamari with saffron aioli, and red pepper-tomato sauce over beef carpaccio and Portobellos with shaved Romano and mustard cream. The onsite bakery whips up delectable desserts. Service is fast and efficient. *2900 McKinney Ave., at Allen St., Uptown, 214/220–1202. AE, MC, V. $$*

12 *f-2*

CHEZ GERARD

Frequented by older, prosperous neighborhood types and regulars, this traditional French restaurant continually maintains a spell of romance, serving classic creations in an intimate, upscale setting. Highlights include scallops with sautéed onions in dark red wine sauce and grilled lamb chops. The hot apple tart accented with rum and whipped cream should not be missed. *4444 McKinney Ave., at Henderson Ave., Highland Park, 214/522–6865. AE, D, MC, V. Closed Sun. No lunch Sat. $$–$$$*

6 *g-6*

CLAIR DE LUNE

Graceful, relaxed surroundings belie this Parisian bistro's strip-mall surroundings. Its classic French menu highlights a spicy gazpacho and crab cakes as starter favorites, and the succulent duck breast bathed in port wine and served with wild rice always impresses. *5934 Royal La., at Preston Rd., North, 214/987–2028. AE, MC, V. No dinner Sun. $$*

12 *f-2*

L'ANCESTRAL

White lace curtains, amply spaced tables, and agreeable service is a welcoming respite from the hectic day at this French bistro. This chef-owned intimate spot skillfully prepares familiar Provence favorites such as cream of mushroom soup, amply flecked with bits of mushrooms, and a mouth-watering grilled orange roughy with lemon butter, moist rice, and a generous portion of grilled vegetables. A leisurely pace matches its reserved setting. *4514 Travis St., at Knox St., Highland Park, 214/528–1081. AE, D, MC, V. Closed Sun. $$*

6 *e-4*

LA MIRABELLE

This classical French jewel serves provincial in a cozy setting. The outstanding menu includes endive and walnut mixed green salad, herb-dusted pasta and shrimp basked in garlicky olive oil, and a pair of large rainbow trout fillets. Its flawless service continually wins high marks. *17610 Midway Rd., at Trinity Mills Rd., North Suburbs, 972/733–0202. Reservations essential. MC, V. Closed Sun.–Mon. No lunch Sat. $$$–$$$$*

6 *g-4*

LAVENDOU

A visit to this cozy eatery, with its Pierre Deux decor, is like dining in Provence. Its classic French fare includes coarse duck pâté, onion soup, rack of lamb, and roast chicken. Be sure to sample the tarts—apricot, with a caramel glaze and sliced almonds, or chocolate, sprinkled with zingy lime zest. *19009 Preston Rd., at Fronkford Rd., Suite 200, North Suburbs, 972/248–1911. AE, D, DC, MC, V. Closed Sun. No lunch Sat. $$$*

12 *e-5*

LE PARIS BISTROT

It took a Frenchman to bring Parisian authenticity to this chic Uptown enclave. Candlelight, murals, and cozy little dining rooms comprise the setting for a bistro menu that's mainstream laced with innovative surprises. Culinary creations such as beef tenderloin in a shallot demi-glaze highlight lunch, while steak au poivre is a favorite dinner entrée. Edible flowers contribute to original frozen treats such as strawberry-basil-vodka sorbet and orchid ice cream. *2533 McKinney Ave., at Routh St., Uptown, 214/720–0225. AE, D, DC, MC, V. $$–$$$*

12 *e-5*

MANGIA E BEVI

Although it styles itself a French bistro, this Uptown spot also serves some Italian delights. Try the baked green *tagliolini*, with chicken, mushrooms, béchamel, and cheese, or the baked champignons (mushrooms) filled with crabmeat. Dessert should not be passed up, especially the dense mousse topped with a grand Grand Marnier sauce. *2504 McKinney Ave., at Fairmount St., Uptown, 214/303–1002. AE, D, DC, MC, V. $$–$$$*

13 *d-1*

WATEL'S

As one of the top French restaurants, this is where you'll find cassoulet, savory pâtés, and Calvados-sauced pork. Dishes are presented in unhurried fashion and spacious tables allow for civilized conversation. A rich creamy sauté of assorted mushrooms begs to be sopped up with bread; any self-respecting French person would do the same. Gallic sweetbreads are presented with mint-chive sauce, the taste of which more than compensates for the odd, almost chartreuse color. Desserts include a wonderfully dense chocolate pâté. *2719 McKinney Ave., at Worthington St., Uptown, 214/720–0323. AE, DC, MC, V. No lunch Sat. $$$*

GERMAN

6 *g-4*

THE BAVARIAN GRILL

This raucous, good-time, family-oriented establishment serves authentic German cuisine, a bevy of fine beers, accordion music, and friendly service, but expect to wait for your table. After tasting the tiny pasta dumplings tossed with mushrooms, sautéed onions, peas, and Black Forest ham in creamy cheese sauce, you might even consider immigrating to Germany. You can also find your favorite wursts and schnitzels in huge quantities with classic sauerkraut on the side. *221 W. Parker Rd. at Hwy. 75, Suite 527, North Suburbs, 972/881–0705. AE, D, DC, MC, V. Closed Sun.–Mon. $$–$$$*

6 *g-7*

HENK'S EUROPEAN DELI AND BLACK FOREST BAKERY

Some Wiener schnitzels are airy and paper-thin; the hefty versions served here will satisfy even a Krupp steel–mill worker. Stick with the "When in Deutschland. . ." theory when selecting one of the hearty entrées. Leave some room for the delectable Black Forest cake—moist and layered with luscious dark cherries. Great take-out deli selections and an ample selection of European beer and German wines are also available. *5811 Blackwell St., at Greenville Ave., East, 214/987–9090. AE, D, MC, V. Closed Sun. $*

6 *f-8*

KUBY'S

A longtime SMU institution, Kuby's persists as the paragon of efficiency, quality, and economy. Many shop at the deli for fresh baked goods, imported cheeses, and meats. At lunchtime the dining room is thronged with regulars needing a fix of mild bratwurst, pudgy knockwurst, or the stouter polish sausage, all available plated with German potato salad and briny kraut. Sunday brunch gets fancier, with specialty egg dishes served with traditional meats—the lean bacon is truly extraordinary. *6601 Snider Plaza, at Daniel Ct., University Park, 214/363–2231. Reservations not accepted. AE, D, MC, V. No dinner Sun.–Thurs. $–$$*

GREEK

6 *g-5*

GREEK ISLES GRILLE AND TAVERNA

This rare Dallas find serves authentic Greek dishes in a comfy setting. From Greek salads to entrées of classic moussaka—a cheese-topped relative of lasagna combining baked macaroni with ground beef and lamb—and herb-dusted redfish fillets, dining here is worth the jaunt. *3309 N. Central Expressway, at Parker Rd., North Suburbs, 972/423–7778. AE, MC, V. Closed Sun. No lunch Sat. $–$$*

12 *f-2*

ZIZIKI'S

This trendy spot has become Dallas's most fashionable and upscale Greek restaurant. Although set in a small space, its eclectic menu, robust flavors, and Herculean helpings more than compensate. Try the marinated shrimp souvlaki, mounded on pita with tomatoes, feta cheese, onions, and basil, or the artichoke dip with chickpeas and garlic. Finish off with one of the icily refreshing sorbets. *15707 Coit Rd., at Arapaho Rd., Suite A, North Suburbs, 972/991–4433. AE, DC, MC, V. $*

12 *f-2*

4514 Travis St., at Armstrong Ave., Suite 122, Highland Park, 214/521–2233.

INDIAN

INDIA PALACE

Widely considered the best Indian restaurant in the city, this quiet, softly-lit establishment appeals to even the ethnically unadventurous. The food is traditional but friendly to the Western palate, with such favorites as chicken curry. Go early for the lunch buffet. *12817 Preston Rd., Far North, 972/392–0190. AE, D, MC, V. $$–$$$*

ITALIAN

12 *c-1*

ALFREDO TRATTORIA

Lace curtains and real plants lend civility to this pleasant venue, set just beyond the Park Cities boundary. House salad, though not extravagant, is splashed with a sprightly dressing and complemented by gratis, crunchy garlic bread. Fettuccini Barones, with shrimp and scallops nestled in velvety light cream sauce, demonstrates the chef's culinary prowess. Instead of the now all-too-common tiramisu or cappuccino pie, try the lemon ice with slices of strawberries. *5404 Lemmon Ave., at Inwood Rd., Oak Lawn, 214/526–3331. AE, D, DC, MC, V. Closed Sun. $$$*

12 *f-1*

AMORE

A comfy home away from home for Park Cities families, this venerable restaurant serves pleasant Italian food in a low-lit setting. The menu is strictly traditional, with cheesy garlic bread, lasagna, and spaghetti topping the list, plus a slew of economical chicken dishes. Linguine, immersed in a garlicky white-clam sauce is so thick it almost qualifies as gravy. *6931 Snider Plaza, University Park, 214/739–0502. Reservations essential. AE, MC, V. Closed Sun. $$*

12 *h-3*

ANGELO'S ITALIAN GRILL

At noon the all-you-can-eat buffet is a lumberjack's fantasy, and it could well be a diner's last productive act of the day. However, at this Italian eatery, cozy booths and soft lights offer Italian romance on a budget, but portions this size and cooked with so much garlic may run counter to the concept of romance. Beware of the fabulous yeast rolls with marinara dipping sauce—they can stuff you before your dinner arrives. *6341 La Vista Dr., at Gaston Ave., East, 214/823–5566. AE, D, MC, V. No lunch weekends. $$*

6 *f-5*

FERRARI'S ITALIAN VILLA

Wood burning ovens and rustic Italian decor amplify the charm of this old standby. Pasta e fagioli, thick with pasta, beans, and vegetables, is definitive Italian comfort food. The veal *piccata al limone* is infused with the forceful flavor and distinctive aroma of white wine sauce and capers. Finish festively with chocolate mousse enveloped within chocolate cake. *14831 Midway Rd., at Belt Line Rd., North Suburbs, 972/980–9898. Reservations essential. AE, D, MC, V. No lunch weekends. $$–$$$*

6 *g-7*

IL SORRENTO

While the palazzo gardenlike decor and soft accordion music can be a bit much, this establishment has been one of the consistently best fine-dining restaurants in Dallas for more than 50 years. The cuisine ranges from such classics as spaghetti with meatballs and veal cutlet parmigiana to more contemporary options such as tortelloni. The extensive wine selection and dark nooks make this an intimate place to celebrate a special occasion. *8616 Turtle Creek Blvd., North 214/352–8759. AE, DC, MC, V. $$–$$$*

6 *g-8*

ISOLA GOZO

Normally, dining in a shopping mall is an act of convenience or desperation, but not so in popular NorthPark, where this elegant and authentic trattoria is a worthy destination. Pizza Margherita with cheese, tomato sauce, and calamata olives is a purist's dream. High marks go to the mixed grilled vegetables and the *pepe e caprino* (semolina-crusted goat cheese baked in a wood-burning oven and served with balsamic-marinated peppers). On a warm, clear night, ask for a table on the patio. *330 NorthPark Center, at Boedecker St., Suite 335, University Park, 214/691–0488. Reservations essential. AE, MC, V. No dinner Sun. $$–$$$*

6 *g-5*

MI PIACI RISTORANTE ITALIANO

Amid soaring ceilings and large glass windows overlooking a small pond with a fountain, this elegant trattoria serves authentic country Italian cuisine by making its own pasta and curing its own meats. Fettucine with fresh peas, lemon, and Parmesan cream is a well focused bull's-eye. The extensive wine list offers many hard-to-find Italian choices. *14854 Montfort Dr., at Belt Line Rd., North Suburbs, 972/934–8424. Reservations essential. AE, D, DC, MC, V. No lunch weekends. $$$*

6 *g-5*

NICOLA'S

Sitting at the painted tables at this snazzy restaurant, you'll quickly forget you're on the top tier of the Galleria shopping complex. The menu is filled with plenty of pizzas and pasta, but the sandwiches garner the most attention. *13350 Dallas Pkwy., at I–635, Galleria, North, 972/788–1177. AE, D, MC, V. No dinner Sun. $$*

12 *d-3*

PARIGI

The sophisticated culinary creations, changed weekly, continually get high marks here. While dining in its cozy, sleek atmosphere, try a salad of frisé lettuce, roasted fig, and bacon with a crunchy Stilton cheese biscuit. The cheese risotto cakes (with ratatouille) and the lovely marinated venison medallions with an amazing carrot-scallion pancake are also highly recommended. *3311 Oak Lawn Ave., at Hall St., Suite 102, Oak Lawn, 214/521–0295. AE, DC, MC, V. No lunch Sat. No dinner Sun. $$–$$$*

10 *f-1*

PATRIZIO

The poshest commercial address in Dallas houses this elegant yet affordable Italian restaurant. Moreover, the people-watching is just as intriguing as the food. Crab claws are awash in drawn butter, and firm grilled Idaho trout luxuriates in a pool of lemon butter sauce. If it gets too noisy, ask for a table on the patio. *25 Mockingbird La., at Preston Rd., Highland Park Village, Highland Park, 214/522–7878. Reservations not accepted. AE, D, MC, V. $$*

POMODORO RISTORANTE ITALIANO

At night the trendy set raises the heat at this chic Eurostyle spot, where one can have a refreshing "grapparita" while munching on *crostini* draped with thinly sliced prosciutto plus mozzarella and pesto. The proprietors frequently visit Italy for new inspiration, and dishes are truly novel and praiseworthy, such as the coarse, tubular *bucatini* paste with lamb in tomato sauce and broad *pappardelle* noodles. Dessert raves include hazelnut gelato with almond biscotti, "drowned in espresso." *2708 Routh St., Turtle Creek, 214/871–1924. Closed Sun. $$$*

12 *e-5*

RUGGERI'S

Twinkling lights, lush plants, and tiers of tables create an intimate, romantic setting where traditional dishes rule. The formidable lasagna, topped with a rich, béchamel-like cream sauce, all but ooze melted ricotta cheese. Ample linguine, with tender clams steeped in an herbed white-wine broth is a light alternative. A wedge of outstanding spumoni will end the meal with a smile. *2911 Routh St., at Cedar Springs Rd., Turtle Creek, 214/871–7377. AE, D, DC, MC, V. $$–$$$*

5348 Belt Line Rd., at Montfort, Addison Town Hall Sq., North Suburbs, 972/726–9555.

13 *c-2*

SALVE!

The experienced owners of several of the city's finest and most prominent restaurants have raised the stakes in this truly fabulous Italian restaurant. The gray-coated staff provides smooth and efficient service, and the menu lists such original concepts as braised venison shank, risotto with 23K gold leaf, and dense herbed gnocchi in wild boar and caramelized onion ragu. All pastas are made fresh in house each day, as are the rich gelati and fruity sorbets. A separate bar serves calzones, pannini sandwiches, and pizza in a more casual setting. *2120 McKinney Ave., at Pearl St., Uptown, 214/220–0070. AE, D, DC, MC, V. No lunch weekends. $$$–$$$$*

12 *f-2*

TORREFAZIONE ITALIA CAFÉ

The serene, comfortable setting of this handsome café is most inviting to solo diners. A "caffetteria" serves a variety of great coffees, including a refreshing iced café mocha, and an assortment of fresh-baked muffins, pastries, and sandwiches. *4527 Travis St., at Knox St., Suite B, Highland Park, 214/521–0886. MC, V. $*

6 *g-7*

TRAMONTANA

If you stop for lunch, expect paper-covered tables and reasonably priced sandwiches and pastas. It's all transformed at dinner by linen cloths, slightly higher prices, and more choices. Those weary of crab cakes will enjoy shrimp cakes with lobster cream sauce. The grilled rib-eye sandwich with grilled onions and cheese is another favorite. Ask about the monthly wine tastings. *8220 Westchester Rd., at Preston Rd., University Park, 214/368–4188. Reservations essential. AE, DC, MC, V. Closed Sun.–Mon. $$$*

JAPANESE

7 *a-4*

AWAJI JAPANESE RESTAURANT

Western palates will enjoy sushi, *gyoza* (meat-filled dumplings, steamed or fried) and grilled chicken teriyaki appetizers, artfully prepared with the sauce brushed on after grilling. Those more experienced in Japanese culinary tradition will find authentic *shabu-shabu*—raw, thinly sliced rib-eye steak and assorted vegetables that are brought to the table with a cauldron of water—boiling on a hibachi. There is plenty of space to relax here, including a large sushi bar and gracious service. *4701 W. Park Blvd., at Preston Rd., Suite 101, North Suburbs, 972/519–1688. AE, D, DC, MC, V. No lunch weekends. $–$$*

6 *g-7*

CHAYA SUSHI AND GRILL

Serene atmosphere adds to the dining experience either at the sushi bar or at a table. Miso soup accompanies most dishes and the wide assortment of sushi is adventurous, especially if you're looking for something beyond the ubiquitous California roll. For more traditional fare, try the charcoal-grilled sirloin served with shiitake mushrooms. *101 Preston Rd., at Royal La., North, 214/361–0220. Reservations not accepted. AE, MC, V. No lunch Sun. $$$*

6 *g-7*

ROYAL TOKYO

Sushi lovers beat a path to Royal Tokyo's door at lunch. Its super special includes miso soup, California rolls (with a crunchy sesame-seed crust), cucumber rolls, and sushi (tuna, yellowtail, shrimp, and salmon) at a bargain fixed price. Add to that a few orders of healthy *edamame* (fresh soybeans in the pod) and addictive gyoza, and you'll have a feast. At night, you can dine amid serene decor, peruse the full Japanese menu, and bask in the gracious service. *7525 Greenville Ave., at Walnut Hill La., East, 214/368–3304. AE, D, DC, MC, V. $$–$$$*

12 *f-2*

SUSHI ON MCKINNEY

A local pioneer in marrying sushi to au courant hipness, this full-service Japanese restaurant with a vibrant sushi bar runs the gamut from piping hot tempura to light and crispy soft-shell crab roll. Velvety blankets of fresh salmon are served at room temperature, heightening their full flavor and buttery texture. The restaurant defers to its upscale neighborhood patrons with such variations as Philadelphia roll—an Americanized flavor competition between cream cheese and rice. The flickering slide show of art and artifacts always adds visual surprise. *4502 McKinney Ave., at Armstrong Rd., Highland Park, 214/521–0969. AE, DC, MC, V. No smoking. No lunch weekends. $$*

12 *f-2*

TEI TEI ROBATA BAR

This sleek contemporary restaurant/bar is considered by many to be the Rolls Royce of Dallas' sushi/sashimi bars. Famous for its fabled Kobe beef—everything from a 10-ounce steak priced at a C-note to sushi with a thin sampling at under $5—it also serves up a fresh assortment of sushi, from silky flounder to an avocado-filled California roll. Innovative blackboard specials are created every night, and an extensive Japanese menu is available for those not desiring fish. *2906 N. Henderson, at Willis Ave., East, 214/828–2400. Reservations not accepted. AE, MC, V. Closed Mon. No lunch. $$$*

12 *g-3*

TEPPO

Catering to a trendy crowd for more than four years now, Teppo shows no sign of going out of style. Sushi and yakitori are its meat and potatoes, and the long list of daily specials leaves plenty of room for experimentation. Impossibly fresh ingredients and definitive flavors make this an excellent choice, whether you are a sushi aficionado or a first-timer. *2014 Greenville Ave., East, 214/826–8989. AE, MC, V. $$–$$$*

6 *f-7*

YAMAGUCHI'S BAR AND SUSHI

Popular with the lunch crowd, this humble eatery serves a steamy assortment of appetizers such as gyoza, skewers of marinated chicken, and puffy shrimp tempura. For lighter fare, try the rainbow of sliced salmon, yellowtail, and tuna sushi. The asparagus roll surprises with its spicy bite, perfectly offsetting the sweet tempura roll. For dessert, the tart plum wine sorbet and green-tea ice cream should not be missed. *7713 Inwood Rd., at Lovers La., University Park, 214/350–8660. Reservations not accepted. AE, DC, MC, V. No lunch Sat.–Mon. $$$*

MEDITERRANEAN

12 *f-2*

ADELMO'S RISTORANTE

This charming, romantic two-story treasure is the perfect spot for a cozy Mediterranean-Italian meal. The best tables are upstairs, although the service can be slower as your waiter must contend with the narrow staircase between you and the kitchen. Look on the blackboard for specials. The veal chop is exceptional. *4537 Cole Ave., Oak Lawn, 214/559–0325. AE, D, MC, V. Closed Sun. $$–$$$*

10 *g-1*

BISTRO A

Innovations abound on this Mediterranean-Middle Eastern menu. Despite complaints about small portions, the sleek and edgy bistro remains a popular hot spot. Named one of Dallas' top 10 new restaurants in 1998. *6815 Snider Plaza, University Park, 214/373–9911. AE, D, DC, MC, V. Closed Sun. $$–$$$*

6 *h-5*

CAFÉ MED

"Mediterranean" achieves its broadest geographical definition here as dishes represent a wide range of countries. The eclectic menu includes a tasty Moroccan lentil soup, Lebanese roasted peppers in an addictive garlicky vinaigrette, and a Turkish *shawarma* (shredded chicken and lamb) stuffed in pillowy pita and drizzled with a tasty yogurt sauce. Dessert is just as diverse. The service is casual and friendly, and belly dancers entertain patrons every Thursday night. *101 S. Coit Rd., at Belt Line Rd., Suite 1, Dal-Rich Village, North Suburbs, 972/671–8188. AE, D, DC, MC, V. $$–$$$*

6 *f-4*

MEDITERRANEO

This wonderful oasis of civility does everything right. Imaginative choices such as chunky white-bean soup, three-cheese ravioli topped with tomatoes, walnuts, and blue cheese, and a heart-healthy sautéed chicken and herb ravioli dish highlight its menu. As with its entrées, desserts are wonderfully eclectic. *18111 Preston Rd., at Frankford Rd., North Suburbs, 972/447–0066. Reservations essential. AE, DC, MC, V. No lunch weekends. $$$*

13 *c-2*

PALOMINO EURO BISTRO

This trendy, high fashion spot is quintessential Dallas good times with its wheeler-dealer-filled bar and a restaurant that serves stylish quasi-Mediterranean cuisine. It's more than just flash and sparkling decor; its innovative menu and attentive service always impress. Sweetly glazed spit roasted chicken arrives hot and juicy and the artichoke dip remains a wonderful indulgence. Smaller lunchtime pasta specials are good values. Choose your pizza toppings carefully. The ever-changing choices have included such bizarre toppings as manchego cheese, fresh mussels, and sherry cream. *500 Crescent Center, at Cedar Springs Rd., Suite 165, Uptown, 214/999–1222. Reservations essential. AE, D, DC, MC, V. No lunch weekends. $$$*

6 *f-8*

THE RIVIERA

Near the top of every "best in town" compilation, the pricey and prominent Riviera careens between the extremes of being either peerless or eccentric. Scallops and wild mushrooms on risotto with sun-dried-tomato pesto clearly occupy the peerless category. At the eccentric end of the spectrum, a balsamic vinegar enriched with foie gras sauce overpowers a monster slab of pepper-herb Cervena elk loin. Service exudes grace and professionalism. *7709 Inwood Rd., at Lovers La., University Park, 214/351–0094. Reservations essential. AE, D, DC, MC, V. No Lunch. $$$–$$$$*

MEXICAN

12 *e-3*

CIUDAD

The fashion set flocks to this casually elegant dining extravaganza for upscale Mexican foods. Innovative choices include ceviche-dressed chunks of octopus, conch, and shrimp with vanilla-pineapple vinaigrette and flavorful raviolis napped with *raja* sauce and studded with sautéed vanilla shrimp. The signature dessert is *edificio ciudad*—a rich architecturally-structured chocolate mousse that's stunning to behold. *3888 Oak Lawn Ave., at Blackburn St., Suite 135, Turtle Creek, 214/219–3141. Reservations essential. AE, D, DC, MC, V. Closed Sun. No lunch Sat. $$$*

7 *a-3*

EL NORTE GRILL

This nicely decorated and homey restaurant is ideal for family dining and prepares Mexican dishes with creative subtleties. The salsa is downright addictive, with its earthy nuance of roasted peppers. For lighter fare, an anomaly for a Mexican restaurant, try the "heart special"—roasted chicken enchiladas with sautéed onions and green sauce, rolled in corn tortillas, plus moist Mexican rice, pico de gallo, and a super house salad. Flan for adults and free sno–cones for children make everybody happy. *2205 W. Parker, at Custer Rd., North Suburbs, 972/596–6783. Reservations not accepted. AE, D, MC, V. $–$$*

12 *d-3*

GLORIA'S

Gloria's introduced Dallas to Salvadoran cuisine, a cousin of Mexican with such delightful differences as pork, black beans, and plantains, and has since grown into an economical and popular alternative with three locations. Favorites include two table salsas: heavy-on-cilantro red and thick-as-molasses black bean. Don't miss the papusas—the Salvadoran national dish, which consists of soft tortillas, stuffed with pork and cheese. *4140 Lemmon Ave., at Douglas Ave., Oak Lawn, 214/521–7576. Reservations not accepted. AE, D, DC, MC, V. $–$$*

10 *e-4*
600 W. Davis St., at Llewellyn St., Oak Cliff, 214/948–3672.

12 *h-1*
3715 Greenville Ave., Matalee Ave., East, 214/874-0088.

12 *f-2*
JAVIER'S

Not to be confused with Tex-Mex, this low-key spot serves sophisticated "Mexico City–style" dishes with a Continental influence. Red snapper, shrimp, steak, and chicken all well represented on the menu, and delicious sauces enhance their flavor. The warm and cozy atmosphere and regal service ensure a full house on most nights. *4912 Cole Ave., at Monticello Ave., Highland Park, 214/521–4211. Reservations essential. AE, D, DC, MC, V. No lunch. $$$–$$$$*

13 *f-3*
LA CALLE DOCE

This Oak Cliff restaurant renowned for its Mexican seafood specialties is no secret, as its framed autographed celebrity photos testify. It impresses patrons with hospitality and originality; it's set in a charming old house, with a warm interior dressed with antique furniture. The hearty house special—a whole marinated, grilled catfish—will make mouths water, but the lighter filleted version is equally tasty and easier to deal with. Meat lovers should try the monster Tampico-style grilled skirt steak with avocado and Mexican cheese. *415 W. 12th St., at Bishop, Oak Cliff, 214/941–4304. AE, D, MC, V. $–$$*

6 *f-5*
LA VALENTINA DE MEXICO

The elegance and eclectic flavors of upscale dining in Mexico City have been cloned in this beautiful north Dallas hacienda. Drawing on the experience of its three siblings south of the border, it serves carefully prepared dishes distinctively spiced with exotic flourishes such as *huitlacoche*, or "corn truffles." Culinary innovations include a mild but complex chile-spiced black sauce that dresses an entrée of huge shrimp, and sea bass basked in a rich butter-parsley sauce. *14866 Montfort Dr., at Belt Line Rd., North Suburbs, 972/726–0202. AE, D, MC, V. No lunch. $$–$$$*

7 *a-7*
MARTIN'S COCINA

The eccentric Mexican food served here is of the low-cal, low-fat variety. Remarkably, dishes such as stuffed zucchini and vegetarian enchiladas are robust and flavorful. Despite its healthful selection, the menu retains plenty of old standards: the combo plate includes a crisp ground-beef taco, creamy soft-cheese taco, enchilada, and salty guacamole. Dessert dictates the "no sugar added" three-berry pie. *7726 Ferguson Rd., at Highland Rd., East, 214/319–8834. AE, D, MC, V. BYOB. $*

13 *g-4*
MONICA'S ACA Y ALLA

This longtime Deep Ellum hangout sustains a cutting-edge profile that keeps the curious interested. "Aunt B's omelet," a brunch dish of a tamale with salsa and black beans, crowned with scrambled eggs, elicits feelings of content. Mimosas—the quintessential brunch spirit lifter are bargain priced. There's even a dish with fat-free beans and steamed rice for health-conscious diners. It's a pleasant place to spend Sunday morning, with the ever-flamboyant proprietor who personally checks to see that all's right with her guests. *2914 Main St., at Malcolm X Blvd., Deep Ellum, 214/748–7140. AE, D, MC, V. Closed Mon. $$*

12 *d-3*
NUEVO LEON

The menu at this upscale Mexican restaurant highlights the unique spices of the Mexican state of Nuevo Leon. Chunky guacamole with tomatoes, onions, and cilantro, and warm, zingy salsa tempts diners to excess, but save room for the three-enchilada special. The cheese and the beef versions both are drenched in red chile con carne, while the exceptional chicken is soused with tangy green tomatillo sauce. The highest praise, however, is earned by the *crepas de mariscos*—seafood stuffed crepes with creamy adobo chile sauce and mango-papaya pico de gallo. All three locations maintain a refined, feel-good ambience. *3211-C Oak Lawn Ave., at Cedar Springs Rd., Oak Lawn, 214/522–3331. AE, D, DC, MC, V. Closed Mon. $–$$*

13 *g-4*

PEPE'S & MITO'S

At this festive café, huge breakfast crowds dine on such favorites as *huevos rancheros* with the tasty scrambled eggs accompanied with almost sweet tomato sauce. For lunch, try the vegetarian quesadillas (onion, tomato, poblano, and parsley) in homemade flour tortillas or chicken chimichangas. *2935 Elm St., at Walton, Deep Ellum, 214/741–1901. Reservations not accepted. AE, D, MC, V. No dinner Mon.–Tues. $–$$*

MIDDLE EASTERN

12 *g-3*

ALI BABA

Dallas diners definitely have a love affair with Middle Eastern food, and Ali Baba serves a wonderful bounty at a small price. Juicy gyro meat, thickly sliced and wrapped in hot grilled pita bread, is lushly anointed with tahini sauce. The assorted appetizer plate comes with tabbouleh (heavy on the parsley, with a secret dose of cilantro); creamy, nutty hummus; and eggplant-based baba ghanouj. Getting a table is the only challenge. *1905 Greenville Ave., at Alta St., East, 214/823–8235. Closed Sun.–Mon. $*

12 *g-1*

CAFÉ IZMIR

Distinctive in its coziness, sophistication, and fixed-price menu, Izmir changes its menu nightly but always includes both vegetarian and meat alternatives. Presentation is colorful and too bountiful to fully describe. Appetizers include lemony tabbouleh mixed with couscous, smoky hummus, and a delicious Russian potato salad enhanced with shredded chicken. Meats include ground beef (in a sausage shape) and kabobs of lamb and chicken. *3711 Greenville Ave., at Martel, East, 214/826–7788. AE, MC, V. No lunch. $$$*

6 *f-8*

FOOD FROM GALILEE AND BARRY'S SANDWICHES

Bring the whole family because this eclectic and humble gem serves peanut-butter-and-jelly sandwiches and chili dogs. More sophisticated diners will relish the spinach-filled *samosas* (deep-fried pastry triangles filled with savory stuffing), and creamy hummus and lemony, parsley-rich tabbouleh on hot pita just couldn't be better or healthier for you. Honey-drenched pistachio baklava is a must-taste dessert. *6710 Snider Plaza, at Hillcrest and Lovers La., University Park, 214/750–0330. AE, D, MC, V. Closed Sun. $*

MOROCCAN

6 *f-8*

MARRAKESH

Though comfy Moroccan-style seating on low divans is available, some spines may prefer seating at tables, especially the ones near the area in which the belly dancers give enthusiastic performances. But if you're here for the food, try the almond-and-prune-flavored lamb stew. You can nibble on earthy black olives and scoop up a garlicky spinach and mushroom appetizer with warm, house-made bread. *5027 W. Lovers La., at Inwood Rd., University Park, 214/357–4104. AE, D, DC, MC, V. Closed Mon. No lunch. $$*

PAN ASIAN

12 *e-3*

CITIZEN

Between the Pan-Asian menu and sophisticated, minimalist decor, this Turtle Creek "in" spot epitomizes "City-Zen." Lunch specialties include fish du jour or pork stir-fry on a mound of textured pan-fried noodles. The sushi chef deftly satisfies requests for off-menu seafood such as flounder. It's hard to choose between banana fritters and wonton napoleon layered with crème brûlée and red berries swimming in intense caramel. *3858 Oak Lawn Ave., at Blackburn St., Suite 145, Turtle Creek, 214/522–7253. AE, D, DC, MC, V. No lunch weekends. $$$*

12 *g-3*

LIBERTY

Dallas's first "noodle shop" is hardly elegant but nonetheless haute fashionable. Dining al fresco is delightful when service is leisurely. Praiseworthy starters include skewered chicken and Thai-West tacos—small tortillas draped with chicken, pork, mushrooms, carrots, onion, and cilantro. Curry lovers should try the *chow fun* noodles with chicken sauced with onion, tomato, and garlic. Portions tend to be large, so come with a hearty appetite. *5631 Alta Ave., at*

Greenville Ave., East, 214/887–8795. Reservations essential. AE, D, DC, MC, V. Closed Mon. No lunch Sun. $$$

PIZZA

6 *f-7*

AL'S PIZZERIA

Started years ago by real New Yorkers (subway map posted on the wall), these guys spin pizzas by hand that will keep a family full and happy. The vegetarian deluxe pizza has a whopping 10 toppings—artichokes, green peppers, black and green olives, mushrooms, onions, jalapeños, garlic, spinach, and fresh tomato slices (not sauce). Standout dinners include lasagna, eggplant Parmigiana, baked ziti, and a large calzone with a good three inches of lavalike cheeses. The pizza slices are purportedly the best in town. *3701 W. Northwest Hwy., between Webbs Chapel and Marsh La., Northwest, 214/350–2714. Reservations not accepted. AE, D, MC, V. $*

12 *g-1*

CAMPISI'S

This 50-year old restaurant has become a Dallas institution by serving up inexpensive but delicious Italian food. And although it's the famous pizza that keeps people coming back, shrimp scampi and various pasta dishes are sure to satisfy as well. *5610 E. Mockingbird La., East, 214/827–0355. AE, D, MC, V. $–$$*

12 *g-1*

GORDO'S

Loyal SMU and near-North types have followed Gordo's pizza and burgers from place to place. This no-frills eatery also serves crusty beer-battered onion rings and traditional Italian fare, such as spaghetti marinara and cheese-coated meatball sandwiches. *4301 Lovers La., at Douglas, University Park, 214/521–5111. Reservations not accepted. AE, D, MC, V. $*

12 *g-3*

LOUIE'S

Louie's is the ultimate neighborhood watering hole with its array of TVs tuned to sporting events. First timers get the once over, as if entering a private club. Inside it is dark, smoky, and lovable—adjectives that also describe its outstanding thin-crusted anchovy and black olive pizza. Meatball sandwiches, pasta, and coconut chess pie are favorite indulgences. *1839 N. Henderson Ave., at Ross St., East, 214/826–0505. Reservations not accepted. AE, MC, V. No lunch. $$*

6 *f-8*

LOVERS PIZZA PASTA

New York-style thin crust pies are the specialty at this family-run pizza place. Fresh ingredients combined with homemade dough and sauce make for a taste better than anything delivered. *5605 W. Lovers La., University Park, 214/353–0509. No credit cards. $$*

6 *f-5*

PASTAZIO'S PIZZA

A huge wedge of pizza, discretely topped with mild anchovies, will satisfy most diners. You can also choose from a variety of other toppings, such as pineapple and pepperoni. Hot dishes such as lasagna, ravioli, and mozzarella-smothered baked ziti are presided over by Mama herself. The chocolate chip cannoli are homemade. *5206 Addison Circle, at Dallas North Tollway, North Suburbs, 972/386–9200. Reservations not accepted. AE, MC, V. $–$$*

SEAFOOD

12 *f-2*

AQUAKNOX

Stephan Pyles' dedication to creativity and perfection is a given: Witness his roasted lobster (scented with canela) on white-truffle risotto. The grilled rack of lamb, which comes with a caramelized-onion tamale topped with ratatouille, is equally delightful and a departure from the primary theme of this high fashion venue—exotic seafood creations. *3214 Knox St., at Cole Ave., Highland Park, 214/219–2782. Reservations essential. AE, D, MC, V. No smoking. No lunch. $$$–$$$$*

12 *g-1*

AW SHUCKS

Mix-your-own sauces, paper towels on the tables, and paying on the honor system are all part of the tradition that keeps this aquatic outpost packed. Come casual for the fried shrimp, catfish, and cold beer. *3601 Greenville Ave., East, 214/821–9449. AE, D, MC, V. $–$$*

12 *f-2*

BIG FISH LITTLE FISH

At this rustic seafooder, your selection of fresh fish is prepared as you like—grilled, fried, sautéed, or blackened—and topped with your choice of elaborate sauces (Chardonnay cream, artichoke-basil, tomato-onion, and more). Or you can go sauceless, squeezing only lemon on an ample plank of lightly battered flounder with emerald-hue broccoli, hearty mashed potatoes, and sweet corn on the cob. The chocolate mousse—a dense brick with caramel, whipped cream, and pecans—will satisfy those with a sweet tooth. *2810 N. Henderson Ave., at Central, East, 214/821–4552. AE, D, DC, MC, V. Closed Sun. $$*

12 *e-1*

CAFÉ PACIFIC

This popular restaurant draws a full house of well-heeled seafood lovers. Always deft at handling off-menu requests, the kitchen will happily prepare a huge plate of crab Louis—bits of tender crabmeat with Thousand Island dressing. For dessert, the pecan-coated, fudge-drenched ice cream ball has no peer. *24 Highland Park Village, at Mockingbird La., Highland Park, 214/526–1170. Reservations essential. AE, D, DC, MC, V. Closed Sun. $$$*

6 *g-7*

DADDY JACK'S LOBSTER AND CHOWDER HOUSE

The lobster special is a real draw, but you can also order a fine flounder plumped up with crabmeat stuffing at this casual, neighborhood hangout. The accompanying fluffy baked potato and ear of corn will satisfy the heartiest appetite, but make sure you leave room for a slice of strawberry-and-rhubarb pie for dessert. Non-piscivores will find pasta and beef dishes on the menu. *5940 Royal La., at Preston Rd., North, 214/378–6767. Reservations essential. AE, D, DC, MC, V. No smoking. No lunch weekends. $$–$$$*

12 *f-2*

FISH BOWL

Fish Bowl stands proudly on its own even though it shares co-tenancy with glitzy AquaKnox. Its contemporary room is both a trendy social venue and an outstanding restaurant. Start with creatively stuffed rock shrimp pot stickers. Green papaya salad provides a refreshing, but tart, foil. Highest kudos go to lemongrass beef satay, paired with pineapple-cucumber salad, and to a heaping bowl of red Thai coconut curry chicken with jasmine rice and basil. *3214 Knox St., at Cole Ave., Highland Park, 214/521–2695. Reservations not accepted. AE, D, DC, MC, V. No lunch. $$$*

6 *f-5*

LOMBARDI MARE

This chic, upscale seafooder prepares fresh seafood and pasta creations that change daily. The kitchen skillfully grills a thin slice of swordfish to the razor's edge of doneness without drying it out. A popular draw here is its Sunday champagne brunch, which includes a salad of organic mixed greens in balsamic vinaigrette, polenta crusted salmon with chive-bourbon sauce and red cabbage, and a key lime pie. All this, including mimosas, is served for a reasonable prix fixe. *5100 Belt Line Rd., at Montfort Rd., North Suburbs, Village on the Parkway, 972/503–1233. AE, MC, V. No lunch Sat. $$–$$$*

6 *g-7*

MAINSTREAM FISH HOUSE

Fresh fish in creative, savory sauces is why crowds mob this unassuming restaurant every day of the week. Stellar crab cakes and Oregon fisherman's stew are favorite appetizers. The lunch "reel deal" may include Canadian salmon, Idaho trout, or Mississippi catfish, cooked to perfection. Any of these pair well with sides of garlicky coleslaw and "Killer Potato Cakes." Wednesday is lobster night, a bargain not to be missed. The efficient and friendly service more than compensate for a small wine list and a noisy ambiance. *11661 Preston Rd., at Forest La., Preston Forest Village Shopping Center, North, 214/739–3474. Reservations not accepted. AE, D, DC, MC, V. No smoking. $$*

13 *c-1*

S&D OYSTER COMPANY

A New Orleans vibe contributes to the longevity of this longtime magnet for fresh seafood lovers. Fried shrimps and robust seafood gumbo are always reliable, and the delicately broiled flounder is a treat. Simmered in an addictive combination of butter, spices, and Worcestershire sauce, the jumbo New Orleans–style barbecued shrimp is rich, spicy and irresistible. A finger bowl, bib, and two cloth napkins are thoughtfully provided. *2701 McKinney Ave., at Boll St., Uptown, 214/880–0111. Reservations not accepted. MC, V. Closed Sun. $–$$*

6 *f-5*

SOHO FOOD, DRINKS, AND JAZZ

This lively restaurant bar lives up to its namesake with New York sophistication and style. The eclectic, but Asian-tinged menu emphasizes seafood, including cornmeal fried calamari, plump tempura shrimp, and peanut-sauced tenderloin satay—all part of the pricey but worthy *pupu* platter. Soft-shell crabs, encrusted in Romano cheese and accompanied by lemon cream sauce, has earned raves as an extraordinary creation. Attentive service and pride in the kitchen elevate SoHo above the pack of trendy, beautiful people places. Live jazz every night. *5290 Belt Line Rd., at Montfort Dr., North Suburbs, 972/490–8686. AE, D, DC, MC, V. $$–$$$*

SOUTHWESTERN

6 *g-8*

BLUE MESA

Crowds flock to this colorful, upscale spot, especially for the impressive entrance. The skewers of steak and chicken rolled up in grilled panna bread (similar to pita) are a perfect foil to roasted Chimayo market corn. Remember to leave room for the almond cookie taco filled with chocolate mousse. The tequila bar is a connoisseur's delight. *7700 W. Northwest Hwy., between Central Expressway and Boedecker, Suite 740, University Park, 214/378–8686. Reservations not accepted. AE, DC, MC, V. $$–$$$*

12 *g-1*

CISCO GRILL

Southwestern decor and food prevail at this café, along with reasonable prices. Its varied menu includes plenty of hearty choices—tacos, black bean quesadillas, Red River rice, and dishes of guacamole, black beans, and salsa. A memorable peach cobbler will easily leave a smile on three faces. *6630 Snider Plaza, at Hillcrest La., University Park, 214/363–9506. AE, MC, V. No smoking. Closed Sun. $*

12 *h-3*

MATT'S NO PLACE

Signless and with a casual Texas vibe, this one-of-a-kind restaurant enjoys cult-like status. If you're a fan of cigar smoke, stout flavors, and deep red wines, you've come to the right place. Upscale Texas chuckwagon best captures this nearly-indescribable cuisine. The special mixed grill is pricey, but includes ostrich, duck, and wild boar. Add wild rice and side choices such as smoky mashed potatoes or fried apples, and you've definitely got a memorable meal. For a gentler experience try farm-raised quail with goat cheese and vinaigrette salad. *6326 La Vista Dr., at Gaston Ave., East, 214/823–9077. AE, D, DC, MC, V. $$–$$$*

12 *d-3*

STAR CANYON

The number one restaurant stop for many visitors is this high temple of Southwestern cuisine. Conservative types will enjoy the huge "cowboy rib-eye" steak, with a heaping tangle of fried onion rings. More adventuresome diners will find on the always-evolving menu offbeat local variations such as *cabrito* (spit-roasted goat) as filling as more familiar quesadillas. The accompanying black beans and salsa complete the earthy-flavored experience. *3102 Oak Lawn Ave., at Cedar Springs Rd., Suite 144, Oak Lawn, 214/520–7827. Reservations essential. AE, D, MC, V. No lunch weekends. $$$–$$$$*

SPANISH

12 *f-2*

CAFÉ MADRID

It's like stepping into another land when you enter Dallas' original tapas bar. The sparse rooms resonate with the passion of an authentic Spanish café. Dishes such as a dense potato omelet with garlic aioli, grilled pork loin, and vinaigrette-dressed white asparagus round out the menu, and blackboard specials, a selection of exotic cheeses, and economically priced wines add to its highlights. *4501 Travis St., at Armstrong Ave., Highland Park, 214/528–1731. Reservations not accepted. MC, V. Closed Sun. No lunch. $–$$*

6 *f-5*

DE TAPAS

While sipping sangria, summer's soul mate, order a variety of little snack platters and get into a tapas state of mind at this cozy Spanish bistro. Choices range from a potato omelet with garlic aioli to grilled shiitake mushrooms, from mussels in a piquant tomato sauce to anchovy-stuffed olives. If the weather's nice, ask for a table on the patio. *5100 Belt Line Rd., at Monfort, Village on the Parkway, North Suburbs, 972/233–8553. Reservations not accepted. AE, D, DC, MC, V. Closed Mon. $*

STEAK

12 *d-3*

BOB'S STEAK AND CHOP HOUSE

This dark, clubby steak house may be upscale—it attracts business-suited men with lofty expense accounts—but the beef and lamb stay loyal to their "down-home" origins. If you are short on embellishments and cigar smoke, you can choose a more casual back room where the dress better matches the meat. The no-nonsense prime beef and the time-honored rack of lamb are among the city's best. *4300 Lemmon Ave., Oak Lawn, 214/528–9446. AE, D, MC, V. Closed Sun. $$–$$$*

13 *c-2*

CAPITAL GRILLE

Powerbrokers are rumored to conspire in booths at the Washington, D.C. mother ship. The low-lit, masculine ambiance of the Dallas outpost has the same feeling of a rendezvous walking the line between intrigue and romance. A well-marbled, flavorful Delmonico steak, easily enough shared by two promises to please. Assorted seasoned mushrooms, tasty and grilled to allow each variety's individual flavor are a fitting, earthy companion. All side dishes are à la carte, but extremely generous. *500 Crescent Court, at Cedar Springs Rd. and Maple Ave., Uptown, 214/303–0500. Reservations essential. AE, D, MC, V. No lunch weekends. $$$$*

6 *f-5*

DEL FRISCO'S DOUBLE EAGLE STEAK HOUSE

Big with the expense account and convention crowd, this nationally prominent steak house serves big steaks, with some chops and fish thrown in for the more timid. Sides are à la carte. Appetizers such as the boiled shrimp are worth their bounty. With huge, boisterous surroundings, excellent service, and decadent desserts, excess has never tasted so good. *5251 Spring Valley, at N. Dallas Tollway, North Suburbs, 972/490–9000. Reservations essential. AE, D, DC, MC, V. Closed Sun. No lunch. $$$$*

6 *f-7*

DUSTON'S STEAKHOUSE

Familiar faces, old Levi's, and low-priced quality steaks can be found at this 43-year-old traditional steakhouse. You won't find waiters in stuffy white suits here, but rather rosy-cheeked waitresses with a knack for good country service. Seafood, including lobster, shrimp, and salmon rounds out the menu. Any selection from the affordable wine list is a good match. *423 W. Lovers La., North, 214/352–8320. AE, D, MC, V. $–$$*

12 *g-1*

KIRBY'S STEAKHOUSE

This favorite institution of longtime Dallasites has an alternative—aged, corn-fed Black Angus. The meat is lean, buttery and expertly grilled. Add low lights, western-theme etched glass, and a gracious staff, and you have a striking, civilized, and economical contrast to the flamboyant big-name steakhouses. Don't just come for the hard-to-beat salad bar: à la carte side dishes such as sautéed button mushrooms and billowy mashed potatoes add to the dining experience. *3525 Greenville Ave., at McCommas Rd., East, 214/821–2122. Reservations essential. AE, D, MC, V. No lunch. $$$*

7 *a-4*

3408 Preston Rd., at Parker Rd., North Suburbs, 972/867–2122.

6 *f-5*

LAWRY'S THE PRIME RIB

Here is a peerless example of a simple concept executed with precision and consistently outstanding results. Prime rib is carved at tableside from imposing rolling silver serving carts. The so-called California cut of standing rib roast is just right for smaller appetites though the Yorkshire pudding and mashed potatoes could sink any diet. The Spinning Salad Bowl fascinates as it evenly anoints humble lettuces with sherry-enhanced dressing. The elegant setting and service is pure Southern courtesy. *14655 Dallas Pkwy., at Belt Line Rd. and Spring Valley Rd., North, 972/503–6688. AE, D, DC, MC, V. No dinner Sun. $$$–$$$$*

13 *b-1*

NICK AND SAM'S

This handsome beef emporium packs in the drinkers and diners. A barrel-vaulted ceiling imparts a casual yet classy feel to the huge open room. Surf-and-turf is imposing, tempting, and pricey. The special Porterhouse is a masterpiece, and sides, desserts, and service are all excellent. *3008 Maple Ave., at Wolf St., Turtle Creek, 214/871–7444. Reservations essential. AE, DC, MC, V. No lunch. $$$$*

13 *c-5*

THE PALM

Its days of surly waiters and sawdust floors have finally been replaced by obliging service and more attractive dark-wood ambiance. Not only are incomparable steak dishes available, but there are sultry lobster, veal, and pasta choices as well. Usually, crab cakes have a lot of filler; but these are crammed with huge chunks of delicious crab. "Heavenly" describes the à la carte sides of hash browns and spinach. *701 Ross Ave., at Market St., West End, 214/698–0470. Reservations essential. AE, DC, MC, V. No lunch. $$$$*

12 *c-2*

RUTH'S CHRIS

The Cedar Springs location of this venerable beef emporium seems intimate and clubby compared with the festive North Dallas location. With otherworldly tenderloins, expansive portions, and efficient service, you get the complete upscale steakhouse experience. The many side dishes (all à la carte) will delight a vegetarian. A halved tomato as sweet as a dessert emerges with form and texture intact, and spinach bathes in a rich cream sauce. Bring your expense account. *5922 Cedar Springs Rd., at Inwood Rd., Oak Lawn, 214/902–8080. Reservations essential. AE, D, MC, V. No lunch. $$$$*

17840 Dallas Pkwy., at Briargrove La., North Suburbs, 972/250–2244.

6 *f-5*

SULLIVAN'S STEAKHOUSE

There is no shortage of glitzy steak houses in Dallas, but Sullivan's brings a little sanity to prices, appropriate familiarity to the service, and an environment that is both vibrant and sophisticated. Beef is served in a variety of cuts and grilled to perfection. Creamed spinach, doubly enriched with cream cheese, easily satisfies two diners, as does deep-dish apple pie. At meal's end, retire to Ringside, the adjoining boxing-theme club, for coffee and jazz. *17795 N. Dallas Pkwy., at Briargrove La., North Suburbs, 972/267–9393. Reservations essential. AE, D, DC, MC, V. Closed Sun. No lunch. $$$–$$$$*

6 *f-5*

III FORKS

Meat-eaters take note: this formidable edifice seats 930 diners at a whack, but you'll still wait. One notable innovation is the demise of its à la carte menu—dishes now come with ample sides. Steak and seafood share roughly equal billing. The beef tenderloin and prime cuts are luscious and satisfying—and the wine list is beyond extensive—but such pleasure comes at a price. *17776 Dallas Pkwy., at Trinity Mills, North Suburbs, 972/267–1776. Reservations essential. AE, D, MC, V. No lunch. $$$$*

6 *e-8*

TRAIL DUST STEAK HOUSE

This cowboy-friendly hangout has live country music, a dance floor for two-steppers, and communal dining tables for big Texas families. For those who want to experience Texas flavor at its best, or have their necktie snipped and pinned to the wall, this is the place. With selections from the cowboy porterhouse to the golden fried jalapeños, you'll be sure to leave with a smile. *10841 Composite Dr., Northwest, 214/357–3862. AE, DC, D, MC, V. $$*

TEX-MEX

12 *d-3*

AVILA'S MEXICAN RESTAURANT

A clean, simple interior makes a great backdrop for fresh Tex-Mex at this reliable family-operated downtown eatery. With Mom and Sis in the kitchen and the boys running the front, who can complain? Don't miss the mole or the chile rellenos. *4714 Maple Ave., Oak Lawn, 214/520–2700. AE, D, DC, MC, V. $*

12 *g-2*

BLUE GOOSE

The cantina atmosphere and aura of a border-town hangout keep the regulars coming back. Hearty appetites are required for the hefty fajita platters; margaritas help to wash it all down. Regulars advise coming in early to avoid the university set. *2905 Greenville Ave., East, 214/823–8339. AE, D, DC, MC, V. $$*

12 *d-3*

CASA DOMINGUEZ

Once a gas station, believe or not, this casual spot is a Tex-Mex old-timer. The near-flawless crispy chips and snappy sauce are *excelente*, and enchiladas filled with sautéed spinach and topped with sour cream and provolone cheese are a lingering favorite. Kick back with a refreshing margarita and let the friendly and accommodating waitstaff take your order. *2408 Cedar Springs Rd., at Fairmont St., Turtle Creek, 214/871–9787. Reservations not accepted. AE, D, MC, V. $–$$*

6 *f-8*

CASA ROSA

Tucked away in Inwood Village, this is one of the most charming places in town for Mexican eats. The menu has plenty of standard and familiar Tex-Mex fare, but also incorporates innovation without going to au courant extremes. Blue corn enchiladas, topped with green chile sauce and stuffed with chicken, are served with a huge plate full of black beans and rice. Mexican apple pie, served sizzling on an iron platter (à la fajitas), with brandy butter and cinnamony ice cream is an extraordinary treat. *165 Inwood Village, at Inwood Rd. and Lovers La., University Park, 214/350–5227. Reservations not accepted. AE, D, MC, V. $–$$*

12 *f-2*

CUQUITA'S

A special favorite, Cuquita's serves food better described as Mex-Mex than Tex-Mex in an attractive, spotless, and efficiently run restaurant. A trio of *chalupas*—cheese, guacamole, and bean—crackle with crispness, while a delicately battered *chile relleno* oozes warm, mild cheese. Burrito fillings may be mixed and matched, while such specialties as tongue and mole appeal to a large and loyal Hispanic clientele. *2326 N. Henderson Ave., at Central, East, 214/823–1859. No credit cards. No smoking. $*

12 *c-2*

HERRERA'S TEX-MEX

Long a favorite for Dallasites, this is where you'll find retro Tex-Mex cuisine. Authentic and funky, legendary cheese-and-onion enchiladas can be washed down with sweet margaritas. Disks of pure sugar and pecans, otherwise known as pralines, is a perfect finish. *5427 Denton Dr., at Inwood Rd., Oak Lawn, 214/630–2599. AE, D, DC, MC, V. Closed Mon. $*

MI COCINA

This local chain serves tasty food in a contemporary setting. The constant crowd chows down on Mama's tacos and pork tamales. For dessert, the flan is a winner. Service is fast and efficient. *77 Highland Park Village, Highland Park, 214/521–6426. AE, D, MC, V. $$*

6 *g-8*

5950 Berkshire La., University Park, 214/750–9892.

6 *g-7*

11661 Preston Rd., North, 214/265–7704.

6 *f-5*

13350 Dallas Pkwy., North Suburbs, 972/239–6426.

6 *h-6*

18352 Dallas Pkwy., North Suburbs, 972/250–6426.

7201 Skillman Rd., East 214/503–6426.

12 *d-3*

MIA'S TEX MEX

The sign says "If Mama ain't happy, ain't nobody happy" and everyone's usually happy after eating at this of Dallas Tex-Mex spots. Try her eponymous appetizer platter of *flautas*, nachos, quesadillas, sour cream, and creamy guacamole, along with powerful margaritas. House specialties include a Miguelito's plate consisting of crisp meat taco and sour cream chicken and cheese enchiladas, and chicken breast smothered in sour cream sauce and jack cheese. Top-notch pralines are all that's needed for dessert. *4322 Lemmon Ave., at Wycliff Ave., Oak Lawn, 214/526–1020. MC, V. Closed Sun. $*

7 *b-6*

MOTHER MESQUITE'S CANTINA

This family-oriented Tex-Mex place has a low-key, upscale look. While waiting for your entrée, sip a margarita and dip the delicate thin chips in bowls of fresh chunky salsa, heavy on cilantro. The tender *carne asada*, mesquite grilled and basted and melded with the flavor of grilled onions, is worth the wait. All entrées come with moist Tex-Mex rice and a choice of pinto or black beans. Creamy praline cheesecake with caramel sauce easily satisfies two. *9210 Skillman St., at I–635, East, 214/348–1217. Reservations not accepted. AE, D, DC, MC, V. $$*

12 *d-4*

OJEDA'S

The lunch line stretches out the door, and with good reason: this Dallas institution provides the quintessential Tex-Mex experience. The only dilemma is whether to order the cheese-and-onion enchiladas (covered with that distinctive and addictive brown gravy) or to hold out for the puffy tacos—huge crisp shells filled with meat, salad, and cheese. *4617 Maple Ave., Oak Lawn, 214/528–8383. AE, D, DC, MC, V. Closed Sun. $*

12 *e-3*

PRIMO'S BAR & GRILL

The easygoing atmosphere at Primo's sets the stage for tasty Tex-Mex and a lively bar. The grilled chicken breast, pounded wafer-thin and served with tomatillo-avocado sauce and jack cheese, is a must. Eggs are served at all hours (a particular favorite is the eggs with potatoes—*papas huevos*), and a variety of standards fill out the menu. *3309 McKinney Ave., at Hall St., Turtle Creek, 214/220–0510. Reservations not accepted. AE, D, MC, V. $*

12 *e-4*

VICTOR'S TAQUERIA

Adventuresome diners, seeking a real taste of authentic south-of-the-border cuisine, can step into another land where the menu splits Tex-Mex fare with Colombian specialties such as *arapas* (which resemble fried corn hush puppies). The reputed hangover cure, *menudo*, made from tripe, is offered "all-you-can-eat" on weekends. *Taquitos* (crisp fried corn shells) can be ordered stuffed with familiar beef, chicken, or pork fillings, but daredevils may elect the more esoteric *barbacoa* of beef head, pork snout, or brains—all with fresh cilantro and onions. *4447 Maple Dr., at Lucas Dr., Oak Lawn, 214/521–0121. Reservations not accepted. No credit cards. No smoking. $*

6 *e-8*

9625 Webb Chapel Rd., Suite 400, Northwest, 214/357–0162.

6 *f-8*

Z-TECA MEXICAN GRILL

This cantina should be praised for using no lard, reducing other animal fats, and assembling dishes as they are ordered. This is indeed "fresh food fast." Burritos are made to order, with rice or a choice of beans as a side; you select salsa and choose between cheese and sour cream on top. You won't go away hungry. *600 W. Lovers La., at Dallas N. Tollway, University Park, 214/352–2277. Reservations not accepted. MC, V. $*

6 *g-5*

1930 N. Coit Rd., at Campbell Rd., Suite 150, North Suburbs, 972/231–6655.

BEST SPOTS FOR SUNDAY BRUNCH

When it comes to Sunday brunch, Dallas offers a host of fine spots that will please every palate.

Beau Nash (Contemporary)
Elegant setting plus creative cuisine equals top drawer choice.

Ciudad, D.F. (Mexican)
Brunch amid a festive south-of-the-border atmosphere in this sophisticated Mexico City–style diner.

Isolo Gozo (Italian)
Rustic country Italian charm lends itself to an array of freshly prepared choices.

The Mansion on Turtle Hill (Contemporary)
The be-all and end-all in elegance and cuisine for those seeking the ultimate brunch.

Samba Room (Brazilian)
Exotic treats inspired by the Caribbean attract late-sleeping weekend revelers.

San Francisco Rose (American Casual)
A pleasant but unassuming place to read the newspaper and dwell over familiar fare.

THAI

6 *f-5*

CHOW THAI

Diners frequently return to this classy Art Deco room for another taste of its quality Thai cuisine. Among other culinary creations, skewered chicken satay, with tasty crushed-peanut sauce and cucumbers, and *bahmee* (a stir-fry of egg noodles and vegetables) are menu favorites. *5290 Belt Line Rd., at Montfort Rd., North Suburbs, 972/960–2999. AE, D, MC, V. No lunch weekends. $$*

6 *g-8*

ROYAL THAI

In a city with limited Thai choices, this handsome restaurant expands your Asian taste horizons amid a congenial ambience. Thai spices prevail in a blazing house sauce, which accompanies the *gai ho bai tong* (grilled marinated chicken wrapped in banana leaves). For milder fare, the garlic shrimp with black peppers and broccoli will cool things off. For a really memorable finish try the strange sounding, but delicious black rice pudding with cream. *5500 Greenville at Lovers La., Old Town Shopping Village, East, 214/691–3555. AE, D, MC, V. No smoking. No lunch weekends. $$*

6 *g-7*

STAR OF SIAM

This modest Thai eatery is part of an unexplored culinary wonderland of countless Asian restaurants stretching from east to west across the northern part of the city. The expansive menu doesn't skimp on selection—plenty of soups, noodle dishes, salads, and house specials—and its economical menu easily suits every budget. *708-B W. Spring Valley Rd., at N. Central Expressway, North, 972/497–9542. Reservations not accepted. AE, D, MC, V. BYOB. No smoking. No lunch Sun. $*

12 *f-3*

THAI TASTE

From salads and soups for starters to pork toast and angel hair noodles with shrimp for entrees, prominent chef Annie Wong lays out a broad spectrum of traditional Thai dishes at this Uptown Thai eatery. For a romantic treat, ask for a table in the glass-walled second floor and relish the awesome view of the sunset. *3101 N. Fitzhugh Ave., at McKinney Ave., Suite 101, Highland Park, 214/521–3513. AE, D, DC, MC, V. No lunch Sun. $$*

BEST RESTAURANTS FOR ROMANTIC DINNERS

If romance is in the offing, one of these venues will ensure a proper setting for starry-eyed patrons.

The Grape (Contemporary)
The Casablanca-like bar is a romantic prelude to cozy, yet casual candlelight dining.

Jennivine (English)
Creative dishes, both British and au courant, served in a quaint and rustic English countryside ambiance.

Lavendou (French)
A spacious and lovely setting, with quintessential Gaelic charm and caring attention to detail and authenticity.

Old Warsaw (Continental)
Flaming desserts, a strolling violinist, classical pianist, and the finest of Continental cuisine highlight this Grande dame of upscale dining in Dallas.

York Street (Contemporary)
A popular spot for special occasions, this cozy, dimly-lit house ensures caring preparation and lavish personal attention.

VEGETARIAN & MACROBIOTIC

12 *d-3*

COSMIC CAFÉ

The earthy decor in this funky vegetarian café draws inspiration from both India and the Middle East. Indian curry dishes, herbal teas, and nourishing fruit smoothies share space on its menu. In keep with its transcendental vibe, poetry readings and Indian tabla music are part of the weekly happenings. *2912 Oak Lawn Ave., at Cedar Springs Rd., Oak Lawn, 214/521–6157. Reservations not accepted. AE, D, DC, MC, V. $*

12 *h-4*

KALACHANDJI'S RESTAURANT

In the mood for relaxing atmosphere and healthy living? This restaurant, attached to an East Dallas Hare Krishna temple, has a peaceful garden patio and vegetarian and vegan food that will fill both your belly and your mind with karmic joy. *5430 Gurley Ave., East, 214/821–1048. AE, D, MC, V. $*

VIETNAMESE

12 *d-3*

GREEN PAPAYA

Find sustenance and reward in this tiny yet popular eatery's namesake salad, which combines lemon-marinated papaya with mint, shrimp, and grilled pork. *Pho*—the "Big Soup" with rice noodles, cilantro, and meatballs—will fill the gap until breakfast. The chicken vermicelli garners high marks, and so does the refreshing Vietnamese soda. *3211 Oak Lawn Ave., at Hall St., Oak Lawn, 214/521–4811. AE, MC, V. No lunch weekends. $–$$*

10 *g-1*

MAI'S ORIENTAL

This chic venue is hot, both in atmosphere and in its Vietnamese cuisine. The hands-down favorite is chicken cooked in a clay pot with banana flowers, mushrooms, and onion. This University Park spot is not to be confused with Mai's in East Dallas. *6912 Snider Plaza, University Park, 214/361–8220. AE, DC, MC, V. Closed Sun. $*

6 *f-7*

MISS SAIGON

With fresh ingredients, courteous service, and a menu that's traditional with a dash of innovation this Vietnamese-Chinese eatery has become a popular spot. The large, impressive selection of entrées includes a flavorful curried chicken with sautéed morsels of juicy white meat with chunky potatoes and a monster Mexican tortilla filled with mixed oriental vegetables. *12300 Inwood Rd., at Forest La., North, 972/503–7110. AE, MC, V. Closed Sun. $$*

BEST VIEWS

Here are some places where heavenly light outshines city light.

Chapparral Club (Contemporary) *Uninterrupted vistas from a city-center location provide breathtaking views of the Dallas prairie while diners indulge in savory Southwestern-inspired dishes.*

Laurel's (Continental) *The spacious room overlooking the city skyline from a northern vantage point boasts a premier kitchen staff.*

Nana Grill (Continental) *The namesake odalisque painting adorning the bar and a strolling violinist provide Continental charm in this penthouse with a sweeping view of the city below.*

restaurants by cuisine: fort worth/mid-cities

AMERICAN

5 *d-4*

BABE'S CHICKEN DINNER HOUSE

As sure as the sun rises each day, throngs of people consistently wait in long lines for Babe's to open its doors, even on 100-degree days. The menu consists of juicy fried chicken and the famous Texas staple, chicken-fried steak. Served family-style, all dinners come with whipped buttery potatoes, corn, salad greens in an oil-and-vinegar dressing, and hot biscuits with sorghum syrup. Babe's is open only for an early dinner, Tuesday through Saturday, and for lunch on Sunday: *104 N. Oak St., near Texas 114 and U.S. 377, Roanoke, 817/491–2900. AE, D, DC, MC, V. BYOB. Closed for dinner Sun., closed Mon. $$*

14 *e-7*

LUCILE'S STATESIDE BISTRO

This sun-filled café is known for its uptown home-cooking—burgers, steaks, pastas, and one of the best wood-burning pizzas in town. The annual September Lobsterama brings lobster in a myriad of combinations with reasonable prices. You can eat, chat with neighborhood locals, or watch a ball game on TV at the bar. The vintage mosaic tile floor is a stunning visual, but can be an acoustical hindrance. *4700 Camp Bowie Blvd., Arlington, 817/738–4761. AE, D, DC, MC, V. $–$$*

14 *h-8*

OL' SOUTH PANCAKE HOUSE

Open 24/7, this sprawling diner is always jumping. It's hard to resist the Dutch babies (thin crepes topped with butter, powdered sugar, and squeezed-at-the-table lemon juice). Lunch and dinner run the blue-plate gamut, from chicken fried steak to Tex-Mex. Service is speedy, but the Sunday post-church crowd can slow things down. *1509 S. University Dr., Fort Worth, 817/336–0311. D, MC, V. $*

5148 Belknap St., Haltom City, 817/834–1291. D, MC, V. $

AMERICAN/CASUAL

14 *h-6*

THE BACK PORCH

The windows of this ultra-casual café provide views of the Kimbell Art Museum and the Will Rogers Auditorium complex. If the pay-by-the-weight salad bar poses too many choices, you can always opt for comforting soups, burgers, sandwiches, or pizza, all baked on the premises. The self-serve policy can help make your visit a quick one, but if you want to linger, go next door for some of the best homemade ice cream in the city, especially the fresh peach when it's in season. *3400 Camp Bowie Blvd., Fort Worth, 817/332–1422. AE, MC, V. No smoking. Closed Mon. $*

9 *e-1*

BAYLEY'S

Breakfast at this sunny shopping center treasure is a ritual in Northeast Tarrant County, with diners crowding in every morning for its generous portions and accommodating service. An enormous menu includes honey granola pancakes, Italian frittata, eggs Benedict, and shirred eggs with Swiss cheese and spinach inside a buttery croissant. *109 Harwood Rd., at Norwood Rd., Hurst, 817/268–5779. AE, D, DC, MC, V. $*

15 *c-6*

FRED'S CAFÉ

By day, Fred's is a hole-in-the-wall dive serving up biscuits and gravy breakfasts and burger lunches to a loyal blue-collar following. By night, owner J. D. Chandler's son Terry takes over the skillets. Hot Friday nights feature cuisine designed to scorch the skin off your tongue. The eclectic background music ranges from Led Zeppelin to Junior Brown, sometimes reaching pulsating decibel levels. *915 Currie St., Fort Worth, 817/332–0083. No credit cards. BYOB. Closed Sun. $*

14 *e-7*

KINCAID'S HAMBURGERS

It started out as a neighborhood grocery store that served hamburgers in the back, but eventually the groceries got in the way, so out went the canned goods and in came the picnic tables and reading material. Stock up on napkins—you'll need them for these juicy, big burgers. The frozen krinkle-cut french fries are a bit of a cop-out, but it hasn't hurt Kincaid's long-standing lock on the top of the burger list. *4901 Camp Bowie Blvd., Arlington, 817/732–2881. No credit cards. No smoking. Closed Sun. $*

5 *h-6*

RAINFOREST CAFÉ

Once you get over the talking trees and jungle noises, and your child has recovered from the near attack by an automated alligator, you'll get down to eating Kalahari safari pot pie (it's chicken, of course), sandwiches, pizzas, pastas, and salads bearing equally goofy names. It's a theme restaurant on steroids, perfectly suited to the overdone, oversized, and overwhelming shopping mall. Be sure to share the bodacious desserts, such as apple crisp. *3000 Grapevine Mills Pkwy., at Texas Hwy. 121, Grapevine, 972/539–5001. AE, D, DC, MC, V. $$*

14 *a-8*

TOMMY'S HAMBURGERS

The rolls of paper towels and dueling televisions keep the ambience loose and loud. Many locals consider Tommy's hamburgers to be the best in town, but the superb catfish and chicken-fried steak are equally tasty. Check out the sides of fried corn and cheddar peppers.

2701 Green Oaks Rd., Fort Worth, 817/735–9651. D, MC, V. $

14 *h-6*

400 Houston St., Fort Worth, 817/334–0999. D, MC, V.

8 *f-2*

3431 W. 7th St., Fort Worth, 817/332–1922. AE, D, DC, MC, V.

15 *c-6*

7028 Navajo Tr., Fort Worth, 817/237–9992. AE, D, DC, MC, V.

BARBECUE

15 *a-5*

ANGELO'S BARBECUE

A veritable international shrine in the barbeque religion, Angelo's fought off the competition by serving what they've always served; tender brisket and pork ribs with a thick sauce that isn't too sweet. The Georges family has made few concessions to the changing times, but they finally relented and added a delicious smoked chicken to the lineup. Waitresses holler in the beer orders tableside, adding to the prevailing raucous atmosphere. *2533 White Settlement Rd., Fort Worth, 817/332–0357. No credit cards. BYOB. Closed Sun. $–$$*

5 *h-6*

BARTLEY'S

Carolinians adore this unadorned, strip-center family-run joint for its barbecued pork loin, something rarely found in Texas. Solid eats here also include smoked beef brisket, baby-back pork ribs, and bologna. Be sure to seek out side dishes of corn fritters and barbecued beans; the peach cobbler is in a category all its own. *413 E. Northwest Hwy., Grapevine, 817/481–3212. AE, D, DC, MC, V. BYOB. Closed Sun. and Mon. $*

9 *g-4*

DAVID'S

A cousin to the famous Red Bryan's barbecue family in Dallas, the family-friendly David's packs in all ages for deeply smoked pork ribs, turkey, beef brisket, and sausage. Service is caféteria style, and everyone sits hunkered over tables where centerpieces consist of big rolls of paper towels. *2224 W. Park Row, Arlington, 817/261–9998. D, MC, V. Closed Sun. and Mon. $*

9 *g-4*

GAYLEN'S

Conveniently near the Ballpark in Arlington, this smokehouse is a popular stop for pork ribs, brisket, beans, slaw, and potato salad prior to seeing the Texas Rangers play nine innings. Loyalists are drawn to the amiable behind-the-counter service almost as much as the food. *826 N. Collins St., Arlington, 817/277–1945. AE, D, MC, V. Closed Sun. and Mon. $*

9 *g-1*

NORTH MAIN BBQ

Racking up awards for its hickory-smoked pork ribs was so much more fun than trucking that the owners of this warehouse-style restaurant decided to quit the road and stick to serving food. This all-you-can-eat stop only operates on Friday, Saturday, and Sunday, serving truckloads of short ribs, brisket, pork shoulder, chicken, and sausage. *406 N. Main St., at Texas Hwy. 183, Euless, 817/267–9101. No credit cards. BYOB. $*

14 *h-8*

RAILHEAD SMOKEHOUSE

Here you'll find a more lively and younger clientele coming for what many diehards think is the city's best BBQ. Decor is picnic table casual with excellent outdoor porch dining. *2900 Montgomery Ave., Fort Worth, 817/738–9808. MC, V. BYOB. Closed Sun. $–$$*

5 *g-7*

5220 Hwy. 121, Colleyville, 817/571–2525. Reservations not accepted. AE, D, MC, V. BYOB. Closed Sun. $–$$

5 *c-6*

UP IN SMOKE

Slow-smoked over a white-oak fire, the beef brisket, pork ribs, sausage, ham, pork tenderloin, and turkey breast at this neighborhood hangout pair nicely with fried okra, potato salad, pinto beans, and corn fritters. The bar side of the business often draws a lively after-work crowd, and the race car memorabilia seems appropriate with Texas Motor Speedway just a short drive west. *134 S. Main St., Keller, 817/431–9091. AE, D, MC, V. Closed Sun. $*

CAFÉS

15 *d-5*

GRAPE ESCAPE

Almost 100 different wines are offered by the glass, or by the flight, at this charming wine bistro. The light menu includes snacks of perfectly prepared *pommes fri*, pâtés, salads, and tenderloin. Across the street from the Bass Performing Hall, this is an ideal pre- or post-performance pit stop. *500 Commerce St., Fort Worth, 817/336–9463. Reservations not accepted. AE, D, MC, V. $$*

9 *b-4*

SAPRISTI!

Borrowing the favorite exclamation of French comic strip character Tin Tin, the gang from St. Emilion restaurant have cooked up a zippy ultra-casual, world-cuisine café. Excellent wines by the glass, reasonable prices, and inventive food combinations will keep the oilcloth-covered tables spinning. Bravo for transforming a former fern bar into such an appealing destination. *2418 Forest Park Blvd., Fort Worth, 817/924–7231. AE, D, MC, V. No dinner Sun., closed Mon. $–$$*

CARIBBEAN

15 *c-5*

CABO MIX-MEX GRILL

Whimsical and fun, this amped-up diner emphasizes neon, chrome, and handsome tuck-and-roll booths. The salsa is very hot and the rock music is very loud. While the highlights are the fish tacos, the menu also includes all the usual Tex-Mex suspects, including zippy chicken enchiladas and black beans topped with cheese and jalapeño pepper mix. The adjacent El Rincon Bar has the same menu in a darker and more decidedly Caribbean atmosphere. *115 W. 2nd St., Fort Worth, 817/348–8226. Reservations not accepted. AE, D, DC, MC, V. $*

CHINESE

9 *g-4*

ARC-EN-CIEL

Although this Chinese-Vietnamese eatery serves a variety of mainstream dishes, the dim sum served daily garners all the attention. Servers stroll past with pushcarts packed with steamed dumplings filled with shrimp and pork, baked eggplant filled with marinated shrimp, and some 80 other selections. Beware the massive crowds on weekends. *2208 New York Ave., at Collins St., Arlington, 817/469–9999. AE, D, MC, V. $*

CONTEMPORARY

8 *h-5*

BISTRO LOUISE

Louise Lamensdorf's neo-Mediterranean menu pulls in an upscale crowd, but the Provence country-style decor of the dining areas is warm and welcoming. The menu changes seasonally, but always includes inspired treatments of fresh fish, meats, salads, and soups. Tapas are served beginning at 5PM, with an array of cheeses in glass cases. *2900 S. Hulen St., Suite 40, Fort Worth, 817/922–9244. AE, D, DC, MC, V. Closed Sun. $$–$$$$*

14 *h-6*

BUFFET RESTAURANT AT THE KIMBELL

Mastermind Shelby Schafer continues to invent sublime salad selections with innovative combinations of beans, vegetables, grains, and meats. Choose from two soups and sandwiches and cap it all off with desserts and fresh whipped cream. Taking in a meal in Louis Kahn's breathtaking masterpiece of a building is worth the trip alone. *Kimbell Art Museum, 3333 Camp Bowie Blvd., Fort Worth, 817/332–8451. AE, D, MC, V. Closed Mon.; no lunch Fri. $*

8 *g-4*

CAFÉ ASPEN

The hodge-podge decor of this contemporary dining room could use some tweeking, but the food is still among the most cosmopolitan in town. The globe-spanning menu includes fondue Suisse, quesadillas, coriander-crusted tuna, and veal chop Portobello with cabernet mashed potatoes. Before the dinner bell rings, the dark Aspen Bar at the back of the restaurant does a brisk business, thanks to the locals who have adopted it as their hangout. *6103 Camp Bowie Blvd., Fort Worth, 817/738–0838. AE, DC, MC, V. Closed Sun.; no lunch Sat. $$–$$$*

5 *d-4*

CLASSIC CAFÉ

Perhaps the biggest surprise in all the Metroplex area is what's within this charming, blue-and-white cottage. Well-heeled patrons fill its dining room to devour Stilton-crusted rib-eye steaks, pan-seared, almond-crusted trout with mint salsa, and comforting favorites such as bourbon pecan pie. It's perfect for business lunches and special occasions. *504 N. Oak St., at Texas Hwy. 114, Roanoke, 817/430–8185. AE, D, DC, MC, V. Closed Sun.; no lunch Sat. $$*

5 *f-6*

621 E. Southlake Blvd., Closed Sun.; no lunch Sat. 621 E. Southlake Blvd., Southlake, 817/410–9001. Closed Sun.; no lunch Sat.

8 *g-4*

MICHEL AT THE BALCONY

The elegant dining rooms at this romantic retreat are a great place to celebrate special occasions, but the prevailing mood is more relaxed since new owner and veteran uberchef Michel Baudouin overhauled the kitchen. Choose among seven sauces and seven vegetables to accompany the grilled steaks, lamb, veal, pork, free-range chicken, venison, or seafood. The nightly live music ranges from intimate cabaret to straight-ahead jazz. *6100 Camp Bowie Blvd., Suite 25, Fort Worth, 817/731–3719. AE, D, DC, MC, V. Closed Sun.; no lunch Sat. $$–$$$$*

15 *d-6*

RANDALL'S GOURMET CHEESECAKE CO.

Chef/owner Randall Wallace made his name baking exquisite cheesecakes, but he expanded his selections to include an eclectic gourmet lunch and dinner menu. The spacious dining room is loaded with romance and character thanks to the two stories of exposed brick walls. The pâté and vegetable cheesecake appetizers are divine, and the wine choices are good, but service can be dodgy. *907 Houston St., Fort Worth, 817/336–2253. AE, D, MC, V. Closed Sun. and Mon.; no lunch Sat. $$–$$$$*

14 *a-8*

ZODIAC

Timelessly elegant, this tearoom in Neiman Marcus continues to be a pleasant place to dine, especially with the ladies-who-lunch crowd. Complimentary puffy popovers served with strawberry butter, followed by a demitasse of chicken consommé, is a tradition that goes all the way back to the 1950s when Helen Corbitt was manning the original kitchen at the Dallas flagship store. Zodiac does a fine job of keeping the menu current, but is careful not to disappoint the traditionalists. *Neiman Marcus at Ridgmar Shopping Mall, 2100 Green Oaks Rd., Fort Worth, 817/738–3581. AE, D. Lunch only. $–$$*

DELICATESSENS

8 *h-5*

CARSHON'S DELI

Craving a Cel-Ray soda and nothing else will do? Head straight to this southside institution that stocks all things kosher: chopped liver, corned beef, lox, and a short but informed list of wines and beers. Enticing daily specials, such as rice artichoke salad and smoked trout plate, have kept loyal customers happy since 1928. Take-home gourmet foods and sumptuous brownies, lemon bars, and other fresh baked goodies fill the large glass cases by the cash register. *3133 Cleburne Rd., Fort Worth, 817/923–1907. No credit cards. Closed Mon. $*

8 *h-5*

YOGI'S BAGEL CAFÉ

Bagels and beyond is the formula at this café, serving plenty of nearby Texas Christian University students. Close to 20 different kinds of bagels and a selection of smears, including peanut butter, are available at the front, along with gourmet coffee concoctions. The caféteria in the back serves sandwiches and omelettes. Breakfast is served until the grill is turned off at 3PM. Be prepared for weekend crowds. The staff tends to be young and inexperienced. *2710 S. Hulen St., Fort Worth, 817/921–4500. AE, D, DC, MC, V. $*

ECLECTIC

15 *d-5*

ANGELUNA

Hip and zoomy, the cloud-painted ceilings and the sleek marble bar of this stunning room have captured the hearts and pocketbooks of locals and tourists alike. Drawing its primary inspirations from Asia and America, this globally eclectic restaurant invented One World plates, including lobster dumplings with ginger sauce and flash-fried giant calamari with sweet and sour chile pepper sauce. Standby favorites are the steak and Popeye's Favorite Pie (pizza with spinach, mushrooms, and goat cheese). *215 E. 4th St., Fort Worth, 817/334–0080. AE, MC, V. $$–$$$*

15 *d-5*

FLYING SAUCER DRAUGHT EMPORIUM

Housed in a beautifully restored 1889 redbrick building, this suds palace stocks close to 200 different kinds of beer, 70 of them on tap. The bratwurst, soup, and sandwiches are beside the point. Commemorative plates of every ilk and color cover the walls of this boisterous joint, and the beer garden hosts live music almost every night. *111 E. 4th St., Fort Worth, 817/336–7468. AE, D, DC, MC, V. $*

8 *h-5*

THE PEGASUS

This welcome new addition to the deluxe dining scene serves "exotic flavors of faraway places" in artfully presented combinations. The menu lists an ambitious number of entrées, most available in half-portion sizes. A standout appetizer is the phyllo-wrapped shrimp served with a tangy sauce of sweet coconut milk and spicy chili. The minimal decor hardly hides the fact that you're in a strip mall, but who cares when the food is this good? *2443 Forest Park Blvd., Fort Worth, 817/922–0808. AE, D, DC, MC, V. Closed Sun. $$–$$$*

FRENCH

9 *h-3*

CACHAREL

Sitting high atop an office building overlooking the Hurricane Harbor water park, Arlington's only French restaurant raises the bar for competitors with such opulent creations as ostrich with satin-textured carrot mousse and steaks in cabernet sauce. A three-course, fixed-price deal, which typically includes lamb, quail, and duck, might seem on the high end, but it's absolutely a great value when you consider the quality. *Brookhollow II Bldg., 2221 E. Lamar Blvd., Suite 910, at Texas 360, Arlington, 817/640–9981. AE, D, DC, MC, V. $$$*

14 *h-6*

ESCARGOT

It's hard to believe that this used to be a bright country French bistro. Sage-color walls metamorphose the space into a chic and elegant formal dining room with dramatic matching drapery to obscure the passing of time. The menu is extensive, the presentations sophisticated, with prices that follow suit. The French wine choices (by the glass or by the bottle) and jazz soundtrack put this place in front of the pack. *3427 W. 7th St., Fort Worth, 817/336–3090. AE, MC, V. Closed Sun., Mon.; no breakfast or lunch. $$–$$$$*

15 *c-5*

LA MADELEINE

Quick service in an amiable atmosphere is the hallmark at this bustling café. The breakfast, lunch, and dinner crowds are sated with baguettes, hearty soups, healthy salads, croissant sandwiches, and tempting desserts served cafeteria-style. The rotisseried rosemary chicken is a bargain and travels well as take-out. Beaujolais season, celebrated with special events here, always brings in crowds. *305 Main St., Fort Worth, 817/332–6099. AE, D, MC. $*

8 *g-4*

6140 Camp Bowie Blvd., Fort Worth, 817/732–4656. AE, D, MC. $

14 *g-6*

SAINT EMILION

Tucked into an inviting brick Tudor house, this bistro offers sophisticated dining in a cozy French countryside atmosphere. The prix fixe menu changes every few months, but always includes duck, rabbit, beef, and fresh fish flown in daily. Nightly blackboard specials allow chef Lawrence Klang to use the freshest ingredients he can get his hands on. The tab can be steep, but Klang usually delivers a home run. *3617 W. 7th St., Fort Worth, 817/737–2781. AE, D, DC, MC, V. Closed Sun., Mon.; no breakfast or lunch. $$–$$$$*

GERMAN

8 *f-5*

EDELWEISS GERMAN RESTAURANT

Bernd Schnerzinger opened this big-as-a-barn restaurant in 1967 because he wanted to have a place to sing. So guess who stars every night in his lederhosen, playing the spoons and tambourine, singing everything from oompah to

Elvis? When you add in his trusty sidekick Helga on organ, accordion, and the saw, it makes for a mighty wacky backdrop to prepared schnitzel, dumplings, and sauerkraut. *3801-A Southwest Blvd., Fort Worth, 817/738–5934. AE, D, DC, MC, V. Closed Sun. and Mon.; no breakfast, lunch. $–$$*

GREEK

14 *g-8*

JAZZ CAFÉ

The white stucco building and the funky patio statuary and fountains transport you to some undiscovered island. Chef Nick Kithas adds his own New World spin to classic Greek favorites, his original sandwich selection, and his own creation *Zardoz* (pastrami, mozzarella, avocado, and Bermuda onion on an onion dill bun). Sunday brunch features live jazz. Service is casual. *2504 Montgomery St., Fort Worth, 817/737–0043. Reservations not accepted. No credit cards. BYOB. No dinner; no breakfast weekdays. $*

9 *f-3*

MYKONOS CAFÉ

Surprisingly cozy and inviting for a place tucked into a run-of-the-mill strip mall, this little isle of pleasure serves smoked salmon appetizer, glorious rack of lamb entrée, soothing *moussaka* and sturdy *spanakopita*. The helpful staff will offer suggestions. *518 Fielder North Plaza, on Fielder St., near I–30, Arlington, 817/795–2962. AE, D, MC, V. BYOB. $*

15 *c-5*

PARTHENON

This spotless Hellenic outpost serves up authentic old country Greek and Mediterranean cuisine. Chef Gus Katzianis's include such specialties as *avgolemono* soup and *spanakopita*; falafel, hummus, tabbouleh, and baba ghannouj also get equal play. For a tempting dessert alternative, go for the *kataifi* or the *baklava*. *401 N. Henderson St., Fort Worth, 817/810–0800. AE, MC, V. Closed Sun. $–$$*

INDIAN

9 *e-1*

INDIA GRILL

For shoppers weary from the beating your wallet took at NorthEast Mall, you can relax and enjoy the curry dishes and grilled chicken, lamb, and beef kabobs in this nearby tiny strip-center haven. The lunch buffet has a nice variety, including nan and vegetable specialties. *8755 Bedford Euless Rd., at Texas Hwy. 121, Hurst, 817/589–9035. AE, D, DC, MC, V. $*

8 *h-6*

MAHARAJAH

Maharajah welcomes you with *pappadum* (wonderfully thin and crispy lentil wafers), accompanied by a cool mint sauce and a luscious brown tamarind sauce. The lamb vindaloo is nicely offset by palate-pleasing basmati rice. Try the stout *mulligatawany muglai* soup (lentil soup melded with rice and chicken), a meal unto itself. While many of the entrées pack heat, the kitchen will turn it up or down a few notches on request. Soothing recorded Indian music and the amiable decor will make you forget you're dining in a strip mall. *6308 Hulen Bend Blvd., Fort Worth, 817/263–7156. AE, D, DC, MC, V. $–$$$*

9 *f-3*

TANDOOR

Immensely popular and dependable for nearly two decades, this blue-lighted room of serenity is a fine choice for a spread of chicken, shrimp, and lamb baked in tandoori ovens. Generous plates of palate-searing chicken vindaloo, lamb curry, and the divine vegetable dishes such as *dahl* (split peas or lentils) and *sag paneer* (cheese with spinach) fill out the menu. Try the samosas (deep fried pastry triangles filled with savory stuffing) and nan, and don't be shy about asking servers for pointers. *532 Fielder Plaza N., Fielder Rd. near I–30, Arlington, 817/261–6604. No smoking. AE, D, MC, V. $–$$*

5 *h-8*

TASTE OF PAKISTAN

Distinguishable from Indian fare only to an expert, the food at this tiny pocket of treasures includes vegetables cooked in tomatoes and spices, beef-filled pastries, and yogurt drinks. For more familiar fare, try the grilled kebobs and cheesecake. *699 E. Harwood Rd., near Main St., Euless, 817/540–2555. No credit cards. $*

ITALIAN

5 *g-7*

A&E ITALIAN DELI

Whether for dining in or taking out, A&E is the best antidote for fast-food monotony. Freshly prepared items in chilly deli cases include vegetable or meat lasagnas; spinach-and-cheese tortellini; eggplant rolls; thick foccacia; and lemony salad with crab, calamari, and shrimp. True Italian panini (small bread or roll sandwich) combine *mortadello* (various cuts of pork and beef formed in one piece and boiled) and salami with provolone. Desserts include tiramisu and cannoli. *3930 Glade Rd., near Texas 121, Colleyville, 817/267–3336. Closed Sun. AE, MC, V. $*

14 *e-8*

BELLA ITALIA WEST

A lovely plant-filled atrium beckons you into this comfortable Westside haunt. Locals flock here for beautifully prepared wild game, including ostrich, elk, antelope, and caribou. Chef Carlo Croci's flavorful sauces complement the quail pasta and buffalo tartare. The wine list is strictly Italian, with a few Argentinian selections. *5139 Camp Bowie Blvd., Fort Worth, 817/738–1700. AE, D, DC, MC, V. Closed Sun. $$–$$$*

LA BISTRO

Unassuming from the outside, this quaint Italian hideout impresses with its heavy table linens, stem crystal, and colorful wall paintings. Good bets are the chicken sautéed with garlic, white wine, and lemon, and linguine pesto with sun-dried tomato. Seafood and veal dishes are plentiful. *722 Grapevine Hwy., near Harwood Rd., Hurst, 817/281–9333. No lunch Sat. AE, D, DC, MC, V. $$*

14 *h-8*

LA PIAZZA

Superb food, high price tag, and an attitude that sometimes unbearable, especially when it comes to enforcing the dress code (no jeans, no athletic shoes, no T-shirts, no shorts): But that doesn't keep Fort Worth's well-heeled set from returning night after night for their sups. The kitchen shines on its entrées of fish, pasta, veal, steaks, and exotic sorbets. Proprietor/chef Vito Cerratze keeps a hushed clubby ambience going, except on the rare occasion when he lets loose with an a cappella aria. *University Park Village, 1600 S. University Dr., Suite 601, Fort Worth, 817/334–0000. AE, MC, V. $$–$$$$*

8 *h-6*

ON BROADWAY RISTORANTE

Don't let the outdated decor of neon and shiny metal unnerve you. The comprehensive menu and the nightly blackboard specials present a dizzying number of choices. The thick pasta e fagioli is a warm respite on a chilly night. This is a handy place to go before or after the movie at the adjacent AMC Hulen 10. *6306 Hulen Bend, Hulen Pointe Shopping Center, Fort Worth, 817/346–8841. AE, D, DC, MC, V. $–$$*

9 *g-3*

PICCOLO MONDO

Once inside this lovely retreat, you'll instantly forget the shopping center and highway outside. Soft lights bathe intimate dining areas and piano music eases diners into a sense of luxury, perfect for feasting on veal tenderloins laced with garlic and wine and on fresh grilled spinach and sea bass. The setting is ideal for business lunch and romantic evening rendezvous. Reservations are a good idea on weekends. *829 Lamar Blvd. E, at North Collins St., Arlington, 817/265–9174. Closed Sat., no lunch Sun. AE, D, DC, MC, V. $$–$$$*

9 *g-3*

PORTOFINO

If there's a client to be won or a companion to be wooed, it is wisely done in the quiet elegance of this upscale shopping center cornerstone. Servers prepare Caesar salads tableside in the old-fashioned manner, and sautéed fish, grilled steak, and lovely veal are memorable meals. *226 Lincoln Sq., at Collins St. and I–30, Arlington, 817/861–8300. Closed Sun.; no lunch Sat. AE, D, DC, MC, V. $$*

JAPANESE

9 *e-5*

I LOVE SUSHI

Madly loyal crowds smitten with creative flavors and combinations of sushi and sashimi keep this place jumping at lunch and dinner. Favorites include spicy tuna and salmon hand rolls, as well as caterpillar, spider, Texas Rangers, and

Philadelphia rolls. Only diners with the sturdiest of sinus cavities can handle the Mach 6 roll, guaranteed to bring tears of joy. Miso soup and dumplings filled with meat or shellfish, chestnuts, scallions, seasonings, then browned and simmered in broth are also highly recommended. *4101 W. Green Oaks Blvd., near I–20, Arlington, 817/483–9090. Closed Mon. AE, D, DC, MC, V. $*

ISSHIN

With great proximity to both Las Colinas and Valley Ranch, this retreat from the urban highway madness serves up plenty of Japanese culinary delights. Yellowtail, octopus, tuna, and a handful of other sushi creations are served over a bowl of rice with veggies, wasabi, and ginger. Beef teriyaki, grilled salmon, shrimp tempura, gyoza, and soft-shell crab are also worth sampling. Plan to spend a little time reveling in the soothing, gray interior. *7600 N. MacArthur Blvd., at I–635, Irving, 972/506–9906. AE, D, DC, MC, V. $$*

JINBEH

Las Colinas crowds adore the L-shape sushi bar; hibachi tables for grilled meats, chicken, salmon, scallops and calamari; and large tatami room, where you kick off your shoes and sit on floor cushions. Noteworthy selections include the conch-filled Caribbean roll, Jinbeh rolls with snow crab and tuna, shrimp tempura, grilled lobster tail, and yakitori. *301 E. Las Colinas Blvd., at O'Connor Rd., Irving, 972/869–4011. AE, D, DC, MC, V. $$*

9 *g-4*

SUSHI ZONE

From the same owners as I Love Sushi, this cheerful Arlington spot near Six Flags wins new devotees every day with its sushi delights. Grilled chicken and salmon teriyaki dishes with sides of fried rice are perfect choices for sushi-squeamish diners. *915 East Rd., near Six Flags and I–30, Arlington, 817/226–4055. Closed Sun.; no lunch Sat. $$*

LEBANESE

8 *g-4*

HEDARY'S LEBANESE RESTAURANT

Antoine Hedary emigrated to Fort Worth in the 1970s and single-handedly converted thousands of Cowtowners to the exotic tastes of the Middle East. With an emphasis on garlic, Hedary's prepares authentic tabbouleh, hummus, and the top selling favorite *Frarej* (broiled garlic chicken with lemon). Mom and the children still run the Camp Bowie location, Dad opened one in Azle, and brother Mario runs Byblos, which serves weekday lunch buffets and belly dancing on the weekends. *3308 Fairfield St., Fort Worth, 817/731–6961. AE, DC, MC, V. No smoking. Closed Mon. $*

MEXICAN

9 *g-4*

CASA JOSE

When nothing but an old-fashioned, home-style plate of Mexican comfort food will do, this unassuming family operation comes to the rescue. Plates of cheesy enchiladas, crunchy tacos, and snappy salsa will set your world right again. A favorite among police officers, the café serves breakfast, lunch, and dinner. *2030 S. Cooper St., Arlington, 817/265–5423. Closed Sun.; no dinner Mon. $*

LA HACIENDA RANCH

Hard to say which is more appealing: the menu of giant steaks, grilled chicken, and enchiladas or the variety of margaritas and the Old West, log-cabin retreat decor. Saddles serve as barstools, fires roar in the stone fireplaces, and old westerns play on black-and-white TVs. Cherry cobbler is served in a sizzling skillet with a cinnamon crumble crust and a wild cherry brandy-butter sauce. *5250 Texas Hwy., 121 at Hall-Johnson Rd., Colleyville, 817/318–7500. AE, D, DC, MC, V. $$*

9 *e-1*

MIGUELITO'S

In a cluster of pink-splashed rooms, happy hordes chow down on chicken fajitas, plump beef enchiladas, and deep bowls of queso, scooped with fresh, crispy tostada chips. The red salsa and the sweetish margaritas keep patrons pleased. *209 W. Bedford Rd., at Norwood Rd., Hurst, 817/268–0404. AE, DC, MC, V. $*

VIA REAL

Tucked into an attractive shopping center next to the Four Seasons Resort at Las Colinas, this restaurant blends New Mexican with dressed-up Mexican fare. Choice results include grilled shrimp with goat cheese and chili con queso packed with spinach. *4020 N. MacArthur Blvd., at Northgate Dr., Irving, 972/650–9001. AE, D, MC, V. $$*

MEDITERRANEAN

5 *f-8*

CAFÉ MEDITERRANEA

Tucked away on the back side of a Tom Thumb shopping center is a little sunny room serving pleasant renditions of dishes from ports around the Mediterranean. Gyros as well as falafel, tabbouleh, couscous, and shrimp in marinara sauce fill its menu. Business is balanced between take-out and dine-in, and service can be a tad slow. *3104 Harwood Rd., near Texas Hwy. 121, Bedford, 817/354–5335. AE, DC, MC, V. Closed Sun. $*

SEAFOOD

8 *h-5*

FISHMONGER'S SEAFOOD MARKET AND GRILL

The rough wood and galvanized tin walls lend a dockside feel to this price-conscious backwater hangout. Regulars, including ex-Speaker of the House Jim Wright, come for the fish—fried, grilled or blackened, especially the catfish and shrimp. Tantalizing gumbo, burgers, chicken, and rib-eye are also favorites. *3468 Bluebonnet Cr., Fort Worth, 817/924–7000. Reservations not accepted. AE, D, MC, V. Closed Sun. $*

9 *g-3*

LONE STAR OYSTER BAR

Gumbo packed with shrimp, snappy Buffalo wings, and the house specialty of oysters Laredo—baked fresh oysters topped with salsa and cheddar and jack cheeses—are great reasons to discover this casual hangout. You can always count on a big beer crowd here, particularly when ball games are on TV. *780 Rd. to Six Flags E at Collins St., Arlington, 817/469–6616. AE, MC, V. $*

ROCKFISH

It's difficult to pinpoint just one or two specialties here, because the casual, family-friendly fish house serves several selections with flair. Maryland crab cakes, cornmeal-coated fried oysters, and a shrimp cocktail that combines baby shrimp with chunks of tomato, avocado, and onion in a cocktail sauce are all worth a taste. *228 State St., at Southlake Blvd., Southlake, 817/442–0131. AE, MC, V. $$*

SOUTH PRAIRIE OYSTER BAR

A petite fish house of the first order, this spot in Grapevine's historic district does a bang-up job with fried oyster po-boy sandwiches, jalapeños stuffed with cheese and shrimp, and oysters on the half shell. You'll find a second order of hush puppies is hard to resist, as is the icy-cold beer. *651 S. Main St., at Hutchins Rd., Grapevine, 817/488–3909. No credit cards. Closed Sun. and Mon. $*

14 *h-8*

WATER STREET SEAFOOD COMPANY

The bar's dramatic black tile counters and glass brick partition create a visual counterpoint to the spacious dining room. This is the place to come for fresh oysters on the half shell, but don't forget the house signature dish of "slap-pin-fresh" mesquite-grilled salmon with lemon-dill sauce, served with a side of fresh vegetables. Choices vary day to day but crab cakes, tilapia, and mahimahi are always available. In case

BEST SPOTS FOR ROMANTIC DINNERS

When it comes to romance, these places can help you get things moving in the right direction.

Bistro Louise (Contemporary)
Sipping good red wine amid a warm and relaxed French decor. Just as inspirational as its cuisine.

Grape Escape (Cafés)
If wine and light fare are your ultimate aphrodisiacs, this cozy bistro is for you.

Michael at the Balcony (Contemporary)
The nightly cabaret and jazz set ensures a romantic mood in its relaxed, elegant dining rooms.

St. Emilion (French)
Let the mood prevail when inside this brick Tudor house. Its sophisticated French countryside dining never fails.

you've got the children in tow, all entrées are offered in two serving sizes. *1540 S. University Dr., Fort Worth, 817/877–3474. AE, D, MC, V. $–$$*

14 *c-8*

ZEKE'S FISH AND CHIPS

If you're still stoked about the 1960s, this might be one of the last places to catch a whiff. They still serve avocado sandwiches on honey-wheat bread, but what's kept the place abuzz is the fried shrimp; catfish; and especially the fried okra, eggplant, zucchini, and mushrooms. For dessert, the Tugboard Annie bars, loaded with chocolate chips and pecans, are a must. The dining area is tiny, so do what the locals do and get take-out. *5920 Curzon Ave., Fort Worth, 817/731–3321. AE, D, DC, MC, V. $*

SOUTHERN

15 *c-5*

ELLINGTON'S CHOP HOUSE

A new addition to the downtown dining scene, this New Orleans–style brasserie is tastefully outfitted in cherrywood and frosted glass. The specialty is the righteous gumbo loaded with sassafras, green pepper, and okra. *301 Main St., Fort Worth, 817/336–4129. AE, D, DC, MC, V. $$–$$$*

15 *c-8*

PARIS COFFEE SHOP

Bee-hived waitresses call you "sugar" while they top off your extra-tall bottomless glass of iced tea. Each day has its own specials at this blue-plate institution, but any day is great for the pan-fried chicken-fried steak or the Arkansas Traveler (sliced beef and brown gravy over corn-bread muffins). The twirling rack of tempting pies is hard to resist. *704 W. Magnolia Ave., Fort Worth, 817/335–2041. Reservations not accepted. AE, D, DC, MC, V. Closed Sun.; no dinner; no lunch Sat. $*

SOUTHWESTERN

14 *h-8*

BLUE MESA GRILL

See Dallas listing above. *University Park Village, 1600 S. University Dr., Fort Worth, 817/332–6372. $$–$$$*

15 *b-2*

LONESOME DOVE WESTERN BISTRO

Holy smokes, who ever thought you'd ever see white tablecloths in the Stockyards? Sounds pretty fancy, but you'll feel right at home wearing your cowboy shirt (better put a spit shine on the old cowboy boots, though). Taking its cues from Reata, this intimate little bistro has well-worn planked oak floors, raw brick walls, and a pressed copper ceiling. The kitchen goes beyond the red meat standards, opting instead for the chipotle and sundried tomato trail. Try the luscious lobster cakes with a freshly prepared corn and black bean salsa. *2406 N. Main St., Fort Worth, 817/740–8810, AE, MC, V, closed Sun., Mon., dinner Thurs.–Sat. only. $$–$$$*

14 *h-6*

MICHAEL'S RESTAURANT & ANCHO CHILE BAR

The starkly modern dining rooms hint at the new wave ranch approach of the kitchen. Chef Michael Thomson's menu highlights imaginative food combinations, including pecan-crusted goat cheese chicken, shrimp pizza with chipotle pesto, and fried chicken salad. Chipotle and ancho-chile sauces accompany such classics as tenderloin, lamb chops, and crab cakes. The fireplace is always roaring in the perpetually hopping Ancho Chile Bar. *3413 W. 7th St., Fort Worth, 817/877–3413. AE, D, DC, MC, V. Closed Sun.; no dinner weekdays. $–$$$*

15 *c-6*

REATA

Perched on top of a 35-story downtown building overlooking the city below, this cowboy-and-ranch eatery is a must-see for tourists. The kitchen posse play it straight, with time-honored renditions of beef, chicken, and fish, served in he-man portions. Three dining rooms, two full bars, and private banquet rooms, all very handsomely appointed, are great fodder for cowboy contemplation. If you're short on time, stop by for a drink. Complimentary valet parking is available at the Throckmorton entrance. *500 Throckmorton St., 35th floor, Fort Worth, 817/336–1009. Reservations essential. AE, MC, V. $–$$$*

STEAK

9 *f-4*

ARLINGTON STEAK HOUSE

Not unlike an old Texas roadside diner, this unpretentious beef joint has been keeping generations of Arlington residents gratified with heavy plates of strip sirloin steaks, T-bones, and massive chicken-fried steak. Day and night, you'll find families, as well as big guys with names such as "Tiny" embossed on their western belts crowding into the place. *1724 W. Division St., at Fielder Rd., Arlington, 817/275–7881. AE, D, DC, MC, V. $–$$*

15 *c-6*

DEL FRISCO'S DOUBLE EAGLE STEAKHOUSE

If you're flush with C-notes, here's a good place to drop them. Steaks, steaks, and more steaks; woe be the vegetarian who passes through this gilded door, although the menu includes lobster and shrimp selections and assorted vegetable sides such as fresh asparagus. *812 Main St., Fort Worth, 817/877–3999. Reservations essential. AE, D, DC, MC, V. Closed Sun. $$–$$$$*

BEST SPOTS FOR OUTDOOR DINING

Air conditioning may be a necessity in Fort Worth/Mid-Cities, but there are eateries for every budget that allow you to bask in fresh, unconditioned air on a warm summer night.

A&E Italian Deli (Italian)
Little café tables under the brick awning make this a pleasant place to linger over a tiramisu and coffee.

Flying Saucer Draught Emporium (Eclectic)
Savor a pint or two from its selection of 200 beers and munch on sandwiches and bratwurst while star-gazing from the beer garden.

Fred's Café (American Casual)
Biscuits and gravy are just as good outside as inside; plus the music isn't as loud.

Jazz Café (Greek)
Dine amid the pleasant respite of its patio statuary and fountains.

15 *b-1*

CATTLEMAN'S STEAKHOUSE

The Fort Worth Stockyards may have long been idle, but Cattleman's is an authentic remnant of the Chisholm Trail era. Not much has changed since the 1950s in this popular tourist stop, including the kitschy monster trophy steer heads that crowd the walls. *2458 N. Main St., Fort Worth, 817/624–3945. Reservations essential. AE, D, DC, MC, V. $$–$$$*

15 *a-1*

M & M STEAK HOUSE

It's easy to drive past this small roadhouse, but you'll never regret making the U-turn. Locals come here for the cold beer, the unpretentious atmosphere, and the great jukebox loaded down with country/western selections. M & M separates itself from the pack by cooking their meats with fresh garlic topping. For something different, try garlic on chicken-fried steak, frog legs, or calf fries. *1106 NW 28th St., Fort Worth, 817/624–0612. No credit cards. Closed Sun. and Mon. $–$$*

15 *c-5*

TEXAS DE BRAZIL

See Dallas listing. *101 N. Houston St., Fort Worth, 817/882–9500.*

TEX-MEX

15 *c-8*

BENITO'S

The "no chips and salsa" policy has run off a few customers, but this little outpost doesn't need to worry about filling its tables. When you've worn out all the Tex-Mex alternatives, this is the place to turn for chicken in red mole sauce or the Yucatan tamale stuffed into a banana leaf. Dinner is served until 2AM on the weekends. *1450 W. Magnolia Ave., Fort Worth, 817/332–8633. D, DC, MC, V. $*

5 *e-8*

EDUARDO'S

Here's a no-frills café with a few colorful Mexican decorations and solid, gratifying Tex-Mex plates of fajitas, enchiladas, chalupas, and nachos. The low prices and friendly service have built a loyal clientele. *240 Grapevine Hwy., near Glade*

Rd., Hurst, 817/485–5942. AE, D, DC, MC, V. $

ESCONDIDO
You'll search hard to find better home-style Tex-Mex fare near the DFW International Airport. Generous plates of homemade tamales, cheese enchiladas, crisp tacos, and fiery salsa keep crowds happy day and night. Service can be a little slow and the decor begs for attention, but the food is worth any inconvenience. *501 N. Main St., near Texas Hwy. 183, Euless, 817/355–1993. AE, DC, MC, V. BYOB. Closed Sun. and Mon. $*

15 *b-2*
JOE T. GARCIA'S
Once a leaning shack with eight tables, Joe T. Garcia's evolved into a Tex-Mex empire capable of serving 3,000 dinners a night. Sprawling across an entire city block, Joe T.'s includes a swimming pool, private party rooms, outdoor fountains, and a garden. There's never been a menu, everything's served family-style, and the dinner hasn't changed since the 1930s (cheese nachos; beef tacos; cheese enchiladas topped with shredded lettuce, refried beans, rice, and especially good guacamole). The margaritas are a must. Be prepared to wait on the weekends. *2201 N. Commerce St., Fort Worth 817/626–4356. Reservations not accepted. No credit cards. No smoking. $–$$*

14 *e-7*
THE ORIGINAL MEXICAN EATS CAFÉ
Generations of Westsiders have made this, the oldest Tex-Mex restaurant in Fort Worth, a weekly tradition since 1926. The hot sauce isn't very hot, but that's not what this place is about. The popular Roosevelt Special (beef taco, chili cheese enchilada, bean chalupa with lettuce and tomato) is close to impossible to finish, but an enchilada omelet is more manageable. The east dining room wall has a rustic mural depicting life in Old Mexico. *4713 Camp Bowie Blvd., Fort Worth, 817/738–6226. AE, D, DC, MC, V. Closed Mon. $–$$*

9 *f-4*
RAMON'S HACIENDA
In addition to old-fashioned, down-home Tex-Mex favorites, including enchiladas and tacos, Ramon's creates favorite renditions from the southwest and the interior of Mexico, such as *nopales* (cactus) with grilled chicken. Affordable and family-friendly, Ramon's supports a stable of regulars who have sworn by the place for years. *1800 W. Division St., Arlington, 817/275–1700. AE, D, MC, V. Closed Sun. $*

THAI

15 *c-8*
BANGKOK CITY
The black and white checkerboard floor tiles belie the traditional Thai kitchen. The weekday lunch buffet includes two kinds of curry, cold beef salad, egg rolls, and fried bananas. Monday and Friday spotlight shrimp, Tuesday and Thursday for mussels, and Wednesday for squid. Annotated "angry" dishes are very, very hot. Catering to a large vegetarian customer base, the restaurant opens its doors once a month for a special Sunday vegetarian lunch. *1109 W. Magnolia Ave., Fort Worth, 817/927–3220. MC, V. Closed Sun. $*

BANGKOK CUISINE
One of the oldest Thai restaurants in the area, Bangkok is much-loved for its chicken soup flavored with coconut milk and lemon grass as well as its green and red curry treatments that enliven beef, pork, chicken, and shrimp plates. Dishes are spiced to your taste. *5095 Broadway*

BEST SPOTS FOR SUNDAY BRUNCH

Sunday brunch has long been a staple of weekend outings for Fort Worth/Mid-Cities diners, satisfying the region's eclectic tastes.

Blue Mesa Grill (Southwestern)
This popular upscale Dallas extension prides itself, like its flagship eatery, on its eclectic brunch.

La Piazza (Italian)
The well-heeled local patrons can't resist its consistently first-rate cuisine. Neither will you.

Zodiac (Contemporary)
Tradition and consistency is the backbone of this timelessly elegant tearoom.

Ave., at Haltom Rd., Haltom City, 817/831–4711. Reservations not accepted. No credit cards. BYOB. Closed Mon. $$

VIETNAMESE

9 *b-2*

MY LAN

How to decide which is best among 157 entrées is impossible, but you'll be happy if you choose one of the vermicelli dishes, topped with char-grilled pork or beef. Also try the pho, the soul-nourishing soup packed with anything from beef or pork to shrimp and egg noodles and fresh herbs and slices of crisp jalapeño. Spring rolls, not the fried variety, are packed with fresh shrimp and grilled pork. *4017 E. Belknap St., at Beach St., Haltom City, 817/222–1471. No credit cards. Closed Wed. $*

9 *g-4*

PHO BO VANG

It's hard to say if the freshly squeezed lemonade, spring rolls, or the noodle dishes are the best at this strip center café. But past patrons agree that comfort is always found in the plate of *com bo nuong xa* (grilled beef deeply marinated with tart lemongrass, served on a bed of fluffy white rice with lightly steamed broccoli). Then again, the *bun cha ha noi* (grilled pork strips over rice vermicelli with a bank of fluffy leaf lettuce, mint leaves, lime leaves, carrot shreds, and cilantro sprigs), leaves lasting memories. *2230 S. Collins St., at Arkansas La., Arlington, 817/277–5525. AE, D, DC, MC, V. $*

15 *h-2*

TUHAI

It's not much to look at, but this tiny strip mall entry serves what patrons think is the best Vietnamese food in the city. The roasted pork is always a good choice, but for something special go for the Saigon pancakes. *3909 E. Belknap St., Haltom City, 817/834–6473. No credit cards. Closed Sun. $*

chapter 2

SHOPPING

Dallas has an international reputation as a first-class place to buy trendy clothes, western apparel, and art. Three major shopping areas compete for designer boutiques: Galleria, NorthPark, and Highland Park Village. Neiman Marcus started here and still has its original Downtown store open, although it has also expanded into shopping malls. You won't find many bargains in any of these areas, unless you're patient enough to wait for sales, but that doesn't keep shoppers from packing the stores on weekends. Art galleries and expensive antique stores are plentiful in the Uptown area. You will find these shops along such streets as McKinney Avenue, Cedar Springs, and Routh. Look to Lower Greenville Avenue and Deep Ellum for fun and funky art, furniture, and collectibles. These two areas have a nice mix of retail shops, restaurants, and nightclubs housed in brick stores built in the early 1900s.

shopping areas: dallas

DEPARTMENT STORES

6 *g-8*

DILLARD'S

Merchandize fits all sizes and price ranges at this fashionable four-floor department store. Among designer women's wear, with such names as Lizwear, Ellen Tracy, and Preston & York, the store has a particularly large selection of Ralph Lauren formal and casual clothing for women. For men, look for formal and casual attire by Roundtree & York, Kenneth Cole, and Muran. You'll also find a limited selection of Wedgwood and Lenox china. *100 NorthPark Center, North, 214/373–7000.*

10 *d-6*

Southwest Center, 3560 W. Camp Wisdom Rd., South, 972/298–4229.

6 *f-6*

Valley View Center, 13343 Preston Rd., North, 972/386–4595.

6 *g-8*

FOLEY'S

Locals know to watch for "Red Apple" sales at this two-story store that is part of the May Department Store chain. This is the chain's largest Dallas store so you will find a bigger selection here—and in most cases higher-end goods—than at other area stores. If you enter from the mall, you must first weave your way through a jungle of cosmetic islands touting such brands as Estee Lauder and Lancome. The friendly sales staff likes to hand out free perfume samples, so you often leave with a new fragrance. Once inside, designer lines are set up in islands with the emphasis on variety rather than depth. Look for Anne Klein, Liz Claiborne, Ellen Tracy, Preston & York for women and Calvin Klein, Kenneth Cole and Murano for men. *8687 North Central Expressway, North Park, 469/232–3600.*

6 *f-6*

2040 Valley View Center, North, 972/385–6533.

10 *d-6*

3550 West Camp Wisdom Rd. 972/780–6700.

6 *f-6*

JCPENNEY

Despite recent sluggish sales, this department chain remains popular with middle-class families. This three-floor store has a large men's department, with a wide selection of casual jeans and shirts, including Levi's and the Penney's Arizona label. In the office casual section, look for Dockers and Haggar. Women's casual dominates the second floor with such designers as Jones Wear and Penney's popular St. John's Bay and Cabin Creek. In home furnishings, you'll find a large selection of table lamps, including crystal and Tiffany. *Valley View Center, 13320 Montford Dr., North, 972/726–1821.*

10 *d-6*

Southwest Center, 7702 Westmoreland Rd., South, 972/296–1461.

6 *g-8*

LORD & TAYLOR

You can find the right accessories to go with that new outfit at this upscale two-story department store, which carries men's and women's clothing. In the American Woman department, you can buy a J Kara black-beaded dress for a party, a Maggy London black leather jacket for play, or an Elisabeth red dress for the office. In the men's wear, Lord & Taylor brand of casual knit and button shirts are popular items. You'll also find a selection of Oshkosh, Genuine Girl and Healthtex playwear for children. *450 NorthPark Center, North, 214/691–6600.*

6 *f-1*
Prestonwood Town Center, 15350 Dallas Pkwy, North, 972/387–0588.

6 *f-6*
MACY'S
You'll find the irresistible urge to redecorate your bedroom when you walk through the bedding section. The best selections are in the Charter Club line where you can choose an antique-looking embroidered quilt, a leopard skin printed comforter, or a Hungarian white goose down comforter. Ralph Lauren and Calvin Klein lines are also well represented. This three-floor store devotes the second floor to women fashions, where you will find Liz Claiborne dressy and casual mix-and-match knits along with smaller selections of Anne Klein, Jones of New York. and INC. The men's department is geared toward the young business professional with Perry Ellis suits. Although the store carries Ralph Lauren and Levi casual wear, Dockers tend to be a popular selling item. *Dallas Galleria, 13350 Dallas Pkwy., North, 972/851–5185.*

7 *b-7*
MERVYN'S
Young families look to this Northern California chain for moderately priced fashion goods. Clothing lines for men and women are geared more toward young professionals. Casual lines in both departments offer a good selection of knit tops, including national and house brands. In addition to clothing, you can also shop for linens and tableware. The bedding section is especially popular for a wide assortment of mix and match sheets and comforters. *1201 Centerville Rd., East, 972/270–8800.*

10 *d-6*
MONTGOMERY WARD
You can shop while having your tires rotated at this department store, which stopped carrying its own store brands several years ago and switched to national brand names. In the furniture section, you'll find such brands as Bassett, La-Z-Boy, and Lane. The sofa selection displays a variety of fabrics and designs, ranging from plaids to florals. The men's clothing section has generous selections of Lee jeans and Urban Works shirts. In women's wear, Gloria Vanderbilt and Northwest Blue dominate casual shirts and jeans area. Upstairs in the appliance center, you can choose from Whirlpool, Frigidare and GE refrigerators, stoves, and dishwashers. *Southwest Center, 3662 W. Camp Wisdom Rd., South, 972/296–6372.*

13 *d-5*
NEIMAN MARCUS
If you're looking for an orange Tahari wool suit with coordinated orange and black plaid spike heels by Cunmetal, then this is where you'll find them. You'll also find more conservative business and social dress attire by Tahari and other top designers, including Kay Unger or Shelli Segal. This internationally known store has been a hit ever since 1907 when it opened in Downtown Dallas. This seven-floor store, adorned with marble floors and red awnings, has the feel of an old-fashioned department store. Neiman's still retains that feel of exclusiveness by keeping merchandise uncluttered and aisles spacious, and employing a friendly and helpful sales staff. In addition to its own line of clothing, the store carries such designers as Anne Klein, Dana Buchman and Ellen Tracy for women and Andrew Marc, Bobby Jones and Bruno Magli for men. At Christmas, the store's popular catalog keeps locals browsing for hours. Although the costly "His and Hers" gifts, such as matching airplanes, receive a lot of media attention, you can also find items priced under $25. You can have Neiman's delicious chocolate chip cookie recipe for free, despite persistent rumors to the contrary. Although you'll find less merchandise Downtown, it is the only Dallas Neiman's that carries bridal clothing. The NorthPark store, the city's largest Neiman's, carries more merchandise than Downtown and houses the Estee Lauder Spa. All Neiman stores have Zodiac restaurants, where the popular item is strawberry butter with popovers. *1618 Main St., Downtown, 214/741–6911.*

6 *g-8*
1618 NorthPark, 400 NorthPark Center, North, 214/691–4499.

6 *f-1*
Prestonwood, 5285 Belt Line Rd., 75240, North, 972/233–1100.

6 *f-6*
NORDSTROM
If you enter this three-floor department store from the parking garage on the first floor, you have to pass by its terrific selection of women's shoes. It's easy to pick out the most popular brands: Lining the isle include such designers as Stuart Weitzman, Donald J Pliner and Taryn Rose. Originally opened a century ago in Seattle as a shoe store, it has one of the best shoe departments in Dallas. The women's and men's department have ample selections of popular designer wear. The fashion department for young teens is especially enticing with one wall covered by 16 TV screens. Retro rules with spandex tops in a rainbow of colors and Maxi red leather flair pants. Perhaps the best part of this store is the classical music played by pianists on the grand piano located by the second-floor escalator. *Galleria, 5220 Alpha, North, 972/702–0055.*

6 *f-6*
SAKS FIFTH AVENUE
After running the maze of displays and racks found in many overstocked department stores, you will appreciate Saks spaciousness. The cosmetic department stocks such hard-to-find, though costly, brands as Sisley, Nars, and Laura Mercier. Locals have taken to this New York store with its trendy merchandise for men (Hugo Boss, John Bartlett, Ermenegildo Zegna) and women (Donna Karan, Michael Kors, Oscar de la Reta). Women's clothing ranges from petite to size 24. You will find women's fashions arranged in designer groups on the second floor. On the third floor is the Holland and Holland section—a British brand sold exclusively at Saks—which includes tweed caps coordinated with jackets. *Galleria, 13550 Dallas Pkwy., North, 972/458–7000.*

6 *f-6*
SEARS
Do-it-yourselfer's head straight for the Craftsman tools while the little ones make a bee-line for Winnie-the-Pooh's domain at this popular department store. In the 1960s, this Sears store stood as a lone retail beacon in the midst of a cow pasture in North Dallas. Today, as one of the anchors for Valley View Center, it is still a major force in the retail market. You'll find clothes for the entire family, although the women's department is by far the largest. In the women's casual wear, Sears continues to stock a wide variety of its own brands—Cross Roads, Classic Elements, Laura Scott—alongside such name brands as Dockers, Lee, and Levi. Upstairs look for Brand Central, the store's popular home appliances area where Sear's Kenmore competes with such brands as Whirlpool. *Valley View Center, 13131 Preston Rd., North, 972/458–3500.*

10 *d-6*
Southwest Center, 3450 W. Camp Wisdom Rd., South, 972/780–4500.

6 *e-8*
TARGET
Mom and the kids know all about the back-to-school bargains in supplies and fun fashions here. You can depend on finding just the right picture frame whether you want a fun design for your pet's photo or a crystal piece for a wedding picture. With a large area devoted to matching towels and rugs, decorating is quick and inexpensive. You'll even have enough left over to buy a favorite Mozart or Garth Brooks CD. *9440 Marsh La., North, 214/357–3980, and other locations.*

MALLS & SHOPPING CENTERS

6 *f-6*
GALLERIA
Inspired by the famed 19th-century Milan, Italy, mall, this shopping complex is one of the top five tourist attractions in the Dallas area. Its tempered glass vault skylight spans the entire quarter-mile length of the pink granite center. More than 200 stores are arranged in a long straight line down both sides of the corridor with Macy's, Nordstrom, and Saks Fifth Avenue serving as anchors. Not much breaks this long span except for the four-story-high atrium, which rises above the ice rink. Some wooden benches, small trees, and tropical plants help warm up an otherwise monoto-

nous length of storefronts. You won't find discount shops at this upscale mall, but you will find a range of prices. It's the kind of mall where you can buy an Ann Taylor dress or Texas T-shirt. You have plenty of choices for gift shopping, whether looking for an expensive fountain pen or a toy. While most of the stores are chains—Old Navy, Victoria's Secret, Gordon Jewelers—you will also find some independently owned shops not found elsewhere in town, including Turquoise Lady. Ever since this mall opened in 1982, it has been a favorite with both residents and visitors. The mall also has restaurants, child care, and five-screen theater. Ample parking is available in parking garages, which link to the mall. *13350 Dallas Pkwy., North, 972/702–7100.*

10 *f-1*

HIGHLAND PARK VILLAGE

This 1931 cluster of Mediterranean Spanish-style shops built facing an interior parking lot is America's first shopping center and the prototype for shopping centers across the country. Today you can walk along brick paths to shop at more than 60 internationally known tony shops. Designers boutiques include Luca Luca and Calvin Klein. Or you can have shoes repaired at Deno's Shoe Service, stop in Doubleday Books for the latest best seller, browse for a new camera at Cooters, or shop for casual pants at Banana Republic. Even though this is an older shopping center, it is still so popular than even on a rainy Sunday afternoon, when many shops are closed, you will find parking a challenge. *Preston Rd. at Mockingbird La., Highland Park, 214/559–2740.*

10 *f-1*

INWOOD VILLAGE SHOPPING CENTER

More than 50 shops and restaurants fill this well-established center where locals have shopped since 1949. Stores include such women apparel shops as Mary Nash and Jo Kelly and Jamba Juice and Le Pasœ antiques. You can stroll from store to store on stone and brick walkways lined with trees, seasonal flowers, and ivy. If you're looking for some respite, stop by the Inwood Theater, which is one of the few places in Dallas that consistently shows foreign and independent films. *West Lovers La. at Inwood Rd., North, 214/745–1701.*

6 *g-8*

NORTHPARK CENTER

When this enclosed center opened in 1965, it forever changed the way the city shopped. Since this was one of the first regional malls in the U.S., it soon attracted the top retail stores, which in turn pulled shoppers from across Texas and the nation. And it still does. The parking lots overflow on weekends with locals turning out to look for the latest fashions at Neiman Marcus, Dilliard's, Lord & Taylor, and Foley's. Restaurants and 160 specialty stores—mostly chains(Banana Republic, Lady Footlocker, Sunglass Hut)—fill its space. Ducks and turtles frolic in the fountain and pool just outside Neiman's entrance. Another fountain near Foley's soothes with sounds of cascading water. Colorful seasonal plants and tropical greenery line the long corridors of polished concrete. Be sure to look for artwork inside the mall. Owner Raymond Nasher has shared his love of art with the public since the center's opening. You can browse for cutlery, stationary, toys, and bath products as well as shoes and clothing to fit all sizes and taste. Eating choices include restaurants, a cafeteria, and bakeries. The mall has a large parking lot and a parking garage. Valet parking is available in front of the mall and at the Neiman's entrance. *8687 N. Central Expressway, North, 214/363–7441.*

10 *d-6*

SOUTHWEST CENTER MALL

Built in 1975, this 1.3-million-square-foot, two-story shopping center is the largest in South Dallas. The center has 75 stores, including anchors Dillard's, Foley's, JC Penney, Montgomery Ward, and Sears. While this shopping center lacks the high profile draw of its wealthier North Dallas counterparts, it still has attracted major retail chains, including Old Navy and Foot Action USA. Besides chain stores, you will also find many independently owned shops with ethnic goods not found elsewhere in the city. Originally called Redbird Mall, the shopping center changed its name in 1997. *I–20 at Hwy. 67, South, 972/296–1491.*

6 *f-6*

VALLEY VIEW CENTER

JC Penney, Dillard's, Sears, and Foley's anchor this one million-plus square-foot shopping center built in 1971 on what was once a large stretch of empty prairie.

All those wide-open spaces, however, have long since been transformed into mile after mile of stores. But it was this shopping center that started the retail momentum in this part of North Dallas. The two-story mall has 170 specialty shops, ranging from the trendy Ann Taylor Loft to discount Lerner New York. You'll also find many national clothing chains here, such as Gap and The Limited, with a smaller mix of home furnishings, eyeglasses, books and luggage stores. El Fenix and Luby's Cafeteria are your only choices of restaurants, but the food court on the lower level offers barbecue and Chinese food in addition to standard fast-food fare such as pizza, hotdogs, and burgers. The marketing department stays busy lining up annual events held. Even though the center has ample parking, it can become crowded on weekends and near holidays. *I–635 at Preston Rd., North, 972/661–2424.*

13 *b-4*

WEST END MARKET PLACE

You may feel like you've stepped back in history when walking around this part of Downtown. The four-story red brick building that serves as a shopping center was originally a cracker and candy factory built in the early 1900s. The interior from top to bottom is subdivided into 50 shops, which primarily house independently owned or small local chain stores. The largest occupies only 10,000 square feet with smaller shops fitting into a cozy 150 square feet. This is the kind of place where you can buy a cowboy hat, a 1960 Life magazine, a jar of hot salsa, or a toe ring. You can move easily from floor to floor by elevator or escalator. Tourists and locals alike find it a fun place to browse. Although eating choices are limited inside, just step outdoors to find a variety of restaurants. Street parking is limited, but large parking lots are available across the street. *603 Munger Ave., at Market St., Downtown, 214/741–7185.*

SHOPPING NEIGHBORHOODS

13 *f-4*

DEEP ELLUM

What once was a rundown part of the city, this three-block stretch of Commerce, Main, and Elm streets a few minutes east of Downtown is quickly being restored to one of the trendiest areas in Dallas. The brick storefronts here were mostly built in the early 1900s in what was a thriving African-American community. Today, those same storefronts have attracted a bohemian mix of antique, jewelry, and furniture shops, as well as a bevy of nightclubs and restaurants. A shopping trip can net you preservative-free sausage from an old-fashioned meat market, a pair of sterling silver earrings, a brightly painted Mexican imported flower pot and an antique oak desk chair. You can also get a tattoo or have your nose (and other body parts) pierced or buy motorcycle parts. These are independently owned businesses where the proprietor is likely to greet you at the door, show you around, and pass along all kinds of history and gossip about the area. During the week, you see Downtown workers dropping in on their lunch hour and tourists all during the day. Some of the shops are closed on Sunday.

10 *g-1*

GREENVILLE AVENUE

What starts as a narrow two-lane street near Downtown widens into a broad avenue north of Mockingbird Lane. Along lower Greenville, brick buildings dating from the 1920s now house antique and gift shops, bars, nightclubs, and restaurants. You can browse for Gloucester cheese and potato scones from England or pick up a pair of 1950s white dress gloves. Parking is available along the street.

10 *g-2*

KNOX HENDERSON

In the mid-1990s, a revitalization effort resulted in a two-mile strip of new life in this area, one of the city's oldest shopping neighborhoods. Along Knox Street, the original 1920's storefronts remain, but the insides have been gutted to accommodate modern businesses, including Weir Furniture, Thomasville, and Crate & Barrel. Although this is all one street, it changes names at Central Expressway, becoming Henderson on the east side of the freeway. With the freeway acting as a divider, the two sides attract totally different businesses. National retail chains specializing in furniture and home furnishings line Knox Street, whereas Henderson Street attracts colorful antique stores, art galleries and import shops. Both sides offer a diverse selection of restaurants. Parking along Knox Street can be tricky, so you may want to park in the large parking lot next to Crate & Barrel.

13 c-2

UPTOWN

Getting around Uptown can be a challenge because the narrow tree-lined streets have a way of intersecting at odd angles. But shopping here is worth the effort. You'll find many cozy antique shops, art galleries, and restaurants. Two shopping malls also offer shopping opportunities. At Crescent Court Shops & Galleries (200 Crescent Court, 214/880–4500), which is part of an opulent hotel and office complex built in 1985, you'll find clothing boutiques, art galleries, and antique stores surrounded by an open atrium at end of the complex. The Quadrangle (2800 Routh St., 214/871–0878), which has been around since 1966, houses shops and galleries including such current occupants as Eclectics (David Marsh handcrafted, colorfully painted furniture and ethnographic arts), Trumeau (custom bedding) and After Image (art gallery). You can stroll through the open-air center of this modern, multi–story complex or linger on a wooden bench that sits near a water fountain. Crepe Myrtle trees and seasonal flowers add plenty of color during summer months. Although Crescent Court and The Quadrangle have ample parking available in lots, parking can be a problem in other areas. Often, the only parking for a particular business is limited to what is available alongside the store. An electric trolley from Downtown runs along McKinney Avenue, carrying shoppers to the mix of restaurants, stores, and art galleries on this street. When the weather is nice, many of the other shops on nearby streets are within walking distance of the trolley.

specialty shops

ANTIQUES

13 b-5

ANTIQUE ANGLE

Expect the unexpected at this large antique store in the West End Market Place. The stock of 500,000 old magazines includes a complete set of *Life* and more than 200,000 copies of *Time* magazine. Owners LeRoy and Sharon Mielke have also rounded up lots of collectible advertisements, conveniently displayed by category. An area of new items include such pop culture icons as Lucy, Betty Boop, and Elvis on such wares as metal cookie cans and salt & pepper shakers. *603 Munger St., West End, 214/954–1864.*

13 f-4

DECO-DENCE

The selection of Art Deco furniture from the 1920s through the 1940s doesn't get any better than this. Owners Justin Burgess and Mark McCay specialize in hand-rubbed lacquer finish to restore many of the pieces to their original sheen and boast the largest collection in the U.S. *2827 Commerce St., Deep Ellum, 214/744–3326. Mon. and Tues. by appointment only.*

13 f-4

DEEP ELLUM GALLERIES

The dozens of wooden file cabinets, rolltop desks, and aging chairs that fill this large warehouse were once movie props for such TV favorites as "Walker, Texas Ranger" and "Dallas." *2646 Main St., Deep Ellum, 214/752–8315. Closed Mon., Tues.*

10 g-1

LINDA'S TREASURES & AFFORDABLE ANTIQUES

It's only fitting that the owner of this shop chose to carry a large selection of English Art Deco armoires dating from the 1920s, since this early 20th century building once housed an iron bed factory. You will also find Depression era glassware and Victorian lamps. *1929 Greenville Ave., 214/824–7915.*

6 e-8

LOVE FIELD ANTIQUE MALL & CLASSIC CAR COLLECTION

More than 200 dealers set up booths in this large building to display their wares. From fine china, books, and mahogany dining room tables and chairs to Coca Cola collectibles, this is an antique lover's paradise. One section is devoted to antique cars where you are apt to find a fully restored 1955 pink Cadillac or a 1929 pickup roadster. *6500 Cedar Springs, Northwest, 214/357–6500.*

6 *e-8*

LOVERS LANE ANTIQUES

Behind the black and white striped awnings lie an upscale group market specializing in 18th and 19th-century furniture, accessories, and collectibles, discovered by more than 35 dealers in the countrysides of England, France , Italy, and New England. Collections of period French and English furniture are particularly strong and include everything from English oak to mahogany pieces. If you're looking for collectibles, you can also find a significant collection of Faience, Majolica, and Stafordshire porcelain, from oyster and asparagus plates to figurines of historical persons, gothic buildings, and animals. *5001 W. Lovers La., 214/351–5656.*

10 *e-2*

CITY VIEW ANTIQUES

In what was once an industrial part of west Dallas, this antique mall has room for 40 dealers, who sell everything from 1950's Fiestaware, Candlewick, and FireKing dishes to mid-1800s furniture and shabby chic pieces from the '30s and '40s. Look for the building with the big red awning. The loading dock has been converted to an entryway. *909 N. Industrial Blvd., West, 214/824–4136.*

6 *d-5*

THE ATRIUM ANTIQUE MALL

An antique mall and auction now occupy the 140,000 square feet of this former warehouse. This is the place to search for Italian and French antique furniture from the 1890s to 1920s. You'll also find early 1900s windows, doors, columns, and mantels. Auctions are held about every six weeks. *3404 Beltline Rd., North, 972/243–2406.*

6 *f-6*

FORESTWOOD ANTIQUE MALL

This antique mall stocks extensive collections of Depression era glassware, first edition books, and English furniture. More than 250 dealers occupy the space, which includes a garden tearoom for shoppers looking for a respite from the wares. *5333 Forest La., North, 972/661–0001.*

10 *h-2*

BUCHANAN'S MARKET

This large antique and collectors market hosts 400 dealers, who bring in just about everything, including the kitchen sink—or dish pan—as the case may be. Furniture ranges from shabby tables and chairs to elegant rolltop desks. You can also browse for toys, books, vintage clothing, baseball cards, and quilts. The market is held either the third or fourth weekend of each month in the Automobile Building at Fair Park (1300 Robert B. Cullum Blvd., 214/670–8400), except for September and October when it moves to Market Hall (2100 N. Freeway, 214/655–6181).

ART SUPPLIES

13 *c-1*

ASEL ART SUPPLY

Amateur to professional-grade quality materials and supplies for fine artists, graphic artists, architects, and amateurs are stocked at this Texas retail fine art store. You'll find discounted acrylic, watercolor and oil brushes and paints, drawing and pastel papers, matte and illustration boards, mechanical and drawing pencils, adhesives, and studio equipment. Grumbacher, Windsor-Newton, Strathmore, Rembrandt are just some of the most popular brands stocked. *2701 Cedar Springs Rd., Oak Lawn, 214/871–2425.*

10 *d-1*

8920 Premier Row, 214/634–1667 Closed Sat. and Sun.

6 *f-6*

BINDERS DISCOUNT ART CENTER

A repository of fine art supplies sold at discounts of up to 20% off retail prices, the store fosters art education through demonstrations, classes, and events scheduled at varying times of day to accommodate even the most rigorous schedule. Membership in the Frequent Buyer Program will earn you extra savings on everything from graphic arts supplies (Pantone colors) to Windsor-Newton and Old Holland paints, pastels, brushes, canvases, and matte boards. *Preston Forest Village, 11661 Preston Rd. 214/739–2281.*

BEADS

6 *h-6*

ROCK BARRELL

Millions of beads fill every corner of this store. The supply of ceramic, bone, jade, sapphire, onyx, glass, and metal seem endless. *13650 TI Blvd., #104, North, 972/231–4809. Closed Sun.*

BEAUTY

fragrances & skin products

6 *f-6*

AVEDA

The world's largest manufacturer of plant-and-flower based hair, skin, makeup, body, and lifestyle products, Aveda sells over 700 products ranging from hair brushes, shampoos, and conditioners to exfoliants, hydrating lotions, deep cleansing masks, and firming fluids. The Galleria location includes a salon that offers hair cuts, manicures, makeup application, massages, and facials. *Galleria, 13350 Dallas Pkwy., North, 972/991–9490.*

6 *e-7*

SALLY BEAUTY SUPPLY

An oasis of professional beauty products and equipment, Sally stocks everything from chemical processors and cutting accessories to chairs and trolleys. You'll also find gallon-size jugs of shampoo, pedicure supplies, lip and nail colors, Revlon cosmetics, and a large selection of ethnic products for skin and hair. Their own generic brand, Ion, replicates bigger brands at lower prices. *Park Forest Shopping Center, 3767 Forest La., Ste. 108, North, 972/247–6186, and other locations.*

6 *f-6*

THE BODY SHOP

You have lots of choices at this store, including a full line of bath and shower products in such myriad fragrances as grape, jasmine, lime, and pink grapefruit. Makeup and hair products are sold here as well. *Galleria, 13350 Dallas Pkwy., North, 972/934–0257.*

6 *e-8*

BATH & BODY WORKS

Match the fruit and floral fragrances of shower gels and bubble bath with those of home sprays and candles. With so many choices, you are sure to find just the right scent. This store's top seller is cucumber melon. *924 North Park Center, North, 214/987–0840.*

6 *f-6*

GARDEN BOTANIKA

This decade-old company prides itself on earth and animal-friendly all-natural body care products. A $10 membership fee in the Garden Club buys you year-round discounts of up to 30% around your birthday. The botanically-based products run the gamut from skin and hair care goods to cosmetics, transparencies (floral fragrances) and oils bearing philosophical names like "clean slate" that you can blend yourself to create your own fragrance. The store also stocks a full line of products for men, such as its signature fragrance "Botanika," shaving creams, hair and skin care products. *Galleria, 13350 Dallas N. Parkway, Galleria, 972/934–1071.*

Preston Oaks. 10720 Preston Rd. Ste. 1005, 214/368–6876.

hair care

6 *f-1*

MATRIX BEAUTY STORE & SALON

Have your hair cut and nails done all at the same time at this salon and beauty store, which also stocks a full line of hair products including sprays, shampoos, and conditioners. Walk-ins are welcome, but an appointment is better. *Preston Park Village, 1900 Preston Rd., North, 972/867–6888.*

6 *e-3*

TONI & GUY

An appointment is the best way to guarantee a haircut at this upscale North Dallas salon, which styles, colors, and treats men and women's hair. The salon carries the Tigi Linea line of haircare and skin products. *1330 N. Dallas Pkwy., North, 972/991–7993.*

BICYCLES

6 *h-8*

CYCLE SPECTRUM

Get free service for life when you purchase a bicycle from this shop, part of the largest bike chain in the United States. You can buy Peugeot, Univega and GT bicycles here. *5521 Greenville Ave., East, 214/369–6140.*

11 *a-1*

JACK JOHNSTON BICYCLES

This 13-year-old moderate to high-end bike shop will accommodate you with same-or next-day repairs even when they're busy. Hybrid, mountain and racing bikes by Raleigh, and Italian- made frames of carbon fiber, steel, and titanium are popular lines sold here. Helmuts by Bell, Pearl Isumi clothing for men and women, and accessories such as hydration packs, Thule and Rhode Gear car racks, and Mavic, Velocity and Spinergy tires and tubes round out the stock. A biking club, Team Jonti, welcomes bikers of all ages from 13 up and all abilities for a nominal annual fee. You can also rent mountain and hybrid bikes on a daily, weekly and monthly basis. *9005 Garland Rd., White Rock Lake, 214/328–5238.*

11 *a-1*

RICHARDSON BIKE MART

In business since 1962, this store carries a variety of bikes from racing and road to recumbent. You'll find a variety of names as well, including Trek, Specialized, Schwinn and Colnago. *9040 Garland Rd., White Rock Lake, 214/321–0705.*

BOOKS

general

6 *g-3*

BARNES & NOBLE

Boasting more than 150,000 titles, this megastore has become the library of the millenium, sprouting clones of varying size and features all over the area. A monthly calendar of events lists readings and signings by authors of both kids and adult books, and a music department carries titles from more than 50,000 artists. You can also have a cup of Starbucks coffee or tea at the café while browsing through books and magazines. *14999 Preston Rd., 972/661–8068, and other locations.*

6 *e-8*

BOOKSTOP

This offshoot of Barnes and Noble has four bays of art and photo books in addition to a range of subjects, and it unilaterally offers 10% discounts off the list price and 20% to holders of the Readers' Choice card. Standard gift wrapping and direct shipping services are available upon request. A smattering of reading-related gift items such as bookmarks, bookends, and booklights make good impulse-buying at the checkout counter. *5550 W. Lovers La., #147, Northwest, 214/357–2697.*

6 *g-7*

BORDERS BOOKS & MUSIC

What germinated 30 years ago in Ann Arbor as a bookstore for serious readers with a customer-friendly library ambience and well-read staff has blossomed into a worldwide phenomenon. Browse through more than 200,000 titles in the café or in library-reminiscent seating throughout the store. Best-selling authors are regulars at book signings. A music department stocks thousands of CDs and DVDs. *10720 Preston Rd., Ste. 1018, North, 214/363–1977.*

6 *h-8*

5500 Greenville Ave., 214/739–1166.

6 *h-5*

15757 Coit Rd.,972/458–0400.

discount

6 *h-8*

HALF PRICE BOOKS

This Dallas-based chain of new and used books carries 500,000 books in its main store. You can't beat the prices with even new books selling at half of retail price. *5801 E. Northwest Hwy., East, 214/379–8000.*

6 *f-6*

75 PERCENT OFF BOOKS

Nothing in this no-frills 3,000 square foot store is over $4.99. Come prepared to spend hours browsing the categories of subjects, ranging from art to technical books; nothing is alphabetized and the stock changes weekly. A particularly large and complete selection of computer and software books is stocked. *13020 Preston Rd., North, 972/702–0414.*

antiquarian

13 *d-2*

ANTIQUARIAN OF DALLAS

This store carries an impressive collection of leather–bound books. You'll find first editions of Hemmingway, Twain, Faulkner, and wide variety of rare books. It specializes in classic novels and first edition Texanna. *2609 Routh St., Uptown, 214/754–0705.*

13 *d-2*

HISTORY MERCHANT

You might just find that rare first edition Civil War title here. Opened in 1989, this store specializes in hardcover books about the Civil War, World War II, and the U.S. presidents. *2723 Routh St., Uptown, 214/742–5487.*

specialty

10 *e-4*

BLACK IMAGES BOOK BAZAAR

This store carries 29,000 titles of African–American nonfiction, fiction, and children's titles. It stocks a limited selection of historical videos and books on tape. Watch for occasional book signings. *230 Wynnewood Village, Oak Cliff, 214/943–0142.*

6 *f-3*

CONSTELLATION BOOKSTORE

Delving into some of these New Age and metaphysical books will give you a new view of life. This Bachman Lake shop stocks more than 12,000 titles, including a limited selection of educational videos. *5100 Beltline Rd., North, 972/385–1200. Closed Mon.*

10 *g-2*

ENCHANTED FOREST BOOKS FOR CHILDREN

You can buy your baby's first book here. In addition to the assortment of titles for ages from infants to teenagers, this store carries book character toys, children's art supplies, and videos. *6333 E. Mockingbird Ln., Ste. 231, East, 214/827–2234. Closed Sun.*

10 *e-1*

MAPSCO & TRAVEL CENTERS

It's hard to lose your way with one of these annually-updated city street guides. You'll also find a variety of local, regional, national and international atlases and maps. *5308 Maple Ave., Oak Lawn, 214/219–6277, and other locations. Closed Sat., Sun.*

6 *g-8*

RAND MCNALLY—MAP AND TRAVEL STORE

Learning about a future destination is easy when you stop by this store for a handy map and guide. Besides scads of maps and books, you will find all kinds of useful travel aids such as adapters, luggage tags, toiletry bottles. *211 NorthPark Center, North, 214/987–9941.*

6 *f-6*

SHAKESPEARE, BEETHOVEN & COMPANY

When this Canadian-owned store decided to venture south of the border, it chose the Galleria as its only U.S. location. You'll not only find a broad selection of books unavailable elsewhere but also foreign and domestic magazines and newspapers, and classical and jazz music. *Galleria, 13350 Dallas Pkwy., Ste. 3200, North, 972/387–1720.*

BUTTONS

6 *f-8*

BENNO'S BUTTON STORE

Hundreds of new buttons—glass, jet, wood—are just waiting to be stitched on the right garment. Lace trim for a blouse or pair of pillowcases is also available. *5611 W. Lovers Ln., Northwest, 214/352–0534. No credit cards. Closed Sun.*

CAKE DECORATING EQUIPMENT & SUPPLIES

7 *b-7*

CELEBRATE CAKES

From bakeware, pastry tips and airbrush equipment to cake and cupcake boxes, you'll find everything you need to create, personalize, and transport your cake at this source of inspiration and instruction for the home baker. You can also enroll in month-long novice to advanced cake decorating classes or day-long classes in wedding cake and cupcake decorating, gingerbread house making, and candy making. But if you don't want to tackle any of the above, you can also order a complete line of wedding, specialty, birthday, digital photo, and company or corporate logo cakes. *4310 Saturn Rd., Garland, 972/271–4396. Closed Sun.*

CANDLES

13 *b-4*

THE FRONT PORCH

With more than 50 scents to choose from, finding the candle with the right scent is a breeze. You can watch many of these handmade candles being cast in sand in all shapes and sizes. Some are even decorated with crystals. *West End Market Place, 603 Munger Ave., Level 4, Ste. 11, Downtown, 214/999–1209.*

6 *f-6*

WICKS 'N' STICKS

Be prepared to linger in this fragrant store. The wax fruit pies smell—and look—good enough to eat. Candles come in a seemingly endless array of scents and shapes. *Galleria, 13350 Dallas Pkwy., North, 972/991–7727.*

CLOTHING FOR CHILDREN

6 *g-8*

ANGEL'S KIDS

Amid the handmade dolls and quilts at this upscale children's clothing store, you'll find infant sizes to size 7 for boys and girls. Clothing ranges from denim to dressy knits. *460 NorthPark Center, North, 214/368–1876.*

6 *f-6*

BABY GAP

The ubiquitous gift source for all baby showers, it stocks bright colored, moderately priced outfits of cottons, fleece, and wool for newborns to toddlers. Standard merchandise includes jeans, one-piece bodysuits and sleepwear, velvet party dresses and velvet footed pants, fleece hats and mittens, wool and cashmere pants, cotton and fleece booties, receiving blankets, and cotton socks in every shade of the rainbow. A Gapcard earns you 10% discounts on purchases at all Gap stores. *Galleria, 13350 Dallas Pkwy., North, 972/934–7656.*

6 *g-8*

728 Northpark Center, 214/369–5498.

6 *f-6*

GAP KIDS

The same moderately-priced jean and khaki outfits sold at the Gap for adults are available here, as well as whatever is currently trendy. For girls, some of the standard fare includes twill jumpers, three-quarter sleeve oxford shirts, ankle zip pants, khakis, micro tights, and sweaters of all fits and patterns; for boys, check out the hooded sweatshirts, khakis, corduroys, flannel pants, oxfords, sport socks, and cotton knit shirts in a variety of colors. *Galleria, 13350 Dallas Pkwy., Ste. 2200, North, 972/991–6818.*

6 *g-8*

728 Northpark Center, 214/369–5498.

6 *f-6*

GYMBOREE

Infants through age 7 can dress in fashionable mix-and-match wear when their moms shop at this clothing store. *Galleria, 13350 Dallas Pkwy., Ste. 2535, 972/233–7199, and other locations.*

10 *d-6*

ELLENE'S KIDS

This is a dress-up shop for kids, with fancy party dresses and lacy socks for girls and tux and ties for boys. *Southwest Center, 3662 W. Camp Wisdom Rd., South, 972/780–1703.*

CLOTHING FOR WOMEN/GENERAL

classic & casual

6 *f-6*

ANN TAYLOR

Popular among career women, this chain retail store sells its own line of moderately-priced professional, dress casual and evening attire. Suits, slacks, blouses, dresses, coats, jackets are mostly made of natural fibers or blends of natural fibers. You'll also find a selection of belts, dress shoes, casual shoes, and hosiery. *Galleria, 13350 Dallas Pkwy., North, 972/386–4548.*

6 *f-6*

BANANA REPUBLIC

What was once a safari-inspired men's and women's clothing store more than 20 years ago has grown into a multifaceted store with casual, professional, and evening attire as well as intimate apparel, shoes, belts, bags and personal care items for both genders. The store carries its own brand of dresses, slacks, skirts, sweaters, shirts, jackets and coats principally in natural fibers such as suede, leather, cotton, silk and wool; though some of the dressy evening attire for women includes blended fabrics. *Galleria, 13350 Dallas Pkwy., North, 972/960–9988.*

10 *f-1*

40 Highland Park Village, 214/536–3269.

10 *f-1*

30 Highland Park Village, 214/443–9485.

6 *g-8*

1030 North Park Center, 214/739–8577.

6 *f-1*

1900 Preston Rd., Plano, 972/612–9966.

6 *f-6*

GUESS?

This national chain exclusively carries its own label of trendy, casual and evening attire for young women and men. The GC label offers more sedate, classic looks for men and women in natural fibers from cotton to wool, and sultry evening ware for young women, including sequined halter tops, leopard double-slit miniskirts, figure-hugging cotton-lycra pants, and leather pants and jackets. *Galleria, 13350 Dallas Pkwy., Ste. 2848, North, 972/490–5616.*

6 *g-8*

320 North Park Center, 214/739–8195.

6 *g-6*

THE LIMITED

Moderately priced classic, modern designs in its own label make this a popular spot for fashionable casual, professional, and formal wear in natural fibers and blends. Merchandise ranges from belts, handbags, and hosiery to a "virtual stretch" line of skirts and pants, leather and mohair coats, and silk blouses. *2273 Valley View Center, #1058, North, 972/386–9037, and other locations.*

13 *c-13*

STANLEY KORSHAK

You'll find the perfect outfit for most occasion amid the racks of contemporary and casual sportswear from American and European designers. You can also pick out matching shoes, handbags, and accessories. The often–overlooked evening wear is worth checking out. *500 Crescent Court, Ste. 100, Uptown, 214/871–3600. Closed Sun.*

6 *f-6*

TALBOTS

The destination for moderately-priced conservative women's casual, evening and professional attire, Talbots exclusively sells its own label of clothing and accessories. Apparel runs in petite to plus sizes, and includes classics like boucle jackets, wool crepe skirts, wool flannel suits, and silk blouses. Accessories include croco-embossed boots, side-zip ankle boots, pins, necklaces, earrings, hosiery, smooth and textured handbags and wallets, dressy evening bags, dress and casual shoes. *Galleria, 13350 Dallas Pkwy., Ste. 1610, North, 972/233–1353.*

6 *g-8*

8687 N. Central Expressway, 214/361–9231.

10 *f-2*

4208 Oaklawn Ave., 214/522–8490.

contemporary

10 *f-1*

MARY NASH

For 50 years, this women's boutique has specialized in casual to work apparel made from a range of fibers from wools to silks and cottons in sizes from 2 to 18. Mary Nash also stocks lines such as Lilly, Da Rue of California, Kasper, Olsen, JSS Knits, San Remo, and Lady Primrose. *5560 W. Lovers La. #248, 214/352–2603. Closed Sun.*

designer

10 *f-1*

CHANEL BOUTIQUE

The ultimate token of success is to own anything from this upscale boutique whose trademark merchandise includes classic tailored tweed suits with fitted jackets, cap toe shoes, and handbags with the telltale interlocking c's. Couture evening wear abounds as well, in every glamorous textile, for a handsome price. The attentive staff know their merchandise, and will make you feel queen for a day. *85 Highland Park Village, Highland Park, 214/520–1055. Closed Sun.*

10 *f-1*

CHRISTIAN DIOR

This pricey women's boutique elegantly and sparsely displays its apparel and accessories such as Lady Dior handbags, shoes, scarves, sunglasses and necklaces. *42 Highland Park Village, Highland Park, 214/252–0049. Closed Sun.*

10 *f-1*

LUCA LUCA

The Southwest's first free-standing Luca Luca boutique opened in 1999 to showcase Milan designer Luca Orlandi's colorful Italian-made clothing expertly crafted made from couture-quality fabrics. He is expanding his design sensibility to include younger silhouettes such as cashmere knits, beaded halter tops, and leather pants. Complimentary delivery and seamstress' services are available for customers. *42A Highland Park Village, Highland Park, 214/219–5822. Closed Sun.*

6 *f-6*

TERRY COSTA

Whether it's a bar mitzvah, a benefit gala, or a black-tie wedding you're shopping for, something among the hundreds of designer-label samples is sure to fit the bill but not break the bank. Bridal department staff will shower you with their undivided attention, gowns by Mori Lee, Alfred Angelo, Eden and Mon Cherie, and lend advice on selecting suitable bridesmaid gowns. *12817 Preston Rd., Ste. 138, North, 972/385–6100.*

discount & off-price

10 *d-6*

BURLINGTON COAT FACTORY

You may have trouble squeezing between the racks crammed with designer and off-brand merchandise, but don't let the name fool you. The store carries a lot more than coats for the entire family. *3107 W. Camp Wisdom Rd., South, 214/337–2660.*

13 *d-6*

BON TON FASHION BOUTIQUE

Snatch up designer samples and business casual fashions by Ellen Tracy, Chandiz, and Doony at wholesale prices at this upscale women's boutique. In addition to an array of slacks, dresses, shirts, blouses and sweaters, the store also carries accessories such as costume jewelry by local designer Anthony Mark Hankis, belts and handbags by Fossil, and sunglasses and hats. *120 Two Bell Plaza, 211 South Acker St., Downtown, 214/741–1510. By appointment only Sat., closed Sun.*

10 *e-2*

KAREN'S FASHIONS

This wholesale women's apparel store carries formal wear by Donna Karan, Carol Little, Liz Claibourne, Armani, and Bob Macki. In addition to sequined tops and gowns, the store also sells slacks, skirts, blouses and sweaters. *2200 Vantage St., Northwest, 214/638–6988. Closed Sun.*

6 *h-8*

K-MART

Decorating is a snap with Martha Stewart's coordinated bedding, towels, and accessories found at this popular discount chain. You'll also find an assortment of clothing for men, women, and children. *6000 Skillman St., East, 214/361–9547, and other locations.*

6 *f-4*

LABELS

Walk in to this upscale boutique that elegantly displays contemporary sportswear, professional, and couture eveningwear attire and you'll be surprised that it's all consignment merchandise offered at 25–30% of its original retail price. Regularly-spotted merchandise includes Escada, St. John, Armani, Gucci, and Prada slacks, skirts, dresses, and jackets. Depending upon the season, you may find Gucci cashmere coats, Donna Karan couture gowns, Armani suits, and Jill Sander wool and angora coats. Accessories include antique jewelry, and Prada, Louis Vuitton, Chanel, and Coach shoes and handbags. Faux handbags sold here include Kate Spade, Prada, Gucci, and Fendi. The star-studded merchandise is matched by the star-worthy treatment you receive from staff who serve you coffee, tea and spiced cider and greet the innumerable regulars by name. *18101 Preston Rd., North, 972/713–8600.*

6 *g-8*

T.J. MAXX

The largest off-price retailer in the nation with more than 600 stores nationwide, TJ Maxx sells brand name and designer fashions for home and family for up to 60% less than department store prices. More than 10,000 new items are available each week. Merchandise is organized in eight departments: men's, women's, teens, kids, home, women's footwear, accessories, and fine jewelry. Grab that pashmina when you see it; there are no tracking or locating services for merchandise. *9100 N. Central Expressway, Ste. 125, North, 214/373–7310, and other locations.*

resale

6 *f-8*

CLOTHES CIRCUIT

The repository for the consigned wardrobes of Dallas' well-heeled ladies, this store stocks more than 8,000 items of merchandise ranging from designer shoes and handbags by Stuart Weitzman, Gucci and Prada to couture gowns, business attire, and weekend sportswear. Browse through such designer labels as Giorgio Armani, Dior, Chanel, DKNY, Jil Sander, Escada, Laundry, and Yves Saint Laurent. Initially priced at 30–40% of original retail, merchandise is often reduced further by sequential markdowns.Twice a year, in late January and July, you can get 50% off prior season's goods on the floor at their Backroom Sale. *6105 Sherry La., North, 214/696–8634.*

unusual sizes

6 *f-7*

CLASSIC WOMAN

This boutique carries contemporary casual, professional, and evening attire for women in sizes 14 to 24 by such designers as Susan Bristol, Nina Wong, and Maggie London. Merchandise ranges from sweaters to sleek evening gowns in a variety of natural (cotton, silk, linen, wools) and blended fabrics. *235 Preston Royal Village, North, 214/265–9111. Closed Sun.*

6 *f-6*

LARGESSE

This upscale boutique carries "after 5" and casual apparel for women sizes 14W to 26W by designers such as Nina Wong, Tohmatsu, and Gallina. The store also sells belts, costume jewelry, and a limited selection of fine jewelry. *5312 Belt Line Rd., North, 972/233–2700. Closed Sun.*

vintage

10 *g-1*

LULA B'S ANTIQUE MALL

Upstairs is where you will find the white beaded 1960s purse, organdy sun hat, and 1950s nylon net prom dresses. *2004 Greenville Ave., East, 214/824–2185.*

10 *g-1*

RAGWEAR

1950s tuxedos, leather jackets, 1960s polyester shirts and pants, chiffon evening dresses, and more fill this store. *2000 Greenville Ave., East, 214/827–4163.*

CLOTHING FOR WOMEN/ SPECIALTIES

furs

6 *f-5*

BIFANO FURS

All facilities—manufacturing, sales, service, storage, cleaning, restructuring—are under one roof of this ultra-service oriented premier furrier that has been selling furs since 1919. Furs run the gauntlet from mink, sable, fox, and chinchilla. They can combine and restyle any furs as you request; if your old coat doesn't fit, they can make it into a vest with zip-out sleeves. You're treated to your own showroom here'the merchandise is brought out as you request it. *4205 Sigma Rd., North, 214/871–1111. Closed Sun.*

6 *g-8*

KOSLOW'S

In business since 1935, Koslow's continue their tradition of storing, cleaning, and selling furs. Sheered mink, beaver, fox, chincilla, and sable coats are the staples here, but they also sell leather coats, jackets hats, earmuffs, mink eyeglass cases, and cashmere sweaters with or without mink trim on cuffs and collars. *9100 N. Central Expressway, Ste. 101, North, 214/361–6400. Closed Sun.*

handbags & gloves

6 *f-6*

BRIGHTON COLLECTIBLES

This upscale accessory shop carries coordinated handbags, belts, wallets, and jewelry. *Galleria, 13350 Dallas Pkwy., Ste. 2500, North, 972/774–1133.*

6 *f-6*

CUL DE SAC ACCESSORIES

Look no further than Cul De Sac for French and Italian leather handbags and briefcases. *Galleria, 13350 Dallas Pkwy., North, 972/661–8629.*

6 *f-6*

FOREVER LEATHER & LUGGAGE

This store stocks a wide selection of Brighton and Brahmin handbags, Ricardo luggage, Jansport backpacks, and Brenthaven briefcases. *2010 Valley View, North, 972/726–8688.*

lingerie

10 *f-2*

SHEERS

Staff at this high-end women's convenience store knows exactly what you need to look ravishing in apparel lingerie and accessories by such designers as Calvin Klein, Donna Karan, Hanna, Cossalini, Earl, and Jon Quil. Sexy black pants, Cavallini tops, honeymoon lingerie, Love Letter thongs, pajamas, designer jeans, bath products by Primal and On Gossamer, Wolford hosiery, and jewlery are just some of the staples. Staff will shop for you, help get your clothes together, and even deliver purchases to homes and hotels. *4266 Oak Lawn Ave., Oak Lawn, 214/528–7292. Closed Sun.*

6 *g-8*

VICTORIA'S SECRET

This ladies lingerie, loungewear, and sleepwear chain has popped up in so many locations nationwide, it's certainly no secret anymore. It's perhaps most known for an overwhelming volume of five lines of bras in nearly a dozen styles such as strapless and underwear, in materials from cotton to silk and colors to match any outfit. Nightgowns, robes, slips, and camisoles range in a variety of styles and materials from natural fibers to microfibers. New lines such as second-skin satin and miracle bra boast luxury and voluptuousness at a relative pittance. *522 NorthPark Center, North, 214/987–9034.*

maternity

10 *f-2*

BETTER MATERNITY OUTLET

Modeled after designer styles in fabrics from natural fibers to microfibers, the casual and professional maternity attire here is 40–50% less than what you'd pay for designer labels. *1644 Irving Blvd., Oak Lawn, 214/742–2229. Closed Sun.*

6 *f-6*

MOTHERHOOD MATERNITY

This upscale maternity store affiliated with A Pea in the Pod sells fashionable clothing for all occasions, including casual, career, and party. Apparel is sized according to women's pre-pregnancy sizes—from 4 to 14—and includes designs by Three Dots, Lily Pulitzer, Vivian Tam, Hue, and Nicole Miller. You can buy dresses, slacks, shirts, leggings, swimwear, lingerie, sleepwear, and activewear. *Galleria, Ste. 2655, 13350 Dallas Pkwy., North, 972/490–6490.*

6 *f-6*

A PEA IN THE POD-MATERNITY REDEFINED

Modern, sleek, designer maternity clothing for professional, casual, and evening occasions fill this store. Apparel is sized according to women's pre-pregnancy sizes, runs from 4 to 14, and includes designs by Three Dots, Lily Pulitzer, Vivian Tam, Hue, and Nicole Miller. You can get dresses, evening dresses, slacks, shirts, leggings, swimwear, lingerie, sleepwear, and activewear. *Galleria, 13350 Dallas Pkwy., Ste. 2530, North, 972/490–7790.*

shoes & boots

6 *f-6*

LOUIS VUITTON

World-famous for the brown-on-brown "LV" monogram, Louis Vuitton sells accesssories only—no clothing. Merchandise includes designer handbags, luggage, scarves, wallets, and belts—not to mention men's and women's shoes, preciously priced as they are crafted. *Galleria, 13350 Dallas Pkwy., North, 972/934–3637.*

6 *f-6*

THE ROCKPORT SHOP

This Galleria shop exclusively carries Rockport shoes—80% of its current line—for men and women in a variety of styles including boots, lace-up shoes, loafers and pumps. *Galleria, 13350 Dallas Pkwy., North, 972/774–9050.*

6 *f-6*

STEVE MADDEN

The footwear created by designer Steven Madden appeals to young women with trendy tastes, targeted by the bizarre-looking characters that hallmark his print ad campaign. All his latest designs come in sizes 5 to 11 from clunky platform shoes and boots to wedge sandals, slippers, loafers, and sneakers. *Galleria, 13350 Dallas Pkwy., North, 972/701–8767.*

6 *g-8*

VIA SPIGA

Accessorize in ostrich, python, crocodile print leather and suede at this tony Italian footwear shop that sells everything from sporty loafers to day and evening pumps, slingbacks and books. Matching handbags in a variety of styles—including the bowling bag and classic shoulder strap—belts, credit card holders and wallets are available in all textiles. *NorthPark Center, North, 214/265–1699.*

swimsuits

6 *f-8*

JUST ADD WATER

This ladies' fashion swimwear and resort retailer carries designs of four international and 20 domestic manufacturers, including Moschino, Karla Colletto, Huit, Calvin Klein, Anne Klein Cole, Robin Piccone, and Adrienne Vittadini. In addition to swimwear in sizes 4–18, it sells specialty suits such as Roxanne and Miracle suits, cruisewear in fabrics from cotton to microfiber, mix and match separates, coverups such as pareos, Tommy Bahamas sportswear, Helen Kiminski and Rafia hats and bags, and beach shoes by Guess, Shicca, and Roxy. *6139 Luther La., North, 214/691–5881.*

CLOTHING FOR MEN/GENERAL

classic & casual

BANANA REPUBLIC

See Clothing For Women, *above.*

6 *f-6*

BROOKS BROTHERS

Since 1818 it has been a fashion innovator, introducing the concept of ready-made suits, wash-and-wear dress shirts, and tailored slacks for women. Men's apparel runs in fabrics from cotton to cashmere, and includes suits, Polo-collar shirts, neckties, cashmere sweaters, tailored slacks, dress shoes, sleepwear, and socks. Women's apparel includes skirt and pant suits, tailored shirts, flannel trousers, cashmere turtleneck sweaters, and non-iron dress shirts. Services include complimentary alternations and monogramming of holiday gift items. *Galleria, 13350 Dallas Pkwy., North, 972/960–6200.*

6 *f-7*

THE GAP

This popular chain appeals to all ages with its reasonably priced jeans, shirts, and athletic wear. Log on to *www.gap.com* for a store locator. *10720 Preston Rd., North, 214/361–6651, and other locations.*

6 *f-7*

KEN'S MAN'S SHOP

Don't be surprised if you happen to run into one of the pigskin carrying Dallas Cowboys at this classy haberdashery opened by Ken Helfman in the 1960s. *309 Preston Royal Shopping Center, North, 214/369–5367. Closed Sun.*

6 *f-6*

LEVI'S

Levi's jeans, shirts, caps, and socks are the mainstay of this Galleria store, which stocks no other brand. You can even have jeans made exactly the way you want them by ordering a custom pair. *Galleria, 13350 Dallas Pkwy., Ste. 2860, North, 972/866–8055.*

6 *f-6*

MARK SHALE

When you revisit this upscale men's and women's apparel store, the staff recall the size and brand of your past purchases from their computer. Casual and dress apparel—from slacks and sport coats to dresses, suits, blouses, and evening wear—come in such textiles as glitter and silk knits, mohair, leather, suede, charmeuse, twills, and microfibers. Designer labels include Zanella, Kenneth Cole, Joseph Abboud, Hugo Boss, Tommy Bahama, Lafayette 148, and Eileen Fisher. *Galleria, 13350 Dallas Pkwy., Ste. 2750, North, 972/458–2428.*

6 *f-5*

OLD NAVY

Inexpensive, trendy, casual clothes in fibers such as cotton, fleece and wool make this the perfect place for college students to build their wardrobes. Standard apparel includes boxers, pajamas, sweats, knit shirts, T-shirts, sweaters, jeans, carpenter pants, hooded and crewneck sweatshirts, jeans, winter jackets, and leather coats. A complete line of similar apparel is also available for kids and babies. *14902 Preston Rd., North, 972/386–6489.*

10 *f-1*

ULTIMO

Known for its niche vendors, such as Miguel Androver, this upscale ladies' boutique designed by Gabelini has bright orange walls and merchandise by Dolce & Gabana, Yoji Yamamoto, Chloe, Galliano, and Pamela Dennis displayed on beautiful Italian racks hung from the ceiling. Browse everything from $25 Three Dot T-shirts to $4,000 ball gowns, fur boas, and Piazza Sempione career suits—all in textiles ranging from cashmere and wool to silk, velvet, leather, and suede. Staff know you by name, order you lunch and a glass of wine, and ask about your lastest travels while you shop. Alterations are done on site, and purchases may be delivered to you. *44 Highland Park Village, Highland Park, 214/520–2066. Closed Sun.*

contemporary

6 *f-6*

ARMANI EXCHANGE

In this contemporary store Armani applies his design sense to a mixture of moderately-priced basic but trendy apparel for men and women, from denim jeans and jackets to leather and suede coats and every kind of natural-fiber knit shirt and casual pant in between. A limited line of accessories such as belts and bags are displayed throughout. *Galleria, 13350 Dallas Pkwy., Ste. 1530, North, 972/701–9743.*

GARIANI MENSWEAR

This shop carries apparel by couture European designers, including Zanetti and Cavelli. Designs include dress slacks, sport coats, jackets, coats, sweaters, shirts, and accessories in natural fibers such as lambswool, cotton, silk, leather, and suede. *15340 Dallas Pkwy., North, 972/661–0104.*

6 *f-6*

MEN'S GALLERY

This upscale store stocks only designer dress and casual wear with such labels as Zanini, Kevoman, Zanier, and Savane. *2240 Valley View Center, North, 972/726–6300.*

6 *f-6*

MILANO

This ultrachic Italian designer caters to the up-and-coming young professionals with suits, casual, and in-store alterations. *2168 Valley View Mall, North, 972/404–9933.*

10 *f-1*

POLO RALPH LAUREN

Warmly appointed and reminiscent of a country manor, this upscale boutique sells classic equestrian and outdoorsmen-inspired apparel for men and women. Its stock ranges from leather jackets, overcoats, and raincoats in a variety of classic styles and natural fabrics to tailored tweed sportcoats, slacks, blazers for women with suede or leather elbow patches, and mohair and lambswool sweaters of every neckline. The store also carries a line of home decorating merchandise including sheets in rich Mediterranean-inspired colors and designs, duvets, and towels. *58 Highland Park Village, Highland Park, 214/522–5270.*

SIGNORI GIOANNI

This men's and women's upscale European clothing boutique carries designer labels such as Versace, Pelo, Canali, Bruno, Lady Zanella and Xacus. *15550 Quorum, Addison, 972/387–2332. Closed Sun.*

custom

6 *f-6*

CUSTOM SHOP

Men can order shirts, sport coats, and suits to fit. Shirts are sewn from Egyptian cotton and suits from high quality wool. *Galleria, 13350 Dallas Pkwy., North, 972/866–0043.*

10 *f-1*

LOMBARDO CUSTOM APPAREL

This full service men's clothing store known for its celebrity clientele specializes in custom-made casual and business attire from traditional to the most fashion-forward styles in virtually every type of fabric. In addition to clothing, you'll find neckwear collections from Europe in iridescent, jacquard and woven fabrics, as well as shoes, belts and sweaters. If you can't get here, traveling consultants will come to you for measurements and fittings. Even when the suit is made and sold, they'll maintain complete wardrobe files containing your pattern so all you need to do for future purchases is select your fabric and style. *8315 Preston Rd., Highland Park, 214/265–8488. Closed Sun.*

discount & off price

6 *g-8*

BIG & TALL FASHIONS FOR LESS

This discount store carries men's casual and business attire in sizes 1X–8X and coat sizes 48 to 70 in labels such as Chaps by Ralph Lauren, DKNY, Levis, Tommy Hilfiger, and Palm Beach. You can save up to 35% on department store merchandise. In addition to suits, sportcoats, slacks, and shirts, you can buy belts, ties, socks sleepwear, and sweaters. *9100 North Central Expressway, Ste. 145, North, 214/360–0422.*

6 *h-4*

K & D MEN'S CENTER

Suits, casual wear, and accessories are available with discounts up to 65% off department store prices on brand-name labels. *1050 N. Central Expressway, Richardson, 972/234–8500. Closed Mon.–Thurs.*

6 *f-8*

MEN'S WAREHOUSE

Moderately-priced brand-name casual and professional attire and attentive, knowledgable service are this store's emphases. Wardrobe consultants work with you to find the right style suit for your body type by such designers as Pierre Cardin, Chaps by Ralph Lauren, Oscar de la Renta, and Givenchy in sizes ranging from 35S to 52XL. Additional attire by the same designers includes sportcoats, slacks, dress and casual shirts. The shoe department stocks formal, professional and casual shoes by Dexter, Florsheim, and the store's line, Vito Rufulo. *8239 Preston Rd., North, 214/369–1841.*

unusual sizes

7 *b-8*

BIG & TALL VALUE CENTER

This men's apparel store stocks moderately priced designer names such as Chaps by Ralph Lauren in sizes from 1X to 6X. You'll also find sweaters, casual and dress shirts, dress and casual slacks, sport coats, suits, and some accessories in natural fibers from cotton to wool. *11312 LBJ Freeway, Ste. 100, Northeast, 214/221–8255.*

5957 Alpha Rd., 972/385–8255.

6 *f-6*

CASUAL MALE BIG & TALL

Men's casual and business attire in designs by Palm Beach, Carhartt, and Savare are sold here in sizes from 1X–6X. Accessories such as belts, socks, and shoes (sizes 11–16W) round out the selection. *13398 Preston Rd., North, 972/934–2376.*

6 *f-5*

HYROOP'S BIG & TALL

In-house tailoring is available here if that designer suit doesn't fit perfectly. *15340 N. Dallas Pkwy., North, 972/239–9181.*

vintage

6 *f-6*

RETHREADS

Suits, slacks, shirts, ties, and other men's wear make budgeting easy when you shop at this consignment store. *411 Preston Valley Shopping Center, North, 972/233–1684.*

CLOTHING FOR MEN/SPECIALTIES

formalwear

6 *f-6*

AL'S FORMAL WEAR

This tuxedo rental and sales shop stocks tuxedos for boys size 2 to men's size 70; it also carries shirts and appropriate accessories in designer brands such as Bill Blass and Adolfo. *Valley View Center, North, 214/712–5609.*

6 *h-5*

7632 Campbell Rd., 972/248–8686.

10 *d-6*

4353 Gannon La., 972/283–1289.

6 *h-8*

6713 W. Northwest Hwy., 214/368–6439.

6 *f-5*

14999 Preston Rd., 972/788–4472.

6 *f-6*

ASCOT TUXEDOS

A subsidiary of Al's Formal Wear, this tuxedo rental and sales shop stocks formalwear by designers such as Bill Blass and Adolfo in boy's size 2 to men's size 70. This company also promises to match competitors' prices. *5850 LBJ Freeway, North, 972/387–3999.*

6 *f-6*

GINGISS FORMALWEAR

You can rent or buy the perfect tuxedo—Pierre Cardin, Adolfo, Bill Blass—for any formal occasion at this Galleria store. *13350 Dallas Pkwy., North, 972/458–7767.*

6 *g-8*

9100 N. Central Expressway, Ste. 107, 214/696–5796.

10 *d-6*

3917 W. Camp Wisdom Rd., Ste. 109, 214/296–2911.

10 *e-2*

2707 Stemmons Freeway, Ste. 100, 214/638–4300.

hats

10 *d-6*

DOBBS THE HAT STORE

Fashion dress hats are the word here, in a variety of styles, Capri, Basino, Centre Dent, El Dorado, Anguila, and Panama, as well as Deion by Dobbs (Silk Homburg, Broadstreet) in a variety of natural colors. *3917 W. Camp Wisdom Rd., Oak Cliff, 972/572–4287. Closed Sun.*

6 *f-6*

LIDS

Caps, fishing hats, visors, and golf hats line the walls at this hat shop. Star athletes even buy their caps here, since the store carries most pro team caps. Forget adjusting a plastic tab; caps are made to fit. *Galleria, 13350 Dallas Pkwy., North, 972/239–7965.*

PAPILLON NECKWEAR

See Ties, *below.*

razors

6 *f-6*

REMINGTON

This store carries a lot of handy personal items, including manicure and grooming sets, but it really specializes in razors. You will find an assortment of electric shavers, including cordless ones, as well as beard and mustache trimmers, and straight razors, complete with brush, cup, and soap. *Galleria, 13350 Dallas Pkwy., North, 972/960–0274.*

shoes & boots

6 *f-6*

CAVENDER'S BOOT CITY

This Texas chain carries Western boots in exotic leathers as well as tough bullhides. *5539 LBJ Fwy., North, 972/239–1375.*

6 *f-6*

JOHNSTON & MURPHY

Regardless of the kind of shoe you need, this store stocks them all from elegant patent leather oxfords to rugged work boots. It also has a good selection of men's hosiery and belts. *Galleria, 13350 Dallas Pkwy., North, 972/387–7934.*

6 *f-5*

LARRY'S SHOES

For more than 50 years, this men's footwear boutique has carried extensive selections and styles of designer professional and casual shoes and boots by Cole Haan, Kenneth Cole, Johnston & Murphy, Timberland, Rockport, New Balance, Nicke, Skechers, Dr. Martens, and Allen-Edmonds. Whether you're buying running shoes or classic dress lace-up shoes, the attentive staff will help you find the right fit. *15340 N. Dallas Pkwy., 972/980–8811, and other locations.*

6 *f-6*

MORGAN-HAYES

Step out in style, with more than a dozen brands of footwear and a variety of styles from which to choose. *Galleria, 13350 Dallas Pkwy., North, 972/458–8510.*

6 *f-6*

OVERLAND TRADING CO.

This is the place to find comfortable and durable shoes—Rockport, Birkenstock, Ecco, and Timberland—for those leisurely afternoon walks or daylong shopping excursions. *Galleria, 13350 Dallas Pkwy., Ste. 2355, North, 972/991–3995.*

13 *b-5*

WILD BILL'S WESTERN STORE

Whether you need boots, belt or buckle, you'll find all kinds of cowboy duds here. *West End Market Place, Ste. 321, Downtown, 214/954–1050.*

ties

13 *b-5*

TIES AND ACCESSORIES

From power ties to fun ties, this may be the ultimate tie shop. *West End Market Place, Downtown, 214/303–0770.*

10 *d-6*

PAPILLON NECKWEAR

With walls lined with ties in all different colors and designs, you are bound to find just the right one to go with that new suit. This store also stocks tie clips and cuff links. Papillon also stocks a full selection of hats, including derbies and fedoras. *3662 W. Camp Wisdom Rd., South, 972/283–8437.*

6 *f-6*

THE TIE SHOP

With 1,200 silk ties to pick from, you can find just the right tie to impress anyone. Texas motif ties add a fun touch for the right business occasion. *Galleria, 13350 Dallas Pkwy., Ste. 2445, North, 972/239–0088.*

COINS

6 *f-7*

DALLAS RARE COINS & JEWELRY

The only full scale coin collector in Dallas, the open showroom displays everything from Greek coins dating from 650 BC to last week's issue. A full line of coin supplies and albums are also sold here. *5211 Forest La., North, 972/458–1617. Closed Sun., Mon.*

6 *e-8*

WALNUT GOLD & SILVER

Collectible coins, gold bullion, and jewelry are sold at this shop. *3720 Walnut Hill La., North, 214/357–1111. Closed Sun.*

COMPUTERS & SOFTWARE

6 *f-8*

OFFICE DEPOT

This chain office supply, furniture and electronics store will match competitor's advertised prices on computers, printers, and other merchandise. Large inventories of paper supplies, filing and storage supplies, writing implements, bookcases, work tables, computers, electronic organizers, phones, printers, software, scanners, and copy machines make it an efficient and economical place to shop. *Greeneville Junction Shopping Center, 5111 Greenville Ave., East, 214/365–9840, and other locations.*

6 *f-5*

OFFICE MAX

Every conceivable organizational tool for the office is stocked at this moderately priced chain office supply, equipment, and electronics store. Brand names of office equipment include Xerox, Canon, Hewlett-Packard, Dell, and Compaq. *15440 Dallas Pkwy., North, 972/386–7770.*

6 *d-5*

RESOURCE CONCEPTS

It's hard to beat the prices of reconditioned computers sold here; most come with guarantees. If the sales staff can't answer your question, he or she will grab a technician from the back who will. *2940 Eisenhower, Carrollton, 972/245–5050. Closed Sun.*

COSTUMES & COSTUME RENTAL

6 *f-5*

COSTUME WORLD

This Florida-based chain has the second largest collection of costumes in the nation, with retail and rental costumes for special occasions. A large collection of costumes for theatrical productions and opera are available, in addition to historical figures, Halloween, theme-related, and character costumes (such as action figures, television personalities, movie stars, and animal characters.) *13621 Inwood Rd., North, 972/404–0584. Closed Sun.*

13 *f-4*

DALLAS COSTUME SHOPPE

Established in the 1930s, this Deep Ellum store only rents costumes. You'll find outfits for reenactments, theatrical productions, parades and special occasions. *3905 Main St., Deep Ellum, 214/428–4613. No credit cards. Closed Sun.*

CRAFT & HOBBY SUPPLIES

6 *e-7*

HOBBY LOBBY

Glue sticks, acrylic paint, grapevine wreaths. Wax crystals, plastic model kits, pony beads. Whatever your hobby, this supply shop probably has what you need. Whatever the season, you can find a good variety of decorations, including plastic pumpkins, Christmas lights, and Easter baskets. *3616 Forest La., North, 214/902–8336.*

CRAFTS

10 *g-2*

CASA CAREYES

Blown glass, ceramics, and wrought iron pieces imported from Mexico are just samples of items found here. *2772 N. Henderson, East, 214/821–2937. Closed Sun.*

13 *b-4*

COSMO UNIVERSAL ART

Martin Martinez decorates license plates, tiles, and other items with unusual space photos. *West End Market Place, Downtown, 214/740–0639.*

13 *f-4*

SILVER FEATHER GALLERY

Shop for Native American jewelry, pottery, and other artifacts at this Deep Ellum store. *2540 Elm St., Deep Ellum, 214/752–7191. Closed Mon.*

CUTLERY & GADGETRY

6 *g-8*

CUTLERY COLLECTION

Carving a turkey just became easier with the popular German brand Wusthof Trident knife. You'll also find a broad selection of serrated knives, pocket knives, French collectibles, knife blocks, and knife sets. *534 NorthPark Center, North, 214/360–9076.*

DISCOUNT

6 *f-6*

DSW SHOES

This help-yourself 20,000 square foot store is filled with boxes of men's and women's dress and casual shoes—all inventory is displayed on the floor by size. You can find savings on name brand shoes, including Bass, Evan-Picone, and Mootsie Tootsies. Savings get even greater if you are lucky enough to find a shoe you like on the clearance rack at the back of the store. Also check out sock, hosiery, and handbag prices. *13548 Preston Rd., North, 972/233–9931.*

6 *f-5*

SAM'S CLUB

You have to purchase an inexpensive membership to shop here, but you soon recover the cost with what you save. You'll especially save on food items, including canned fruits and vegetables and frozen meats. However, be prepared to buy industrial-sized quantities to reap the savings benfefit. You can also pick up fresh flowers, usually for a fraction of what you pay elsewhere. *4150 Belt Line Rd., 972/934–9274.*

10 *f-1*

TUESDAY MORNING

This store opens four times a year for 40 to 80 days to sell housewares at 50–80% off the original retail price of brand-name merchandise such as Wedgwood, Samsonite, Steinbach, Imoges, and Lego. Merchandise includes bed linens, crystal and glassware, area rugs, luggage, toys, cookware, and bath accessories. *Hillside Shopping Center, 6465 Mockingbird, 214/828–1708.*

ELECTRONICS & AUDIO

6 *g-7*

BEST BUY

The largest volume specialty retailer of consumer electronics, personal computers, entertainment software and appliances, this megastore offers competitive prices on brand names such as Sony, Panasonic, Bose, JVC, Cannon, Olympus, Dell, and Compaq. Merchandise includes personal computers, phones, and fax machines for home office, stereo components, speakers, video games, photography equipment, and camcorders. Installation service of mobile electronics such as car stereos is available. *9378 N. Central Expressway, North, 214/696–2089, and other locations.*

10 *g-2*

RADIO SHACK

This national electronics chain mostly sells its own brand of electronic equipment and accessories, including batteries and adaptors, calculators and electronic office equipment, securing and home automation devises, telephones, pagers, wire, cable, hardware and tools. It also stocks some other name brand produces such as RCA televisions and speakers, Sony portable CD players, and a variety of brands of cellphones including Qualcom and Nokia. It offers extended warranties on many items. The repair department will service most major brands of audio equipment, telephones, computers, and all brands of VCRs. *Cityplace Market, 2415 N. Haskell Ave., Ste. 109, 214/824–3600.*

6 *f-6*

STEREO 2000

In business since 1982, this Galleria electronic and photographic store stocks all major brands of cameras, lenses, electronics, and telephones. Cameras range from Canon, Nikon and Olympus point-and-shoot 35mm lines to the same brands of professional models. Electronic merchandise ranges from Bose lifestyle speakers and Sony and Panasonic portable stereos to Uniden radar dectectors, and Panasonic portable palm theater DVDs. *Galleria, 13350 Dallas Pkwy., North, 972/387–8356.*

ETHNIC ITEMS

10 *d-6*

AFRICAN IMPORTS

African-American authors, including Michael Baisden and Melvin Williams, and artists, including Bibbs and Wak, are well represented here. The store also stocks CDs, clothing, and handmade scented candles. *3662 W. Camp Wisdom Rd., South, 972/296–9861.*

10 *f-4*

BLACK IMAGES BOOK BAZAAR

Founded in 1977, this store may be the oldest African-American book store in Texas. More than 29,000 titles ranging from black histories to fiction by black authors fill its shelves. The store also carries Kwanzaa supplies: kinara, unity cup and mat. *230 Wynnewood Village, Oak Cliff, 214/943–0142.*

6 *f-6*

RUSSIAN ISLAND

You will enjoy the warmth of these handmade Russian pieces, including brightly painted nested dolls, straw boxes, and flax dolls. *Galleria, 13350 Dallas Pkwy., North, 972/387–3310.*

EYEWEAR

6 *f-6*

EYEMASTERS

If you're in a hurry, stop here where you can get glasses in an hour. You can find designer frames—Polo, DKNY, Calvin Klein, Laura Ashley—as well as lightweight lens with scratch resistant and UV protection built in. Watch for frequent sales. *Valley View Center, North, 972/392–7570, and other locations.*

6 *g-7*

OPTICAL MART

This discount eyewear store stocks more than 400 colors and styles, including such designers as Oleg Cassini, Michael Jordan, and Cosmopolitan. You can save over 50% on eyeware, but it takes about a week to get your glasses. *10455 N. Central Expressway, #116B, North, 214/363–2988, and other locations.*

FABRICS

6 *f-6*

CALICO CORNERS

Adding a new look to your home just became easier with this store's ample fabric selection for slipcovers, draperies, upholstery, and bedspreads. Fabrics include cotton, damask, chenile, sheers, and silk. *12370 Inwood Rd., North, 972/ 386–5081.*

6 *e-5*

CUTTING CORNERS

This store carries thousands of different fabrics—cotton, sheers—to brighten any home décor. The store also stocks cord, polyester fill, and other needed supplies. *13720 Midway Rd., Farmers Branch, 972/233–1741.*

6 *e-7*

HANCOCK FABRICS

Whether shopping for satin or sailcloth, you'll find it here. This fabric store carries everything from knits to drapery materials. You can also find a variety of buttons, thread, and lace. A scissors sharpener visits the store monthly. *11888 Marsh La., North, 972/243–6094.*

6 *h-8*

JO-ANN FABRICS & CRAFTS

With all the colorful patterns and weaves found here, you will want to rush home to sew a new outfit. Fabrics include wool, silk, satin, cotton, and flannel. Expect a monthly visit from the scissor sharpener. *10233 E. Northwest Hwy., East, 214/503–8332.*

6 *f-8*

RICHARD BROOKS COUTURE FABRICS

You'll want to sew a really creative design from these fine fashion fabrics, including imported silk, cotton, and wool. *6131 Luther La., North, 214/ 739–2772. Closed Sun.*

FLOWERS & PLANTS

6 *g-5*

CALLOWAY'S

Brighten your landscape with this shop's selection of seasonal annuals, shrubs, trees, and other colorful flowers and plants. Free delivery within 10 miles of store with purchase of $50 or more. *8152 Spring Valley Rd., North, 972/ 994–0134.*

13 *e-4*

DALLAS FARMERS MARKET

Domestic and exotic flowers and plants for your garden can be found at this Downtown landmark. Seasonal produce from Texas farms runs the gamut from vine-ripened tomatoes to herb plants. Some vendors accept credit cards, while others do not. *1010 S. Pearl, Downtown, 214/939–2808.*

6 *e-8*

I LOVE FLOWERS

This florist specializes in bouquets of a wide variety of exotic, tropical and Holland flowers. The staff also provides decorating services for weddings and parties. *4347 W. Northwest Hwy., North, 214/357–9577. Closed Sun.*

6 *g-7*

NORTH HAVEN GARDENS

This garden shop is a North Dallas institution, having been in business since 1951. Colorful perennials, fragrant herbs, even aquatic plants are available here. You can also buy fresh flower arrangements. The store provides free delivery within a 5-mile radius and presents free lectures on weekends. *7700 Northaven Rd., North, 214/363–5316.*

FOOD & DRINK

bread & pastries

6 *g-8*

BLACK FOREST BAKERY

The Swiss Madrissa is the most popular cake, but you can't go wrong with any of the great tasting European creations topped with yummy whipped icing. You can buy a slice or the whole cake. Besides cakes and cookies, the bakery also sells breads, including German rye, French round, and Italian round. *5811 Blackwell St., North, 214/987–9090. Closed Sun.*

11 *a-1*

CHEESECAKE ROYALE

Kahlua cake and cheesecakes can be mailed anywhere in the United States, as can a Cheesecake Royale sampler containing two slices each of the following flavors: Amaretto, Chocolate, New York Plain, Strawberry, Black Forest, White Chocolate, Key Lime and Raspberry. *9016 Garland Rd., East, 214/328–9102. Closed Sun.*

13 *b-5*

THE COOKIE JAR

Eight varieties of cookies are available for gift giving or your own consumption in 2–pound tins: chocolate chip with or without pecans, white chocolate macadamia, Texas pecan cookies, peanut butter, oatmeal raisin, snickerdoodles, and pure sugar cookies. You can select from a variety of seasonal and holiday-theme tins or have one personalized by a resident artist for shipping anywhere in the United States. *223 West End Market Place, Downtown, 214/871–2166.*

10 *f-2*

LA MADELEINE FRENCH BAKERY

What once started as a boulangerie specializing in pastries and European breads on Mockingbird Lane has grown into a bakery/café serving authentic French country cuisine. The décor and furnishings resemble a French provincial village, with exposed beams, wood floors, and rustic earthenware. The bakery sells European rustic breads, French pastries, tarts, tartines, croissants, and French roast coffee. Staple café menu items include omelettes and French egg dishes for breakfast; Tomato Basil soup, sandwiches, and quiche for lunch; rosemary rotisserie chicken, soups, and caesar salad for dinner. *3906 Lemmon Ave. #110, Oak Lawn, 214/521–0183, and other locations.*

cheese

10 *f-2*

MARTY'S FOOD AND WINE INC.

This gourmet food and wine store stocks hundreds of different cheeses, including Brie, Morbier, and Raclette, sold by the pound or slice. It also has other gourmet items, including caviar, paté, smoked meats, smoked fish, takeout meals in its Café Tugogh, gift baskets including cheeses and wines, pastries, and cakes. Among its myriad wine selection, the wine store specializes in burgundies and hosts wine tastings and classes on Chardonnay, Burgundies, and Champagnes. *3316 Oak Lawn, Oak Lawn, 214/526–4070.*

chocolate & other candy

6 *f-6*

CANDY BARREL

Sure this store has delicious chocolates—coconut clusters, pecan clusters, peanut cluster, chocolate almonds—and former President Ronald Reagan's favorite, Goelitz jelly belly, but its specialty is salt water taffy. You can buy it by the pound. *Galleria, 13350 Dallas Pkwy., North, 972/980–8183, and other locations.*

13 *d-3*

DARVEAUX CONFECTIONNAIRE

These mouth-watering goodies, including chocolate covered raisins and peanuts and chocolate malted balls, will have you coming back for more. *Plaza of the Americas, 700 N. Pearl, Ste. N207, Downtown, 214/953–1120. Closed Sat., Sun.*

13 *b-5*

THE FUDGERY

This confectionery exclusively sells fudge in such flavors as chocolate, chocolate walnut, vanilla nut, vanilla, rocky road, chocolate caramel, peanut butter, praline, and low fat chocolate. *West End Market Place, 603 Munger Ave., Downtown, 214/880–0078. No credit cards.*

coffee & tea

10 *g-1*

COFFEE HAUS

This shop sells 50 different coffees by the pound and 60 different teas by the ounce. Near SNU, it's a favorite spot for the university crowd. *6411 Hillcrest Ave., Highland Park, 214/521–5282.*

6 *f-5*

THE CULTURED CUP

Choose from 40 different kinds of coffee and 95 different teas here. You can also attend a tea tasting or learn tea etiquette. *5346 Belt Line Rd., North, 972/960–1521. Closed Sun.*

10 *d-2*

STARBUCKS

This popular Seattle export is still the place for a quick or leisurely cup of java. You'll find coffee from about 20 different regions, including Guatemala, Ethiopia, and Kenya. *3715 Greenville Ave., East, 214/826–3912, and other locations.*

ethnic foods

6 *h-7*

ASIAN GROCERY

This Asian specialty market mostly carries hard-to-find Thai and Indonesian products including curry pastes, coconut milk, spices, and rice noodles; it also has a small section of Asian produce including fresh lemongrass, sprouts, Thai basil, Chinese broccoli, and Chinese parsley (cilantro). *9191 Forest La., East, 972/235–3038. No credit cards.*

6 *h-5*

ASIA WORLD SUPERMARKET

Since 1989, this market has served the oriental community by stocking as much as 4,000 items, including chile paste, tofu, 30 different kinds of fish (red snapper, trout, cod), sushi rice, and green tea. *400 N. Greenville Ave., Richardson, 972/235–3888.*

10 *h-1*

CARNIVAL FOOD STORES

The produce department is always heaped with fresh limes, papayas, avocados, and cacti leaves. Also look for fruit drinks and other items from Mexico. *6015 Lindsley Ave., East, 214/821–5327, and other locations.*

10 *f-3*

DALLAS TORTILLA & TAMALE FACTORY

This family-owned factory, where the corn is still hand ground, remains a favorite place to pick up tortillas, tamales, and other traditional Mexican dishes. *309 N. Marsalis Ave., South, 214/943–7681, and other locations.*

10 *g-2*

JIMMY'S FOOD STORE INC.

The homemade Italian sausage is a bestseller at this family owned market, which specializes in Italian and Caribbean meats and food products from Jamaica, Cuba, and Trinidad. Jimmy's also stocks more than 30 imported cheeses and pastas. *4901 Bryan St., East, 214/823–6180.*

10 *g-1*

WORLD SERVICE UK

When American substitutes just won't do, folks can head to this Lower Greenville Avenue shop for such British favorites as Gloucester cheese, potato scones, Heinz white beans, biscuits and HP sauces. During holidays, you can also find Christmas pudding and British Easter eggs. The six-year-old shop also has teapots and British videos. *1923 Greenville Ave., 214/827–8886.*

fish & seafood

10 *g-5*

BOB DAVIS SEAFOOD MARKET

This Oak Cliff shop sells hard-to-find fish, such as buffalo and drum fish, and favorites like perch and catfish. *3834 Lancaster Rd., Oak Cliff, 214/374–3215. Closed Sun.*

6 *f-7*

TJ'S FRESH SEAFOOD MARKET

The signature specialty is the cooked shrimp, but you'll also find 17 kinds of fresh fish—from salmon, trout and catfish to swordfish, halibut, sole, and tuna. *11661 Preston Rd., Ste. 149, North, 214/691–2369. Closed Sun.*

health food

7 *b-1*

FAMILY HEALTH FOOD STORE

Organically grown produce, breads, cooking oil, and tofu are favorites here. *121 N. Greenville Ave., Allen, 972/390–1148. Closed Sun.*

10 *d-1*

WHOLE FOODS MARKET

This store is well stocked with antibiotic-free meats, organically grown produce, and organic milk. Locals love the rice milk and salad bar. You can also buy vitamins and herbs. *2218 Greenville Ave., East, 214/824–1744, and other locations.*

herbs & spices

6 *d-5*

THE HERB MARKET

You'll find a lot more than sage, rosemary, and thyme here. The Herb Market sells 200 different herbs and spices, in bulk or dried. Plants are sold as well, if you want to grow your own. *1002 4th Ave., Carrollton, 972/446–9503. Seasonal hours: 7 days a week in the spring; otherwise closed Sun.*

meats & poultry

6 *e-8*

HONEYBAKED HAM CO.

Spiral-sliced hams ranging from 7-pound halves to 16-pound whole hams make this national chain the food source for holiday entertaining. A variety of side dishes, such as sweet potato souffle, spinach souffle, broccoli au gratin and potatoes au gratin round out the meal. To top everything off, you can choose from a small variety of seasonal pies, including apple, pecan and pumpkin. *4343 W. Northwest Hwy., Northwest, 214/351–1414. Closed Sun.*

6 *g-8*

KUBY'S SAUSAGE HOUSE INC.

Locals go to this well-stocked Highland Park meat store for such favorites as homemade sausage and beef tenderloin. *6601 Snider Plaza, Highland Park, 214/363–2231.*

6 *f-7*

OMAHA STEAKS

The filet mignon is tops, but you can also buy poultry, veal, lamb, and seafood in addition to steaks. *10854 Preston Rd., North, 214/368–7597, and other locations.*

13 *f-4*

RUDOLPH'S MARKET & SAUSAGE FACTORY

This old-fashioned meat market has been at this location since 1895. Locals rave about the homemade, preservative-free sausage and chili as well as pork chicken and beef cut to order. It is still family owned, although it changed families in 1947. *2924 Elm St., Deep Ellum, 214/741–1874. Closed Sun.*

nuts & seeds

13 *f-6*

HINES NUT CO.

You can buy fresh pecans here for your homemade pie, and pick up cashews, walnuts, sunflower seeds, and other nutty goodies for the drive home. *990 S. St. Paul St., Downtown, 214/939–0253. Closed weekends.*

6 *d-6*

TEXAS PECAN CO.

Raw or roasted, salted or unsalted, this store sells all kind of nuts as well as trail mixes and dry fruits. *2850 Satsuma Dr., North, 972/241–7878.*

produce

13 *e-4*

DALLAS FARMERS MARKET

You'll soon have your car loaded with fresh fruits and vegetables after strolling through the three drive-through sheds where 150 vendors set up shop. The market started in 1941 when area farmers came to the city to sell freshly harvested produce. If it's in season anywhere in the U.S., you'll find it here. Credit card acceptance is subject to each vendor's policy. *1010 S. Pearl St., Downtown, 214/939–2808.*

wines & spirits

13 *c-2*

GINO'S VINO WINE EMPORIUM

This wine store offers services such as tasting seminars and presentations at your home, personal wine cellar consulting, and traveling wine dinners for home or business. The wide selection of wines more or less equally represents worldwide vineyards such as South Africa, Australia, New Zealand, France, California, and Argentina. *2603–A Routh St., Uptown, 214/303–1616.*

10 *f-1*

MARTY'S

This store specializes in collector wines, but stocks about 2,000 wines, many available in half bottles, for more ordinary tastes. About 50% of the wine is French, 30% Californian, 10%, Italian, and the remainder various domestics and imports. *3316 Oak Lawn Ave., Oak Lawn, 214/526–7796. Closed Sun.*

6 *e-8*

POGO'S WINE & SPIRITS

The owners constantly travel, searching for new vintages of European and domestic wines. Beer-lovers will also find their favorite imports here. The store stocks 2,500 different wines and 300 brands of beer. *5360 W. Lovers La., Northwest, 214/350–8989. Closed Sun.*

10 *f-1*

TONY'S WINE WAREHOUSE & BISTRO

With 2,400 different wines to choose from, you'll surely find the perfect bottle to fit your taste. This shop specializes in handmade wines. You may have to take more than one class to sample them all. *2904 Oak Lawn Ave., Oak Lawn, 214/520–9464. Closed Sun.*

FRAMING

6 *f-8*

CHRIS' CRAFT CUSTOM FRAMING

No memorabilia is too large or small for this frame shop. From baptismal gowns and swords to such traditional items as photographs and artwork, this shop can frame nearly anything. For a suitable frame, choose from 5,000 samples. *5655 W. Lovers La., Park City, 214/351–4093. Closed Sun., Mon.*

6 *f-7*

EMPTY WALLS

This art gallery and framing store sells contemporary, traditional, abstract, aboriginal, and southwestern works of art, including original canvas paintings, signed and limited editions, and monoprints. You can choose from a thousand different frames, moldings, liners, mats, fillets, and fabrics. *217 Preston Royal Village, North, 214/369–9989. Closed Sun.*

6 *d-5*

THE FRAMING WAREHOUSE

With the help of professional framers, you can choose from dozens of selections of mat styles and frames such as Amante, Kingsford, Marquis, Renaissance, and Windswept. Standard turnover for framing is about a week, but staff can rush orders upon request. If you need to get something to fill that frame, check out the more than one thousand prints by artists such as Robert Bateman and Terry Isaac. *2760 E. Trinity Mills Rd., Carrollton, 972/416–3626. Closed Sun.*

10 *g-2*

FRITZ'S PICTURE FRAMING

In business since 1948, this frame shop specializes in triple mats and glass floating but can frame any size photo or poster with any kind of mat and wood, plexi, or metal frame within two weeks, even during the holiday season. *3426 Greenville Ave., East, 214/823–8974. Closed Sun.*

10 *g-2*

FRAMES MASTERS

Despite its upscale location, this shop's prices can easily compete with mass market frame shops. You can get any kind of framing done here. *5014 McKinney Ave., Uptown, 214/526–1700.*

GIFTS & SOUVENIRS

6 *g-8*

AMERICAN IMAGES

This small shop celebrates American's fascination with sports by selling such novelty items as golf bookends, sport-theme picture frames, and baseball clocks. *447 NorthPark Center, North, 214/361–5940.*

6 *f-6*

THE ANGEL GARDEN

Finding an angel is easy when shopping at this small boutique. From small lapel pins to foot-high statues, angels come in all sizes and prices. *Galleria, 13350 Dallas Pkwy., North, 972/387–8088.*

6 *f-6*

BEST OF DALLAS

If you're looking for a Texas icon, this store has a complete selection, including armadillo images in all shapes, sizes, and materials, from brass to glass. *Galleria, 13350 Dallas Pkwy., North, 972/385–1308.*

6 *f-6*

THE DOG COMPANY

Your canine friends will love this shop and you will you. You'll find snacks, bowls, and fancy collars for Fido, and dog calendars, picture frames, and stationery for you. *Galleria, 13350 Dallas Pkwy., North, 972/233–3647.*

6 *f-6*

FIELD OF DREAMS

From autographed jerseys and baseballs to basketballs, footballs, and hockey pucks, this is the ultimate collection store. Naturally, you'll find a large assortment of trading cards and autographed photographs. *Galleria, 13350 Dallas Pkwy., North, 972/934–9688.*

13 *f-4*

GIFTED

Chrome nightlights and replicas of 1950s pop art fill this retro-shopper's paradise. *2903 Elm St., Deep Ellum, 214/752–7839. By appointment on Mon.*

6 *f-6*

GUITARS & CADILLACS

You can find all your favorite Lone Star State icons—from bluebonnets to cowboy boots—emblazoned on everything from aprons to cuff links. It's also a good place to pick up a jar of hot salsa or chili fixings. *Galleria, 13350 Dallas Pkwy., North, 972/490–1311, and other locations.*

6 *f-6*

IN THE WIND

Whichever way the wind blows is just fine when you own a colorful wind sock, flag, or wind chimes from this shop. These colorful nylon pieces for all occasions brighten any Texas landscape. *Galleria, 13350 Dallas Pkwy., North, 972/233–3707.*

6 *f-6*

MARY ENGELBREIT

The old-fashioned characters of this St. Louis illustrator adorn her popular line of sentimental greeting cards, cookbooks and holiday books, figurines, calendars, T-shirts, and mugs—all of which can be purchased at her stores nationwide. *Galleria, 13350 Dallas Pkwy., North, 972/716–0644.*

6 *g-8*

THE MUSEUM COMPANY

Finding a gargoyle in Dallas isn't always easy, but here's a good place to start looking. There's also stained glass, stationary, cards, framed prints, and even Egyptian cat and the Loch Ness Monster replicas. *526 NorthPark Center, North, 214/987–3332.*

6 *g-8*

NATURAL WONDERS

This is the place to find a lava lamp or agate bookends. You'll also find a terrific assortment of science and nature items, including space blankets, fossils, water fountains, New Age music, and wildlife books. *919 NorthPark Center, North, 214/692–1766.*

6 *g-8*

OUR CHILDREN'S STORE

The money you spend here goes to 50 local agencies—such as Child Protective Services Community Partners, Inc. and Head Start of Greater Dallas—which provide basic needs and services to children in crisis. The store stocks an eclectic assortment of gift items, including hand-painted children's furniture, baby gifts, vases, frames, candles, Italian pottery, and designer lamps. All items are tagged by the participating agencies so you know who is benefiting from your sale. *437 NorthPark Center, North, 214/691–9411.*

6 *f-6*

THINGS REMEMBERED

You can mark special occasions with a gift that will last forever, including such favorites as an engraved silver picture frame for a wedding photo or a silver tree ornament for baby's first Christmas. *Galleria, 13350 Dallas Pkwy., North, 972/490–8196.*

6 *g-8*

TEXAS OUTPOST

From a Marilyn Moore autographed picture to your favorite college team, this store has all kind of stuff for you or a friend. Also included is any kind of Texas memorabilia imaginable. *736 NorthPark Center, North, 214/696–5998.*

6 *f-7*

YOGA FOR LIFE

In addition to yoga-related accessories such as tapes, mats, and workout clothes, this studio offers beginning, intermediate, prenatal, and advanced (yoga vinyasana) classes to fit any schedule. A gift shop sells unrelated collectibles such as ornaments and decorative porcelain pieces. *12835 Preston Rd., Ste. 427, North, 972/392–9642. Closed Sun.*

HOME FURNISHINGS

architectural artifacts

10 *g-3*

HMI ARCHITECTURAL SALVAGE & ANTIQUES

This antique store has one of the largest collections of architectural antiques in the Southwest, such as mantels, columns, corbels, fencing, cupolas, and decorative mouldings. It also carries gardenalia, handcrafted furniture, period reproductions, and unique metalwork. Period antiques include pieces such as 18th century hand-carved teak columns from India in the English colonial style and 19th century solid brass English bank doors. *200 Corinth St., South, 214/428–1888. Open Thurs.–Sat. only; other days by appointment.*

10 *f-2*

WRECKING BARN

This 16,000–square-foot building sells salvaged items dating from the 1850s. You'll find a good selection of stained glass windows, claw-foot bathtubs, barn beams, and columns. *1421 N. Industrial Blvd., #102, Northwest, 214/747–2777. Closed Sun., Mon.*

carpets & rugs

6 *h-7*

PEEK'S CARPET

The floor-covering market meets all your flooring needs, with thousands of high-end wool carpet samples—including hard to find floral and print designs—Oriental rugs, and wood and ceramic tiles. You can also arrange for carpet cleaning. *9780 LBJ Freeway, Ste. 110, North, 214/503–1324. Closed Sun.*

6 *d-5*

RUSSELL'S CARPET

This store sells first quality 100% nylon carpeting from Mohawk, Shaw, Ebbings, and Aladdin, and some area rugs. The attentive and knowledgeable staff will refer customers to cleaning services. *1609 S I–35E, Carrollton, 972/242–8556. Closed Sun.*

ceramic tiles

10 *d-1*

CERAMIC & MARBLE TILE OUTLET

This imported tile specialty store has one million square feet of tiles in a variety of colors and textures. Italian tiles dominate the selection, but you'll also find Mexican and Spanish tile—and all are priced at nearly half of the original retail price. Staff are familiar with the stock and advise customers on quantity, style, decoration, and installation. *909 Regal Row, Northwest, 214/951–9525.*

6 *d-7*

CERAMIC TILE INTERNATIONAL

You don't have to be a contractor to purchase tile here. The designer showroom displays 16–17 vignettes of room areas to demonstrate the various patterns and colors of ceramic tile available, from rustic to marblesque. Discontinued tiles can be purchased at 25% off their original price. Personnel have interior design backgrounds and give advise on care, installation, sealants, and contractor referrals. *2682 Forest La., North, 972/243–4465, and other locations. Closed Sun.*

china, glassware, porcelain, pottery, silver

6 *f-6*

BACHENDORF'S

Just looking at the hand-painted porcelain is reason enough to stop by this store. You can find a selection of Herend porcelain—the dinnerware of nobility—in such popular patterns as Windsor Garden, Poisson, and Chinese Bouquet. *Galleria, 13350 Dallas Pkwy., Ste. 1415, North, 972/392–9900, and other locations.*

6 *f-6*

CRATE & BARREL

Cast your eye on all kinds of glassware and dinnerware, including earthenware, stoneware and porcelain. Houseware accessories include woven clothes hampers and assorted baskets. *5221 Alpha Rd., North, 972/934–1800, and other locations.*

6 *f-5*

MIKASA HOME STORE

This spacious moderate to high-end dinnerware and crystal store with 30–foot ceilings displays hundreds of patterns of Mikasa dinnerware to fit any lifestyle or taste, from contemporary to traditional. Guest services help you match stemware with patterns, and a huge shipping and handling department will ensure that they get where they're going in one piece. Exclusive Mikasa brands include Christopher Stuart, Studio Nova, Home Beautiful, and Savoir Vive. They're the exclusive US carrier of French Sia silk flowers at outlet prices. *13710 Dallas Pkwy., North, 972/385–6183.*

6 *f-8*

SILVER VAULT

This eclectic silver shop sells everything from baby rattles, cigar cutters, antique trays, and to picture frames, tea sets, wine coasters, and wine coolers. Engraving and gift-wrapping serves are also offered. *5655 W. Lovers La., at Devonshire, 214/357–7115. Closed Sun.*

furniture & accessories

13 *f-4*

THE DESIGN COLLECTION

Need a wall sconce to finish your dining room? This eclectic gift, accessory and furniture store resembles an antique market. Discover treasures such as glass or brass vases and mirrors in a variety of sizes, chandeliers, lamps, and leather furniture by Highland House and Distinction Leather. The owner also operates an interior design business, Glen Boudreaux and Associates, on the second floor studio. You can arrange a consultation with him by appointment. *2614 Elm St., Deep Ellum, 214/752–0997. Closed Sun.*

6 *f-6*

FOREIGN OBJECTS

This store is know for its selection of Mexican home accents, including clay figures, vases, and handcrafted and hand-painted furniture. *Galleria, 13350 Dallas Pkwy., North, 972/702–0775, and other locations.*

6 *f-6*

FURNITURE FOREVER

Owner, designer Tony Villarreal uses only natural materials—limestone, marble, granite, wood, glass and metal—in these large one-of-a-kind pieces. Even accessories are custom made with pictures created from limestone dust. *2048 Valley View Center, 972/392–3609.*

13 *f-4*

HOME CONCEPTS

Its large selection of futons and frames can't be beat. You'll also find lamps, room screens, and coffee tables. *2900 Main St., Deep Ellum, 214/761–1872. Closed Mon.*

13 *f-4*

MARK & LARRY'S STUFF

This is the place to find modern designs—such as a Blue Phosphorus Electra lamp and a Milano chair and ottoman—that fit with any contemporary décor to Victorian replicas, including Tiffany-inspired lamps and natural horn cups. *2614 Elm St., Deep Ellum, 214/747–8833.*

6 *f-8*

RUTHERFORD'S DESIGN

With thousands of yards of fabric at your fingertips, brightening a window or covering a chair has never been easier. Many of the fabrics—woven, chintz, and silk—and trims are from Europe. Designers will help you pick the right color and texture for any décor. Furniture, lamps, and gift items are also available. *5647 W. Lovers La., 214/357–0888.*

13 *f-4*

THIRTY 60

If you prefer a modern décor, this Deep Ellum shop has vintage Herman Miller and Knoll pieces from the mid-20th century to funky new Panton chains, which are instant conversation pieces. *2924 Main St., Ste. 101, Deep Ellum, 214/742–3060. Closed Mon., Tues.*

6 *f-6*

TREES OF THE FIELD

This store is an affordable treasure chest of European luxuries for your home. Paintings, tapestries, bronzes, clocks, swords, and chess sets come from such places as France, Belgium, Italy, Spain, Hungary, and England. *Galleria, 13350 Dallas Pkwy., North, 972/701–0107.*

lamps & lighting

6 *d-8*

BERL'S LAMP & CHANDELIER SERVICE

Since the 1950s, this family-owned store has specialized in stocking hard-to-find lamps, such as Tiffany or Quzell. You can also have your antique lamps repaired here. *10760 Shady Tr., Ste. 200, 972/991–2000. Closed weekends.*

10 *h-1*

LAKEWOOD LIGHTING

Sue Sinclair, who started this lamp store in 1978, will answer your questions and help you pick out a lamp shade. For lamps, you can choose from one of the 500 discounted manufacturer's lamp samples. Lamp repair is also available. *341 Hillside Village, North, 214/826–5980. Closed Sun.*

paint & wallpaper

6 *f-6*

THE WALLPAPER SOURCE & MORE

This emporium stocks more than 1,200 wallpaper, and has a large library of wallpaper catalogs for custom ordering. You can also pick out matching fabric for curtains or furniture. *612 Preston Forest Shopping Center, North, 214/987–2369. Closed Sun.*

HOUSEWARES & HARDWARE

6 *h-8*

THE CONTAINER STORE

A godsend for the time and space challenged, this 22,000 square foot store stocks thousands of innovative and multifunctional products to organize and streamline your life. During their first year salespersons receive 185 hours of training which helps them to work with customers and assess their organization needs. The store is organized in nine departments including closet, kitchen, home office, garage, laundry room (such as chrome clothes hampers and mesh wash bags), the media store, drawer systems, shelving (such as birch Skandia), and Elfa , a popular multifunctional design of mix-and-match flexible wire shelving. *7700 W. Northwest Hwy., North, 214/373–3131, and other locations.*

6 *e-8*

ELLIOTT'S HARDWARE

If you're stuck with a repair problem, seek advice from the friendly folks at this store. They also carry all the tools and supplies you'll need to repair a plumbing problem or add a new light switch. *4901 Maple Ave., Northwest, 214/634–9900, and other locations. Closed Sun.*

6 *e-8*

THE HOME DEPOT

From the smallest nails to the largest table saws, this massive warehouse excels in home improvement supplies. You can buy your wallpaper here, then take classes to learn how to hang it. Indeed, this store stocks just about everything you need to build a house—lumber, bathroom fixtures, kitchen cabinets, lighting—and landscape it—tree, plants, flowers, fencing and stepping stones. *6110 Lemmon Ave., Northwest, 214/654–9939, and other locations.*

JEWELRY

13 *d-5*

FARRAR JEWELRY

Platinum and diamond duos are a tough pair to resist at this high-end store, in business since 1947. *1226 Commerce St., Downtown, 214/748–4391. Open Tues.–Fri, Sun., and second Sat. of each month.*

6 *f-6*

HELZBERG DIAMONDS

This Missouri-based jeweler carries necklaces, rings, and earrings made of diamonds, precious and semi-precious stones, including sapphires, emeralds and rubies. Many staff members are certified diamontologists and certified gemologists and can advise the novice purchaser about cut, clarity, color, and carat weight. Service includes free professional jewelry repair, inspection and refurbishing for up to a year after purchase. *Valley View Center, North, 972/934–0794.*

6 *f-6*

THE TURQUOISE LADY

Native American Indians leave no stone unturned when crafting sterling silver jewelry, adding turquoise, coral, lapis, and onyx to fine crafted necklaces, bracelets, earrings, and rings. There's also an assortment of Native American arts and crafts. *Galleria, 13350 Dallas Pkwy., North, 972/934–2855.*

LEATHER GOODS & LUGGAGE

6 *f-6*

BAG 'N BAGGAGE

This upscale chain stocks a full line of leather luggage, billfolds, desk sets, and travel accessories, and hard-to-find items such as opera glasses, manicure sets, and magnifying glasses. *2142 Valley View Center, 972/233–6216, and other locations.*

6 *f-6*

FOREVER LEATHER & LUGGAGE

A hefty selection of Brighton handbags, Ricardo luggage, Jansport backpack, and Brenthaven briefcases line the wall of this store. *2010 Valley View Center, 972/726–8688.*

LINENS

6 *g-8*

APRIL CORNELL

In addition to table and bed linens, ironware and furniture, pottery and glassware, this women's store carries five apparel collections: a classic collection with signature floral prints; April Too, with plus sizes; the Pudding shop for petites; Cornelloki, a little girls' clothing line; and Mother and Daughter outfits. April Cornell fabrics include crinkled crepe, boucle, brocade, jacquard, panne velvet, organdy, and satin stripe georgette, to name a few. *1014 NorthPark Center, North, 214/750–8338.*

6 *f-8*

THE LINEN GALLERY

Fine European bed and table linens is this upscale boutique's specialty. You'll also find a variety of tabletop accessories—plate stands, candles, candlesticks, and frames—and bathroom accessories—wastebaskets, shower curtains, towels, and soap dishes. *7001 Preston Rd., Park Cities, 214/522–6700. Closed Sun.*

6 *f-7*

LINENS N' THINGS

Give your bedroom a new look with matching sheets and a comforter or brighten up the bath with new towels. All kinds of home accessories—soap dishes, wastebaskets, shower rods—are available here in the latest designer colors. *10720 Preston Rd., North, 214/265–8651, and other locations.*

10 *g-1*

PEACOCK ALLEY

This small specialty store carries fine European bed linens, duvets, covers, and coverlets primarily in natural shades: white, ivory, and taupe. Aside from their line of 350-thread Egyptian cotton sheets you'll also find Greenhorn Linens. *3210 Armstrong, Knox-Henderson, 214/520–6736. Closed Sun.*

MAPS

10 *e-1*

MAPSCO & TRAVEL CENTERS

Dallas is a big city. Having one of these easy-to-use maps will help you negotiate your way through the "Big D." The store also stocks national and international maps. *5308 Maple Ave., Oak Lawn, 214/219–6277, and other locations. Closed weekends.*

6 *g-8*

RAND MCNALLY MAP AND TRAVEL STORE

A household name in travel aids, Rand sells maps, guidebooks, and travel accessories. *NorthPark Center, North, 214/987–9941.*

MEMORABILIA

6 *h-4*

BRASS REGISTER

Jukeboxes, slot machines, and coke machines give this collectibles store a retro feel. *610 James Dr., Richardson, 972/231–1386. Closed Sun.*

6 *f-5*

FORESTWOOD ANTIQUE MALL

One booth specializes in airline memorabilia and another in Coke stuff. You'll also find plenty of other all-American nostalgia pieces scattered among other booths. *5333 Forest La., 972/661–0001.*

10 *g-1*

LULA B'S ANTIQUE MALL

Lulu's selection of records will really send you—right back to the 50s, 60s and 70s. Look for other collectible items including costume jewlery from the 1950s. *2004 Greenville Ave., East, 214/824–2185.*

MINIATURES

13 *b-5*

AMERICAN MUSEUM OF MINIATURE ARTS

From pieces of fruit to tiny books, everything needed to turn a dollhouse into a home is available in miniature. *West End Market Place, 2001 N. Lamar, Downtown, 214/969–9311. Closed Mon.*

6 *f-6*

THROUGH THE KEYHOLE

This emporium is filled with millions of tiny items, including accessories to build a dollhouse. *625 Preston Forest Shopping Center, North, 214/691–7467. Closed Sun.*

MISCELLANY

6 *e-7*

MAGIC LAND

This store, in business since 1915, is packed with magic tricks, costumes, wigs, and gag gifts. *603 Park Forest Shopping Center, North, 972/241–9898. Closed Sun.*

13 *b-5*

MAGIC MAX

This full-line magic shop sells card tricks, stage tricks, pranks and gags, such as light bulbs that light up in your hand or mouth. Many items are available by mail order off the store's website, www.magicmax.com. *West End Market Place, Downtown, 214/922–0004.*

MUSIC

cds, tapes & vinyl

6 *f-6*

RECORD TOWN

With all kinds of music in stock, you will find whatever suits your taste among the thousands of CDs and tapes. *Galleria, 13350 Dallas Pkwy., North, 972/385–7089, and other locations.*

6 *f-6*

SAM GOODY

This national music and small electronics chain sells CD and cassette recordings of rock, R&B, gospel, country, jazz, new age, classical, and latin artists. Other merchandise includes blank cassettes and CDs, films on videotape and DVD, portable CD players by Sony and Aiwa, and sports and recreational headphone sets. *Galleria, 13350 Dallas Pkwy., North, 972/386–8017, and other locations.*

6 *f-6*

SHAKESPEARE, BEETHOVEN & COMPANY

Classical and jazz music is more than an afterthought at this 5,000 square foot store that lives up to its moniker with an extensive selection of recordings on both CD and DVD. A full line of books in a library setting of green carpeting and wood shelving runs the gamut of subjects from fiction and nonfiction to philosophy. An annual "opera karaoke" in August draws amateur singers, judges from the Dallas Opera, as well as spectators. *Galleria, 13350 Dallas Pkwy., Ste. 3200, North, 972/387–1720.*

7 *b-7*

MEMORIES RECORDS

If you're a music collector, you're sure to find something appealing in this store's selection of vintage records, 78s, CDs, 8–track tapes, and cassette tapes of jazz, rhythm and blues, rock, comedy, showtunes, soundtracks and reggae. Keep an eye out for sales. *112 E. Centerville Rd., Garland, 972/864–5698. Closed Sun., Mon.*

musical instruments

6 *f-5*

BROOK MAYS MUSIC CO.

This retailer carries a wide variety of musical instruments, including Yamaha, Ibanez and Martin guitars and amplifiers, band and orchestra instruments such as Bach Stradivarius trumpets and clarinets, professional keyboards, professional audio and recording equipment, drums and percussion. They also stock piano vocal sheet music; the LBJ store carries guitar, band and orchestra sheet music. *5100 Beltline, Ste. 864, Dallas, 972/991–4496.*

6 *f-6*

5756 LBJ Freeway, 972/233–9633.

10 *d-6*

6960 Marvin D. Love Freeway, 214/330–0453.

8605 Carpenter Freeway, 214/631–0923.

6 *h-7*

DALLAS PIANO WAREHOUSE

In addition to grand and upright pianos by Bosendorfer, Schimmel, Pranberger, Bergmann, and Young Chang, this full-service piano store also sells Kurzweil, Technics and Van Koevering digital pianos, and Technic electronic keyboards. Seven full-time technicians will rebuild and service all merchandise, and all prices include delivery. *9292 LBJ Freeway, North, 972/231–4607.*

6 *h-8*

MARS SUPERSTORE

This 35,000 square foot chain retailer carries a full line of musical instruments, including brass, woodwind, percussion, recorders, keyboards, and Gibson and Fender guitars. In addition, it sells GBL, Roland, and Yamaha speakers and amplifiers, and recording and sound equipment. *8081 Walnut Hill La., North, 214/361–8155.*

NEEDLEWORK & KNITTING

6 *h-8*

KEY STITCHES

Look here for silk ribbon as well as yarn, needles, and patterns. The shop also offers needlepoint classes. *6333 E. Mockingbird La., Ste. 151, East, 214/826–2101. Closed Sun., Mon.*

6 *f-8*

NEEDLE IN A HAYSTACK

Come here for the yarn selection and hand-painted canvases. You can also have your piece blocked and finished here. *6911 Preston Rd., North, 214/528–2850. Closed Sun.*

NEWSPAPERS & MAGAZINES

6 *e-7*

ROY'S WEBB & FOREST LANE NEWSSTAND

Dallas' largest newsstand of 4,000 titles stocks not only out-of-state newspapers but also hard-to-find British and Canadian magazines. *3128 Forest La., North, 972/241–0280.*

PETS & PET SUPPLIES

6 *h-8*

PETSMART

Stop here and treat your pet to a corduroy dog bone or a container of spray catnip. The store stocks dog, cat, fish and bird food, and offers obedience classes and veterinary and grooming services. *6301 Abrams Rd., East, 214/349–9071.*

6 *e-8*

PETCO

Whether you own dog, cat, reptile, or other small animals, stop here for your supplies and pet treats. *4325 Lovers La., North, 214/522–4893.*

PHOTO EQUIPMENT

6 *g-8*

COOTER'S VILLAGE CAMERA STORE

This family-owned and -operated store, in business since 1941, stocks all major brands of cameras from point-and-shoot 35mm to professional single-lens reflex cameras, and camera accessories for both traditional and electronic formats including Cannon, Nikon, Lyca and Olympus. It also carries a full line of Cannon digital video cameras and a full line of telescopes. The store offers in-house processing services, takes passport photos, and will ship merchandise out of state. *12 Highland Park Village, Highland Park, 214/521–4553. Closed Sun.*

6 *d-7*

WOLF CAMERA

Besides stocking popular brand cameras, including digital and camcorders, it's also a good place to make an instant reprint of a favorite photo. They also will match competitors' prices. *11171 Harry Hines Blvd., Northwest, 972/241–0582, and other locations.*

PORTRAITS

6 *f-6*

ZOOM IN ZOOM OUT PHOTOS

This portrait studio takes speedy color and black and white portraits against a variety of trendy backdrops, from a big heart to daisies to butterflies. Depending upon the size of your photos (as large as 11 × 14) and volume of your order, they'll have your photos ready within the same day. *2040 Valley View Center, Ste. 2034, 972/934–9010. No credit cards.*

POSTCARDS

13 *b-4*

LITTLE TASTE OF TEXAS

The destination of choice for Texas memorabilia, including Texas-shape magnets, postcards, shotglasses, ceramic armadillos, and Texas-shaped ornaments, mugs, and ash trays. You can also buy gourmet gift baskets filled with tortilla chips and any of 100 varieties of hot sauces. *West End Market Place, 603 Munger Ave.. Downtown, 214/754–0877.*

POSTERS

6 *f-6*

DECK THE WALLS

Every cranny is filled with affordable art, including posters, limited edition prints, and originals. Look for such Southwest favorites as Ansel Adams and G. Harvey. Art pieces can be purchased framed or unframed. Custom framing is also available. *Galleria, 13350 Dallas Pkwy., North, 972/991–6004, and other locations.*

6 *f-6*

PRINTS PLUS

Framed and unframed posters and prints ranging from sports to fine arts fill this small shop. If you need a picture framed in a hurry, this store also provides same day service. *Galleria, 13350 Dallas Pkwy., North, 972/233–7560.*

SPORTING GOODS & CLOTHING

6 *f-5*

OSHMAN'S SPORTING GOODS

Headquartered in Houston, this sporting goods store carries equipment apparel and accessories for virtually every sport there is including archery, camping, hiking, fishing, football, in-line skating, hockey, paint ball, skiing, tennis, and volleyball. *15490 Dallas Pkwy., North, 972/991–3533.*

6 *f-5*

PLAY IT AGAIN SPORTS

You'll find discounted prices on new sports equipment at these independently-owned franchises. This branch specializes in ice hockey, baseball, golf and fitness equipment. *14902 Preston Rd., Ste. 506, North, Dallas, 972/720–9666, and other locations.*

boating

6 *f-7*

WEST MARINE

Ropes, anchors, sailboat hardware, fishing equipment, water skis: You'll find everything you need here except the boat. It's the largest of its kind in Dallas. *10400 N. Central Expressway, North, 214/265–7776.*

bowling

11 *a-1*

AMF BOWLING CENTERS

Helping you find a ball that's the perfect fit and weight for you is the staff's specialty. You can also pick out a bag and shoes to go with your new ball. *11336 Jupiter, East, 214/327–4616, and other locations.*

camping

6 *f-8*

MOUNTAIN HIDEOUT

Open since the 1970s, this shop stocks sleeping bags, stoves, tents, camping equipment, and backpacks. *5643 W. Lovers La., North, 214/350–8181.*

6 *h-8*

WHOLE EARTH PROVISION CO.

All you need is a wilderness after shopping for supplies here. The store caters to backpackers, stocking a good selection of tents, stoves, clothes, and shoes. *5400 E. Mockingbird, North, 214/824–7444.*

fishing & tackle supplies

6 *f-8*

FISHIN' WORLD

After getting outfitted with just the right tackle, you may not even need a fish story the next time you go fishing. You'll find a big assortment of fresh and saltwater tackle here. *4609 W. Lovers La., Northwest, 214/358–4941. Closed Sun.*

6 *f-7*

ORVIS CO.

Hooks, rod and reels, flies, and rugged clothing fill this shop's shelves. For novice fisherman, fly-fishing classes are offered. *10720 Preston Rd., North, 214/265–1600.*

6 *f-8*

WESTBANK ANGLERS

This shop doesn't guarantee you'll land a big one, but you can leave here with the right equipment to haul in a whopper. You'll find rods by Sage, Scott and Abel, and Simms wading jackets and boots. *5370 W. Lovers La., Ste. 320, Northwest, 214/350–4665.*

golf

10 *e-2*

EDWIN WATTS GOLF SHOP

Pro-line clubs, bags, balls, shoes, belts, and everything else you need to play the game is available. *2320 Stemmons Tr., Northwest, 214/352–9431.*

6 *e-6*

GOLFSMITH GOLF CENTER

Custom-made golf clubs and repair are the specialties of this superstore that also carries golf club components, shoes and apparel, and bags and gloves all in major brands such as Callaway and Cobra. Before you buy test the clubs out in the indoor hitting area. *4141 LBJ Freeway, North, 972/991–9255.*

6 *f-5*

PLAY IT AGAIN SPORTS

These two stores carry a fine assortment of golf equipment—clubs, putters, bags—at discounted prices. *14902 Preston Rd., North, 972/720–9666, and other locations.*

6 *d-7*

WALLY'S DISCOUNT GOLF SHOP

Wally's doesn't skimp when it comes to golf clubs. You'll find both Callaway and Cobra clubs, and a complete line of shoes, apparel, bags and gloves for both men and women by Footjoy, Adidas, Nike, Lady Fair, and Dexter. All of the staff are avid golfers and can advise you on equipment and apparel. *9090 N. Stemmons, North, 214/637–2944. Closed Sun.*

running

10 *f-2*

LUKE'S

What started as a hobby is now a huge business with thousands of brand-name running shoes just waiting for the right feet. Besides shoes, the store also stocks running gear and accessories, including reflective vests. *3607 Oak Lawn Ave., Oak Lawn, 214/528–1290.*

skating

6 *h-8*

SUN & SKI SPORTS

This water and snow skiing specialty store stocks slalom skis by K2 and Solomon and skiwear by K2 , Rossignol, Solomon and Nordica. In season, you'll also find a full stock of water-skis by HO and Connolly in addition to wetsuits, goggles, and gloves. The store also carries bicycles and in-line skates by Bauer, Rollerblade, and Obermeyer; you can even try the skates before you buy in the store's inline skating demo area. All skis and bindings, and skate bearings and wheels are serviced at the store. *5500 Greenville Ave., East, 214/696–2696.*

skiing

7 *a-4*

FLATLANDERS SKI & SPORTS

This store rivals Warming Hut Ski & Skate as the oldest ski stores in Texas. Both opened in 1976. You'll find brand names at discounted prices. You will find snow skis, snow boards, and ski clothing. *1750 Alma Rd., Richardson, 972/690–4579. Closed Sun., except March–Oct. when open 7 days a week.*

6 *h-8*

SUN & SKI SPORTS

With its knowledgeable staff, this shop ensure you know everything about snow and water skis before you buy. *5500 Greenville Ave., East, 214/696–2696.*

7 *a-4*

WARMING HUT SKI & BOARD

Despite the name, you won't find any skates here. The store only carries snow and water skis, snow and water boards, and accessories for both winter and summer sports. *331 N. Central Expressway, Richardson, 972/234–6088.*

swimwear

6 *f-6*

SPEEDO AUTHENTIC FITNESS

The Speedo brand of body-hugging swimwear is a favorite with Olympic and recreational swimmers. But the Australian swim wear company has gone beyond swimming by stocking a selection of workout wear. *Galleria, 13350 Dallas Pkwy., Ste. 2280, 972/404–7450, and other locations.*

STATIONERY & OFFICE SUPPLIES

office supplies

6 *f-6*

FRANKLIN COVEY

This is the store to get organized. With such helpful gadgets as an electronic organizer, leather planner and whimsical reminders, you will always stay on schedule. *Galleria, 13350 Dallas Pkwy., North, 972/980–7345, and other locations. Closed Sun.*

6 *f-6*

SUCCESSORIES

Motivation is this store's specialty. Leaders can find plenty of props to build team spirt: positive thinking themes are found on cups, notepads, mouse pads, pens, clocks, and just about every imaginable item that fits in an office. *Galleria, 13350 Dallas Pkwy., North, 972/980–1050.*

pen & pencils

6 *f-6*

COLORADO PEN COMPANY

Write with flair after selecting the right pen. Look for such hard-to-find brands as Cartier, Pelikan, and Aurora. *Galleria, 13350 Dallas Pkwy., North, 972/991–4110, and other locations.*

stationery

6 *g-8*

CRANE & CO.

This story carries its own brand of 100% cotton fiber paper. You can also order custom invitations as well as engraved stationery. It's also a good place to find bookmarks and letter openers. *401 NorthPark Center, North, 214/696–1291.*

6 *f-6*

PAPERTREE, LIMITED

The friendly staff at this Galleria store will personalize stationary and print invitations while you shop. The store also carries handmade cards and picture frames. *Galleria, 13350 Dallas Parkway, North, 972/980–1113.*

TOBACCONISTS

6 *h-8*

UP IN SMOKE

Even if you don't use tobacco products, you will still enjoy the rich aroma of this shop with its handmade pipes, mahogany humidors, blended pipe tobacco, and imported cigars. *7700 W. Northwest Hwy., North, 214/368–0433, and other locations.*

TOOLS

6 *f-6*

BROOKSTONE

Hard-to-find-tools—a one-piece multiple wrench set, branch rachet loppers, trash funnel—are an anomaly here. You'll soon wonder how you ever did without some of the nifty items that promise to make your life simpler. *2251 Valley View Center, North, 972/788–0514, and other locations.*

TOYS & GAMES

6 *f-6*

DOLL HAVEN

From $15 machine-washable dolls to $2,500 collectibles, this doll shop brings out the little girl in most women. Mother and daughter team Sharon Hanson and Stacey Purcell opened the cozy store in 1991, and stacked it to the ceiling with such popular favorites as Lee Middleton baby dolls and Daddy's Long Legs African American dolls. *Galleria, 13350 Dallas Pkwy., North, 972/404–9501.*

6 *f-6*

GAME CHEST

This store's assortment of puzzles are bound to make you think twice about their solutions. Puzzles come in all types of materials—wood, paper, foam, plastic, wire—and for all ages from youngsters to adults. You'll also find such traditional favorites as playing cards, dominoes, checkers, and chess. *2137 Valley View Mall, North, 972/490–7814.*

6 *f-6*

NOODLE KIDOODLE

Tell the kids touching is permitted. The staff here actually encourages kids to try out toys. The emphasis is on non-violate, educational toys, such as music blocks, tabletop easels, and computer software for youngsters. *Galleria, 13350 Dallas Pkwy., North, 972/404–4550.*

6 *f-6*

TEDDY BEAR DEPOT

Dangling from key chains, clinging to drinking straws, and perched on shelves, bears are everywhere. Some bears are soft and cuddly, just waiting for a hug; others are pretty ceramic or plastic figurines perfect for decorating. *2228 Valley View Center, North, 972/934–2327.*

VIDEOS

7 *a-8*

BLOCKBUSTER

With more than 10,000 video and DVD movie titles to rent and buy, this national chain is found within a 10–minute drive of nearly every neighborhood in the country. Current releases line the periphery of the store, which also carries science fiction, classics, comedies, dramas, horror, biographies, foreign films, and children's videos. On a weekly basis, selected new releases on video are guaranteed to be in stock and available for rental. *6760 Abrams Rd., 214/340–4133, and other locations.*

STARLIGHT VIDEO

When you tire of the same old movies, stop by this store for hard-to-find classics, including silent films and foreign flicks. The store stocks 13,000 titles, so make a big bowl of popcorn for your private film fest. *13378 Preston Rd., North, 972/702–9477.*

WATCHES & CLOCKS

6 *f-6*

FOSSIL

This store has lots of watches to choose from, including D-Teq and Bit Tic. You can also find an assortment of leather belts, purses, and handbags. *Galleria, 13350 Dallas Pkwy., North, 972/386–4212.*

6 *f-6*

WATCH STATION

Shopping for the perfect watch just became easier. This store sells sport, designer, classic, and pocket watches. Prices range from $50 to $1,200. *Galleria, 13350 Dallas Pkwy., North, 972/851–7238.*

6 *f-6*

WORLD TIME

Jaguar, Swiss Winger, and Hamilton are among the 22 brands of watches stocked here. The store also repairs watches. *Galleria, 13350 Dallas Pkwy., North, 972/980–7202.*

shopping areas: fort worth/ mid-cities

While the Fort Worth/Mid-cities area doesn't have the depth of shopping found in Dallas, its supply of retailers is growing as steadily as Tarrant County's real estate is booming. All the major chains are here, as well as good, home-grown shops. In recent years, attention has come back to downtown Fort Worth from the suburbs, thanks to the booming success of Sundance Square, home to a bevy of boutiques, and to the growing popularity of the Cultural District, where shops specialize in everything for the home. Along University Drive and in such malls as Ridgmar, Hulen and The Parks at Arlington, shoppers can find all the Ann Taylor, Williams-Sonoma, Pottery Barn, and Nine West goodies they need. For Neiman Marcus, look to Ridgmar; for Nordstrom, it's NorthEast Mall. The surrounding Mid-cites are following suit. Many major chains are springing up in this quickly growing area.

DEPARTMENT STORES

14 *a-7*

DILLARD'S

See Department Stores: Dallas. *Ridgmar Mall, 2060 Green Oaks Blvd., Fort Worth, 817/731–0856, and other locations.*

8 *g-5*

FOLEY'S

See Department Stores: Dallas. *Hulen Mall, 4800 S. Hulen St., Fort Worth, 817/294–1200, and other locations.*

9 *e-2*

JC PENNEY

See Department Stores: Dallas. *North-East Mall, 1101 Melbourne Rd., Hurst, 817/731–0856, and other locations.*

9 *f-5*

MERVYN'S

See Department Stores: Dallas. *The Parks at Arlington, 3811 S. Cooper St., Arlington, 817/467–0200, and other locations.*

8 *g-5*

MONTGOMERY WARD

See Department Stores: Dallas. *Hulen Mall, 4800 S. Hulen St., Fort Worth, 817/294–1200, and other locations.*

14 *a-7*

NEIMAN MARCUS

See Department Stores: Dallas. *Ridgmar Mall, 2060 Green Oaks Rd., Fort Worth, 817/738–3581.*

9 *e-2*

NORDSTROM

See Department Stores: Dallas. *North-East Mall, 1101 Melbourne Rd., Hurst, 817/284–3427.*

9 *f-5*

SEARS

See Department Stores: Dallas. *The Parks at Arlington, 3811 S. Cooper St., Arlington, 817/467–0200, and other locations.*

MALLS & SHOPPING CENTERS

15 *c-6*

FORT WORTH OUTLET SQUARE

The lower level of downtown Fort Worth's Tandy Center has been renovated into an outlet shoppers' paradise. Find deep discounts on Factory Brand Shoes, London Fog, Mikasa, Nine West, Samsonite, Spiegel, and a lot more. Several fast dining choices are here, too, as is an ice-skating rink. *Thockmorton St. at 2nd St., Fort Worth, 817/415–3720.*

5 *h-5*

GRAPEVINE MILLS

A monument to outlet shopping, 1.5 million square feet of retail space near DFW Airport is home to more than 200 popular stores. Bed, Bath & Beyond, Old Navy, Mikasa, Virgin Records, Guess, Warner Bros., The Icing, Books-A-Million, J.C. Penney Outlet, all reside here. There's a 30–screen movie complex, numerous theme restaurants, and the high-tech wonderland, Gameworks. *3000 Grapevine Mills Pkwy., Grapevine, 972/724–4900.*

8 *g-5*

HULEN MALL

Fort Worth's first upscale, specialty mall has Foley's, Dillard's, Montgomery Ward, and all the requisite stores, such as the Gap, Victoria's Secret, and the Body Shop. *4800 S. Hulen St., Fort Worth, 817/294–1200.*

9 *e-2*

NORTHEAST MALL

This mall at the junction of the Airport Freeway and Loop 820 is home to Nordstrom, Dillard's, and Sears. *1101 Melbourne Rd., Hurst, 817/284–3427.*

9 *f-5*

THE PARKS AT ARLINGTON

This giant but attractive spread of stores includes Dillard's, Mervyn's, Sears, Foley's, and J.C. Penney. Near restaurants and freeways, it's become quite a busy spot. *3811 S. Cooper St., Arlington, 817/467–0200.*

14 *a-7*

RIDGMAR MALL

Newly renovated and vigorously upgraded, the specialty center in west Fort Worth is home to Neiman Marcus, Foley's, and Dillard's, and numerous specialty stores. Valet parking is a perk during Christmas shopping. *2060 Green Oaks Rd., Fort Worth, 817/731–0856.*

8 *h-4*

UNIVERSITY PARK VILLAGE

Red-bricked walls and exteriors encase this western-styled center, appropriately adorned with steer head, silver star design details, and a copper cupola. Retailers include Pottery Barn, Williams Sonoma, Ann Taylor, Nine West, Barnes & Noble, Banana Republic, and Mi Mi Maternity. Good dining is found at Blue Mesa and La Piazza. *1612 S. University Dr., Fort Worth, 817/332–5700.*

specialty shops

ANTIQUES

flea markets & antique dealers

14 *h-8*

MONTGOMERY STREET ANTIQUE MALL AND TEA ROOM

Hundreds of booths fill this old warehouse with everything from stained glass window inserts and lovely old armoires to vintage glass and tin-fronted pie safes. The onsite dining rooms serves soups, salads, and sandwiches. *2601 Montgomery St., Fort Worth, 817/735–9685.*

TRADER'S VILLAGE

This year-round weekend flea market is the largest in Texas, where more than 1,800 dealers gather every Saturday and Sunday to sell a variety of furniture, dishware, antique and newly-crafted clothing, quilts, ceramics, porcelain, and more. Rides for kids and food and beverage vendors make it appealing to spend an afternoon sifting through the masses for buried treasures. *2602 Mayfield Rd., Fort Worth, 972/647–2331.*

ART SUPPLIES

15 *a-6*

ASEL ART SUPPLY

You'll find a fine selection of paints, canvases, drafting materials, and graphic art tools here. *3001 W. 7th St., Fort Worth, 817/335–8168.*

14 *h-6*

3204–D Camp Bowie Blvd., Fort Worth 817/335–8168.

9 *g-4*

827 Oram St., Arlington, 817/274–8282.

BASKETS

8 *e-5*

GRISSOM'S BASKET CASE

This off-the-beaten path stocks thousands of baskets from around the world in every shape, size, and color. *9524 Hwy. 80 W., Fort Worth, 817/244–2237.*

BEAUTY

fragrances & skin products

15 *c-5*

MARIE ANTOINETTE PARFUMERIE

Lavish yourself with the pleasures of Caswell-Massey goods, or find a new favorite fragrance from among numerous European lines. Massage therapy services and aromatherapy goods are also available. *101 W. 2nd St., Fort Worth, 817/332–2888.*

hair care

14 *b-8*

SALLY BEAUTY SUPPLY

This chain of stores throughout Texas offers everything you need in salon-quality hair products, such as Paul Mitchell and Sebastian and numerous other lines. Those funky crimping irons are here, too, as are OPI nail goods, paraffin waxes for baby-soft feet, and manicure tools. *6228 Camp Bowie Blvd., Fort Worth, 817/731–6501, and other locations.*

BICYCLES

8 *h-6*

BICYCLES INC.

One of the largest bike retailers in Texas, Bicycles stocks and repairs Trek, Schwinn, Diamondback, Merlin, Kelir, Waterford, Lemond, and many others. *5039 Granbury Rd., Fort Worth, 817/292–2911, and other locations.*

BOOKS

general

15 *c-5*

BARNES & NOBLE

The national chain has one of its largest stores in downtown Fort Worth's Sundance Square, with two stories of hundreds of thousands of titles. A faux cowboy bronze dominates the escalator area, where kids spend a lot of time riding up to their own section. Peruse your favorite titles in one of the several reading areas or enjoy a coffee at the spacious, adjacent Starbucks. *401 Commerce St., Fort Worth, 817/332–7178, and other locations.*

8 *g-5*

BORDERS

What germinated 30 years ago in Ann Arbor as a bookstore for serious readers with a customer-friendly library ambience and well-read staff has blossomed into a worldwide phenomenon. Browse through more than 200,000 titles in the café or in library-reminiscent seating throughout the store. Best-selling authors are regulars at book signings. A music department stocks thousands of CDs and DVDs. *4613 S. Hulen St., Fort Worth, 817/370–9473.*

ethnic

9 *b-5*

BLACK BOOK WORM

Works by African-American writers exclusively fill the shelves of this specialty bookstore. Subjects include everything from fiction and history to self-help and poetry. *605 E. Berry St., Fort Worth, 817/923–9661.*

discount

9 *f-5*

THE BOOK RACK

More than 100,000 used books are found on these shelves, which also hold discounted new books as well as comics and audio books. *2304 W. Park Row Dr., Arlington, 817/274–1717, and other locations.*

8 *g-5*

HALF PRICE BOOKS

At this bookstore chain you can sell books you've read and pick up new and used books, software, and music. Unlike the big chains complimentary coffee is available for customers. *5264 S. Hulen St., Fort Worth, 817/294–1166.*

CANDLES

8 *f-4*

DEEJAY'S CANDLES BY DIANE

Inside this tiny house in an industrial area, find hundreds of kinds of candles, from votives and pillars, in myriad scents. Diane also stocks appropriate holders and containers. Ask about gift baskets that incorporate other decorative items. *4333 W. Vickery Blvd., Fort Worth, 817/737–2355.*

CHARITABLE COMPANIES

8 *h-5*

BERRY GOOD BUYS

Clothing donated to this shop directly benefits the Women's Haven, a shelter for abused women and their children. *1701 W. Berry St., Fort Worth, 817/921–2793.*

CLOTHING FOR CHILDREN

9 *f-6*

GADZOOKS

This store is a must for teenagers and college students. Racks abound with trendy clothes, accessories, and shoes made of leather, glittery fabrics, and natural fibers for casual weekend wear and club hopping. Girls' attire by Candie's runs in junior sizes from 0 up; boys' waist sizes are from 27″ to 44″. Shoes include Dr. Martens, Skechers, and Candie's. *3811 S. Cooper St., Arlington, 817/467–5585.*

Hulen Mall, 4800 S. Hulen St., Fort Worth, 817/370–2208.

CLOTHING FOR MEN & WOMEN/ GENERAL

classic & casual

8 *h-4*

BANANA REPUBLIC
What was once a safari-inspired men's and women's clothing store more than 20 years ago has grown into a multifaceted store with casual, professional, and evening attire as well as intimate apparel, shoes, belts, bags and personal care items for both genders. The store carries its own brand of dresses, slacks, skirts, sweaters, shirts, jackets and coats principally in natural fibers such as suede, leather, cotton, silk and wool—though some of the dressy evening attire for women includes blended fabrics. *1604 University Dr., Fort Worth, 817/885–8229, and other locations.*

8 *g-5*
4800 So Hulen, Fort Worth, 817/263–5602.

14 *a-7*
Ridgmar Mall 2060 Green Oaks Rd., Fort Worth, 817/569–8800.

conservative

8 *h-4*

TALBOT'S
The destination for moderately-priced conservative women's casual, evening and professional attire, Talbots exclusively sells its own label of clothing and accessories. Apparel runs in petite to plus sizes, and includes classics like boucle jackets, wool crepe skirts, wool flannel suits, and silk blouses. Accessories include croco-embossed boots, side-zip ankle boots, pins, necklaces, earrings, hosiery, smooth and textured handbags and wallets, dressy evening bags, dress and casual shoes. *1540 S. University, Fort Worth, 817/336–6111.*

contemporary

8 *h-4*

THE GAP
As the hip TV ads indicate, the coolest in casual clothes are found at this trendy chain. Jeans, khakis, sweater, tops, and jackets are mainstays, while the occasional skirt, dress, topcoat, and hat are frequent seasonal offering. Look also for accessories, including socks, stockings, belts, bags, fragrances, sunblock, and candies. *1620 S. University Dr., Fort Worth, 817/332–9089, and other locations.*

resale

14 *b-8*

BAUBLES AND BEADS
Consignment and resale are key here, where fashions range from cocktail attire to maternity clothing and wedding gowns. The inventory changes frequently, so it's fun to visit this place often. *6387 Camp Bowie Blvd., Fort Worth, 817/732–5451.*

vintage

14 *h-6*

PAST PERFECT
The entire cast from *That 70s Show* could be outfitted for several seasons with goodies from this shop. In fact, a complete reenactment of *Laugh In* could be costumed here, too. Everything in the way of used clothing, housewares, furniture, records, and books from six decades is stocked here, and most are priced fairly cheap. *3210 W. 7th St., Fort Worth, 817/870–1088.*

COINS

15 *a-6*

FORT WORTH COIN COMPANY, INC.
A dealer in rare coins and precious metals, this small, service-oriented shop does appraisals, stocks coins from around the world, and sells coin jewelry. *2822 W. 7th St., Fort Worth, 817/336–1782.*

COMPUTERS & SOFTWARE

14 *f-8*

COMPUTER DEPOT
Buy computer software, hardware, systems, and upgrades. Also, have your

computer serviced or get parts. Need training? They'll do it here. *4997 S. Hulen St., Fort Worth, 817/370–0071.*

14 *h-6*

UNIVERSITY COMPUTERS

This shop specializes in setting up networks, repairs, and personalized training. It carries a small stock of IBM compatible personal computers, and can special-order Compaq and Toshiba laptops. Rentals on nearly every model are available. *3334 W. 7th St., Fort Worth, 817/870–2921.*

COSTUMES & COSTUME RENTAL

15 *a-6*

HARRIS COSTUMES

Whether you're going as Count Dracula, Bo-Peep, or Austin Powers, this shop has the wigs, clothing, make-up, masks, and other accessories you'll need. *3001 Bledsoe St., Fort Worth, 817/332–7465.*

CRAFTS

14 *a-6*

M J DESIGNS

The aspiring Martha Stewart and the child artist alike can be found in droves at this Texas Chain. Everything needed to do faux painting on walls, acrylic painting on canvas, fancy gift wrap, needlework, picture-framing, wreath creations, flower arrangements, junk jewelry making, and birthday party inspiration is found right here. *Ridgmar Town Square at Green Oaks Blvd., Fort Worth, 817/737–3668.*

DISCOUNT

15 *d-7*

DICKIE'S FACTORY OUTLET

Discounted jeans, overalls, flannel shirts and T-shirts are the staples at this outlet store that exclusively carries its own label of casual attire. This store is next door to the factory, which offers similar discounts on all merchandise. *521 W. Vickery Blvd., Fort Worth, 817/877–0387.*

8 *g-4*

DSW SHOES

Phenomenal savings are found on nearly every major shoe name, from Nine West to Joan & David to Rockport. Men and women's selections are extensive, and accessory items include handbags, socks, and stockings. *3000 S. Hulen St., Fort Worth, 817/377–9902.*

ELECTRONICS & AUDIO

14 *e-8*

JIM GUNTER

This longtime neighborhood electronics store specializes in sales and service of major brands in televisions and home entertainment centers such as Sony, Panasonic, RCN and JVC. *4904 Camp Bowie Blvd., Fort Worth, 817/731–2731.*

8 *g-4*

MARVIN ELECTRONICS

Inside this mammoth state-of-the-art, 20,000 square foot audio/video store, service center, and custom installation facility, you'll find a large selection of stereo systems, audio visual furniture, flush mount speakers, pool and patio speakers, televisions, and DVDs. The knowledgeable staff will discuss your requirements in a consultation room and set up appointments for custom design and installation of audio/video systems for your home or office. Some of the most popular brands stocked include Boston Acoustics, JVC, Mitsubishi, Nakamichi, Sharpvision, and Yamaha. *2750 S. Hulen St., Fort Worth, 817/927–5311.*

ETHNIC ITEMS

15 *c-6*

EARTHBONES

Masks from Thailand, handbags from Guatemala, wrought iron tables from Mexico, and beaded necklaces from India are just a few of the thousands of gift items stocked in this upbeat shop. Aromatherapy soaps and candles, T-shirts and buttons bearing funny messages, and pewter picture frames fill the various nooks and crannies. *108 E. 4th St., Fort Worth, 817/332–2662, and other locations.*

EYEWEAR

14 *c-8*

ADAIR OPTICAL

This is the first choice for people requiring the most fashionable eyewear styles from Europe. Service is extraordinary, as it should be for the highest prices in town. *3210 Winthrop Ave., Fort Worth, 817/377–3500, and other locations.*

8 *g-4*

LUCK OPTICAL

Outstanding discounts are guaranteed at this family business, where eye exams are done on site and prescriptions for contact lenses and eyeglasses are filled quickly. Sometimes the cattle-call feel can be a nuisance on weekends. *7108 Camp Bowie Blvd., Fort Worth, 817/738–3191.*

FABRICS

15 *b-3*

J & D FABRICS

Claiming the largest selection of decorative fabrics in the Metroplex area, this huge design center has more than 8,000 bolts in stock and a wide selection of tassels and fringes. *2015 N. Main St., Northside, Fort Worth, 817/626–2365.*

FLOWERS & PLANTS

15 *c-6*

FLOWERS ON THE SQUARE

When something exceedingly creative in floral design is desired, this is your shop. True artistry goes into the flower arrangements, which are unlike any you've seen at the traditional florists. *311 Main St., Fort Worth, 817/336–8400.*

8 *f-5*

PLANT SHED

Hundreds of kinds of bedding plants, shrubs, and trees of every description are found at this huge lot. Everything you could need in the way of dirt, mulch, grass, and ground cover is here, too. Prices are some of the best in North Texas. *5050 Hwy. 377 S., Fort Worth, 817/244–2109.*

FOOD & DRINK

9 *a-5*

FIESTA MART

Where else can you grocery shop while serenaded by mariachi bands? The store's motto, "a store for all," has particular resonance in its eight other area locations which carry mainstream grocery products, Hispanic specialty items and brands, and an array of worldwide ethnic specialty items from wonton wrappers to kimchee. This location specializes in Hispanic goods and has more than 20 varieties of peppers and hard-to-find produce such as 15 varieties of jicama root, as well as maseca (used to make tortillas), specialty sweet rolls and everything in between. *4200 South Freeway, Fort Worth, 817/920–1930.*

8 *g-4*

RONNIE'S

More than 200 specialty food items from around the world make this store a gourmand's dream come true. The beverage selection alone is staggering, with thousands of wines, hundreds of liquors, domestic and imported beers to choose from. Gourmet foods include more than 50 cheeses including top sellers such as St. Andre, Parmesan Reggiano, Huntsman and Rublichon stocked by the wheel, and excellent take-out fare including sandwiches made from gourmet breads baked on-site each morning. They also do a big lunch sandwich tray business for companies. Gift baskets like the "Italian Lovers Gift Basket" of pasta, sauces, cheese, biscotti, and crostini are a popular holiday item. And for after dinner, there are 25 kinds of Dominican, Honduran and Mexican cigars. *2701 S. Hulen St., Fort Worth, 817/927–0101.*

ethnic

9 *c-2*

NGUYEN LOI ORIENT SUPERMARKET

Every supply needed to make Thai, Vietnamese, and Japanese dishes is found within this large grocery store. Prices on woks, fresh and frozen fish, Asian vegetables, dried herbs, noodles, and canned goods are exceptionally low. *5302 Belknap St., Haltom City, 817/831–4778.*

health food

14 *c-8*

SUNFLOWER SHOPPE

Every fathomable natural food item, organic produce, soy product, and vitamin is found inside this airy, 8,000-square-foot store. In addition, largely-organic health and beauty aids, hair products, essential oils, and cosmetics are also carried. Staff are qualified to advise novices what to buy; all associates are educated in Bastryl, a nutritional course. You can make an appointment with a nutritionist on staff for a 3–session hair analysis and consultation that determines what vitamins and minerals you're lacking in. *5817 Curzon Ave., Fort Worth, 817/738–9051.*

9 *g-3*

WHOLE FOODS

This national chain, begun as a little natural foods grocery during the hippie days in Austin, offers the best in organic, natural foods. The gigantic produce area is matched by superb selections stocking the freshest meats, fish, and cheese, and shelves between are jammed with the finest in condiments, cereals, grains, hair and skin products, and natural cleaning agents. An excellent salad bar, deli department, and juice/coffee bar fill an entire side of the store. Plenty of ready-made meals await you after a long day. *801 E. Lamar Blvd., Arlington, 817/461–8324.*

meats & poultry

14 *e-8*

ROY POPE GROCERY

Whether your menu calls for veal shank, emu, or bison, this is the meat market with all the exotic and hard-to-find fare. Ready-made dishes include good meatloaf, lasagna, and homemade pies, and a good, if small, wine selection is on hand. *2300 Merrick St., Fort Worth, 817/732–8202.*

wine & spirits

14 *h-6*

CHICOTSKY'S

Since 1950 this mid to high-end liquor and wine merchant has carried wines from all over the world, emphasizing French, Chilean, Italian, and Californian labels. Specializing in the best liquors, they have more than 100 single malt scotches and more than 40 high-end vodkas. They also have an extensive selection of domestic and imported beers. If you're looking for advice on which and how much alcohol to serve at your wedding, you're in luck: the owner plans parties and events. *3429 W. 7th St., Fort Worth, 817/332–3566. Closed Sun.*

KING'S

Wine consultants have been here for 35 years dispensing advice on which one of the thousand selections will compliment your meal. They also stock an extensive selection of imported beers, liquors, and some party supplies such as napkins, plates and cups. Closed Sun. *2810 W. Berry St., Fort Worth, 817/923–3737.*

FRAMING

14 *e-8*

BOWIE ON BOWIE

Gene Bowie does an expert job in framing paintings, old photos, and diplomas, and he's fast and congenial. *4821 Camp Bowie Blvd., Fort Worth, 817/737–3313.*

GIFTS & SOUVENIRS

15 *b-1*

STOCKYARDS DRUG STORE

The destination of choice for anything that represents or says "Fort Worth" or "Texas" t-shirts, cups, shot glasses, ash trays in the shape of Texas, caps, armadillos, and long horns. About half of the store is filled with souvenirs, and the other half sells over-the-counter drugstore items. *104 E. Exchange Ave., Fort Worth, 817/624–1626.*

HOME FURNISHINGS

14 *h-6*

DOMAIN

Need a couple hundred gorgeous, elegant things for the home? This is your destination. Lovely, handcrafted and hand-painted dinnerware from Provence, handmade linens from Peacock Alley, tiny desk lamps, wall sconces, baroque paintings, pretty porcelain creations, milled soaps, antiques and much more are found in floor-to-ceiling arrangements in this tony store. *3214 Camp Bowie Blvd., Fort Worth, 817/336–1994.*

15 *c-5*

PIER 1

This is home base, ground zero. The national chain's flagship store has everything necessary for outfitting a stylishly casual home. Dish and glassware selections are numerous, as are table linens, candles, bath soaps and sponges, rugs, pillows, lamps, dining tables, mirrors, picture frames, desk accessories, and garden decor. Best of all, lots of things are on sale. *501 Houston St., Fort Worth, 817/878–7845.*

HOUSEWARES & HARDWARE

5 *h-6*

ELLIOT'S HARDWARE

Originated in Dallas long ago, this fabulous repository of fix-it and decorative goods is a giant blessing in Northeast Tarrant. From the best in plumbing gadgets, screwdriver sets, and lighting needs to mailboxes and Texas flags, this store can take you right to it. *108 W. Northwest Hwy., Grapevine, 817/424–1424.*

15 *d-8*

OLD HOME SUPPLY

Vintage light fixtures, doors, bathroom sinks and toilets, and much more are found in three buildings full of treasures. *1801 College Ave., Fort Worth, 817/927–8004.*

JEWELRY

fine jewelry

14 *c-8*

HALTOM'S

Fine watches, rings, bracelets, and necklaces are sold at this homegrown business. *6102 Camp Bowie Blvd., Fort Worth, 817/738–6511.*

MAPS

14 *c-8*

MAPSCO

Unless you know every inch of Tarrant County like the back of your hand, you'll need a Mapsco book to find addresses in every commercial and residential area. These stores also supply fold-out city and state maps, as well as driving maps and atlases of all varieties. *6353 Camp Bowie Blvd., Fort Worth, 817/731–1666, and other locations.*

8 *h-4*

VOYAGER TRAVEL STORE

This one-stop-shopping for the time-challenged, efficient-minded traveler offers a mind-boggling range of quality Briggs and Riley and Andiamo luggage, travel accessories and gadgets, converters for phones and modems globes, books, maps, and language tapes. To help you weed through the possibilities, the well-traveled staff provide knowledge about the products and give customers an honest assessment of what's practical. They also take passport photos and have passport applications on hand. *1600 S. University Dr., Fort Worth, 817/335–3100.*

MISCELLANY

15 *c-5*

NATURE COLLECTION

Small, artistic fountains crafted from stone and metal make corners of your home, office, and garden infinitely more peaceful, and aromatherapy candles make your world a bit more pleasant. This store has plenty to offer, as well as Burt's Bees skin care products, and science and nature toys for young and old. *406 Houston St., Fort Worth, 817/335–0999.*

14 *h-6*

STRINGS

Wedged into a small 1950s shopping center in the Cultural District, this stylish and upscale home furnishings boutique offers a variety of contemporary designs in everything from clocks and salad bowls to chairs and lamps. It's the perfect gift store, but it's hard to leave without buying something for yourself. *3425 W. 7th St., Fort Worth, 817/336–8042.*

MUSIC

musical instruments & sheet music

5 *f-8*

MR. E'S MUSIC SUPERSTORE

Buy or rent a Kimbal piano, outfit your child's school band needs, or pick up a new set of drums or a Yamaha or Fender guitar. Everything to help your playing progress is here, including the sheet music. *1320 Airport Freeway, Bedford, 817/545–1103, and other locations.*

NEEDLEWORK & KNITTING

14 *e-7*

FRENCH KNOT

All the requisite goods for needlepoint, embroidery, knitting, and such are found in this upscale nook. *4706 Bryce, Fort Worth, 817/731–3446.*

NEWSPAPERS & MAGAZINES

8 *g-4*

SUPERSTAND

If it's the French *Vogue*, the Spanish *Elle*, the city magazines for Sedona and Providence, or today's issue of *International Herald Tribune*, this store carries it. *3000 S. Hulen St., Fort Worth, 817/989–8880.*

PETS & PET SUPPLIES

14 *a-6*

PETSMART

Buy cat and dog food by the case, an Australian bearded dragon and the crickets to feed it, a new toy and dog house, a book to help you understand your cat, a new aquarium and hundreds of fish, or simply a box of hamster food. It's all here in this warehouse-like space, where you're welcome to bring Fido (on a leash, of course) for your shopping trip. *1300 Green Oaks Rd., Fort Worth, 817/377–8669.*

9 *g-5*

1040 W. Arkansas La., Arlington, 817/860–2067.

9 *e-2*

WINNIE'S FISH & PETS

Not the tiny, neighborhood shop you'd think, this one has a full supply of pet goods, as well as fish, lizards, birds, ferrets, and puppies. *528 W. Pipeline Rd., Hurst, 817/282–2572.*

SPORTING GOODS & CLOTHING

5 *h-5*

BASS PRO SHOPS

Fresh from Springfield, Missouri, this monument to outdoorsy pursuits stocks everything for the angler, hunter, golfer, and camper. You'll also find an aquarium Big Buck Brewery and Restaurant. *2501 Bass Pro Dr., Grapevine, 972/724–2018.*

15 *c-5*

MAIN STREET OUTFITTER

A full-line Orvis dealer, this shop has plenty of fly rods and reels, fly-tying goods, knives, binoculars, outdoor wear, and travel accessories. *501 Main St., Fort Worth, 817/332–4144.*

STATIONERY & OFFICE SUPPLIES

stationery

14 *e-8*

THE LETTER

Exceptional, fine writing papers, as well as wedding gifts in silver, crystal, and porcelain, are found in this gorgeous little store. *5122 Camp Bowie Blvd., Fort Worth, 817/731–2032.*

TOYS & GAMES

new

14 *e-8*

DESIGNS FOR CHILDREN

Educational toys, puzzles, books, and games are great finds at this store in a vintage shopping center. *4804 Camp Bowie Blvd., Fort Worth, 817/732–6711.*

VIDEOS

14 *h-6*

BLOCKBUSTER

The mega-chain video store stocks all new releases in multiple copies, as well as hits throughout filmdom in two to three copies each. Videos are divided into comedy, drama, action, and family. Workout and travel tapes are stocked, too. *709 University Dr., Fort Worth, 817/ 338–4670, and other locations.*

WATCHES & CLOCKS

antique & contemporary

14 *f-7*

JEWELERS ON THE BOULEVARD

A small family operation, this shop is packed with antique and modern clocks, and a few choice pieces of antique furniture, vintage table linens, a scattering of crystal items, and picture frames. Good, quick jewelry and watch repair is done on-site, and the service is particularly friendly. *3911 Camp Bowie Blvd., Fort Worth, 817/763–0441.*

WESTERN WEAR

15 *b-1*

M. L. LEDDY'S

For 80 years they've been manufacturing and selling custom boots, hand-creased hats, saddles, and clothing for men and ladies, such as contemporary and western style suits, shirts, slacks, and sportcoats. You'll also find plenty of natural fiber apparel (wool, cotton) and leather accessories such as belts, wallets, and purses. Specialized salespeople and clothing coordinators know everything there is to know about the apparel they sell. *2455 N. Main St., Fort Worth, 817/ 624–3149.*

15 *d-6*

PETERS BROS. HATS

Since 1911, this family operation has repaired, created, and sold hats to generations of ranchers, oilfield families, and tourists from a little shop in Downtown. Today the third generation of Peters runs the outfit, where cowboy hats in all prices and styles are found. The Peters also run the oldest retail booth at the annual Southwestern Exposition and Stock Show in January and February at Will Rogers Memorial Coliseum. *909 Houston St., Fort Worth, 817/ 335–1715.*

chapter 3

PARKS, GARDENS & SPORTS

parks: dallas

Dallas parks may be this city's best-kept secret. Within its network of 336 parks, you'll find just about every kind of park imaginable. For a sense of history, head to the older parks where Work Progress Administration (WPA) stonework furniture and shelters still exist from the 1930s. Walkers, joggers, and cyclists can choose from paved trails in residential parks to primitive paths in natural reserves. There are also seven natural areas owned by the city and designated as parks. Since the area is blessed with favorable weather most of the time, Dallasites have plenty of opportunity to enjoy the outdoors. During July and August, when daytime temperatures often soar above 100 degrees, most locals usually head for parks either early in the morning or after sundown. Dallas is such a sports city, with professional teams in football, basketball, hockey, and soccer, that when locals aren't at the games, they're playing the games in parks from one end of the city to the other.

park information

The Dallas Park & Recreation Department oversees more than 300 athletic and multipurpose fields, six golf courses, five tennis centers, 22 swimming pools, and 45 neighborhood recreation centers across the city. You won't have to travel more than a few blocks to find at least a small neighborhood park, if not a major green area. City parks cover 21,000 acres with another 17,000 acres reserved as greenbelts. Most city-owned recreation centers have an indoor gym and offer a variety of classes for all ages. Sports and classes offered at each location vary so call the center nearest you for more information. To reserve a picnic shelter, call 214/670–8243. The park department has two regional offices: East (214/670–8847) and West (214/670–1923).

permits

Admission to most parks is free, but permits are required for special events. For details about permits, call or stop by the Park & Recreation Department (8100 Doran Circle, 75238, 214/670–8748). For general information and picnic area reservations call 214/670–8243. Alcohol consumption is illegal in all city-owned parks.

6 *e-8*

BACHMAN LAKE PARK

From this 206-acre expanse, you can watch aircraft land and take off at Love Field. The park is actually set at the end of the runway, with aircraft landing lights built on park property. When you tire of watching planes zoom in overhead, you can feed friendly ducks or take advantage of a paved path for walking, jogging, or roller-blading. In the center of the park is Bachman Lake, a favorite spot for birthday parties and picnics. *3500 Northwest Hwy., Northwest Dallas.*

7 *a-7*

B.B. OWENS

An 18-hole Frisbee® golf course is the draw for this 27-acre park. You will also find a playground and picnic tables. *10700 Kingsley Rd., North Dallas.*

6 *c-8*

CALIFORNIA CROSSING

This park was once the spot where hundreds of wagons crossed the Elm Fork of the Trinity River on their way to California. Those deep ruts left behind by wagon wheels more than 100 years ago are still visible today. In fact, this 390-acre park hasn't changed all that much. It's a great place to observe wildlife, including watching the flocks of migratory birds pass overhead each year. *1400 California Crossing Rd., Northwest Dallas.*

13 *g-3*

CENTRAL SQUARE PARK

A redbrick walkway leads to a small gazebo at this quiet sanctuary, a few minutes from Downtown. Nestled in the heart of historic Swiss Avenue, this 1¼-acre neighborhood park is surrounded by early 20th-century Victorian homes. A pleasant respite amid mostly modern surroundings. *3000 Swiss Ave., East Dallas.*

10 *e-3*

KIDD SPRINGS

With an exotic Oriental garden easing down the side of a low hill to the shore of a small lake, this is one of Dallas's prettiest parks. A paved walkway meanders up the hill under cypress, willow, and oak trees to a covered shelter on top. Benches invite you to stay awhile in order to enjoy the tranquil surroundings. Don't be surprised when ducks waddle up to greet you. While at the 31-acre park, be sure to stop by the natural-spring fountain. The park also has outdoor basketball courts, a pool, baseball diamond, and recreation center. *700 W. Canty St., Oak Cliff, 214/670–7535.*

10 *e-4*

KIEST PARK

Jogging, walking, or playing a sport are popular activities here. A paved trail runs through the 263-acre park, which has basketball and volleyball courts, 10 soccer fields, seven softball diamonds, and a baseball diamond. A recreation center offers even more activities, including karate and aerobics classes. *3080 S. Hampton Rd., Oak Cliff, 214/670–1918.*

10 *e-3*

LAKE CLIFF

Cypress and cottonwood trees outline a lake in this 44½-acre park, set inside historic Oak Cliff. Picnic under the trees or in one of the covered shelters built in the 1930s by the WPA. In the spring, azalea beds add dashes of color to the landscape. With its lighted basketball courts, a football field, and two multi-purpose fields, this community park is a popular spot for sport enthusiasts. *300 E. Colorado Blvd., Oak Cliff.*

LEE PARK

Bronze statues of Confederate General Robert E. Lee and a young aide dominate the green common area of this 14.61-acre neighborhood park built in 1909. Pure Southern elegance emanates throughout the park, with its massive shade trees, a 2½–acre lake, and a scaled replica of the general's elegant Virginia plantation house, Arlington Hall. *3400 Turtle Creek Blvd., Turtle Creek, 214/670–8242.*

13 *a-1*

REVERCHON PARK

A concrete dolphin reclines under huge pecan trees in this quiet park near Turtle Creek. In 1999 when city workers cleaned away a mass of overgrowth they discovered a stonework treasure trove—benches, fountain, barbecue pits—constructed in the 1930s by the WPA. This shady 36-acre park, built in 1915 and named after French pioneer and botanist Julien Reverchon, is popular for walkers, who enjoy its winding paved path and hillside stone steps. The newly constructed hike-and-bike Katy Trail runs adjacent to the park. *3505 Maple Ave., Turtle Creek, 214/670–7720.*

10 *h-1*

SAMUELL-GRAND

In the summer, hundreds of people bring lawn chairs or quilts to this 78-acre park for an evening of the Bard at the annual Shakespeare Festival. Its hilly terrain, large oak trees, and a rose garden is dotted with sculptures, including the hard-to-miss, bright orange "Guardian II, Skywatcher" and the elusive "Mirror Images." A favorite spot for picnics and sports, the park has 24 picnic tables, baseball diamonds, a swimming pool, and a recreation center. At one end of the park is Tenison Golf Course and Samuell-Grand Tennis Center. *6200 E. Grand Ave., East Dallas, 214/670–1383.*

other green places

BOTANICAL GARDENS

11 *a-1*

DALLAS ARBORETUM & BOTANICAL GARDEN

Set on the southeast corner of White Rock Lake, only minutes from Downtown, these 66 acres of giant trees, fragrant flowers, and soothing waterfalls provide a quiet respite from the noise and clamor of the busy city. In 1970, two estates were purchased for a public arboretum: The 1940 DeGolyer house is now used as a gift shop and the 1938 Camp Home is headquarters to the Dallas Arboretum and Botanical Society. The acreage is divided into gardens, each providing a different setting, from a Southern-theme garden with wisteria and magnolias to an English countryside filled with shade-loving ferns. *8525 Garland Rd., 214/327–8263. Admission: $6 adults, $3 children (6–12); $3 parking.*

Open Nov.–Feb., daily 10–5; Mar.–Oct., daily 10–6.

10 *g-2*

DALLAS HORTICULTURE CENTER

Seven acres of native plants thrive at Texas's second oldest botanical garden, where each year 300,000 visitors discover the beauty of nature. It has 14 small, intimate gardens, including one filled with plants that attract colorful butterflies. Inside the William Douglas Blachly Conservatory, the first built in the Southwest, is a 6,800-square-ft, climate-controlled glasshouse containing more than 253 African plants. *3601 Martin Luther King Blvd., Fair Park, 214/428–7476. Tues.–Sat. 10–5; Sun. 1–5.*

LAKES

When nature neglected to provide North Texas with any natural lakes, the government constructed some by building dams across creeks. Although their original purpose was to guarantee the city a permanent water source, they soon became popular recreation areas for water sports, picnicking, and nature watching.

7 *f-8*

LAKE RAY HUBBARD

This Dallas-owned lake is a favorite for sailing, water skiing, and fishing. Just east of Dallas, the 22,745-acre lake has three public boat ramps, four commercial boat ramps, picnic areas, and two nature areas. No swimming is allowed. *East on I–30 to Rockwall. 214/670–8061.*

6 *b-1*

LEWISVILLE LAKE

In the 1950s, Lewisville Lake swallowed Lake Dallas, but some longtime locals still aren't used to the name change. This 30,000-acre lake is one of the largest lakes in North Texas and the busiest with 2½ million visitors annually. Although water skiing is one of the most popular activities, you'll also find plenty of people fishing from boats or along the shore. You can swim just about anywhere on the lake, except near boat ramps, but some favorite spots are Westlake and Lewisville Lake Park. Hunting is allowed in selected places from September through February. All hunters need a hunting license and hunter education card. The three campgrounds fill up quickly around holidays, so reservations are a good idea. Call 877/444–6777 for reservations at Oakland, Pilot Knoll, and Hickory Creek campgrounds. *1801 N. Mill St., north on I–35E, Lewisville, 972/434–1666.*

10 *h-1*

WHITE ROCK LAKE

Just east of Downtown, this shallow lake is a favorite with those who jog, cycle, fish, picnic, sail, bird-watch, or just lull away an afternoon daydreaming. The one thing you can't do is swim, as is the case with all city-owned lakes. Much of the lake's history is still here including the aging redbrick pump station and the white Art Deco boathouse, now a favorite spot for fishermen. After heavy rains, the spillway turns into a roaring waterfall. The dam area also serves as a nature reserve and a bird-watching spot. You can park alongside the spillway at Garland Road or hike to the top of the spillway through the reserve. More than 9 mi of hike-and-bike trails circle the lake. You'll also find plenty of picnic areas, playgrounds, and rest-rooms. *8300 Garland Rd., East Dallas.*

NATURE WALKS

10 *c-7*

DALLAS NATURE CENTER

This unspoiled hilly wilderness area is a reminder of what this part of Dallas looked like 100 years ago. You are likely to see squirrels scampering among mesquite and oak trees and, if you're lucky, an elusive armadillo. Owls are more likely to be heard than seen. But expect the unexpected when you walk along one of the nine trails meandering through a habitat rich in native plants and animals. Trails offer different views and vary in length and physical difficulty. For an easy walk, head to the colorful butterfly garden or for a more strenuous hike, go to Cattail Pond, where you might see beavers at play. Joe Pool Lake is located at the foot of the 633-acre nature center. The center has something different to see each season, including an abundance of wildflowers in spring and brightly colored leaves in autumn. *7171 Mountain Creek Pkwy., South Dallas, 972/296–1955. Admission: $3 donation per car. Open Tues.–Sun. 7–sundown.*

10 *g-2*

THE LEONHARDT LAGOON NATURE WALK

Just outside the Dallas Museum of Natural History in Fair Park, this nature walk has 25 numbered markers and four descriptive panels of birds, insects, plants, trees, fish, and other wildlife that live in the lagoon. A printed walking guide has information about the flora and fauna in each area. Built in 1936 by the WPA, the lagoon is filled with native Texas plants and attacts more than 70 species of birds. At the south end, a sculpture resembles an enormous snake sliding through the water. Made of terracotta color gunite, a type of concrete sprayed over a metal frame, the sculpture curls at one point to form an arched pedestrian bridge. The controversial piece—some think it detracts from the natural beauty of the lagoon—winds, curls, and weaves its way across and around the water area. Others see the sculpture as erosion prevention, as well as a bridge for crossing the lagoon. *3535 Grand Ave., East Dallas.*

zoos, aquariums & animal preserves

10 *g-2*

DALLAS AQUARIUM

Expect the unexpected at the Dallas Aquarium. Its Art Deco structure houses 5,000 aquatic animals, from an upside-down jellyfish and batfish to a nearly invisible glass catfish. The newest, and largest, exhibit is the spectacular Amazon Flooded Forest. The 10,500-gallon tank holds 30 species found in the Amazon River, including prehistoric-looking black armored catfish and the acrobatic arawanna. Animal feeding time is at 2:30 PM when you can safely watch sharks and piranha dine. The aquarium opened with a freshwater section in 1936 as part of the state's centennial celebration. Saltwater tanks were added in 1964. Numerous conservation and research projects are held here, including breeding such critically endangered Texas species as the blind salamander and several desert fishes. *1462 1st Ave., Fair Park, 214/670–8443. Admission: $3 adults, $1.50 children (11–3), children under 3 enter free, preregistered school groups $1 per person. Open daily 9–4:30.*

13 *c-4*

THE DALLAS WORLD AQUARIUM

This aquarium provides a world of exotic, aquatic adventures. Take time out for a tropical excursion through a rain forest, where you will follow a bamboo path through exotic plants that are the home to toucans, pink spoonbills, and monkeys. The path descends to the crescendo of roaring waterfall. Beware: the walkway can be slippery. The area simulates a rain forest so the humidity leaves everything damp. Your journey ends in the ground-level aquarium, where you'll find exotic underwater creatures such as glowing moon jellyfish, South Australia seadragons, small African penguins, and plenty of bright yellow, blue, and purple tropical fish. There's also find a gift shop and restaurant at this level. *1801 N. Griffin St., Downtown, 214/655–1444, 214/720–2224. Open daily 10–5.*

10 *f-4*

DALLAS ZOO

Sometimes you wonder who's watching whom at the Dallas Zoo. At a glass viewing area, it's easy to come face to face with a tiger as it prowls in a rain forest. You can also watch gorillas frolic in their special 2-acre home, with heated rocks and fog nozzles to simulate the warmth of a rain forest, through a camouflaged viewing area. Opened in 1888, the zoo moved a couple of times before settling into its present Oak Cliff location in 1912. Soon afterward, it made its first major acquisition, "Queenie" the elephant, purchased with coins donated by schoolchildren. Today the 85-acre zoo is home to about 1,900 animals. Of the 370 species, 29 are part of the national Species Survival Plans. Newer exhibits are specially designed to ensure animals feel right at home and to give visitors a feel for native habitats. Glide through a wilderness area on a 1-mi monorail tour through six African habits. Walk along a winding 1,500-ft nature trail to get up close and personal with termite mounds and birds' nests. The zoo recently opened an endangered tiger habitat, which includes a private area for a breeding pair of Sumatran tigers. You won't miss the zoo's entrance: a giant giraffe, standing at 67½-ft tall, is Texas's tallest statue. *650 S. R.L. Thornton Free-*

way, Oak Cliff, 214/670–5656. Admission: $6 adults, $3 children (11–3), children under three and Dallas Zoological Society members enter free, $4 seniors 65-plus. $3 parking. Open daily 9–6.

11 *c-2*

SAMUELL FARM

Young city slickers can get a feel for farm life at this 340-acre park. Although many activities are limited to groups of 15 or more, you can still pet the animals—sheep, goats, and even longhorn steer—and inspect antique farm equipment. You can also fish in five ponds, which are stocked with bass, brim, and catfish. Young families pack a picnic basket for an all-day outing. Groups can opt for a full tour, including barnyard chores, candle making, and hayride. Horseback rides cost extra. *100 E. Hwy. 80, Mesquite, 214/670–7866. Admission: $3 adults, $2 children (11–3), children under 3 enter free. Open weekdays 9–5.*

stadiums

13 *a-4*

AMERICAN AIRLINES CENTER

This year the Mavericks and Stars make the move from the smaller, aging Reunion Arena to this new state-of-the-art facility. Built on 12 acres just north of West End and Woodall Rogers Freeway and east of I–35, the new sports center seats about 18,000 hockey fans and 19,200 basketball fans. It features 144 suites, private club restaurant and bar, public restaurant and sports bar, and team stores. In 1998 Dallas voters, after being wooed by opponents and proponents, narrowly approved $125 million in public funds to help build the new Downtown arena.

10 *g-2*

COTTON BOWL

Two annual football games attract overflowing crowds for this 71,000-seat stadium. Each October is reserved for the traditional Texas/Red River shootout between University of Texas Longhorns and University of Oklahoma Sooners. New Year's Day is the Southwestern Bell Cotton Bowl Classic, which is broadcast to millions across the nation. The Dallas Burn pro soccer team also plays here. *3750 Midway Plaza, 214/939–2222.*

sports & outdoor activities

BASEBALL & SOFTBALL

where to watch

The Texas Rangers play in Arlington (*see* Baseball & Softball: Fort Worth, *below*).

where to play

There are numerous of municipal baseball facilities in the city. The Park & Recreation Department's slow-pitch softball program for adults is so popular that it fields about 300 teams for each of three playing seasons—spring, summer, and fall. About half the teams play at Fair Oaks with the other half playing at diamonds in various parks throughout the city. For more information, call 214/670–8898. For details on permits, *see* Permits *under* Parks, *above*.

BASKETBALL

where to watch

11 *c-2*

DALLAS MAVERICKS

What the Mavericks lack in wins they make up for in optimism. Even with all the ingredients for a winning season—top draft picks, star players, and top coaches—this pro team just can't seem to put it all together. During its first season in 1980–81 with the 1970–1971 Chicago Bull's NBA Coach of the Year Dick Motta as leader, the team appeared headed for greatness. But the early '90s saw the Mavericks rapidly decline as losses approached the NBA's worst single-season record. Perhaps the team's most noteworthy accomplishment was when forward A.C. Green played in his 907th consecutive game, setting an NBA record during the 1997–98 season. In 2001, the team moves from Reunion Arena to American Airlines Center. *214/748–1808.*

Ballpark in Arlington

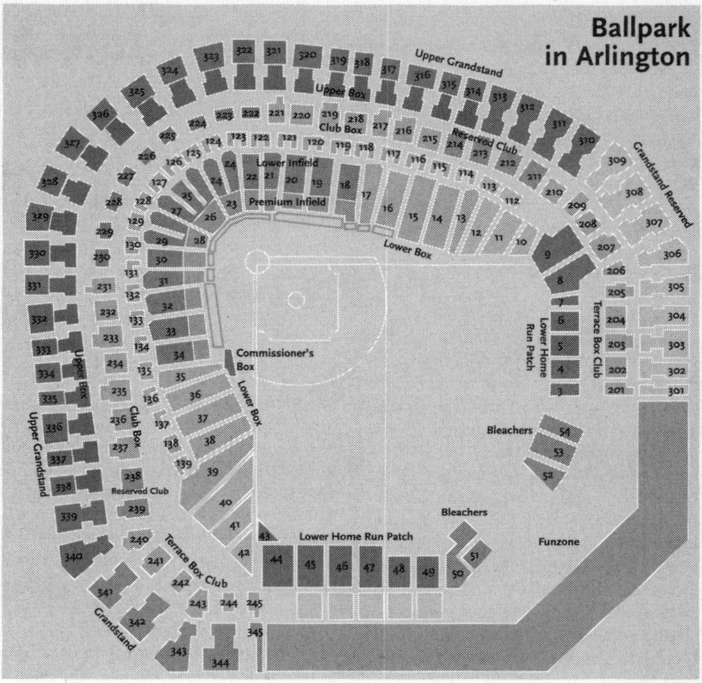

Texas Stadium

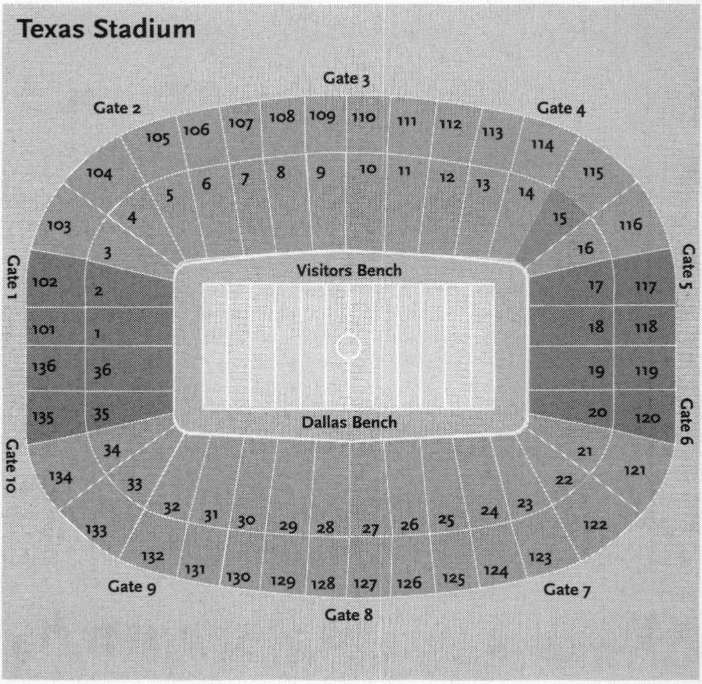

where to play

Just about every neighborhood park has a basketball hoop and many of the city recreation centers have gyms. The Park & Recreation Department (214/670–8847) has no citywide basketball league, but many of the recreation facilities have neighborhood leagues. Some health gyms and YMCA facilities (214/826–9922) have basketball leagues or pick up games.

BICYCLING

The city has 500 mi of streets designated as bike routes. You can ride from the far northern suburb of Plano to the far southern suburb of Duncanville, and from the eastern suburb of Grand Prairie to the western suburb of Mesquite. These streets usually have little motor traffic. For bike trails and map information call 214/670–4039. Paved cycling and walking trails, plus at least 61 mi of natural trails, wind through Dallas parks with the city busily constructing more. Cyclists who like hills, though, often drive to rural areas south of Dallas to ride along country roads. Call 214/670–4039 for bike trail and map information.

Whether riding on a busy street or down a country road, safety is the first rule for cyclists. Make sure you are visible and above all ride defensively. Not all motorists believe cyclists have as much right on the streets as they do. Nonetheless, cyclists must obey the same traffic laws as motorists. You must ride with the traffic, stop for signal lights, and signal for turns. Even though Dallas has plenty of hike and bike trails, it is often safer for you to ride on streets with lighter traffic. Popular paved trails are usually no wider than 6 ft and tend to be congested with walkers, joggers, and other cyclists. For safety reasons, slow down on these trails. Traveling 15–25 mph is too fast for pedestrian traffic. Remember to ride on the right hand side of the trail and announce when passing on the left. You must also wear a helmet. For more information on bicycle regulations and safety tips, call 214/670–4039.

places to ride

White Rock Lake Park is a favorite cycling spot where you can enjoy the view without worrying about automobile traffic. Many cyclists prefer to ride along **Lawther Drive,** which also circles the lake but avoids joggers. Depending on your starting point, the trail varies from 9.3 mi to 10.2 mi as it winds around the lake. You can stop at the park office (830 E. Lawther Dr., 214/670–8281) for a free map. Ardent cyclists often pedal from far North Dallas to the lake along **White Rock Creek Trail.** You can enter this 7½-mi-long, 8-ft-wide trail at 7000 Valley View Road. The scenic **Katy Trail** runs along what was once an old railroad bed from Southern Methodist University to the new Downtown sports arena, passing Lee Park and Reverchon Park on the way.

Popular mountain bike trails are in **L.B. Houston Park** (1600 California Crossing, 214/670–4100), **Boulder Park** (3200 Red Bird La., 214/670–6880), and **Cedar Hill State Park** (Joe Pool Lake, 972/291–3900). The terrain in L.B. Houston Park is flat. For a more challenging ride, opt for Boulder Park with its slick creek banks. Racers also head to nearby Frisco for weekly races at the Superdrome (9700 Wade Blvd., 972/731–1100, www.superdrome.com), a world-class velodrome, which hosts such major events as the 2000 Olympics trials and the 1999 World Cup of Cycling.

bicycle organizations

DALLAS OFF ROAD BICYCLE ASSOCIATION

Founded in 1988, this group holds monthly meetings to help newcomers get acquainted and learn about upcoming events. A weekly Friday night ride around White Rock Lake ends with burgers and beer at a nearby restaurant. Check out their web site at www.dorba.org. *1775 California Crossing, Northwest, 214/827–6599.*

GREATER DALLAS BICYCLISTS

This is Dallas's largest cycling club. It's for people who like to ride, not race, their bikes. The club holds weekly bike rides at various locations on Saturday, Sunday, and Tuesday nights. Rides vary from 15 to 40 mi. Cyclists usually eat afterward. Members receive discounts at some bike shops. *214/946–2453.*

6 *g-5*

MATRIX CYCLE CLUB

This group races in weekly events held throughout the year except winter. The

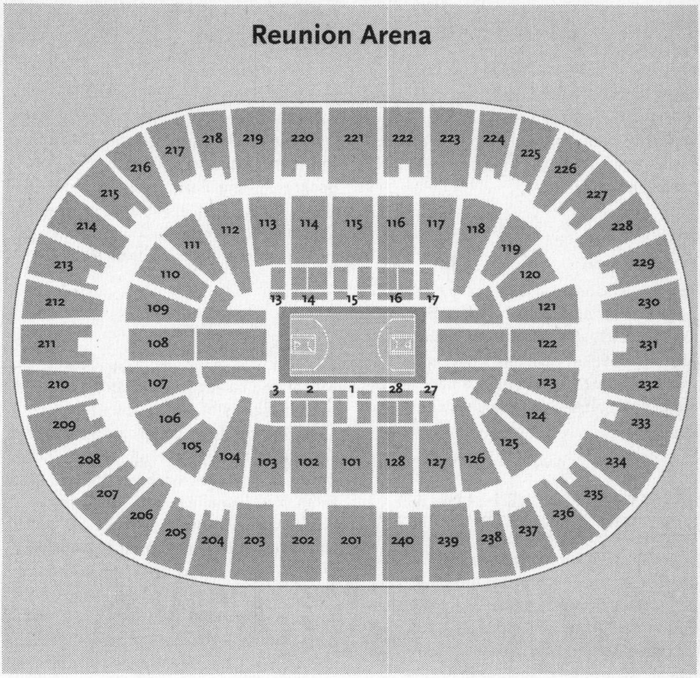

organization holds monthly meetings, except in December. *Richardson Bike Mart, 1415 W. Campbell Rd., Richardson, 972/231–3993.*

RECUMBENT-BIKE ENTHUSIASTS OF NORTH TEXAS

This loose-knit organization has no elections and no dues—just group rides. Diamond-frame bikers are welcome. The organization has an official fourth Saturday ride and impromptu outings. Favorite trails include White Rock Lake and Joe Pool Lake. The group conducts other rides along routes in Richardson and Garland, among other suburbs. *972/285–4935 or 972/285–4935.*

bike rental

Bike Exchange *(11716 Ferguson, Northeast Dallas, 972/270–9269).*

6 *g-5*

Bike Mart *(9040 Garland Rd., East Dallas, 214/321–0705; 1451 W. Campbell Rd., Richardson, 972/231–3993).*

11 *a-1*

Jack Johnston Bicycles *(9005 Garland Rd., East Dallas, 214/328–5238).*

BILLIARDS

Trends come and go, but pool remains a recreational mainstay in Dallas. Multiple rates are available at most halls, depending on day of week and time of day. Rates also tend to change frequently, so call ahead.

7 *a-7*

CLICKS

You'll often see the same faces week after week at these popular billiard parlors. Each location sponsors weekly pool and dart tournaments and leagues. You can also play foosball or video games. *9247 Skillman St., Northeast, 214/343–2184.*

7 *a-7*

11111 Kingsley Rd., Northeast, 214/340–7360.

6 *h-1*

19049 Marsh La., North, 972/306–3935.

6 *g-6*

HAWLEY'S

This north Dallas hall sells pool cues, cases, and billiard accessories and hosts four weekly tournaments. Besides shooting pool, you can also throw darts and play foosball. *5623 Alpha Rd., North Dallas, 972/239–4846.*

6 *h-7*

O'RILEY'S

You can shoot pool free every day until 7 PM at this billiard hall, where players rack up balls every Saturday at 4 PM for a tournament. Thursday night is karaoke night for those with an urge to sing. *8989 Forest La., North Dallas, 972/235–2781.*

BIRD-WATCHING

Hundreds of birds migrate through or spend the winter in and around Dallas each year. Peak migration months are April, May, September, and October. The Dallas Audubon Society can fill you in where to watch: InfoLine (972/498–8930), Metro Rare Bird Alert (972/480–5370), Rehabilitation Hotline (972/480–5370). The following spots offer the best bird-watching in Dallas.

10 *c-7*

DALLAS NATURE CENTER

You'll see cedar waxwings, cardinals, and red-tailed hawks in winter; black-chinned hummingbirds, painted buntings, and perhaps roadrunners in summer. *7171 Mountain Creek Pkwy., South, 972/296–1955.*

7 *f-8*

LAKE RAY HUBBARD

Thousands of Bonapart's gulls and ring-gilled gulls winter near the dam. Loons also like this area but tend to settle in deeper water. *East on I–30 to Rockwall. 214/670–8061.*

6 *b-1*

LEWISVILLE LAKE DAM

Song sparrows and swamp sparrows favor this area in the winter months. *1801 N. Mill St., north on I–35E, Lewisville, 972/434–1666.*

10 *h-1*

WHITE ROCK LAKE DAM

In the wooded area off Winston Road, just below the dam, you will likely spot white-throated sparrows (different from the house sparrow commonly seen in this area), chickadees, red belly woodpeckers, grebes, and Eastern phoebes. Wood ducks nest in the area during the summer. On rare occasions, you might spot an eagle. *8300 Garland Rd., East Dallas.*

BOATING

Motorized boating is a favorite pastime for thousands of Dallasites who can enjoy the thrill of speeding across a lake throughout the year. High winds, more than any other factor, keep boaters off lakes. You'll see less activity during colder winter months when most water-skiers, except for the most zealous who wear wet suits, find the water too cold. Area lakes have public boat ramps so most people keep their boats at home. Most lakeside marinas provide berths should you choose to leave your boat at the lake. Some marinas also rent boats during summer months. Favorite lakes for recreational boating include Joe Pool Lake, Lewisville Lake, and Lake Ray Hubbard (*see* Lakes, *above*).

BOWLING

This is one sport that seems to attract people of all ages from youngsters to senior citizens. Some bowling centers even have leagues for two-year-old children. But bowling alleys aren't just for bowling anymore. Many also have game rooms, restaurants, and bars.

AMF BOWLING CENTERS

This family-oriented company dominates the Dallas bowling scene, with 12 centers in Dallas and its surrounding suburbs. Some locations even have a dance floor. *214/328–3266.*

6 *d-7*

DON CARTER'S ALL-STAR LANES

Bowling in the dark can be fun at this 58-lane alley. Only the lights along the lane during "lightning strikes" provide the guiding glow. Forget cuddling during league play, though, because the lights always stay on. *10920 Composite Dr., Northwest Dallas, 214/358–1382.*

BOXING

Although many people box primarily for physical fitness in Dallas, you can still find gyms for professional training and sparring. Each February, Dallas Golden Gloves matches are held at Fair Park Coliseum (1300 Robert B. Cullum Blvd., East Dallas, 214-670-8400). Boxing is also offered for youth and young adults at two Dallas Park & Recreation centers: Anita Martinez (3212 N. Winnetka Ave., West Dallas, 214/670–7773) and Pike (2807 Harry Hines Blvd., Oak Lawn, 214/670–1491).

13 *e-5*

DOUG'S GYM

Owner Doug Eidd started personal training long before it became trendy. This gym has no fancy frills, just lots of personal attention. Boxing is limited to focus mittens—no sparring—and heavy bag punching. Rope jumping and weight lifting help members stay in shape. Scenes for Chuck Norris's popular TV show, "Walker Texas Ranger," are often shot here. *2010½ Commerce St., Downtown, 214/742–3758.*

10 *e-4*

HOME OF CHAMPIONS GYM

1966 World Champion Welter Weight boxer Curtis Coke owns this gym where professionals, including two world champs, and amateurs go to train. *111 E. Saner Ave., Oak Cliff, 214/941–5744.*

6 *g-4*

TRAINERS ELITE

You can spar for professional training or go the non-contact route for conditioning. Ex-pro boxer Ron Browning also teaches martial arts training to some area police departments. Cameras shooting fight scenes for the TV series "Walker Texas Ranger" are familiar sights. *17370 Preston Rd., Suite 450, North Dallas, 972/931–0867.*

TROY DORSEY INTERNATIONAL KARATE & SELF-DEFENSE

Owner Troy Dorsey, who holds world championship titles in boxing and kick boxing, opened this gym in the early 1980s. With all his titles, he's bound to know the right kicks, punches, and moves. *10918 Garland Rd., East, 214/327–8585.*

10 *h-1*

WHITE COLLAR BOXING

You're sure to get a good workout from former world-ranked kickboxer Jeff Overturf, who also knows his boxing. Overturf started using boxing techniques as a means to get into shape in 1989. *Lakewood Gym, 6434 E. Mockingbird La., Suite 210, East, 972/851–5656.*

FENCING

6 *h-7*

DALLAS FENCERS CLUB

Classes are available for all levels, regardless of your age or experience. Open fencing is also available. *Lake Highlands North Recreation Center, 9440 White Rock Trail, East, 214-670–7794.*

6 *d-7*

LONE STAR FENCING CENTER

Class are offered for youngsters and adults. *2636 Walnut Hill La., Suite 301, North, 214/352–3733.*

FISHING

It's not unusual during favorable weather to see young and old alike lined up along the shores of creeks and lakes just hoping to hook a catfish or bass for dinner. However, if you are older than 17 and younger than 65, you'll need a fishing license. Most sporting goods stores and bait shops carry them, but the cost varies depending on the type you buy. The only day you can fish without a license in Texas is the first Saturday in June. You can fish in most public waters except those posted. During December and January, locales get a special treat when the Texas Parks & Wildlife stocks some area lakes and rivers with rainbow trout. Texas water is too warm for trout except during winter months, so this is the only opportunity for anglers to catch the cold-water loving fish. A special freshwater trout stamp is required. To find the trout-fishing location nearest you, go to www.tpwd.state.tx.us or call 800/792–1112.

Fishing is also permitted in any creek or lake within Dallas city limits, including those in Dallas parks. Expect plenty of company, but even the most devoted fishermen usually don't mind a little conversation if the fish prove unfriendly. You'll most likely catch catfish, crappie, bass. Dallas has no fishing restrictions on park lakes, which stay well stocked.

7 *f-8*

LAKE RAY HUBBARD

Sand bass and hybrid stripers are the best catch at this lake. Even without a boat, you can find good fishing around bridges and near the power plant on the west shore. For general lake information, call 214/670–8061; for boat rentals, bait, and tackle, call 972/771–8865. *East on I–30 to Rockwall. 214/670–8061.*

6 *b-1*

LEWISVILLE LAKE

Although more of a recreational boating lake than a fisherman's paradise, this is still a good place to haul in a catfish, crappie, or bass. If you don't have a boat and get tired of untangling your line while casting from shore, drop by the Lewisville Lake Fishing Barge, on the east side of the lake. Opened in 1957, the barge is open 24 hours a day, 7 days a week, and is heated so even during the coldest winter days you can fish in comfort. For general lake information, call 972/434–1666; for bait, call Lewisville Lake Fishing Barge, 972/436–9341; for boat rentals, call Just for Fun, 972/370–7700. *1801 N. Mill St., north on I–35E, Lewisville, 972/434–1666.*

10 *h-1*

WHITE ROCK LAKE

If fishing from shore, your best bet is to toss your line where feeder creeks enter the lake. Any place reeds grow are always favorite spots for bass, catfish, and crappie. No boat rentals or bait/tackle shops in the area. *8300 Garland Rd., East Dallas, 214/670–8281.*

FLYING

6 *e-5*

CLASSIC AVIATION

This aviation school has seen a lot of changes since it started training pilots in the 1940s. This FAA approved FAR61 flight school instructs novice and commercial pilots at Addison Airport. *4511 Eddie Rickenbacker St., Addison, 972/661–8086.*

6 *e-5*

HENLEY'S AIRCRAFT SERVICES

You can get your private pilot and commercial certificates at this FAA approved FAR61 flight school. Daily flight instructions are available at Addison Airport. *15841 Addison Rd., Addison, 972/934–0875.*

FOOTBALL

where to watch

The Dallas Cowboys play at Texas Stadium in Irving (*see* Football: Fort Worth, *below*).

where to play

All you need is a football and 11 players—or fewer—for a great afternoon of fun at just about any city park. If you want something a little more organized, then sign up for one of the city's flag football leagues (214/670–8898). About 30 teams, including half a dozen women's teams, regularly play in fall and winter leagues. Each team is comprised of eight men or women. All games are played at Fair Oaks Park. Dallas Sports & Social Club (214/821–4611) has co-ed touch and flag football every Saturday, men's flag football every Tuesday.

GOLF

Why pay expensive private club fees when you can play on city-owned golf courses for a fraction of the cost? The city owns five expertly designed and carefully maintained 18-hole golf courses. Reservations aren't required, but are recommended. Courses open at sunup and close at sunset and all have a clubhouse, pro shop, restaurant, and golf pro, who is available for private lessons. Some clubs also have driving ranges and putting and chipping greens. Fees vary.

10 *g-4*

CEDAR CREST

Opened in 1917, this 6,550-yard course just south of Downtown tests your skills with plenty of challenges. You have great view of the Dallas skyline, but don't look for any water: the golf course is dry. *1800 Southerland, 214/670–7615.*

11 *a-3*

GROVER C. KEETON

All 6,511 yards of this award-winning course are a challenge. The numerous lakes and heavily wooded fairway found here demand accuracy from the tee. *2323 N. Jim Miller Rd., 214/670–8784.*

6 *c-7*

L.B. HOUSTON

This is the city's most popular course. Its 6,705 yards of tight fairways, rolling greens, and plenty of water traps challenge even the best golfer. *11223 Luna Rd., 214/670–6322.*

10 *e-3*

STEVENS

Even though this is the city's shortest course at 6,305 yards, don't be deceived by its length. The elevated greens and winding layout provide plenty of competition. *1005 N. Montclair Ave., 214/670–7506.*

10 *h-1*

TENISON

This is the city's only double course. Both courses have small, fast greens and plenty of trees guarding the fairways. Water and trees populate the 6,762-yard east course; at 6,872 yards, the west course is wooded and hilly. *3501 Samuel Blvd., 214/670–1402.*

HANDBALL

You can still find handball courts at some YMCA facilities and health clubs. The Downtown YMCA (214/954–0500) has a handball league.

HOCKEY

where to watch

DALLAS STARS

In 1999, the Dallas Stars finally got hot. Ken Hitchcock guided the team to its first Stanley Cup win, and center Joe Nieuwendyk walked away with the 1999 NHL Most Valuable Player trophy. Dallas sport fans, who love a winner, were jubilant. The city paraded the team through Downtown streets packed with cheering fans. The Stars shifted south from Minnesota to Dallas in 1993 to become the state's first NHL franchise. This year, they'll move play from Reunion Arena to American Airlines Center. *817/273–5222.*

where to play

You might think that ice hockey is more of a northern sport than southern but many locals disagree. Although the city is still short on ice rinks, players travel to the nearest rink in order to play in a hockey league or pick up games.

7 *a-3*

ICE BOUND ENTERTAINMENT CENTER

Amateurs learn to shoot the biscuit in the basket at this double-rink facility, which hosts hockey teams ranging in age from 5 to 55. The pro shop stocks plenty of hockey equipment. *4020 W. Plano Pkwy., Plano, 972/758–7528.*

6 *e-4*

ICEOPLEX

This ice rink has youth and adult hockey leagues. The pro shop carries sticks, pucks, and other hockey equipment. *15100 Midway Rd., Addison, 972/991–7539.*

HORSEBACK RIDING

Dallas long ago transferred its horsepower from the stable to the garage. It's hard to find a place to ride in the city, so most locals head out of town.

7 *c-1*

JOLABEC RIDING STABLES

You can rent horses by the hour for a nice ride along trails through 400 wooded acres. Call for directions to stables. *Hwy. 380 W, 972/562–0658.*

11 *c-2*

SAMUELL FARM

The rides here are for children willing to let others lead their horses in a circle. *100 E. Hwy. 80, Mesquite, 214/670–8551.*

6 *a-5*

WAGON WHEEL RANCH

Hourly guided trail rides lead you through 300 scenic wooded acres. *153 State Rd., Coppell, 972/462–0894.*

HORSE RACING

LONE STAR PARK

Watch world-class Thoroughbred and quarter horse racing at this upscale park, with fine dining and luxurious box seating. See the mid-South's top Thoroughbreds run from April to July and the world's best quarter horses from September to December. You can also wager on races nationwide year round. *1000 Lone Star Pkwy., Grand Prairie, 972/263–7223.*

ICE-SKATING

If you're new to Dallas then be forewarned: it rarely gets cold enough to freeze even shallow ponds. It is unsafe to walk on any pond that appears frozen because the ice is rarely thick enough to support your weight. Still, you don't have to give up ice-skating. Plenty of locals find the following indoor rinks good places to skate, even though the ice sometimes gets crowded.

13 *d-3*

AMERICAS ICE GARDEN

You can get a great workout during your lunch hour at this Downtown ice rink, which has Friday night specials for the yuppie set. The rink also offers broomball and classes. *Plaza of the Americas, 700 N. Pearl St., Downtown, 214/720–8080.*

6 *f-6*

GALLERIA

Set in the center of this internationally known shopping mall, this rink is a favorite for youngsters who entertain themselves skating while mom shops. You can also take lessons and play broomball. *13350 Dallas Pkwy., North, 972/392–3363.*

7 *a-3*

ICE BOUND ENTERTAINMENT CENTER

Skaters of all ages like to glide across the ice at this twin-rink facility, which also has a pro shop stocked with all the latest in skating apparel. *4020 W. Plano Pkwy., Plano, 972/758–7528.*

IN-LINE & ROLLER SKATING

Most adults in-line skate for exercise. They share the same paved trails found in city parks with cyclists, runners, joggers, and walkers. Younger skaters usually prefer streets and parking lots. Aggressive skaters who like to grind along rails and race up steep walls can find a workout at Eisenbergs Skate Park (930 E. 15th St., Plano, 972/509–7725). Skateboarders and BMX bikers can also use the facility. The park offers two levels of competition, one for beginners and the other for more experienced skaters. In-line skating is more popular, but some people still prefer roller skates. For indoor skating, try the following:

11 *c-5*

SUPER SKATE

This rink offers skating sessions for youngsters on weekday mornings and hosts theme-night skating sessions on the weekend. *13953 C. F. Hawn Freeway, South, 972/286–8055.*

11 *a-1*

WHITE ROCK SKATE CENTER

Sunday is family day where parents skate free with their children. There is open skating all day Saturday and Friday night, but no skating during the week. *10055 Shoreview Rd., East, 214/341–6660.*

MARTIAL ARTS

The martial arts are an Eastern mix of physical training and philosophy for self-defense techniques—karate, ju jitsu, tae kwon do, tai chi, and judo. Dozens of places offer classes, including the YMCA and some Park & Recreation centers. Consult the Yellow Pages for a complete listing.

7 *a-7*

DALLAS ACADEMY OF MARTIAL ARTS

Owner Bobby Autry opened this center in 1980. Classes are geared toward all age groups and skill levels. *9644 Plano Rd., Northeast, 214/343–3000.*

6 *f-7*

JI MU DO MARTIAL ARTS

Ji Mu Do means to learn wisdom through martial arts. Private instruction and group classes are available. *14902 Preston Rd., North, 972/991–0918.*

MINIATURE GOLF

6 *g-7*

FAMILY GOLF CENTER

This is a fun place for the entire family. Youngsters will enjoy walking through the waterfall and cave to reach the next hole. In addition to three 18-hole miniature golf courses, you will also find a 4-hole course. *8787 Park La., North, 214/341–9600.*

7 *a-4*

PUTT-PUTT GOLF & GAMES

Caves and ponds on all three 18-hole courses enhance the miniature golfing fun. Some players, regardless of age, are convinced that Course 2 is the most challenging because of bank shots. *17717 Coit Rd., North, 972/248–4966.*

RACQUETBALL

Keeping your eye on the ball is a must in this fast-paced game, which is a sure way to stay physically fit. Most health clubs have at least one court.

10 *e-4*

KIEST RECREATION CENTER

This is the only Park & Recreation facility with a racquetball court. Membership fees for Dallas residents cost $7, then pay $10 monthly or $1 for each time you play. Day passes for non-residents cost $2. *3080 S. Hampton Rd., South, 214/670–1918.*

6 *f-3*

SIGNATURE ATHLETIC CLUB

This club has league play on four racquetball courts. Club members play free. Guests pay $12 a day. *14725 Preston Rd., North, 972/490–7777.*

13 *d-6*

YMCA DOWNTOWN

The Downtown crowd fully takes advantage of the 14 racquetball courts here. Club members play free; guests pay $10 a day. *601 N. Akard St., Downtown, 214/954–0500.*

RODEO

Being a cowboy is one tough profession. If you doubt that, watch the bucking matches at the Mesquite Championship Rodeo, an internationally famous rodeo. The 6,000-seat arena hosts performances every Friday and Saturday night from April to October. *1818 Rodeo Dr., Mesquite, 972/285–8777.*

RUNNING & WALKING

Runners and walkers are all over town. Some prefer neighborhood parks, others head for longer paved trails found in green belts, which connect one park to another. The paved trail around **White Rock Lake** remains a popular spot. Another favorite is the scenic 2.3-mi **Turtle Creek Trail,** which winds from Reverchon to Stonebridge. **Keist Park** also has a 3-mi trail (*see* park information, *above*). Watch out for cyclists who often share trails. Indoor malls are favorite spots for walkers who can enjoy exercising in air-conditioned comfort.

CROSS COUNTRY CLUB OF DALLAS

This is the city's largest running organization. It holds monthly races as well as several social events yearly. Walkers are also welcome. Log on to their website at www.cccd.org. *214/855–1511.*

7 *b-3*

DALLAS TREKKERS

This non-competitive walking group sponsors several walking events throughout the year for athletes and non-athletes. Walks lead you through a scenic or historic district. You don't have to be a member to participate. *2800 Oak Grove Dr., Plano, 972/578–9746.*

SAILING

White Rock Lake is a favorite with sailors because no large motorboats leave behind churning wakes. Those with large yachts often sail at **Lake Ray Hubbard,** considered one of the best inland sailing lakes in Texas.

7 *g-5*

CHANDLERS LANDING YACHT & TENNIS CLUB

Chandlers Landing is one of the nation's largest inland yacht clubs. Weekly races and special regattas keep sailors in top sailing form. The club's North Texas Sailing School teaches those who want to learn how to sail or just sharpen their skills. For more information, log on to their website at www.chandlerslanding.com. *501 Yacht Club Dr., Rockwall, 972/771–2051.*

11 *a-1*

CORINTHIAN SAILING CLUB

Formed in 1939, this is Dallas' oldest and largest yacht club. It holds weekly races on White Rock Lake. This organization offers lessons for adults and sailing camps for juniors. Kelley Gough, 1998 National Champion of Champions, is a current member. Check out their website www.csc.sailing.org. *441 E. Lawther Dr., East Dallas, 214/320–0841.*

SOCCER

where to watch

13 *c-2*

DALLAS BURN

It is little wonder that this professional soccer team regularly clinches a play-off berth with such stellar players as forward Jason Kreis, who became the first player in professional soccer history to score 18 goals and 15 assists. The team plays 16 regular-season home games from March through October. Remember, Texas summers are hot, so ask for tickets on the shady side of the Cotton Bowl. *2602 McKinney Ave., Suite 200, Downtown, 214/979–0303.*

13 *b-6*

DALLAS SIDEKICKS

With such able players as Sidekicks superstar turned player-coach Tatu, it is no surprise that this team has won three championships. Tatu, who took the indoor soccer lead in 1996 with the most points, goals, and assists, has five Most Valuable Player awards. Baskin-Robbins even named an ice cream flavor after him—Tatu Toffee. Part of the World Indoor Soccer League, the Sidekicks have been in Dallas since 1984. *Reunion Arena, 777 Sports St., 214/653–0200.*

where to play

More than 3,000 youngsters ages 6–16 sign up each year for the Park & Recreation Department's highly successful youth soccer program. The 65 teams are divided into six districts and play in city parks across town. In January, the city hosts an indoor soccer festival in the massive Automobile Building in Fair Park. The building has enough space for up to 10 soccer fields, plus room for spectators. Some recreation centers also have indoor soccer programs. For more information, call 214/670–0577. Youngsters can also play for private soccer associations, many of them organized by neighborhood. The city has no soccer program for adults. Most adults play for North Texas Co-Ed Soccer Association (972/323–1323).

SQUASH

Although not as popular as racquetball, many fitness clubs have courts.

13 *e-1*

PREMIER CLUB

To guarantee one of three courts, you need to make reservations. Guest fee is $10 a day. *5910 N. Central Expressway, North, 214/891–6600.*

6 *f-5*

SIGNATURE ATHLETIC CLUB

This club has three squash courts, but no league play. Guest fee is $12.99 a day. *14725 Preston Rd., North, 972/490–7777.*

13 *d-6*

YMCA DOWNTOWN

The four squash courts here are popular with those who work and live in the Downtown area. Guest fee is $10 a day. *601 N. Akard St., Downtown, 214/954–0500.*

SWIMMING

One of the best ways to cool off during the city's balmy summer months is a quick dip in a pool. The city's 22 outdoor pools are open from June through August. The Park and Recreation Department (214/670–4100) has information about swimming lessons, aquatic exercises, pool rentals, and pool locations. For indoor pools open year round, consult private fitness centers or YMCA locations.

13 *h-3*

BAYLOR-TOM LANDRY CENTER

A 25-meter, 10-lane indoor training pool has sophisticated aquatic training equipment, including an underwater video camera to monitor technique. The Lone Star Masters program (214/794–7946) offers structured swim practices that are professionally coached to anyone 19 years and older. *411 N. Washington St., East, 214/820–7860.*

YMCA

All YMCA locations have outdoor pools and some locations have indoor pools. They all offer swim lessons and water aerobics. Both the Downtown Y (601 N. Akard St., 214/954–0500) and Town North (4332 Northhaven Rd., North, 214/357–8431) have eight-lane 25-meter indoor pools.

TENNIS

where to play

Tennis pros run all five city-owned tennis centers. You can find amenities here that private centers have, including lessons, ball machines, racket repair, and full-line pro shops. All courts are outdoors, and have high-quality surfacing. These centers are popular, so be sure to call 24 hours in advance for a reservation. Court fees range from $3 to $6 for 1½ hours, depending on the center and time of day. Centers are open from 9 AM–10 PM daily, but close during bad weather. In addition to the tennis centers, the city also has 250 neighborhood courts in parks throughout the city.

6 *h-7*

FAIR OAKS

A shady grove of pecan trees provides a welcome relief during a hot summer day at this tennis center on White Rock Creek. Built in 1980, it has 16 lighted tennis courts. *7501 Merriman Pkwy., 214/670–1495.*

6 *g-6*

FRETZ

This convenient North Dallas location has 15 lighted courts. Watch for plenty of league activity at this popular facility. *14700 Hillcrest Rd., 214/670–6622.*

10 *e-4*

KIEST

This center promotes all levels of play on its 16 lighted courts. *2324 W. Kiest Blvd., Oak Cliff, 214/670–7618.*

6 *c-8*

L.B. HOUSTON

This city-owned facility in northeast Dallas has the feel of a country club with a combined golf course and tennis center. Built in 1990, the 16-court lighted center is the city's newest. *11225 Luna Rd., 214/670–6367.*

10 *h-1*

SAMUELL-GRAND

The city's oldest tennis center is in historic W.W. Samuell Park. With 20 lighted courts, this center specializes in tournaments. *6200 E. Grand Ave., 214/670–1374.*

VOLLEYBALL

Although volleyball isn't a big sport in town, you can always organize your own game in a city park. You can find volleyball leagues at some Park & Recreation Department centers as well as the YMCA and a few health clubs.

10 *g-1*

CENTRUM SPORTS CLUB

This sports club has an open league when it can field enough teams. You don't have to be a member of the club to play volleyball. *3102 Oak Lawn Ave., Oak Lawn, 214/522–4100.*

13 *d-6*

YMCA DOWNTOWN

This popular Y offers indoor and outdoor volleyball games. *601 N. Akard St., Downtown, 214/954–0500.*

YOGA

Some people find yoga a great antidote for stress. Many fitness centers and YMCA locations offer yoga classes.

10 *f-1*

DALLAS YOGA CENTER

With 30 classes to choose from, you are bound to find one that fits your schedule. *4525 Lemmon Ave., Suite 305, Oak Lawn, 214/443–9642.*

fitness centers, health clubs & spa services

CLUBS

Dallas is a physical fitness town. Finding a place to help you stay fit has never been easier. In addition to the dozens of private health clubs, YMCA locations also have weight equipment, gyms, pools, and tracks. Even though YMCAs more likely offer the lowest price membership, you may prefer a private clubs for convenience. Fitness centers are also a good place to meet others of similar interests and many health clubs offer socials. Membership fees vary.

6 *h-7*

24 HOUR FITNESS

Whenever you feel the urge to work out, this club is always open. The club has cardiovascular equipment, including stationary bikes and steppers. There's a Kids Club, where there youngsters can play while their parents workout. *10025 Royal La., North, 214/340–4200.*

7 *a-4*

7622 Campbell Rd., North, 972/248–2900.

BALLY'S TOTAL FITNESS

If you travel often, you will never be far from one of these national chains. There are 14 in the Dallas area. The fitness centers have everything from running tracks to personal training. Call for a location nearest you. *800/695–8111.*

13 *h-3*

BAYLOR-TOM LANDRY CENTER

Named after legendary Dallas Cowboys football coach Tom Landry, the center's outdoor track winds through a 7-acre landscaped garden. It also has weights, a pool, racquetball, indoor track, and aerobics. *411 N. Washington St., East, 214/820–7870.*

6 *f-6*

COOPER AEROBICS CENTER

Founded in 1970 by preventive medicine pioneer Kenneth Cooper after publishing his first book, the center attracts people from across the globe. A physical examination includes instructions on diet and exercise. The center, set on 30 wooded acres, has all the essentials needed to get into shape: walking; jogging tracks; swimming pools; weight training; and basketball, volleyball, tennis, and racquetball courts. Exercise classes, seminars, and lessons are also available. *12100 Preston Rd., North, 972/233–4832.*

6 *f-6*

COOPER FITNESS CENTER

Founder Dr. Kenneth H. Cooper has sold 30 million copies of his 16 books on physical fitness, and the fitness center lives up to his reputation. You can row, climb, cycle, or walk your way through an extensive cardiovascular workout. *12200 Preston Rd., North, 888/964–8875.*

13 *c-2*

LARRY NORTH FITNESS FACTORY

North's name alone is enough to draw admirers to his chain of clubs. Besides state-of-the-art equipment, you also find aerobics, tanning, and day care for your youngsters. *2425 McKinney Ave., Turtle Creek, 214/871–0708.*

DAY SPAS

If you haven't pampered yourself in a while, maybe now is the time. A visit to one of the following will make you feel like royalty:

6 *f-6*

THE SPA AT THE COOPER AEROBICS CENTER

This spa offers facials, waxing, body wraps, and mud masks, priced by individual services or packages. *12100 Preston Rd., North, 972/386–0306.*

13 *c-3*

THE SPA AT THE CRESCENT

Visit this upscale spot for its facials, massages, saunas, steam room, and whirlpools. *400 Crescent Court, Turtle Creek, 214/871–3232.*

6 *g-8*

ESTEE LAUDER SPA

Inside Neiman Marcus, this is one of only two Estee Lauder Spas in the nation. You need an appointment for facials, waxing, and body wraps. You can even take lessons to learn makeup tricks used by the pros. *400 NorthPark Center, North, 214/891–1280.*

6 *f-5*

GRAND SPA INTERNATIONAL

The largest spa in Dallas, with 13,000 square ft, has plenty of room for clients who come for body wraps, massages, and facials. Sessions vary from 1 to 10 hours. *5100 Belt Line Rd., North, 972/392–9393.*

13 *c-2*

MOOD SPA

Emmy Award-winning television personality Paula McClure, whose expertise is mind and body treatment, owns this trendy facility. You can select a package that best suits your needs, including a custom day-retreat for you and your partner. Specialties include massages, body wraps, and facials. *2723 McKinney Ave., Turtle Creek, 214/303–1223.*

MASSAGES

This is a terrific way to unknot those tense muscles at the end of a stressful day. A massage can be expensive but devotees swear they're worth every penny. Many massage schools offer great rates for massages by interns, who are required to have 50 hours of supervised massages to fulfill a state-licensing requirement. Most spas also offer massages as part of their service.

10 *f-2*

MASSAGE INSTITUTE & HEALING ARTS CENTER

Schools like this one are a good place to have your first massage. Licensed instructors teach the students Swedish massage techniques. *3626 N. Hall St., Suite 826, Turtle Creek, 214/443–0060.*

6 *f-6*

HEALTHY HABITS

Opened in 1991, this facility gives massages daily. You can drop in without an appointment for a Swedish or sports massage. *12250 Inwood Rd., Suite 1, North, 972/458–7184.*

6 *h-8*

TEXAS MASSAGE

You can't beat the price of a Swedish massage at this school. *6102 E. Mockingbird La., Suite 401, East , 214/828–4000.*

parks: fort worth/ mid-cities

Northeast Texans love their parks and gardens. The beauty of Fort Worth/Mid-Cities—actually with most of North Texas—is that winter only lasts a few minutes. Temperatures in the 70s are not uncommon in January, so time spent outdoors is something taken for granted. The active people who hike, bike, fish, jog, and enjoy outdoor life in general have a variety of places to catch a breath of fresh air.

park information

The parks and recreation departments for each city in the Fort Worth/Mid-Cities have information about the parks in their respective communities and can help you locate the one nearest you. These departments are responsible for maintaining the facilities, renting gazebos and pavilions, and educating citizens on the proper use of area parks. The following are general information numbers: Fort Worth Parks & Community Services Department (817/871–5700), Arlington Parks & Recreation Department (817/459–5474), North Richland Hills Parks & Recreation Department (817/427–6620), and Colleyville Parks & Recreation Department (817/498–4749).

permits

Call the local park department nearest you for information about permit requirements. Admission to most parks is free, but large groups of people and alcohol require premits.

arlington

The city's 72 parks provide space for almost every activity, from hiking and inline skating to cycling, fishing, swimming, golf, and tennis.

CEDAR HILL STATE PARK

On the eastern shore of Joe Pool Lake (*see* Lakes, Arlington, *below*) is a 1,850-acre park spread with cedar-shaded hills, crisscrossed with hiking and mountain biking trails, and sprinkled with picnic areas and camping sites. Although it's close to freeways, the feel is remote and rugged. *Farm Rd. 1382, due south of I–20, 972/291–3900.*

9 *g-2*

RIVER LEGACY

Unrolling along the Trinity River is a 400-acre spread of natural lands with self-guided nature trails, and trails for hiking, cycling, and skating. Check at the Living Science Center for maps and schedules for guided nature walks. *703 N.W. Green Oaks Rd., 817/860–6752.*

fort worth

15 *a-7*

TRINITY PARK

Among dozens of parks, this popular spot hosts plenty of joggers, cyclists, in-line skaters, and dog walkers at morning, noon, and after work on the 2 mi of paved trails that follow the curve of the Trinity River from downtown. Filled with oak, hackberry, and dozens of other old trees, the park has numerous picnic sites and benches for watching sunrises and sunsets. On the first weekend in May, the park is packed with revelers enjoying the annual family festival called Mayfest; in June, the park hosts Shakespeare in the Park. *Entrances on 7th St., Crestline Rd., and University Dr., Fort Worth, 817/871–5700.*

irving

NORTHWEST PARK

One of the city's 43 parks, this jewel has an outdoor swimming pool, jogging trail, picnic area, recreation center, gym, lighted tennis courts, and sandlot softball field. *2800 Cheyenne Park, 972/721–2501.*

amusement parks

9 *h-3*

HURRICANE HARBOR

Facing Six Flags right across Interstate 30, this 47-acre expanse includes a 1-million gallon wave pool with a 4-ft-high surf, six water flumes, a towering water slide, tube slide with strobe lights, and a river raft ride. There is a 2-acre section for smaller children, too. *I–30 at Ballpark Way, Arlington, 817/265–3356. Admission: $27 adults, $14 children and seniors, $5 parking.*

9 *h-3*

SIX FLAGS OVER TEXAS

Easily one of Texas' most popular attractions and the prototype for hundreds of parks, Six Flags has all the roller coasters and musical shows you could want. The park is also home to a musical amphitheater, which books a variety of national acts. During the winter, the park is open for a holiday extravaganza. *Texas Hwy. 360 and I–30, Arlington, 817/530–6000. Admission: $39 adults, $20 children and seniors, $8 parking.*

other green places

BOTANICAL GARDENS

14 *h-8*

FORT WORTH BOTANIC GARDEN

The oldest botanic garden in Texas, this creation from the Depression era evolved into an "outdoor library of plants." The rose gardens, established in 1933, were the first public relief project in Tarrant County and today have more than 3,400 roses that peak in late April and October. Of particular significance is the Republic of Texas Rose Garden, filled with antique roses. Other sites include the fragrance garden, perennial garden, the Conservatory, the greenhouse, the trial garden, and the Japanese Garden (*see below*). *3320 Botanic Garden Blvd., at University Dr., Fort Worth 817/871–7689. Open daily 8 AM–sundown.*

15 *d-6*

FORT WORTH WATER GARDENS

This oasis, in the midst of downtown Fort Worth, offers a serene respite from the surrounding urban trappings. Designed by New York architects Philip Johnson and John Burgee, the 4.3-acre water gardens is made of stone carved into thousands of angles to symbolize mountains and valleys, through which thousands of gallons of waterfalls and streams cascade around the clock into a series of pools. The hundreds of steps down to the pools are surrounded by plants and trees, including coastal live oak, bald cypress, Bradford pear, azaleas, junipers, Indian Hawthorne, and English ivy. *1502 Commerce St., Fort Worth.*

14 *h-8*

JAPANESE GARDEN

Within the Botanic Garden is this retreat of beauty and solitude. Patterned after Japanese models, the tea garden is a place for meditation, relaxation, and reflection, augmented by the blooms of trees and shrubs in spring and the coloring of maple trees in fall. You'll enjoy pools of koi, a moon viewing deck, and a pagoda. A gift shop is on site, and tea ceremonies are offered during special celebrations. *3320 Botanic Garden Blvd., Fort Worth, 817/871–7685. Admission: $2 adults weekdays, $2.50 weekends and holidays. Nov.–Mar., daily 10–5; Apr.–Oct., daily 9–7.*

LAKES

arlington

9 *h-8*

JOE POOL LAKE

This 7,470-acre spread along the Dallas/Tarrant County line is easily accessible from Arlington and Grand Prairie. Hauling in largemouth bass attracts plenty of anglers, while water-skiers and other water sports types find splashy fun. Call or stop by Lynn Creek Marina (5700 Lakeridge Pkwy., 817/640–4200) for information on recreational activities.

9 *d-4*

LAKE ARLINGTON

Boaters, water-skiers, and other water jocks find the 2,250-acre lake in south Arlington a gem to treasure. Anglers like these waters for crappie, catfish, sand bass, hybrid stripers, and largemouth bass. Bowman Springs Park, one of several parks, has boat launches, picnic areas, barbecue grills, and rest rooms. *7001 Poly Webb Rd., 817/451–6860.*

fort worth

4 *e-6*

EAGLE MOUNTAIN LAKE

This 9,200-acre reservoir on the west fork of the Trinity River, surrounded by gently rolling topography, appeals to every sort of water enthusiast. Fishing spots for striped bass and smallmouth bass have been reported, and various marina businesses keep sailing and waterskiing fans happy. Twin Points Resort (10200 Ten Mile Bridge Rd., 817/237–3141) has a sandy beach. *12 mi northwest from Fort Worth via Farm Road 1220, also called Boat Club Road.*

grapevine

5 *g-4*

GRAPEVINE LAKE

One mile north of downtown Grapevine is the fourth busiest lake in Texas, with 60 mi of shoreline and 7,380 acres of water attracting wind surfers, sailors, and anglers. Among the several parks surrounding the lake are Murrell Park, with a playground, rest rooms, picnic sites, and access to hiking trails; Oak Grove Park, with camping, boat ramps, playground, and picnic areas; Meadowmere Park, with a boat ramp and swimming beach; and Marshall Creek, with an off-road vehicle area, boat ramp, and picnic sites. There are also more than 30 mi of natural surface hiking trails. *Lake office: 110 Fairway Dr., 817/481–4541; trail hot line: 817/481–3576.*

zoos, aquariums & animal preserves

fort worth

4 *f-8*

FORT WORTH NATURE CENTER

A complex preserve of prairie, marshes, forest, and the Trinity River includes a 25-mi trail system on which visitors can see native wildlife and plants, including buffalo, white-tailed deer, armadillo, and Texas wildflowers. Spreading over 3,500 acres, the sanctuary offers canoe lessons and trips, nature studies, wildflower walks, and natural history classes. *9601 Fossil Ridge Rd., 817/237–1111. Open daily 9–5. Visitor Center open Tues.–Sat. 9–4:30, Sun. noon–4:30.*

8 *h-4*

FORT WORTH ZOO

Ranked among the top zoos in the nation, this collection of natural-habitat exhibits is home to more than 5,000 exotic and native animals. Areas include World of Primates, where gorillas, orangutans, chimpanzees, and colorful birds await; Asian Falls, a spread of habitats that tigers, sun bears, elephants, deer, and rhinos call home; and Raptor Canyon, the domain of birds of prey. Other areas to visit include the koala-kangaroo habitat, the aquarium, and herpetarium. A gift shop and several snack places are on site. The zoo also offers day school, overnight, and summer programs for children. *1989 Colonial Pkwy., 817/871–7050. Admission: $7 adults, $4.50 children 3–12, $3 seniors 65-plus. Half price on Wed. Parking $4. Open daily 10–5.*

stadiums

9 *g-3*

THE BALLPARK IN ARLINGTON

Home to the Texas Rangers of the American League, the stadium seats about 49,000. Tours are offered during the off-season and in the mornings when the team is playing at home. *1000 Ballpark Way, Arlington, 817/273–5100.*

TEXAS STADIUM

Tours of 60,000-seat home of the five-time Super Bowl champion Dallas Cowboys are offered daily. *2401 E. Airport Freeway, Irving, 972/554–1804.*

sports & outdoor activities

AUTO RACING

5 *c-3*

TEXAS MOTOR SPEEDWAY

The second-largest sports facility in the nation, TMS hosts one NASCAR race early in the season, two Indy Racing League races, two NASCAR truck races, and Legends racing events. It's also home to race driving schools. *I–35 W at Texas Hwy. 114, Fort Worth, 817/215–8500.*

BASEBALL & SOFTBALL

where to watch

9 *g-3*

TEXAS RANGERS BASEBALL

The American League West Champions in Major League Baseball for a few years, the Rangers attract huge crowds from April through September when playing here. The Rangers have enjoyed great press in recent years, thanks to the Golden Glove of catcher Ivan "Pudge" Rodriguez, American League MVP Juan Gonzalez, and the association of the club with pitching Hall of Fame inductee Nolan Ryan. Too bad the Rangers can't seem to get past the curse of the New York Yankees, who send the Rangers back home early in the playoffs nearly every year. *1000 Ballpark Way, Arlington, 817/273–5100. Tickets usually $37.50–$50.*

where to play

Find a few friends and head to a green space near you for a game. Check local sporting goods stores for postings of like-minded folks looking to play ball.

NATIONAL ADULT BASEBALL ASSOCIATION

League play is divided into groups for 18 and over, 30 and over, and 40 and over in the Tarrant County area. *817/792–3532.*

BASKETBALL

where to watch

TEXAS SHOOTING STARS BASKETBALL CLUB

Games are usually held in area schools. Call to find out the location of the next game. *817/534–5281.*

where to play

15 *c-6*

YMCA

Pick-up games and scheduled leagues are always on tap at the downtown YMCA. *512 Lamar St., Fort Worth, 817/332–3281.*

BICYCLING

DALLAS OFF-ROAD BICYCLING ORGANIZATION
See Dallas: Bicycling, *above.*

BILLIARDS

9 *g-6*
RUSTY'S BILLIARDS
This club is open 24 hours and has 17 tables, which cost $8 per hour. *3151 S. Cooper St., Arlington, 817/468–9191.*

BIRD-WATCHING

14 *g-6*
FORT WORTH AUDUBON SOCIETY
This group organizes bird-watching events, and meets the second Thursday of the month at the University of North Texas Health Science Center. *817/292–5274.*

BOATING

4 *e-6*
EAGLE MOUNTAIN LAKE
This 9,200-acre impoundment on the West Fork of the Trinity River has plenty of launching ramps and room for sailing, skiing, and boating. The marina (9290 Herring Dr., Fort Worth, 817/236–8362) provides boat rentals, storage, and repair. *12 mi northwest of Fort Worth via Farm Road 1220.*

8 *f-7*
LAKE BENBROOK
The 3,770-acre impoundment on the Clear Fork of the Trinity River is a Corps of Engineers work that is popular with water skiers and windsurfers. Boat storage and rentals are available at Rocky Creek Marina (6199 Rocky Creek Park Rd., Benbrook Lake, Crowley, 817/346–2199). *Lake Shore Drive off U.S. 377 near Benbrook.*

5 *g-4*
LAKE GRAPEVINE
Another Corps of Engineers reservoir, this 7,380-acre lake has nearly 150 mi of shoreline and excellent skiing, sailing and windsurfing. *817/481–4541.*

BOWLING

8 *g-5*
DON CARTER'S ALL-STAR LANES
One of the newer bowling centers in Tarrant County, this one has 64 lanes, league play, family days, a pro shop, and café. *6601 Oakmont Blvd., Fort Worth, 817/346–0444.*

BOXING

15 *b-5*
GOLDEN GLOVES YOUTH ASSOCIATION
For decades this program has trained children to box. It's one of the primary youth training centers in the nation. *1040 N. Henderson St., Fort Worth, 817/332–0552.*

CANOEING

9 *e-1*
DOUBLE M CANOE
This retailer not only sells canoes but rents them as well. *317 Baker St., Hurst, 817/282–3135.*

4 *f-8*
FORT WORTH NATURE CENTER AND REFUGE
Canoeing techniques and safety are taught here around Lake Worth and on the Trinity River. Trips are offered in spring and fall. *Texas 199, Fort Worth, 817/237–1111.*

NORTH TEXAS RIVER RUNNERS
This group promotes river safety, preservation, recreation, and organizes trips. The Runners hold monthly meetings in the Tarrant County area. Call for meeting times and locations. *817/485–4443.*

FISHING

4 *e-6*
EAGLE MOUNTAIN LAKE
This 9,200-acre impoundment on the West Fork of the Trinity River has plenty of launching ramps and is a favorite with anglers in search of white bass, stripers, and smallmouth bass. The lake is 12 mi northwest of Fort Worth via

Farm Road 1220. Lake Country Marina has boat rentals, storage, bait, and gear. *9290 Herring Dr., Fort Worth, 817/236–8362.*

8 *f-7*

LAKE BENBROOK

Anglers flock to this 3,770-acre reservoir on the Clear Fork of the Trinity River for largemouth and smallmouth bass and stripers. Boat storage and rentals, gear, and bait are available at Rocky Creek Marina (6199 Rocky Creek Park Rd., Benbrook Lake, Crowley, 817/346–2199). *Lake Shore Drive off U.S. 377 near Benbrook.*

9 *h-8*

LAKE JOE POOL

The record largemouth bass caught at this lake along the Tarrant-Dallas county line is nearly 11 pounds. The 7,470-acre lake is served by Joe Pool Marina in Cedar Hill State Park (972/299–9010).

FLYING

9 *g-6*

ALAMO AVIATION

Alamo offers flight instruction, helicopter training, aircraft rental, and pilot supplies. *5070 S. Collins St., Arlington, 817/472–8307.*

FOOTBALL

where to watch

DALLAS COWBOYS

Often called America's Team, this NFL team has five Super Bowl championships but hasn't gone far in the playoffs in several years. Frequent coaching changes and aging heroes haven't tarnished the famous silver stars in fans' eyes, though. Find the Boys at home at Texas Stadium. *2401 E. Airport Freeway, Irving, 972/785–5000.*

8 *h-5*

TEXAS CHRISTIAN UNIVERSITY

The mighty Horned Frogs, whose annals are filled with such gridiron dignitaries as Bob Lilly, Sammy Baugh, and Abe Martin, struggled mightily for glory in the '70s and '80s, wrapping up the 1990s with victories at the Sun Bowl and the Mobile Alabama bowl. New competition awaits as the Frogs move into the USA Conference. Home games are played at the vintage Amon G. Carter Stadium. *Stadium Dr. at Cantey St., Fort Worth, 817/257–6588.*

where to play

Check local sporting goods stores for seasonal flyers and information on local games.

GOLF

9 *g-4*

CHESTER W. DITTO GOLF COURSE

Operated by the Arlington parks department, Ditto's 18-hole, par 72 course matches tight and open shots with sand and water hazards. There's also a full line pro shop and driving range. *801 W. Brown Blvd., Arlington, 817/275–5941.*

9 *d-4*

MEADOWBROOK

Listed among the 25 best municipal courses in Texas, this beautifully-landscaped course has 18 holes, a par 71 course, and a pro shop. *1815 Jenson Rd., Fort Worth, 817/457–4616.*

8 *d-7*

PECAN VALLEY

Possibly the favorite among locals playing the courses, Pecan Valley consists of two 18-hole courses separated by the Clear Fork of the Trinity River. The River Course plays about 6,100 yards from the white markers and the Hills Course plays about 150 yards shorter. Golf architect Dave Bennet designed the back nine of the Hills. There's a snack shop and an outdoor patio with tables. *6400 Pecan Valley Dr., Fort Worth, 817/249–1845.*

HOCKEY

where to watch

FORT WORTH BRAHMAS

A relatively young team, this Western Professional Hockey League contender made the playoffs twice in its first two years. Look for wild and wacky promotions that bring spirited fans to games

at the Fort Worth Convention Center and Will Rogers Coliseum in Fort Worth. *817/336–4423.*

where to play

8 *f-4*

SKATIN' TEXAS COWTOWN ICE ARENA

Both league play and public skate times are offered. Skate times change seasonally, so call ahead for the most current schedule. *3600 Hwy. 377 S., 817/560–7465.*

HORSEBACK RIDING

8 *f-5*

BENBROOK STABLES

The most complete selection of equestrian offerings is found here, on the southwestern corner of Tarrant County. Guided trail rides on gentle horses follow scenic paths along the shores of Lake Benbrook. For birthday parties, count on pony rides and entertainment. Riding lessons are available. *10001 U.S. Hwy. 377 S., 817/249–1001.*

ICE-SKATING

15 *c-5*

THE ICE

The Ice has daily public skating times, and skate rentals are plenty cheap. *Fort Worth Outlet Sq., 100 Throckmorton St., Fort Worth, 817/415–4800.*

IN-LINE SKATING

9 *d-1*

MOUNTASIA

In-line hockey league play is found at this amusement center. *8851 Grapevine Hwy., Fort Worth, 817/788–1051.*

MARTIAL ARTS

8 *g-4*

KARATE'S BEST

Learn American karate, tae kwon do, aerobic kick boxing, and more from police officers. *6970 Green Oaks Rd., Fort Worth, 817/737–4650.*

MINIATURE GOLF

9 *d-1*

MOUNTASIA

Go-karts, batting cages, bumper boats, in-line skating, and miniature golf among waterfalls, dinosaurs, and palm trees are among the oodles of fun at this family center. *8851 Grapevine Hwy., Fort Worth, 817/788–0990.*

ROLLER-SKATING

8 *g-4*

ROLLERLAND WEST

Free skating time and skating parties are this rink's big draw. *7325 Calmont Ave., Fort Worth, 817/244–8290.*

RUNNING & WALKING

running organizations

ARLINGTON RUNNERS CLUB

Running events are scheduled January through August and are open to all levels. *817/460–1055 or 817/461–2281.*

FORT WORTH RUNNERS CLUB

All levels of runners, including walkers, are invited to join events in Fort Worth and across North Texas. Weekly runs are organized. *817/654–5390.*

LAKE GRAPEVINE RUNNERS AND WALKERS

Fitness events, competitions, and community service events are regularly scheduled. *817/488–9719.*

SCUBA DIVING

8 *f-4*

DIVERS SCUBA SUPPLY

This shop provides instruction courses, service and equipment departments, monthly trips, and individual diving travel planning. *3807 Southwest Blvd., Fort Worth, 817/732–5761.*

8 *g-4*

SCUBA SPHERE

PADI-certified training is booked at this fully stocked Scuba shop. *6703 Camp Bowie Blvd., Fort Worth, 817/731–1461.*

SOCCER

where to watch

9 *f-4*

ARLINGTON SOCCER ASSOCIATION

Watch games played by soccer enthusiasts ages 5–18. Schedule for league play changes seasonally. Call for complete details. *3630 Pioneer Pkwy., Arlington, 817/261–0242.*

where to play

8 *h-6*

FORT WORTH ADULT SOCCER ASSOCIATION

This group sponsors league play for men and women. Schedules and venues vary; call for detailed information. *5043 Trail Lake Dr., Fort Worth, 817/346–0150.*

SWIMMING

EMLER SWIM SCHOOL

Swimming classes are taught for ages six months to adults in group or private classes in indoor, heated pools by certified instructors. *Colleyville, 817/481–7946; Arlington, 817/275–7946.*

9 *d-1*

NRH2O

This landscaped spread of water slides, wave pool, water playground, and inner-tubing river promises a day of splashy fun. *9001 Grapevine Hwy., Fort Worth, 817/656–6500.*

YMCA

Area Y locations have swimming pools and swim programs. Call the Metropolitan YMCA (817/335–9622) for the location nearest you.

TENNIS

where to play

FORT WORTH TENNIS ASSOCIATION

Tournaments and league change seasonally. Call for most current schedule. *817/795–4015.*

9 *f-4*

ARLINGTON TENNIS CENTER

A grand facility with 12 lighted tennis courts and a 3,000-square-ft clubhouse, this tennis haven has a pro shop, concession area, and locker rooms. Certified host programs and provide lessons. *500 W. Mayfield Rd., Arlington, 817/557–5683.*

YOGA

8 *g-5*

BODY, MIND, SPIRIT

Enroll in one of the weekly yoga, Tai Chi, or stretching classes. *5521 Bellaire Dr., Fort Worth, 817/738–7284.*

15 *a-8*

WELLNESS CONNECTION

Yoga for all experience levels is offered daily. *2481 Forest Park Blvd., Fort Worth, 817/926–9642.*

fitness centers, health clubs & spa services

CLUBS

BALLY'S TOTAL FITNESS

You'll find an assortment of activities and amenities, including aerobics program, personal training, indoor pool, cardiovascular training machines, free weights, tracks, and racquetball. Call for the location nearest you. *800/695–8111.*

8 *g-5*

FIT FOR LIFE

This club has more than 80 cardiovascular stations and personal, circuit, and weight training. *Cityview Shopping Center, 6125 I–20, Suite 144, Fort Worth, 817/292–8101.*

8 *g-5*

HEALTH & FITNESS CONNECTION

Among such amenities as an indoor pool, free weights, and recumbent bikes, this facility offers programs in yoga, water fitness, circuit boxing, karate, personal trainers, and aerobics. *6242-A Hulen Bend Blvd., Fort Worth, 817/346–6161.*

15 *d-5*

J'S PERSONALIZED TRAINING

This small, friendly club has free weights, weight circuits, cardiovascular machines, personal training, and nutritional counseling. *711 Commerce St. #G-200, Fort Worth, 817/338–4046.*

15 *c-6*

YMCA

Aerobics classes, cardiovascular machines, free weights, training circuits, running track, indoor pool, water aerobics, sauna, massage, and more highlight this national club. *512 Lamar St., Fort Worth, 817/332–3281.*

DAY SPAS

14 *c-8*

EUROPEAN SKINCARE INSTITUTE

Facials, an assortment of massage therapies, hydrotherapy, nail treatments, and gift certificates are available. *6038 Camp Bowie Blvd., Fort Worth, 817/731–0707.*

14 *e-8*

GOLDWAVES

An Aveda Concept Spa, this comfortable salon offers numerous hair, nail, skin, and body treatments. Whole-day packages are available. *5137 El Campo St., Fort Worth, 817/731–8888.*

MASSAGES

14 *h-6*

CYNTHIA BUCHANAN

Swedish, sports, Shiatsu, reflexology, chair, Reiki, and polarity massages are offered. *3230 Camp Bowie Blvd., Fort Worth, 817/996–4325.*

9 *c-2*

WELLNESS SKILLS

Learning center offers affordable, 55-minute massages. *6301 Airport Freeway, at Minnis Dr., Haltom City, 817/838–3363.*

chapter 4

PLACES TO EXPLORE

galleries, museums & more

where to go: dallas

Getting stuck in a routine is so easy. When was the last time you really looked at the Dallas skyline? Dallas has many magnificent buildings. Sure, you always make the big exhibitions at the Dallas Museum of Art but you probably haven't taken the time to give more than a cursory glance to all the superb sculptures scattered about the city in parks, plazas, and sculpture gardens. This weekend, instead of wrapping around a good book or surfing the net, spend the day visiting some place you've never been before. Take a drive through the city and visit the many plazas and historic buildings. And if you favor a more rural setting, visit one of the dozens of small communities surrounding the city. Here, you'll find everything from farm museums to Victorian homes to flea markets to festivals.

ARCHITECTURE

Nothing evokes Dallas more than its skyline at night, when bright neon lights illuminate Downtown into a prism of color. At different times of the day and from different directions, the view is ever-changing but never any less spectacular. Here you'll find the city's most significant achievements in urban architecture. Each site is introduced with the name of the architect and the year the project was completed. A telephone number is given if the building is open to the general public beyond its lobby and other pubic areas.

13 *d-5*

ADOLPHUS HOTEL

(Barnett, Haynes & Barnett, C.D. Hill, 1912) The architects just kept adding frills to the upper stories of this ornate Edwardian grand hotel built by beer magnate Adolphus Busch. Hundreds of celebrities have stayed here since the hotel opened. *1321 Commerce St., Downtown.*

13 *c-5*

BANK OF AMERICA PLAZA

(JPJ Architects, 1986) The green neon lights outlining this modern building, coupled with it being the tallest in Downtown, create a structure that is hard to miss at night. During the day, the green lights disappear, leaving 72 stories of silver glass. Keeping up with its name is a challenge. This is the fifth moniker for this bank and office tower. *901 Main St., Downtown, 214/209–1373.*

13 *e-5*

BANK ONE CENTER

(Philip Johnson, John Burger, 1987) The copper-top arched rooftops of this 60-story glimmering pink granite and glass building lend a distinctive texture to the skyline. A vaulted glass roof covers the banking hall. *1717 Main St., Downtown, 214/290–2000.*

13 *d-4*

BELO MANSION

(Herbert M. Greene, 1890s) Prominent newspaper publisher A.H. Belo had this classical revival house built for his family in what was then the city's most elegant neighborhood. Greene included many features from the Belo family home in North Carolina. *2101 Ross Ave., Downtown, 214/220–0239.*

13 *d-3*

CATHEDRAL GUADALUPE

(Nicholas J. Clayton, 1902) This fine example of Victorian Gothic design contrasts its ultra modern neighbor, the Morton H. Myerson Symphony Center. In 1898, workers placed the first cornerstone as they began constructing the church from red Thurber brick. Designer Clayton was the state's first registered architect and considered by many to be one of the best. *2215 Ross Ave., Downtown, 214/871–1362. Open daily 9–3:30.*

10 *f-2*

THE CENTRUM

(Rossetti Associates, 1987) The green glass clock tower perfectly compliments this pink granite office building. Inside, you'll find the popular Star Canyon Restaurant. *3102 Oak Lawn Ave., Oak Lawn.*

13 *d-3*

CHASE BANK TOWER

(Skidmore, Owings & Merrill, 1987) Like a giant needle puncturing the sky, this 55-story building of brown solar glass has a five-story eye that extends from the 41st floor to 49th floor. That "hole," as locals call it, is a structural design that reduces wind load. *2200 Ross Ave., Downtown.*

13 *c-3*

THE CRESCENT

(Philip Johnson, 1985) This lavish complex of offices, hotel, and retail shops became an instant Dallas landmark, although not considered one of Philip Johnson's better designs. Its post–modern design includes mansard roofs, arched entrances, and dormer windows. The hotel is a favorite with celebrity visitors. *400 Crescent Court, Uptown, 214/871–3200.*

13 *d-6*

DALLAS CITY HALL

(I.M. Pei, 1978) This abstract building is hard to forget because it looks like it was built upside down. The cast concrete structure stands on a 12-acre site that includes a Henry Moore bronze abstract, "The Piece," especially designed for this location. The sparse outside design falls apart inside the building, where the original open-concept interior is now a labyrinth of office cubicles. *1500 Marrilla St., Downtown, 214/670–3011.*

13 *d-7*

DALLAS CONVENTION CENTER

(George Dahl, 1957) The Dallas Convention Center keeps going and going and going. This sprawling building—two million square ft—defies description; its 1973 and 1993 expansions resulted in a hodgepodge of designs. The first structure, built in 1957, was classic modern, which is in sharp contrast to the 1993 deconstructionist design of steel and glass. It has a heliport on the roof and a DART station nearby. *650 S. Griffin St., Downtown, 214/939–2700.*

13 *b-5*

DALLAS COUNTY CRIMINALS COURT BUILDING

(H.A. Overbeck, 1913) You cannot escape the enduring legacy of The John F. Kennedy assassination in Dallas. Jack Ruby, the infamous nightclub owner who shot assassin Lee Harvey Oswald before thousands of TV viewers, was tried in one of the courtrooms in this elegant Renaissance Revival jail and courts building. *501 Main St., Downtown, 214/653–7011.*

13 *d-3*

DALLAS MUSEUM OF ART

(Edward Larrabee Barnes; Pratt, Box & Henderson, 1984) This sprawling limestone museum, with its sloping central hallway, anchors one end of the Arts District. The structure is probably best known for the barrel vault that serves as the Flora Street entrance. *1717 N. Harwood St., Downtown, 214/922–1200.*

13 *d-5*

DALLAS POWER & LIGHT BUILDING

(Otto Lang, Frank Witchell, 1931) This art deco building has leaded, stained-glass windows with a Zifzag Moderne style. *1506 Commerce St., Downtown, 972/791–2888.*

13 *d-5*

DAVIS BUILDING

(C.D. Hill, 1926) You will likely wonder what creative muse urged the architect to add a gilded cupola to the roof of this Classic Revival building. Actually, the original owner, Republic Bank, needed the cupola's extra height to make the building taller than an unknown competitor's. *1309 Main St., Downtown, 972/288–6411.*

13 *c-3*

FEDERAL RESERVE BANK OF DALLAS

(Kohn Pedersen Fox; SJKB, 1992) The nation's spare change is safe inside this multi-level high-tech complex of stone and glass. While most locals will never have a reason to enter this building, it is a familiar sight to those who visit the trendy Uptown area. *2200 N. Pearl St., Uptown, 214/922–6000.*

13 *c-4*

FOUNTAIN PLACE

(I.M. Pei, Henry Cobb, New York,1986) From a distance, this shimmering bluish-green glass tower looks like a rocket to some, a 60-story pyramid to others. Up close, its appearance changes again, causing newcomers to wonder if they are indeed at the right place. The building is an integral part of a 6-acre plaza and water garden. *1445 Ross Ave., Downtown.*

10 *f-2*

INFOMART

(Martin Growald, 1985) This eight-story glass and white metal building is modeled after Great Britain's 19th-century Crystal Palace. The Old-World Victorian design contrasts with the futuristic aesthetic of the telecommunication and internet companies within. *1950 Stemmons Freeway, Northwest, 214/746–3500.*

10 *f-2*

INTERNATIONAL APPAREL MART

(Pratt, Box & Henderson, 1964) This is the largest building of its kind in the world. The huge facility covers four square blocks, with space for at least 1,500 exhibitors. It is one of six buildings that comprise Dallas Market Center, the world's largest wholesale mart. Fountains, tropical plants, and artwork warm the otherwise impersonal structure. *2300 Stemmons Freeway, Northwest, 214/879–8300.*

13 *c-5*

JOHN F. KENNEDY MEMORIAL

(Philip Johnson, 1970) This 50-ft-square memorial to the slain president stands isolated in the center of a plaza. Built of four concrete slabs, the empty tomb contains only a single large basaltic slab inscribed "John Fitzgerald Kennedy." Thousands visit the site each year. *600 block Main St., Downtown.*

10 *f-2*

KALITA HUMPHREYS THEATER

(Frank Lloyd Wright, 1959) One of three theaters Wright designed, this architectural shrine appears to have grown from a small hill on which it rests. Since nature has no right angles, neither does the theater. Even the windows and door frames are slightly askew. Wright also disliked elevators, so the freight elevator used to move sets from the stage to the basement was secretly added without his knowledge after his last visit. He died before the theater's premiere performance. *3636 Turtle Creek Blvd., Turtle Creek, 214/522–8499.*

13 *d-5*

KIRBY BUILDING

(Barnett, Haynes & Barnett, 1913) This U-shape building, dubbed by locals as "Old Girl," was financed by beer magnet Adolphus Busch. The French Gothic revival design of this 17-story building includes rooftop finials. *1509 Main St., Downtown, 214/748–6246.*

13 *d-5*

MAGNOLIA BUILDING

(Alfred C. Bossom, 1922) In 1999 the Magnolia Building, once headquarters for Magnolia Oil Co. (predecessor of Mobil Oil), reopened as a hotel. This 29-story Renaissance Revival building, the tallest in Dallas until after World War II, has a limestone façade, arches, and columns. An arch ties together separate wings. The 30-ft-high neon revolving Flying Red Horse placed on the building's roof in 1934 quickly became a Dallas landmark. *108 S. Akard St., Downtown, 214/915–6500.*

13 *e-5*

THE MAJESTIC THEATRE

(John Eberson, 1921) Karl Hoblitzelle built the Majestic to serve as headquarters of his Interstate Amusement Company. It was one of seven theaters Eberson designed. During the early 1980s, the Renaissance Baroque exterior, the Roman Gardens interior, and the overhead trellis at the entrance were restored to their original appearance. *1925 Elm St., Downtown, 214/880–0137.*

13 *d-3*

MORTON H. MEYERSON SYMPHONY CENTER

(I.M. Pei, 1989) Inside this modern glass-and-marble structure, natural light flows through a skylight in the circular glass lobby. The McDermott Concert Hall dominates the facility, which includes 74 thick concrete doors weighing 2½ tons each, 56 acoustic curtains, and a 42-ton canopy system suspended above the stage. *2301 Flora St., Arts District, 214/670–3737.*

13 *d-5*

NEIMAN MARCUS

(Herbert M. Greene, 1914) Years after most large retail centers abandoned Downtown for the suburbs, this internationally known department store still thrives among the high-rises. After the original store burned in 1913, the business moved to this location. Since then, several renovations have doubled its size. The seven-story building is unembellished except for red awnings. *1618 Main St., Downtown, 214/741–6911.*

13 *d-5*

RENAISSANCE TOWER

(Harwood K Smith & Partners, 1973) This glass tower—Dallas's first and the tallest in Texas until 1981—stands out at night because of the lighted "X" pattern and brightly illuminated rooftop spires. The building is less impressive during the day when the spires look oddly out of place and the "X" pattern, created by structural bracing, is only slightly noticeable. Fans of the "Dallas" TV series will recognize this 56-story building as the place where J.R. worked. *1201 Elm St., Downtown.*

13 *d-4*

REPUBLIC CENTER

(Harrison & Abramovitz, 1955) You'll recognize this 36-story building from its distinctive gray aluminum siding with embossed star designs. A sculpture shaped like a rocket was added to make the structure taller. *325 N. St. Paul St. (at Pacific St.), Downtown, 214/965–8600.*

13 *b-6*

REUNION TOWER

(Beckett & Associates, 1978) This 50-story tower topped with a geodesic dome serves as an internationally recognized landmark of Dallas. A computer system creates an infinite number of lighting patterns with the 260 lights that cross the dome's face. Built of four concrete cylinders, the center tube holds elevators that whisk visitors to the top in 68 seconds. Built on the western edge of Downtown near the original site of La Reunion, a 19th-century French utopian colony, the tower and adjacent blue glittering glass Hyatt Regency Hotel are part of a 30-acre Reunion development. *300 Reunion Blvd., 214/651–1234.*

13 *d-4*

SCOTTISH RITE CATHEDRAL

(Herbert M. Greene, 1913) This neo-classical building remains a standout in Downtown. Immediately visible is the elegant gold double eagle that adorns a portico with six stately columns. *500 S. Harwood St., Downtown, 214/748–9196.*

7 *a-8*

ST. JOHN'S EPISCOPAL CHURCH

(O'Neil Ford, Arch Swank, 1963) What looks like a chain of silos is really 12 areas designed for Stations of the Cross in this modern church. A carving symbolizing Christ's journey stands in each area. *848 Harter Rd., East, 214/321–6451.*

13 *d-5*

THANKS-GIVING SQUARE

(Philip Johnson, John Burgee, 1977) In this small recessed triangle, you can relax among trees, grass, and cascading fountains. The spiral chapel, built of white marble aggregate, has a colorful stained glass ceiling. From the central courtyard, you can visit the Hall of Thanksgiving for details of this annual American holiday. The triangle opened in 1977 in observance of the 200th anniversary of Thanksgiving Day. *1627 Pacific Ave. (at Ervay St.), Downtown, 214/969–1977. Open weekdays 9–5.*

13 *d-3*

TRAMMELL CROW CENTER

(Richard Keating, 1984) At the base of this granite and glass high-rise is a public sculpture garden. The building is easily recognizable by the pyramid atop the building. *2001 Ross Ave., Downtown, 214/979–6441.*

13 *b-6*

UNION STATION

(Jarvis Hunt, 1916) When five stations consolidated into one central terminal, it made catching a train much easier after 1916. By 1969, the Golden Age of Rail had passed and the grand station closed. The building re-opened in 1974 as an AMTRAK station. In 1996, this beaux-arts style building with a vaulted waiting room became Downtown's terminal for the DART light-rail line. *400 S. Houston St., Downtown.*

10 *h-2*

VIETNAM MEMORIAL

(Richard Matrix, 1989) This memorial is chiseled from pink and gray Texas granite, an appropriate material for walls honoring the 3,271 Texans killed in Vietnam and the 156 Texans still missing in action. Names are engraved on four pink granite walls, which run along a gray granite rectangular pool. *Fair Park, 3809 Grand Ave., East, 214/553–9688.*

13 *d-5*

WILSON BUILDING

(Sanguinett & Staats, 1903) This eight-story Victorian-era office building with its round corners contrasts its glimmering modern neighbor, Bank One Center. Built by wealthy rancher and banker J. B. Wilson, its series of stone eagles along the fifth floor keep watch on the streets below. *1623 Main St., Downtown, 214/741–2112.*

ART EVENTS

april

13 *f-4*

DEEP ELLUM ART FESTIVAL

More than 60 artists set up booths along Main Street in Deep Ellum to display such creative efforts as paintings, photographs, and sculptures. Music and tasty goodies are part of the fun. Dates change from year to year. *214/748–4332.*

may

10 *h-2*

ARTFEST 2000

Since 1970, artists from around the U.S. come to sell their creations at the city's largest art festival. More than 25,000 people attend the three-day event to talk with such favorites as landscape artist Gregory Strachov and Southwest artist Amando Peña. Dates change from year to year. *Fair Park, 214/361–2011.*

september

GALLERY WALK

Members of the Dallas Arts Dealers Association kick off the fall buying season with the opening of special exhibits in galleries throughout the city on the Saturday after Labor Day. *214/925–9558.*

october

13 *d-3*

ANNUAL AMERICAN INDIAN ART FESTIVAL & MARKET

Native Americans from tribes across the nation perform traditional dances and sell arts and crafts. *Annette Strauss Artist Square, 1800 Leonard St., Downtown, 214/891–9640.*

6 *g-5*

COTTONWOOD ARTS FESTIVAL

This shady park is transformed into an art mart when artists from across Texas set up booths for this annual outdoor festival. *Cottonwood Park, Richardson, 972/231–4798.*

EAST DALLAS ARTISTS STUDIO TOUR

You can watch a potter turn a lump of clay into a vase and an artist transform white canvas into a landscape when artists open their studios to the public during an annual one-day tour. Locations and dates vary from year to year. *214/320–1275.*

ART GALLERIES

13 *c-4*

ART DISTRICT GALLERY

This standout gallery shows colorful contemporary fine art on canvas. *Fairmont Hotel, 1717 N. Akard St., Downtown, 214/220–3266.*

13 *f-4*

CASA MEXICANA

You can buy those wonderful clay figures created by the Aguliar sisters of Oaxaca, Mexico, at this gallery that specializes in Latin American and Mexican folk art. *2616 Elm St., Deep Ellum, 214/747–7227.*

13 *f-4*

CONDUIT

When this gallery opened in 1984, it helped kick off the Deep Ellum revival. The gallery exhibits paintings, sculptures, and photographs from Texas artists, including Robert Barsamian, Arthur Koch, and Susie Phillips. *3200 Main St., Suite 25, Deep Ellum, 214/939–0064.*

13 *c-2*

CRAIGHEAD-GREEN

Budding artists rub elbows with established ones at this gallery that displays landscapes, still life, and abstracts. Works include wall hangings by Marla Ziegler, oil on linen by Winston McGee, and oil on canvas by Susan Sales. *2404 Cedar Springs, Suite 700, Arts District, 214/855–0779.*

13 *d-2*

DAVID DIKE FINE ART

David Dike showcases 19th- and early 20th-century European and American oil paintings, including works by Julian Onderdonk, Robert Wood, and Porsirio Salinas, among others. *2613 Fairmount St., Art District, 214/720–4044.*

6 *h-6*

DOZIER'S OF DALLAS

This is one of the few galleries in Dallas that displays a large selection of Southwest art, including paintings by Tony Abeyta, G. Harvey, and Donald Vann. *10750 Forest La., East, 214/340–5350.*

10 *g-1*

DUNN & BROWN CONTEMPORARY

This gallery represents Lone Star artists in the midst of their careers. Exhibits include photography by Nic Nicosia, oil paintings and bronzes by David Bates, and oil paintings by Vernon Fisher. *5020 Tracy St., Uptown, 214/521–4322.*

13 *c-2*

EDITH BAKER GALLERY

Opened in 1978, this is one of Dallas's oldest contemporary art galleries. It displays mostly works by Texas artists, including paintings on tar paper by Denise Brown, assemblages by Norman Kary, and printmaking by Judy Youngbood. *2404 Cedar Springs Rd., Uptown, 214/855–5101.*

13 *c-2*

ELIZABETH STATE THOMAS GALLERY

Elizabeth State Thomas exhibits such diverse works as Russian realism by Mikhail and bronze sculptures by Dallas artist Charles Rice. *2315 Routh St., Art District, 214/754–5905.*

6 *g-8*

ELLIOTT YEARY GALLERY

American and French contemporary artists are represented in an extensive collection of original oils, acrylics, watercolors, and ceramics. *6817 Snider Plaza, Highland Park, 214/265–1565.*

6 *f-7*

EMPTY WALLS

Rare posters from artists such as Thomas Pradzynski, Issa Shojaei, and Elizabeth Estivalet are displayed. You can also choose from thousands of moldings to frame your art piece. *217 Preston Royal Village, North, 214/369–9989.*

13 *c-2*

FLORENCE ART GALLERY

This gallery's eclectic collection of contemporary fine art, including impressionists and abstracts, features works by Jay Miller, Henrietta Milan, and Vladimir Ryklin. *2500 Cedar Springs, Art District, 214/754–7070.*

6 *f-6*

FREE FLIGHT GALLERY

You will find one of the largest collections of kaleidoscopes in the Southwest here. These entertaining tubes filled with bits of colorful glass, feathers, or wood cost from $50 to $3,000. *Dallas Galleria, 13350 Dallas Pkwy., Suite 2390, North, 972/701–9566.*

603 Munger Ave., East, 214/720–9147.

6 *g-8*

IVANFFY-UHLER GALLERY

Contemporary European paintings, drawings, sculptures, or collages are the order of the day, including works from Pal Gerzson, Janos Kass, and Tamas Vigh. *4623 W. Lovers La., Northwest, 214/350–3500.*

6 *f-6*

THE OLD WORLD

Elegant Fabergé eggs, Gosset ducks, and Refuge music boxes are just a few of the collectibles you will find at this North Dallas gallery. *Dallas Galleria, 13350 Dallas Pkwy., Suite 2480, 972/385–8919.*

13 *d-2*

PILLSBURY & PETERS FINE ART

The newly formed partnership of Edmund Pillsbury, former director of the world renown Kimbell Art Museum in Fort Worth, and long-time gallery owner Gerald Peters promises a continued emphasis on contemporary art from Texas artists as well as novel exhibits. Works include sculptures by George Segal, photo collage by David Hockney, and mixed-media pieces by Al Souza. *2913 Fairmont St., 214/969–9410. Closed Sun.*

13 *c-1*

RIDDELL RARE MAPS & PRINTS

U.S. history is represented through this gallery's collection of antique maps, globes, and fine prints. Periods include the Civil War, Western expansion, and Texas republic years. *2607 Routh St., 214/953–0601.*

6 *f-6*

SOUTHWEST GALLERY

This 16,000-square-ft gallery showcases more than 100 artists—from Russian impressionists to American traditionalists—such as R.C. Gorman, W.A. Slaughter, Rufino Tamayo, and A.D. Greer. *4500 Sigma Rd., 972/960–8935. Closed Mon.*

13 *f-4*

STEPHANIE'S COLLECTION

Brick walls and hardwood floors of this 19th-century building contrast nicely with a large collection of contemporary abstracts, primitive African masks, and mud cloth African fabric. *2546 Elm St., 214/752–5588. Closed Sun.*

6 *f-5*

VALLEY HOUSE GALLERY

The five-acre, tree-shaded sculpture gardens and gallery beckon visitors to enjoy 19th- and 20th-century American and European originals with a focus on Texas regional artists. You will find oil paintings by Texas artist Donald S. Vogel, mixed-media pieces by Spanish artist Miguel Zapata, and photos by Texas artist David Gibson. It is one of only three Texas galleries that maintains a membership in the prestigious Art Dealers Association of America, Inc. *6616 Spring Valley Rd., 972/239–2441. Closed Sun.*

ART MUSEUMS

10 *h-2*

AFRICAN AMERICAN MUSEUM

This is the only museum in the Southwest dedicated to the life, culture, and art of African Americans. Founded in 1974 as part of Bishop College, the museum holds permanent collections of masks, sculptures, gold weights, textiles, folk art, and fine art. The museum also houses the history collection for *Sepia* magazine, Texas Black Women's History Archives, and Dallas County Black Political Archives. A variety of courses relating to African American history and cultures are offered. *3536 Grand Ave., 214/565–9026. Free except for special exhibitions. Closed Mon.*

6 *g-8*

BIBLICAL ARTS CENTER

Locals often stopped to watch artist Torger Thompson during the two years it took him to paint one of the world's largest murals, "Miracle at Pentecost." Upon completion, the piece measured 124 ft wide by 20 ft tall and had more than 200 Biblical characters, many of them life-size. Thompson spent 10 years in Biblical research before he ever started painting. His work of art is now the centerpiece of the museum's theater presentation. The museum also owns hundreds of paintings with Biblical themes. *7500 Park La., North, 214/691–4661. Admission: $7, $6 children 6–18, under 6 free. Open Sun. 1–5, Tues.–Sat., 10–5.*

13 *d-4*

DALLAS MUSEUM OF ART

Since opening in 1903, the museum has built a permanent collection of some of the world's finest pieces, representing various ages and cultures. The museum includes the Wendy and Emery Reves Collection, which comprises their lifetime collections of impressionist paintings by such artists as Renoir, Cézanne, Gaugin, Van Gogh, and Monet. In other parts of the museum, you will find classic works from all European periods; funerary sculpture and gold jewelry from the late classical Greek and Roman periods; and a 16th and 19th-century collection of fine paintings including works by Canaletto, Bernet, and Turner. The 20th century is represented through Picasso, Braque, Gris, Mondrian, Brancusi, and Malevich. From ancient America are ceramics, textiles, gold objects, and stone sculptures from such diverse cultures as the Paracas, Olmec, Maya, Aztec, Mimbre, and Anasazi. Other highlights include an extensive collection of ancient Egyptian and Nubian sculptures of gods and kings, funerary objects, and jewelry. The Mayer Library has general information about art and art history and the museum's collection. In addition to 30,000 volumes, the museum has art magazines; auction catalogs; artist files; and 400,000 slides, photographs, and transparencies. When you are ready for a break, stop by the museum's Seventeen Seventeen Restaurant or Atrium Café. *1717 N. Harwood St., Downtown, 214/922–1200. Admission is free except for special exhibits. Free public tours daily start from the Visitor Service Desk. Open Tues.–Wed. and Fri.–Sun. 11–5, Thur. 11–9.*

Dallas Museum of Art

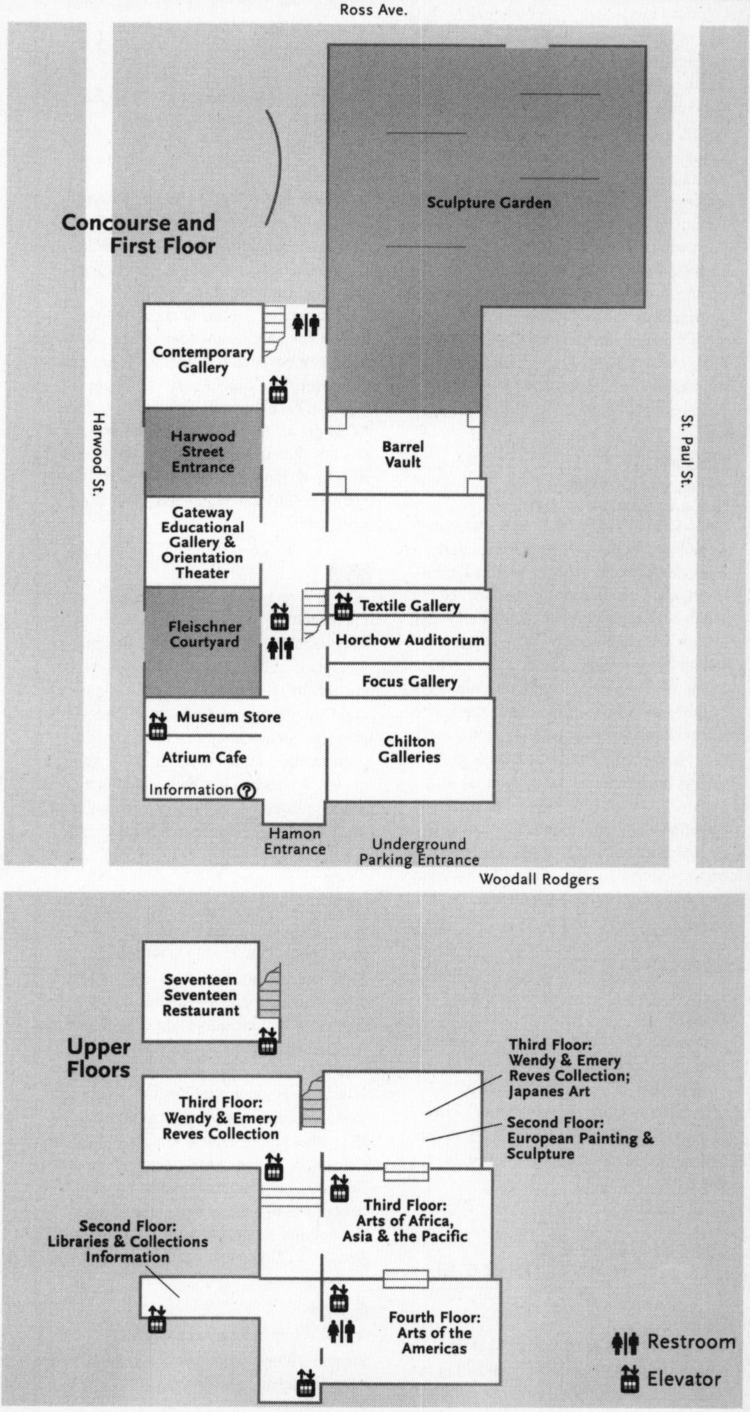
Ross Ave.
Concourse and First Floor
Sculpture Garden
Contemporary Gallery
Harwood Street Entrance
Barrel Vault
Harwood St.
St. Paul St.
Gateway Educational Gallery & Orientation Theater
Textile Gallery
Fleischner Courtyard
Horchow Auditorium
Focus Gallery
Museum Store
Atrium Cafe
Chilton Galleries
Information
Hamon Entrance
Underground Parking Entrance
Woodall Rodgers
Seventeen Seventeen Restaurant
Upper Floors
Third Floor: Wendy & Emery Reves Collection; Japanes Art
Third Floor: Wendy & Emery Reves Collection
Second Floor: European Painting & Sculpture
Third Floor: Arts of Africa, Asia & the Pacific
Second Floor: Libraries & Collections Information
Fourth Floor: Arts of the Americas
Restroom
Elevator

6 *f-8*

MEADOWS MUSEUM

"The Three Graces," a sculpture by Aristide Maillol greets visitors and art students at this museum tucked into a corner of the Meadows School of Art at Southern Methodist University. Other sculptures, including pieces by Henry Moore and Claes Oldenberg, are part of the sculpture garden. Inside, the museum houses 738 Spanish art pieces, including paintings and sculpture by such artists as El Greco, Valazquez, Goya, and Picasso. A magnificent 1762 Portuguese Baroque organ and brightly painted Eucharistic cabinet (1375–1400) hang in the foyer. *Bishop Blvd. at Binkley Ave., University Park, 214/768–2516. Admission: free. Open Sun. 1–5, Mon.–Tues. and Fri.–Sat. 10–5, Thurs. 10–8.*

13 *d-3*

THE TRAMMELL & MARGARET CROW COLLECTION OF ASIAN ART

A quiet reflection among Asian deities is a quick refresher from bustling Downtown. This permanent collection of Asian art—all from the Trammell family's private collection—showcases works from Japan, China, and India. Some of the most impressive pieces are of jade, created by Chinese artists who often toiled for years on large elaborate pieces. Outside follow the pink granite walkway shaded by oak, cypress, and sycamore trees to view works by such European sculptors as Rodin, Bourdelle, and Maillol. *2010 Flora St., 214/979–6430. Admission: free. Open Tues.–Wed. and Fri.–Sun. 11–6, Thurs. 11–9.*

BRIDGES

13 *b-7*

HOUSTON STREET VIADUCT

(Hedrick & Cochrane, Kansas City, 1912) This bridge of 51 concrete arches crosses the Trinity River to link Downtown with Oak Cliff. When built, it was one of the longest arched viaducts in the United States.

CHURCHES & SYNAGOGUES

13 *d-3*

CATHEDRAL GUADALUPE

The Roman Catholic Diocese of Dallas, established in 1890, uses this cathedral as the mother church. The church is Victorian Gothic built of red brick with white stone accents. It has the fourth largest Catholic congregation in the United States and is the only one named for Our Lady of Guadalupe. *2215 Ross Ave., Downtown, 214/871–1362. Open daily, 9–5; daily 7 PM mass.*

13 *d-4*

FIRST BAPTIST CHURCH

Designed by Albert Ulrich, this Victorian-era church built in 1890 is the only Downtown church still at its original site. The congregation is one of the largest in the United States, having grown for 46 years under the leadership by the Reverend W.A. Criswell, now pastor emeritus. The Criswell College, which offers degrees in ministry, and KCBI 90.9 FM radio are also part of the church. For many years, the Reverend Billy Graham kept his membership here. *1707 San Jacinto St., Downtown, 214/969–0111.*

13 *g-7*

FIRST PRESBYTERIAN CHURCH

Architect C.D. Hill designed the present structure of the city's first Presbyterian church in 1912 with a fan-shape sanctuary, Corinthian columns, and stained-glass windows. A gold cross stands on a gold-topped cupola, which crowns a green tile dome. Inside, church artifacts are displayed in its Hall of History. *408 Park Ave., 214/748–8051. Open weekdays 8:30–5.*

13 *d-2*

ST. PAUL UNITED METHODIST CHURCH

Bible scenes are depicted in 35 magnificent stained-glass windows in this Gothic and Victorian-style church, which was designed by African American architect William Sidney Pittman in 1912. The altar and pews are laid out in a rarely used diagonal pattern. Organized in 1873, this is the oldest African American church in Dallas. At the time, it served as both a church and a school, becoming one of the few places in town for African Americans to obtain an education. *1816 Routh St., Downtown, 214/922–0000.*

6 *g-7*

TEMPLE EMANU-EL

Howard Meyer designed this award-winning synagogue with an outdoor courtyard, which is ideally suited for receptions. This is the fourth temple for Dallas's oldest and largest Jewish congregation. *8500 Hillcrest Rd., North, 214/706–0000.*

10 *f-2*

THIRD CHURCH OF CHRIST SCIENTIST

A red-tile roof tops this Romanesque-style church designed in 1932 by Mark Lemmon. Church members voted to build a third church on Oct. 29, 1929, "Black Friday," the day of the stock market crash. Construction of the church became one of the city's major building projects, providing work for many left jobless during the Depression. The cornerstone was laid on Thanksgiving Day, November 27, 1930. *4419 Oak Lawn Ave., Oak Lawn, 214/526–7783.*

GRAVEYARDS & CEMETERIES

10 *g-2*

FREEDMAN'S CEMETERY

From 1861 to 1925, thousands of African Americans were buried in this cemetery. Many of these graves were paved over in the 1940s during construction of North Central Expressway. In the 1990s, during preparation to widen the freeway, archaeologists relocated 1,500 graves. A $2 million memorial was dedicated in 1999. *S.W. corner of Lemmon Ave. and N. Central Expressway.*

13 *d-1*

GREENWOOD CEMETERY

Many of the city's most prominent citizens rest in this historic spot. The cemetery was founded as Trinity Cemetery in 1874 on part of a Republic of Texas land grant. The Greenwood Cemetery Association assumed operation in 1896. You'll also find graves of soldiers from all military battles since the Civil War, including a special section for Union soldiers. *3020 Oak Grove Ave., Oak Lawn.*

13 *c-6*

PIONEER CEMETERY

At one time, this area contained three cemeteries: Independent Order of Odd Fellows, Hebrew Benevolent Association, and Old City Cemetery, which dates back to 1871. Many of the city's leaders are buried here including John Henry Long, who was buried here in 1870. The last burial was in the 1920s. The cemetery is showing wear with many stone markers broken. It is next to the Dallas Convention Center and adjoins Pioneer Plaza. *Young and Griffin Sts., Downtown.*

6 *h-6*

RESTLAND MEMORIAL PARK

What once began as a small family burial plot in the mid-19th century developed into one of the area's largest as the population grew. Nestled in the heart of this large cemetery is the one-acre Floyd Pioneer Cemetery, created by the John B. Floyd family in the 1860s. Restland adjoined the pioneer cemetery in 1924. A sculpture of Christ, whose eyes appear to watch you regardless of where you stand, has long been a favorite of locals. *9220 Restland Rd., North.*

13 *d-1*

TEMPLE EMANU-EL CEMETERY

Established in 1884, this is Dallas's second oldest Jewish cemetery. It holds graves from the city's first Jewish cemetery, on Akard Street, which were then moved to their present location in 1956 when the Dallas Convention Center was built. In the mausoleum, which opened in 1998, crypts surround a triangular courtyard. *3430 Howell St., Oak Lawn.*

HAUNTED PLACES

10 *h-2*

CENTENNIAL BUILDING

Some say an unnamed ghost walks the corridors of the old WRR studio, which was housed at the end of this building. It's never seen, only heard. Others who work in the building dismiss such stories. *Fair Park, 1300 Robert B. Cullum Blvd., East.*

6 *h-8*

LADY OF WHITE ROCK LAKE

The story goes that this urban ghost of a young woman in a dripping white gown flags down a motorist late at night. The motorist gives her a ride, but when he stops at her home, no one is in the backseat. Another version is the motorist returns to the house the next day to see how the woman is only to have her mother say her daughter drowned years earlier. The story dates from the 1930s. *Lawther Dr.*

13 *e-5*

MAJESTIC THEATRE

Some claim this friendly ghost is none other than Karl Hoblitzelle, the theater's original owner. He is blamed—or credited—for causing telephone lines to light up when not in use and for mysteriously causing the stage's backdrop to descend. *1925 Elm St., Downtown, 214/880–0137.*

13 *f-7*

MILLERMORE HOUSE

Old City Park employees, guides, and visitors often sense an unseen presence on the second floor of this antebellum house built by William Brown Miller. Before the house was completed, his wife, Minerva, died in the log cabin next door. Some say they have seen her likeness standing in front of a second-floor window. She seems to prefer the master bedroom and nursery area on the second floor. *Old City Park, 1717 Gano St., South, 214/421–5141.*

10 *g-1*

SNUFFER'S RESTAURANT & BAR

This ghost, who some say is a woman who was fatally stabbed years ago when the building was a bar, tosses glasses and ashtrays across the room and moves chairs at this popular hamburger café. After closing the café, employees claim to have seen flashing lights, watched a woman's figure floating through a locked door, felt a hand on their right shoulder, and heard their names whispered three times by a hoarse voice. *3526 Greenville Ave., East, 214/826–6850.*

13 *f-4*

SONS OF HERMANN HALL

These ghosts don't care if it's night or day. They like to make noise in this 1911 building that is owned by a German fraternal order. Employees report doors slamming and children laughing. When they look, no one is there. They also find tables and chairs rearranged and see people walk down the hall toward the door but never hear them leave. Some say it is deceased caretaker Louis Barnhardt who used to yell at children for playing the stage piano. *3414 Elm St., Deep Ellum, 214/747–4422.*

HISTORIC STRUCTURES & STREETS

6 *h-8*

BATH HOUSE CULTURAL CENTER

(Carson & Linskie, 1929) Built in 1929, this bathhouse is one of the earliest Art Deco structures in Texas. It was closed in 1953 when the city banned swimming at White Rock Lake in response to a polio outbreak. In 1981, the building reopened as a community cultural center. *521 E. Lawther Dr., East, 214/670–8749.*

13 *d-4*

BELO MANSION

A.H. Belo moved to Texas after the Civil War, buying a Galveston newspaper that would later become *The Dallas Morning News*. After the Belo family sold the house in 1922, it became a funeral home for 50 years. The mansion has nine meeting rooms that will accommodate 10–400 guests. The house is on the National Register of Historic Places and is designated a Texas Historic Landmark. *2101 Ross Ave., 214/220–0239.*

13 *b-5*

DALLAS COUNTY COURTHOUSE

(Orlopp & Kusener, H.H. Richardson, Little Rock, 1892) Better known as "Old Red," this red sandstone and Arkansas gray limestone Romanesque revival–style courthouse was built on the site of the first log courthouse. The imposing structure has arched windows, turrets, and four red gargoyle-like figures on the roof. In 1919, a central clock tower was removed. It now houses the Dallas Visitors Information Center. *500 Main St., Downtown, 214/571–1301.*

13 *c-5*

DALLAS COUNTY HISTORICAL PLAZA

In this area are such historical buildings as "Old Red" courthouse, a log cabin, Kennedy Memorial, and Dallas County terrazzo map. (*See* individual listings.) *Market, Elm, Commerce, and Houston Sts., Downtown.*

13 *b-5*

DEALEY PLAZA

The assassination of President John F. Kennedy made this Dallas landmark a household name. Built in 1836 by the National Youth Administration, Dealey Plaza is actually the birthplace of Dallas. On this site, the first home, post office, and store were built in what would eventually become a thriving metropolitan city. A larger-than-life bronze statue of George Bannerman Dealey—founder of *The Dallas Morning News*—stands on one side of the plaza. Across the street are three commemorative markers inscribed with a description of the Kennedy assassination. *Elm, Main, and Commerce Sts. at Houston St., Downtown.*

10 *h-2*

FAIR PARK

This is the largest collection in the world of 1930s Art Deco exposition style architecture. Most of the buildings were built for the 1936 Texas Centennial Exposition under the direction of chief architect George Dahl. More than six million people attended the centennial celebration, and thousands still turn out annually for the fair, summer musicals, and sporting events held here. Buildings constructed in 1936 include the Hall of State, Tower Building, Dallas Aquarium, and Agricultural Building. Preparation for the centennial also sparked the beginning of the Dallas cultural district with a fine arts museum and band shell. Fair Park Music Hall, Cotton Bowl, and Centennial Building were all renovated for the celebration. *1300 Robert B. Cullum Blvd., East, 214/421–9600.*

13 *c-5*

JOHN NEELY BRYAN CABIN

This one-room cedar log cabin was built shortly after John Neely Bryan founded the settlement of Dallas in 1841. Floods washed away his first log cabin, which was built on the east banks of the Trinity River. This is believed to be half of his third cabin. *600 block of Elm St., Downtown.*

13 *e-5*

THE MAJESTIC THEATRE

At one time, theaters stretched down Elm Street, illuminating the streets with their neon marquees. Today, only the Majestic is left. Vaudeville great Olga Petrova opened the theater in 1921. Ginger Rogers began her career here, and Duke Ellington and Kate Smith performed on its stage. Unable to compete with suburban flight and multi-theater complexes, the grand theater closed in 1973. It reopened in 1983 after extensive renovations as a performing arts center. *1925 Elm St., 214/880–0137.*

13 *g-3*

SWISS AVENUE HISTORIC DISTRICT

This district was part of the Munger Place development, an early 1900s real estate venture with deed restrictions that required a house to be two stories and cost at least $10,000. Early marketers claimed the area had more paving than anywhere else in Dallas. Many of Dallas's leaders built substantial homes here in such diverse styles as Georgian, Spanish, Mediterranean, English Tudor, and Prairie School. The district includes Swiss Avenue, portions of Bryan Street, La Vista Avenue, Live Oak Street, Swiss Avenue, and Bryan Parkway. *East.*

13 *b-5*

TEXAS SCHOOL BOOK DEPOSITORY

While other early 20th-century buildings have long ago disappeared into anonymity, this structure received historic status the day Lee Harvey Oswald perched in a sixth floor window to shoot President John F. Kennedy. Before becoming a textbook warehouse, the building housed a plow company. It is now a museum dedicated to the assassination. *411 Elm St., Downtown, 214/747–6660. Admission: $9; $8 seniors, students, and children; $3 children under 6. Open daily 9–6.*

13 *g-3*

WILSON HISTORIC DISTRICT

In the 1980s the Meadow Foundation saved a number of 19th-century houses in the 2900 block of Swiss Avenue, known as the Wilson Block. Frederick P. Wilson built his Queen Anne–style home here in 1899. He later built six other houses, which he rented to prominent Dallas leaders. Wilson's original house is now headquarters for Preservation Dallas. Renovation of this block of homes proved so successful that the Meadow Foundation moved other Victorian and Queen Anne homes destined for demolition to the 2800 block of Swiss Avenue. This is known as the Beilharz Block, named after Theodore Beilharz, who built his house Shingle style in 1902. The Meadow Foundation restored the houses's original exteriors, then rented the buildings to non-profit organizations for use as offices. Although the inside of the houses are closed to the public, the area is worth driving through to see the fancy wooden homes that once housed Dallas's elite. *2800–2900 Swiss Ave., East, 214/826–5746 or 214/826–9431.*

HISTORY MUSEUMS

10 *h-2*

AGE OF STEAM RAILROAD MUSEUM

Steam engines—those puffing, smoke-belching iron horses of the movies—now sit quietly at this Fair Park museum as train buffs of all ages pay homage to the golden days of rail travel. If the Union Pacific's "Big Boy"—the world's largest steam locomotive at 1.2 million pounds—looks familiar, that's because it's now on a postage stamp. To reach the trains, visitors must first buy a ticket in Dallas's oldest train depot; a bright yellowish-orange wooden structure built in 1903. The historic building also houses a gift shop. *1105 Washington St., 214/428–0101. Admission: $4, $2 children under 12. Open Wed.–Sun. 10–5.*

13 *c-5*

CONSPIRACY MUSEUM

This museum contains information about various U.S. assassinations and alleged cover-ups from 1835 to the present. Weekend admissions include a guided walking tour of Dealey Plaza with insight into the assassination of John F. Kennedy. *110 S. Market St., 214/741–3040, Downtown. Admission: $7, $6 seniors, $3 children 9–12, children under 9 free. Open daily 10–6.*

10 *h-2*

DALLAS FIREFIGHTERS MUSEUM

You can have a cup of coffee while you monitor the Dallas Fire Department radio or learn about "Old Tigue," a horse-drawn pumper purchased by the city in 1883. The museum is set in the Old No. 5 Hook & Ladder Co. station, which housed firefighters from 1907 to 1978. A gift shop stocks a variety of items with fire themes. *3801 Parry Ave., East, 214/821–1500. Open Wed.–Sat. 9–4.*

6 *g-7*

DALLAS HOLOCAUST CENTER

Photographs, artifacts, documents, film, and memorabilia of the Holocaust pay tribute to the six million Jewish people who perished in Nazi Germany. The museum, which opened in 1984, has an extensive library of audio-visual materials. *Jewish Community Center, 7900 Northhaven Rd., North, 214/750–4654. Admission: free. Open Mon.–Wed. and Fri. 9:30–4:30, Thurs. 9:30–9, Sun. noon–4.*

13 *f-7*

OLD CITY PARK

All ages will find this outdoor museum, just north of Downtown, an entertaining way to spend an afternoon. Originally, this was Dallas's first city park, built on land donated to the city by John J. and Ophelia Eakins. Now the Dallas County Heritage Society has transformed the 13 acres into a 19th-century village, with brick streets and 37 restored historic homes, buildings, and shops. Artisans are often on hand to demonstrate candle making, weaving, and printing. Volunteers give guided tours of most buildings. The two oldest structures are log cabins dating to the 1840s. A two-room log cabin served the Miller family for nearly 20 years until a more elegant two-story antebellum home was completed. During the winter holidays, the historic homes take on a festive touch with Christmas and Hanukkah decorations. Hundreds of hurricane lamps illuminate the paths through the Victorian village, lighting the way for Christmas visitors. This is a popular time for people to visit the park, so purchase tickets in advance for the Christmas tour. *1717 Gano St., 214/421–5141. Admission: $6. Open Sun. noon–4, Tues.–Sat. 10–4.*

13 *b-5*

THE SIXTH FLOOR MUSEUM

From the sixth floor of the infamous Texas School Book Depository (now Dallas County Administration Building), you can look down onto Dealey Plaza and imagine President John F. Kennedy's motorcade slowly driving past on November 22, 1963. Then the crisp morning air of that now historic day is shattered by the explosion of gunshots, fired from near where you are standing by assassin Lee Harvey Oswald. That same sixth floor is now a museum with a historical exhibition of the life, times, death, and legacy of the late president. His assassination is documented with nearly 400 photographs, a 45-minute film, and other interpretative materials. Artifacts include the Zapruder camera, which captured the only moving pictures of the event, and the FBI model of Dealey Plaza used by the Warren Commission. The tragic event draws millions of visitors to this area annually with two million taking time to stop by the museum for a tour. *411 Elm St., 214/747–6660. Admission: with audio guide, $9 adults, $8 seniors and students, $3 children under 6. Open daily 9–6.*

10 *h-2*

THE WOMEN'S MUSEUM

From high-tech interactive displays to primitive tool artifacts, this museum is one of a few in the United States that is devoted to women's history. The three-story museum has such popular electronic displays as a listening room, where you hear the words of poets by leaning against a wall. A loop DBD allows you to hear such comediennes as Lucille Ball or Judy Tenuta. While these electronic gadgets tell about women today, more traditional exhibits tell about the past including biographies, photographs, and artifacts from some of this country's trailblazers. Well known achievers such as Amelia Earhart (you can see her Postal Service flight suit) and lesser-known but equally important figures such as Meggie Lena Walker, the first female bank president, are all represented. A time line traces women's history from 1500 to the present with such artifacts as a certificate for wife, required by women in the North seeking Civil War benefits, and a helmet worn by women working in defense factories during World War II. *3800 Parry Ave., 214/915–0860. Admission: $5, $4 students. Open Tues.–Sun., 1–5.*

LIBRARIES

6 *b-8*

FONDREN LIBRARY CENTER

(Roscoe DeWitt, 1940) More than 3.2 million volumes are housed in the four libraries at this central location on the campus of Southern Methodist University. The Fondren Library (214/768–7378) has the largest general reference collection on campus with more than a million volumes. The DeGolyer Library (214/768–3231) houses a special collection of Western Americana that includes 90,000 rare books, 350,000 photographs, and 4,000 cubic ft of manuscripts. *5700 Bishop Blvd., University Park, 214/768–2323.*

10 *h-2*

G.B. DEALEY LIBRARY

(Texas Centennial Architects; Adams & Adams, San Antonio, 1936) Following the 1986 renovation of the Hall of State Building, the Dallas Historical Society opened this library to house its extensive collection of Dallas and Texas-related documents and artifacts. The library holds more than 10,000 books and three million historic documents, including Sam Houston's handwritten account of the decisive battle at San Jacinto that led to Texas becoming a republic. *3939 Grand Ave., at Hall of State at Fair Park, 214/421–4500, ext. 112. Open Wed.–Fri. 1–5, by appointment only.*

13 *d-6*

J. ERIK JONSSON CENTRAL LIBRARY

(Fisher & Spillman, 1982) This is the centerpiece of the city's library system, which includes 22 branches. The central library houses more than one million books including local and state history collections of more than 45,000 books; 1,500 newspaper and periodical titles; more than 5,000 maps; 500,000 photographs; and 300 oral history interviews. The seventh floor has one of the 23 original copies of the Declaration of Independence, printed July 4, 1776, and "The First Folio," a 1623 printing of William Shakespeare's plays. Scattered throughout the library is a large collection of Navajo rugs, paintings, and sculptures. You will also find a children's center, government publications, and a business and technology center. *1515 Young St., Downtown, 214/670–1400. Open Sun. noon–4, Mon.–Thurs. 9–9, Fri.–Sat. 9–5.*

SCHOOLS

13 *h-3*

BAYLOR COLLEGE OF DENTISTRY

This once private, nondenominational college is now part of the Texas A&M University System. It offers degrees in dental hygiene, dentistry, and highly specialized dental treatment. More than

117,000 patients, many low income, receive care at the college each year. *3302 Gaston Ave., East, 214/828–8100.*

13 *h-3*

BAYLOR UNIVERSITY SCHOOL OF NURSING

Offering bachelor and master degrees in nursing, this is a privately supported, two-year school. Affiliated with Baylor University, it was founded in 1909. *3700 Worth, 214/820–3361.*

13 *h-3*

CRISWELL COLLEGE

Students can earn associate, bachelor, and graduate degrees at this four-year Bible seminary college. Affiliated with the Southern Baptist Convention, the school has courses in such studies as the Bible, missionary, counseling, evangelism, pastoral ministry, urban ministry, New and Old Testaments, and theology. *4010 Gaston Ave., 214/821–5433.*

10 *c-5*

DALLAS BAPTIST UNIVERSITY

Affiliated with the Baptist General Convention of Texas, this privately funded university has undergraduate and graduate programs in Biblical studies, business administration, and education. It also provides a special tutorial program for deaf students. *3000 Mountain Creek Pkwy., 214/331–8311.*

DALLAS COUNTY COMMUNITY COLLEGE DISTRICT

More than 55,000 students annually enroll on the seven campuses of this two-year college to pursue a variety of programs. Credits earned transfer to universities. An additional 70,000 locals enroll for noncredit classes. *214/860–2135.*

13 *h-3*

DALLAS THEOLOGICAL SEMINARY

Established in 1924, this private school offers a variety of graduate and doctoral programs in ministry, theology, and Biblical studies. *3909 Swiss Ave., East, 214/824–3094.*

10 *g-4*

PAUL QUINN COLLEGE

Founded in 1872 by the African Methodist Episcopal Church in Austin, this is the oldest African American college west of the Mississippi River. The college moved to Waco in 1881, then to Dallas in 1990. Set on the former campus of Bishop College, this college has bachelor programs in liberal arts and sciences, including business management, protective services, and an innovative adult degree-completion program in organizational management. *3837 Simpson Stuart Rd., 214/376–1000.*

6 *d-8*

SOUTHERN METHODIST UNIVERSITY

Founded in 1911 by what is now the United Methodist Church, SMU is an upscale private university offering undergraduate and graduate degrees in all major areas of study, including law and theology. The Caruth Institute of Owner-Managed Business is one of the United States's oldest entrepreneurial programs. Bishop Avenue runs through the heart of the campus where you will find an eclectic array of architecture, from the Classical Revival Dallas Hall (Shepley, Rutan, & Coolidge, Boston, 1915) to the Modernist Science Information Center (O'Neil Ford, A. B. Swank, 1961). A popular summer get-away is at the university's Taos, New Mexico, campus where students can take a variety of classes or participate in the excavation of a 13th-century Native American pueblo. *Bounded by Mockingbird La., Hillcrest Ave., Daniel Ave., and Airline Rd., University Park, 214/768–2000.*

13 *e-5*

UNIVERSITIES CENTER AT DALLAS

Locals can take courses from universities scattered across North Texas without ever leaving the city. A renovated Downtown building serves as classrooms for the following universities: Dallas County Community College, Texas A&M University at Commerce, Texas Woman's University, University of Texas at Arlington, University of Texas at Dallas, and the University of North Texas. *1901 Main St., Downtown, 214/915–1900.*

10 *f-10*

UNIVERSITY OF TEXAS SOUTHWESTERN MEDICAL CENTER AT DALLAS

Founded in 1943, this medical school is now considered a top international research and teaching facility with four Nobel laureates on staff. Competition for admission is high with the school annually accepting only 200 new students, 90% of those from Texas. Each year, 3,000 students graduate from this school. In 1999, the school built its first student housing. Faculty and residents annually treat more than one million patients at numerous area hospitals. *5323 Harry Hines Blvd., Northwest Dallas, 214/648–3111.*

7 *a-5*

UNIVERSITY OF TEXAS AT DALLAS

About 9,000 students attend this university, which started as a graduate school in 1961. In 1989, it began offering undergraduate degrees in a variety of studies. Alum Jim Reilly, who earned three degrees from the university, was part of the space shuttle team that transferred material and supplies to the Mir Space Station in 1998. *2601 N. Floyd Rd., Richardson, 972/883–2111.*

STATUES, MURALS & MONUMENTS

Dallas has a public art collection that is the envy of many museums. You will find hundreds of sculptures scattered about the city. Many are privately owned but publicly displayed for everyone's enjoyment. The city alone owns more than 200 pieces of art. Thanks to a public art program, the city continues to acquire new pieces as part of capital improvement projects.

10 *h-2*

BIG TEX

(Jack Bridges, 1952) No visit to the State Fair is complete without a greeting from Big Tex, which started out as the world's largest Santa Claus in Kerens, Texas, in 1949. He became a cowboy, complete with size 70 cowboy boots and a 75-gallon hat in 1952. Standing 52 ft tall, Big Tex makes his appearance only during the State Fair, where you will find him waving and greeting folks with a friendly "howdy" at the main entrance. *1300 Robert B. Cullum Blvd.*

13 *d-7*

CONFEDERATE MEMORIAL

(Frank Teich, 1896) Dignitaries from across the state turned out for the 1897 dedication of this Confederate memorial in City Park. Life-size statues of four Southern leaders (Lee, Jackson, Johnson, and Davis) surround the Confederate private standing atop the granite obelisk. The memorial was moved to Pioneer Cemetery in 1962. *1400 Marilla St.*

13 *d-7*

THE DALLAS PIECE

(Henry Moore, 1978) Is this piece sitting, standing, or reclining in front of Dallas City Hall? You be the judge. Internationally acclaimed sculptor Henry Moore designed this 27,000-pound bronze especially for its present location. It's actually comprised of three sections and a favorite of locals who like to stroll through the pieces. *1500 Marilla St.*

13 *d-3*

DE MUSICA

(Eduardo Chillida, 1989) Chillida worked with architect I.M. Pei to design this abstract of two 15-ft vertical columns for the Morton H. Meyerson Symphony Center. Appendages near the top of each column represent music, architecture, and sculpture. *2301 Flora St., Downtown.*

13 *d-5*

FOREVER EAGLES

(Gerald Balciar, 1993) In front of Thanksgiving Tower sits this large bronze eagle perched on a red granite base. The plaza and water fountains are also granite, the same used in many buildings Downtown. *1601 Elm St., Downtown, 214/922–4022.*

13 *d-4*

FOUR CHROMATIC GATES

(Herbert Bayer, 1984) These aluminum-plate gates in colors of white, yellow, bright blue, and red add a dash of color to all the concrete, granite, marble, and glass found in Downtown Dallas. The Atlantic Richfield Company donated the abstract gates to the city in 1985. *1600 Bryan St., Downtown.*

13 *d-3*

GENESIS, THE GIFT OF LIFE

(Miguel Covarrubias, 1954) Measuring 12 ft by 60 ft, this colorful Venetian glass

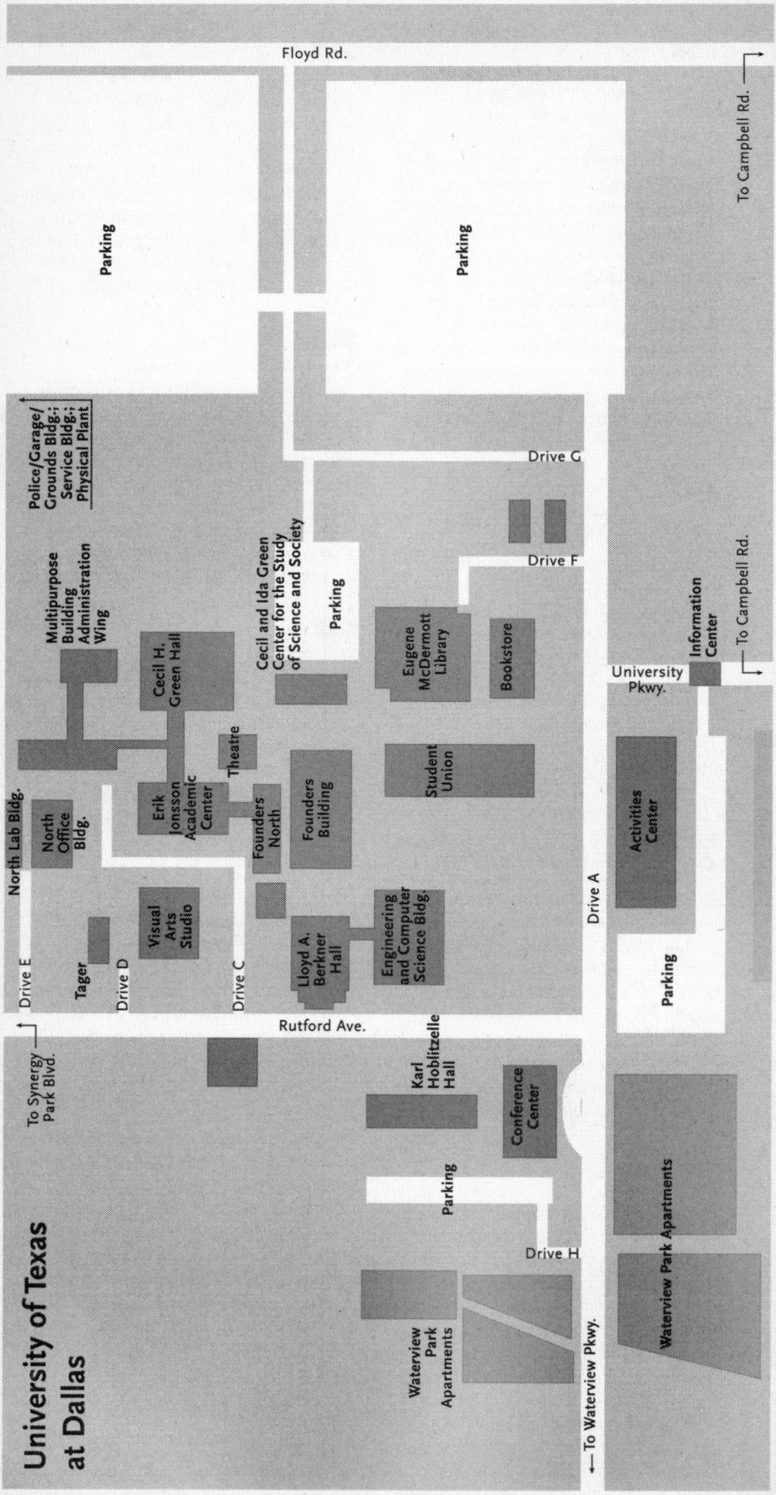
University of Texas at Dallas
Floyd Rd.
To Campbell Rd.
Parking
Parking
Police/Garage/ Grounds Bldg.; Service Bldg.; Physical Plant
Multipurpose Building Administration Wing
Cecil and Ida Green Center for the Study of Science and Society
Parking
Drive G
Drive F
Cecil H. Green Hall
Eugene McDermott Library
Bookstore
Information Center
To Campbell Rd.
University Pkwy.
Theatre
North Lab Bldg.
North Office Bldg.
Erik Jonsson Academic Center
Founders North
Founders Building
Student Union
Activities Center
Drive A
Visual Arts Studio
Tager
Drive E
Drive D
Drive C
Lloyd A. Berkner Hall
Engineering and Computer Science Bldg.
Parking
Rutford Ave.
To Synergy Park Blvd.
Karl Hoblitzelle Hall
Conference Center
Parking
Drive H
Waterview Park Apartments
Waterview Park Apartments
To Waterview Pkwy.

mosaic is hard to miss. It is filled with life and movement as the blues, reds, oranges, and yellows almost leap toward you. *Dallas Museum of Art, 1717 N. Harwood St., 214/922–1200.*

10 *h-2*

THE GULF CLOUD

(Clyde Giltner Chandler, 1916) This popular sculpture east of the Music Hall at Fair Park is an allegorical composition of four figures representing Texas's diverse geographical climates: coastal plains, tablelands, mountains, and gulf breezes. Chandler, one of Dallas's first professional female sculptors, considered this her best work. *1200 Second Ave.*

10 *e-2*

A LONG ROAD HOME

(Ghelardini Pietrasanta, 1985) Cattle rustlers aren't likely to make off with these five cows as they graze along the Trinity River—each cow weighs three tons. Their names are Lucy, Margaret, Ruth, Elsa, and Annette. *Trinity Park, Wycliff Ave. and Sylvan Dr. at the Trinity River.*

10 *f-1*

MULE DEER

(A. Durenne, 1985) This life-size cast-iron doe and her fawn remind daily commuters along Turtle Creek Boulevard of an earlier time when this part of Dallas was still rural. *William B. Dean Park, 3636 Turtle Creek Blvd., Turtle Creek.*

10 *f-2*

OUR HISPANIC ROOTS

(Juan Manuel Campos, 1988) This brightly colored mural resulted from a proposal by the Art in Public Places Committee to donate artwork to the Pike Recreation Center. It depicts the Hispanic influences in Texas from the state's colonial period to present. *2807 Harry Hines Blvd., Oak Lawn.*

10 *h-2*

PAIR OF PYLONS WITH PEGASUS AND SIRENS

(Pierre Bourdelle, 1936) These raised cement frescoes have a winged horse on one side and a siren on the other side. Each pylon stands at opposite ends of a pool at the entrance to the Esplanade of State at Fair Park. Soon after graduating from the Sorbonne, French sculptor Pierre Bourdelle moved to New York where his murals caught the attention of Texas Centennial architects. He has three other raised cement frescoes at Fair Park. *1200 Second Ave., East.*

13 *d-5*

PEGASUS (FLYING RED HORSE)

(J.B. McMath, 1934) Since being hoisted to the top of the Magnolia Building in 1934, Pegasus's red neon lights have served as a beacon to those near Downtown. Engineer J. B. McMath created the Flying Red Horse, as locals call the sign, for Magnolia Oil Co. The creation turned out to be a designing feat of two signs, 14 ft apart, that hid unsightly bracing necessary to cope with high winds 29 stories up. For at least 20 years the sign stood dark until needed repairs returned Pegasus to its original splendor at midnight on January 1, 2000, to the cheers of 35,000 millenium celebrators. *108 S. Akard St., Downtown.*

13 *c-6*

PIONEER PLAZA CATTLE DRIVE

(Robert Summers, 1994) Celebrating the legendary cattle drives of the old west, three bronze cowboys herd 40 large bronze longhorn steers, weighing 1,000 pounds each, down a grassy hill in Downtown Dallas. The 4-acre park, between Pioneer Cemetery and the Dallas Convention Center, is set on the old 1854 cattle trail route, amid mesquite trees, yucca, and purple sage. *Griffin St. and Young St., Downtown.*

13 *e-4*

PORTAL PARK PIECE

(Robert Irwin, 1979–1981) Depending on whom you ask, people either love or hate these three sections of thin steel that twist through Carpenter Plaza in Downtown Dallas. The metal wall varies from 2-ft to 10-ft tall. *2201 Pacific Ave.*

10 *h-2*

PROSPERO BERNARDI/ HALL OF HEROES

(Pompeo Luigi Coppini, 1936) A bust of Bernardi, an Italian hero in the Texas fight for independence in 1836, is one of six other statues of Texas heroes at Fair Park created by Coppini, who eventually produced 35 public monuments, 16 portrait statues, and 75 portrait busts throughout the United States and Mexico. *Fair Park, 3939 Grand Ave., East.*

10 *f-2*

ROBERT E. LEE & THE CONFEDERATE SOLDIER

(Alexander Phimster Proctor, 1936) Confederate General Lee, riding his beloved horse Traveller, and a young aide look anything except defeated in this bronze monument in Robert E. Lee Park. *3400 Turtle Creek Blvd., Turtle Creek.*

13 *d-4*

SLICKER SHY

(Herb Mignery, 1999) This 18-ft bronze sculpture of a horse spooked by a cowboy wearing a slicker during a rainstorm dominates the lobby at Adam's Mark Hotel. *400 N. Olive St., Downtown.*

10 *h-2*

SPIRIT OF THE CENTENNIAL

(Raoul Josset, 1936) This concrete and plaster sculpture of a nude woman standing on a saguaro cactus was created for the Texas Centennial. After weathering the sun and rain since 1936, this huge statue, weighing 15 tons and standing 19 ft high, was restored in 1998. A 16-year-old Dallas teen modeled for the statue's face after artist Raoul Josset spotted her in a beauty contest. A colorful untitled mural with a map of Texas and indigenous plants and animals serves as the statue's backdrop. *Fair Park, 3809 Grand Ave., East.*

6 *e-8*

SPIRIT OF FLIGHT

(Charles Julius Umlauf, 1959–60) Standing at the entrance to Dallas Love Field, this bronze figure with outspread wings atop a granite plinth, surrounded by six groups of birds in flight, serves as a memorial to the aviation industry. *8008 Cedar Springs Rd., Northwest.*

13 *c-5*

TERRAZZO MAP

This map inlaid in concrete just east of John Neely Bryan's log cabin depicts the pioneer settlements in 1846 Dallas County. The map, however, shows wear from thousands of footsteps that annually walk cross it. *Dallas County Historical Plaza at Market, Elm, Commerce, and Houston Sts., Downtown.*

10 *h-2*

TOWER EAGLE

(Raoul Josset, 1936) After 62 years of weathering high winds, hail, and countless lightning strikes, this golden eagle was falling apart. In 1998 it was removed from its perch at the top of the 175-ft Tower Building at Fair Park. After being carefully rebuilt and gilded with gleaming gold leaf, the eagle has since returned to its lofty perch. *1200 2nd Ave., East.*

10 *f-4*

UNTITLED

(Bob Cassilly, 1996) From toe to tip of tongue, this 67-ft tall giraffe is the tallest statue in Texas. The winsome piece has the look of bronze but is really urethane foam and fiberglass over a metal skeleton. The metallic look results from a coating of gel containing 80% bronze. Look for the giraffe at the entrance to the Dallas Zoo. *650 S.R.L. Thornton Freeway (I–35E), South.*

10 *d-4*

WITH THE WIND

(Mary Dickson Albrecht, 1970) The artist created this piece by welding 49 steel rods into a design depicting wind movement. It resembles a Tinker-toy set with cylinders going in different directions, often at odd angles. It was originally painted black for an invitational exhibition, then painted red. For its current location in Martin Weiss Park, it is painted bright yellow. *1111 Martindell, South.*

SCULPTURE GARDENS/SPECIAL COLLECTIONS

13 *b-5*

DALLAS ALLEY

Texan William Easley designed these 10 modern sculptures to salute Texans who made significant contributions to popular music. Honored are Buddy Holly, Blind Lemon Jefferson, Sam "Lighting" Hopkins, William Orville "Lefty" Frizzell, Jiles Perry "Big Bopper" Richardson, Tex Ritter, T-Bone Walker, Scott Joplin, Roy Orbison, and Bob Wills. *Dallas West End Market Pl., 2019 N. Lamar St., Downtown, 214/748–4801.*

DALLAS AREA RAPID TRANSPORTATION (DART)

When you travel by DART, you get more than a ride. Artists worked with architects and engineers to design rail stations with spaces for a variety of art work. Below is a partial listing of art found at rail stations. *214/979–1111.*

Carousel (Tom Stancliffe) Three free-standing conical forms of sheet bronze represent cedar trees, which once grew profusely in this area. *Cedars Station, 1505 Wall St., South.*

Cycles of Life (Eliseo Garcia and Roberto Mungia) Four limestone bas-relief images representing Hispanic heritage top a concrete foundation reminiscent of a Mayan pyramid. *Westmoreland Station, 2626 S. Westmoreland, South.*

Full Circle Merrit (Frances Thompson) This lighted piece is a collage of photographic digital mural prints, which traces the city from frontier days to modern times. *Convention Center Station, 727 S. Lamar St., Downtown.*

Images of Community Life (Johnice I. Parker) Everyday activities, including a jazz club scene, are hand painted on these hand-fired tiles. *Corinth Station, 1740 E. 8th St., South.*

Recalling Dallas Milestones & Historic Murals (Philip Lamb) This series of 12 terrazzo panels is a partial recreation of panels installed in City Hall during the Depression. The original panels were destroyed in 1954, but artist Philip Lamb includes the mural's original themes in his creation. *Union Station, 401 S. Houston St., Downtown.*

Sun/Moon (Michael Brown) This steel, copper, and glass piece includes a functional clock. *St. Paul Station, 1800 Bryan St., Downtown.*

Untitled (Edwin McGowin) Cast in bronze, this circular form depicts images of animals and fish indigenous to Elmwood Creek, a popular neighborhood family-outing spot. *Hampton Station, 2202 S. Hampton, South.*

13 *d-3*

DALLAS MUSEUM OF ART

A sign at the entrance to the sculpture garden urges children not to climb on the 12 pieces, many of which likely appeal to youngsters's sense of exploration. Such sculptures include Henry Moore's 1961 "Two Pieces Reclining No. 3," Barbara Hepworth's 1960 "Figure for Landscape," and Kenneth Snelson's 1969 untitled suspension piece created of iron, steel, and cable. You'll also find sculptures by Ellsworth Kelly, Tony Smith, Mac Whitney, James Surls, Beverly Pepper, Matt Mullican, and Bryan Hunt. *1717 N. Harwood, Downtown, 214/922–1200.*

10 *f-4*

DALLAS ZOO

Art lovers will find the sculptures, ranging from life-size to amusing, as interesting as the animals. Visitors are greeted at the entrance by the tallest statue in Texas, a 67–ft–tall giraffe created in 1997 by artist Bob Cassilly. Below are some of the more prominent sculptures. *650 S. R.L. Thornton Fwy., South, 214/670–5656. Admission: $6, $4 seniors and children 3–11, children 2 and under free.*

Acrobatics on a Kudu (David Cargill,1969) A bronze kudu seems to leap from its base.

African Elephant Calves (Lorenzo Ghiglieri, 1985) This bronze fountain piece has young elephants playfully spewing water from their trunks.

The Elephant Child (Tom Tischler, 1988) Although it weighs 800 pounds, this bronze piece depicts a baby elephant.

Galapagos Tortoise (Tom Tischler, 1988) This giant turtle weighs 900 pounds.

Giraffe with Swing (David Cargill,1969–1971) This bronze piece includes a child swinging from a giraffe's neck.

Porcellino (unknown, 1985 recast) This is a bronze replica of a Florence, Italy, fountain sculpture designed in 1639 by Pietro Tacca.

Rhinoceros with Children (David Cargill, 1970) This playful bronze piece has five children clinging to a rhino's back.

10 *h-2*

FAIR PARK

Dallas spared no expenses when commissioning art for the Texas Centennial in 1936. More than 50 statues and paintings are scattered in buildings and plazas. Finding them all could constitute a treasure hunt. At various times some pieces are inaccessible because of renovation work (*see* Sculptures, *above*). Other works include Italian artist Pompeo Luigi Coppini's five bronzes of Texas heroes William B. Travis, Thomas J. Rusk, Mirabeau B. Lamar, Sam Houston, and Stephen F. Austin. French artist Pierre Bourdelle created five raised cement frescoes: "Pair of Pylons with Pegasus & Sirens," "Man Taming Wild

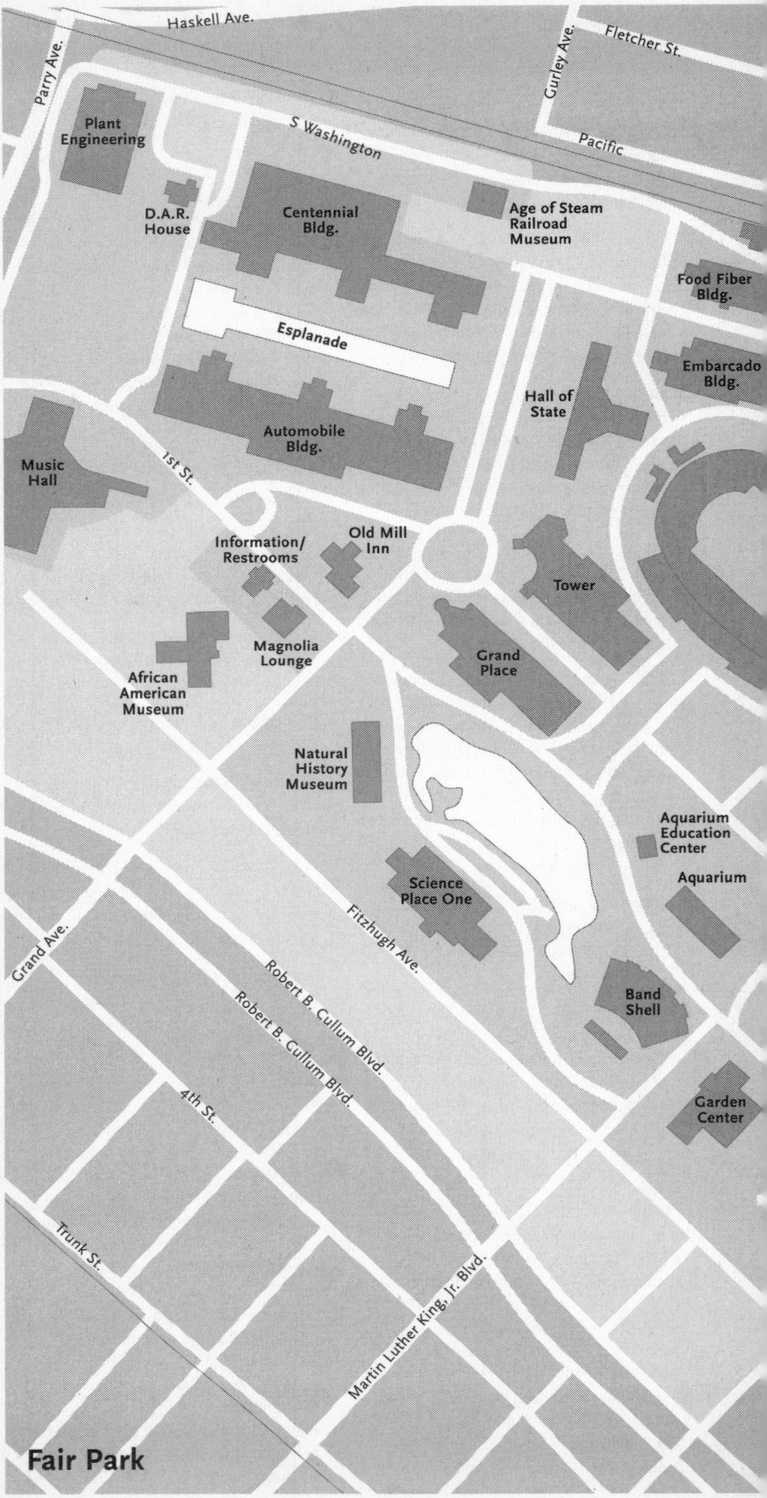
Haskell Ave.
Fletcher St.
Parry Ave.
Gurley Ave.
Plant Engineering
S Washington
Pacific
D.A.R. House
Centennial Bldg.
Age of Steam Railroad Museum
Food Fiber Bldg.
Esplanade
Embarcado Bldg.
Hall of State
Automobile Bldg.
Music Hall
1st St.
Information/ Restrooms
Old Mill Inn
Tower
Magnolia Lounge
Grand Place
African American Museum
Natural History Museum
Aquarium Education Center
Aquarium
Science Place One
Fitzhugh Ave.
Grand Ave.
Robert B. Cullum Blvd.
Robert B. Cullum Blvd.
Band Shell
4th St.
Garden Center
Trunk St.
Martin Luther King, Jr. Blvd.
Fair Park

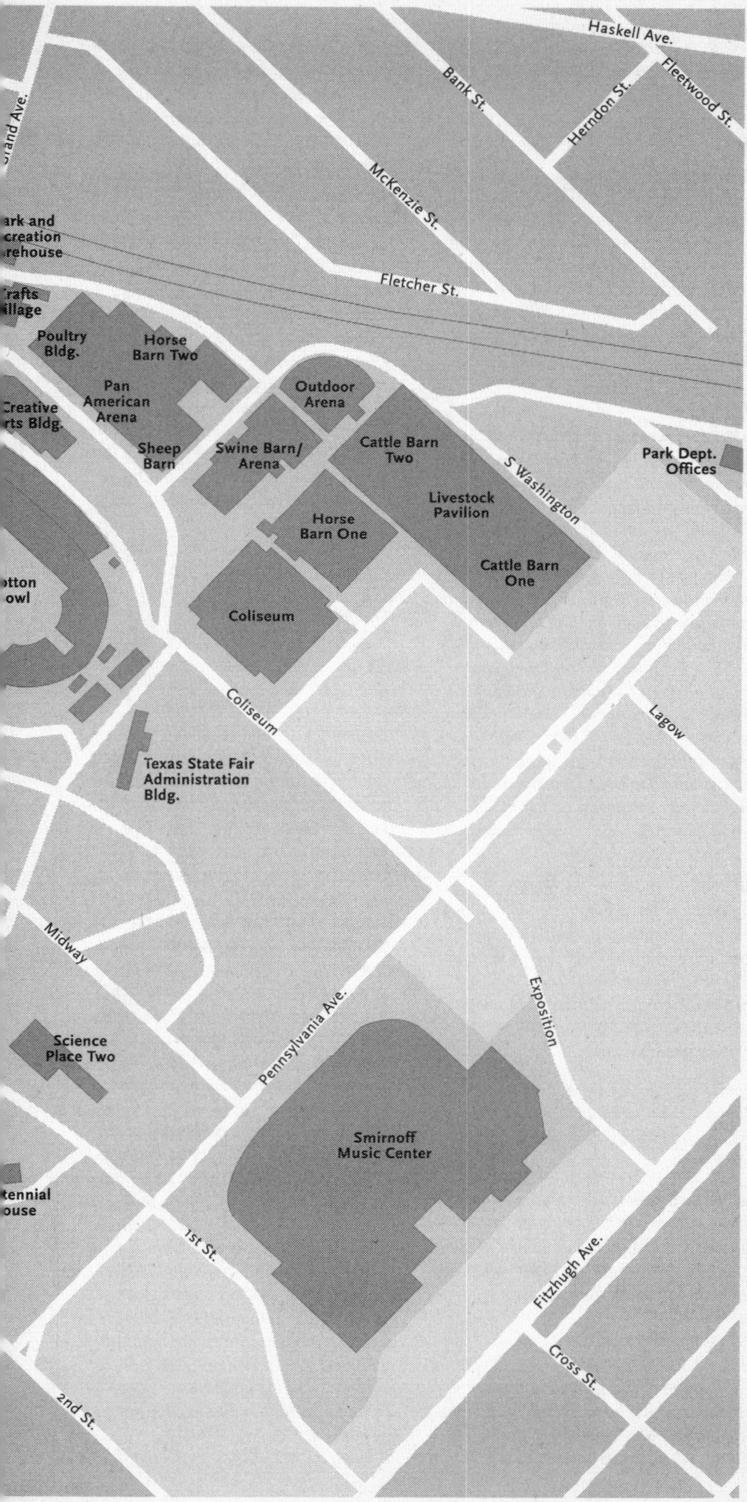

Haskell Ave.
Bank St.
Herndon St.
Fleetwood St.
rand Ave.
McKenzie St.
ark and
creation
rehouse
Fletcher St.
rafts
illage
Poultry
Bldg.
Horse
Barn Two
Pan
American
Arena
Outdoor
Arena
Creative
rts Bldg.
Sheep
Barn
Swine Barn/
Arena
Cattle Barn
Two
S Washington
Park Dept.
Offices
Livestock
Pavilion
Horse
Barn One
Cattle Barn
One
otton
owl
Coliseum
Coliseum
Lagow
Texas State Fair
Administration
Bldg.
Midway
Exposition
Pennsylvania Ave.
Science
Place Two
Smirnoff
Music Center
tennial
ouse
1st St.
Fitzhugh Ave.
Cross St.
2nd St.

Horses," "Streamline Cougar & Bison," "Locomotive Power," and "Speed." *3809 Grand Ave., East, 214/421–9600.*

10 *f-6*

FIVE MILE CREEK SCULPTURE WALK

Sculptor Michael Pavlovsky created five bronze pieces in 1994 for the greenbelt trail. On your walk, watch for "Archway," "River Column I," "Circle of Life," "River Column II," and "Little Circle." *East of Marsalis Avenue to Hortense Avenue, South.*

10 *g-1*

FREEDMAN'S MEMORIAL

(David Newton, 1996) This memorial is dedicated to the thousands of African Americans whose graves were covered or lost during construction of North Central Expressway. David Newton, who won the honor during a national search, designed the 20-ft granite entryway and five bronze sculptures. On the front of the arched entry stand "The Sentinel" and "The Prophetess," representing African Americans prior to slavery. On the back of the entry are "Violated Soul" and "Struggling Soul," depicting slavery. "Dream of Freedom" is a large bronze of an African American couple freed from slavery. *Southwest corner of Lemmon Ave. and N. Central Expressway.*

13 *c-6*

LUBBEN PLAZA

A.H. Belo Corporation deeded this urban park to the City of Dallas in 1985 to commemorate *The Dallas Morning News* centennial. The following sculptures can be found here. *400 S. Market St., Downtown.*

Harrow (Linnea Glatt, 1992) Every 24 hours, this motorized cone of rusted-looking steel leaves concentric rings in a bed of sand.

Journey to Sirius (George Smith, 1992) The paintings and carvings of mythical ancestors found on the African Bandiagara cliffs along the Niger River inspired these welded black metal plates.

PEGASUS PLAZA

(Brad J. Goldberg, 1994) Perhaps water cascading over stone is the best part of this plaza, which loses much of its artistic appeal when viewed from the ground. A bird's eye view shows a serpentine design of limestone and granite. One pond has a large chunk of rose crystal. Scattered around the plaza are large pieces of granite carved with sayings by different muses. *1401 Commerce St., Downtown.*

13 *d-3*

TRAMMEL CROW CENTER

This outdoor collection of 19 sculptures stands in a public plaza that wraps around a 50-story office tower. Shaded by cypress, sycamore, magnolia, and oak trees, this sculpture garden offers a pleasant respite from bustling Downtown streets. Such artists as Maillol, Carton, Rodin, Bourdelle, Bernard, Wlerick, and Buxin created the pieces. Other sculptures can be found inside the lobby. *2001 Ross Ave., Downtown, 214/979–6492.*

SCIENCE MUSEUMS

10 *h-2*

DALLAS MUSEUM OF NATURAL HISTORY

Youngsters visiting this museum are less impressed by its massive collection—more than 280,000 specimens—than by the neat exhibits that provide a close-up view of animals that crawl, fly, slither, swim, and walk in Texas. Founded in 1936, the museum collects, researches, and exhibits a vast diversity of life from fossils of extinct species to living animals. You can go behind the scenes for talks with field scientists or visit a simulated archaeological site. There are also art classes for sketching nature and programs that explore Texas ecosystems. If you want a really hands-on experience, then volunteer to help prepare fossils or care for the collections. The wildlife dioramas show animals in their native habitats. Birds and crickets chirp a greeting to the rising sun and at the close of day an alligator bellows a farewell to the setting sun. While at the museum take time for the Leonhardt Lagoon nature walk, with numbered markers keyed to a printed walking guide. While outside, be sure to check out the large dinosaur sculptures. *3535 Grand Ave., 214/421–3466. Admission: $5, $3 seniors and children, free admission from 10–1. Open daily 10–5. Free parking.*

Dallas Museum of Natural History

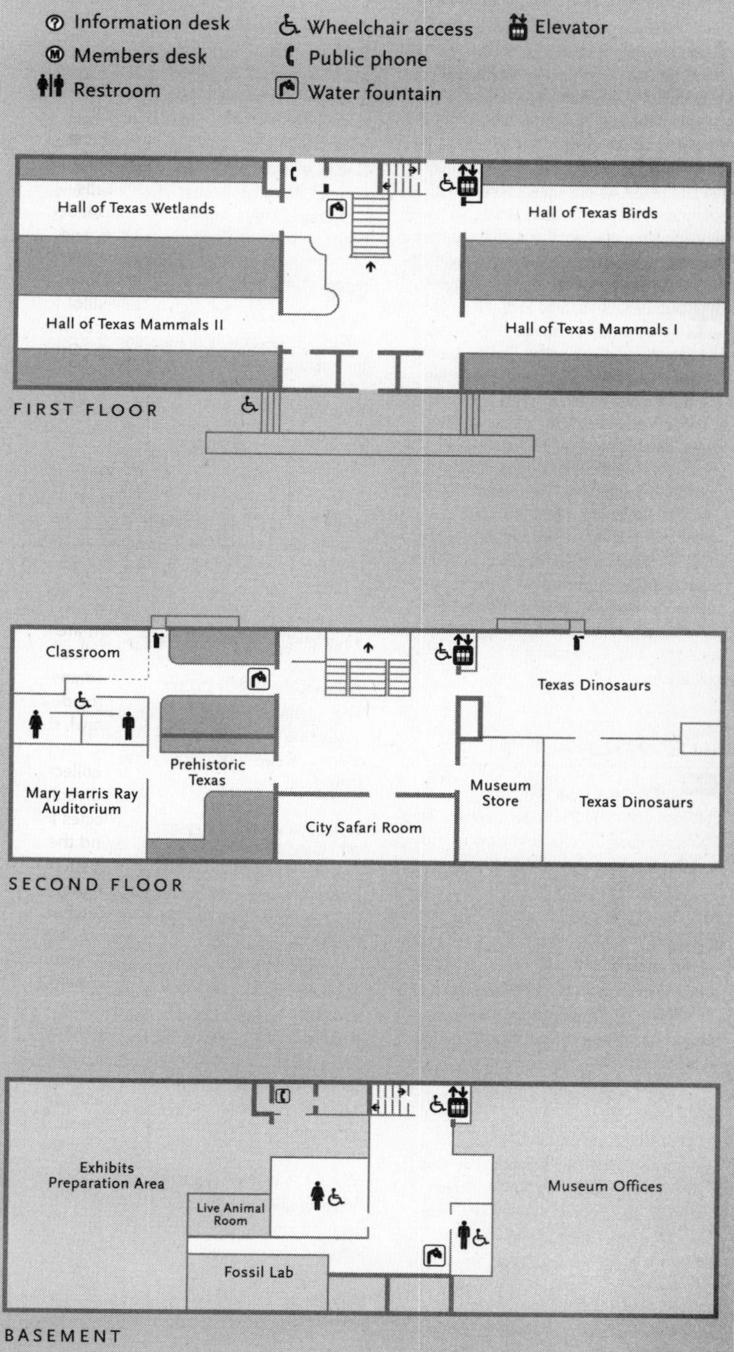

Information desk
Members desk
Restroom
Wheelchair access
Public phone
Water fountain
Elevator
Hall of Texas Wetlands
Hall of Texas Birds
Hall of Texas Mammals II
Hall of Texas Mammals I
FIRST FLOOR
Classroom
Texas Dinosaurs
Prehistoric Texas
Mary Harris Ray Auditorium
Museum Store
Texas Dinosaurs
City Safari Room
SECOND FLOOR
Exhibits Preparation Area
Museum Offices
Live Animal Room
Fossil Lab
BASEMENT

10 *h-2*

THE SCIENCE PLACE & TI FOUNDERS IMAX THEATER

One million people annually visit here to view science in the works. If you ever wondered what makes an arm bend, then stop by the Medical Gallery. In the Electric Theatre, you can watch a lightning bolt strike across the room. Children younger than eight have their own special place where they can build a playhouse or float a boat. You can also visit the planetarium for a close-up view of the night skies or take in a movie at the IMAX theater. The museum store sells puzzles, toys, and kits. The 1936 building originally housed the Museum of Fine Arts. In 1946, the Dallas Health Museum was founded and displayed exhibits focusing on such health issues as allergies, communicable diseases, and cancer. Since 1957, the museum has included all types of educational programs and exhibits on science. The IMAX theater was added in 1996. *Fair Park, 1318 2nd Ave., East, 214/428–5555. Exhibit center admission: $6, $3 children 3–12, children under 3 free; Imax movies admission: $10, $9 seniors, $8 children 3–12. Admissions vary, but package rates are your best buy, Open daily 9:30–8; call for holiday hours.*

VIEWPOINTS

INTERSTATE-30

You can view the Reunion Tower, a popular spot for film crews shooting movies and TV shows, while driving east on this major highway.

13 *f-7*

OLD CITY PARK

Look north to see the ultra-modern Dallas skyline while standing among buildings constructed in the 1800s and early 1900s. *1717 Gano St., Downtown.*

13 *c-6*

PIONEER PLAZA

For a good view of Pegasus, the Red Flying Horse, park on Young Street. No tall buildings impede your view from this location. *Griffin St. & Young St., Downtown.*

13 *b-6*

REUNION TOWER

Stroll around a public observation deck atop the tower for a panoramic view of Dallas and surrounding areas. Look west for the white dome of Texas Stadium, home of the Dallas Cowboys; east to the world's largest Ferris wheel at Fair Park; north for a spectacular view of the Dallas skyline; south for a bird's eye view of Reunion Arena. The view from 560 ft up always impresses, day or night. *300 Reunion Blvd., 214/651–1234.*

10 *h-1*

WHITE ROCK LAKE

Although several spots around the lake give you a view of the Dallas skyline, the east shore probably has some of the best vantage points. *Lawther Dr., White Rock Lake.*

guided tours

SPECIAL INTEREST TOURS

CEMETERY TOUR

The "cemetery lady" Frances James leads this fall tour of historic burial places of some of the city's early founders. *214/381–0445.*

DALLAS HISTORICAL SOCIETY TOURS

The society conducts five annual tours—three in the spring and two in the fall. The five-hour tours include lunch. *214/421–4500.*

DALLAS LANDMARKS TOUR

This tour takes you from prairie-style homes of the 1800s to today's skyscrapers as you learn how Dallas grew from a single log cabin on the Trinity River to a modern business center. *972/263–0294, ext 108.*

DALLAS MARKET CENTER

Visit the heart of Dallas's wholesale market where thousands of vendors and buyers come together every year. This tour takes you through the World Trade Center and International Apparel Mart during non-market times. *214/749–5473.*

EAST DALLAS TOUR

Led by historian Darwin Payne, this spring outing begins with the 1930s Art Deco buildings in Fair Park and continues to McCommas Bluff and Swiss Avenue. *214/503–0738.*

HOLLY JOLLY TROLLEY TOUR

This festive seasonal tour takes you to a few Dallas neighborhoods where homes are lavishly adorned in holiday decorations. *972/263–0294.*

JFK HISTORICAL TOUR

See the places connected to President Kennedy's assassination. Key sites associated with assassin Lee Harvey Oswald include the boardinghouse where he lived and the Texas Theater where he was arrested. A walking tour of Dealey Plaza and a stop at the Sixth Floor Museum is included. *972/263–0294.*

WALKING TOURS

WEST END HISTORIC DISTRICT

Take a guided tour of the West End via cyberspace. You can also print your own copy of this Web site tour to carry with your while actually making the walk. *www.dallaswestend.org/history.*

WILSON DISTRICT TOUR

Preservation Dallas hosts this 45-minute tour of a two-block area of Victorian homes. The tour starts with a short film in the Wilson Carriage House. You can bring a picnic lunch to enjoy at nearby Central Square Park. *214/821–3290.*

events

JANUARY

10 *h-2*

SOUTHWESTERN BELL COTTON BOWL CLASSIC

Two of the nation's best college football teams battle to win this televised New Year Day's favorite gridiron classic. *214/467–8277.*

FEBRUARY

13 *d-7*

DALLAS BOAT SHOW

Thousands of boats ranging from fishing boats to yachts are part of the largest boat show in North Texas. Children can try to hook a catfish at the fish-a-rama. *Dallas Convention Center, 972/714–0177.*

13 *b-4*

WEST END MARKETPLACE'S ANNUAL MAGIC OF ICE

Professionals chisel giant ice blocks into spectacular ice sculptures as you watch. Wander from ice block to ice block to see the different techniques used. *West End Market, 214/741–7180.*

MARCH

13 *d-7*

DALLAS HOME & GARDEN SHOW

You will leave this annual event with all kinds of new decorating ideas for inside and outside your home. *Dallas Convention Center, 800/654–1480.*

ST. PATRICK'S DAY PARADE

Even the beer is green when the Irish turn out to celebrate this special day. Head Downtown for a parade of all things Irish along Main Street to West End. *972/991–6705.*

APRIL

ANNUAL USA FILM FESTIVAL

International filmmakers screen and discuss movies for film enthusiasts at this annual film festival that attracts about 70 filmmakers from around the world. Each spring, this eight-day event brings together artists and audience while premiering a diverse selection of film. Location varies. *214/871–3456.*

10 *f-2*

DALLAS BOOK & PAPER SHOW

At this biannual show, you can find a variety used books and rare, signed first editions. *Market Hall, 281/496–7827.*

11 *a-1*

EGGSTRAVAGANZA

Easter festivities include an Easter Egg Hunt at the Dallas Arboretum & Botanical Garden. *214/327–8263.*

MAY

ARTFEST 2000

(*See* Art Events).

10 *h-2*

CINCO DE MAYO CELEBRATION

Celebrates Dallas's rich Mexican heritage with traditional food and dance. *Fair Park, 214/670–8400.*

JUNE

13 *f-7*

AFRICAN-AMERICAN HERITAGE FESTIVAL

Juneteenth, now a popular national African-American celebration, started when Texas slaves learned of their freedom. In Dallas, the festival includes entertainment and arts and crafts activities, including quilting. *Old City Park, 214/421–5141.*

10 *h-2*

DALLAS SUMMER MUSICALS

This month kicks off the start of the Broadway musical season. Past performances included Julie Harris and Charles Durning starring in *The Gin Game* and Toni Tennille in *Victor/Victoria. Fair Park, 214/691–7200.*

HOOP IT UP

This is the nation's largest 3-on-3 basketball tournament, held by Streetball International, the sports marketing arm of NBC Sports. The event attracts thousands of local participants. *972/392–5700.*

10 *h-1*

SHAKESPEARE FESTIVAL OF DALLAS

Time to head to Samuell-Grand Park for a night under the stars with the Bard. Past performances have included *Romeo & Juliet* and *King Lear. 214/559–2778.*

JULY

13 *b-4*

TASTE OF DALLAS

Join thousands of locals for this outdoor food festival in the West End where restaurants and retailers set up booths. *West End Market, 214/741–7180.*

AUGUST

11 *a-1*

CELEBRATION OF CULTURES

Enjoy dance, music, art, and food from different ethnic groups at the Dallas Arboretum & Botanical Garden. *214/327–4901 or 214/327–8263.*

13 *d-3*

DALLAS MORNING NEWS DANCE FESTIVAL

This free festival features emerging and professional dance companies in the Annette Strauss Artist Square. *214/953–1977.*

SEPTEMBER

6 *g-6*

ANNUAL GREEK FOOD FESTIVAL

Have an extra helping of baklava, then enjoy toe tapping music and lively folk dancing during this three-day event. *Holy Trinity Greek Orthodox Church, 13555 Hillcrest Rd., 972/991–1166.*

MONTAGE

More than 15,000 locals turn out for this weekend that showcases Dallas's performing arts. With 150 artists selling their work, it is also a good place to find an affordable original. *214/361–2011.*

OCTOBER

13 *d-3*

ANNUAL AMERICAN INDIAN ART FESTIVAL & MARKET

Native Americans perform traditional dances and sell handmade jewelry, pottery, and other traditional goods in Annette Strauss Artist Square. Tribes from across the nation are represented. *214/891–9640.*

10 *h-2*

STATE FAIR OF TEXAS

Wave howdy to "Big Tex" as you head for exhibit buildings to taste homemade jams and try out the latest computer technology. The livestock exhibits and carnival rides are always popular stops. *Fair Park, 214/565–9931.*

NOVEMBER

13 *d-7*

CHI OMEGA CHRISTMAS MARKET

More than 130 merchants set up booths at the Dallas Convention Center to give you an early start on holiday shopping. *214/890–8131.*

13 *b-4*

HOLIDAY TREE-LIGHTING FESTIVAL

The lighting of a huge holiday tree is part of day-long family entertainment at West End Market Place. *214/741–7180.*

TURKEY TROT

Running this popular 10K event on Thanksgiving morning is a sure way to work up an appetite for Thanksgiving dinner. The run starts and ends Downtown. *214/954–0500.*

DECEMBER

13 *f-7*

CANDLELIGHT TOUR OLD CITY PARK

Take a step back to Christmas past with a tour of historic buildings decorated in 19th-century Victorian style. Avoid lines by purchasing tickets early. *214/421–5141.*

11 *a-1*

HOLIDAY AT THE ARBORETUM

Decorators transform the stately DeGolyer mansion at White Rock Lake into a holiday wonderland. *214/327–4901 or 214/327–8263.*

NEIMAN MARCUS ADOLPHUS CHILDREN'S CHRISTMAS PARADE

Thousands of locals line Dallas streets to watch this televised parade capture the season's spirit with floats, marching bands, and costumed characters. It starts at Lamar St. and Commerce St., turns on Ervay St. and ends at City Hall Plaza. *214/742–8200.*

WHITE ROCK MARATHON

This is considered one of the world's premier marathons. Runners start in Downtown and finish at White Rock Lake. *214/467–3369.*

day trips out of town

NORTH ON INTERSTATE 35: PLANO

This trendy city of million-dollar homes grew from a farming community to a major urban center during the population drift in the 1970s. For three days each September, the city hosts Southwestern Bell Plano Balloon Festival (972/867–7566), where 100 colorful hot-air balloons are launched twice daily. About 250,000 people turn out for balloon competitions, arts and crafts, concerts, and children's activities. Plano has preserved its historic downtown, which reflect the city's agricultural roots. The original brick streets were restored in 1986 as part of the state's Sesquicentennial celebrations. Renovated early 20th-century buildings now house antiques shops and boutiques. The Heritage Farmstead (972/424–7874), a restored 1890s farmhouse has octagonal garden structure once used for seedlings and cuttings, a smokehouse for curing hams, and barns that once housed sheep, hogs, horses, and mules. Efforts to replicate the Victorian farm include growing antique roses in the yard and heirloom vegetables and herbs in the garden. While in Plano, remember to visit SouthFork (972/442–7800), probably the world's best-known ranch, thanks to the long-running TV series, "Dallas." When filming first started on the series in 1978, the original ranch owners still lived here. A need for privacy from hordes of fans sent the family packing in 1985 when they donated the house and grounds to the TV series and its fans. A tour guide, who is usually a treasure trove of "Dallas" trivia, walks you through the famous Ewing mansion and around the ranch grounds.

MCKINNEY

Just up the road from Plano is another town that has turned its Victorian charm into a pleasant getaway. Filmmakers discovered the wholesome appeal of the town with the filming of *Benji* in 1973. The movie's haunted house (1104 S. Tennessee St.), built in 1870, is now a bed and breakfast. Collin County Farm Museum (972/548–4793), while not as large as the one in Plano, has plenty of antique farm machinery and household items. Although the town has a calendar full of annual events, one of the most popular is "Dickens of a Christmas," held in historic Downtown Square the Friday and Saturday after Thanksgiving. This salute to the Victorian era includes vendors and carolers in period dress, carriage rides, Santa visits, and live reindeer. You will want to find time to visit the Heard Natural Science Museum (972/562–5566), which includes a 287-acre wildlife sanctuary with more than 5 mi of nature trails through wooded areas, prairies, and wetlands; a science museum with large collections of butterflies, seashells, and minerals; and a bird rehabilitation center. You can take a guided tour along the nature trails or hike alone. An observation deck and boardwalk allow you to get up close to plants and animals that call the 50 acres of wetlands home.

WEST ON INTERSTATE 30: FORNEY

If you're an antiques lover or just a casual browser, be sure to peruse the shops scattered up and down Highway 80 about 25 mi from Dallas. With more than 200 antiques dealers in town, it is little wonder that this place is dubbed the Antique Capital of Texas. It all started in the late 1960s when "Red" Whaley opened his first antiques shop in a large metal warehouse. His location proved so popular that a Tennessee antiques dealer, Clements, bought all of Red's antiques and leased the building. So Red built another metal warehouse and another until he had about 50 buildings for antiques. He still has an antiques shop, Red's, and so does his son, Little Red's. The area has about 25 large stand-alone shops as well as antiques malls. Mammoth warehouses—some as big as 100,000 square ft—stock large selections of antique furniture not usually found in smaller stores.

TERRELL

If you're an aviation buff, drive another few miles to Terrell. Silent Wings Museum (972/563–0402) has a restored World War II glider, one of only two in existence. The museum also has a video theater with glider films. The Terrell Heritage Museum (972/526–6082) showcases a large collection of British Flying Training School memorabilia from World War II days when the school trained Royal Air Force and some U.S. Army pilots in Terrell. Although a farming community, Terrell still has plenty of historic buildings, including the R.A. Terrell home, set on the campus of Southwestern Christian College. This eight-sided house built in 1864 is one of only 20 surviving Round Houses left in the nation.

CANTON

If you're looking for a bargain, join the more than 300,000 other bargain hunters who head to this small town of 3,000 residents every month for First Monday Trade Days. Just 60 mi from Dallas, this giant flea market attracts more than 6,000 dealers who sell everything from antiques to crafts to new merchandise to animals. Wear comfortable shoes and plan to spend the day. This monthly event has roots to the 1850s when farmers came to town on the first Monday of each month to buy, sell, and trade stock. The flea market is so popular that it now covers 380 acres. It actually starts on Thursday and ends on the first Monday with weekends being the busiest times. Toward the end of June, bluegrass bands and fans take over First Monday Trade grounds for the annual Texas State Bluegrass Festival. Music is played from 10–10 during this five-day event. *903/567–2991. Admission: $18 per day, $50 all days, $3 parking.*

SOUTH ON INTERSTATE 35: HILLSBORO

This quaint country town, 58 mi from Dallas, is a contrast of eras. Downtown, with its late 19th-century courthouse square, remains much like it was during the town's heydays as one of the world's cotton capitals. But the town's eastern edge, anchored by a large outlet mall, is pure 21st century. You can shop at more than 90 outlet stores, which discount prices on such big-names as Jones New York, Liz Claiborne, Savane, Bass, Nike, and Chicago Cutlery. When you tire of trendy fashions, drop by some of the town's numerous antiques stores. Even if shopping is your main intent, you really should take time for a quick history lesson at town square. Built in 1890, Hill County Courthouse (254/582–0409) was destroyed in disastrous fire in 1993; it was rebuilt in 1999. The original county jail, built in 1893, is still there but now is known as Cell Block Museum. Elvis Presley once spent the night in jail here. A new addition houses memorabilia of popular country singer Willie Nelson, who grew up a few miles down the road at Abbott. Willie still comes to town to play dominoes and cards with local buddies. And while you're learning history, you might as well head east of the outlet mall to the hilltop setting of Hill College, home of Harold B. Simpson History complex. Here you will find the Texas Heritage Museum and Confederate Research Center, both of which specialize in Civil War artifacts and information. The Texas Heritage Museum (903/856–0463) includes an exhibition for actor Audie Murphy, a native Texan and decorated soldier in World War II, and a collection of Civil War artifacts, including diaries, letters, maps, and photographs.

WAXAHACHIE

Just 17 mi from Downtown Dallas, this farm community with its many Victorian buildings is a favorite spot for shooting movies and TV shows, including *Bonnie and Clyde, Tender Mercies,* and *Places in the Heart.* The Ellis County Courthouse, built of red sandstone in 1895, has a central tower containing the stairway around which radiate government offices. This imposing Romanesque revival structure is the centerpiece of 40 buildings that makeup the downtown historic district. A fully restored 1800s Chautauqua, believed to be the last such octagonal auditorium left in the United States, is still used for plays. In June, many of the elegant gingerbread, Gothic revival, and Queen Anne–style homes are open for tour. A few of these homes are also B&Bs. While in town, peruse the antiques shops and little boutiques. Scarborough Fair brings thousands to town each spring on weekends during April through mid-June. The Renaissance Festival—where you'll find 16th-century entertainment, crafts, food, and games, and hundreds of vendors and entertainers in period costumes—is one of the largest in the United States.

where to go: fort worth/mid-cities

Fort Worth's rich history is abundant throughout Downtown, the Stockyards National Historic District, and the Cultural District. Markers designating state and national historical significance can be found nearly everywhere within these districts, so allow plenty of time to see it all.

ARCHITECTURE

15 *d-6*

BLACKSTONE HOTEL

(Mauran, Russell, & Crowell, 1929) Designed by a renowned St. Louis firm, this 23-story structure with its stepped and spired top was a popular hotel in its day. Closed and rundown from the late 1970s until 1999, it reopened as a Courtyard by Marriott after extensive renovation. *601 Main St., Fort Worth.*

15 *d-6*

BURK BURNETT BUILDING

(Sanguinet & Staats, 1914) Declared the city's first skyscraper, this neoclassical building once housed the State National Bank. The white terra-cotta base is marked with granite columns, and the middle of the building is made of red-brick with a band of terra-cotta separating each floor. *500 Main St., Fort Worth.*

15 *c-5*

CITY NATIONAL BANK BUILDING

(Haggard and Sanguinet, 1884–85) Although this building retained its original façade, the interior was renovated and rebuilt during the Sundance Square development of the 1980s. A Second Empire design of four stories, the building had a mansard roof and was just 25 ft wide. In 1910, the building width was doubled. *315 Houston St., Fort Worth.*

15 *b-6*

EDDLEMAN-MCFARLAND HOUSE

(Messer, Sanguinet, & Messer, 1899) Built on a bluff overlooking the Trinity River in the Quality Hill neighborhood, this former cattle baron's home has a Victorian design, including turrets, spires, and rounded marble porch. *1110 W. Penn St., Fort Worth, 817/332–5875. Weekday tours.*

15 *c-5*

FIRE STATION NO. 1

(Sanguinet & Staats, 1907) A functional fire station until 1980, the building was renovated in 1982 and now houses informative exhibits on 150 years of Fort Worth history. *Commerce St. (at 2nd St.), Fort Worth. Admission: free. Open daily 9–7.*

15 *d-6*

FLATIRON BUILDING

(Sanguinet & Staats, 1907) Modeled after New York's Flatiron building, built five years earlier, this was one of the premiere steel-frame structures in town and was once among the taller commercial buildings in North Texas. *1000 Houston St., Fort Worth.*

15 *c-5*

KNIGHTS OF PYTHIAS CASTLE HILL

(Sanguinet & Staats, 1901) A favorite among the gems in Sundance Square, this building has medieval detailing, with a gable roof and turreted corner. *Main St., Fort Worth.*

15 *d-5*

LAND TITLE BLOCK

(Haggard and Sanguinet, 1889) Influenced by the Romanesque revival style, this redbrick jewel with red sandstone trim, stained glass windows, and multi-hue glazed brick has been home to a bank and investment firm, and a law firm. *111 E. 4th, Fort Worth.*

15 *d-5*

SINCLAIR BUILDING

(Wiley G. Clarkson, 1930) An outstanding exhibit in Art Deco design, this building's specific style is called Zigzag Moderne and has elaborate angular detailing in doorways, windows, and walls. *512 Main St., Fort Worth.*

15 *d-6*

ST. PATRICK CATHEDRAL

(James J. Kane, 1888–92) This is the oldest continuously used church in the city. Built of limestone, its Gothic Revival design includes twin towers. *1206 Throckmorton, Fort Worth.*

15 *c-5*

TARRANT COUNTY COURTHOUSE

(Gunn and Curtiss, 1895) This pink-granite, American beaux-arts designed structure was modeled after the state capitol in Austin and was among the earliest structural steel frame buildings in the American Southwest. *100 E. Weatherford St., Fort Worth, 817/884–1457.*

15 *d-6*

TEXAS & PACIFIC RAILWAY TERMINAL

(Wyatt Hedrick, Herman C. Koeppe, 1931) Another structure of Zigzag Moderne style in Art Deco design, this building was originally a railroad passenger terminal, an office building, and a warehouse facility. Note the eagle in a zigzag motif guarding the front entrance. *1600 Throckmorton St., Fort Worth.*

15 *d-6*

U.S. POST OFFICE

(Wyatt Hedrick, 1933) This building's native limestone work is a blend of beaux arts and classical styling. with Texas longhorn and polled Hereford cattle column capitals. The interior is worth a trip in itself for the ornate cornice work and gold-leaf detail. *251 W. Lancaster Ave., Fort Worth, 817/870–8102.*

15 *d-6*

W.T. WAGGONER BUILDING

(Sanguinet & Staats, 1919–20) This 20-story masterpiece might have been crafted after the famous Equitable Building in New York. The classical design is built on a two-story marble base, with a two-story white brick and terra-cotta top. Look inside the ornate lobby for its restored vaulted elevator and banking halls. *810 Houston St., Fort Worth.*

ART EVENTS

september

14 *h-6*

GALLERY NIGHT

One Saturday evening in mid-September is set aside for galleries to keep doors open until 9 PM or 10 PM. Strollers wind their way through what is sort of a roving cocktail party, as many galleries entice visitors with wine and champagne. Look primarily along the 7th Street and Camp Bowie art gallery corridors. *817/737–9566.*

ART GALLERIES

14 *h-6*

CAROL HENDERSON GALLERY

An open and airy space with plenty of natural light, this friendly gallery showcases contemporary work in mixed media, sculpture, and paintings, and hand-blown glasswork by Jim Bowman. Colorful pen and ink drawings and jewelry are also displayed. *3409 W. 7th St., Fort Worth, 817/737–9910. Closed Sun.–Mon.*

14 *h-6*

EDMUND CRAIG GALLERY

You'll find a variety of Texas and other regional artists' work in photography, paint, and sculpture on display. *3550-C W 7th St., Fort Worth, 817/732–6663. Closed Sun.–Mon.*

14 *h-6*

EVELYN SIEGEL GALLERY

Contemporary and post-modern exhibits in various media by such artists as Rene Alvarado, Carol Anthony, Betsy Bauer, and Alexandra Nechita are displayed in this intimate gallery on the edge of the upscale Monticello neighborhood. *3700 W. 7th St., 817/731–6412. Closed Sun.*

14 *e-7*

WILLIAM CAMPBELL CONTEMPORARY ART

Exhibits here have showcased the work of Ed and Linda Blackburn, Richard Thompson, David Keens, Francis X, Tolbert II, and others. Outlandish and entertaining, the creations in this large, long-loved gallery are always worth a stop. *4935 Byers Ave., 817/737–9566.*

ART MUSEUMS

14 *h-6*

AMON CARTER MUSEUM

Devotees of this museum's collection of American art will have to wait until 2002 to see the legions of artworks accumulated over the past 40 years. The building is currently undergoing an extensive expansion. In the meantime, the Carter Downtown gallery in Fort Worth—conveniently across the street from the Bass Performance Hall—has donated a large space to exhibit major pieces from the permanent collection. The gallery also has a museum store, architectural renderings, and site elevations of the expansion project. The gallery includes such paintings as Frederic Remington's "The Fall of the Cowboy," William J. McCloskey's "Wrapped Oranges," and William Michael Harnett's "Attention, Company!" The gallery will host tours for groups of 10–25, but arrangements must be made well in advance. Until the museum expansion is complete, you are urged to visit the Carter's Web site at www.cartermuseum.org to learn more about the significant collection that began with the personal acquisitions of *Fort Worth Star-Telegram* publisher and local philanthropist, Amon G. Carter (1879–1955). It has grown to more than 300,000 works of American art, including paintings, drawings, prints, sculpture, and photographs. *500 Commerce St. (at 5th St.), Fort Worth, 817/738–1933. Admission: free. Open Tues.–Wed. 10:30–5, Thurs–Sat. 10:30–8, Sun. noon–5.*

9 *g-4*

ARLINGTON MUSEUM OF ART

While there's no collecting done by this museum, the exhibits showcase traveling works from Texas and the Southwest. *201 W. Main St., Arlington, 817/275–4600. Admission: free. Open Wed.–Sat. 10–5.*

14 *h-6*

KIMBELL ART MUSEUM

Known as one of the richest privately-endowed museums in the world, the Kimbell was built upon an art collection amassed from the 1930s until the 1960s by Kay Kimbell, an entrepreneur who made his fortune in grain, retailing, real estate, and petroleum, and his wife, Velma Fuller Kimbell. The museum was opened in 1972 and is home now to an extraordinary range of holdings, including masterpieces from Fra Angelico and Caravaggio to Cézanne and Matisse. The museum also displays an expansive collection of Asian arts and Mesoamerican, African, and Mediterranean antiquities. Louis I. Kahn (1901–1974) created its classic modern design, and his use of light and space renders a soothing and airy ambiance. The reflecting pools and large, shady lawn outside are easily as compelling, and are an ideal setting for contemplation. A full schedule of programs includes guest speakers, gallery talks, films, storytelling for children, and musical events. *3333 Camp Bowie Blvd. (near University Dr. and W. 7th St.), Fort Worth, 817/332–8451. Admission: free, except for special exhibits. Open Tues.–Thurs. and Sat. 10–5, Fri. noon–8, Sun. noon–5.*

14 *h-6*

MODERN ART MUSEUM OF FORT WORTH

The city's oldest museum specializes in American and European art from the 20th century. Touring and local exhibits augment the Modern's active collecting program. The museum, however, is bursting at the seams and a new building is expected to open in 2003. *1309 Montgomery St., Fort Worth, 817/738–9215. Admission: Free. Open Tues.–Fri. 10–5, Sat. 11–5, Sun. noon–5.*

15 *c-5*

SID RICHARDSON COLLECTION OF WESTERN ART

Inside a restored turn-of-the-20th-century building in Sundance Square, this small museum houses the collection of one of Texas's great legendary oil barons and philanthropists, Fort Worth's Sid W. Richardson. From 1942 until his death in 1959, he amassed an amazing 55 paintings by the great Frederic Remington and Charles M. Russell. These dramatic and often heart-touching works aptly capture the rugged, sometimes painful, beauty of the Wild West that the spectator at once understands how the world came to engage in its never-ending romance with this time of history. All ages enjoy roaming through the collection, taking in the lonesome sadness of Remington's 1909 "The Luckless Hunter," the breathless, windblown excitement in his 1909 "Buffalo Runners, Big Horn Basin," and the back-breaking exhaustion of Russell's 1904 "The Bucker." A small museum bookstore sells prints, postcards, and books. *309 Main St., Fort Worth, 817/332–6554. Admission: free. Open Tues.–Wed. 10–5, Thurs.–Fri. 10–8, Sat. 11–8, Sun. 1–5.*

CHURCHES & SYNAGOGUES

15 *d-7*

BROADWAY BAPTIST CHURCH

Inside this massive church is the Cliburn Organ, the largest organ in Texas, named for the late Rildia Bee Cliburn, the mother and primary teacher of the renowned pianist Van Cliburn, who lives in Fort Worth. The organ has 10,615 pipes and can be heard at special concerts, such as Handel's *Messiah*, performed early in the Christmas season. *305 W. Broadway St., Fort Worth, 817/336–5761.*

15 *c-6*

FIRST UNITED METHODIST CHURCH

A Gothic revival design by Fort Worth architect Wiley G. Clarkson, this massive structure has been added onto several times. *800 W. 5th St, Fort Worth, 817/336–7277.*

GRAVEYARDS

15 *b-4*

OAKWOOD CEMETERY

With a scenic hilltop setting overlooking downtown, this cemetery is the final resting place of many of Cowtown's benevolent residents. Headstones mark the graves of cattle barons such as Fountan Goodlet Oxsheer, who once owned more than one million acres of ranchland, and W.T. Waggoner, who gave each of his three children 90,000 acres of land and 10,000 head of cattle. *701 Grand Ave., Fort Worth, 817/624–3531.*

15 *d-4*

PIONEER REST CEMETERY

Begun in 1850 to bury the children of the founder of Camp Worth, Pioneer Rest holds the graves of several Fort Worth pioneers, including General Edward H. Tarrant, for whom the county is named, and Ephraim Daggett, often called the Father of Fort Worth. *626 Samuels Ave., Fort Worth, 817/332–8515.*

9 *d-4*

SHANNON ROSE HILL CEMETERY

Without a doubt, the most notorious person buried here is Lee Harvey Oswald. At his burial in November 1963, members of the press acted as impromptu pallbearers because there were no other people in attendance to perform the duty. His grave is unmarked, however, and the funeral home–cemetery staff has a policy of not disclosing the location. *7301 E. Lancaster Ave., Fort Worth, 817/451–3333.*

HISTORIC STRUCTURES & STREETS

15 *b-6*

EDDLEMAN-MCFARLAND HOUSE

One of several mansions that once blanketed the near-downtown neighborhood formerly called Quality Hill, this 1899 home escaped the neglect and demise of its many neighbors. Built by a cattle baron family and designed by the English architect Howard Messer, the self-billed "Victorian Lady" has belonged to only two families. Its parquet floors, elegant dining room, slate-tile roof, and porches of red sandstone and marble are truly something to behold. The home is often used for weddings and parties. *1110 Penn St. (near W. 7th St.), Fort Worth, 817/332–5875. Admission: $2.50. Open Tues. and Thurs. 10–1, or by appointment.*

15 *b-1*

STOCKYARDS NATIONAL HISTORIC DISTRICT

North from Downtown about 3 mi is another of Cowtown's crowning glories, a lovingly restored 19th-century neighborhood with original brick and stucco buildings. The boomtown of cattle-drive days, this district has saddle and boot makers, saloons and cafés, souvenir shops and hotels, a rodeo arena, a vintage train station, and antiques shops along wooden sidewalks and brick streets. Weather permitting, the Fort Worth Herd is a group of pure-bred Texas longhorn cattle that is driven every day, between March 15 and November 15, from the Stockyards to the Trinity River at 11:30 AM, then back again at 4 PM. The Stockyards is also the place to catch the Tarantula Railroad for trips to south Fort Worth and Grapevine. *N. Main St., Fort Worth.*

15 *c-8*

THISTLE HILL

A notation in the National Register of Historic Places calls this 1903 masterpiece "one of the few remaining examples of Georgian Revival architecture in the Southwest," but that hardly does justice to the grandeur found inside and out. Built also on the one-time Quality Hill, the mansion was designed by Marshall Sanguinet (a partner of Messer, who built the Eddleman-McFarland House, *see above*) for A.B. and Electra Waggoner Wharton. On the guided tour, you can learn about the lives of famous ranchers and other local history, as well as the sensational detail found in the house, such as the 14-ft-wide staircase, the variations of crafted woods used throughout the interior, and collections of Havilland and Limoges china. The common rooms downstairs and the wide, wraparound porches and expansive lawns are used for weddings and receptions. *1509 Pennsylvania Ave., at Summit Ave., Fort Worth, 817/336–1212. Admission: $4, $2 senior citizens and children 7–12. Open weekdays 11–2, Sun. 1–3.*

HISTORY MUSEUMS

9 *h-1*

AMERICAN AIRLINES C.R. SMITH MUSEUM

A restored DC-3 serves as the centerpiece alongside some 1,000 items of this exhibit that illustrates the history of aviation in North Texas. *4601 Hwy. 360 (at FAA Rd.), Fort Worth, 817/967–1560. Admission: free. Open Tues.–Sat. 10–6, Sun. noon–5.*

15 *c-6*

CATTLE RAISERS MUSEUM

Preservation of the heritage of ranch life is the objective at this admirable, small museum near downtown. The lives of people who built empires on ranching are detailed in the museum. It also holds the world's largest documented collection of branding irons, a pair of boots worn by Western artist Charles Russell, some 50 pairs of spurs, and historic photographs. *1301 W. 7th St., near Summit St., Fort Worth, 817/332–7064. Admission: $3, $2 seniors, $1 children 4–12. Open Mon.–Sat. 10–5, Sun. 1–5.*

9 *g-4*

FIELDER MUSEUM

Children will relish in the once-simple American life when they see the old-fashioned country store, barber shop, bedroom, and photography exhibit that detail turn-of-the-20th-century Arlington. *1616 W. Abram St., Arlington, 817/460–4001. Admission: $3, $1.50 senior citizens. Open Wed.–Sat. 10–2, Sun. 1:30–4:30.*

9 *g-3*

LEGENDS OF THE GAME BASEBALL MUSEUM

Inside the Ballpark at Arlington, legions of baseball memorabilia—some on loan from the Hall of Fame at Cooperstown—and historical artifacts from the Negro League are displayed. You can also learn about the history of the Texas Rangers Baseball Club. *1000 Ballpark Way, Arlington, 817/273–5600. Admission: $6, $5 seniors and college students with ID. Open Fall, Mon.–Sat. 9–6:30, Sun. noon–4, Spring, Mon.–Sat. 9–4, Sun. noon–4.*

8 *h-4*

LOG CABIN VILLAGE

Late 19th and early 20th-century cabins fill this village where guides in period costume demonstrate weaving, quilting, candle making, and other activities of the day. *2100 Log Cabin Village La., Fort Worth, 817/926–5881. Admission: $2. Open Tues.–Fri. 9–5, Sat. 10–5, Sun. 1–5.*

9 *a-1*

VINTAGE FLYING MUSEUM

You'll find a variety of airplanes on display, including the B-17 Flying Fortress, AT-6, PT-17, L-5, L-3, Convair, Korean War, and Vietnam War-era jets. *505 N.W. 38th St., Hangar 33S, Fort Worth, 817/624–1935. Admission: $4. Open Tues.–Fri. 9:30–4:30, Sat. 10–5, Sun. noon–5.*

LIBRARIES

15 *c-5*

FORT WORTH PUBLIC LIBRARY

Supported for decades by the Friends of the Library organization, Fort Worth's central library is known for its genealogy department. You'll find numerous branches and regional libraries around town. *300 Taylor St., Fort Worth, 817/871–7701. Open Mon.–Thurs. 9–9, weekends 10–6.*

SCHOOLS

8 *h-5*

TEXAS CHRISTIAN UNIVERSITY

Established in 1873, this small, private university with more than 100 undergraduate and graduate programs offers degrees in arts and sciences, nursing, fine arts, communication, business, and education. On the 237-acre campus, you'll find the Robert Carr Chapel with Williamsburg styling, Jarvis Hall with a neo-Georgian design, and the Walsh Center for Performing Arts. *2800 S. University Dr., Fort Worth, 817/257–7800.*

9 *b-4*

TEXAS WESLEYAN UNIVERSITY

Originally called Polytechnic College when established in 1890 by the Methodist Episcopal Church South, this fine little university has around 3,000 students pursuing degrees in business, education, humanities, law, dentistry, and nurse anesthesia. *1201 Wesleyan St., Fort Worth, 817/531–4444.*

9 *g-4*

UNIVERSITY OF TEXAS AT ARLINGTON

By far the most internationally attractive school in the metro area, UTA has an enrollment of some 27,000 from 80 countries studying in 80 buildings. On campus, you'll find several music department theaters, a planetarium, and art collections. *701 W. Nedderman Dr., Arlington, 817/272–2222.*

SCIENCE MUSEUMS

14 *h-7*

FORT WORTH MUSEUM OF SCIENCE AND HISTORY

More than one million visitors, old and young, visit the eight galleries to see such exhibits as "Lone Star Dinosaurs," which explores Texas' prehistoric past; "DinoDig," a place to hunt for Texas fossils; and the computer gallery, where your problem-solving skills are tested and the internet is explored. For sensory overload, be sure to see one of the films showing day and night at the Omni Theater, an 80-ft domed room where you can experience thundering elephant herds, oceans, Mount Everest, or space ships. Taking a trip through the stars is the objective at Noble Planetarium, where astronomical stargazing programs are held regularly. *1501 Montgomery St., near Camp Bowie Blvd., Fort Worth, 817/732–1631. Admission: $5, $4 seniors citizens, $3 children 3–12. Omni admission; $6, $4 senior citizens and children under 12. Planetarium admission: $3. Open Mon.–Thurs. 9–5:30, Fri.–Sat. 9–8, Sun. noon–5:30.*

STATUES, MURALS & MONUMENTS

15 *b-1*

THE BULLDOGGER

Full of energy and drama, this sculpture honors Bill Pickett, the bulldogger rodeo star who was the first black cowboy inducted into the Cowboy Hall of Fame and whose trademark technique was that of biting the upper lip of the steer he was wrestling to the ground. *Cowtown Coliseum, 130 E. Exchange Ave., Fort Worth.*

15 *d-5*

CHISHOLM TRAIL MURAL

On the backside of the Jett Building in Sundance Square, you will see a mural depicting cattle painted by artist Richard Haas. It almost looks as if the cattle are stepping off the wall and onto your path. *400 Main St., Fort Worth.*

15 *b-1*

TEXAS GOLD

In front of Billy Bob's Texas you can't miss this giant bronze of seven longhorn steers. These represent the seven families who are credited with preserving the endangered breed in the early 1900s. *2520 Rodeo Plaza, Fort Worth.*

14 *h-7*

WILL ROGERS STATUE

The *Sweet Will Rogers Riding into the Sunset* bronze statue, crafted in 1947 by Electra Waggoner of Fort Worth, stands in front of the Will Rogers Memorial Coliseum. The beloved humorist, who was a close friend of Fort Worth philanthropist Amon Carter and a frequent visitor to Fort Worth, sits atop his beloved horse, Soapsuds. *3300 W. Lancaster Ave., Fort Worth.*

guided tours

WALKING TOURS

15 *b-1*

STOCKYARDS TRAILS

Historians with a flair for the dramatic lead a fun and informative tour through the sensational Stockyards National Historic District. Allow about an hour. *130 E. Exchange Ave., Fort Worth, 817/625–9715. Admission: $6, $5 senior citizens. Open Mon.–Sat. 10–4, Sun. 11–4.*

events

JANUARY

14 *h-7*

SOUTHWESTERN EXPOSITION AND LIVESTOCK SHOW AND RODEO

Hundreds flock this annual stock show and rodeo, now in its second century. More than 30 performances of the world's oldest indoor rodeo are included in the fun from mid-January to early February. *Will Rogers Memorial Center, 3301 Lancaster Ave., Fort Worth, 817/877–2400.*

FEBRUARY

15 *b-1*

COWTOWN MARATHON

For the past 23 years this, Cowtown has hosted this marathon, which winding 3K and 10K races through downtown and Stockyards National Historic District. *Fort Worth, 817–735–2033, fax 817–735–2449.*

MARCH

15 *b-1*

COWTOWN GOES GREEN

Lots of blarneys are on tap for an Irish parade and a St. Patrick's Street Dance in the Stockyards National Historic District. *Fort Worth, 817/625–9839.*

APRIL

15 *c-5*

MAIN ST. ARTS FESTIVAL

Eight blocks of Main Street in Sundance Square, from the courthouse to the convention center, are blocked off for four days of art exhibits and every sort of musical presentation imaginable. Usually held in mid-April. *Fort Worth, 817/ 336–2787.*

MAY

14 *h-7*

MAYFEST

Trinity Park is filled with happy family revelry, clowns, games, food, arts, crafts, and live music and dance in a party that benefits the parks department. *Fort Worth, 817/332–1055.*

JUNE

15 *b-1*

CHISHOLM TRAIL ROUNDUP

This horseback trail ride is a salute to the military that ends in a BBQ cook off. Bring your own horse, of course. *Fort Worth, 817/625–7005.*

14 *h-7*

CONCERTS IN THE GARDEN

Fort Worth Symphony Orchestra and guest artists play three weeks of evening concerts in the Botanic Gardens, culminating with July 4th festivities. *Fort Worth, 817/665–6000.*

SHAKESPEARE IN THE PARK

Two weeks of the bard's best work is presented in Trinity Park, under the stars. *Fort Worth, 817/923–6698.*

SEPTEMBER

15 *b-1*

PIONEER DAYS

The Stockyards National Historic District celebrates its early period with street dances, food, arts and crafts, and entertainment. *Fort Worth, 817/626–7921.*

OCTOBER

15 *d-6*

OKTOBERFEST

The Fort Worth Symphony Orchestra holds a weekend-long party downtown to raise money. *Fort Worth, 817/332–2560.*

day trips out of town

GRANBURY

This 19th-century country town has a courthouse square that serves as a blueprint for the Main Street restoration efforts across the state. Reached by driving southwest of Fort Worth about 40 minutes via U.S. 377, the Hood County seat is filled with antique shops, bed-and-breakfast lodgings, casual cafés, and a photogenic spread of native limestone buildings. The old jail is worth exploring, as is Elizabeth Crockett's gravesite, a few miles north in the town of Acton. *817/573–5548.*

DENTON

Due north of Fort Worth along Interstate 35 is the Denton County Seat, and home to the University of North Texas and Texas Woman's University. This courthouse square in vintage downtown has art galleries, home decor boutiques, charming restaurants and bars, a great used book and record store, and more, all set in restored turn-of-the-20th-century buildings. Nearby are historic neighborhoods and a few B&Bs. *940/ 382–7895.*

GLEN ROSE

About an hour's drive southwest of Fort Worth along U.S. 377 and Texas 144, this bucolic little escape is nestled at the meeting point of the Paluxy and Brazos rivers. The quietly growing town saw its heyday during the 1920s when people journeyed here to take the healing waters and rest at area sanitariums. One of those institutions is now the Inn on the River, a B&B. Nearby is Fossil Rim Wildlife Ranch, a refuge for exotic and endangered beasts. *888/346–6282.*

chapter 5

ARTS, ENTERTAINMENT & NIGHTLIFE

performing arts: dallas

Dallas continues to raise its standards in the performing arts by supporting a variety of culture to fit all moods. Theater is a mixed bag of traditional and avant-garde, guaranteeing a year-round assortment of plays and musicals. Big D may lack the reputation enjoyed by some big cities as being a performance town, but those who know the city soon discover plenty of small theater companies, which consistently present quality entertainment. You'll also find an internationally recognized orchestra as well as small ensembles. Dance companies range from ballet to tango.

CHORAL & CHAMBER GROUPS

DALLAS BACH SOCIETY

Considered one of the nation's premiere baroque and classical music ensembles, the Dallas Bach Choir and Orchestra performs lively renditions of Bach, Handel, Mozart, and friends at several Dallas locations. The ensemble is led by artistic Director James Richman, who was knighted by the French government for his contributions to the field of music. *214/320–8700.*

DALLAS CHAMBER MUSIC SOCIETY

For six decades, this organization has brought outstanding chamber music to Dallas. Internationally known chamber ensembles perform every Monday night at Caruth Auditorium on the Southern Methodist University campus. *972/392–3267.*

DALLAS SYMPHONY CHORUS

Founded in 1977, this 240-member chorus is the official vocal ensemble of the Dallas Symphony Orchestra (*see* Orchestras & Ensembles, *below*). *214/871–4000.*

TURTLE CREEK CHORALE

Led by Timothy Seeling, known for his humor as well as musical direction, the 225 singing members perform season concerts at the Morton H. Meyerson Symphony Center (*see* Performance Venues, *below*). The award-winning group performs music ranging from Bach to Broadway. *214/526–3214.*

CONCERTS IN CHURCHES

Churches play a quiet but crucial role in Dallas's music scene. You'll hear talented choral groups and musicians perform a variety of music from spiritual and classical to jazz.

13 *d-3*

CATHEDRAL GUADALUPE CHURCH

This Gothic cathedral hosts musical programs as varied as a solo piano recital to a handbell choir. The concert series Suites Before Lunch presents classical music each Wednesday during May and October at noon. *2215 Ross Ave., Downtown, 214/871–1362.*

10 *g-1*

CHURCH OF INCARNATION

Choral groups or pianists from the Dallas Bach Society (*see* Choral and Chamber Groups, *above*) perform monthly at this Gothic-revival church. *3966 McKinney Ave., Uptown, 214/521–5101.*

6 *f-8*

LOVER'S LANE UNITED METHODIST CHURCH

Duke Wellington protégé Randall Horton directs the church's jazz band ministry, whose 20-piece band is lead by SMU Mustang bandleader Tommy Tucker. On Good Friday, Christmas, and Music Sunday, in October, the Sanctuary Choir performs. *9200 Inwood Rd., North, 214/691–4721.*

6 *f-8*

NORTH PARK PRESBYTERIAN CHURCH

Groups and solo performers play folk, bluegrass, country, and other types of music at Uncle Calvin's Coffee House, tucked into a corner of the church. Members and guests mingle while soaking up the sounds at tables with checkered tablecloths and candles. *9555 N. Central Expressway, North, 214/363–5457.*

6 *f-7*

SHEARITH ISRAEL SYNAGOGUE

Pianist Jeffrey Siegel's "Keyboard Conversations" peppers music with talk five times throughout the year. Musical selections vary. *9401 Douglas Ave., North, 214/827–2225.*

13 *d-3*

ST. MATTHEW'S CATHEDRAL

The St. Matthews Cathedral Choir performs here each Sunday. It also frequently performs at the Morton H. Myerson Symphony Center (*see* Performance Venues, *below*). *5100 Ross Ave., East, 214/823–8134.*

13 *d-2*

ST. PAUL UNITED METHODIST CHURCH

This church sponsors regular performances by its four choirs. *1816 N. Routh St., Uptown, 214/922–0000.*

10 *h-1*

ST. THOMAS AQUINAS CHURCH

The Dallas Bach Society and Orpheus Chamber Singers are among this churches featured performers. *6306 Kenwood Ave., East, 214/821–3360.*

DANCE

Ballet and modern dance thrive in Dallas, and its dance community is the fourth largest in the United States. Both SMU and Texas International Theatrical Arts Society have strong dance departments, and have exposed Dallas to some of the world's finest troupes and dancers, including Mikhail Baryshnikov. You'll find several society sponsored performances at the McFarlin Auditorium (*see* Performance Venues, *below*).

companies

ANITA N. MARTINEZ BALLET FOLKORICO

What started as an informal children's dance group in 1975 became a full-blown dance company in 1990. Specializing in traditional Mexican dances, this group of 20 professional dancers now perform internationally, with local productions in May and September at the Majestic Theater (*see* Performance Venues, *below*). *214/828–0181.*

DALLAS BLACK DANCE THEATRE

The Dallas Black Dance ensemble brings contemporary dance to the Majestic Theatre (*see* Performance Venues, *below*). Thirteen professional dancers perform a mix of modern, jazz, ethnic, and spiritual works by well-known choreographers. Ann Williams, artistic director, founded the group in 1976. *214/871–2376.*

festivals

13 *d-3*

DANCE FOR THE PLANET

You can see all kinds of dances—African American, Latino, and tap at this annual event held in April. The audience is invited to participate in workshops and a variety of dance classes. *Annette Strauss Artist Square, 1800 Leonard St., Downtown, 214/775–1238.*

13 *d-3*

DALLAS MORNING NEWS DANCE FESTIVAL

Each September, 8–16 dance companies perform ballet, modern, ethnic, tap, and jazz dances. *Annette Strauss Artist Square, 1800 Leonard St., Downtown, 214/219–2290.*

13 *e-2*

NATIONAL TAP DANCE CELEBRATION

Held each Memorial Day weekend, this annual event brings in such legendary tappers as Gregory Hines, Debbi Dee, and Patricia Swayze (Patrick's mom) to hold tap dancing jams and workshops. *Booker T. Washington High School, 2501 Flora St., Uptown, 214/953–1977.*

FILM

theaters & programs

6 *e-7*

CINEMARK IMAX

The nation's first IMAX, this 261-seat theater has a busy weekend crowd, so go early. You'll need a reality check during the frequent 3-D screenings to remind yourself that the dinosaurs about to pounce on you are just images on the five-story high screen. *11819 Webb Chapel Rd., North, 972/247–8172.*

13 *d-3*

DALLAS MUSEUM OF ART

This museum screens film as varied as Italian neorealism, cinematic explorations of D.H. Lawrence's writings, and such classics as *Women in Love* each Sunday at 2 PM in the Horchow Auditorium. *1717 N. Harwood St., Downtown, 214/922–1200.*

6 *f-8*

INWOOD THEATER

Diversity is this theater's forte, as evidenced by its consistent screenings of foreign and independent films. Its noirish, yesteryear decor will make you feel like you're watching a film in Paris. *5458 W. Lovers La., North, 214/352–6040.*

10 *h-2*

LAKEWOOD THEATER

Movie theater mogul Karl Hoblitzelle opened this now-historic theater in 1938 by showing *Love Finds Andy Hardy*. The theater still specializes in vintage movies on the second Tuesday and Wednesday each month; admission is still 15¢ and popcorn is still 25¢ cents. On some nights, the Robert-Morton organ, built in 1927 with eight huge racks of 72 pipes, is played prior to movies. The first Thursday of each month is reserved for "All About Art," an open forum where artists, musicians, and filmmakers show and discuss their works. *1825 Abrams Rd., East, 214/827–5253.*

10 *h-2*

TI FOUNDERS IMAX THEATER

By the time you're blasted with the 15,000-watt sound system and surrounded with images from the 79-ft dome screen, you'll actually feel like you are dangling from an icy rock cliff or snorkeling through a coral reef. It's a great spot for a mini-vacation. *1318 Second Ave., Fair Park, 214/428–5555.*

10 *g-1*

UNITED ARTISTS CINEMA

A favorite spot to view foreign and independent film, this theater provides more modern amenities such as comfortable seats, not often found in older theaters. *5540 Yale Blvd., North, 214/369–5308.*

festivals

13 *d-3*

CHILDREN'S HOLIDAY FILM FESTIVAL

Favorite videos such as *How the Grinch Stole Christmas* and *Adventures of Curious George* in this video series will thrill children and parents alike. Films are shown in the Orientation Center during December and January. *Dallas Museum of Art, 1717 N. Harwood St., Downtown, 214/922–1200.*

10 *f-2*

DALLAS VIDEO FESTIVAL

Presented each March, this festival presents more than 200 videos produced worldwide, from dramatic and animation to experimental and documentaries. Each year the Video Association of Dallas presents the Kovacs Award—named for TV personality Ernie Kovacs—for innovation. Past recipients include Paul Reubens, aka Pee Wee Herman, and Terry Gilliam of Monty Python fame. More information is available at www.videofest.org. *Dallas Theater Center, 3636 Turtle Creek, Uptown, 214/948–7300.*

13 *f-4*

DEEP ELLUM FILM FESTIVAL

It's no telling what you will see at this annual festival. But plan on having a good time, despite the dubious quality of some of the films. Screenings take place on rooftops, bars, and anywhere a group can set a projector. Event sponsors, DEFMAN (Deep Ellum Film, Art, Music and Noise), also host a summer series where local filmmakers have had the opportunity to talk to such guest speakers as *Southpark* executive producer Anne Garefino. *214/752-6759*

6 *g-8*

JEWISH FILM FESTIVAL

Sponsored by the Jewish Community Center of Dallas, this September festival screens foreign films rarely shown in this area. Past selections include the Israeli Academy Award winner, *Yana's Friends*, and the Argentina drama, *Poor Butterfly*. *AMC Glen Lakes 8, 9450 N. Central Expressway, North, 214/739–2737.*

USA FILM FESTIVAL/DALLAS

Dallas's annual film festival attracts as many as 70 filmmakers from around the world. Each spring, this eight-day event brings together artists and audiences while premiering a diverse selection of film. During January, the organization holds a 12-day Kidfilm Festival, which includes presentations by animators and puppeteers, plus daily screenings of contemporary and classic films. Location varies. *214/871–3456.*

OPERA

companies

DALLAS OPERA

From its inception in 1957, the Dallas Opera has enjoyed an international reputation as one of America's leading opera companies. It continues to emphasize innovative productions and contemporary repertoire. Its Puppet Opera Theater, aimed at kindergarten through third grade, is especially popular with area children. *214/443–1000.*

ORCHESTRAS & ENSEMBLES

performing groups

DALLAS CLASSICAL GUITAR SOCIETY

From September to April, the society hosts at least one concert a month, showcasing guitarists in the International Series and lesser-known virtuosos in its Master Series. Past classical guitar virtuosos include Pepe Romero, Manuel Barrueco, and Chet Atkins. *214/528–3733.*

DALLAS JAZZ ORCHESTRA

Under the guidance of founder and artistic director Galen Jeter, the world-renowned Dallas Jazz Orchestra performs original and traditional big-band jazz. The 20-piece unit has performed at the prestigious Montreux Jazz Festival in Switzerland, and its recordings are known worldwide. Each year, some of the best jazz students in the country accompany the band during its numerous live performances around the city, including free summer concerts. *972/644–8833.*

13 *d-3*

DALLAS SYMPHONY ORCHESTRA

Celebrating its 100th anniversary, this world-class orchestra, let by Andrew Litton, regularly performs classical, pop, and special concerts showcasing some of the world's best known musical artists. *Morton H. Meyerson Symphony Center, 2301 Flora St., 214/871–4000.*

13 *d-3*

DALLAS WIND SYMPHONY

From Bach to Sousa, this musical group performs an eclectic blend of musical styles. The 50 woodwind, brass, and percussion players, led by Jerry Junkin, perform year-round, including outdoor summer concerts in the Fair Park Bandshell (3809 Grand Ave., 214/670–8400). *Morton H. Meyerson Symphony Center, 2301 Flora St., 214/528–5576.*

PERFORMANCE VENUES

13 *d-3*

BRONCO BOWL

This 3,000-seat venue is part of a bowling alley, arcade, and banquet hall complex. Past performers have included Bruce Springsteen and Patti LaBelle. *2600 Fort Worth Ave., South, 214/943–1777.*

6 *g-8*

MCFARLIN MEMORIAL AUDITORIUM

Since 1926, this formal chapel has hosted an eclectic mix of famous entertainers, from Elton John, Beverly Sills, and Bob Hope to Carl Sandburg, Ogden Nash, and Salvadore Dali. It is the oldest and largest of Southern Methodist University's three auditoriums. The 2,398-seat facility also is a popular spot for classical music concerts, dance performances, and guest lecturers. It is also home of the Texas Theatrical Arts Society, which brings internationally known musical and dance groups to the city for classical music concerts, dance performances, and guest lecturers. *6405 Boaz La., University Park, 214/768–3129.*

13 *d-3*

MORTON H. MEYERSON SYMPHONY CENTER

Since opening in 1989, few concert halls in the country can equal the beauty or acoustic quality of the Meyerson. Its centerpiece, Eugene McDermott Concert Hall, is a European-style music chamber with seating for 2,062 music lovers. Seasonal performances include family pop concerts and the Christmas Celebration Series. The Meyerson also has a gift shop and two restaurants. Preconcert lectures are available. *2301 Flora St., 214/670–3600.*

13 *b-6*

REUNION ARENA

With the opening of the new sports arena, the future is uncertain for this 15,520-seat facility. In the past, it's been a favorite indoor arena for such performers as Tina Turner, AC/DC, and the Dixie Chicks. It also hosted the Dallas Stars, Dallas Mavericks, Dallas Sidekicks, and the annual Ice Capade and circus performances. *777 Sport St., Downtown, 214/939–2770.*

10 *h-2*

SMIRNOFF MUSIC CENTRE

Dozens of live performances from rock groups to country singers annually sell out this 20,000-seat amphitheater, formerly the Coca Cola Starplex Amphitheater. The music center draws some of the nations top performers, including Clint Black, The Moody Blues, and Pearl Jam. *1818 First Ave., Fair Park, 214/428–8365.*

THEATERS

Dallas has a surprisingly wide mix of theater to fit all tastes—children's, musicals, avant-garde, ethnic. The theaters are equally diverse, ranging from stages housed in elegant centers to those squeezed into close quarters. Most theater companies are small, but devoted to putting on the best performances possible. Besides, all that talent on Broadway has to start somewhere.

13 *d-3*

ARTS DISTRICT THEATER

Housed in a corrugated metal warehouse, the theater's industrial exterior is in sharp contrast to the large flexible performance space found inside. Originally an expansion of the Dallas Theater Center, the 750-seat theater stages such large musical productions as *Guys and Dolls* and annual Christmas performances of Dickens's *A Christmas Carol. 2401 Flora St., Downtown, 214/522–8499.*

6 *h-8*

BATH HOUSE CULTURAL CENTER

Along the shore of White Rock Lake, northeast of Dallas, this Art Deco bathhouse began a new life in 1981 as a community cultural center. Today, the 120-seat theater hosts multicultural visual and performing arts throughout the year. Each July, the center stages the annual Festival of Independent Theaters, where diverse theater groups perform new, original, and avant-garde works. *521 E. Lawther Dr., East, 214/670–8749.*

10 *h-2*

MUSIC HALL AT FAIR PARK

Since opening in 1925, this Dallas landmark has recently enlarged its lobby and improved its acoustics. The 3,420-seat hall is home to the Dallas Summer Musicals and is frequently used by the Dallas Opera and Fort Worth Dallas Ballet. *909 First Ave., 214/565–1116.*

10 *f-2*

KALITA HUMPHREYS THEATER

The Dallas Theater Center uses this now-legendary 497-seat theater for many of its performances. Opened in 1959, this is one of three theaters designed by Frank Lloyd Wright. The architecturally rich setting enhances plays written by the famous—Shakespeare, Oscar Wilde, Dylan Thomas—and the not yet so famous—Preston Jones. A series of discussions that brings together the theater cast with the audience takes place following the opening of all productions. The popular annual Big D Festival of the Unexpected is also held here. *3636 Turtle Creek Blvd., 214/522–8499.*

6 *g-8*

LA THEATRE DE MARIONETTE

A favorite spot with local children, this special theater presents marionette performances of classic stories and fairy tales in the traditional European style. A small shop in the lobby sells finger and hand puppets and small puppet stages. Performances are on weekends with special birthday party performances during the week. *462 NorthPark Center, North, 214/369–4849.*

13 *e-5*

THE MAJESTIC THEATRE

The historic Majestic is *the* performing arts center of Dallas, staging work from the finest theater, dance, and music organizations as well as Southwest premieres of Broadway touring productions. Its supreme acoustics, lighting, stage areas, and 1,648 seats—a result of extensive renovations in 1983—enliven modern dance, opera, symphonies, touring productions, and conventions. *1925 Elm St., Downtown, 214/880–0137.*

13 *f-4*

PEGASUS THEATRE

Housed in a converted warehouse in Deep Ellum, this cozy theater presents year-round comedy productions. *3916 Main St., Downtown, 214/821–6005.*

13 *d-2*

THEATRE THREE

An intimate theater-in-the-round set in the Quadrangle Courtyard is the place to see musicals, classics, dramas, and comedy. With more than 300 performances a year, this is truly a year-round in-the-round theater. *2800 Routh St., 214/871–3300.*

THEATRE TOO!

This small, flexible theater space inside Theatre Three stages performances from 30 different local theater groups who lack their own facility. It seats 30–60, depending on stage set up. *2800 Routh St., 214/871–3300.*

13 *f-4*

UNDERMAIN THEATER

Avant-garde and literary adaptations provide a welcome change to other theatrical venues in town. *3200 Main St., 214/747–5515.*

companies

BEARDSLEY LIVING THEATRE

Founded in 1987 by alumni of Austin College, this theater group annually presents two new works at the Bath House Cultural Center (see Theaters, above). Most productions are written by local playrights and explore spirituality and cultural diversity. Each performance runs for three weekends. *214/328–7764.*

13 *c-1*

DALLAS CHILDREN'S THEATER

This nationally respected theater produces family-oriented plays that address serious social issues, including race, coming of age, and foster care. Founded in 1984, the theater produces 10 plays each season. It also offers acting classes for children ages 3–8. *2215 Cedar Springs Rd., Oak Lawn, 214/978–0110.*

6 *f-6*

DALLAS PUPPET THEATER

Children sit spellbound as the magic of puppetry introduces them to such fairy tales as *Beauty and the Beast* and *Sleeping Beauty*. Performances are held Wednesday through Sunday. Reservations are required for afternoon performances. *2040 Valley View Center, 972/716–0230.*

DALLAS THEATER CENTER

More than 100,000 theater lovers annually attend this center for diverse plays ranging from classics and musicals to new works. Since 1959, the Center has staged more than 8,300 performances of nearly 400 plays. The most popular play is *A Christmas Carol*, produced 16 times. In 1964, the center represented the United States at the theater of Nations in Paris, becoming the first theater outside New York to perform at the annual event. Performances are held at either the Kalita Humphreys Theater or the Arts District Theater. *214/522–8499.*

13 *c-1*

KITCHEN DOG THEATER

Formed in 1990 by five Southern Methodist University students, this critically-acclaimed 100-seat theater group stages original plays and classics, such as *Romeo and Juliet* and *Who's Afraid of Virginia Wolfe*. *McKinney Avenue Contemporary Art Gallery, 3120 McKinney Ave., Uptown, 214/953–1055.*

TEATRO DALLAS

Performing seasonal productions and representing the United States at international festivals keeps this professional theater group busy. Established in 1985, Teatro Dallas stages works by classical and contemporary Latino playwrights. Each October, the theater group selects a play that honors the traditional Latino holiday Day of the Dead. *2204 Commerce St., Downtown, 214/741–6833.*

festivals

10 *f-2*

BIG D FESTIVAL OF THE UNEXPECTED

This festival enables local writers, actors, and performers to showcase their works. The popular festival started in the early 1990s as a seasonal grand finale. Focus is thought-provoking new plays and new interpretations of the classics. *Kalita Humphreys Theater, 3636 Turtle Creek Blvd., 214/522–8499.*

10 *h-2*

DALLAS SUMMER MUSICALS

Since 1941, music lovers have seen some of Broadway's most popular hits performed by national touring companies, and an annual local production of *Oklahoma*. Performances are held at the Music Hall at Fair Park (see Theaters, above) from June through August. The organization also stages fall and winter musicals geared toward avant-garde performances. *214/421–5678.*

6 *h-8*

FESTIVAL OF INDEPENDENT THEATERS

During July, independent theater companies that lack a permanent home present a variety of performances. *Bath House Culture Center, 521 E. Lawther Dr., East, 214/670–8749.*

10 *h-1*

SHAKESPEARE FESTIVAL OF DALLAS

About 100,000 Bard lovers head to Samuell-Grand Park each summer for an evening under the stars with the nation's second oldest Shakespeare theater company. Whether you bring a blanket to toss on the ground or rent sand chairs, arrive early for the best view. *Samuell-Grand Park, 6200 E. Grand Ave., East, 214/559–2778.*

TICKETS

The best advice you will likely receive from a ticket broker is to buy early. Popular shows sell out immediately. And even if you can find a ticket, it will hardly be the best seat in the house. For convenience, order early over the phone, then have it mailed to you. If you'd rather buy tickets in person, stop at any Foley's (972/385–6533), Dillard's (800/654–9545), or Albertson's (972/660–8300) stores. All have either Ticketmaster or Star Tickets outlets. Foley's also sells half-price tickets for evening performances on the day of the show. To order by phone, call Ticketmaster (214/373–8000) or visits its website at www.ticketmaster.com. *You can also have tickets left at the arena's Will Call window. You'll find seating charts for most major venues in the front of Southwestern Bell's Yellow Pages; some ticket sellers also have charts. Nearly all ticket vendors add a service charge of $2–$4.*

nightlife

Dallas nightlife ranges from sophisticated clubs with cigar lounges to neighborhood bars that are long on friendliness but short on decor. Club sizes range from mega nightspots with multiple bars and dance floors to cozy little spots that seem full with only a few people inside. Hours vary with some open only on weekends. So whether you want to dress up or down, to see or be seen, you'll find the perfect night spot that fits your mood.

Nightclubs tend to cluster in neighborhoods, enabling you to club hop from one spot to another. Lower Greenville Avenue and Deep Ellum are two of the most popular areas. Deep Ellum is an especially appropriate spot for nightclubs since it is credited with turning out some of the nation's best known blues performers in the 1920s and '30s.

Crowds follow the music and most clubs host a variety of sounds, so how you dress and whom you see will be influenced by the music playing that night. Dress is often mixed, but most places lean toward the casual. Of course, folks do stop by after a big party still decked out in tux and satin or after the rodeo in boots and jeans. Cover charges, if any, generally range from $4 to $10. Live music usually begins after 9 PM. Most bars are open until 2 AM Friday night and 3 AM to 4 AM on Saturday night.

BARS & LOUNGES

13 *f-4*

ART BAR

DJs spin house music for the fashion-oriented and artist types who hang out here to chat and admire the artwork adorning the walls. The bar doubles as an art gallery, with works changing every five weeks. Each opening is kicked off with a reception. *2806 Elm St., Deep Ellum, 214/939–0077.*

10 *g-1*

ACROSS THE STREET BAR

The university crowd relishes the $1.25 pitchers of beer. A psychedelic drum jam happens each Wednesday. *5625 Yale Blvd., East, 214/363–0660.*

6 *f-2*

BEGGAR CLUB

The Dallas version of "Cheers," so dubbed by locals. They toss darts, shoot pool, and dance to Top 40 rock hits on the weekends. *17449 Preston Rd., North, 972/732–8801.*

13 *b-4*

DALLAS ALLEY

This West End space houses seven bars under one roof. *See* individual listings for Alley Cats, 110 Neon Beach, Kats, Roadhouse Saloon, Tilt, Stogies, and Plaza Bar. *2019 N. Lamar St., West End, 214/720–0170.*

13 *f-4*

GREEN ROOM

The only remnant of this former pre-gig band hangout is the band memorabilia on its walls. Today, white tablecloths, fine food, and a wine list appease an indifferent, casually-dressed crowd. During warm weather, the crowds populate on the outside deck for drinks and pizza. The view from the roof is one of the best around of Downtown. *2715 Elm St., Deep Ellum, 214/748–7666.*

13 *b-4*

KATS

You get to be the singing star at this karaoke bar, except the weekends when local hip-hop, pop or jazz bands perform. *Dallas Alley, 2019 N. Lamar St., West End, 214/720–0170.*

6 *f-8*

INWOOD TAVERN

The din of lively chatter resonates in this cozy neighborhood bar, where regulars congregate for drinks and discourse. *7717 Inwood Rd., Central, 214/353–2666.*

13 *f-4*

MAIN STREET INTERNET

Dot.com guys and gals come here to cyber-surf the night away on flat computer screens while sipping beer or coffee. Many of the regulars work in the area, since Deep Ellum has become the in-spot for Internet and software-related companies to open shop. This is a blue jeans and T-shirt crowd. But don't be fooled by the dress. The person sitting next to you might be a dot.com information architect with his or her own company. *2656 Main St., Deep Ellum, 214/237–1308.*

13 *b-4*

PLAZA BAR

Enjoy a variety of live music while people-watching at this beer-only outdoor bar. *Dallas Alley, 2019 N. Lamar St., West End, 214/720–0170.*

10 *g-1*

ZUBAR

Arrive early or expect to stand in line at this popular nightspot on Lower Greenville Avenue. This 25-plus crowd goes for the well-heeled look of designer couture, especially on weekends. DJs on Friday and Saturday spin jazz, samba, and other sounds. A lounge in back is a favorite hangout for cigar lovers. *2012 Greenville Ave., East, 214/887–0071.*

BLUES

13 *f-4*

BLUE CAT BLUES

All kinds of local and international talent plug in at this Chicago-style blues joint. Festival posters line the walls, autographed by the itinerant musicians who play here. In fact, during the 1920s and '30s, the area thrived with clubs hosting many great blues singers, including Leadbelly and Blind Lemon Jefferson. *2612 Commerce St., Deep Ellum, 214/744–2287.*

13 *f-4*

THE BONE

Be prepared to stand in line with other twenty-somethings for entrance into this popular blues club. Weather permitting, mix the night stars with great live blues by local bands by hanging out on the roof. *2724 Elm St., Downtown, 214/744–2663. No cover.*

6 *d-7*

HOLE IN THE WALL

This roadhouse is known for live local blues and juicy hamburgers. Sometimes the band plays outdoors on the wood deck. *11654 Harry Hines Blvd., Northwest, 972/247–2253.*

BREWPUBS & MICROBREWERIES

13 *f-4*

COPPER TANK BREWERY

If you're searching for a varied selection of beers and a burger, some conversation, and a game of pool, you'll find like-minded folks here. With six specialty beers always on tap, this award-winning microbrewery has just the right flavor for most taste. Try them all—fruit, stout, or lager—during specials on Wednesday ($1 a pint), Friday ($2 for all), and Saturday (spin the wheel). *2600 Main St., Downtown, 214/744–2739.*

13 *b-4*

STOGIE'S

You can buy cigars priced from $6 to $20, and listen to live blues on the weekends. *Dallas Alley, 2019 N. Lamar St., West End, 214/720–0170.*

COFFEEHOUSES

13 *f-4*

INSOMNIA

Sip the popular coffee shake or try one of the other 14 espresso flavors. The crowd tends to be young; it's a favorite spot for the teen set, since this is one of the few places in Deep Ellum where they are allowed to hang out. Tuesday is poetry night, Thursday is open mike, and Friday and Saturday local groups play live rock or techno on the patio. *2640 Elm St., Deep Ellum, 214/761–1556.*

13 *f-4*

NEW AMSTERDAM COFFEE HAUS

This coffee house serves two flavors of the day, but if you want others then buy the beans and brew your own at home. Local bands play folk and jazz on Friday and Saturday nights. *831 Exposition Ave., Deep Ellum, 214/824–5301.*

COMEDY

13 *e-3*

AD-LIBS THEATER

As fast as the lively audience shouts topics, this hometown improv troupe pops back a funny line. Make your reservations early, as Friday and Saturday shows usually sell out by Wednesday. A light menu includes sandwiches, nachos, soft drinks, beer, and wine. *2613 Ross Ave., Downtown, 214/754–7050.*

THE IMPROV

Nationally-known comedians including Tommy Davidson and Brian Reagan keep audiences chuckling. The club has a full restaurant and bar. *4980 Belt Line Rd., Addison, 972/404–8501.*

13 *f-4*

LATE NIGHT KRAZY

This interactive music and comedy set is only for late nighters. The show starts Friday at midnight and runs until 5 AM. *3200 Main St., Deep Ellum, 214/662–5600.*

COUNTRY & WESTERN

6 *d-8*

COUNTRY 2000

With 40,000 square ft, this Texas-size club is country with pizzazz. Country and western lovers can strut their stuff on a 3,500-square-ft dance floor, mingle at six different bars—three upstairs, three downstairs—or shoot pool. Most of the time DJs spin the sound, but the club also hosts an occasional Friday night concert featuring such popular singers as Sammy Kershaw, Ty Herndon, or Wade Hayes. Free dance lessons are available Wednesday and Thursday nights, 7:30 PM–8 PM, and Sunday, 4:30 PM–8 PM. *10707 Finnell St., 214/654–9595.*

6 *d-8*

COWBOYS RED RIVER

When they tire of boot scootin' songs, locals head to the mechanical bull for a little bucking action. You can learn all the latest in country dances when you show up to Wednesday's dance lessons from 7 PM to 8 PM. Merle Haggard and Pat Green perform twice monthly, with local groups performing other times. DJs spin tunes between sets. Evening buffets are catered, so you may have barbecue one night and Mexican food another night. *10310 Technology Blvd., West, 214/352–1796.*

13 *b-4*

ROAD HOUSE SALOON

Dance indoors or outdoors at this West End bar, while soaking up its Texas ambiance. DJs spin the latest country hits nightly. Wednesday nights feature 75¢ beer until 10 PM. *2019 N. Lamar St., West End, 214/720–0170.*

DANCE CLUBS

13 *f-4*

BLIND LEMON

Gen Xers dance to DJ-spun funk and old school at this Deep Ellum club, which is part of the Club Clearview complex. If you're the voyeuristic sort, watch from the multi-color shag bar. *2804 Elm St., Deep Ellum, 214/939–0077.*

13 *f-4*

CLUB RED

Unlike the other three clubs that are part of the Club Clearview complex, Red is smaller and has a separate street entrance. DJs spin high-energy house and techno music on Thursday, Friday, and Saturday night. A poetry slam is held each Friday night from 8:30–10. *2806 Elm St., Deep Ellum, 214/939–0077.*

13 *f-4*

LIQUID LOUNGE

This is another club within a club, but has its own entrance. You can dance to live local jazz, pop, and hip-hop, or pop into the larger Curtain Club and check out live rock music. *2800 Main St., Deep Ellum, 214/742–2336.*

10 *g-1*

RED JACKET

House, techno, funk, and disco keep locals dancing. A 1999 addition created the Ruby Room, a memorial to Dallas' infamous nightclub owner, Jack Ruby, who killed Kennedy assassin Lee Harvey Oswald. The room includes photos of Ruby and the assassination. *3606 Greenville Ave., East, 214/823–8333.*

13 *f-4*

SEVEN

You had better be in shape to keep up with the high-energy '80s dance music played here. DJs spin the music for the well-dressed crowd, who know to leave their blue jeans at home. *2505 Pacific Ave., Downtown, 214/887–8787.*

13 *f-4*

SONS OF HERMANN HALL

Live music—from blues to country to swing—upstairs keeps your feet moving at this 1911 building that still serves as a club to a German fraternal order, but welcomes the public to drop by anytime. Downstairs crowds can still belly up to the large carved wood bar. Remember to stop by the first Friday of each month for $1 pizzas. Mingle with the very young to the very old. *3414 Elm St., Deep Ellum, 214/747–4422.*

DINING & DANCING

11 *a-4*

LONE STAR CAFÉ & CLUB

You can belly-up to this horseshoe-shape bar and stare at pictures of some of your favorite singers—Willie Nelson, Merle Haggard, Waylan Jennings—while deciding if you want to join the other two-steppers and dance to the nightly local and regional bands. If all that dancing makes you hungry, the club's restaurant serves up tasty Americana, from hamburgers to steaks. Karoke night revs up the crowds on Sunday and Monday, while songwriters from all over sing their tunes at Wednesday's pickin' parties. *11277 E. Northwest Hwy., Northeast, 214/341–3538.*

10 *g-2*

SIPANGO

After dining, you can dance off the extra calories with the pumping sounds of disco music from the late '70s and early '80s in the backroom club. Local bands perform Thursday through Sunday, but DJs spin the sounds other nights. Top off the evening with a cigar and cognac on the patio. Expect a mixed crowd with ages varying from 20 to 60. *4513 Travis St., off University Ave., Uptown, 214/522–2411.*

FOLK & ACOUSTIC

10 *g-1*

POOR DAVID'S PUB

Americana country and folk music are mainstays, although you will also hear plenty of rock and blues at this pub housed in a 1919 building that once was a barber's college. Local, regional and national players—including Steve Fromholz and Bugs Henderson—perform four nights a week. *1924 Greenville Ave., East, 214/821–9891.*

GAY AND LESBIAN BARS & PUBS

10 *f-2*

THE BRICK BAR

You'll find a sunken dance floor and high-tech light show at this popular gay dance club, open nightly Wednesday through Sunday. *4117 Maple Ave., Oak Lawn, 214/521–2024.*

10 *f-2*

JR

You'll be assured a lively night out at this lesbian and gay club. There's dance contests every Thursday and Sunday night, pool tournaments on Wednesday, and drink specials Friday and Saturday. *3923 Cedar Springs Rd., Oak Lawn, 214/559–0650.*

10 *f-2*

SUE ELLEN'S

Classic rock, eight-ball pool, an open mike—not for karoke—sand volleyball, and a patio are the right ingredients for fun-packed evenings at this lesbian club in the heart of Oak Lawn. Local bands play Monday, Wednesday, and Friday nights. *3903 Cedar Springs Rd., Oak Lawn, 214/559–0707.*

10 *f-2*

VILLAGE STATION

Dance nightly to your favorite disco sounds or check out a drag show in the Rose Room. *3911 Cedar Springs Rd., Oak Lawn, 214/559–0650.*

HOTEL BARS

13 *b-6*

AT THE TOP OF THE DOME

Drink and dance nightly, while savoring a full view of the city below in this slowly revolving lounge atop the Reunion Tower. If hunger persists, sample some fruit and cheese, chicken wings, or nachos. *300 Reunion Blvd., Downtown, 214/651–1234.*

13 *c-3*

BEAU NASH

This large wood-panel bar courts an international reputation as being *the* spot in Dallas for drinks. The bar menu includes a soup-of-the-day special. *Hotel Crescent Court, 400 Crescent Court, Uptown, 214/871–3200.*

10 *f-2*

NANA BAR

Located on the 27th floor of the Wyndham Anatole Hotel, this bar has it all: great view, cigar list, scotch menu, and live jazz on Wednesday and Thursday. Yummy appetizers include shrimp cocktail and chicken fingers. *2201 Stemmons Freeway, North, 214/761–7479.*

13 *c-4*

PYRAMID ROOM

Dine on prime rib, T-bone and tuna steaks, and sole while listening to the nightly classical piano tinklings. *Fairmont Hotel, 1717 N. Akard St., Downtown, 214/720–5249.*

JAZZ

13 *c-1*

AVANTI

This Italian eatery serves up tasty entrées while local bands play jazz, creating a mellow dining ambience. A midnight favorite is eggs Benedict. *2720 McKinney Ave., Uptown, 214/871–4955.*

THE BALCONY CLUB

Plenty of regulars visit to soak of the sounds of Big Al Dupree, Dallas's legendary jazz and blues pianist. Dupree, born in 1923, has been part of the city's music scene since the 1930s. *1825 Abrams Rd., East, 214/826–8104.*

13 *f-4*

SAMBUCA

This supper club and jazz bar serves up Mediterranean food and live music by local bands nightly to the well-heeled martini crowd. *2618 Elm St., Deep Ellum, 214/744–0820.*

10 *g-1*

TERILLI'S

The wine and martini set packs this Lower Greenville Avenue restaurant, dining on Italian favorites and listening to live jazz from Thursday through Sunday. *2815 Greenville Ave., Central, 214/827–3993.*

festivals

13 *d-3*

DALLAS JAZZ FESTIVAL

Featuring a mix of national performers, including McCoy Tyner and David "Fathead" Newman, and local talent, this outdoor festival in October serves up barbecue and beer while you enjoy the music. *Annette Strauss Artist Square, 1800 Leonard St., Downtown, 214/520–7789.*

6 *d-8*

SAMMONS JAZZ

Hear local artists perform swing to bebop and Dixieland to fusion during this festival's monthly performances, from September to December and the first Wednesday from February to May. Ticket price includes wine, beer, coffee, light appetizers, and valet parking. Performances usually sell out so get tickets early. *Sammons Center for the Arts, 3630 Harry Hines Blvd., Oak Lawn, 214/520–7789.*

PIANO BARS

13 *b-4*

ALLEY CATS

This is no place to be shy. This popular dueling piano sing-a-long bar expects plenty of audience participation. It can be noisy and rowdy at times. *Dallas Alley, 2019 N. Lamar St., West End, 214/720–0170.*

10 *f-2*

LIBRARY BAR

Going to the library takes on a whole new meaning at this combination library and bar in the Melrose Hotel. Although books line the walls at this cozy bar, dry martinis—not the literature—are the attraction. *3015 Oak Lawn Ave., Turtle Creek, 214/521–5151.*

13 *c-4*

LOBBY PIANO BAR

Listen to jazz, sip an expensive port, and smoke a cigar in the Fairmont Hotel's lobby. *1717 N. Akard St., Downtown, 214/720–5249.*

10 *f-2*

MIRAGE BAR

Listen to classical piano every night except Sunday at this bar on the first floor of the Wyndham Anatole Hotel. The hotel caters to the business crowd so expect 40s-plus decked out in suits and ties. *2201 Stemmons Freeway, Northeast, 214/761–7429.*

POP/ROCK

10 *h-2*

BAR OF SOAP

Linger over an icy mug of Shiner Bock, shoot some pool, listen to a punk or rock band, and do your laundry all at the same time. *3615 Parry Ave., East, 214/823–6617.*

13 *e-1*

BARLEY HOUSE

Local bands playing rock 'n' roll, loud punk, grunge, and Top 40 rock and innovative mixed drinks made with beer and other flavors keep the crowd returning for more. Admission is usually free. *2916 N. Henderson St., Oak Lawn, 214/824–0306.*

13 *b-4*

BELLBOTTOMS

Travel back in time and dance to hits from the '70s, '80s, and '90s. *Dallas Alley, 2019 N. Lamar St., West End, 214/720–0170.*

13 *f-4*

CLUB CLEARVIEW

This former window factory now houses four clubs (Clearview, Blind Lemon, Art Bar, and Club Red) under one roof. Clearview, the oldest club in Deep Ellum, dating to 1985, hosts live rock for a crowd of musicians and music fans. Finger-painted murals from visiting rock bands adorn the walls. A roof deck provides a good view of Downtown. *2806 Elm St., Deep Ellum, 214/939–0077.*

13 *f-4*

CLUB DADA

Sunday is open-mike night at this Deep Ellum club that features live rock, country, or blues five nights a week on three stages, including one on the huge outdoor patio. Go prepared for a crowd, or stay home and tune in Thursday night to a live broadcast at www.broadcast.com. *2720 Elm St., Deep Ellum, 214/744–3232.*

13 *f-4*

CURTAIN CLUB

You name it, they play it at this Deep Ellum club. Big rock shows—Brother Kane, Space Hog—blast your ears from the larger stage. The smaller stage in the Lizard Lounge (*see* Bars & Lounges, *above*) hosts national and local groups playing an assortment of sounds, from folk and punk to hip-hop. *2800 Main St., Deep Ellum, 214/742–2336.*

13 *f-4*

GALAXY CLUB

This Deep Ellum club is a haven for those who like loud punk rock and rock. Some local performers have gone on to national fame, including Matchbox 20, Eagle-eye Cherry, and No Doubt. Local talent performs Wednesday through Sunday. *2820 Main St., Deep Ellum, 214/742–5299.*

13 *f-4*

GYPSY TEA ROOM

This is a strange name for a nightclub that features rock, country, and folk music. Then again, it's in Deep Ellum, where the unexpected becomes the expected. It's usually crowded, so expect to be jostled. A smaller room has cushy chairs, when you can find one empty. *2548 Elm St., Deep Ellum, 214/744–9779.*

13 *f-4*

JULY ALLEY

A painted mural on a conveyor belt depicts the history of Deep Ellum. As the belt rotates under the glass-top bar, you can learn all about this part of the city. A jukebox plays pop, rock, and country music. A 1,000-ft long wall is lined with art that changes monthly. If you're not into art, then shoot pool, watch a fashion show, or take in an independent film without ever leaving the building. *2809 Elm St., Deep Ellum, 214/747–2809.*

13 *b-4*

110 NEON BEACH

Twenty-somethings dance to Top 40 rock hits spun by DJs at this nonstop nightspot. If you tire of dancing, you can always watch sports on the big-screen TV. On Wednesday, 75¢ taps are served until 10. *Dallas Alley, 2019 N. Lamar St., West End, 214/720–0170.*

13 *f-4*

TREES

Regardless where you stand or sit in this club—including the upstairs area—every spot is a good vantage point for seeing local and national bands, such as Suicidal Tendencies and Yo La Tango. The sound system—one of the best in town—makes up for dingy decor. The music starts at 10 PM. *2709 Elm St., Deep Ellum, 214/748–5009.*

PUBS & TAVERNS

10 *d-1*

THE DUBLINER

This small, intimate Irish pub serves plenty of imported beer, including Guinness and Murphy's as well as English ale and a full selection of whiskey and scotch. The menu is limited to sandwiches. *2818 Greenville Ave., East, 214/818–0911.*

10 *d-2*

TIPPERARY INN

Wash down a stomach-filling shepherd's pie or smoked Irish salmon with a creamy pint of stout, ale, or lager. Be sure to check out their scotch selection. *5815 Live Oak St., East, 214/823–7167.*

13 *b-4*

WEST END PUB

It gets packed and crazy here when the Stars hockey team plays in town. Fans like to drop in before and after the game for a few rounds. With seven beers on tap—four domestic and three imported—and a selection in bottles, you will surely find one that you like. If hungry, try the chicken salad. *211 N. Record, St. West End, 214/748–5711.*

SPORTS BARS

6 *f-8*

DAMON'S

With four big-screen TVs and six sets, it's impossible to miss the big game any place you sit. Each table has speakers for selective listening, so you can turn the volume up or down for whichever TV you are watching. Food ranges from barbecue to steaks to sandwiches, and the bar serves plenty of beer and wine to wash it down. *10650 N. Central Expressway, North, 214/373–4246.*

10 *d-1*

1ST & 10 SPORTS BAR

The bar's two large-screen TVs and six smaller screen TVs are popular with the neighbors when the Cowboys or Stars play. A full bar, including imported and domestic beers, serves plenty of beverage choices. During the half or a blowout, you can devour one of their renowned juicy hamburgers, play shuffleboard, or shoot pool. Go early on game day; the bar fills in a hurry. *6435 Mockingbird La., North, 214/828–0055.*

6 *d-8*

MILO BUTTERFINGERS

This sports bar had its moment of fame when scenes for Oliver Stone's *Born on the Fourth of July* were shot here. Since then, crowds show up to watch their favorite teams play on the two big-screen TVs and the nine smaller sets scattered around the bar. To keep fans in the proper mood, college pennants and posters decorate the walls. After—and before—the game, you can shoot pool, plays foosball, throw darts, or play video games. The bar serves a variety of beer, both imported and domestic. The kitchen serves up burgers, salads, cheese fries, and nachos. *5645 Greenville Ave., East, 214/368–9212.*

WINE BARS

CORK

With more than 150 wines from around the world on its wine list, this upscale bar is a favorite for wine enthusiasts. And you don't always have to order a bottle; the bar serves 68 wines by the glass. *2709 McKinney Ave., Uptown, 214/303–0302.*

performing arts: fort worth/mid-cities

Fort Worth has long been known for its superb symphony, opera, and ballet companies. The Van Cliburn piano competition is a world-famous event based right here in Cowtown. The opening of the extraordinary Bass Performance Hall in downtown Fort Worth—lauded by *The New York Times*—drew attention anew to this old Chisholm Trail stop, placing an unprecedented depth of cultural emphasis almost on top of a spot once called Hell's Half-Acre.

Also in the wild, woolly downtown, out-and-about types find a significant selection of theaters for drama and comedy. Performing arts aren't limited to downtown, however. You'll find plenty of happenings in the Mid-Cities, from Arlington and Grapevine to Irving.

CHORAL & CHAMBER GROUPS

CHAMBER MUSIC SOCIETY OF FORT WORTH

Leading musicians from the Fort Worth/Dallas area and guest artists from around the world—such as Harvey Boatright, Schwang Lin, and Carter Enyeart—perform at the Texas Boys Choir's Great Hall (2925 Riverglen, Fort Worth). *817/332–1610.*

FORT WORTH CIVIC CHORUS

A volunteer choral society performs theme concerts of classical and popular music, including Broadway melodies, at various locations. *817/740–5742.*

SCHOLA CANTORUM OF TEXAS

This internationally acclaimed 60-voice, all-volunteer chorus performs a winter-spring series of Christmas music, 19th-century classical choral music, and masterworks with members of the Fort Worth Symphony. The Irons Recital Hall in Arlington, various area churches, and Bass Performance Hall all host performances. *817/737–5788.*

CONCERTS IN CHURCHES

15 c-6

ST. ANDREW'S EPISCOPAL

Arguably the city's most beautiful church, this downtown Gothic Revival masterpiece serves as a performance space for the Fort Worth Early Music presentations. Local professional groups perform baroque music in historically authentic presentations. *Taylor St., Fort Worth, 817/923–2789.*

DANCE

Although Fort Worth boasts the nation's third-largest cultural district, it still comes as something of a surprise that Fort Worth and Tarrant County support a healthy variety of dance companies, from classical to contemporary.

companies

BALLET ARLINGTON

Directed by Paul Mejia, this company stages performances featuring local musicians, students at Texas Hall at the University of Texas at Arlington (703 West Nedderman Drive), and such international stars as Anna Antoicheva and Dmitri Belogolovtsev. *817/459–1410.*

BALLET CONCERTO

Local dance professionals who teach in outreach programs at schools present an annual holiday performance for school children and outdoor summer concerts during July. *3803 Camp Bowie Blvd., Fort Worth, 817/738–7915.*

CONTEMPORARY DANCE/FORT WORTH

You will enjoy a full season of modern dance performances at Orchestra Hall (4401 Trail Lake Dr., near Texas Christian University) and other venues from this local dance company. *817/922–0944.*

FORT WORTH/DALLAS BALLET

Under the innovative and exciting leadership of artistic director Benjamin Houk, this company stages subscription series ranging from *The Nutcracker* in its most traditional finery to modern interpretations destined to become masterpieces. Performances are at Bass Performance Hall and Music Hall at Fair Park in Dallas (*see* Theaters: Dallas, *above*). *817/763–0207.*

JUBILEE AFRICAN AMERICAN DANCE ENSEMBLE

With an emphasis on African-American heritage, this modern dance company cultivates younger dancers. *817/535–4715.*

FILM

theaters

15 d-6

SUNDANCE SQUARE 20

Downtown's Sundance Square has two movie theater complexes. The Sundance 11, housed in one of the historic redbrick buildings, shows first-run films on 10 screens and top indie, foreign, and repertory films on another screen; the Palace 9, set in an Art Deco revival building, screens major films and an occasional indie. *Fort Worth, 817/870–1111.*

festivals

15 d-6

THE FORT WORTH FILM FESTIVAL

Promoters describe this popular film event as a non-competing showcase for any and all films that explore new frontiers in cinematic storytelling. Hosted annually in late October in Sundance Square (*see* Film, *above*), the festival has brought movie legends from Gregory Peck and Tippi Hedren to John Waters to town for lectures. A schedule of seminars and repertory screenings is part of the fun. *817/237–1008.*

OPERA

companies

FORT WORTH OPERA

The oldest continuing opera company in Texas first performed in 1946 to a sold-out performance of *La Traviata* at Will Rogers Memorial Auditorium. Among artists who debuted with the Fort Worth Opera are Placido Domingo and Beverly Sills. Today the Opera hosts such stars as Frances Ginsberg, Mikhail Svetlov

Krutikov, Robynne Redmon, Louis Otey, Jane Thorngren, Allan Glassman, and Frank Hernandez. Performances are at Bass Performance Hall (see Performance Venues, below). During the show, English translations are projected above the stage, and free opera lectures are offered to season ticket holders before for each performance. *817/731–0200.*

ORCHESTRAS & ENSEMBLES

15 *d-5*

performing groups

FORT WORTH SYMPHONY ORCHESTRA

Organized in 1925, the FWSO has grown into one of the most successful in the United States. The 40-musician ensemble performs nine sets of classical concerts and seven pops concerts in a season, and hosts Concerts in the Garden, its annual summer music festival. The symphony is the principal orchestra for the Fort Worth Opera and Fort Worth/Dallas Ballets. *817/665–6000.*

PERFORMANCE VENUES

15 *d-5*

NANCY LEE AND PERRY R. BASS PERFORMANCE HALL

Called the last great hall built in the 20th century, this elegant performance hall was named one of the world's 10 best opera houses by *Travel & Leisure* in 1999. It resembles the classic European opera houses with an 80-ft diameter Great Dome topping the Founders Concert Theater. Superb acoustics and six seating levels arranged in horseshoe-shape tiers with two piano boxes set it apart from all others in the nation. Past shows have included performances by Lyle Lovett, James Galway, Mandy Patinkin, Russian folk dancers, and a touring production of *Rent.* Bass Hall is home to the Van Cliburn International Piano Competition, the Fort Worth Symphony Orchestra, the Fort Worth Opera, the Fort Worth/Dallas Ballet, and others. *555 Commerce St., Fort Worth, 817/212–4200 or 888/597–7827.*

THEATER

Theater in Fort Worth long ago left behind the reputation as simply a place where Broadway favorites are frequently performed. You can still see such touring productions as *Phantom, Rent,* and *Chicago,* but the diversity and sophistication of Fort Worth's theater scene has grown to support African-American theater and contemporary and controversial works as well.

companies

14 *h-7*

CASA MANANA

The famous theater-in-the-round established by Billy Rose in 1936 for the Texas Centennial continues to present a full bill of musical comedies, plays, and concerts. The Bass Performance Hall (*see* Performance Venues, *above*) stages most productions. *W. Lancaster St., at University Dr., Fort Worth, 817/332–2272.*

15 *c-6*

CIRCLE THEATRE

One of Fort Worth's most intimate venues, this 125-seat theater in the basement beneath the Sanger Lofts in Sundance Square stages a variety of performances, including premieres of new plays. *230 W. 4th St., Fort Worth, 817/877–3040.*

9 *g-4*

CREATIVE ARTS THEATER AND SCHOOL

Known simply as CATS, this children's and family theater presents original plays and contemporary interpretations of classics, starring students from the company's school. *1100 W. Randol Mill Rd., Arlington, 817/861–2287.*

8 *h-5*

FORT WORTH THEATRE

Known mostly for its Hispanic Outreach and Labor of Love series, the city's oldest live theater group also stages such adult-theme works as *Boys in the Band* and *Love! Valour! Compassion! Orchestra Hall, 4401 Trail Lake Dr., near Texas Christian University, Fort Worth, 817/921–5300.*

8 *f-2*

HIP POCKET THEATRE

This innovative, eclectic, and often outrageous group performs a wide range of original musicals, comedies, and dramas at various locations. From June through October, it presents its theater under the stars at the company's outdoor amphitheater. *1620 Las Vegas Tr., at 820 North, Fort Worth, 817/246–9775.*

15 *d-5*

JUBILEE THEATER

Known as the premier African-American theater in the Southwest, Jubilee is two decades old and presents a full season of comedy, drama, and musical presentations. Past performances include *The Grandmama Tree*, a folk fable by Bernard Cummings; *To Be Young, Gifted & Black*, the biography of Lorraine Hansberry, adapted by R. Nemroff; and *The Book of Job*, a gospel musical by Joe Rogers and Rudy Eastman. *506 Main St., Fort Worth, 817/338–4411.*

5 *f-8*

ONSTAGE IN BEDFORD

The Trinity Arts Theater at the Bedford Boys Ranch is the Mid-Cities site for musical, comedy, and drama works from this community theater group. *2821 Forest Ridge Dr., Bedford, 817/354–6444.*

5 *h-6*

RUNWAY THEATRE

This northeast Tarrant County community theater group performs a variety of family-oriented shows such as Broadway musicals and classic comedies. *215 N. Dooley St., Grapevine, 817/488–4842.*

8 *h-5*

STAGE WEST

Its superb presentations of drama and comedy, and the rare musical, are a popular favorite in Fort Worth. Performances are staged in a renovated movie house, facing the Texas Christian University campus. Stage West is partnered with Shakespeare in the Park to present two outdoor Shakespeare productions during the summer (*see below*). *3055 S. University Dr., Fort Worth, 817/784–9378.*

9 *g-4*

THEATRE ARLINGTON

This well-established community theater presents a variety of challenging productions, from award-winning plays to musicals. *305 W. Main St., Arlington, 817/275–7661.*

festivals

15 *b-6*

SHAKESPEARE IN THE PARK

This annual summer theater event, staged by Allied Theatre Group from early June through early July, showcases such Shakespeare classics as *King Lear, Midsummer Night's Dream, Taming of the Shrew,* and *Much Ado About Nothing* at Trinity Park. *817/784–9378.*

TICKETS

Tickets bought by phone are by far the most convenient to obtain, but you'll usually pay a $3 or more surcharge. Both Ticketmaster (972/647–5700) and Star Tickets (888/597–7827) sell tickets for most events. Call the venue for other options.

nightlife

You'll find much more than country & western bars in the Fort Worth/Mid-Cities area. Most shows start between 8 PM and 10 PM; cover charges are typically between $3 and $20, depending on day of the week and headliner. Bars usually stay open until 2 AM; a few dance clubs stay open later on the weekends, but alcohol isn't served after 2 AM.

BARS & LOUNGES

15 *b-6*

A BAR

Given an artful, upscale look with low, contemporary lighting, couches, candles, flowers, and photo exhibits, this little watering hole in the Cultural District is a pleasant place for a heart-to-heart and to meet new people. *2308 W. 7th St, Fort Worth, 817/336–1410.*

15 *c-5*

BLARNEY STONE

A popular Downtown bar, this pool hall attracts an after-work, twenty-something crowd. Sandwiches are above average, and plenty of patrons order in pizzas. *904 Houston St., Fort Worth, 817/332–4747.*

15 *c-5*

8.0

The drinks and companionship here are more special than the food. Drink one of the signature Blue Things—basically, a blue daiquiri—and everything seems a little rosier. If the weather's nice, snag a table on the brick patio and watch the street theater. *111 E. 3rd St., Fort Worth, 817/336–0880.*

14 *c-8*

HOME PLATE

Still called the Su-Su, its former name for decades, this neighborhood hangout has a cast of regulars who drink everything from Bud in the bottle to Dom Perignon. A dozen TVs accommodate the sports nuts. *5922 Curzon Ave., Fort Worth, 817/377–0188.*

15 *d-5*

SPRING BOK PUB

There are plenty of bar stools for the throngs of after-work and post-college regulars, who may or may not play pool while checking out the opposite sex. It's rather hard to find, thanks to its obscure parking garage location. *600 Houston St., Fort Worth, 817/878–4284.*

BLUES

15 *b-5*

J&J BLUES BAR

Since the mid-'80s, this warehouse has been home to every sort of regional and touring blues and rock act. You'll find college students, blue-collar types, and after-work professionals stopping in to see who's playing. Acts range from Robert Ealey to Bugs Henderson. Cover charge ranges from about $5 to $10. *937 Woodward St., Fort Worth, 817/870–2337.*

BREWPUBS & MICROBREWERIES

15 *c-5*

FLYING SAUCER DRAUGHT EMPORIUM

Tucked into a fabulous Art Deco relic downtown, this libation hangout serves hundreds of beers from around the world, both on draught and in bottles. If conversation lags, you can peruse the hundreds of kitschy and antique plates that adorn the walls and ceilings; listen to a folk, rock, or blues guitarist; or find somebody interesting to chat with on the couches or on the patio. *111 E. 4th St., Fort Worth, 817/336–7468.*

CIGAR BARS

14 *h-6*

ANCHO CHILE BAR

Attached to the Southwestern restaurant Michaels, this is a favorite among the famous "trust-fund babies," and other fashionable types from the west side. Ask to see some of the better cigars, perfect for pairing with a glass of Knob Hill or Glen Fiddich. *3413 W. 7th St., Fort Worth, 817/877–3413.*

COFFEEHOUSES

14 *h-6*

FOUR STAR COFFEE BAR

Latte-sipping, chess-playing, newspaper-reading regulars pack this cool, calm java joint day and night. Decorated with paintings by local artists, it's also the place to hear folk music on Friday and Saturday evenings or to catch a light breakfast and lunch. *3324 W. 7th St., Fort Worth, 817/336–5555.*

15 *c-5*

HUMAN BEAN

Open at 6 AM daily, this tiny but hip coffee shop is distinctive for the pool table sitting at its center. Cappuccinos, mochas, and mini-pizzas are popular, as are the alternative newspapers scattered around. *904 Houston St., Fort Worth, 817/332–7788.*

COMEDY

15 *c-5*

CARAVAN OF DREAMS

This club is home to the widely acclaimed Four-Day Weekend comedy troupe, which has won a loyal following with a strong team and brilliant, fresh writing. *312 Houston St., Fort Worth, 817/226–4329.*

15 *c-5*

HYENA'S COMEDY CLUB

From open mike night for amateurs to national headliners, this is the place for lots of laughs—and perhaps a few groans. *604 Main St., Fort Worth, 817/877–5233.*

COUNTRY & WESTERN

9 *g-4*

ARLINGTON MUSIC HALL

LeAnne Rimes started her career at this favorite family entertainment center patterned after the Grand Ol' Opry in Nashville. *224 N. Center St., Arlington, 817/226–4400.*

15 *b-1*

BILLY BOB'S TEXAS

Still and likely forever, this cavernous complex of bars and dance floors is known as the world's largest honky-tonk. Anchoring one end of the legendary Stockyards National Historic District, Billy Bob's books regional bands such as Pat Green but you'll often find Pam Tillis, Tanya Tucker, Merle Haggard, or Willie Nelson on stage. You'll also find a gigantic pool hall and video arcade, a rodeo, gift shops, and snack bars. *2520 Rodeo Plaza, Fort Worth, 817/624–7117.*

15 *b-1*

WHITE ELEPHANT SALOON

The old-fashioned barroom seems right out of Dodge City, so belly up to the bar and drink a couple of cold ones. You can dance most nights to live county-western music, shoot pool, or settle back in the shady beer garden. *106 E. Exchange Ave., at N. Main St., Fort Worth, 817/624–1887.*

OUTDOOR DRINKING SPOTS

On sunny afternoons and temperate evenings, sipping beneath the wide-open sky is a Texas birthright.

The Bone Blues
Music and black skies make a great color combo on the roof of this club.

Club Clearview
The rooftop deck features a DJ, bar, and small dance area.

Club Dada
Hang out on the large landscaped patio and listen to the sounds from the stage.

Flying Saucer Draught Emporium
Nightly after-work revelers fill the long picnic tables on the brick patio.

Hole in the Wall Hamburgers
Sip a cold one on the wood deck while listening to the soothing sounds of water trickling from the fountain.

Plaza Bar
Enjoy live music and drinks on the patio.

White Elephant Saloon
A shady side yard next to one of the state's premier historical watering holes provides a comfortable beer-drinking arena.

DANCE CLUBS

14 *a-8*

ALAN'S ROCK 'N' ROLL

Cut the rug to DJ-spun hits from the '70s through the '90s on Friday night and to the true oldies on Saturday night. *Texas 183 S at Calmont St., Fort Worth, 817/560–2526.*

9 *g-1*

EL PARAISO

This Caribbean restaurant doubles as the premier Tarrant County place to learn and practice the salsa and the merengue. *1363 W. Euless Blvd., Euless, 817/267–3434.*

14 *d-1*

STARDUST BALLROOM

The old-fashioned, Friday-night dance center requires that ladies wear dresses and men don coats and ties for cutting the rug. *3316 Roberts Cut-Off Rd., Fort Worth, 817/624–1361.*

9 *a-6*

SWINGTIME CENTER

Square dance until your heart's content, Thursday through Sunday evenings. *5100 S. Loop 820, Fort Worth, 817/478–9959.*

HOTEL BARS

15 *c-5*

THE RENAISSANCE WORTHINGTON HOTEL

This quiet intimate spot in the lobby is the ideal place for an aperitif or for a snifter of brandy after the opera. Its impressive list of single-malt whiskeys is worth a look. *200 Main St., Sundance Square, Fort Worth, 817/870–1000.*

JAZZ

15 *d-5*

BLACK DOG TAVERN

A jazz jam keeps patrons tapping their toes on Sunday evening, an acoustic jam happens on Wednesday evening, and a live swing band heats up on Thursday evening. *903 Throckmorton St., Fort Worth, 817/332–8190.*

14 *g-6*

SARDINE'S

Local musician Johnny Case tinkles the ivory solo and accompanied, Tuesday through Sunday, at this favorite Italian restaurant. *3410 Camp Bowie Blvd., Fort Worth, 817/332–9937.*

POP/ROCK

14 *b-8*

RIDGLEA THEATER

This landmark, 1940's movie house has been transformed into a live music venue, featuring heavy rock from such local groups as Zion and Buddha Toe. *6025 Camp Bowie Blvd., Fort Worth, 817/738–9500.*

14 *g-6*

WRECK ROOM

The just-out-of-college and more radical twenty-somethings hang out here to listen to local alternative rock shows. *3208 W. 7th St., Fort Worth, 817/870–4900.*

SPORTS BARS

9 *e-1*

BRONCO'S

Boasting the largest collection of sports memorabilia—jerseys, gloves, bats, etc.—in Fort Worth, this loud, gregarious hangout is a giant space with dozens of TVs tuned to every sports event. The burgers and nachos are good diversions. *900 Airport Freeway, Hurst, 817/498–0600.*

9 *f-6*

BOBBY VALENTINE'S SPORTS GALLERY CAFÉ

Named for and owned by a former Texas Rangers manager, this Arlington landmark and memorabilia-jammed sports haunt pulls in as many fans of baseball, football, basketball, and hockey as it does hungry civilians in need of a club sandwich and a cold brew. *4301 S. Bowen Rd., at I–20, Arlington, 817/467–9922.*

WINE BARS

15 *c-5*

GRAPE ESCAPE

Dozens of flights of wines allow sippers to taste four or five small servings with similar descriptions and attributes at once. You may discover some new favorites from the United States, Europe, South America, and Australia. Snacks range from miniature pizzas to olives and cheeses. *500 Commerce St., Fort Worth, 817/336–9463.*

chapter 6

HOTELS

Without question, the Metroplex—Dallas, Fort Worth, Mid-Cities—is as popular among its residents as its visitors. Lodging is no exception. Whether you need a place to stay while renovating your house or to put up visiting friends and family, you will find hotels to fit all budgets. Some are marvelously furnished with antiques and original art; others are homier, but with many of the same amenities found at more expensive hotels.

In Dallas, hotels tend to cluster around major business areas. The largest concentration of hotels is in Downtown, Uptown, Market District, and North Dallas. In Downtown, hotels tend to be pricier than those in the suburbs. However, if Downtown is where you're going to spend your time, the convenience usually offsets any additional costs. For upscale hotels that know how to pamper guests with deep pockets, follow the rich and famous to Uptown, just north of Downtown but only minutes away by car. Chain hotels flourish in the Market District, home to dozens of annual national conventions, and North Dallas, an area rich in high-rise office towers. These hotels cater to business travelers with simple rooms for those on a limited expense account and suites for executives.

Dallas is a popular spot for conventions, but don't let that discourage you if you need accommodations at short notice. Although it's always good to make reservations as far in advance as possible, you can find a room most months without booking too far ahead. In January and July, however, Dallas hosts the National Home Builders convention and the Mary Kay Cosmetics convention, respectively. Hotels and restaurants across the city fill up during these two popular conventions, which draw visitors from across the nation.

Fort Worth and Mid-Cities have recently become popular destinations, so much so that a rush to provide adequate lodgings has ensued. Cowtown is becoming a choice destination for convention folks, so don't be surprised to find downtown hotels sold out. However, plenty of choices can be found in Arlington, Grapevine, and Irving, which all provide close proximity to Dallas/Fort Worth International Airport.

When you book a room, ask for a confirmation number. Most hotels hold rooms until 6 PM and most guarantee your reservation regardless of when you arrive, as long as you reserve the room with a credit card. Cancellation policies vary, so inquire when booking your room. If you should cancel, keep the cancellation number to insure you receive proper credit. A significant discount is often available for bulk bookings through no-fee discount hotel-reservation services. Call Hotel Reservations Network for more information (214/361–7311).

Most amenities are free, but some hotels charge extra. Ask when making a reservation. In Texas, even budget-priced hotels have swimming pools. On-site exercise rooms are common at even moderately priced facilities. Cable or satellite TV is standard with free or pay-for-view movie channels. Room service, dry cleaning, and laundry are usually available. Many hotels, even some moderately priced, cater to business travelers by providing at the very least fax, copiers, and meeting rooms.

price categories

CATEGORY	COST
very expensive	over $200
expensive	$150–$200
moderate	$100–$149
budget	under $100

All prices are for a standard double room weekday rate. Hotel taxes vary from city to city: Arlington 13%, Irving 13%, Fort Worth 15%, Grapevine 12%, Dallas 15%.

dallas lodging

VERY EXPENSIVE LODGINGS

13 *d-3*

ADAM'S MARK

Texas's largest hotel pays homage to the state's ranching culture with Western decor running throughout. On the outside, the stucco-like finish on original blue tile surface was part of its transformation from office building to luxury hotel. Inside, a towering 18-ft bronze bronc bucking off a cowboy dominates the spacious lobby. This downtown hotel is conveniently just blocks from the arts and financial districts and on the DART Light Rail Line. In addition to the hotel's five restaurants and four lounges, a small food court, in the Plaza of the Americas, is readily available via skywalk. The 38th floor Chaparral Club—one of Dallas's Top 10 fine dining restaurants—overlooks the city below. *400 N. Olive St., Downtown, 214/922–8000 or 800/444–2326, fax 214/922–0308. 1,842 rooms, 211 suites. 5 restaurants, no-smoking floors, indoor pool, pool, health club, dry cleaning, laundry service, business services, meeting rooms, parking (fee). AE, D, DC, MC, V.*

13 *d-5*

ADOLPHUS HOTEL

This richly furnished 21-story grand dame of grand hotels never ceases to dazzle guests with its unabashed elegance. Each nook and cranny in the warmly welcoming lobby beckons with discovery: fabulous Flemish tapestries, 19th century lacquered chinoiserie, a Napoléon III oval mirror. Tea is served each weekday and notes played on the 1893 Steinway signal the cocktail hour. Dining in The French Room is a feast for mind and palate. All this splendor is a prelude to the rooms, decorated in English, Queen Anne, and Chippendale furniture, and accented with a touch of lace. The Terrace Suites include party-size outdoor patios. Built in 1912 by a Missouri beer baron, the Adolphus Hotel was once the tallest building in Texas. *1321 Commerce St., Downtown, 214/742–8200, fax 214/651–3563. 432 rooms, 25 1-bedroom suites, 100 junior 1-room suites. 46 rooms, 16 suites. 2 restaurants, bar, grill, minibar, laundry service, concierge, parking (fee). No pets. AE, D, DC, MC, V.*

13 *c-4*

FAIRMONT HOTEL

A small art gallery off the lobby sets the mood if you're headed to the Art District, just minutes away. Built in the late 1960s, the twin towers—one with 19 stories, the other with 24—of this beige brick hotel provide plenty of space for exercise facilities and a rooftop swimming pool. You can start and finish your day in the Lobby Bar with Continental breakfast in the morning and drinks and piano music at night. The Pyramid Grill serves such favorites as lobster and steak. The clean, modern rooms provide a homey feel. *1717 N. Akard St., Downtown, 214/720–2020 or 800/527–4727, fax 214/720–5282. 500 rooms, 50 suites. 2 restaurants, in-room data ports, in-room safes, minibar, pool, exercise room, laundry service, concierge, parking (fee). AE, D, DC, MC, V.*

13 *c-3*

HOTEL CRESCENT COURT

This small prestigious hotel is the centerpiece of an office and shopping complex just north of Dallas in the Turtle Creek section of the city. With 24-hour room service, twice-daily maid service, and a European-style setting, you are coddled in luxury. Some of the suites are two stories with spiral staircases, hardwood floors, and dining rooms. On the 17th floor, the opulent Crescent Club offers a splendid view of Downtown. The club also has a bar and private dining rooms. For more informal dining, you can dine downstairs in Beau Nash, a bar and grill. If you really want to pamper yourself, enroll at The Spa, a state-of-the-art fitness center, focusing on physical and mental health. Memberships are required for the Crescent Club and the Spa, but guests can pay by the day. *400 Crescent Court, Turtle Creek, 214/871–3200 or 800/654–6541, fax 214/871–3245. 218 rooms. 2 restaurants, bar, grill, in-room fax, in-room safes, minibar, pool, beauty salon, massage, health club, laundry service, concierge, meeting rooms, parking (fee). AE, D, DC, MC, V.*

13 *b-1*

HOTEL ST. GERMAIN

Proprietor Claire Heymann decorated this former 1906 mansion with antiques from France and New Orleans and transformed it into opulent accommodations.

Each suite has a fireplace and canopied feather bed, and a complimentary breakfast awaits you each morning. The hotel opened to rave reviews in 1991 and has since garnered accolades for accommodations, service, and its restaurant. You're also a block away from McKinney Avenue, which is filled with restaurants, galleries, and antiques shops. The New Orleans–style courtyard is a favorite with guests, who have included such celebrities as Martha Stewart and Prince Albert of Monaco. *2516 Maple Ave., Turtle Creek, 214/871–2516. 7 suites. Bar, hot tub, concierge. AE, MC, V.*

13 *b-6*

HYATT REGENCY DALLAS

Upon arrival, you'll enter a magnificent 18-story atrium lobby, an introduction visitors have come to expect from this Dallas landmark. A recent renovation and expansion program enlarged meeting space, doubled the size of the health club, and added guest rooms, some with parlors and balconies. It is minutes away from the Convention Center, DART Light Rail Line, and the Central Business District. *300 Reunion Blvd., Downtown, 214/651–1234, fax 214/742–8126. 1,123 rooms. Restaurant, bar, in-room data ports, laundry service, concierge, parking (fee). No pets. AE, D, DC, MC, V.*

13 *d-3*

LEMERIDIEN

Regardless of your room, you're bound to relish the view of either the Dallas skyline or the 15-story atrium. The hotel is part of a chain originally created by Air France when its pilots complained about accommodations worldwide. Like the rest of the hotel, rooms are decorated in modern European with Old World flair. The 650 North Restaurant adds a French touch to such Texas favorites as steak and salmon. *650 N. Pearl St., Downtown, 214/979–9000 or 800/543–4300, fax 214/953–1931. 407 rooms, 18 suites. Restaurant, bar, in-room data ports, in-room fax, exercise room, laundry service, concierge, business services. AE, D, DC, MC, V.*

13 *d-5*

MAGNOLIA

Once the tallest structure west of the Mississippi River, this former 1922 office building was recently converted to a first-class hotel. The conversion meant gutting the building, which resulted in a blend of yester-year's elegance—including the original ornate gold-leaf ceiling—with modern conveniences. The exterior remains the same: two identical office wings joined at the 17th floor by an arch. Rooms adorned in warm earth tones, modern artwork, and comfortable furniture help you unwind at the end of the day. You'll have no problem finding this Dallas landmark. Just look for Pegasus, the red flying horse, on top of a 29-floor building. *1401 Commerce St., Downtown, 214/915–6500 or 888/915–1110, fax 214/253–0053. 200 rooms, 130 suites. In-room data ports, refrigerators, exercise room, dry cleaning, laundry service, parking (fee). No pets. AE, D, DC, MC, V.*

10 *f-2*

MANSION ON TURTLE CREEK

Terrific service, creative cuisine, and Old World splendor combine to make this the only five-star, five-diamond hotel in the Southwest. You'll find a restaurant, bar, and private dining rooms in the restored 1925 Italian Renaissance estate, which retains such elegant touches as inlaid wood ceilings, stained glass, and a marble stairway. Guest rooms are in the nine-story tower. Of course, some things have changed in the once private residences of a cotton magnate. The silver vault is now a wine cellar, often used for intimate private dining, and the veranda is now glass-enclosed for all-weather enjoyment. You'll be pampered in your lavishly furnished rooms with fresh flowers, bottled water, and all-cotton bed and bath linens. Complimentary sedan service within a 5-mi radius includes shopping excursions to the Galleria and NorthPark. *2821 Turtle Creek Blvd., Turtle Creek, 214/559–2100, fax 214/528–4187. 141 rooms, 15 suites. Restaurant, bar, beauty salon, fitness center, pool, business services, concierge, parking (fee). AE, D, DC, MC, V.*

6 *f-6*

WESTIN GALLERIA DALLAS

If shopping is your favorite pastime, you'll discover staying at the 22-story Galleria is the perfect location. Attached to the west side of the famed shopping center, it is only minutes from your room. For those who prefer an alternate exercise to shopping, try the jogging track on the roof. This hotel caters to business executives by providing large rooms with comfortable sitting areas and a balcony.

For a full-course dinner, make reservations at the Huntington Restaurant. For a quick sandwich, try the Options Lounge. *13340 Dallas Pkwy., North, 972/934–9494 or 800/937–8461, fax 972/851–2869. 432 rooms, 13 suites. 2 restaurants, 2 bars, in-room data ports, in-room safes, jogging, dry cleaning, laundry service, concierge. AE, D, DC, MC, V.*

EXPENSIVE LODGINGS

13 *b-5*

AMERISUITES DALLAS WEST END

This 10-story redbrick hotel, only minutes away from the historic West End District, fits right in with the surrounding century-old brick warehouses filled with specialty shops, restaurants, and bars. In each suite the sleeping area is separate from the living area and comes equipped with mini-refrigerator, microwave, and wet bar. Tapestry sofas and cherry-wood furniture lends a homey ambiance to each suite. *1907 N. Lamar St., Downtown, 214/999–0500, fax 214/999–0501. 149 suites. In-room data ports, refrigerators, pool, dry cleaning. AE, D, DC, MC, V.*

6 *g-7*

Dallas Park Central, 12411 N. Central Expressway, North, 972/458–1224, fax 972/458–2887.

13 *e-5*

ARISTOCRAT HOTEL

This beaux-arts influenced structure is the second hotel built by Conrad Hilton in 1925 and the first to bear his name. You can't beat the location, which is within walking distance of the Central Business District, Arts District, West End, and Convention Center. The hotel is connected to an extensive skywalk and tunnel system that links office buildings, banks, and shops in Downtown. Dark wood paneling, crown molding, etched glass, and period furniture exudes an intimate, European setting. *1933 Main St., Downtown, 214/741–7700, fax 214/939–3639. 172 rooms, 73 suites. Restaurant, bar, exercise room, business services, meeting rooms. AE, D, DC, MC, V.*

10 *f-2*

COURTYARD BY MARRIOTT/MARKET CENTER

This five-story hotel is ideal for those with business in the Market District, but equally convenient to Downtown. A comfortable sitting area in each room provides the perfect spot to relax after a hectic day. *2150 Market Center Blvd., Northwest, 214/653–1166 or 800/321–2211, fax 214/653–1892. 184 rooms. In-room data ports, pool, exercise room, laundry service, concierge, business services, meeting rooms, free parking. No pets. AE, D, DC, MC, V.*

10 *e-2*

2383 Stemmons Trail, Northwest, 214/352–7676 or 800/321–2211, fax 214/352–4914.

10 *e-2*

DALLAS MARRIOTT SUITES MARKET CENTER

The jewel-tone red carpet, mahogany furniture, and modern art of the lobby of this 12-story contemporary hotel will surely catch your eye. The same deep rich colors carry through into the rooms. French doors separate the sleeping area in the two-room suites from the bedroom so you can watch TV without disturbing your mate. *2493 N. Stemmons Freeway, Northwest, 214/905–0050 or 800/228–9290, fax 214/905–0060. 266 suites. Restaurant, bar, in-room data ports, refrigerators, pool, exercise room. AE, D, DC, MC, V.*

6 *g-8*

DOUBLETREE HOTEL

The complimentary chocolate chip cookies sweeten the day at this 21-floor hotel. In fact, the chain's cookies are so popular you can buy extras for the trip home. Many of the room amenities here are also found at pricier hotels, including sofas, desk areas, and coffeemakers. For the best view of Dallas, select a premium corner room. *8250 N. Central Expressway, North, 214/691–8700, fax 214/706–0186. 300 rooms, 21 suites. Restaurant, bar, hot tubs, exercise room, laundry service, meeting rooms, free parking. No pets. AE, D, DC, MC, V.*

6 *f-6*

5410 LBJ Freeway, North, 972/934–8400, fax 972/701–5244.

10 *e-2*

EMBASSY SUITES, MARKET CENTER

Arrive at your meetings ready to go after eating a complimentary full breakfast, and then unwind at the end of the day with complimentary cocktails. The suites in this popular hotel chain have microwaves, refrigerator, coffeemaker, and two television sets. *2727 Stemmons Freeway, Northwest, 214/630–5332 or 800/362–2779, fax 214/630–3446. 244 suites. Refrigerators, indoor pool, exercise room, meeting rooms. No pets. AE, D, DC, MC, V. BP.*

6 *f-5*
14021 Noel Rd., North, 972/364–3640, fax 972/364–3642.

6 *h-6*

EMBASSY SUITES, PARK CENTRAL

Since you are only minutes away from meetings in the North Dallas Business District, you have plenty of time to eat a complimentary made-to-order breakfast at this hotel. When you return at the end of the day, mingle with the other guests over complimentary cocktails in the garden atrium. Greenery and a fountain with koi fish fill the lobby. Each suite has a separate sitting area, two phones, two televisions, and a vanity sink in the bedroom. All rooms have ironing boards, irons, and hair dryers. *13131 N. Central Expressway, North, 972/234–3300, fax 972/437–9863. 279 suites. Restaurant, in-room data ports, pool, exercise room, laundry service, meeting rooms, free parking. AE, D, DC, MC, V.*

6 *f-6*

THE GUEST LODGE AT COOPER AEROBICS CENTER

Actually part of the world famous Cooper Aerobics Center, this luxurious North Dallas hotel has 62 large rooms and suites with private balconies and French doors. Rates include access to the 40,000-square-ft health club, tennis courts, sauna, and whirlpool. A spa provides massages and body treatments, and restaurant emphasizes healthy eating. A 74-seat amphitheater with state-of-the-art audio and visual equipment is available for meetings. *12230 Preston Rd., North, 972/386–0306, fax 972/386–5415. 62 rooms, 16 suites. Restaurant, in-room data ports, hot tub, massage, sauna, 4 tennis courts, health club, meeting rooms, parking. No pets. AE, D, DC, MC, V.*

13 *c-5*

HAMPTON INN

Featuring a Nintendo in every room, this Downtown hotel near the West End is sure to be a hit with families, especially since children stay free. The floral-motif rooms have such homey touches as framed art, comfortable chairs, coffeemaker, and ironing board. *1015 Elm St., Downtown, 214/742–5678, fax 214/744–6167. 311 rooms. In-room data ports, pool, exercise room, laundry service. AE, D, DC, MC, V.*

10 *f-2*

MELROSE HOTEL

Since opening in 1924, this landmark hotel still retains its Old World charm while including all modern amenities associated with luxurious hotels. Mahogany furnishings are used throughout the hotel, including the lobby and popular Library Bar, which is adjacent to the Landmark Restaurant, a convivial meeting place. The Presidential Suite, which includes a large dining area, has a terrific view of Dallas. *3015 Oak Lawn Ave., Turtle Creek, 214/521–5151 or 800/635–7673, fax 214/521–2470. 184 rooms. Restaurant, bar, in-room data ports, in-room safes, laundry service, meeting rooms. No pets. AE, D, DC, MC, V.*

6 *c-6*

OMNI DALLAS HOTEL PARK WEST

This 12-floor luxury hotel with an opulent marble lobby overlooks a 125-acre lake surrounded by trees. The concierge level includes a lounge area where guests are served complimentary evening cocktails and breakfast. Room amenities include minibars, coffeemakers, irons, ironing boards, and hair dryers. The Presidential Suite has a large living area complete with piano and two balconies, both with views of the lake. *1590 LBJ Freeway, North, 972/869–4300, fax 972/869–3295. 337 rooms, 28 suites, 1 penthouse. Restaurant, 2 bars, in-room data ports, pool, sauna, exercise room, concierge, meeting rooms, parking (fee). No pets. AE, D, DC, MC, V.*

6 *f-6*

RENAISSANCE DALLAS NORTH HOTEL

A tropical feel emanates from this hotel, regardless of the season. While relishing the eight-story atrium with fountain and palm trees, unwind with a cocktail and absorb the soothing sounds of the nearby waterfall. Just minutes east of upscale Galleria Mall or Valley View Center, this hotel is popular with out-of-town shoppers. Mahogany furnishings adorn the rooms with luxury, along with tables, coffeemakers, irons, hair dryers, and two-line phones with data ports. Both Love Field and Dallas/Fort Worth International Airport are only 20 minutes away. *4099 Valley View La., North, 972/385–9000 or 800/468–3571, fax 972/458–8260. 289 rooms, 7 suites. In-room data ports, pool, exercise room. No pets. AE, D, DC, MC, V.*

10 *f-2*

2222 Stemmons Freeway, 75207, Northwest, 214/631–2222 or 800/468–3571, fax 214/905–3814.

10 *f-2*

WYNDHAM ANATOLE HOTEL

Billing itself as the largest convention resort in the Southwest, this 27-story redbrick hotel towers over the Dallas Market Center. The elegantly furnished resort rates high with art and antique lovers who enjoy the hotel's impressive collection, which includes 10 Picassos, a Louis XIV bronze sculpture, and rare malachite urns. The no-nonsense comfort of these rooms target business travelers with easy desk chairs, voice mail, coffeemakers, minibars, hairdryers, and irons and ironing boards. *2201 Stemmons Freeway, Northwest, 214/748–1200 or 800/695–8284. 1,620 rooms, 129 suites. 5 restaurants, 4 bars, grill, in-room data ports, in-room safes, pool, 2 tennis courts, croquet, exercise room, indoor track, jogging, racquetball, squash, dance club, laundry service, concierge, meeting rooms, free parking. AE, D, DC, MC, V.*

MODERATELY PRICED LODGINGS

10 *e-1*

CROWNE PLAZA

Whether in town alone or with your family, you'll think you are staying in a much pricier hotel, thanks to the European-flair decor and modern amenities—hair dryers, coffeemakers, irons, and ironing boards—found in each room. European travel posters dominate the walls. Your children can play on the Nintendo game center in each room, while you watch the Cowboys on the big screen television in the lobby. Later, you can take the family to Bristol Bar & Grill for some Tex-Mex or barbecue. *7050 Stemmons Freeway, Northwest, 214/630–8500 or 800/227–6963, fax 214/630–9486. 352 rooms, 2 suites. Restaurant, in-room data ports, indoor pool, hot tub, exercise room, laundry service, meeting rooms. AE, D, DC, MC, V.*

14315 Midway Rd., North, 972/980–8877, fax 972/991–2740.

6 *d-6*

7815 Alpha Rd., North Dallas, 972/233–7600, fax 972/788–0947.

6 *f-6*

DALLAS PARKWAY HILTON

Don't be surprised if you hear a variety of languages at this North Dallas hotel; it's a popular spot with international travelers. A two-story atrium off the check-in area hosts occasional parties and receptions. Overstuffed chairs and framed floral pictures exude homey ambiance in all the rooms, which include coffeemakers, irons, ironing boards, and hair dryers. Just minutes away from two major shopping malls and 75 restaurants. *4801 LBJ Freeway, North, 972/661–3600, fax 972/385–3156. 310 rooms. Restaurant, bar, in-room data ports, indoor-outdoor pool, exercise room, laundry service. No pets. AE, D, DC, MC, V.*

6 *f-4*

HOTEL INTER-CONTINENTAL DALLAS

Regulars to this 15-floor, pale gray-brick hotel still call it Grand Kempi's, even though it changed its name in 1997. It's only minutes away from posh North Dallas, where you'll find plenty of restaurants and shops. Of course, you don't have to dine out. Three restaurants on site provide plenty of choices for casual or fine dining. Afterward, linger in the piano bar or stop by Kempi's nightclub for some high-energy dancing. Rooms are decorated with three themes: Oriental, French, or English. Each room has a wing-back chair or sofa and chair with desk. *15201 Dallas Pkwy., Addison, 75001, 972/386–6000, fax 972/991–6937. 508 rooms, 20 suites. 3 restaurants, indoor-outdoor pool, 4 tennis courts, sauna, racquetball, bicycles, laundry service, business services, concierge, parking (fee). No pets. AE, D, DC, MC, V.*

13 *b-6*

PARAMOUNT HOTEL

Styled after small European inns, this minimalist, no-frills hotel provides clean rooms and a comfortable place to sleep.

Executives and culture seekers will love its close proximity to the Arts District and Convention Center. Constructed in 1920, the single-story building originally housed a factory before it was converted to a hotel a few years later. Fish, an upscale restaurant just off the lobby, serves such favorites as sesame-crusted tuna and Lake Victoria snapper. *302 S. Houston St., Downtown, 214/761–9090, fax 214/761–0470. 118 rooms, 7 junior suites. Restaurant, refrigerators, meeting rooms. AE, D, MC, V.*

13 *b-1*

STONELEIGH HOTEL

You never know who you will see in this elegant brick hotel. Both Hollywood director Oliver Stone and Elvis Presley, among other celebrities, have spent time here. Touted as the "Pride of Dallas" when it opened in 1923, the hotel still retains its original charm with such amenities as a barber shop, roof garden, billiard room, and ballroom. The sign with the red letters atop the building is a historic landmark, having glowed since 1938. Discerning diners have three restaurants from which to choose: The Lion's Den, which opened in 1923, still cooks up such regional lunch favorites as meat loaf, corn bread, and black-eyed peas; lighter appetites may opt for sushi at Stoneleigh; and Seville serves European and Spanish dishes, including a variety of tapas. *2927 Maple Ave., Turtle Creek, 214/871–7111 or 800/255–9299, fax 214/880–0820. 154 rooms, 9 suites. 3 restaurants, barbershop, billiards, laundry service, concierge, parking (fee). AE, D, DC, MC, V.*

10 *f-2*

WILSON WORLD HOTEL & SUITES

By staying at this centrally-located hotel, you can quickly drive Downtown and conveniently shop wholesale in Market District. If you prefer not to drive, then take advantage of the hotel's complimentary shuttle service. A Southwest theme, including Native American and cowboy designs, permeates the eight-floor atrium lobby. All guest rooms have sitting areas, with leather love seat and chair. Room amenities include microwaves, mini-refrigerators, coffeemakers, and hair dryers. *2325 N. Stemmons Freeway, Northwest, 214/630–3330 or 800/945–7667, fax 214/689–0420. 173 rooms, 67 suites. Restaurant, bar, in-room data ports, refrigerators, pool, exercise room, laundry service, concierge. AE, D, DC, MC, V.*

BUDGET LODGINGS

10 *f-2*

BEST WESTERN MARKET CENTER

Convention goers and corporate vagabonds will find this small hotel fits most travel budgets. Decorated in Southwest motif, you'll find many of the same amenities as found in more expensive accommodations. This hotel is popular with those shopping in the Market District. *2023 N. Market Center Blvd., Northwest, 214/741–9000 or 800/275–7419, fax 214/741–6100. 98 rooms. In-room data ports, in-room safes, pool, business services, free parking. No pets. AE, D, DC, MC, V.*

6 *g-7*

HOLIDAY INN SELECT

Whether you are in town for business or pleasure, this affordable chain offers lots of amenities for the money. The Business Resource Center has computers, printers, fax, and copier. And regardless of why you are visiting, a dip in the indoor pool is a pleasant respite after a day filled with meetings. *10650 N. Central Expressway, North, 214/373–6000 or 800/465–4329, fax 214/373–1037. 282 rooms, 2 suites. Restaurant, in-room data ports, indoor pool, exercise room, laundry service, business services, meeting rooms, free parking. No pets. AE, D, DC, MC, V.*

2645 LBJ Freeway, North, 972/243–3363 or 800/465–4329, fax 972/484–7082.

6 *f-6*

TERRA COTTA INN

This small independently owned inn is only minutes from North Dallas shopping, the North Dallas Business District, and a plethora of restaurants. One of Dallas's best kept secrets, this hotel provides luxury accommodations at budget prices. From the moment you enter the lobby, adorned with Mexican antiques and warrior masks, you'll know you've found something special. Mexican antiques flavor each room. *6101 LBJ Freeway, North, 972/387–2525 or 800/533–3591, fax 972/387–3784. 98 rooms, 1 suite. In-room data ports, pool, free parking. No pets. AE, D, DC, MC, V.*

10 *f-2*

WYNDHAM GARDEN HOTEL, DALLAS MARKET

Italian marble, Asian art, and a reading room give the deceptive impression of an expensive hotel. The niceties carry through to the guest rooms, where you can relax in a recliner chair after a busy day. *2015 Market Center Blvd., Northwest, 214/741–7481, fax 214/747–6191. 217 rooms, 11 suites. Restaurant, bar, in-room data ports, pool, exercise room, laundry service, free parking. No pets. AE, D, DC, MC, V.*

B & B RESERVATION SERVICES

Sometimes, staying at a bed and breakfast can be the next best thing to staying with family or friends when visiting. Most B&B hosts are a friendly sort, who enjoy pointing out interesting sights—including some that don't make the local tourist's list—and mentioning shortcuts to the freeway or the best spot for a good lunch. Before you know it, you forget you are paying strangers to sleep in their house and start to feel right at home. Even the most accommodating hotel can never quite capture that sort of homey feeling.

Most B & B's are booked through Bed & Breakfasts Texas Style (701 Honeysuckle La., College Station, TX, 77845, 409/696–9222 or 800/899–4538, fax 409/696–9444). This helpful service will tell you all you need to know about various places to stay. The following are a few recommended B&Bs. Those with no address can be booked through B&B Texas Style.

13 *e-6*

AMELIA'S PLACE

Amelia Jenkins opened this hostelry in 1998 in a three-story warehouse, setting up accommodations on the lower floor. Guests are invited to join Jenkins in her living room for a game of Scrabble or to play the piano. She stocks her shelves with lots of books, ranging from philosophy to classics to mysteries. Each guest room is decorated differently with themes reflecting the heritage of the female Dallas advocate whose name is on the room. Depending on the room, you may find a Mexican piñata or African American artifacts or ruffles and lace. *1775 Young St., Downtown, 214/651–1775, 888/651–1775. 5 rooms, 4 with bath, 1 suite. AE, D, DC, MC, V. Budget.*

THE CLOISTERS

For visitors who like outdoor activities, this large ranch-style brick home is in an ideal spot. Set in a wooded area only a block from White Rock Lake, you are minutes away from a 10-mi bike and hiking trail. The host even provides bikes. One bedroom is decorated in hand-painted Mexican antiques, the other in Texas oak antiques. *800/899–4538. 2 rooms with bath. Bicycles. AE, D, MC, V. Budget.*

6 *h-8*

COURTYARD ON THE TRAIL

Guests are just 15 minutes from Downtown and North Dallas when staying at this two-story stucco home tucked away

CELEBRITY SPOTTING

If you're a star seeker, here are some prime places for celebrity sightings.

Adolphus Hotel (very expensive)
Since opening in 1912, this hotel's registry has included such dignitaries as Franklin D. Roosevelt, Lyndon B. Johnson, George Bush, Bill Clinton, Charles Lindberg, Rudolph Valentino, John Glenn, Sean Penn, and Maya Angelou.

Hotel Crescent Court (very expensive)
Celebrity watching can get a bit tiresome at this favorite hangout of the rich and famous. A popular spot for rock stars, the hotel's guests have included Rod Stewart, Tony Bennet, Tony Randall, Whitney Houston, and Phil Collins.

Hotel St. Germain (very expensive)
Martha Stewart stayed here, so that must say something about the decor of this elegant small hotel. Oscar de la Renta, Prince Albert of Monaco, and Jeff Bridges have also been seduced by its charm.

Melrose Hotel (expensive)
Watch for such musicians as John Tesh, Patti LaBelle, and The Hansons at this elegant hotel. Other celebrity guests such as Elizabeth Taylor, Andi MacDowell, and Leonard Nemoy have also signed the registry.

in the woods near White Rock Lake. Walk around the lake or relax by the private pool. Three guest rooms, including two suites with king- or queen-size beds, have private entrances and gardens. Enjoy oriental antiques as well as Southwest decor. *8045 Forest Trail, 214/553–9700, fax 214/553–9700. 3 rooms with bath. AE, MC, V. Expensive.*

FAN ROOM

Two guest rooms with double beds share a bath in this North Dallas ranch-style house, near the Galleria. An antique fan—just one of many fans in the host's collection—is the focus in one guest room; wild animal prints serve as accents in the second. A full country breakfast includes jalapeño muffins. *800/899–4538. 2 rooms, 1 with bath. AE, D, MC, V. Budget.*

10 *f-2*

INN ON FAIRMONT

What was once a stylish doctor's building in the 1930s now houses equally stylish lodgings in this classy Turtle Creek neighborhood. Two blocks north of this white brick Federal-style building is Turtle Creek with its scenic walkway. All rooms include televisions and telephones. *3701 Fairmount St., 214/522–2800, fax 214/522–2898. 7 rooms with bath, 2 mini-suites with bath, 1 suite with bath. AE, D, MC, V. Moderate.*

HAVE DRINK WILL TRAVEL

Hotel Crescent Court (very expensive)
This hotel's popular Beau Nash was recently voted the best place for drinks in the Metroplex.

Mansion on Turtle Creek (very expensive)
A hunting-theme decor, with trophies and 18th century paintings on its walls, sets the tone for The Bar, where modern-day business titans, old money, and the newly rich dot-com set stalk the best deals in town.

Melrose Hotel (expensive)
For decades, this historic hotel's Library Bar, known for its extra-dry martini, has been a favorite meeting spot for local wheelers and dealers, including Ross Perot and Cowboys owner Jerry Jones.

Wyndham Anatole Hotel (expensive)
A 35-plus business crowd tends to fill the Nana Bar, where favorite drinks include the martini and a cranberry juice and vodka creation dubbed a kamikaze.

THE SOUTHERN HOUSE

Surrounded by historic homes, this new three-story prairie-style abode blends right in with the neighborhood, conveniently only a mile from the downtown Arts District. Two elegantly decorated guest rooms share a bath. The computer and fax are made available to guests. A full gourmet breakfast is served. *800/899–4538. 2 rooms with shared bath. AE, D, MC, V. Expensive.*

fort worth/ mid-cities lodging

EXPENSIVE LODGINGS

FOUR SEASONS RESORT AND SPA

This sprawling conference resort is known both for its European-style spa and sports club, as well as the TPC championship golf course that hosts the annual Byron Nelson Golf Classic. Accommodations go beyond the luxury room selection and include suites and 50 fabulous villa-style rooms adjacent to the golf course, with outdoor balconies and patios. Café on the Green is a delightful restaurant serving fine New American cuisine. About 7 mi east of DFW Airport, the hotel has twice-daily maid service and complete pro shops for tennis and golf. *4150 N. MacArthur Blvd., Irving, 972/717–0700 or 800/332–3442, fax 972/717–2550. 357 rooms, 12 suites. Restaurant, bar, beauty salon, spa, 2 18-hole golf courses, 12 tennis courts, concierge, business services, meeting rooms, free parking, parking (fee). AE, D, DC, MC, V.*

OMNI MANDALAY HOTEL AT LAS COLINAS

Right in the heart of the Las Colinas Urban Center, adjacent to Lake Carolyn and the Mandalay Canal, this 27-story luxury hotel is less than 15 minutes east of DFW Airport. Sooth those aching joints in the adjacent Spa Atelier, relish in the 24-hour room service, and suites with balconies. *221 E. Las Colinas Blvd., Irving, 972/556–0800 or 800/843–6664, fax 972/556–*

0729. 410 rooms, 96 suites. Restaurant, café, bar, no-smoking rooms, room service, concierge, meeting rooms, free parking, parking (fee). AE, D, DC, MC, V.

15 *c-5*

RENAISSANCE WORTHINGTON HOTEL

Spanning three city blocks, this contemporary, 12-story complex anchors the north side of Sundance Square and attaches to the Tandy Center, home of Radio Shack headquarters and the Fort Worth Outlet Center shopping complex. A recent renovation added guest rooms, ballrooms, exhibition halls, and nearly two dozen meeting spaces. Reflections is the hotel's upscale restaurant, and Star of Texas Grill serves a casual breakfast, lunch, and dinner. The Lobby Bar is a favorite spot for sipping drinks. The Club Level has personalized concierge services, and the amenity-rich Athletic Club schedules regular aerobics classes. *200 Main St., Fort Worth, 817/870–1000, fax 817/335–3847 or 800/468–3571. 504 rooms, 44 suites. 2 restaurants, bar, in-room data ports, no-smoking rooms, room service, indoor pool, massage, sauna, 2 tennis courts, exercise room, dry cleaning, laundry services, concierge, concierge floor, business services, meeting rooms, parking (fee). AE, D, DC, MC, V.*

MODERATELY PRICED LODGINGS

9 *g-3*

ARLINGTON WYNDHAM

Formerly the Arlington Marriott, this spacious high-rise hotel sits adjacent to the Arlington Convention Center and within walking distance to Six Flags Over Texas and the Ballpark in Arlington, home of Major League Baseball's Texas Rangers. *1500 Convention Center Dr., Arlington, 817/261–8200, fax 817/548–2873. 310 rooms, 18 suites. Restaurant, bar, room service, pool, laundry service, exercise room, concierge floor, meeting rooms. No pets. AE, D, DC, MC, V.*

15 *d-6*

COURTYARD FORT WORTH DOWNTOWN

Marriott breathed new life into the abandoned, decaying art deco–style Blackstone Hotel in 1999, bringing 1930s beauty in downtown Fort Worth back to life. Its 20 floors house 203 rooms designed for businesspeople, including desks with lamps, two-line phones and weekday morning newspapers. The Corner Bakery on the ground floor serves breakfast, lunch, and dinner, and sells wine and beer, and all the delights of Sundance Square are a few footsteps away. *601 Main St., Fort Worth, 817/ 885–8700, fax 817/885–8303. 203 rooms. Restaurant, in-room data ports, room service, pool, business services, coin laundry, laundry service, meeting rooms. No pets. AE, D, DC, MC, V.*

15 *d-6*

RADISSON PLAZA HOTEL FORT WORTH

Listed on the National Register of Historic Places, this neo-Gothic hotel holds the tragic distinction of being the last place where John F. Kennedy spent the night before making the fateful trip to Dallas on November 22, 1963. That aside, the 517-room hotel (382 are nonsmoking) stands on the redbrick Main Street, which connects the city's convention center with Sundance Square and the courthouse eight blocks north. On site are two restaurants and a bar, and plenty of dining and nightlife are in quick walking distance. *815 Main St., Fort Worth, 817/870–2100, fax 817/882–1300. 517 rooms. 2 restaurants, bar, room service, pool, exercise room, meeting rooms, free parking, parking (fee). No pets. AE, D, DC, MC, V.*

9 *g-3*

RESIDENCE INN

Conveniently near Six Flags Over Texas and Hurricane Harbor, this all-suite lodging sits in a pleasant woodsy stretch facing an expanse of upscale business complexes. Inside each apartmentlike room is a kitchenette. *1050 Brookhollow Plaza Dr., Arlington, 817/ 649–7300, fax 817/649–7600. 114 suites. Bar, kitchenettes, pool, tennis court, exercise room, health club, meeting rooms. AE, D, DC, MC, V.*

15 *b-1*

STOCKYARDS HOTEL

Named in 1999 to the National Trust Historic Hotels, this 1907 hotel has hosted cattle barons, outlaws, and country music legends. Room decor styles range from elegant Victorian to ranch rugged to Native American artful, while cowhide chairs, bronze sculptures, and rough-hewn wood detail adorn the common areas. Meeting rooms can be reserved for wedding receptions, training seminars, business lunches, and special buffet gatherings. *103 E. Exchange Ave., Fort Worth, 817/625–6427, fax 817/624–2571. 52 rooms. Restaurant, bar, meeting rooms. No pets. AE, D, DC, MC, V.*

BUDGET LODGINGS

15 *d-2*

COUNTRY INN & SUITES

Designed to be comfortable and homey, the hotel's suites have separate bed and living rooms. All rooms include coffeemakers, irons and ironing boards, and HBO. An expanded continental breakfast, local telephone calls, fax and copy service, and weekday morning newspaper are included with your room. Downtown Fort Worth and the Stockyards National Historic District are nearby. *2200 Mercado Dr., Fort Worth, 817/831–9200, fax 817/838–7567. 46 rooms, 22 suites. Pool, hot tub, exercise room, meeting room. No pets. AE, D, DC, MC, V. CP.*

9 *b-1*

HOMEWOOD SUITES HOTEL

"Home away from home" is the slogan of this attractive new chain arrival. The comfortable apartment-style suites have one or two bedrooms with roomy, sunny living areas. Each suite has a kitchenette, data port, video player, sofa sleeper, hair dryer, iron, and ironing board, and you can call local for free. Continental breakfast is served daily, and you can unwind during the free cocktail hour offered from Monday through Thursday evenings. *3801 Tannacross Dr. at Fossil Creek, 817/834–7400, fax 817/834–3701. 137 suites. In-room data ports, kitchenettes, exercise room, coin laundry, meeting rooms. No pets. AE, D, DC, MC, V.*

15 *b-1*

HOTEL TEXAS

A recent renovation brought this 1939 former Exchange Hotel back to life. This two-story brick hotel in the Stockyards National Historic District in easy walking distance to all area attractions. This 20-room inn includes king and queen beds, a honeymoon suite, and the four-room Bob Wills suite. *2415 Ellis Ave., at W. Exchange Ave., Fort Worth, 817/624–2224, fax 817/624–7177. 21 rooms. Meeting room. No pets. AE, D, DC, MC, V.*

B & B RESERVATION SERVICES

B&B lodgings in Fort Worth are booked directly and not through services. These lodgings provide personalized service and homelike comforts you can't find in hotels. Innkeepers at B&Bs are well-acquainted with attractions and restaurants, and will often recommend off-the-beaten path attractions and dining spots.

15 *e-2*

AZALEA PLANTATION

Settled amid 1½ acres of oak-studded land about 10 minutes north of downtown Fort Worth, this Southern-style home bears the beauty of rock terracing and the grace of a gazebo and fountain. Spacious guest rooms and cottages are filled with antiques and have private baths. The Magnolia Cottage is a good romantic getaway, thanks to a large, two-person whirlpool. Cottage amenities include microwaves, refrigerators, and coffeemakers. By request you can have a stay that includes roses, chocolates, and massages. *1400 Robinwood Dr., Oakhurst, Fort Worth, 817/838–5882 or 800/687–3529, fax 817/838–5882, 4 rooms. Kitchenettes, no-smoking rooms, refrigerators, dry cleaning, meeting rooms, business services. No pets. AE, D, MC, V. Moderate.*

15 *c-6*

ETTA'S PLACE

This residential-style B&B is smack in the middle of Sundance Square, amid theaters, upscale dining, movie houses, bars and nightclubs, and galleries and shops. Antiques from the American West, private baths, cable TV, and luxury bed and bath linens adorn each of the 10 rooms. Some suites have kitchenettes attached. Available-by-request services include wine or champagne upon arrival, picnic basket preparations, Swedish massage, meeting facilities and catering, flower arrangements, and dry cleaning. *200 W. 3rd St., Sundance Square, Fort Worth, 817/654–0267, fax 817/878–2560. 10 rooms. Kitchenettes, business services, meeting rooms, free parking. No pets. AE, D, DC, MC, V. Moderate.*

15 *b-1*

MISS MOLLY'S

From prim boarding house to a 1940's bawdy house to cozy B&B, this 1910 building above the Star Cafe in the Stockyards National Historic District defines the word landmark. Appropriately, the rooms are outfitted with some period furniture pieces as well as western-style decor, shutters, and lace curtains. *109½ W. Exchange Ave., near N. Main St., Fort Worth, 817/626–1522 or 800/996–6559, fax 817/625–2723. 8 rooms, 1 with bath. No-smoking rooms. No pets. AE, D, DC, MC, V. Budget.*

15 *b-8*

TEXAS WHITE HOUSE

The 1910 home with its Texas historical marker, period decor, and specialty elements such as claw-footed bathtubs, wrap-around porch, and breakfast served on heirloom china is convenient to downtown and the city's medical centers. Three guest rooms are furnished with queen-size beds, sitting areas, and private baths. Breakfast, which can be served in either the dining room or your bedroom, includes such pleasures as fresh fruit or baked fruit in compote, egg casseroles, and homemade breads and muffins. Make sure to leave the youngsters at home: adults only here. *1417 Eighth Ave., Fort Worth, 817/923–3597, fax 817/923–0410, 800/279–6491. 3 rooms. No-smoking rooms, laundry service. No pets. AE, D, DC, MC, V. Moderate.*

hotels near the airport

NEAR LOVE FIELD

CLARION SUITES

If you need to divide your time between North Dallas and Downtown, this hotel is convenient and only minutes from Love Field and the Market District. Unwind at the end of a busy day with complimentary beer, wine, and soft drinks. You'll find plenty of dining options with prices and food to fit all tastes. *2363 Stemmons Trail, Northwest, 214/350–2300, fax 214/350–5144. 96 suites. In-room data ports, coin laundry, free parking. No pets. AE, D, DC, MC, V. Budget.*

EMBASSY SUITES, LOVE FIELD

Start your day with a complimentary cooked-to-order breakfast and end the day with complimentary cocktails. It's all part of the service at this hotel, which has suites with separate sitting and sleeping areas. You can catch a free shuttle to Love Field or NorthPark Center. *3880 W. Northwest Hwy., Northwest, 214/357–4500 or 800/326–2779, fax 214/357–0683. 248 suites. In-room data ports, indoor pool, exercise room, laundry service, free parking. No pets. AE, D, DC, MC, V. BP. Expensive.*

RADISSON HOTEL DALLAS

Health-conscious travelers appreciate this hotel's exercise facilities, complete with whirlpool, racquetball courts, outdoor track, and outdoor swimming pool. It also is conveniently near shopping, dining, and entertainment. *1893 W. Mockingbird La., Northwest, 75235, 214/634–8850, fax 214/630–8134. 305 rooms. Restaurant, bar, in-room data ports, pool, hot tub, jogging, racquetball, coin laundry, laundry service, free parking. AE, D, DC, MC, V. Moderate.*

SHERATON DALLAS BROOKHOLLOW HOTEL

This 13-story stucco hotel is perfect for business travelers, with two telephones in each room, data ports, and a business center. A complimentary shuttle service is available within a 5-mi radius. *1241 Mockingbird La., 75247, Northwest, 214/630–7000, fax 214/638–6943. 348 rooms, 7 suites. In-room data ports, in-room fax, business services, meeting rooms, exercise room. AE, D, DC, MC, V. Very Expensive*

NEAR DFW INTERNATIONAL

DALLAS/FORT WORTH MARRIOTT

Large and well-geared for business types, this bustling giant has everything including a business center, two dozen meeting rooms, sports bar, steak house, and coffee kiosk. The hotel also provides complimentary 24-hour transportation to the airport. *8440 Freeport Pkwy., Irving, 972/929–8800 or 800/228–9290, fax 972/929–6501. 491 rooms, 5 suites. 2 restaurants, bar, coffee shop, in-room data ports, business center, meeting rooms, no-smoking rooms, health club, pool, hot tub, sauna, spa. No pets. AE, D, DC, MC, V. Expensive.*

EMBASSY SUITES

Connected to Bass Pro Shops Outdoor World, this all-suite facility accommodates everyone from sports nuts and shopping fiends (Grapevine Mills is a stone's throw) to business travelers and families with infants and toddlers in tow. Rooms have microwave ovens and small refrigerators. *2401 Bass Pro Dr., Grapevine, 972/724–2600 or 800/362–2779, fax 972/724–5145. 329 suites. Room service, refrigerators, pool, sauna, exercise room, dry cleaning, laundry service, concierge, business services, meeting rooms. AE, D, DC, MC, V. Expensive.*

HARVEY HOTEL DFW AIRPORT

At the north entrance of DFW Airport, this 15-story hotel has at its center a four-story atrium crafted from salmon-color marble and glass. Solid teak furnishings, executive desks, and overstuffed sofas are standard in each room. Benton's, the specialty restaurant, serves mesquite-broiled fresh seafood and steaks. The hotel has a courtesy airport shuttle, an airline desk, and car rental services. *4545 W. Carpenter Fwy. (Texas 114), Irving, 972/929–4500 or 800/922–9222, fax 972/929–0733. 506 rooms, 64 suites. Restaurant, bar, café, pool, hot tub, exercise room, dry cleaning, business services, meeting rooms. AE, D, DC, MC, V. Expensive.*

HILTON DFW LAKES

Spread over 27 woodsy acres just north of DFW Airport and within shouting distance of the mammoth Grapevine Mills Mall and Bass Pro Shops, this huge conference center hotel is loaded with amenities, including an extensive computer center. Meritage, its upscale eatery, serves New American cuisine, including seafood, chops and pasta. A 24-hour complimentary airport shuttle is at your service. *1800 Texas Hwy. 26 E, Grapevine, 817/481–8444, fax 817/481–3160. 395 rooms, 16 suites. Restaurant, café, bar, room service, pool, basketball, exercise room, jogging, fishing, meeting rooms, free parking, parking (fee). AE, D, DC, MC, V. Moderate.*

chapter 7

CITY SOURCES

getting a handle on the city

basics of city life: dallas

BANKS

Commercial banks are generally open weekdays from 9 AM until 3 PM, with drive-thru hours from 7 AM to 6 PM weekdays and from 9 AM to noon on Saturday. A few banks also have Saturday morning lobby hours and extended hours at major grocery stores. Call the following for branch locations.

Chase (800/235–8522).

Wells Fargo (800/869–3557).

Coamerica (214/630–3030).

Compass (800/266–7277).

NationsBank (800/247–6262).

State National (972/771–7555).

DRIVING

Some people manage to get by without a car in Dallas, but it can be a trying experience. While mass transportation is improving in the city, many places are not accessible by bus or light rail. Most people have a car and freeways are often packed with traffic not only during rush hour but late into the night. Freeway speeds are usually set at 60 mph. Right turns are permitted except where noted.

licenses

You must get a driver's license within 30 days of moving to the state, and you can get one by stopping by any Texas Department of Public Safety office. You'll need proof of car registration, a copy of your birth certificate or a valid out-of-state driver's license, your social security number, and proof of insurance. Be prepared to pass a vision test, written exam, and driver's test if your driver's license has expired.

You must also register your car within 30 days with the Motor Vehicle Registration office Downtown. Bring your title, a sales or tax use affidavit, your current Texas driver's license, and a vehicle identification certificate indicating your car has passed a safety inspection. All vehicles must have a safety inspection every 12 months. Inspections are available at many gas stations, service centers, and dealers. Cost varies by year and make of your car. The state of Texas requires that all drivers have liability insurance.

DEPARTMENT OF MOTOR VEHICLES

For vehicle registration, call the Motor Vehicle Registration (500 Elm St., 214/653–7621). Driver's Licenses are obtained from the Texas Department of Public Safety (214/861–2000). Call for a location nearest you.

traffic

Dallas is rapidly upgrading its freeway system, but not fast enough to keep pace with the traffic. Freeways and streets are packed during rush hour, which is 7–10 AM and 4–6 PM on weekdays. Traffic is lighter on weekend mornings, but becomes more congested during the day. Traffic in HOV lanes moves much faster than the other freeway lanes but is only for cars with more than one occupant. A north-south toll road also speeds traffic along, so it is often worth the extra cost.

GAS STATIONS

Gas stations are plentiful in Dallas, except in the Downtown area. Be sure you have plenty of fuel before heading to such Downtown areas as the Arts District or West End.

GEOGRAPHY

Getting around Dallas can be a challenge. The city is a mishmash of streets that are best conquered with a good map. At least half of what is now Dallas started as other towns. Although the city eventually incorporated these small towns, the original streets and numbering systems remained. The multiple plats often result in the same street having more than one name. For example, heading northeast from Downtown, Grand Avenue becomes East Grand at Fair Park then Garland Road at White Rock Lake.

Downtown is a six-block grid, which includes Elm, Main, and Commerce streets. North-south street numbers ascend as you move either north or south from Downtown. East-west streets ascend as you move away from

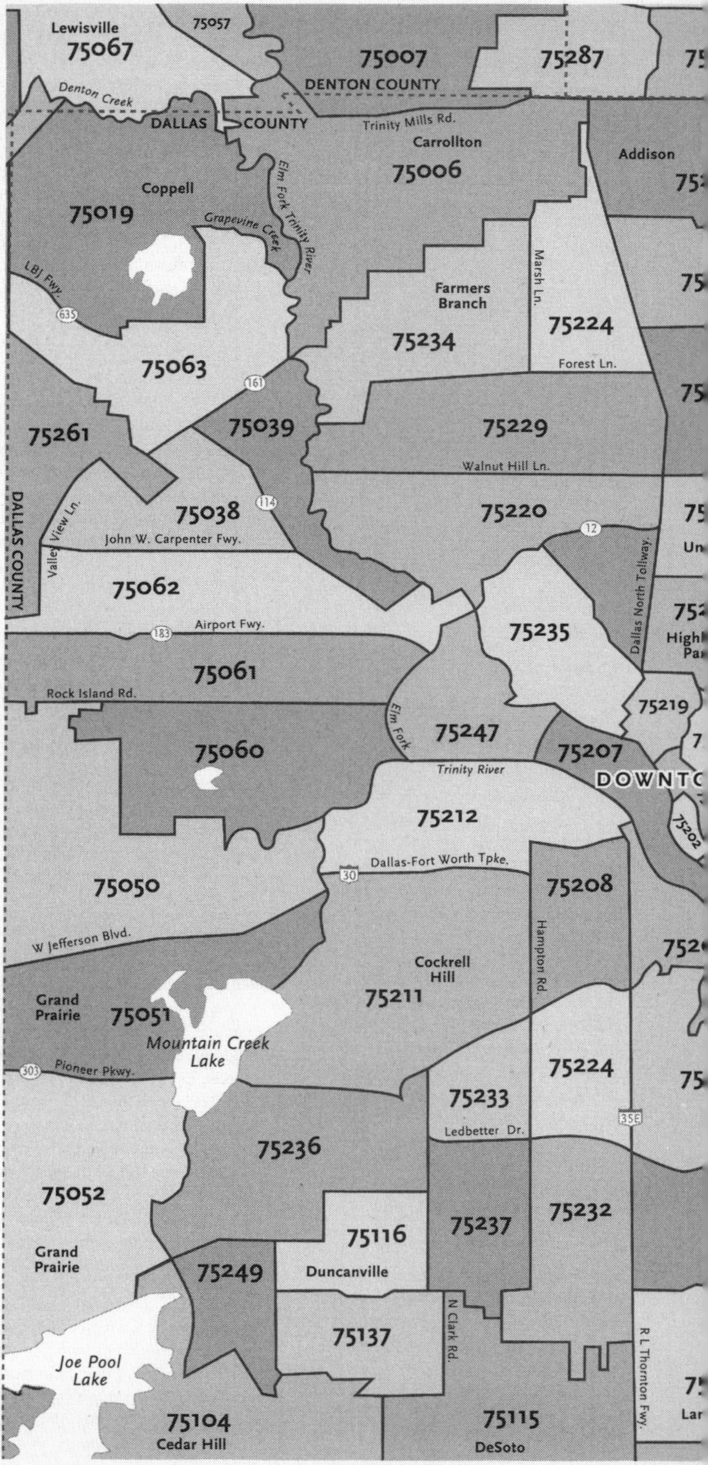
Lewisville
75067
75057
75007
DENTON COUNTY
75287
Denton Creek
DALLAS
COUNTY
Trinity Mills Rd.
Carrollton
75006
Addison
Coppell
75019
Grapevine Creek
Elm Fork Trinity River
LBJ Fwy.
635
Farmers Branch
Marsh Ln.
75224
75234
Forest Ln.
75063
161
75039
75229
75261
Walnut Hill Ln.
114
75038
75220
12
DALLAS COUNTY
Valley View Ln.
John W. Carpenter Fwy.
Dallas North Tollway
75062
75235
Airport Fwy.
183
75061
Rock Island Rd.
75219
Elm Fork
75247
75060
75207
Trinity River
75212
75202
75050
Dallas-Fort Worth Tpke.
30
75208
W Jefferson Blvd.
Hampton Rd.
Cockrell Hill
Grand Prairie
75051
75211
Mountain Creek Lake
303
Pioneer Pkwy.
75224
75233
35E
Ledbetter Dr.
75236
75052
75237
75232
75116
Grand Prairie
75249
Duncanville
N Clark Rd.
75137
R L Thornton Fwy.
Joe Pool Lake
75104
Cedar Hill
75115
DeSoto

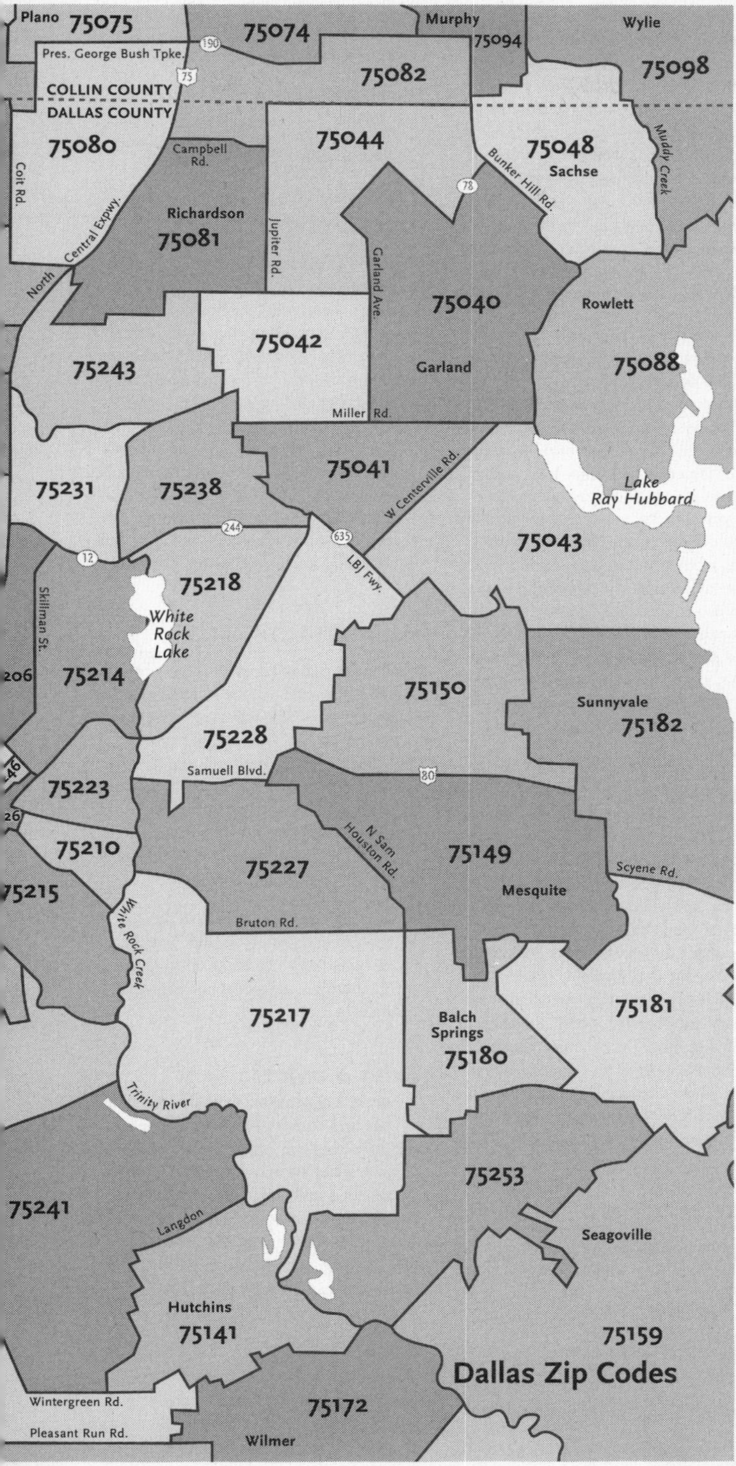
Dallas Zip Codes
Plano 75075
75074
Murphy
75094
Wylie
75098
Pres. George Bush Tpke.
190
75
75082
COLLIN COUNTY
DALLAS COUNTY
75080
Coit Rd.
Campbell Rd.
75044
75048
Sachse
Bunker Hill Rd.
Muddy Creek
78
Richardson
75081
North Central Expwy.
Jupiter Rd.
Garland Ave.
75040
Rowlett
75042
75243
Garland
75088
Miller Rd.
75041
W Centerville Rd.
75231
75238
Lake Ray Hubbard
244
635
75043
12
LBJ Fwy.
75218
Skillman St.
White Rock Lake
206
75214
75150
Sunnyvale
75182
75228
Samuell Blvd.
80
75223
N Sam Houston Rd.
75149
75210
75227
Scyene Rd.
Mesquite
75215
White Rock Creek
Bruton Rd.
75217
Balch Springs
75180
75181
Trinity River
75253
75241
Langdon
Seagoville
Hutchins
75141
75159
75172
Wintergreen Rd.
Pleasant Run Rd.
Wilmer

the Trinity River. Be aware, though: the numbering systems change the farther you head away from Downtown. Contrary to its city streets, Dallas's freeways are easily navigable—it's almost impossible to get lost within the intricate system that threads through the city. Downtown is bounded by Interstate Highway 30 in the south, U.S. Highway 75 (Central Expressway) in the east, Interstate Highway 35 East in the west (Stemmons Freeway), and Woodall Rodgers Freeway on the north edge.

Dallas is a city of neighborhoods whose boundaries shrink and expand as surrounding areas take on the similar characteristics or shift emphasis. Restored redbrick houses populate West End, just west of Downtown. Just minutes southwest of Downtown is Oak Cliff, one of the city's oldest and most scenic sections with houses nested among rolling hills and large trees. On the eastern fringes of downtown is Deep Ellum, an industrial neighborhood turned avant garde with nightclubs, galleries, and restaurants. Continuing northeast, you'll pass a plethora of Victorian homes in various stages of restoration on your way to White Rock Lake, a favorite spot for jogging, picnicking, and boating.

Heading north from Downtown, within an area bounded by the Dallas North Tollway and Central Expressway, you'll enter what is increasingly called Uptown, which includes the McKinney Avenue/Oak Lawn/Turtle Creek area of posh shops, art galleries, and elegant homes. Nearby is Southern Methodist University with plenty of youth-oriented bars and shops. The university is between Highland Park and University Park, both small affluent neighborhoods surrounded by Dallas. Continuing north, a few miles south of Love Field airport, is the Dallas Market Center, where thousands of retailers converge monthly to buy seasonal goods from thousands of wholesalers.

HOLIDAYS

City offices observe the following holidays.

New Year's Day (January 1).

Martin Luther King Jr., Day (3rd Monday in January).

President's Day (3rd Monday in February).

Memorial Day (last Monday in May).

Independence Day (July 4).

Thanksgiving Day (4th Thursday in November).

Christmas Day (December 25).

LIQUOR LAWS

The drinking age in Texas is 21. Dallas has more than 60 different liquor licenses, which dictate hours of operation. Bars can sell drinks as early as 7 AM, but must stop selling alcohol by 2 AM, even though some stay open as late as 4 AM, depending on its city liquor license. Liquor stores cannot sell hard liquor after 9 PM or on Sunday. Convenience stores can sell beer and wine from 7 AM until 1 AM Monday–Saturday, and noon until midnight on Sunday. A restaurant's particular license specifies what it may serve and when.

NO SMOKING

Like most major cities, it is becoming increasingly difficult for smokers to find a place in public to light up. Smoking is not permitted in most public areas, including stores, theaters, and shopping malls. Most restaurants offer non-smoking areas. All government-owned buildings are smoke free.

PARKING

Parking is usually no problem outside of Downtown with most schools, stadiums, and special events providing adequate lots.

rules & enforcement

When in Downtown, read signs posted on parking meters carefully. Some do not allow parking during rush hours. Others allow free parking after certain hours on certain days. Prices paid at meters vary with rates as high as a $1 an hour at four-hour meters. Be sure to follow parking rules because parking tickets and towing are costly.

parking lots

The following are just a few of the numerous parking lots and parking garages available Downtown. Be sure to check the closing time, or you might lose your car for the night.

Classified (1115 Commerce St., 214/741–3641 or 704 Ross Ave., 214/741–3641).

Metropolitan Garage (1310 Elm St., 214/748–1293).

One Main Place (1201 Main St., 214/651–1160).

PERSONAL SECURITY

Dallas is a big city, so take the same precautions you would take in any metropolitan area. Most neighborhoods are safe during the day, but it's best to stay in well-lighted areas at night and to know where you are and where you are going. It's always better to travel with a companion late at night. Keep your car locked and valuable items out of sight. Let common sense be your guide. Anytime you feel uncomfortable in an area, leave.

PUBLIC TRANSPORTATION

Dallas has been slow developing a mass transportation system. Although travel by bus and light rail is improving, many areas of the city are still unavailable by public transportation. DART (Dallas Area Rapid Transit) provides bus and light rail service throughout Dallas. Fares vary from 50¢ to $2, but you can buy bonus packs, one-day passes and monthly passes. A $2 day pass allows unlimited rides on trains and buses. Seats near the boarding doors are usually reserved for senior citizens or disabled riders. Strollers are allowed if they do not block the aisle. Loud music without headphones, smoking, drinking, eating, gambling, and littering are prohibited. You may want to avoid traveling during rush hour, when buses and trains are crowded with commuters. You can pick up monthly passes and bus and rail information at the DART Store (Akard Station, 214/749–3282 or Elm and Ervay Streets, 214/749–3800) or some area grocery stores. Taxis are available, but don't expect to hail one on the street. You usually have to call ahead for taxi service.

buses

DART buses run more than 130 routes across Dallas and into 12 nearby suburbs, an area totaling 700 square mi. Buses can be slow but are an inexpensive way of reaching some areas of town. Express buses have fewer stops and are much faster than regular buses, which stop about every block. Bus hours vary, but they generally begin operation at 4:50 AM and run until 10 PM. Duration of operation on some routes vary, with some ending as early as 6 PM while others run until midnight. A Downtown trolley bus, complete with wooden seats and clanging bell, runs every 10 minutes along routes linking the West End, Arts District, and City Hall. Trolley buses also zip passengers from the Park Lane Rail Station to NorthPark Center for shopping. DART Customer Information (214/979–1111) will help you plan the most convenient route for any destination.

light rail

Although rapidly expanding but still limited in the areas served, DART's light rail system has become popular with commuters traveling from North Dallas to Downtown and Oak Cliff. Many rail stations offer free parking. If you don't want to drive to catch the train, you can catch a bus to the nearest rail station. Downtown has six rail stations. Light Rail service operates from 5 AM to midnight, with trains running every 5–10 minutes during peak hours and every 10–20 minutes during off-peak times. The Trinity Railway Express, which links Dallas to Fort Worth, Dallas-Fort Worth International Airport, Irving, and the Dallas Market District operates weekdays every 20–25 minutes during peak hours, hourly during off-peak hours and on Saturday. Trinity Railway Express connects with Dallas's other light rail service Downtown at Union Station. For more information, call DART Customer Information (214/979–1111).

taxis

Taking a cab usually requires advance planning since you will probably have to call one. Although some hotels have a taxi stand, it's unlikely you'll be able to hail one on the street. Make sure you allow plenty of time for the taxi to get to your location as well as to take you to your destination. Base fare is $2, plus $1.60 per mile, plus $2 for each addition pas-

DART
Dallas Area Rapid Transit

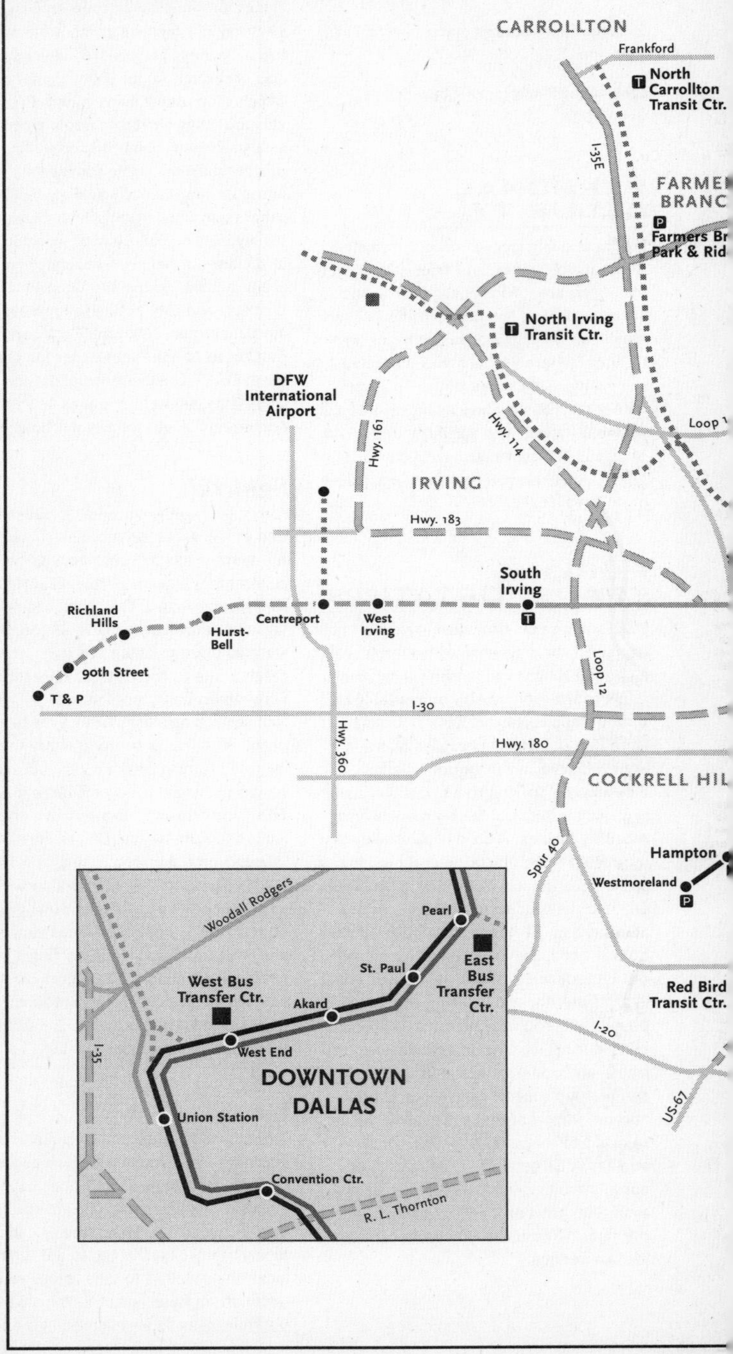

CARROLLTON
Frankford
North Carrollton Transit Ctr.
I-35E
FARME
BRANC
Farmers Br
Park & Rid
North Irving Transit Ctr.
DFW International Airport
Hwy. 161
Hwy. 114
Loop
IRVING
Hwy. 183
South Irving
Richland Hills
Hurst-Bell
Centreport
West Irving
90th Street
T & P
Loop 12
I-30
Hwy. 360
Hwy. 180
COCKRELL HIL
Spur 40
Hampton
Westmoreland
Red Bird Transit Ctr.
I-20
US-67
Woodall Rodgers
Pearl
East Bus Transfer Ctr.
St. Paul
West Bus Transfer Ctr.
Akard
West End
I-35
DOWNTOWN DALLAS
Union Station
Convention Ctr.
R. L. Thornton

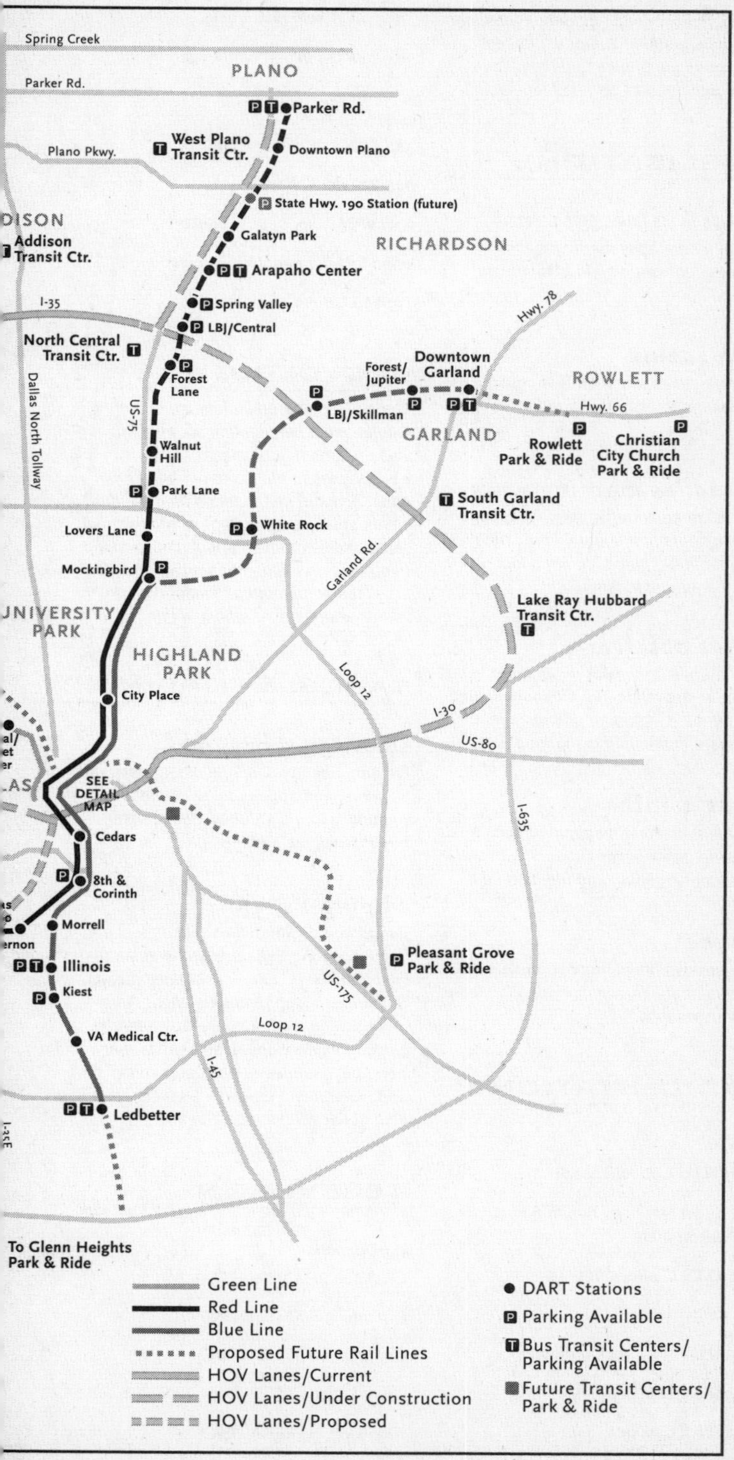

Spring Creek
PLANO
Parker Rd.
Parker Rd.
West Plano Transit Ctr.
Plano Pkwy.
Downtown Plano
State Hwy. 190 Station (future)
Addison Transit Ctr.
Galatyn Park
RICHARDSON
Arapaho Center
I-35
Spring Valley
Hwy. 78
LBJ/Central
North Central Transit Ctr.
Forest Lane
Downtown Garland
Forest/ Jupiter
ROWLETT
LBJ/Skillman
Hwy. 66
US-75
Dallas North Tollway
GARLAND
Walnut Hill
Rowlett Park & Ride
Christian City Church Park & Ride
Park Lane
South Garland Transit Ctr.
White Rock
Lovers Lane
Garland Rd.
Mockingbird
Lake Ray Hubbard Transit Ctr.
UNIVERSITY PARK
HIGHLAND PARK
Loop 12
City Place
I-30
US-80
SEE DETAIL MAP
I-635
Cedars
8th & Corinth
Morrell
Illinois
Pleasant Grove Park & Ride
Kiest
US-175
Loop 12
VA Medical Ctr.
I-45
Ledbetter
To Glenn Heights Park & Ride
Green Line
Red Line
Blue Line
Proposed Future Rail Lines
HOV Lanes/Current
HOV Lanes/Under Construction
HOV Lanes/Proposed
DART Stations
Parking Available
Bus Transit Centers/ Parking Available
Future Transit Centers/ Park & Ride

senger. Pay only what's on the meter, plus 15%–20% gratuity. Two of the largest companies are Choice Cab (972/222–2000) and Yellow Cab (214/426–6262).

PUBLICATIONS

dallas business journal
Weekly newspaper that focuses on the business community. Published on Friday.

d magazine
Monthly magazine with feature articles and extensive entertainment and restaurant listings.

the dallas morning news
Pulitzer prize-winning daily newspaper known for its investigative reporting. Its Friday insert, "guide," covers local events and restaurants.

dallas observer
Free alternative weekly newspaper featuring in-depth stories, extensive entertainment listings, and pop-culture coverage. Published on Thursdays.

texas monthly
A general interest magazine about texas covering politics, music, sports, travel, restaurant reviews, and lifestyle.

the met
Free weekly entertainment guide with reviews of art, movies, music. Published on Wednesdays.

RADIO STATIONS

fm
88.1 KNTU Jazz, classical

90.1 KERA National Public Radio, talk, adult alternative

96.3 KSCS Country, Top 40

97.1 KEGL Rock

98.7 KLUV Pop, rock oldies

99.5 KPLX Country

101.1 WRR Classical

103.7 KVIL soft pop, rock

104.5 KKDA urban contemporary

am
570 KLIF talk

730 KKDA soul, gospel

820 WBAP news, talk, sports

1080 KRLD news, talk, sports

1190 KLUV rock oldies

RECYCLING

The city's residential curbside recycling service picks up plastics, aluminum, and tin cans in a blue plastic bag and newspapers in brown paper bags once a week. The day of the week depends on where you live. Igloo-type containers for glass and aluminum are placed outside in some areas. Businesses that recycle must use a private contractor. For more information, call 214/670–4475.

TAXES & TIPPING

sales tax & beyond
Dallas sales tax is 8.25%, a standard rate in Texas, and applies to all purchases excluding items shipped out of state. Hotel taxes are a steep 15%.

tipping
Dallas is a tipping town with 15%–20% fast becoming the standard in restaurants and bars. Leave a tip even if you only order a cup of coffee. Most restaurants add at least a 15% gratuity to the bill for large parties. Hair-stylists, barbers, pet groomers, caddies, taxi drivers, and others who perform a service are also generally tipped 15%–20%.

TELEVISION

network
Channel 4—KDFW (FOX)

Channel 5—KXAS (NBC)

Channel 8—WFAA (ABC)

Channel 11—KTVT (CBS)

Channel 13—KERA (PBS)

cable
Local channel numbers vary according to the cable system used.

VOTER REGISTRATION

Once a resident of Texas, it takes 30 days from the date of application to become a registered voter. You don't need to register again as long as you vote at least once every three years. To obtain a registration form, call the Dallas County Elections Department (214/653–7871).

WEATHER

Dallas's favorably mild climate is conducive for those who enjoy outdoor activities. January is the coldest month with an average temperature of 43.4 degrees; July the warmest with an average of 85.3 degrees and 66% humidity. Texas weather at its best is unpredictable. The area receives little snow or ice, but when moisture does freeze, the city is only equipped to sand roadways, so driving can be risky in these conditions. Local weather reports include information about the humidity index, chill factor, sunburn index, and air pollution. Such information is helpful when deciding whether to limit outdoor activities. For weather information, call 214/787–1111 or 214/787–1701.

resources for challenges & crises

BABY-SITTING SERVICES

AAA Sitters (972/272–8556).

Baby Sitters of Dallas (214/692–1354).

Helping Parents, Inc. (972/424–8993).

Mom's Best Friend (214/357–8018).

CATERING

general parties
Dewell Events (940 Belt Line Rd., Richardson, 972/6690–0368).

Food Glorious Food (2121 San Jacinto St., Suite 3100, Downtown, 214/754–1861).

Gourmet Dallas (10836 Grissom La., North, 972/484–4954).

Two Sisters (2633 Gaston Ave., East, 214/823–3075).

kids' parties
Food Glorious Food (2121 San Jacinto St., Suite, 3100, Downtown, 214/754–1893).

CHARITIES

Donate your old clothing, computers, furniture, and toys at the following locations. You can drop off goods or have items picked up at your home. Receipts are given for tax deductions.

Goodwill Industries (2800 N. Hampton Rd., 214/638–2800).

Salvation Army (5554 Harry Hines Blvd., 214/630–5611).

CHILD CRISIS

Child Abuse Hotline (800/252–5400).

Child Protective Services (2355 N. Stemmons St., 214/951–7902).

Battered Women's Family Place Hotline & Shelter (214/941–1991).

CITY GOVERNMENT

complaints
Dial 311 for city information and non-emergency requests concerning water, sanitation, animal control, and code enforcement. For emergencies, call 911.

other useful numbers
City Council Office (1500 Marilla St., Suite 5EN, 214/670–4050).

Mayor's Office (1500 Marilla St., Suite 5EN, 214/670–4054).

CONSUMER PROTECTION

Better Business Bureau (214/220–2000).

Consumer Product Safety Messages (214/767–0841).

Federal Trade Commission (214/979–0213).

Food and Drug Administration (214/655–5310).

Texas Attorney General Consumer Protection Division (214/969–5310).

COUNSELING & REFERRALS

aids

Aids/Hiv Testing & Counseling (214/819–1980).

Aids Hotline Counseling Service (214/969–1818).

Aids Services of Dallas (214/941–0523).

alcoholism

Al-Anon & Alateen Information Center (5533 Dyer St., Suite 103, 214/363–0461).

Alcoholics Anonymous (4300 Alpha Road, Bldg. 2, Suite 211, 972/239–4599).

Soul's Harbor Alcoholism Rehabilitation Center (13134 Nile Dr., 972/286–1940).

Tough Love International (972/558–1762).

Welcome House II (214/421–3948).

crime

Victim's Outreach (3530 Forest La., 214/358–5173).

Victim-Witness Division (214/653–3838).

drug abuse

Gateway Foundation (732 S. Peak St., 214/827–2870).

Greater Dallas Council on Alcohol & Drug Abuse (4535 Lemmon Ave., Suite 300, 214/522–8600).

Narcotics Anonymous (972/699–9306).

Nexus Inc. (2519 Oaklawn Ave., 214/321–0156).

Tough Love International (972/558–1762).

Welcome House, Inc. Substance Abuse & HIV Counseling (921 N. Peak St., 214/887–0696).

gambling

Texas Council on Problem & Compulsive Gambling (2480 Promenade Shopping Center, 972/889–2331).

mental health

Mental Health Association (13633 Omega Rd., 214/871–2420).

Suicide Prevention (214/828–1000).

rape

Rape Crisis Center. Counseling and emotional support is available (4917 Harry Hines Blvd., 214/590–0430).

DOCTOR & DENTIST REFERRALS

Dallas County Dental Society (13633 Omega Rd., 972/386–5741).

Dallas County Medical Society (104 E. 12th St., 214/948–3622).

Dallas County Pediatric Medical Society (214/521–9221).

EMERGENCIES

ambulance

Dallas Fire Department (Dial 911).

hospital emergency rooms

Baylor (3500 Gaston Ave., East, 214/820–0111).

Children's (1935 Motor St., Hospital District, 214/640–2000).

Dallas Southwest (2929 S. Hampton Rd., South, 214/330–4611).

Doctors (9440 Poppy Dr., East, 214/324–6100).

Medical City (7777 Forest La., North, 972/661–7000).

Methodist (1441 N. Beckley Ave., Oak Cliff, 214/947–8181).

Parkland (5201 Harry Hines Blvd., Hospital District, 214/590–8000).

Presbyterian (8200 Walnut Hill La., North, 214/345-6789).

St. Paul (5909 Harry Hines Blvd., Hospital District, 214/879-1000).

Tri-City (7525 Scyene Rd., Dallas, 214/381-7171).

poison control center

Poison Control Center (800/764-7661).

suicide prevention

Suicide & Crisis Center (214/828-1000).

FAMILY PLANNING

INDIVIDUAL AGENCIES

Dallas Pregnancy Resource Center (12959 Jupiter Rd., Northeast, 214/343-7283).

Downtown Pregnancy Center (525 N. Ervay St., Downtown, 214/969-2433).

Planned Parenthood of Dallas (7035 S. Greenville Ave., Allen, 214/368-1485).

Prestonwood Pregnancy Center (308 Spanish Village, North, 972/386-4015).

GAY & LESBIAN CONCERNS

Dallas Gay & Lesbian Alliance (2701 Reagan St., Oak Lawn, 214/528-4233).

HOUSE CLEANING HELP AGENCIES

Merry Maids (214/748-0686).

INTERIOR DESIGN & ARCHITECT REFERRALS

American Institute of Architects (2811 McKinney Ave., Suite 20, 214/871-2788).

LANDLORD/TENANT ASSISTANCE

Housing Crisis Center (3108 Live Oak St., 214/828-4244).

LEGAL SERVICES

ACLU (214/939-8089).

Dallas Bar Association Lawyer Referral Service (214/220-7444).

Legal Services of North Texas (214/748-1234).

LOST & FOUND

at airlines & airports

For property lost on a plane, contact the airline (*see* Airlines in Vacation and Travel Information *below*). If loss occurred at the airport, call:

Love Field (214/670-6155). Also call the airline on which you traveled.

Dallas/Fort Worth International Airport (972/574-4454). Also call the airline on which you traveled.

on other public transportation

TRAINS

Amtrak (214/670-5869).

LONG-DISTANCE BUSES

Greyhound Bus Lines (214/655-7092).

METROPOLITAN BUSES

DART (214/749-3810).

TAXI CABS

For items lost in a cab, contact the taxi company. (*See* Taxis in Basics of City Life, *above.*)

lost animals

If your pet is lost, place notices in area shops (include only your phone number) and in the local newspaper. Be sure your pet always wears the identification tags provided by a veterinarian at the time of yearly vaccinations. The tag will assist the person who finds your pet. Report the missing animal to City Animal Shelters (525 Shelter Pl., Oak Cliff, 214/670-7430; 8414 Forney Rd., East, 214/670-8226), which are open Monday through Saturday, 8-5.

lost credit cards

American Express (800/528-4800).

Master Card (800/307-7309).

Visa (800/336-8472).

lost traveler's checks

American Express Company Travel Service (800/221-7282).

Citicorp Travelers Checks (800/645-6556).

ON-LINE SERVICES

Digital Highway (972/256-6336).

Internet America (800/232-4335).

PETS

adoptions

Operation Kindness (3201 Earhart Dr., Carrollton, 972/418-7297).

SPCA of Texas (362 S. Industrial Blvd., West, 214/651-9611).

grooming

Bark & Purr (6336 Greenville Ave., East, 214/361-7566).

Best Pet (8320 Lake June Rd., Southeast, 214/398-6840).

The Grooming Table (12300 Inwood Rd., North, 972/960-7171).

Petco (11910 Preston Rd., North, 972/490-9168).

training

The Dallas Dog Trainer (2000 LBJ Fwy., 972/241-9144).

Petco (1152 N. Buckner Blvd., East, 214/320-9116).

veterinary hospitals

East Dallas Veterinary Clinic (8541 Ferguson Rd., East, 214/328-9935).

Lovers Lane Animal Medical Center (4660 W. Lovers La., North, 214/350-5696).

Preston Road Animal Hospital (6060 LBJ Fwy., North, 972/239-1309).

Summertree Animal & Bird Clinic (12300 Inwood Rd., Suite 102, North, 972/387-4168).

veterinarian referrals

Dallas County Veterinary Medical Association (972/669-9237).

PHARMACIES OPEN 24 HOURS

Walgreens (3732 W. Northwest Hwy., Northwest, 214/956-0113).

Eckerd (1235 S. Buckner Blvd., East, 214/391-2151; 703 Preston Forest Shopping Center, North, 214/363-1571; 3012 Mockingbird La., North, 214/363-5525; 10455 N. Central Expressway, North, 214/369-3872).

POLICE

Dial 911 for emergencies.

Dial 311 for nonemergency police services—including reporting a burglary, automobile theft, or anything that does not pose an imminent danger—general information, and the location and phone number of the patrol division nearest you.

patrol divisions

Central Business District (334 S. Hall St., Downtown, 214/670-4413).

Northeast District (9915 E. Northwest Hwy., East, 214/670-4415).

North Central District (6969 McCallum Blvd., North, 214/670-7253).

Northwest District (2828 Shorecrest Dr., Northwest, 214/670-6178).

Southeast District (725 N. Jim Miller Rd., Southeast, 214/670-8345).

Southwest District (4230 W. Illinois Ave., South, 214/670-7470).

POSTAL SERVICES

post offices

Dallas Main Office, 75260, is open 24 hours a day, 7 days a week. Call for general information, including zip codes, express mail tracking, post offices, and more (401 DFW Airport Tpke., 800/275-8777).

NEIGHBORHOOD BRANCHES

The following post offices are open Mon–Sat. Hours may vary. Call 800/275-8777 for hours.

Airline Station 75235 (2310 Stats Dr.).

Apparel Mart Finance Station 75258 (2300 Stemmons Fwy.).

Belmont Finance 75372 (5650 Belmont Ave.).

Bent Tree Station 75287 (4475 Trinity Mill Rd.).

Beverly Hills Station 75211 (2202 S. Cockrell Hill Rd.).

Brookhollow Station 75247 (5055 Norwood Rd.).

Casa View Station 75228 (2345 Oates Dr.).

Downtown Station 75201 (400 N. Ervay St.).

Eastside Finance Station 75371 (502 N. Haskell St.).

Highland Hills Station 75241 (3655 Simpson Stuart Rd.).

Inwood Station 75209 (7611 Inwood Rd.).

Joe Pool Station 75224 (5521 S. Hampton).

Juanita Craft Station 75215 (3055 Grand Ave.).

Lake Highlands Station 75238 (10502 Markison Rd.).

Lakewood Station 75214 (6120 Swill Ave.).

Main Place Finance Station 75250 (Level B One Main Pl.).

Merchandise Mart 75201 (500 S. Ervay St.).

North Branch Station 75244 (2008 E. Belt line Rd.).

Northhaven Station 75229 (2736 Royal La.).

Northlake Finance Station 75238 (333 Northlake Shopping Center).

Northwest Station 75220 (2341 N. Northwest Hwy.).

Oak Lawn Station 75219 (2825 Oak Lawn Ave.).

Olla Podrida Finance Station 75251 (12215 Coit Rd.).

Parkdale Station 75227 (7720 Military Pkwy.).

Pleasant Grove Station 75217 (230 Pleasant Grove Shopping Center).

Preston Royal Finance 75230 (539 Preston Royal Shopping Center).

Preston Station 75225 (8604 Turtle Creek).

Prestonwood Station 75248 (5995 Summerside Dr.).

Richland Station 75243 (9130 Markville Dr.).

Royal Lane Carrier Station 75231 (8231 Park La.).

South Oak Cliff 75216 (1502 E. Kiest Blvd.).

Spring Valley Station 75240 (13770 Noel Rd.).

Station A 75208 (515 Centre St.).

Station C 75202 (1100 Commerce St.).

University Carrier Station 75206 (5606 Yale Blvd.).

Vickery Station 75218 (1351 N. Buckner Blvd.).

World Trade Center Finance 75258 (2050 Stemmons Fwy.).

federal express

For pick-ups and general information, call 800/463–3339.

NEIGHBORHOOD BRANCHES

1999 Bryan St., 75201.

1201 Main St., 75202.

901 Main St., 75202.

5650 Greenville Ave., 75206.

2050 N. Stemmons Fwy., 75207.

2300 N. Stemmons Fwy, 75207.

5301 W Lovers La., 75209.

411 W. Commerce St., 75212.

2920 Oaklawn Ave., 75219.

10440 Olympic Dr., 75220.

2949 Walnut Hill La., 75229.

7927 Forest La., 75230.

1625 W. Mockingbird La., 75235.

5420 Lyndon B. Jonson Fwy., 75240.

7516 Campbell Rd., 75248.

12770 Merit Dr., 75251.

2963 N. Airfield Dr., 75261.

united parcel service

For pick-ups and general information, call 800/742-5877.

NEIGHBORHOOD BRANCHES

10155 Monroe St., 75229.

325 N. St. Paul St., 75201.

2200 Ross Ave., 75201.

400 N. Olive St., 75201.

1700 Pacific Ave., 75201.

900 S. Jackson St., 75201.

7500 N. St. Paul St., 75201.

2515 McKinney Ave., 75201.

201 Bryant St., 75201.

1600 Pacific Ave., 75201.

201 Ross Ave., 75201.

2651 N. Harwood St., 75201.

350 N. St. Paul St., 75201.

2305 Cedar Springs Rd., 75201.

2727 N. Harwood St., 75201.

1907 N. Lamar St., 75201.

700 N. Pearl St., 75201.

717 N. Harwood St., 75201.

2121 San Jacinto St., 75201.

3102 Maple Ave., 75201.

2414 N. Akard St., 75201.

1909 Woodall Rogers Fwy., 75201.

2602 McKinney Ave., 75202.

1910 Pacific Ave., 75201.

500 N. Akard St., 75201.

1717 Main St., 75202.

1845 Woodall Rogers Fwy., 75202.

200 Crescent Court, 75209.

1700 Pearl St., 75209.

SENIOR CITIZEN SERVICES

Aging Information Office (214/741-5244).

American Association of Retired Persons (AARP) (214/265-4060).

Area Agency on Aging (214/379-4636 or 800/548-1873).

Parks & Recreation Senior Programs (214/670-6266).

Senior Citizens of Greater Dallas (214/823-5700).

TELEVISION CABLE COMPANIES

AT&T Cable Services provides service for Dallas. (1565 S. Chenault St., 214/328-5000)

UTILITIES

Call the following for new customers, reporting problems, and general information.

gas

Lone Star Gas (214/741-3750).

electric

TU Electric (972/791-2888).

telephone

Southwestern Bell (800/464-7928).

water

Dallas Water Utilities (214/651-1441).

VOLUNTEERING

The Volunteer Center of Dallas County. The volunteer center conveniently links volunteers, young and old, with such diverse places as art museums and medical centers. You can also contact organizations that you are interesting in helping, such as hospitals, libraries, health foundations and associations, and youth groups (1215 Skiles St., East, 214/826-6767).

ZONING & PLANNING

Historic Preservation/Landmark Commission (214/670-4538).

Zoning Department (214/670-4209).

Planning & Development (214/670-4118).

City Planning Commission (214/670–3086).

learning

ACTING SCHOOLS

KD Studio Actors Conservatory. Specializes in on-camera acting for TV commercials and film for ages four years and older. (2600 Stemmons Freeway, West, 214/638–0484).

STAGE. For the beginner as well as pro, classes include on-camera, stage, and audition techniques for adults only. (7906 Brookhollow Rd., Northwest, 214/630–7722)

ART & PHOTOGRAPHY SCHOOLS

Art Institute of Dallas (8080 Park La., Northeast, 800/275–4243)

Art Academy of Dallas offers a variety of classes, each limited to 10 students, teen-age and older. (8222 Douglas Ave., North, 214/526–7862)

Creative Arts Center/School of Sculpture. Classes are given in sculpting, painting, drawing, and pottery for adults. (2360 Laughlin Dr., East, 214/320–1275)

Richland Community College. Offers a two-year associate degree in art. (12800 Abrams Rd., Northeast, 972/238–6100)

FunEd (5100 Beltline Rd., North Dallas, 972/960–2666)

Southern Methodist University. Offers four-year degree programs in a variety areas of study. (6425 Boaz La., 214/768–2000)

BALLROOM DANCING

Dancemasters (10675 E. Northwest Hwy., Northeast, 214/553–5188).

Metroplex International Ballroom Dancesport Club (972/727–4825).

Preston Center Dance (6162 Sherry La., North, 214/739–1737).

COLLEGES

Central Texas Commercial College (9400 N. Central Expressway, North, 214/368–3680).

American Trades Institute (6627 Maple Ave., Northwest, 972/263–5066).

COMPUTER TRAINING

Ace Computer Training (5550 LBJ Fwy., 972/419–1717).

CompuEdge Technology (1950 N. Stemmons Fwy., 214/747–0333).

ExecuTrain (12201 Merit Dr., Suite 350, 972/387–1212).

World Com (2100 N. Hwy. 360, 972/206–0066).

COOKING SCHOOLS

Aims Academy Culinary Arts (3300 Oak Lawn Ave., Oak Lawn, 214/520–6848).

FunEd (5100 Beltline Rd., 972/960–2666).

Cuisine International (6211 W. Northwest Hwy., Suite 1404, North, 214/373–1161).

U Tou-Can Cook (624 Preston Royal Village, North, 214/346–9090).

DANCE

DanceMasters Social Dance Studio (10675 E. Northwest Hwy., Northeast, 214/553–5188).

Dance Zone (10163 Shoreview Dr., East, 214/221–2000).

FunEd (13608 Midway Rd., North, 972/960–2666).

LANGUAGE SCHOOLS

chinese

Berlitz (17194 Preston Rd., North Dallas, 972/991–6379).

Liaison Language Center (3500 Oak Lawn Ave., Oak Lawn, 214/528–2731).

esl

Threshold to Communication (5931 Ross Ave., East, 214/341–9810).

Dallas International School (6039 Churchill Way, North, 972/991–6379).

french

Berlitz (17194 Preston Rd., North, 972/991–6379).

Liaison Language Center (3500 Oak Lawn Ave., Oak Lawn, 214/528–2731).

german

Berlitz (17194 Preston Rd., North, 972/991–6379).

Liaison Language Center (3500 Oak Lawn Ave., Oak Lawn, 214/528–2731).

italian

Berlitz (17194 Preston Rd., 972/991–6379).

Liaison Language Center (3500 Oak Lawn Ave., Oak Lawn, 214/528–2731).

japanese

Berlitz (17194 Preston Rd., North, 972/991–6379).

Liaison Language Center (3500 Oak Lawn Ave., Oak Lawn, 214/528–2731).

spanish

Berlitz (17194 Preston Rd., North, 972/991–6379).

Liaison Language Center (3500 Oak Lawn Ave., Oak Lawn, 214/528–2731).

MUSIC SCHOOLS

Allen School of Music (705 Greenville Ave., Richardson, 972/359–1600).

American Institute of Musical Studies (6621 Snider Plaza, North, 214/363–2638).

Dallas School of Music (2650 Midway Rd., Carrollton, 972/380–8050).

Dallas Suzuki Academy (4200 Herschel Ave., Turtle Creek, 214/526–6169).

Piano Moderne School of Music (2512 Regal Rd., Plano, 972/596–1173).

vacation & travel information

AIRLINES

Aeromexico (800/237–6639).

Air Tran (800/247–8726).

American Airlines/American Eagle (800/633–3711).

America West (800/235–9292).

Atlantic Southeast (800/221–1212).

British Airways (800/247–9297).

Canadian (800/426–7000).

China Airways (800/227–5188).

Continental (972/263–0523).

Delta (800/221–1212).

Frontier (800/432–1359).

Grupo TACA (800/535–8780).

Japan Air (800/525–3663).

Korean Air (800/438–5000).

Lufthansa (800/645–3880).

Midwest (800/452–2022).

Northwest (800/225–2525).

Southwest (800/435–9792).

TWA (800/221–2000).

United (800/241–6522).

US Airways (800/428–4322).

Vanguard (800/826–4827).

AIRPORTS

Dallas/Fort Worth International Airport. Serves all major airlines. (International Pkwy., Grapevine, 214/574–6701)

Love Field. Home to Southwest Airlines. Direct flights from Love Field are limited to states bordering Texas, but Southwest flies to cities across the United States. (8008 Cedar Springs, Northwest Dallas, 214/670–6073)

getting there by public transportation

A DART bus will take you from Downtown to Love Field in about 30 minutes for $1 and to DFW International Airport in about 40 minutes for $2. Buses run as frequently as every 15 minutes during rush hour and as seldom as every hour during off-peak hours. The Trinity Railway Express takes about 20 minutes for $2. For more details, call DART (214/979–1111).

A taxi from Downtown to Love Field costs about $20 and to DFW Airport about $45. Many area hotels offer free shuttle service to and from Love Field. Call Discount Shuttle (817/267–5150) to pick you up and take you to DFW Airport for $11 from Downtown.

getting there by car

Traffic dictates how long it will take you to get to either airport. Unless you are traveling really early in the morning, prior to 6:30 AM or after 10 PM, be sure to allow extra time for traffic congestion.

To reach Love Field from Downtown, take either Stemmons Freeway or Dallas North Tollway and exit at Mockingbird Lane. A covered walkway connects a four-story covered parking garage to the Love Field terminal. Parking ranges from 50¢ for 1/2 hour to $7 for 24 hours. You can also park 24 hours for $5 in an adjacent outdoor parking lot.

When traveling to DFW Airport from anywhere other than North Dallas, you can take Interstate 30 west to Highway 360, then north on Highway 360 to the airport. You can also take Stemmons Freeway or North Central Expressway north to LBJ Freeway, then west on LBJ Freeway to Highway 121 and the airport. For parking information, *see* Airports: Fort Worth.

CAR RENTAL

major agencies

Alamo (800/327–9633).

Avis (800/831–2847).

Budget (927/527–0700).

Enterprise (877/736–8222).

Hertz (800/704–4473).

limousine services

Alpha Omega (972/503–1190).

Noble Transportation (972/690–4671).

Ambassador Limousines (972/407–9323).

First Executive Transportation (972/578–5700).

CURRENCY EXCHANGE

American Express Travel Agency (8317 Preston Center Plaza, North, 214/363–0214).

Order Express (508-A Jefferson Blvd., 214/943–4364; 9526 Webb Chapel Rd., North, 214/350–0095).

Thomas Cook Currency Service (DFW Airport, Terminal 2E; 2911 Turtle Creek Blvd., Suite 125, Turtle Creek, 214/559–3564).

EMBASSIES & CONSULATES

Belgium (6000 Legacy Dr., Plano, 972/801–4391).

British (2911 Turtle Creek Blvd., Turtle Creek, 214/521–4090).

Canada (750 N. St. Paul St., East, 214/922–9806).

Chile (3500 Oak Lawn Ave., Suite 110, Oak Lawn, 214/528–2731).

Czech Republic (7979 Inwood Rd., Suite 217, Northwest, 214/351–2074).

El Salvador (1555 Mockingbird La., Northwest, 214/637–1018).

France (750 N. St. Paul St., East, 972/789–9305).

Germany (5580 Peterson La., North, 972/239–0707).

Italy (6255 W. Northwest Hwy., Northwest, 214/368–4113).

Korea (12720 Hillcrest Rd., North, 972/934–8644).

Malta (500 N. Akard St., Downtown, 214/855–9897).

Mexico (8855 N. Stemmons Fwy., North, 214/630–7341).

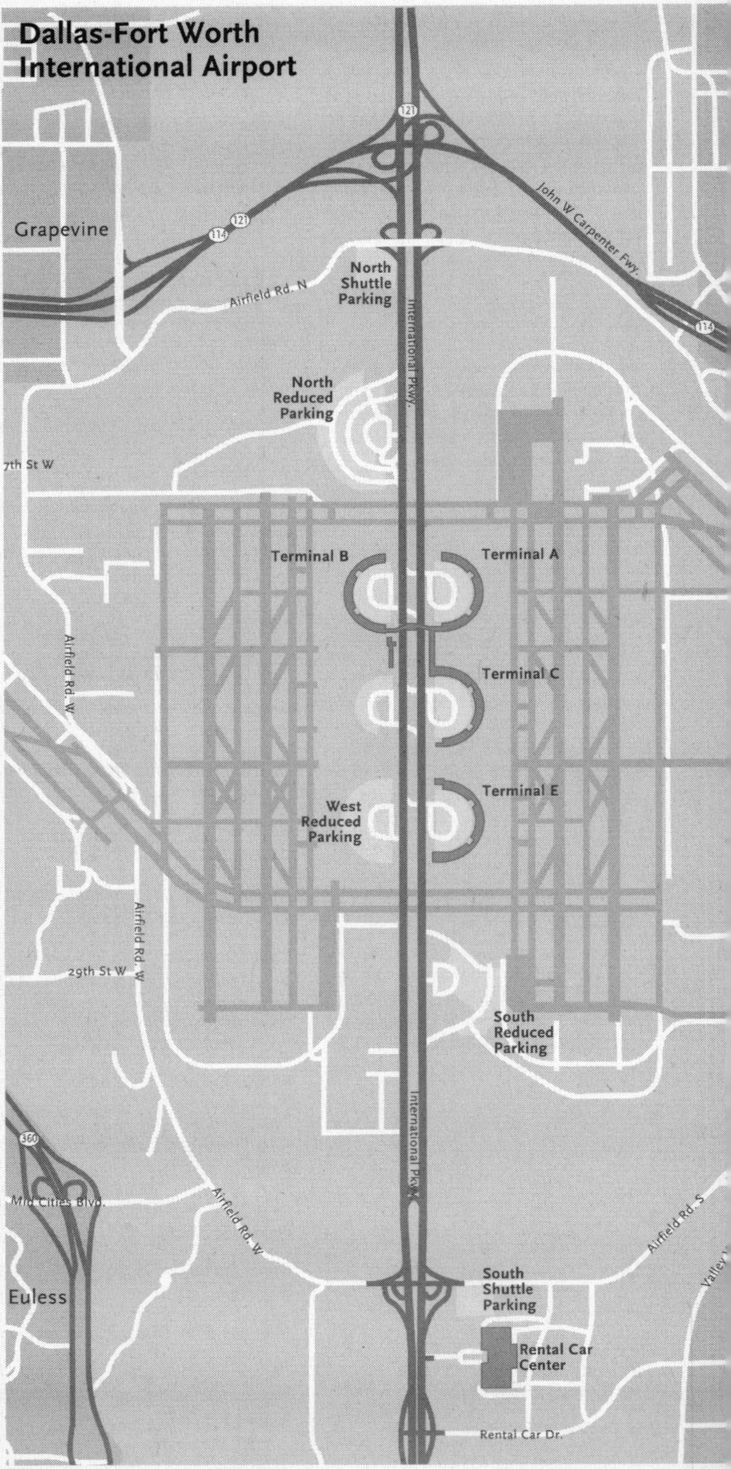
Dallas-Fort Worth
International Airport
Grapevine
121
114
John W Carpenter Fwy.
North
Shuttle
Parking
Airfield Rd. N
International Pkwy.
North
Reduced
Parking
7th St W
Terminal B
Terminal A
Terminal C
Terminal E
Airfield Rd. W
West
Reduced
Parking
29th St W
South
Reduced
Parking
360
Mid Cities Blvd.
Euless
Airfield Rd. S
South
Shuttle
Parking
Rental Car
Center
Rental Car Dr.

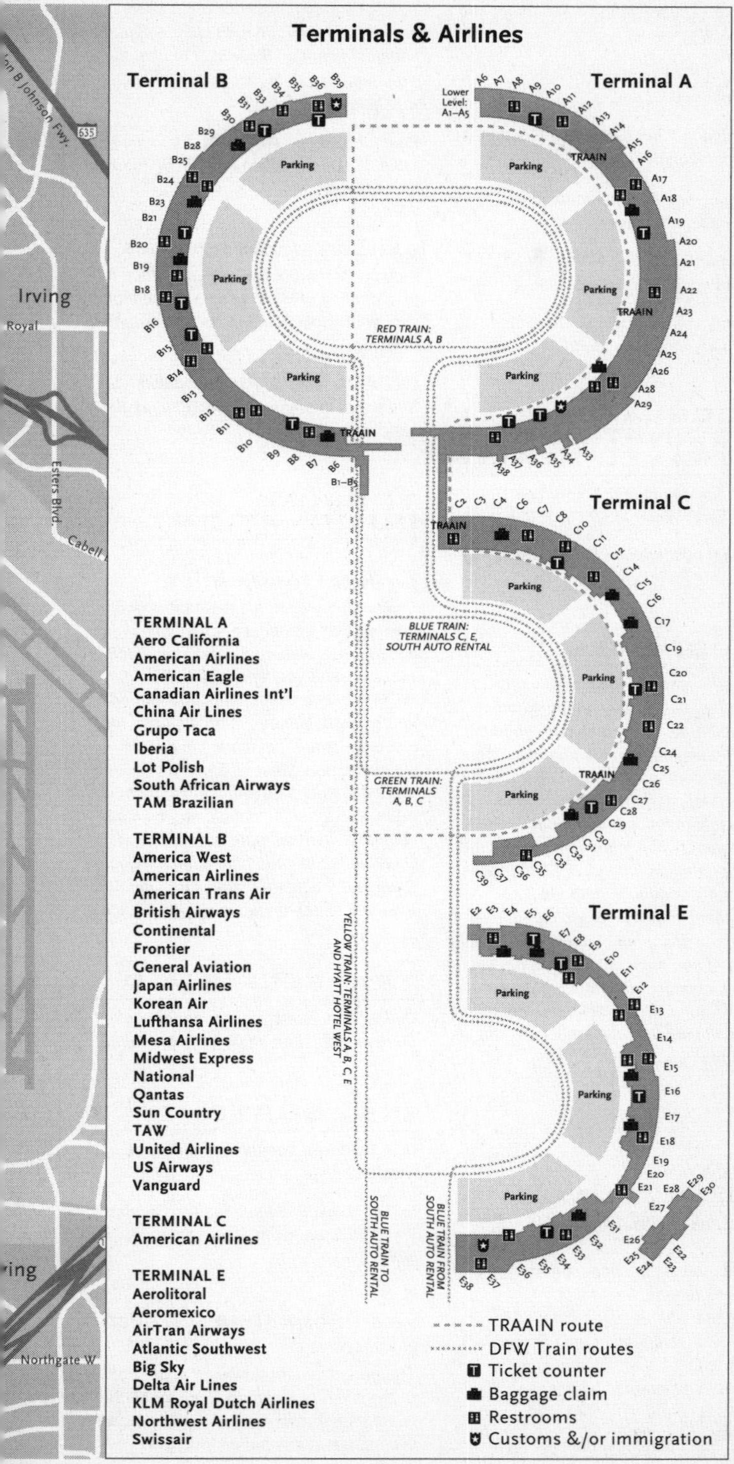
Terminals & Airlines
Terminal B
Terminal A
Lower Level: A1–A5
B1–B5
Terminal C
Terminal E
Parking
TRAAIN
RED TRAIN: TERMINALS A, B
BLUE TRAIN: TERMINALS C, E, SOUTH AUTO RENTAL
GREEN TRAIN: TERMINALS A, B, C
YELLOW TRAIN: TERMINALS A, B, C, E AND HYATT HOTEL WEST
BLUE TRAIN TO SOUTH AUTO RENTAL
BLUE TRAIN FROM SOUTH AUTO RENTAL
Irving
Royal
Esters Blvd.
Cabell
Northgate W
635
TERMINAL A
Aero California
American Airlines
American Eagle
Canadian Airlines Int'l
China Air Lines
Grupo Taca
Iberia
Lot Polish
South African Airways
TAM Brazilian
TERMINAL B
America West
American Airlines
American Trans Air
British Airways
Continental
Frontier
General Aviation
Japan Airlines
Korean Air
Lufthansa Airlines
Mesa Airlines
Midwest Express
National
Qantas
Sun Country
TAW
United Airlines
US Airways
Vanguard
TERMINAL C
American Airlines
TERMINAL E
Aerolitoral
Aeromexico
AirTran Airways
Atlantic Southwest
Big Sky
Delta Air Lines
KLM Royal Dutch Airlines
Northwest Airlines
Swissair
TRAAIN route
DFW Train routes
Ticket counter
Baggage claim
Restrooms
Customs &/or immigration

Monaco (4700 St. John's Dr., Highland Park, 214/521–1058).

Norway (4605 Live Oak, Turtle Creek, 214/826–5231).

Spain (5499 Glen Lakes Dr., Northeast, 214/373–1200).

Sweden (1341 W. Mockingbird La., Northwest, 214/630–9112).

Switzerland (2651 N. Harwood St., Downtown, 214/871–0871).

Taiwan (1168 W. Main St., Suite E, Lewisville, 972/436–4242).

INOCULATIONS, VACCINATIONS & TRAVEL HEALTH

Dallas County Health Clinic (2377 Stemmons Fwy., West, 214/819–2162).

National Information Hotline (404/639–2572).

PASSPORTS

Before you apply for a passport, call any of the Dallas County Passports offices to find out what documentation you will need. Passport applications must be made in person, but renewals can often be done by mail. Applications and renewal forms are available at both the main and DFW Airport post offices. Passports costs $45, plus a $15 processing fee. Renewals by mail are $40. Remember that passports take longer to receive during peak travel times, so plan ahead. If you need to obtain a passport quickly, contact the National Passport Information Center (900/225–5674). This emergency service will cost you an additional $35.

Dallas County Passports (600 Commerce St., Downtown, 214/653–7691; 10056 Marsh La., Suite 137, North, 214/904–3030; 3443 St. Francis St., East, 214/904–3030).

Post Offices (DFW Airport, 2300 W. 32nd St., Irving; Main, 401 DFW Tpke., Downtown).

passport photo agencies

Passports require two identical recent photos. Any photographer can take photos; see the application for specific specifications.

Global Passport & Visa Expeditors (811 S. Central Expressway, North, 972/907–9450).

TOURIST INFORMATION

for local information

Dallas Convention & Visitors Bureau Information Center provides general information and brochures. The DCVB will also send you free information packets in advance of your trip. You can also find many brochures in hotels. Information booths are located at Love Field, Union Station, West End Market Place, and "Old Red" Courthouse. To learn more about the city, check out the Convention & Visitors Bureau web site at www.dallascvb.com (100 S. Houston St., Downtown, 214/571–1300; Hot line: 800/232–5527; Special Events 214/939–2701).

TRAVELER'S AID

Dallas/Fort Worth International Airport (Terminal B, Gate 28, 972/574–4420).

U.S. CUSTOMS

U.S. Customs Service (DFW Airport, 972/574–2170).

Immigration & Naturalization Service (8101 N. Stemmons, Downtown, 214/767–1814).

visa information & travel advisories

The embassy, consulate, or tourist office of the country you plan to visit has the most recent information on visa requirements, travel advisories, and service

ESSENTIAL NUMBERS/DALLAS

Dallas Public Library (214/670–1400).
Park & Recreation Department Activity Line (214/670–7070).
Postal Service (800/275–8777).
Reunion Arena Event Line (214/948–4100).
Time & Temperature (214/349–8367, 214/844–6611).
Weather (214/787–1701).

strikes. The U.S. State Department (202/647–5225) has travel advisories on specific countries.

American Express Global Assist provides travel advisories and emergency doctor referral to American Express cardholders traveling abroad. (800/554–2639)

Ask Immigration provides information about citizenship, visas, and relatives abroad. (800/375–5283)

U.S. Customs Service directs you to appropriate agency for information about importing specific goods. (800/697–3662)

basics of city life: fort worth/ mid-cities

BANKS

Banks are generally open from 9 AM until 4 PM, Monday through Thursday, and until 6 PM on Friday. Some banks stay open later and offer drive-through hours on Saturday morning.

Bank One (817/884–4000).

Bank United (972/263–3222).

Frost Bank (817/420–5200).

Summit National Bank (817/336–8383).

DRIVING

Having a car in Fort Worth and throughout Tarrant County is absolutely necessary. Bus service is available from downtown Fort Worth to most city neighborhoods; however, there is no bus or rail service in the nearby suburbs (Grapevine, Hurst, etc.). Ample parking is available downtown in paid lots and at meters. Speed limits are between 30 mph and 45 mph in the city and 55 mph to 60 mph on the freeways. Right turn on red is permitted except where noted.

licenses

The same requirements to obtain a license in Dallas apply to Fort Worth (*see* Dallas: Driving, *above*).

To register your vehicle, stop at the Motor Vehicle Registration office in the county court offices or at one of the subcourthouses listed below. All vehicles must have a safety inspection every 12 months. Inspections are available at many gas stations, service centers, and dealers. Cost varies by year and make of the car. Texas requires that all drivers have liability insurance.

DEPARTMENT OF MOTOR VEHICHLES

For license plates and vehicle registration, call the Tax Assessor-Collector, County Courts, nearest you: Downtown (100 E. Weatherford St., Fort Worth, 817/884–1100); Arlington Sub-courthouse (724 E. Border St., Arlington, 817/548–3935); Northeast Sub-courthouse (645 Grapevine Hwy., Hurst, 817/581–3635); Southwest Sub-courthouse (6551 Granbury Rd., Fort Worth, 817/370–4535).

Driver's Licenses are obtained from the Texas Department of Public Safety. Choose the location nearest to you: Arlington (3901 W. Arkansas La. #111, 817/274–1818); Fort Worth (6316 Lake Worth Blvd., 817/238–9197; 6413 Woodway Dr., 817/294–1075); Hurst (624 Northeast Loop 820, 817/284–1490).

traffic

Driving around Fort Worth and Mid-Cities requires tolerance. The freeways are as frustrating and annoying as you allow them to be. You can either avoid them during rush hours—between 7 AM and 9 AM and between 4:45 PM and 6:30 PM—or you can drive through the city. The most congested freeways in early morning and late afternoon in Tarrant County are I–820 north and south from I–30 and west of Texas Highway 121; Texas 121 from I–820 in Richland Hills/Hurst to Texas 114 in Grapevine; and I–30 from I–820 in Fort Worth west to University Drive in Fort Worth.

GEOGRAPHY

In Fort Worth proper, downtown has at its heart a renovated section of Victorian buildings and brick streets called Sundance Square. Downtown, which is largely filled with historic buildings and a smattering of bold, contemporary architecture, is bordered on the north by Belknap Street, on the west by the Trinity River, on the east by I–35W, and on the south by I–30. Within the confines of downtown are several loft apartment developments in vintage buildings and giant new, upscale complexes on Henderson Street.

The Hospital District lies south of downtown, bordered on the west by Eighth Avenue, the north by I–30, the east by I–35, and the south by Berry Street. The Fairmont District within is filled with older homes and apartment buildings, some of which are currently being renovated. Medical complexes and a few shopping strips are found here as well.

Forest Park, Texas Christian University, and Southwest Fort Worth (FP/TCU/SW) encompasses a general area southwest from downtown that includes the Fort Worth Zoo, the university, and Cityview. Boundaries are I–30 on the north, Forest Park Boulevard on the east, I–20 on the south, and Loop 820 on the west. Large, elegant homes and modest bungalows are sprinkled throughout on tree-lined streets. More upscale shopping and dining areas are found here, too.

The Cultural District extends west from downtown and encompasses the museums. West from this area is simply called the Westside, which includes the largest and most expensive homes in town, as well as upscale shopping strips along Camp Bowie Boulevard. The Trinity River borders the east, White Settlement Road the north, I–30 the south, and Texas 183 the west. The Northside and Stockyards areas comprise the Hispanic cultural neighborhood and the National Historic District north of downtown. North Main Street runs through the middle of this section, which is bordered on the east by I–35, the west by Meecham Field, the south by the Trinity River, and the north by 28th Street.

The balance of the Metroplex includes a few smaller communities: Arlington, home to the University of Texas, east of Fort Worth is bordered by the West Fork of the Trinity River on the north, Texas 360 on the east, U.S. 287 on the south, and Village Creek on the west. Grapevine lies northeast of Fort Worth and wraps around the northwestern corner of DFW International Airport. Irving, home to the Dallas Cowboys, the Boy Scouts of America, and the mega-business center known as Las Colinas, sits adjacent to DFW Airport's eastern side and on the northwest corner of Dallas. Other communities that make up northeast Tarrant County, with hundreds of dining and shopping options for residents and workers in the Fort Worth area, are Colleyville, Keller, Hurst, Euless, Bedford, and Haltom City. Northwest Tarrant cities and communities include Lake Worth, Eagle Mountain Lake, and River Oaks.

HOLIDAYS

Government offices, banks, and some schools observe the following holidays:

New Year's Day (January 1)

Martin Luther King Jr., Day (3rd Monday in January)

President's Day (3rd Monday in February)

Memorial Day (last Monday in May)

Independence Day (July 4)

Thanksgiving Day (4th Thursday in November)

Christmas Day (December 25)

LIQUOR LAWS

The drinking age in Texas is 21. Liquor stores are open from 10 AM until 9 PM. Beer can be sold at convenience stores until midnight. No hard liquor is sold on Sunday, and no beer or wine can be purchased before noon on Sunday. Bars cannot sell beer, wine, or liquor after 2 AM. In Arlington, grocery and convenience stores sell beer, but wine must be purchased at a liquor store. Beer and wine can be purchased in grocery and convenience stores in Grapevine, and you can buy mixed drinks in restaurants, but no stores sell hard liquor in Grapevine.

NO SMOKING

Many Fort Worth, Grapevine, and Irving restaurants provide smoking sections, and some are exclusively non-smoking. Arlington does not allow smoking in restaurants. Most public buildings in the area—including malls, stores, banks, hospitals, and theaters—have banned smoking.

PARKING

rules & enforcement

The Fort Worth Police Department takes its parking meters seriously. If you have three outstanding meter violations ($12 if paid within 10 days), you are subject to having your car booted. That's a $75 fine, plus the impounding fee of $100 per day and the original ticket's payment. Most parking meters take quarters, dimes, and nickels: 10 minutes for every 5¢, up to two hours. Some meters cost a penny a minute. Within a block west of the public library downtown, you'll find some 10-hour meters. Call Traffic Citation (817/871–6700) for more information.

parking lots

Parking lots in downtown Fort Worth are numerous and somewhat reasonable. Cost is typically $10 for eight hours. Some lots around Sundance Square offer free parking after 5 PM but these spots go quickly, especially on weekends.

Allright Parking (210 W. Sixth St., 817/332–3719).

Central Parking Systems (three downtown locations, 817/334–0436).

Sundance Square Parking (201 Commerce St., 817/390–8763).

PERSONAL SECURITY

As you would in any large city, take precautions to ensure your safety. Use common sense when touring, just as you would in any unfamiliar city. Always lock your car and keep your belongings close to you. Stick to well-lit areas when outside at night. Trust your instinct. Parts of Fort Worth are rough and other parts are not, but crime can occur anywhere.

PUBLIC TRANSPORTATION

bus

The T, Fort Worth's city bus line, operates from 5 AM to midnight weekdays and from 6 AM to midnight Saturday. Sunday service is available on eight routes from 7 AM to 7 PM. Regular city bus service is available on routes in Fort Worth, Lake Worth, and Richland Hills. Eight Express routes allow virtually non-stop travel weekdays from designated park-and-ride lots to downtown Fort Worth and Downtown Dallas. The T provides park-and-ride locationsand free all-day parking. In downtown Fort Worth, a Downtown Free Zone provides free transportation to restaurants, shopping, and offices within the area bounded by Henderson, Jones, Belknap, and Lancaster streets. Basic bus fares are 50¢ for children and seniors and $1 for adults; Park and Ride is $2, and Dallas Express is $3. For general information, call 817/215—8600.

taxis

Fort Worth has a limited taxi supply. Sometimes it's easy to get a taxi within 20 minutes of a call, but often that's not the case. Call Yellow or Checker cabs (817/534–5555).

PUBLICATIONS

fort worth star-telegram

This Knight-Ridder daily newspaper prints three editions: one for Fort Worth, one for Arlington and one for Northeast Tarrant County. The Sunday edition has expanded business, arts, travel, community, and classifieds sections.

arlington morning news

Daily edition published by the *Dallas Morning News.*

fw weekly

The alternative weekly for Tarrant County, this paper has an amusing, biting tone, and often prints stories the *Star-Telegram* is hesitant to touch. Published on Wednesday, it was bought in mid-2000 by New Times, a giant, national chain of weeklies.

texas monthly

A general interest magazine about Texas covering politics, music, sports, travel, restaurant reviews, and lifestyle.

RADIO STATIONS

fm

88.7 KTCU Texas Christian University

94.1 KLTY Christian

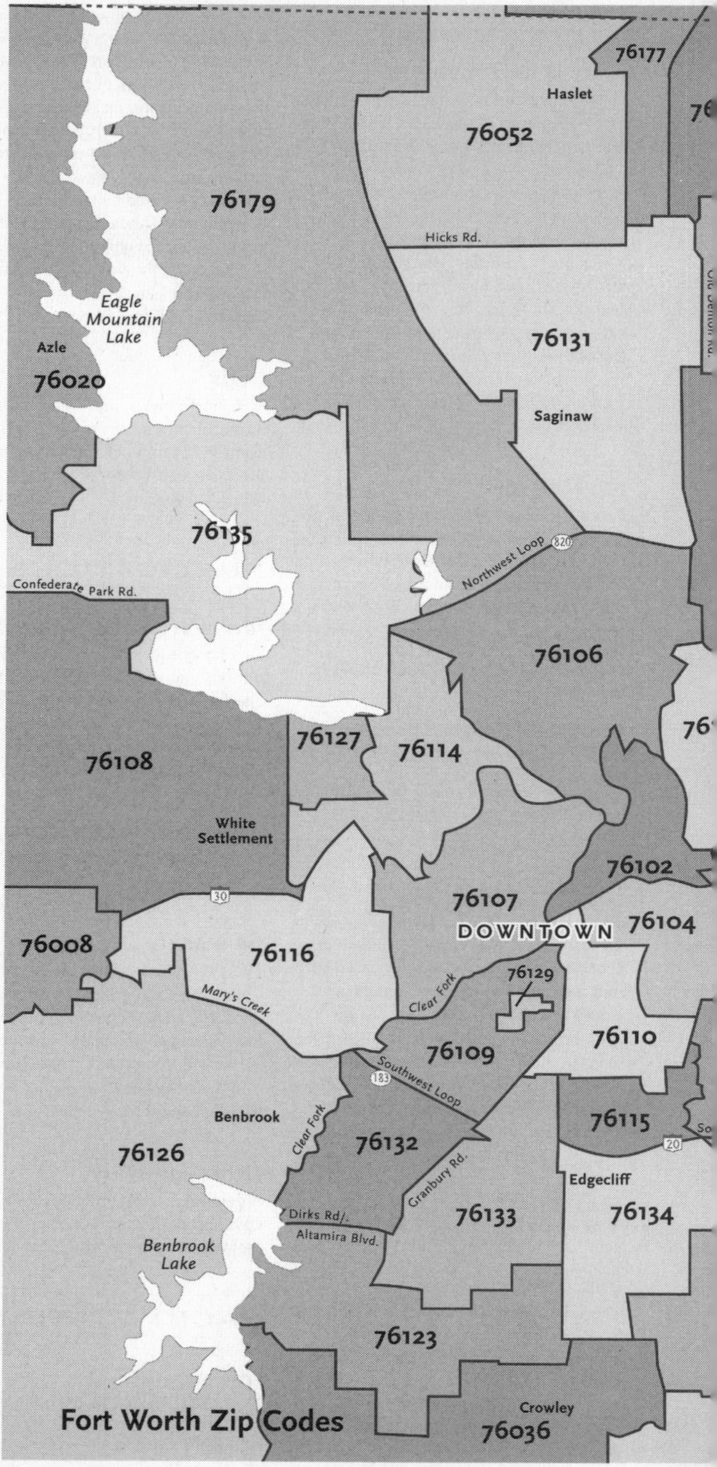

Fort Worth Zip Codes
76177
Haslet
76052
76179
Hicks Rd.
Eagle Mountain Lake
Azle
76020
76131
Saginaw
76135
Northwest Loop
820
Confederate Park Rd.
76106
76127
76114
76108
White Settlement
76102
30
76107
DOWNTOWN
76104
76008
76116
76129
Mary's Creek
Clear Fork
76110
76109
Southwest Loop
183
76115
20
Benbrook
Clear Fork
76132
76126
Granbury Rd.
Edgecliff
76133
76134
Dirks Rd./
Altamira Blvd.
Benbrook Lake
76123
Crowley
76036

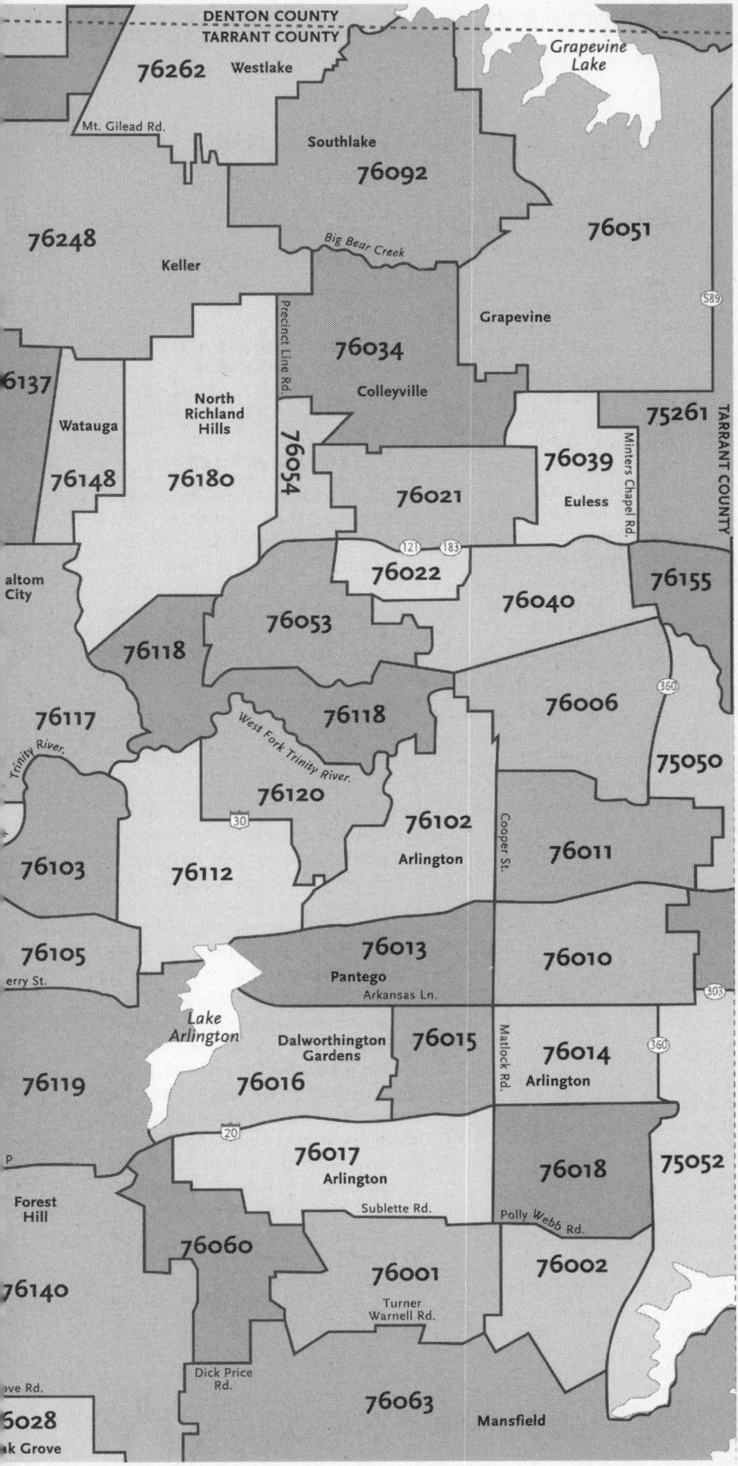

DENTON COUNTY
TARRANT COUNTY
76262
Westlake
Mt. Gilead Rd.
Southlake
76092
Grapevine Lake
76051
Big Bear Creek
76248
Keller
Precinct Line Rd.
76034
Grapevine
589
Colleyville
6137
North Richland Hills
Watauga
75261
TARRANT COUNTY
76148
76180
76054
76039
76021
Minters Chapel Rd.
Euless
121
183
76022
altom City
76155
76040
76053
76118
360
76006
76118
76117
West Fork Trinity River
Trinity River
75050
76120
30
76102
Arlington
Cooper St.
76011
76103
76112
76013
76010
76105
Pantego
erry St.
Arkansas Ln.
303
Lake Arlington
Dalworthington Gardens
76015
Matlock Rd.
360
76014
Arlington
76119
76016
20
76017
Arlington
76018
75052
Forest Hill
Sublette Rd.
Polly Webb Rd.
76060
76001
76002
76140
Turner Warnell Rd.
Dick Price Rd.
ve Rd.
76063
6028
Mansfield
k Grove

97.1 KEGL Classic and modern rock

98.7 KLUV Oldies

105.7 KRNB Jazz

am

820 WBAP News, talk radio

1310 KTCK Sports

RECYCLING

Most Tarrant County cities pick up recyclable items such as clear, green, and amber glass (no mirrors, plate glass, or light bulbs); plastic containers of various grades; newspapers, magazines, clean household paper, and phone books; and aluminum cans and metal food cans. Remember to wash out food and drink containers and throw away caps. Cities have varying rules on pickup of heavy or bulky items such as furniture, appliances, and brush. Call Waste Management of Fort Worth, Inc. (817/332–7329) for more information.

Curbside pickup is available for small piles of brush or wood, cut into 4-ft lengths and tied. Fort Worth operates a disposal center for residents' hazardous waste. Several other cities have arranged for their residents to use the Fort Worth site as well. For more information call: Arlington (817/459–6771, curbside pickup twice a week); Fort Worth (817/332–7329, curbside pickup twice weekly in most areas); Grapevine (817/410–3363, curbside pickup, twice weekly).

TAXES & TIPPING

sales tax and beyond

The Texas sales tax is 8.25%. This applies to food but not alcohol in restaurants and to out-of-state shipping.

tipping

Tipping at restaurants is typically 15%–20% of your bill. Tip bell hops at least $1 per bag, hairstylists 10%–20% of your total bill, and hotel maids $3 or more per day of your stay.

TELEVISION

network

Channel 4—KDFW (FOX)

Channel 5—KXAS (NBC)

Channel 8—WFAA (ABC)

Channel 11—KTVT (CBS)

Channel 13—KERA (PBS)

cable

Local channel numbers vary according to the cable system used.

VOTER REGISTRATION

For information and voter registration cards, contact the Tarrant County Election Administrator (817/884–1115). You can register by mail or at almost any bank, some libraries, and all city halls and sub-courthouses in Tarrant County. You also can log on to the Texas secretary of state website at www.sos.state.tx.us and go to "Functions of the Office."

WEATHER

Fort Worth, like all North Texas, has a mild climate that appeals to outdoor enthusiasts. January is the coldest month with an average temperature of 43.4 degrees; July the warmest with an average of 85.3 degrees. However, July daytime temperatures often soar above 100 degrees and January night temperatures often drop to freezing or below. But Texas weather at its best is unpredictable. If you don't like the present weather just wait a few minutes: it will probably change. The area receives little snow or ice, but when moisture does freeze, the city is only equipped to sand roadways and many drivers handle the conditions poorly. Schools frequently close on icy days. Humidity tends to be very high in the rainy spring season, and warm weather lasts usually from May through September. For more information, call the National Weather Service (817/787–1701).

resources for challenges & crises

BABY-SITTING SERVICES

Day Care Association of Fort Worth and Tarrant County (3000 E. Belknap St., 817/831–9893).

Nanny & Elder Care Professionals (817/226–2669).

CATERING

BK's Creative Catering (275 University Dr., 817/810–0888).

Just Catering (817/877–3770).

Tray Chic (5801 Curzon Ave., Suite L, 817/731–4980).

CHARITIES

The following accept clothing, furniture, housewares, and computer donations. Call to request a pickup, and remember to ask for a receipt.

ARC of Texas (2456 Jacksboro Hwy., 817/624–7001).

Goodwill (4005 Campus Dr., 817/536–8730).

Salvation Army (2901 N.E. 28th St., 817/834–6271).

CHILD CRISIS

Abuse/Protective Services Hotline (800/252–5400).

Child Protective Services (2700 Ben Ave., 817/255–8700).

Women's Haven of Tarrant County Emergency shelter for battered women and their children (24-hour hot line, 817/535–6464).

Women's Shelter Inc. Emergency housing, counseling, and support groups for battered women and their children (24-hour hot line, 817/460–5566).

CITY GOVERNMENT

City Council Office (817/871–6193).

Complaints (817/871–8900).

Mayor's Office (817/871–6118).

CONSUMER PROTECTION

Better Business Bureau (817/332–7585).

Consumer Product Safety Commission (800/638–2772).

Medicare Patient Complaints (800/725–8315).

COUNSELING & REFERRALS

aids

AIDS Interfaith Network (1425 Pennsylvania Ave., 817/870–4800).

AIDS Outreach Arlington (401 W. Sanford St., Suite 1100, Arlington, 817/275–3311).

AIDS Outreach Center (801 W. Cannon St., 817/335–1994).

HIV Street Outreach (129 Harmon Rd., Hurst, 817/569–5760).

Samaritan House (2200 Ephriham Ave., 817/626–9398).

alcoholism

Adult Children of Alcoholics (817/265–1281).

Alcoholics Anonymous (817/332–3533).

Tarrant Council on Alcoholism and Drug Abuse (817/332–6329).

crime victims

United Way's First Call Victim outreach center (210 E. Ninth St., 817/258–8100).

Women's Center of Tarrant County (817/927–2737).

Women's Haven of Tarrant County (817/535–6464).

Women's Shelter Inc. Arlington (817/460–5566).

YWCA-Supportive Living for Transitionally Homeless Women (817/332–6191).

drug abuse

Narcotics Anonymous Helpline (817/624–9525).

mental health

Jewish Family Services (4801-B Briarhaven Rd., 817/569–0898).

Life After Loss (3301 West Fwy., 817/737–9990).

Mental Health and Mental Retardation Tarrant County (3840 Hulen Tower N, 817/565–4300).

The Warm Place (1510 Cooper St., 817/870–2272).

rape

Rape Crisis Center. Counseling and emotional support are offered day and night. (817/927–2737)

DOCTOR & DENTIST REFERRALS

Baylor Helpline Grapevine (800/422–9567).

Care Link (817/735–3627).

Dental Referral Service (800/577–7320).

Well Call Physician Referral Service (817/654–9355).

EMERGENCIES

ambulance

For emergencies, dial 911 for a city ambulance.

Med-Star Ambulance (817/922–3150).

hospital emergency rooms

Arlington Memorial (800 W. Randol Mill Rd., 817/548–6100).

Baylor Grapevine (1650 W. College St., 817/329–2523).

Cook Children's Medical Center (801 7th Ave., 817/885–4000).

Family Service Crisis Intervention Hotline (817/927–5544).

Harris Methodist Fort Worth (1301 Pennsylvania Ave., 817/882–3333).

FAMILY PLANNING

Planned Parenthood of North Texas Inc. (1555 Merrimac Cr., Suite 200, 817/882–1155).

HOME HEALTH

Visiting Nurse Association (6300 Ridglea Pl. #801, 817/738–2273).

HOUSE CLEANING HELP AGENCIES

Maid Brigade (817/263–6243).

Merry Maids (817/568–2244).

LEGAL SERVICES

Legal Line (1315 Calhoun St., 817/335–1239).

Tarrant County Law Library (100 W. Weatherford St., Room 420, 817/884–1481).

West Texas Legal Services (817/336–3943).

LOST & FOUND

at airlines & airports

For property lost on a plane, contact the airline (*see* Airlines in Vacation and Travel Information, *below*) or the one of the following airports.

Love Field (214/670–6155).

Dallas/Fort Worth International Airport (972/574–4454).

on other public transportation

TRAINS

Amtrak (214/670–5869).

LONG-DISTANCE BUSES

Greyhound Bus Lines (214/655–7092).

METROPOLITAN BUSES

T (817/215–8600).

TAXIS

For items lost in a cab, contact the taxi company. (*See* Taxis in Basics of City Life, *above.*)

lost animals

If a pet is lost, contact the following offices or run a classified advertisement in the *Star-Telegram*. (*See* Publications, *above*.)

Animal Control (4900 Martin St., 817/561–3737).

Humane Society of North Texas (1840 E. Lancaster Ave., 817/332–5367).

ON-LINE SERVICES

Cowtown Net (817/293–9353).

Startext/Star-Telegram (817/390–7905).

PETS

adoption

Humane Society of North Texas (1840 E. Lancaster Ave., 817/332–5367).

grooming

Petco (1250 William D. Tate Ave., Grapevine, 817/424–8460).

Petsmart (4800 SW Loop 820, 817/731–2963).

training

Man's Best Friend (5615 Rufe Snow, 817/788–9688).

Ring Leaders (5932 Curzon Ave., 817/732–8886).

veterinary hospitals

Central Animal Hospital (300 N. University Dr., 817/332–3518).

Fort Worth Animal Medical Center (2020 S. Las Vegas Tr., 817/246–2431).

PHARMACIES 24 HOURS

Walgreen's (780 W. Bedford-Euless Rd., Hurst, 817/282–0308; 8600 Hwy. 80 W, Fort Worth, 817/244–0465).

Kroger (3612 North Belt Line Rd., Irving, 972/252–6450).

POLICE

Dial 911 for emergencies.

For non-emergencies such as reporting a theft or burglary, general information, and the location of the substation nearest you, call : Arlington (817/274–4444); Grapevine (817/410–8127); Fort Worth (817/335–4222); Irving (972/721–2661).

POSTAL SERVICES

Arlington (300 E. South St., 800/275–8777).

Fort Worth (251 W. Lancaster Ave., 800/275–8777).

Grapevine (1251 William D. Tate Ave., 800/275–8777).

overnight mail

FedEx (800/463–3339).

UPS (800/742–5877).

SENIOR CITIZEN SERVICES

Area Agency on Aging (210 E. Ninth St., 817/258–8081).

Arlington Senior Recreation (1000 Eunice St., Arlington, 817/277–8091).

Grapevine Senior Activities Center (421 Church St., Grapevine, 817/410–8130).

Senior Citizen Services of Tarrant County, Inc. (1000 Macon St., 817/338–4433).

UTILITIES

Call the following 24-hour automated service numbers for a new account or reporting problems.

gas

TXU Electric and Gas (800/817–8877).

electricity/gas

TXU Electric and Gas (972/791–2888).

telephone

GTE Southwest (800/483–4400).

Southwestern Bell (800/464–7928) .

WATER

Arlington (817/275–5931).

Fort Worth (817/871–8210).

Grapevine (817/410–3173).

VOLUNTEERING

national organizations

Volunteer Center of Tarrant County (805 W. Magnolia Ave., 817/926–9001).

Volunteers of America (2225 E. Randol Mill Rd., Arlington, 817/649–7491).

local organizations

Beautiful Ministry Soup Kitchen (1709 E. Hattie St., 817/536–0505).

Habitat for Humanity (3345 S. Jones St., 817/926–9219).

Meals on Wheels (320 South Fwy., 817/336–0912).

Metroplex Food Bank (3200 Yuma Ave., 817/924–3333).

Metroport Meals on Wheels (504 N. Oak St., Roanoke, 817/491–1141).

Mission Arlington (210 W. South St., Arlington, 817/ 277–6620).

Presbyterian Night Shelter of Tarrant County (2400 Cypress St., 817/336–1781).

Susan G. Komen Breast Cancer Foundation, Tarrant County Chapter, (817/732–1800).

Tarrant Area Food Bank (2600 Cullen St., 817/332–9177).

learning

ACTING SCHOOLS

Creative Arts Theater and School. Acting and musical theater classes and productions for youths. (1100 W. Randol Mill Rd., Arlington, 817/861–2287)

ADULT EDUCATION

Fort Worth Independent School District, Adult Education Center. Finish high school as an adult or take continuing education classes. (1400 Circle Dr., 817/531–4300)

ART & PHOTOGRAPHY SCHOOLS

Artsmart. Learn to create and not just take a picture. (5817 Polo Club Dr., Arlington, 817/467–5511)

BALLROOM DANCING

The Dance Centers. From the tried and true, such as fox trot and waltz, to the more contemporary, such as salsa and merengue, this is the place to start moving your feet. (917 University Dr., Fort Worth, 817/332–8880; 209 Bedford Rd. #145, Bedford, 817/285–7001)

COLLEGES

Tarrant County College. Offers associate degrees in dozens of study areas at five campus locations. (1500 Houston St., 817/515–5100)

COOKING SCHOOLS

Cuisine Concepts. Classical cooking in one- and multi-class offerings. (1406 Thomas Pl., 817/732–4758)

DANCE

Karen O'Brien Dance Studio. Jazz, ballet, and tap. (1114 Norwood St., 817/335–5570)

Nite on the Towne Dance Studio. Learn to move gracefully on the floor. (3100 W. Arkansas La., Arlington, 817/274–1372)

LANGUAGE SCHOOLS

Most language classes are available at the following locations. Call for more information.

Berlitz Language Centers. Demystify the world of travel and learn any language for business and pleasure. (1231 Greenway Dr. #100, Irving, 972/580–3435)

Global Language Center. Spanish, Italian, French, German, Russian, Japanese, and others are taught. (1101 University Dr. #100, 817/332–5872)

MUSIC SCHOOLS

The Guitar Studio (4455 Camp Bowie Blvd. #230, 817/737–8328).

Heavenly Sounds Piano and Voice Studio (100 Valley Spring Dr., Arlington, 817/467–6381).

Ridglea Music Co. (6323 Camp Bowie Blvd., 817/731–1831).

vacation & travel information

AIRLINES

See Airlines in Dallas Vacation & Travel Information, *above.*

AIRPORT

getting there by public transportation

The cheapest way from Fort Worth to DFW International Airport is by The Airporter Bus operated by The T, Fort Worth's public bus system. Fare is $8 one way and departs a downtown terminal at 1000 E. Weatherford Street, Fort Worth. Call 817/215–8600 for schedules and general information.

Super Shuttle (817/329–2000) is the shared-ride van service that picks you up at your home or business and takes you to the airport terminal of your choice. Fares are $25–$50, one-way. Taxi rides are about $30 from downtown to the airport and can be $50–$75 from your home to the airport. Transportation is higher to Love Field (*see* Public Transportation: Taxis, *above*).

getting there by car

The northern entrance to DFW International Airport is reached via Texas Hwy 114 and Texas Hwy 121. The southern entrance is on Texas Hwy. 183, and can also be accessed from Texas Hwy 360. Allow plenty of time for traffic delays. To get to Love Field in Dallas from downtown Fort Worth, take I–30 east to Dallas and I–35 north to Mockingbird Lane. Turn right on Mockingbird Lane and continue to Cedar Springs Road, and turn left into the entrance to Love Field. Expect heavy traffic.

CAR RENTALS

major agencies

See Major Agencies in Dallas Vacation & Travel Information, Car Rental, *above.*

local

Aardvark Used Car Rental (2907 W. 7th St., 817/332–7521).

E-Z Auto Rentals (1665 W. Hurst Blvd., Hurst, 817/284–2277).

CURRENCY EXCHANGE

Most banks do not exchange foreign currency, so be sure to have some American dollars with you.

Thomas Cook Currency Exchange Service (Terminal D, DFW Airport, 972/574–2814; Terminal B, DFW Airport, 972/574–3878).

INOCULATIONS, VACCINATIONS & TRAVEL HEALTH

Tarrant County International Travel Clinic (1800 University Dr., 817/871–7360).

ESSENTIAL NUMBERS/ FORT WORTH & MID-CITIES

Fort Worth Movie Line (817/444–3456).

Star-Telegram Sports Scoreline (817/336–7827, code 1290).

Tickets

Central Tickets (theater and music) (817/335–9000).

Star Tickets (888/597–7827).

Ticketmaster (972/647–5700).

Time (817/844–6611).

Weather (817/787–1701).

PASSPORTS

To apply for a passport, you will need your birth certificate or a certified copy, or your old passport if it has not expired. You'll also need two passport-size photographs. The following post offices have forms and additional information, as well as representatives who can answer every question. Be sure to allow at least four weeks for the application process.

Arlington (800/275–8777).

Fort Worth (817/317–3634).

Grapevine *(800/275–8777)*.

passport photo agencies

T&G Identification (505 S. Henderson St., 817/336–4282).

Kinko's (6020 Camp Bowie Blvd., Fort Worth, 817/737–8021; 1400 E. Copeland Rd., Arlington, 817/543–0833; 415 E. Hwy. 114 E, Grapevine, 817/329–7766).

TOURIST INFORMATION

for local information

Call the following offices to request a packet of information. Stop by to pick up brochures, magazines, and flyers.

Arlington Convention & Visitors Bureau (1905 E. Randol Mill Rd., Arlington, 817/461–3888).

Fort Worth Convention & Visitors Bureau (415 Throckmorton St., 817/336–8791).

Fort Worth District County Office (817/370–6500).

Grapevine Convention & Visitors Bureau (One Liberty Park Plaza, Grapevine, 817/410–3185).

Irving Convention & Visitors Bureau (3333 N. MacArthur Blvd., Irving, 972/252–7476).

Texas Department of Economic Development Tourism Division (800/888–8839).

Texas Department of Transportation Road Repairs for Texas (800/452–9292).

Texas Parks and Wildlife (800/792–1112).

DIRECTORIES

alphabetical listing of resources & topics

restaurants by neighborhood

shops by neighborhood

resources & topics

A

B

T

U

V

W

restaurants by neighborhood

shops by neighborhood

GARLAND

GRAPEVINE

GREENVILLE AVENUE

HALTOM CITY

HIGHLAND PARK

HURST

KNOX-HENDERSON

NORTH DALLAS

NORTH PARK

NORTHEAST DALLAS

NORTHWEST DALLAS

OAK CLIFF

OAK LAWN

PARK CITY

PLANO

PRESTON ROAD

RICHARDSON

SOUTH DALLAS

UPTOWN DALLAS

WEST DALLAS

WEST END

WHITE ROCK LAKE

CITY NOTES

CITY NOTES

CITY NOTES

CITY NOTES

CITY NOTES

CITY NOTES

CITY NOTES